COUNTERTERRORISM

DR. MARIE-HELEN MARAS

Assistant Professor of Criminal Justice
State University of New York-Farmingdale
and
Adjunct Assistant Professor
New York University

JONES & BARTLETT
LEARNING

World Headquarters
Jones & Bartlett Learning
5 Wall Street
Burlington, MA 01803
978-443-5000
info@jblearning.com
www.jblearning.com

Jones & Bartlett Learning books and products are available through most bookstores and online book-sellers. To contact Jones & Bartlett Learning directly, call 800-832-0034, fax 978-443-8000, or visit our website, www.jblearning.com.

Substantial discounts on bulk quantities of Jones & Bartlett Learning publications are available to corporations, professional associations, and other qualified organizations. For details and specific discount information, contact the special sales department at Jones & Bartlett Learning via the above contact information or send an email to specialsales@jblearning.com.

Production Credits
Publisher: Cathleen Sether
Acquisitions Editor: Sean Connelly
Editorial Assistant: Caitlin Murphy
Production Manager: Tracey McCrea
Production Assistant: Alyssa Lawrence
Marketing Manager: Lindsay White
Manufacturing and Inventory Control Supervisor: Amy Bacus
Composition: Paw Print Media
Cover Design: Kristin E. Parker
Cover image: © Jag_cz/ShutterStock, Inc.
Printing and Binding: Edwards Brothers Malloy
Cover Printing: Edwards Brothers Malloy

Library of Congress Cataloging-in-Publication Data
Maras, Marie-Helen, 1979–
    Counterterrorism / Marie-Helen Maras.—1st ed.
        p. cm.
    Includes bibliographical references and index.
    ISBN 978-1-4496-4860-2 (pbk.)—ISBN 1-4496-4860-6 (pbk.)
    1. Terrorism—Prevention. I. Title.
    HV6431.M36267 2013
    363.325'16—dc23
                                    2012011855
6048

Printed in the United States of America
16 15 14 13 12   10 9 8 7 6 5 4 3 2 1

Dedication

To my mother, Dimitra—

For all the years of love and support. I am truly grateful to have you as a parent.

Ο υπερούσιος και τρισήλιος εις και μόνος Θεός ο μόνος αίτιος του είναι τα πάντα αι του ευ είναι έχειν ο κρατών απάντων τους οίακας και άγων ως βούλει.

Brief Contents

Contents

Preface

The available textbooks on terrorism and counterterrorism focus extensively on al-Qaeda at the expense of other domestic terrorist groups and responses to them worldwide. To fully comprehend the evolution and current state of terrorism, students must look at its history on a global scale. This global perspective enables students to think sensibly about terrorism and better understand what works and what does not work in counterterrorism. This text seeks to fill this void in available literature by focusing on domestic terrorist groups from Europe, Asia, Africa, the Middle East, South America, and North America. It will also critically evaluate the counterterrorism measures implemented in response to these terrorist groups. Finally, and most importantly, this text compares terrorist groups; assesses the factors that are conducive to certain groups' sustainability and those that led to other groups' demise; notes counterterrorism measures that were successfully used in the past to combat terrorists and terrorist groups worldwide; and incorporates efficient policies into a counterterrorism strategy that can be used to effectively deal with the current threat of terrorism by al-Qaeda operatives, affiliates, and homegrown terrorists inspired by al-Qaeda's cause.

This text is intended to serve as a comprehensive resource for terrorism and counterterrorism graduate courses. It can also be used for upper-level undergraduate students. This text will also appeal to a wide range of different groups. By steering away from an exclusive focus on al-Qaeda and terrorism after the September 11, 2001 attacks, it will be of interest to a much broader audience of writers and researchers working on terrorism and counterterrorism. Moreover, by providing a detailed account of the most significant terrorist groups and counterterrorism practices and their implications for a number of different fields such as law, public policy and administration, security, and criminology, it is likely to be an extremely useful resource for academicians, practitioners, and graduate and undergraduate students in these areas. Criminal justice, socio-legal, history, and political science scholars and professionals should also find food for thought in this work.

Given that this textbook covers global terrorism and counterterrorism practices, it will be of interest to law enforcement agencies, terrorism and counterterrorism officials, and researchers in the field. Specifically, this text is intended for:

- law enforcement agents seeking to expand their knowledge of who terrorists are and what terrorists can do;
- students and professionals seeking a career in counterterrorism
- counterterrorism specialists seeking to expand their knowledge of terrorism beyond al-Qaeda;
- law students and legal professionals seeking to understand counterterrorism legislation and its implications on human rights; and
- students, academicians, researchers, and practitioners seeking a firmer grasp on the nature and extent of terrorism and what can be done to effectively combat the threat posed by terrorists and terrorist groups.

Probable users of the book also include security, government, and intelligence agencies. Anyone interested in learning about terrorism and counterterrorism will also benefit from this book.

Moreover, this field has gained prominence because of the attacks on September 11, 2001, and current global media coverage of terrorism and measures governments use to combat terrorists. Accordingly, this book will also be relevant to civil liberties groups and professional associations as the extradition of suspected terrorists, their torture in foreign and U.S. military prisons, and indefinite detention around the globe are becoming more of a common practice.

SUPPLEMENTS

This book is accompanied by a series of valuable supplements. An Instructor's Manual, PowerPoint Lecture Outlines, and a Test Bank are available to assist instructors in teaching terrorism and counterterrorism courses. The Instructor's Manual also includes case studies, discussion questions, and recommended topics for student research papers.

Acknowledgments

I would like to warmly thank Sean Connelly, Caitlin Murphy, and Alyssa Lawrence at Jones & Bartlett Learning for their direction and assistance during the development and production of this textbook. Additionally, I would like to thank the editor who helped me during the developmental stage of my book, Deya Saoud Jacob. Moreover, I am grateful to my former DPhil thesis supervisor at the University of Oxford, Dr. Lucia Zedner, for all of her assistance and support long after my graduation. Last and by no means least, I am especially grateful to my friends Katie Norton, Mel Sinclair, Alex Chung, Stephen Noguera, Jessica Black, Roy Hasson, Jamie Lee, and Patrice Rodriguez for making my time at the University of Oxford truly memorable.

Thank you to the following individuals for reviewing this text:

Kristian P. Alexander, *Zayed University, Abu Dhabi, United Arab Emirates*

James David Ballard, *California State University, Northridge*

Derek Charles Catsam, *University of Texas of the Permian Basin*

Edward T. Croissant, *Hillsborough Community College*

James L. Feldkamp, *George Washington University*

Gerald M. Kosicki, *The Ohio State University*

William W. Newmann, *Virginia Commonwealth University*

John L. Padgett, *Capella University*

Cara Rabe-Hemp, *Illinois State University*

Mitchel P. Roth, *Sam Houston State University*

Larry Salinger, *Arkansas State University*

David Sobek, *Louisiana State University*

Nicholas J. Steneck, *Florida Southern College*

Max Wise, *Campbellsville University*

Steve A. Young, *Sam Houston State University*

part one

Understanding Terrorism and Terrorists' Mindset

The success of counterterrorism largely depends on the understanding of terrorism and terrorists' objectives. Therefore, it is imperative that one comprehend how and why individual terrorists and terrorist groups do what they do. Accordingly, the focus of this part is on analyzing the way that terrorist actors think in order to be able to better understand, explain, and possibly predict actions and nonactions of terrorists in future situations.

To achieve this, first, this part explores what terrorism is and what terrorists do (Chapter 1). It also introduces different types of terrorism. Here, particular emphasis is placed on area of operation, tactics, and targets of terrorists. Special attention is paid to the most prominent domestic and international terrorist groups in Europe, Asia, Africa, South America, North America, and the Middle East. Second, it seeks to determine the primary reasons why individuals and groups commit a terrorist attack by focusing on existing theories and hypotheses (Chapter 2). Third, it examines the strategic, social, and individual goals of terrorists (Chapter 3). It further assesses the factors that are conducive to the sustainability of certain groups and those that led to the demise of other groups.

chapter one

Terrorism: An Introduction

On September 11, 2001, four U.S. commercial airliners loaded with jet fuel were hijacked by 19 Islamic terrorists, who used the planes as missiles. The attacks targeted the two towers of the World Trade Center in New York City, the Pentagon in Arlington, Virginia, and an unidentified building in Washington, DC (possibly the U.S. Capitol Building or the White House), although the fourth plane never reached its target due to passengers attacking the hijackers and causing the plane to crash into a field in southwestern Pennsylvania. These events, which resulted in approximately 3,000 deaths and more than $17 billion in damages, were covered worldwide by media and were universally labeled as acts of terrorism. On the fifth anniversary of 9/11 (September 11, 2006), David McMenemy crashed his vehicle, which was doused in gasoline, into the Egerton Women's Health Center in Davenport, Iowa, with the intent of causing an explosion. McMenemy attacked the facility because he believed that the center was providing abortion services to women. No national newspaper, magazine, or network newscast covered the incident (with the exception of an Associated Press wire story).[1] Even when this incident was covered, it was not labeled an act of terrorism.

Between 1997 and 2010, there have been 6,349 incidents of violence against abortion providers in the United States and Canada.[2] Of these incidents, 41 were

---

[1] Pozner, J. L. 2006, October 8.The terrorists who aren't in the news: Anti-abortion fanatics spread fear by bombings, murders and assaults, but the media take little notice. *Women in News and Media*. http://www.wimnonline.org/WIMNsVoicesBlog/?p=286

[2] National Abortion Federation. 2011. *NAF violence and disruption statistics: Incidents of violence and disruption against abortion providers in the U.S. and Canada*. http://www.prochoice.org/pubs _research/publications/downloads/about_abortion/stats_table2010.pdf.

bombings, 662 were anthrax threats, and 100 were butyric acid attacks. Despite this, the media and certain politicians refer to the perpetrators of these incidents as activists and not terrorists.[3] This occurrence may in part be due to misperceptions of what constitutes terrorism. What further complicates matters is the lack of a universally accepted definition of terrorism. This following text seeks to shed some light on this issue by examining definitions of terrorism, identifying the different types of terrorism worldwide, and determining the viability of creating a universally accepted definition of terrorism.

DEFINING TERRORISM

Numerous definitions of terrorism exist. The Federal Bureau of Investigation (FBI) defines terrorism as the "unlawful use of force or violence to intimidate or coerce a government, the civilian population, or any segment thereof, in furtherance of political or social objectives or goals."[4] Terrorism is also defined in national legislation. In the United States, federal law defines terrorism as

> activities that involve . . . violation(s) of the criminal laws of the United States or of any State and . . . appear to be intended (i) to intimidate or coerce a civilian population; (ii) to influence the policy of a government by intimidation or coercion; or (iii) to affect the conduct of a government by mass destruction, assassination, or kidnapping.[3]

In addition, the Code of Federal Regulations defined it as "the unlawful use of force and violence against persons or property to intimidate or coerce a government, the civilian population, or any segment thereof, in furtherance of political or social objectives" (28 CFR Section 0.85). Other countries, such as the United Kingdom, define it as "the use of threat of action . . . [that is] designed to influence the government or to intimidate the public or a section of the public, and . . . is made for the purpose of advancing a political, religious or ideological cause" (Section 1, UK Terrorism Act of 2000); whereas, in Canada, "terrorist activity" is defined as

> an act or omission . . . that is committed in whole or in part for a political, religious or ideological purpose, objective or cause and in whole or in part with the intention of intimidating the public, or a segment of the public, with regard to its security, including its economic security, or compelling a person, a government or a domestic or an international organization to do or to refrain from doing

---

3 Marcotte, A. 2001.The terrorism taboo. *Slate,* July 11, 2011. http://www.slate.com/blogs/xx_factor /2011/07/11/how_is_anti_abortion_violence_not_terrorism_.html; Agence France-Presse (AFP). 2008. Anti abortion bombs not terrorism: Palin. *The Sydney Morning Herald,* October 25, 2008. http://news.smh.com.au/world/anti-abortion-bombs-not-terrorism-palin-20081025-58gy.html

4 Federal Bureau of Investigation. 2005. Terrorism 2002–2005. *US Department of Justice.* http://www.fbi.gov/stats-services/publications/terrorism-2002-2005/terror02_05.pdf.

any act, whether the person, government or organization is inside or outside Canada.[5]

To classify as a terrorist activity in both the United Kingdom and Canada, the act must also, among other things, seek to intentionally cause death, serious bodily harm and/or property damage, endanger lives, or gravely threaten public safety and health.[6]

Moreover, terrorism has been defined in international legislation. For instance, the EU defines terrorist acts as those that "may seriously damage a country or an international organization" when the objective is to "seriously intimidat[e] a population, or . . . unduly compel . . . a Government or international organization to perform or abstain from performing any act, or . . . seriously destabiliz[e] or destroy . . . the fundamental political, constitutional, economic or social structures of a country or international organization."[7] Furthermore, international conventions on terrorism exist that criminalize some of the most significant terrorist acts, including

1. *Offenses against aircrafts and airports.* UN Convention on Offences and Certain Other Acts Committed on Board Aircraft (1963); UN Convention for the Suppression of Unlawful Seizure of Aircraft (1970); UN Convention for the Suppression of Unlawful Acts against the Safety of Civil Aviation (1971); and the UN Protocol on the Suppression of Unlawful Acts of Violence at Airports Serving International Civil Aviation, supplementary to the Convention for the Suppression of Unlawful Acts against the Safety of Civil Aviation (1988), which supplemented the 1971 Convention.
2. *Hostage taking.* UN International Convention against the Taking of Hostages (1979).
3. *Offenses against internationally protected persons, such as state officials and representatives of international organizations.* UN Convention on the Prevention and Punishment of Crimes against Internationally Protected Persons, including Diplomatic Agents (1973).
4. *The international transportation of nuclear material and the domestic use, storage, or transport of nuclear material.* UN Convention on the Physical Protection of Nuclear Material (1980).
5. *Offenses committed aboard or against ships' navigation facilities.* UN Convention for the Suppression of Unlawful Acts against the Safety of Maritime Navigation (1988).

---

[5] Section 83.01(1)(b)(i) of the Canadian Anti-Terrorism Act of 2001.

[6] Section 2 UK Terrorism Act of 2000; Section 83.01(1)(b)(ii) of the Canadian Anti-Terrorism Act of 2001.

[7] Council Framework Decision (EC) of 13 June 2002 on combating terrorism (2002/475/JHA) [2002] OJ L164/3.

6. *Offenses committed in relation to a "fixed platform," which is defined as "an artificial island, installation or structure permanently attached to the sea-bed for the purpose of exploration or exploitation of resources or for other economic purposes."* UN Protocol for the Suppression of Unlawful Acts against the Safety of Fixed Platforms located on the Continental Shelf (1988).

7. *Manufacture of unmarked plastic explosives within each state.* UN Convention on the Marking of Plastic Explosives for the Purpose of Detection (1991).

8. *The intentional and unlawful delivery, placement, discharge, or detonation of an explosive device.* UN International Convention for the Suppression of Terrorist Bombings (1997).

9. *Financing of terrorist acts.* International Convention for the Suppression of the Financing of Terrorism (1999).

The League of Arab Nations also considers the crimes in the majority of the above conventions as terrorist acts,[8] except if the contracting states have not ratified the conventions and if these states have legislation that excludes (some of) these crimes. Examples of crimes that are considered as acts of terrorism are assassinations, bombings, rocket attacks, and the beheading of victims. Terrorism cannot be considered separate from other crimes that are often committed in pursuit of it. Crimes often connected to terrorism include human smuggling; drug trafficking; illicit arms trade; human trafficking; smuggling of nuclear, chemical, biological, and radiological materials; money laundering; identity theft; robberies; and arson.

Terrorism is not a new phenomenon. Throughout history, acts of terrorism have endangered, injured, and killed individuals, "jeopardized fundamental freedoms, and seriously impaired the dignity of human beings."[9] Terrorism has been perpetrated by domestic and international terrorists. Domestic terrorism involves the commission of acts intended to threaten or actually cause harm to persons and property, which are conducted primarily within the territorial jurisdiction of the target country. Therefore, domestic terrorists usually operate only within their host country. Examples of such terrorists are the Revolutionary Struggle (Greece), the First of October Antifascist Group (Spain), Moroccan Islamic Combatant Group (Morocco), Japanese Red Army (Japan), and Revolutionary Armed Forces of Colombia (Colombia). If they are occupied by another country, they can also operate within the occupying country's borders. On the other hand, international terrorism involves dangerous or violent illegal acts that transcend national boundaries or are committed primarily outside the territorial jurisdiction of the target

---

[8] Council of Arab Ministers of the Interior and the Council of Arab Ministers of Justice. *Arab Convention for the Suppression of Terrorism* (1998).

[9] von Schorlemer, S. 2003. Human rights: Substantive and institutional implications of the war against terrorism. *European Journal of International Law* 14 (2): 266.

country. Al-Qaeda engages in international terrorism as it operates in the Middle East, North America, Europe, Africa, and Asia. Another example is the Mujahedine Khalq, whose reach extends beyond the Middle East to include associates and supporters throughout North America and Europe.

DESIGNATING TERRORIST GROUPS

Countries differ in terms of their designations of terrorist groups. The U.S. Department of State has a list of designated foreign terrorist organizations (**Table 1-1**). To be designated as a terrorist organization, the group "must engage in terrorist activity . . . [under] section 212(a)(3)(B) of the Immigration and Nationality Act [of 1952] . . . or terrorism as defined by section 140(d)(2) of the Foreign Relations Authorization Act, Fiscal Years 1988 and 1989 . . . or retain the capacity and intent to engage in terrorist activity or terrorism."[10] Other countries maintain their own list of terrorist groups; for example, Canada and the United Kingdom. The EU also has a list of terrorist organizations. In particular, the European Council adopted a common position on the application of specific measures with which to combat persons, groups, and entities that engage in terrorism (**Table 1-2**).[11] By contrast, the United Nations does not maintain a list of designated terrorist organizations. However, the UN 1267 Committee does maintain a consolidated list of individuals associated with the Taliban and al-Qaeda.[12]

A UNIVERSAL DEFINITION OF TERRORISM: A SISYPHEAN TASK?

Definitions that seek to explain what terrorism is have focused on the tactics and goals of terrorists. Terrorists seek to coerce a civilian population and influence policy of the target government or otherwise affect its conduct. Their attacks are aimed at causing specific reactions in governments and populations. The tactics used to achieve this have involved the use of reflexive control, which seeks to control the target government's decision-making process and compel them to act according to a predetermined plan favorable to the controller. This tactic (developed by Lefebvre in the early 1960s) was learned from the Soviet Union, where it was used by the Soviet military establishment to manage information and get an

---

[10] The Immigration and Nationality Act of 1952 is codified in 8 USC § 1182(a)(3)(B) and the Foreign Relations Authorization Act, Fiscal Years 1988 and 1989 is codified in 22 USC § 2656f(d) (2). U.S. Department of State. 2012, January 27. Foreign Terrorist Organizations. *Office of the Coordinator for Counterterrorism.* http://www.state.gov/j/ct/rls/other/des/123085.htm.

[11] Council Common Position (EC) 2009/67/CFSP of 26 January 2009 updating Common Position 2001/931/CFSP on the application of specific measures to combat terrorism and repealing Common Position 2008/586/CFSP [2009] OJ L 023/37.

[12] United Nations. n.d. The list established and maintained by the 1267 Committee with respect to individuals, groups, undertakings and other entities associated with Al-Qaida. *Security Council Committee Established Pursuant to Resolution 1267 (1999).* http://www.un.org/sc/committees/1267/aq_sanctions_list.shtml.

Table 1-1 U.S. Designation of Foreign Terrorist Organizations

1. Abu Nidal Organization (ANO)
2. Abu Sayyaf Group (ASG)
3. Al-Aqsa Martyrs Brigade (AAMS)
4. Al-Shabaab
5. Ansar al-Islam (AAI)
6. Asbat al-Ansar
7. Aum Shinrikyo (AUM)
8. Basque Fatherland and Liberty (ETA)
9. Communist Party of the Philippines/ New People's Army (CPP/NPA)
10. Continuity Irish Republican Army (CIRA)
11. Gama'a al-Islamiyya (Islamic Group)
12. HAMAS (Islamic Resistance Movement)
13. Harakat ul-Jihad-i-Islami/Bangladesh (HUJI-B)
14. Harakat ul-Mujahidin (HUM)
15. Hizballah (Party of God)
16. Islamic Jihad Union (IJU)
17. Islamic Movement of Uzbekistan (IMU)
18. Jaish-e-Mohammed (JEM) (Army of Mohammed)
19. Jemaah Islamiya (JI)
20. Kahane Chai (Kach)
21. Kata'ib Hizballah (KH)
22. Kongra-Gel (KGK, formerly Kurdistan Workers' Party, PKK, KADEK)
23. Lashkar-e Tayyiba (LT) (Army of the Righteous)
24. Lashkar i Jhangvi (LJ)
25. Liberation Tigers of Tamil Eelam (LTTE)
26. Libyan Islamic Fighting Group (LIFG)
27. Moroccan Islamic Combatant Group (GICM)
28. Mujahedin-e Khalq Organization (MEK)
29. National Liberation Army (ELN)
30. Palestine Liberation Front (PLF)
31. Palestinian Islamic Jihad (PIJ)
32. Popular Front for the Liberation of Palestine (PFLP)
33. PFLP-General Command (PFLP-GC)
34. al-Qaeda in Iraq (AQI)
35. al-Qaeda (AQ)
36. al-Qaeda in the Arabian Peninsula (AQAP)
37. al-Qaeda in the Islamic Maghreb (formerly GSPC)
38. Real IRA (RIRA)
39. Revolutionary Armed Forces of Colombia (FARC)
40. Revolutionary Organization 17 November (17N)
41. Revolutionary People's Liberation Party/Front (DHKP/C)
42. Revolutionary Struggle (RS)
43. Shining Path (Sendero Luminoso, SL)
44. United Self-Defense Forces of Colombia (AUC)
45. Harakat-ul Jihad Islami (HUJI)
46. Tehrik-e Taliban Pakistan (TTP)
47. Jundallah
48. Army of Islam (AOI)

opponent to perform certain actions.[13] Through this tactic, a pattern is created or partial information is provided that causes an opponent to react in a predetermined fashion without realizing that he or she is being manipulated. A well-known example of this is the U.S. military's use of reflexive control in Operation Desert Storm. By feeding Saddam Hussein specific information that led him to

---

[13] Lefebvre, V. A., and Farley, J. D. 2007. The torturer's dilemma: A theoretical analysis of the societal consequences of torturing terrorist suspects. *Studies in Conflict and Terrorism* 30 (7): 636.

Table 1-2 EU Designation of Terrorist Groups and Entities[1]

1. Abu Nidal Organisation (ANO)
2. Al-Aqsa Martyr's Brigade
3. Al-Aqsa e.V.
4. Al-Takfir and Al-Hij ra
5. *Cooperativa Artigiana Fuoco ed Affini—Occasionalmente Spettacolare (Artisans' Cooperative Fire and Similar —Occasionally Spectacular)
6. *Nuclei Armati per il Comunismo (Armed Units for Communism)
7. Aum Shinrikyo
8. Babbar Khalsa
9. *CCCCC—Cellula Contro Capitale, Carcere i suoi Carcerieri e le sue Celle (Cell Against Capital, Prison, Prison Warders and Prison Cells)
10. Communist Party of the Philippines, including New People's Army (NPA)
11. *Continuity Irish Republican Army (CIRA)
12. *Epanastatikos Agonas (Revolutionary Struggle)
13. *Euskadi Ta Askatasuna/Basque Fatherland and Liberty (ETA)
14. Gama'a al-Islamiyya (a.k.a. Al-Gama'a al-Islamiyya, IG)
15. Islami Büyük Dogu Akıncılar Cephesi — IBDA C (Great Islamic Eastern Warriors Front)
16. *Grupos de Resistencia Antifascista Primero de Octubre/Antifascist Resistance Groups First of October (GRAPO)
17. Hamas
18. Hizbul Mujahideen (HM)
19. Hofstadgroep
20. Holy Land Foundation for Relief and Development
21. International Sikh Youth Federation (ISYF)
22. *Solidarietà Internazionale (International Solidarity)
23. Kahane Chai (Kach)
24. Khalistan Zindabad Force (KZF)
25. Kurdistan Workers' Party (PKK)
26. Liberation Tigers of Tamil Eelam (LTTE)
27. *Loyalist Volunteer Force (LVF)
28. Ejército de Liberación Nacional (National Liberation Army)
29. *Orange Volunteers (OV)
30. Palestine Liberation Front (PLF)
31. Palestinian Islamic Jihad (PIJ)
32. Popular Front for the Liberation of Palestine (PFLP)
33. Popular Front for the Liberation of Palestine-General Command, (PFLP-General Command)
34. *Real IRA
35. *Red Brigades
36. *Red Hand Defenders (RHD)
37. Revolutionary Armed Forces of Colombia (FARC)
38. *Epanastatiki Pirines ("Revolutionary Nuclei)
39. *Dekati Evdomi Noemvri (Revolutionary Organisation 17 November)
40. Devrimci Halk Kurtulu Partisi-Cephesi (DHKP/C)
41. Shining Path (SL) (Sendero Luminoso)
42. Stichting Al Aqsa (a.k.a. Stichting Al Aqsa Nederland, a.k.a. Al Aqsa Nederland)
43. Teyrbazen Azadiya Kurdistan (TAK) (a.k.a. Kurdistan Freedom Falcons, Kurdistan Freedom Hawks)
44. *Brigata XX Luglio (Twentieth of July Brigade)
45. *Ulster Defence Association/Ulster Freedom Fighters (UDA/UFF)
46. Autodefensas Unidas de Colombia/United Self Defence Forces/Group of Colombia (AUC)
47. F.A.I.—Federazione Anarchica Informale (Unofficial Anarchist Federation)

---

[1] Groups and entities marked with an * are subject to Article 4 of Common Position 2001/931/CFSP only.

make military decisions favorable to allies and their plans, the war ended in an Allied victory.[14]

Al-Qaeda's strategy also reveals the use of reflexive control tactics. In *Stealing Al-Qa'ida's Playbook*, Brachman and McCants (2006) analyzed various al-Qaeda strategy documents.[15] Their analysis of Abu Bakr Naji's (a well-known jihadi leader) *The Management of Barbarism* revealed that al-Qaeda calls for terrorists to use tactics that will bleed Western governments' economies and militaries, leading to social unrest in these countries and ultimately, defeat of these governments. What is sought is an extreme overreaction, one that seeks to make governments spend all of their resources trying to protect everyone and everything. This strategy is not original; it has been used throughout history and is even found in both Carlos Marighella's (1969) *The Mini-Manual of the Urban Guerrilla* and the Irish Republican Army's (1979) *Green Book*.[16]

The overreaction of governments to terrorist attacks both in terms of military intervention and draconian counterterrorism measures (such as indefinite detention) provides an incentive to terrorists to conduct further attacks in hopes of provoking similar reactions. Military intervention in Afghanistan and Iraq and Western counterterrorism measures are used by Islamist extremists as propaganda to gain sympathy for their cause.[17] Terrorists seek indirectly to modify the behavior of their opponent to their advantage by manipulating the opponent's beliefs and emotions about the terrorists they are confronting—instilling fear in them in order to force their opponents to retaliate in ways that might increase support for the terrorists' cause.

When the target is a democratic government, provoking them into draconian responses also serves another purpose. It aims to demonstrate to the rest of the world that these governments really are the evil powers that terrorists believe them to be.[18] For example, in the 1970s, Germany's Red Army Faction thought that West Germany disguised its true nature as a fascist state behind the veil of democracy.[19] The Red Army Faction believed that West Germany would resort to its "true" character in response to terrorist attacks by employing violent counterresponses.[20]

---

[14] Kramer, X. H. et al. 2003. From prediction to reflexive control. *Reflexive Processes and Control* 2 (1): 89.

[15] Brachman, J. M., and McCants, W. F. 2006, February. Stealing al-Qa'ida's playbook. *Combating Terrorism Center (CTC) Report*. http://www.ctc.usma.edu/posts/stealing-al-qaidas -playbook.

[16] See especially Chapter 16, "Objectives of the Guerrilla's Actions," which notes the desired overreaction by governments (getting them to try to protect every asset and person), in Marighella, C. 1969. The mini-manual of the urban guerrilla. *Marighella Internet Archive*. http://marxists.org/archive /marighella-carlos/1969/06/minimanual-urban-guerrilla/index.htm; Sinn Fein/Irish Republican Army. 1979. *Green book*. http://www.residentgroups.fsnet.co.uk/greenbook.htm.

[17] Stock, J., and Herz, A. 2007. The threat environment created by international terrorism from the German police perspective. *European Journal on Criminal Policy and Research* 13 (1/2): 88.

[18] Richardson, L. (2006). *What terrorists want*. New York: Random House, 99.

[19] Gardner, D. (2008). *Risk: The science of politics and fear*. London: Virgin, 293.

[20] Ibid.

However, the West German government refused to play the Red Army Faction's game—to be goaded into overreacting.[21]

Terrorists often want the response of the government to be an overreaction, not least because an overreaction can discredit the government in the eyes of its population. Indeed, such actions can cause the government to lose legitimacy and can help make sections of the public sympathetic to the terrorists' cause. The goal is to convince the public that the real evildoers and terrorists are governments and that the terrorists are the victims, not the governments. It is easier to make the public sympathize with the terrorists if the public is also feeling victimized by the government. Hence, terrorists need an overreaction by governments in order to further their goals.

The objective of a terrorist can range from censorship to the removal of foreign military forces from what the terrorist sees as their national homeland. The latter was seen in the aftermath of the assassination of Theo Van Gogh, an outspoken critic of Islam and descendant of the 19th-century painter Vincent Van Gogh. He was targeted by terrorists after he broadcast "a short TV movie titled Submission . . . which aimed at exposing the sufferings of women under Islam . . . One scene [that] particularly outraged Holland's Islamists shows Quranic verses justifying violence against women written on the naked body of a young woman."[22] Van Gogh received numerous death threats before being brutally assassinated by Mohammed Bouyeri, a member of the Hofstad group (Dutch militant Islamics). As Bouyeri and supporters later confirmed, his murder was designed to intimidate and silence those who criticized or mocked their religion. Since his assassination, numerous Islamist extremists have claimed that those ridiculing their religion would be killed in a manner similar to Theo van Gogh. This became evident with Lars Vilks, a Swedish cartoonist who had published an offensive cartoon drawing of the Prophet Mohammed. Following the publication of his drawing, a bounty was put on Vilks and his publisher by al-Qaeda groups inside Iraq. Since then, very few magazines and newspapers have been willing to reprint the cartoons for fear of retaliation by terrorists or their supporters.[23]

By and large, academicians, state agencies, legislators, and others view terrorism as the use of coercive tactics, such as the threat or use of violence, to promote control, fear, and intimidation within the target nation or nations for political, religious, or ideological reasons. Individuals who are classified as terrorists are, therefore, those who employ methods of terror. The targets of terrorists are usually those who oppose or criticize the terrorists' ideology and those who are viewed by the terrorists as outsiders, undesirables, or enemies.

---

21 Ibid., p. 294.

22 Vidino, L. (2006). *Al-Qaeda in Europe: The new battleground of international jihad.* New York: Prometheus, 347.

23 Messner, E. 2006. The debate: Should U.S. media reprint the cartoons? *Washington Post,* February 8, 2006. http://blogs.washingtonpost.com/thedebate/2006/02/cartoon_controv.html.

Unsuccessful attempts have been made by the United Nations to propose a definition of terrorism that could be accepted by all countries and embedded in international law. The failure of the universal acceptance of a single definition for terrorism could be attributed to the existence of several different types of terrorism, some countries' refusal to accept a definition that portrayed national liberation movements or armed revolutionaries as terrorists, and the rejection of including the possibility of state agencies being found guilty of terrorism by others. Framing the study of the possibility of a universal definition requires a three-pronged analysis. First, it analyzes the different types of terrorism. Second, it considers the similarities and differences between national liberation movements and terrorists. The motivating questions for this analysis are: how does one differentiate between the two? Are they distinct groups? Or do they overlap in some respects? Finally, a study of a universal definition must explore the nature and extent of state terrorism. The main focus of this section is to answer the following questions: Does state terrorism exist? Should international law criminalize state acts of terrorism?

Types of Terrorism

Terrorism can be classified in two different ways. First, terrorism can be classified according to the means terrorists use to achieve their goals. Examples of these categories are cyberterrorism, bioterrorism, and nuclear terrorism. Cyberterrorism involves the use of computers as weapons or attacks on computer or information systems linked to critical infrastructure (e.g., public safety, traffic control, medical and emergency services, and public works) with the intent to inflict grave harm, such as loss of life or significant economic damage, in order to influence an audience or cause the target government to change its policies. Bioterrorism occurs when biological toxins (such as ricin, anthrax, or smallpox) are intentionally introduced into the air, food, or water in an attempt to inflict massive casualties. Aum Shinrikyo, a Japanese terrorist group, engaged in a bioterrorist attack in 1993 when they released anthrax from an industrial sprayer on the roof of one of their facilities in Kameido (a suburb of Tokyo). The attack was a failure and no people were injured or killed. Nuclear terrorism involves the use of nuclear materials or the attacking of nuclear facilities with the intention of causing significant harm to people and property.

Second, terrorism can be classified according to the end sought. Specifically, to terrorists, the end justifies the mean. The end sought, however, differs according to the type of terrorist group. Virtually all terrorists strive to justify their goals and behaviors by subscribing to some ideology (e.g., socialism, communism, or Marxism). As such, terrorists can also be distinguished and categorized according to their ideology and goals. Some types of terrorism are further explored in the next sections.

Nationalist–Separatist Terrorism

Nationalist–separatists use violence to establish an independent homeland for an ethnic or religious group that is persecuted (or believes it is persecuted) by the majority. These types of terrorists seek to cause fragmentation within the country and establish a "new" state within it. Examples of groups that fall under this category include the Irish Republican Army (IRA) and its splinter groups. The IRA was formed in 1922 after the Anglo-Irish War (1919–1921). When the war ended, a treaty was signed in 1921 by the United Kingdom and the Irish separatists led by Sinn Fein (a political party). Under this treaty, the 26 Catholic counties of the South of Ireland (Eire) would gain their independence from the UK, whereas the remaining six Protestant counties of the North (Ulster) would remain under the control of the UK. The IRA sought to both end British rule in Northern Ireland and to unite Ireland and Northern Ireland as one single, sovereign nation. In 1969, due to differing ideologies and objectives, the IRA was split into two rival groups, the Official IRA and the Provisional IRA. The Official IRA declared a cease-fire in 1972. The Provisional IRA ended its armed struggle with the United Kingdom on April 10, 1998, with the Good Friday Agreement, signed in Belfast, Northern Ireland. Splinter groups—the Real IRA and the Continuity IRA—were subsequently formed from members of the Provisional IRA that were opposed to the peace and ceasefire agreement. The Real IRA and the Continuity IRA both claim to have similar goals to the IRA—to end British sovereignty and reunite Ireland into one sovereign nation. Both of these groups are still active today and continue to engage in terrorist attacks. These two groups have been known to work together. The United Kingdom, the United States, and the European Union have designated the Real IRA and the Continuity IRA as terrorist organizations.

Another group in this category is the Basque Fatherland and Liberty or Euskadi Ta Askatasuna (ETA). In the 1930s, Spain experienced a civil war led by dictator General Francisco Franco, who believed in one unified Spain and opposed regionalism. At the time, the Basque country was culturally different from the rest of Spain, and individuals within this region spoke their own language and had their own unique traditions. General Franco punished the Basque region, which was made up of provinces in Spain and France, for its opposition during the war by declaring them traitors and banning their language of Euskara. In 1959, the Basque Fatherland and Liberty, a radical separatist organization, was formed, which sought national self-determination for the Basque region (i.e., it sought to create an independent Basque state). The ETA is still active today and has engaged in multiple terrorist attacks in Spain. The United States, Spain, and the European Union have designated the ETA as a terrorist organization.

Another nationalist terrorist group is the Liberation Tigers of Tamil Eelam (LTTE) or the Tamil Tigers. In 1949, in Sri Lanka, the United National Party stripped Indian Tamils of their citizenship and right to vote. The majority ethnic group in Sri Lanka was Sinhalese and in 1956, the Sinhala Only Act was passed, which mandated that the language of the Sri Lanka majority, Sinhalese, be the sole official language of the country. Opponents of this law viewed this act as an attempt by the majority to oppress minorities in Sri Lanka such as the Tamils. The Tamils responded to these acts by carrying out nonviolent demonstrations. Many of the Tamil demonstrators were attacked by the Sinhalese, while the police stood idly by and watched. In 1957, the Bandaranaike pact was passed, which sought to grant the Tamils a certain level of autonomy and give them more rights. However, Buddhist monks pushed to get rid of the pact, because they wanted to promote unity and Buddhism. Prime Minister Sirimavo Bandaranaike pursued policies in Sri Lanka that promoted the Sinhalese and Buddhist culture, and the Buddhist religion. In 1972, the protection for the minority Tamils was taken away by Bandaranaike. A new constitution was subsequently drafted that favored Buddhists, and limits were also mandated by the government on how many Tamil students could be accepted into universities. As a result, the Tamil Student Movement formed to protest the limitation of access of Tamil students to universities. This movement subsequently became the Tamil Tigers and began to engage in terrorist activities, many of which were suicide bombings. The goal of the Tamil Tigers is to create a separate state in Sri Lanka for the Tamils. This Tamil state would be in the areas of Sri Lanka that are mostly populated by the Tamils; namely, its northern and eastern provinces. Canada, the United States, the United Kingdom, and the European Union have designated the Tamil Tigers as a terrorist organization.

Furthermore, the Al-Aqsa Martyrs Brigade falls under this category. This terrorist group emerged at the beginning of the Second Intifada (or al-Aqsa Intifada), the second Palestinian Arab uprising, in September 2000. The Al-Aqsa Martyrs Brigade, which operates in Israel, the West Bank, and Gaza, seeks the creation of a Palestinian nation-state by expelling Israelis from these areas. The Al-Aqsa Martyrs Brigade initially focused only on the Israeli military and settlers in the Palestinian-occupied regions of the West Bank and Gaza. However, this group soon expanded its targets to include Israel and even Palestinians who were believed to be working with Israelis. This group is composed primarily of terrorists who belong to al-Fatah, a secular Palestinian nationalist organization that was a faction of the Palestine Liberation Organization (PLO). The PLO, al-Fatah, and other factions of the PLO renounced terrorism as part of the 1993 Oslo Accords. However, factions of these groups, such as the Al-Aqsa Martyrs Brigade, have been suspected of and implicated in engaging in terrorist attacks. Canada, the United States, and the European Union have designated the Al-Aqsa Martyrs Brigade as a terrorist organization.

Left-Wing Terrorism

Left-wing terrorism involves the use of violence by individuals or groups in order to destroy a capitalist system and replace it with a communist or socialist regime. Frequently, banks and other financial centers that are seen as symbols of capitalistic oppression are the targets of left-wing terrorists. This was evident in the acts committed by the Weather Underground, a domestic terrorist group in the United States, which robbed and bombed banks, mostly during the 1970s. The Red Army Faction was also known to target bank and private industry officials. The Revolutionary Organization November 17 (17N), a domestic terrorist group in Greece, similarly targeted businessmen, among others (e.g., American, British, and Turkish diplomats; and Greek policeman and politicians).

These types of terrorists seek to attack the established systems in order to abolish social classes. Karl Marx and Vladimir Lenin advocated for the abolition of the class structure whereby all means of production would be commonly owned by members of society. According to Marx, there are two main social classes within any capitalist society: the proletariat and the bourgeoisie. The proletariat, the working class, is without power and must earn a living by selling their labor (this group is known as the "have-nots"). In contrast, the bourgeoisie are the capitalists or wealthy owners of the means of production (the "haves"). These groups are engaged in an ongoing conflict or class struggle, the outcome of which, as Marx believed, would be the overthrow of the capitalist social order and the birth of a communistic (classless) society. Similar to Marx, Lenin advocated for the abolition of the class structure whereby all means of production would be commonly owned by members of society. Nevertheless, Lenin moved beyond Marx by claiming that a vanguard party of professional revolutionaries was needed in order to succeed in the proletariat revolution. Moreover, the teaching of Mao Zedong (Mao Tse-Tung) provided a variation of Marxism-Leninism known as Maoism (or Mao Zedong Thought). In Maoism, the main source of revolution is the peasantry in the countryside, who Mao believed could be led by the proletariat and the Communist Party of China (its vanguard).

Many left-wing terrorist groups are motivated by Marxist, Marxist-Leninist, or Maoist ideologies. A terrorist group in this category is the Red Army Faction (RAF), which was founded in the 1960s and was motivated by a Marxist-Leninist ideology. The RAF vehemently opposed capitalism and sought to attack the bourgeois values of West Germany.[24] These intentions were made clear in the communiqués of the group. The RAF, active from the 1970s to 1998,[25] engaged in terrorist attacks against West Germany using pistols, machine guns, bazookas, rocket-propelled grenades (RPGs), remote-control bombs, and airplane hijackings as tactics.

Another European group in this category is the Red Brigades (RB), otherwise known as the Brigatte Rossi or Brigatisti. The RB was founded in Milan, Italy, by a group of students. The RB, motivated by Marxist-Leninist ideology, sought the separation of Italy from the North Atlantic Treaty Organization (NATO) and the creation of a revolutionary state in Italy through the armed struggle of its operatives. To gain recognition for their cause from the Italian Communist Party, this left-wing terrorist group engaged in nonviolent demonstrations and protests. When the RB did not get the recognition from the Italian Communist Party that they desired, they conducted a bombing campaign between 1970 and 1974 that resulted in approximately 100 dead and 2,800 wounded. When the group folded in 1984, a splinter group known as the New Red Brigades was created, which had similar

---

24 At least, this is how RAF perceived West Germany.

25 In 1998, the RAF faxed an 18-page letter to the Reuters news agency stating that they were ending their terrorist acts against society.

goals as the RB. The European Union has designated the New Red Brigades as a terrorist organization.

A final example of a terrorist group in this category is the Shining Path or Sendero Luminoso (SL). The SL is a terrorist group in Peru motivated by Maoist ideology. The SL opposes all foreign influences on Peru and seeks to reorder the Peruvian society by destroying all existing Peruvian institutions and replacing them with ones based on communist ideals.[26] This group is well-known for its brutal terrorist campaign against Peruvian government officials and foreign diplomats. However, as Henderson argued, "ironically, although the group has attacked Peruvian officials and foreign diplomats, the majority of its violence has been directed against the very peasants its claim[ed] to be fighting for, brutally punishing people suspected of collaborating with the authorities."[27] It is estimated that this terrorist group has been responsible for approximately 30,000 deaths. Canada, the United States, and the European Union have designated the Shining Path as a terrorist organization.

Some terrorist groups in this category subscribe to more than one ideology. For instance, nationalist–separatist terrorists may also identify with left-wing ideology. A case in point is the Kurdistan Workers Party or Partiya Karkeran Kurdistan (PKK) in Turkey. This group is designated as a Marxist–Leninist separatist organization.[28] This group has been designated as such because it seeks to establish an independent Kurdish state within Turkey.[29] Canada, Australia, the United Kingdom, the United States, Turkey, and the European Union have designated the PKK as a terrorist organization. Another example of a nationalist–separatist terrorist group that identifies with left-wing ideology is the Popular Front for the Liberation of Palestine (PFLP). The PFLP, founded after the Arab defeat in the Arab–Israeli war in 1967, has been identified as a Marxist–Leninist nationalist movement.[30] This group envisions the "Palestinian nationalist movement as part of a broader movement to transform the Arab world along Marxist–Leninist lines. [In addition, although] the PFLP is committed to destroying Israel, it also

---

[26] This terrorist group's organization profile was retrieved from the collection of the National Consortium for the Study of Terrorism and Responses to Terrorism, Center for Excellence of the U.S. Department of Homeland Security based at the University of Maryland. Available at http://www.start.umd.edu/start/data_collections /tops/terrorist _organization_profile.asp?id=111.

[27] Henderson, H. 2001. *Global terrorism: The complete reference guide.* New York: Checkmark, 62.

[28] Kurdistan Workers' Party. 2011. *GlobalSecurity.org.* http://www.globalsecurity.org/military /world/para/pkk.htm.

[29] U.S. Department of State. 2007, April 30. Country reports on terrorism 2008. *Office of the Coordinator for Counterterrorism.* http://www.state.gov/s/ct/rls/crt/2006/82738.htm; Bruno, G. 2007, October 19. Inside the Kurdistan workers' party. *Council on Foreign Relations.* http://www.cfr.org/turkey/inside-kurdistan-workers-party-pkk/p14576.

[30] Katzman, K. 2000, August 17. Terrorism: Middle Eastern groups and state sponsors, 2000. *CRS Report for Congress.* http://www.globalsecurity.org/security/library/report/crs/crsterr3.htm.

opposes conservative Arab regimes, seeking to replace them with Marxist–Leninist states."[31] Canada, the United States and the European Union have designated the PFLP as a terrorist organization.

Right-Wing Terrorism

Right-wing terrorism usually involves individuals or groups that attack liberal democratic governments. Terrorists here are motivated by racism as well as antigovernment and antiregulatory beliefs. Some terrorists in this category believe that the country must rid itself of foreign elements within its borders to protect its rightful citizens. Individuals within these groups believe that their value systems are under attack and in need of protection. This form of terrorism is often perpetrated by persons holding extremist views about race or immigrants. They are prone to using intimidation and violence against select racial and ethnic groups. Right-wing terrorists "frequently desire to return to a time of past glory, which in their belief system has been lost or usurped by an enemy group or culture."[32]

Right-wing groups include white supremacist groups such as the Ku Klux Klan (KKK). This group, however, has not been officially designated by any country as a terrorist group, even though it operated as one. The KKK was founded in the United States by former Confederate soldiers after the Civil War to terrorize individuals they believed to be enemies of white, Christian, heterosexual Americans, including African Americans, Jewish Americans, and even Caucasians who sympathized with the Klan's targets. KKK members have also targeted homosexuals and immigrants. Factions of the KKK, along with other right-wing extremists, formed the Aryan Nation. Similar to the KKK, the Aryan Nation advocates anti-Semitism and the establishment of a white racist state.[33] White supremacist groups exist in other countries as well. In South Africa, a group known as National Warriors (*Nasionale Krygers*) was responsible for a series of terrorist attacks perpetrated against the black neighborhood of Soweto.[34]

Apart from hatred toward certain racial, religious, and ethnic minority groups, these terrorists are motivated by opposition to international organizations, governments, and government regulation and taxation. According to the FBI, one such domestic terrorist group that is currently active in the United States is the

---

[31] This terrorist group's organization profile was retrieved from the collection of the National Consortium for the Study of Terrorism and Responses to Terrorism, Center for Excellence of the U.S. Department of Homeland Security based at the University of Maryland. Available at http://www.start.umd.edu/start/data_collections/tops/terrorist _organization_profile.asp?id=85.

[32] Martin, G. 2003. *Understanding terrorism: Challenges, perspectives and issues.* London: Sage, 23.

[33] This terrorist group's organization profile was retrieved from the collection of the National Consortium for the Study of Terrorism and Responses to Terrorism, Center for Excellence of the U.S. Department of Homeland Security based at the University of Maryland. Available at http://www.start.umd.edu/start/data_collections/tops/terrorist_organization_profile.asp?id=29.

[34] Ibid., http://www.start.umd.edu/start/data_collections/tops/terrorist_organization_profile.asp?id=3647.

Sovereign Citizens. This group is motivated by an antigovernment ideology. Its members believe that even though they physically reside in the United States, "they are separate or 'sovereign' from the United States. As a result, they believe [that] they do not have to answer to any government authority, including courts, taxing entities, motor vehicle departments, or law enforcement."[35]

Right-wing terrorist groups may also subscribe to more than one ideology; for instance, a nationalist ideology. The Macedonian Revolutionary Organization is one such example. The Internal Macedonian Revolutionary Organization or *Vnatresno-Makedonska Revolucionerna Organizacija* (VMRO) is a right-wing nationalist terrorist group that operates in Greece and F.Y.R.O.M. This group believes that a greater Republic of Macedonia should be created, which will incorporate ethnic Macedonians residing in other countries such as Greece and Bulgaria.[36] This group, however, is also anti-Albanian and supports ethnic cleansing for the removal of Albanians in its territories. Another group motivated by multiple ideologies (nationalist–separatist, right-wing, and religious) is Kahane Chai, which operates in Israel, the West Bank, and Gaza. This terrorist group, using violent means, seeks to reinstate the ancient Biblical kingdom in Israel, expel all Arabs from Israeli territories, and create a Jewish theocracy.[37]

Religious Terrorism

Religious terrorism involves the use of violence by individuals or groups to further what they believe to be divinely commanded purposes. With this form of terrorism, the ultimate goal of the group is religiously defined. For instance, Jemaah Islamiya (JI), a Southeast Asia-based radical Islamic terrorist group, seeks to establish an Islamic state that spans Indonesia, Malaysia, Singapore, Brunei, southern Thailand, and the southern Philippines.[38] Another radical Islamic terrorist group is the Abu Sayyaf Group (ASG) or Abu Sayyaf, which operates in the southern Philippines and Malaysia. The goal of the group is the establishment of an Islamic state that will encompass parts of southern Thailand and the Philippines.[39] A further example is al-Qaeda, a radical Sunni Muslim organization that was founded in the 1980s by Osama bin Laden. Al-Qaeda's proclamation of the "The International Islamic Front for Jihad" the goal of which is to turn the Western world into part of the Islamic

---

35 Federal Bureau of Investigation (FBI). 2010, April 13. *Domestic terrorism: The sovereign citizen movement.* http://www.fbi.gov/news/stories/2010/april/sovereigncitizens_041310.

36 This terrorist group's organization profile was retrieved from the collection of the National Consortium for the Study of Terrorism and Responses to Terrorism, Center for Excellence of the U.S. Department of Homeland Security based at the University of Maryland. Available at http://www.start.umd.edu/start/data_collections/tops/terrorist_organization_profile.asp?id=3989.

37 Ibid., http://www.start.umd.edu/start/data_collections/tops/terrorist_organization_profile.asp?id=3750.

38 Ibid., http://www.start.umd.edu/start/data_collections/tops/terrorist_organization_profile.asp?id=3613.

39 Ibid., http://www.start.umd.edu/start/data_collections/tops/terrorist_organization_profile.asp?id=204.

nation that will govern according to *Sharia* (Sunni Islamic religious laws),[40] attests to this. *Sharia* maintains that the world is divided into *Dar al-Islam* (*The House of Islam*), which is composed of the lands where Islamic rule prevails, and *Dar al-Harb*, which consists of all of the remaining lands ruled by infidels.[41] Al-Qaeda believes that those in *Dar al-Harb* must be converted to Islam in a holy war (*jihad*) through the use of force.[42] This group is officially designated as a terrorist organization by Canada, Australia, Russia, the United Kingdom, and the United States.

With this form of terrorism, religion (Catholicism, Christianity, Sikhism, Hinduism, Judaism, Islam, and others) plays some role in defining or determining the methods of the group. Religious terrorists like Jamaat Ul Fuqra (Fuqra)—an organization created in Pakistan, which consists almost entirely of African American extremists who live in communal environments (called *jamaats*) in the United States—commit murders, bombings, white-collar crimes, cybercrime, and identity theft to serve Islam through violence.[43] In addition, al-Qaeda's members are "extremists who have no compunction about killing thousands of civilians . . . They do not feel constrained by any moral or humanitarian limits,"[44] because they "perceive violence to be a sacramental act, or divine duty, executed in direct response to some theological demand or imperative."[45] The religious ideology of al-Qaeda—the belief that it is the divine duty of its members (and those who wish to join them) to participate in the holy war between Islam and the lands of infidels—demonstrates this. The "lands of infidels" includes all persons and nations who do not share the same beliefs as al-Qaeda and all those who refuse to take up arms and join them, Muslims included. The sense of higher purpose and alienation from the rest of the world that arises from the distinction between Islam and all other lands ruled by infidels operates as a sanction for terrorists to use extremely violent measures against a more open-ended category of enemies; that is, anyone who is not a member of their faith.[46] Accordingly, this group views all of those who are not devout Muslims as legitimate targets for elimination.

---

40 Schweitzer, Y., and Shay, S. 2003. *The Globalization of terror: The challenge of al-Qaida and the response of international community.* London: Transaction, 3.

41 Ibid., pp. 3–4.

42 Ibid.

43 Kane, J. and Wall, A. 2005. *Identifying the links between white-collar crime and terrorism.* U.S. Department of Justice, Office of Justice Programs, National Institute of Justice. http://www.ncjrs.gov/pdffiles1/nij/grants/209520.pdf.

44 Urquhart, F. 2003. US links put Britain in front rank for dirty bomb attack by al Qaeda. *The Scotsman*, October 9, 2003, p. 7; Burnett, J. and Whyte, D. 2005. Embedded expertise and the new terrorism. *Journal for Crime, Conflict and the Media* 1 (4): 5.

45 Gurr, N. and Cole, B. 2000. *The new face of terrorism: Threats from weapons of mass destruction.* London: I.B. Tauris, 30.

46 Hoffman, B. 1998. *Inside terrorism.* London: Indigo, 48–49; Schweitzer, Y. and Shay, S. 2003. *The globalization of terror: The challenge of Al-Qaida and the response of international community.* London: Transaction, p. 3.

Religious terrorist groups may also subscribe to more than one ideology, for instance, with nationalist ideologies. For example, the Palestinian Islamic Jihad "believes that the annihilation of Israel and liberation of all of Palestine are prerequisites for recreating [sic] a pan-Islamic empire" and "that the Arab–Israeli conflict is not a national dispute over territory but rather a fundamentally religious conflict."[47] Another terrorist group in this category is Hamas, which operates in the West Bank, Gaza, and Israel and was formed as an outgrowth of the Palestinian branch of the Muslim Brotherhood. This group, combining Palestinian nationalism and religious fundamentalism, seeks to create an Islamic state based on *Sharia* by expelling Jewish Israelis from Israel. Likewise, Hezbollah, which operates in Lebanon, advocates for and operates toward the destruction of Israel. It further seeks "the establishment of a Shiite theocracy in Lebanon . . . and the elimination of Western influences from the Middle East."[48] Other religious groups have also sought the creation of an independent state in their country. Specifically, Babbar Khalsa International (BKI) is an organization of Sikh separatists that seeks to establish a sovereign state for Sikhs in northern India, which they refer to as Khalistan.[49] Furthermore, the Lord's Resistance Army, which operates in the Democratic Republic of Congo, Sudan, and Uganda, seeks to overthrow the government of Uganda and replace it with a theocracy based on the Ten Commandments and Acholi tradition.[50]

Special Interest Terrorism

As the name implies, special interest terrorism focuses on a single specific issue that individuals within the group believe has resulted from government action or inaction and requires immediate attention (e.g., environment, animal rights, and abortion). For that reason, it differs from other groups in that it lacks a broader revolutionary agenda. These groups have been known to use terrorist tactics when its members believe that the issue of which they are promoting awareness is becoming too urgent to be addressed through the usual slow progress of traditional campaigns. Accordingly, terrorists in this group engage in violent acts to gain publicity for their cause, force segments of the population and government to change their attitude toward the issue, and/or modify existing laws.

---

47 This terrorist group's organization profile was retrieved from the collection of the National Consortium for the Study of Terrorism and Responses to Terrorism, Center for Excellence of the U.S. Department of Homeland Security based at the University of Maryland. Available at http://www.start.umd.edu/start/data_collections/tops/terrorist_organization_profile.asp?id=82.

48 Ibid., http://www.start.umd.edu/start/data_collections/tops/terrorist_organization_profile.asp?id=3101.

49 Ibid., http://www.start.umd.edu/start/data_collections/tops/terrorist_organization_profile.asp?id=4568.

50 The Lord's Resistance Army. 2011. *GlobalSecurity.org.* http://www.globalsecurity.org/military/world/para/lra.htm; This terrorist group's organization profile was retrieved from the collection of the National Consortium for the Study of Terrorism and Responses to Terrorism, Center for Excellence of the U.S. Department of Homeland Security based at the University of Maryland. Available at http://www.start.umd.edu/start/data_collections/tops/terrorist_organization_profile.asp?id=3513.

A well-known example of a form of special interest terrorism is environmental terrorism (ecoterrorism). Ecoterrorism involves the infliction of economic damage and personal harm to those who profit from the development and destruction of environmental resources, such as the logging industry, fur companies, laboratories that test products on animals, and restaurant chains that are perceived to be harmful to animals. Ecoterrorists, such as the Animal Liberation Front, Earth Liberation Front, and Earth First!, use terrorist methods—especially arson and vandalism—to promote radical environmentalism. Usually, ecoterrorists sabotage the property of industries to inflict economic damage on those who they perceive as harming the natural environment or animals. However, they have also been known to engage in bombings, intimidation, assault, and the murder of individuals they believe are harming the environment or animals.

The Animal Liberation Front (ALF) and Earth Liberation Front (ELF) are examples of groups that engage in this form of terrorism. In both the United States and the United Kingdom, the ALF "are clandestine in operation . . . [and] amorphous in organization and membership."[51] Individuals are considered part of ALF when they are a vegetarian or vegan and engage in direct action according to the group's guidelines, which usually involves engaging in criminal activities designed to cause economic loss or otherwise disrupt the target's operations. Examples of direct action include breaking into research facilities and removing the animals as well as intimidating executives, management and/or employees of the target by placing fake bombs in buildings or sending hoax anthrax letters. Similarly, individuals are considered part of ELF when they take action according to the group's guidelines, such as property destruction and industrial sabotage (e.g., arson and disabling logging equipment) to halt the destruction of the environment.[52] As such, like ALF, ELF is made up of autonomous groups of individuals.

In addition to ecoterrorism, another form of special interest terrorism is engaged in by anti-abortion extremists. Like ecoterrorists, their primary tactic is arson, yet they have been known to intentionally inflict harm on individuals (by bombing or shooting). Indeed, anti-abortion extremists target abortion clinics and their doctors and staff. A case in point is the Army of God, a domestic anti-abortion terrorist group in the United States. This group believes that the use of violence and intimidation are appropriate tools in the fight against abortion. This group's primary targets are abortion providers and homosexuals, and it has a "how to" manual for its members on engaging in violence against these targets. One passage of this manual reads,

---

[51] U.S. Department of Justice. (1993). Report to Congress on the extent and the effects of domestic and international terrorism in animal enterprises. *The Physiologist* 36 (6): 249.

[52] This terrorist group's organization profile was retrieved from the collection of the National Consortium for the Study of Terrorism and Responses to Terrorism, Center for Excellence of the U.S. Department of Homeland Security based at the University of Maryland. Available at http://www.start.umd.edu/start/data_collections/tops/ terrorist_organization_profile.asp?id=41.

Our Most Dread Sovereign Lord God requires that whosoever sheds man's blood, by man shall his blood be shed. Not out of hatred of you, but out of love for the persons you exterminate, we are forced to take arms against you.[53]

Some of the tactics included in the manual include using butyric acid against facilities (this causes disruption of operations and property damage, often requiring the replacement of furniture, carpeting, and extensive clean-up of the facilities), committing arson, building bombs, and bombing facilities. The Army of God has claimed responsibility for bombing clinics and bars frequented by homosexuals. After the bombings of a gay nightclub and an abortion clinic in Atlanta, Georgia, media outlets received letters claiming credit for the attacks that were purported to be from the Army of God. Individuals seeking abortions and physicians and staff in Planned Parenthood and abortion facilities have also been assaulted, harassed, stalked, intimidated, and in some instances, killed by anti-abortion extremists. The most recent murder of a physician, Dr. George Tiller, involved anti-abortion extremist Scott Roeder. Specifically, in March 2009, Roeder went to Dr. Tiller's church in Wichita, Kansas, and shot and killed him. The Army of God has additionally been implicated in bioterrorist attacks in the United States. About a month after 9/11, Clayton Waagner sent more than 550 hoax anthrax letters to over 250 abortion and family planning clinics in seventeen U.S. states and the District of Columbia.[54]

Revolutionaries, Terrorists, or Both?

The determination of whether someone is a terrorist also depends on who is engaging in this activity. Throughout history, in some countries, groups have been labeled as terrorists, whereas in others they are classified as freedom fighters, urban guerrillas, armed rebels, revolutionaries, and activists. For instance, Carlos Marighella, in his manual *Urban Guerrilla*, defined an urban guerrilla as "a revolutionary and an ardent patriot, he is a fighter for his country's liberation, a friend of the people and of freedom." Islamic extremists believe that their *jihad* against Americans is justified as a form of legitimate self-defense in retaliation for what they perceive to be the war on Islam in the United States.[55] The label given to the individual or group thus depends on the person or country providing it and their interpretation of the group. That is, if an individual or state identifies with the victim (or victims) of an attack, then the individual is more likely to identify the act as that of terrorism; whereas, if an individual or state identifies with the

---

[53] Ibid., http://www.start.umd.edu/start/data_collections/tops/terrorist_organization_profile.asp?id=28.

[54] National Abortion Federation. 2010. *Anti-abortionist extremists/Clayton Waagner.* http://www.prochoice.org/about_abortion/violence/clayton_waagner.html; National Abortion Federation. 2010. *Anti-abortionist extremists/The Army of God and justifiable homicide.* http://www.prochoice.org/about_abortion/violence/army_god.html.

[55] This has been expressed by multiple al-Qaeda leaders and operatives (Osama bin Laden, Adam Gadahn, and Abu Musab al-Zarqawi, to name a few) on numerous occasions.

Box 1-1   Narcoterrorism

Narcoterrorism is a term that was originally used to describe the use of terrorist tactics by drug traffickers to influence the government and prevent them from engaging in efforts to stop the drug trade. According to Hartelius, "the concept of 'narcoterrorism' was introduced in 1983 by Peruvian President Belaunde Terry to designate terrorist-like attacks against his country's drug enforcement police. Drug criminals utilized methods from political assailants to influence the politics of the country by causing terror and obstructing justice."[1] This term has been used by others to describe the use of drug trade and trafficking to fund the operations of certain governments and terrorist groups.[2] The Revolutionary Armed Forces of Colombia (FARC) engages in narcotics trafficking to fund its operations; so too does the Taliban, which gains a "significant amount of funds from the Afghan opium trade, whether actually trafficking or engaging in protection rackets."[3]

---

[1] Hartelius, J. 2008, February. Narcoterrorism. *The East-West Institute & the Swedish Carnegie Institute,* iii, http://www.ewi.info/system/files/reports/Narcoterrorism.pdf; Pacheco, F. C. 2008. Narcofearance: How has narcoterrorism settled in Mexico? *Studies in Conflict & Terrorism* 32 (12): 1023.

[2] Ackerman, R. K. 2010, October. Intelligence Key to Counterdrug Efforts. *Signal* 65(2): 51; Ehrenfeld, R. 1990. *Narco-terrorism* . New York: Basic, xiii; Hollis, A. 2007. Narcoterrorism: A definitional & operational transnational challenge. In *Transnational threats,* ed. K. L. Thachuk, 24. Westport, CT: Praeger.

[3] Ackerman, R. K. 2010, October. Intelligence key to counterdrug efforts. *Signal* 65 (2): 51.

---

perpetrator (or perpetrators) of an attack, then the act is more likely not to be characterized as a terrorist attack and to be "regarded in a more sympathetic, if not positive (or, at the worst, ambivalent) light; and it is not terrorism."[56] For example, according to the U.S. Department of State, the Lebanese government and the majority of the Arab world view Hezbollah as a legitimate resistance group and political party.[57] Other countries and their citizens also view certain terrorists favorably. For instance, the majority of those surveyed in Jordan viewed Hamas favorably.[58] The perception of who constitutes a terrorist differs even between sectors or regions within countries. An example of this was seen is Nicaragua, where the "Nicaraguan elite regarded the Sandinista National Liberation Front (FSLN) as a terrorist group, while much of the rest of the country regarded the FSLN as freedom fighters."[59]

---

[56] Hoffman, B. 1998. *Inside terrorism.* London: Indigo, 31.

[57] U.S. Department of State. 2009, April 30. Country reports on terrorism. *Office of the Coordinator for Counterterrorism.* http://www.state.gov/s/ct/rls/crt/2008/122449.htm.

[58] Pew Research Center. 2010, December 2. Most embrace a role for Islam in politics: Muslim public divided on Hamas and Hezbollah. *Pew Global Attitudes Project.* http://www.pewglobal.org/2010/12/ 02/muslims-around-the-world-divided-on-hamas-and-hezbollah/.

[59] Hudson, R. A. 1999. *The sociology and psychology of terrorism: Who becomes a terrorist and why?* 5. A report prepared under an Interagency Agreement by the Federal Research Division, Library of Congress. http://www.loc.gov/rr/frd/pdf-files/Soc_Psych_of_Terrorism.pdf.

At times, insurgencies and guerrilla warfare are assumed to be synonymous with terrorism; the reason being is that often guerrillas and insurgents use similar tactics as terrorists. They both use actual violence or the threat of harm to persons and/or property. According to Carlos Marighella,

> [i]n Brazil, the number of violent actions carried out by urban guerrillas, including executions, explosions, seizures of weapons, ammunition and explosives, assaults on banks and prisons, etc., [was] significant enough to leave no room for doubt as to the actual aims of the revolutionaries; all are witnesses to the fact that [the urban guerrillas were engaged] in a full revolutionary war and that this war can be waged only by violent means.[60]

Guerrillas often engage in terror tactics, which are used to create mayhem and instill widespread fear in the target government and its population. To succeed, the terror campaign has to bring about support for the guerrillas' cause by sympathizers. Much the same as terrorists, the guerrillas' terror campaign also seeks to reveal the government's repressive nature in order to gain the public's sympathy and support for their cause.

The difference between these two terms—terrorism and guerrilla warfare—essentially boils down to the intent of the actor engaging in the act or acts that appear to be "terroristic." If guerrillas deliberately target civilians in their attacks, then their actions will be labeled as a terrorist attack. Conversely, if guerrillas primarily target military and security personnel of the target country, their actions will be considered a guerrilla attack. Indeed, a violent political, religious, or ideological group often becomes labeled as a terrorist as soon as its actions claim the lives of civilians or noncombatants. Yet the line that seeks to distinguish these two topics is essentially blurred because history shows that guerrillas have attacked both military and nonmilitary targets to achieve their goals (see Box 1-2). In other situations, extensive property damage alone can prompt a government to label a group of dissidents as terrorists; this was seen in the United States with certain extremist animal rights and environmental groups.[61] Yet this distinction further complicates matters, as both guerrillas and terrorists often target civilians and seek to damage property.

A better distinction between guerrillas and terrorists is that the former often fight according to the conventions of war, something that is not seen in the case of terrorists. In fact, those who engage in an armed struggle against a state are not considered terrorists if they operate according to the principles of international law. Specifically, in Article 2 of the *Convention on the Suppression of Terrorism*, the League of Arab States has explicitly stated that "all cases of struggle by whatever means, including armed struggle, against foreign occupation and aggression

---

60 Marighella, C. 1969. How the urban guerrilla lives. *Marighella Internet Archive*. http://www.marxists.org/archive/marighella-carlos/1969/06/minimanual-urban-guerrilla/ch03.htm.

61 Although nowadays, extremist animal rights and environmental groups also target civilians in their attacks.

Box 1-2 Food for Thought—Chechen Groups: Freedom Fighters or Terrorists?

Chechens, an ethic minority group from the North Caucasus region, seek independence from Russia. The Chechens have claimed that Russia is depriving them of basic human rights. Many of the attacks by Chechens have been aimed at Russia's occupying force; however, they have also engaged in indiscriminate attacks against civilians in non-Chechen Russia. For instance, in September 2003, Chechens seized control of a school in Beslan. In this incident, over 350 individuals were killed, more than 150 of which were children. Another incident occurred in November 2009, in which Chechens detonated explosives on the Nevsky Express, causing it to derail and kill 27 individuals. A further example involved two female Chechen suicide bombers, who detonated explosives in Russia's subway stations (Lubyanka and Park Kultury) in March 2010, killing 39 people.

Some argue that Chechens are freedom fighters. Others argue that they are terrorists. What do you think? And why?

for liberation and self-determination, in accordance with the principles of international law, shall not be regarded as" terrorism.[62] This was reiterated in Article 2(a) of the *Convention of the Organization of the Islamic Conference on Combating International Terrorism*.[63] Accordingly, guerrillas, revolutionaries, and the like who follow the conventions of war and adhere to the principles of international law should not be considered terrorists.

State Terrorism: Myth or Reality?

History has shown that both individuals and governments engage in terrorist acts. Thus, to be complete, discussions of terrorism must also include terrorist tactics used by governments. States may sponsor terrorists or engage in terrorism themselves. State-sponsored terrorism involves the use of violence by governments (or factions within governments) against the citizens of the country, factions within the government, or foreign groups or governments. With regard to this form of terrorism, according to the UN *Declaration on Measures to Eliminate International Terrorism*,[64]

> States, guided by the purposes and principles of the Charter of the United Nations and other relevant rules of international law, must refrain from organizing, instigating, assisting or participating in terrorist acts in territories of other States,

---

[62] Council of Arab Ministers of the Interior and the Council of Arab Ministers of Justice. (1998). *The Arab Convention for the Suppression of Terrorism*.

[63] UN *Convention of the Organisation of the Islamic Conference on Combating International Terrorism* (1999).

[64] Part II, paragraph 4 of the UN *Declaration on Measures to Eliminate International Terrorism* (1994).

or from acquiescing in or encouraging activities within their territories directed toward the commission of such acts.

This declaration also holds that states must

refrain from organizing, instigating, facilitating, financing, encouraging or tolerating terrorist activities and to take appropriate practical measures to ensure that their respective territories are not used for terrorist installations or training camps, or for the preparation or organization of terrorist acts intended to be committed against other States or their citizens.[65]

According to the U.S. Department of State, one of the most active state sponsors of terrorism is Iran. This country has supported the Taliban (a militant fundamentalist Islamic group that established a government in Afghanistan) and terrorist groups such as the Palestinian Islamic Jihad, the Popular Front for the Liberation of Palestine-General Command, Hezbollah, and Hamas.[66] The United States has also labeled Cuba, Sudan, and Syria as states that sponsor terrorism.

Some countries may be labeled as engaging in terrorism, while other countries engaged in similar behavior may not be. Instead, the latter may be viewed as repressive regimes, authoritarian systems, and dictatorships. The determination of whether a state engages in acts of terrorism also depends on who is classifying them. If a country or state is using violence, it is usually considered as a legitimate act of war or reprisal for harm done that is necessary to protect and defend its citizens and territory. However, history shows that this is not always the case. Infamous leaders of governments have killed millions of innocent victims and not opponents of their regimes. For example, Adolph Hitler sought to eliminate the non-Aryan race from Germany by killing Jews and Gypsies en masse. However, he, and other leaders who engaged in similar conduct, were not classified as terrorists nor described as engaging in terrorist acts. Instead, they were said to have conducted acts of genocide.

Genocide is the systematic destruction of a particular group of people on the basis of their ethnicity, nationality, political affiliation, culture, religion, race, sex, or disability. This mass killing can be carried out by a national leader, usually a government, against its people or a dominant group against a minority group. A disproportionate number of the 20th-century genocides occurred as a result of the efforts of regimes to counter major guerrilla insurgencies or to defeat internal enemies of the regime. The ongoing civil war in the Democratic Republic of Congo is a classic example. The government effort to defeat guerrilla insurgencies resulted in the mass killing of civilians and guerrillas alike. Leaders who had engaged in genocide to stabilize their rule in the past include "Hitler of Germany, Stalin of [the] former Soviet

---

65 Part II, paragraph 5(a) of the UN *Declaration on Measures to Eliminate International Terrorism* (1994).

66 Bruno, G. 2010, October 7. State sponsors: Iran. *Council on Foreign Relations*. http://www.cfr.org /iran/state-sponsors-iran/p9362.

Union, Mao [Zedong] of China, and Pol Pot of Cambodia."[67] Other countries have also experienced genocide. For example, in Rwanda, the Hutu majority attempted to completely annihilate a victim population composed almost entirely of the Tutsi minority. Rwanda, along with other countries (e.g., Burundi, Pakistan, and Sri Lanka), have utilized their military and paramilitary forces to commit mass murder with the intention of exterminating subgroups within their territory.[68]

Nevertheless, this form of collective punishment is similar to terrorism. Consider the definition of genocide provided by the United Nations in the *Convention on the Prevention and Punishment of the Crime of Genocide*. According to Article 2 of this convention, genocide occurs when acts (e.g., killing members of a group and/or inflicting serious bodily or mental harm on members of a group) are committed with the "intent to destroy, in whole or in part, a national, ethnical, racial or religious group." This type of behavior has been seen with terrorists. In fact, Abu Musab al-Zarqawi (a well-known al-Qaeda operative who died in 2006) had stated al-Qaeda's intent of engaging in the mass killing of Shia Muslims. Al-Qaeda has perpetrated and verbalized similar acts against Jews, Americans, and their allies. Indeed, on February 23, 1998, Osama bin Laden (former leader of al-Qaeda who died in May 2011) issued a *fatwah* (a religious ruling), which stated that killing "Americans and their allies—civilians and military—is an individual duty for every Muslim who can do it in any country in which it is possible to do it." Despite these similarities, genocide is not used to describe al-Qaeda's actions, even though its resemblance to this term is apparent.

The problem with defining terrorism is not so much that existing attempts have been inaccurate, but that they are not complete enough to encompass all forms of terrorism and explain how terrorism relates to other forms of violence. Coupled with the divergent opinions of individuals and states as well as beliefs on what constitutes terrorism, the creation of a universally accepted, single definition is akin to the task of Sisyphus. The quest for it seems just as futile as the belief of Sisyphus that at some point the boulder he rolled up the steep hill[69] would eventually reach the top without being plunged back down.

HYPOTHETICAL SCENARIO

A terrorist group exists in Xanthi, Greece, which has assassinated government officials and engaged in a spree of bombing campaigns against Greek military installations and soldiers. This group seeks to liberate itself from Greece and form an independent Islamic state.

What type(s) of terrorism is (are) described above? Why do you think so?

---

[67] Colaresi, M., and Carey, S. C. 2004. To kill or to protect: Security forces, domestic institutions, and genocide. *Journal of Conflict Resolution* 52 (1): 46.

[68] Ibid., p. 43.

[69] According to Greek mythology, this was the eternal punishment imposed upon him by the gods.

CHAPTER SUMMARY

Numerous definitions of terrorism exist concerning who terrorists are and what terrorists do. These definitions tend to overlap with other forms of violence such as guerrilla warfare and genocide. The existence of terrorism depends on the individual, group, or state defining it. Some individuals, groups, or states view certain individuals as freedom fighters, while others view the same people as terrorists. Terrorism can be classified according to the means terrorists use to achieve their goals and the ends they seek. Several types of terrorism exist, including nationalist–separatist, left-wing, right-wing, religious, and special interest terrorism. States have also been known to either engage in terrorism or sponsor terrorists. Due to the different forms of terrorism, its relationship with other forms of violence, and the differing perspectives on what it constitutes, the creation of a universal definition of terrorism is highly unlikely.

REVIEW QUESTIONS

1. How is terrorism defined?
2. Why do nationalists–separatists engage in terrorism? Religious terrorists?
3. Who do left-wing terrorists target?
4. What motivates right-wing terrorists?
5. What do special interest terrorists seek?
6. What are the differences between a terrorist and a guerrilla? A terrorist and a freedom fighter?
7. What are the differences between terrorism and genocide?

chapter two

Perspectives on Terrorism: Hypotheses and Theories

Before embarking on an analysis of counterterrorism strategies and policies, a fundamental question needs to be addressed: Why do individuals engage in terrorism? This chapter seeks to answer this very question by examining the psychological, sociological, and criminological perspectives on terrorism. In particular, it considers the individual and group processes involved in individuals joining terrorist groups and engaging in terrorist attacks. It additionally explores the factors that motivate individual and group terrorist activity. This chapter further seeks to answer the following questions: What "type" of person is more likely to engage in terrorist attacks or suicide attacks? Is there a terrorist personality? Are terrorists rational actors, or do they suffer from a psychological disorder? Do terrorists share common identifiable characteristics or traits? Is there a terrorist profile that can be used to identify potential terrorists?

BECAUSE THEY ARE POOR

Some theorists and researchers hold that poverty causes individuals to engage in terrorism. For example, from her study of terrorists in Pakistan, Stern concluded that most of the individuals that join terrorist groups are poor.[1] Hudson offered a

---

[1] Stern, J. 2000. Pakistan's jihad culture. *Foreign Affairs* 79 (November/December): 115–126; Koseli, M. 2007. The poverty, inequality, and terrorism relationship: An empirical analysis of some root causes of terrorism. In *Understanding terrorism: Analysis of sociological and psychological aspects*, eds. S. Ozeren, I. D. Gunes, and D. M. Al-Badayneh, 111. NATO Science for Peace and Security Studies (Vol. 22). Oxford, UK: IOS Press.

similar conclusion from his study of terrorist groups.[2] Specifically, he found that "terrorists in much of the developing world tend to be drawn from the lower sections of society. The rank and file of Arab terrorist organizations include substantial numbers of poor people, many of them homeless refugees."[3] Likewise, in their study of the Kurdistan Workers' Party (PKK) in Turkey, Barkey and Fuller found that this terrorist group drew its membership from the lowest social classes.[4] Nevertheless, while poverty might explain why some individuals or groups engage in terrorism, it is not evident in all terrorists and terrorist groups.

Actually, available evidence suggests little validity in the claims that terrorists come from impoverished backgrounds.[5] In particular, in some regions, terrorists are more likely to be middle class and educated.[6] Hudson also noted that "European and Japanese terrorists are more likely the products of affluence and higher education than of poverty."[7] In addition, terrorists associated with al-Qaeda who were captured in Southeast Asia did not come from impoverished backgrounds.[8] Moreover, Krueger and Malecková,[9] along with others,[10] challenged the notion

[2] Hudson, R. A. 1999. *The sociology and psychology of terrorism: Who becomes a terrorist and why?* A report prepared under an Interagency Agreement by the Federal Research Division, Library of Congress. http://www.loc.gov/rr/frd/pdf-files/Soc_Psych_of_Terrorism.pdf.

[3] Ibid.; Malecková, J. 2006. Terrorists and the societies from which they come. In *Tangled roots: Social and psychological factors in the genesis of terrorism*, ed. J. Victoroff, 36. NATO Security Through Science Series (Vol. 11). Oxford, UK: IOS Press.

[4] Barkey, H. J., and Fuller, G. E. 1998. *Turkey's Kurdish question.* Lanham, MD: Rowman & Littlefield.

[5] Atran, S. 2003. Genesis of suicide terrorism. *Science* 299 (March 7): 1534–1539.

[6] Post, J. M. 2007. *The mind of the terrorist.* New York: Palgrave Macmillan, 134; Malecková, K. 2005. Improverished terrorists: Stereotype or reality? In *Root causes of terrorism*, ed. T. Bjørgo, 33–43. London: Routledge; Victoroff, J. 2005. The mind of the terrorist: A review and critique of psychological approaches. *Journal of Conflict Resolution* 49 (1): 3–42; Agnew, R. 2010. A general strain theory of terrorism. *Theoretical Criminology* 14 (2): 134.

[7] Hudson, R. A. 1999. *The sociology and psychology of terrorism: Who becomes a terrorist and why?* A report prepared under an Interagency Agreement by the Federal Research Division, Library of Congress. http://www.loc.gov/rr/frd/pdf-files/Soc_Psych_of_Terrorism.pdf; Malecková, J. 2006. Terrorists and the societies from which they come. In *Tangled roots: Social and psychological factors in the genesis of terrorism*, ed. J. Victoroff, 36. NATO Security Through Science Series (Vol. 11). Oxford, UK: IOS Press.

[8] Singapore Ministry of Home Affairs. 2003, January. *White paper: The Jemaah Islamiyah arrests and the threat of terrorism.* http://www.mha.gov.sg/publication_details.aspx?pageid=35&cid=354.

[9] Krueger, A. B., and Malecková, J. 2002. *Education, poverty, political violence and terrorism: Is there a casual connection?* NBER Working Paper 9074; Krueger, A. B., and Malecková, J. 2003. Poverty and terrorism: Is there a casual connection? *Journal of Economic Perspectives* 17:119–144; Malecková, J. 2006. Terrorists and the societies from which they come. In *Tangled roots: Social and psychological factors in the genesis of terrorism*, ed. J. Victoroff, 35. NATO Security Through Science Series (Vol. 11). Oxford, UK: IOS Press.

[10] Sageman, M. 2004. *Understanding terror networks.* Philadelphia: University of Pennsylvania Press.

that poverty prevails among the Middle Eastern terrorist groups.[11] For instance, Krueger and Malecková compared 129 terrorists from Hezbollah's military wing with the general Lebanese population from which these individuals were drawn, which revealed that the Hezbollah terrorists did not come from the most impoverished groups of Lebanon.[12] Other terrorist groups in the Middle East that were compared and studied provided similar results. A case in point is a study that was conducted on the biographical information of 285 militants from the Palestinian Islamic Jihad and Hamas compared with the Palestinian population.[13] This study revealed that the terrorists came from affluent backgrounds. Another study that was conducted that reviewed the biographies of 27 members of the Jewish underground also did not support the claim that terrorists come from economically disadvantaged groups; in fact, many held respectable and reputable positions in society.[14] A study of suicide terrorists further revealed that neither poverty nor a lack of education has a causal relationship with suicide terrorism.[15]

BECAUSE THEY ARE DENIED ACCESS TO OPPORTUNITIES

It is clear that material conditions do not account for all forms of terrorism. If they did, terrorism would be committed only by underprivileged individuals living in the poorest regions in the world. This, however, is not the case. Actual material deprivation is thus not an accurate predictor of terrorism. Other theorists argue that a better predictor of terrorism is perceived or relative deprivation.[16] Relative deprivation can be defined as the discrepancy between what one expects in life and what one gets. Specifically, it is "defined as actors' perception of discrepancy between their value expectations and their environment's apparent value capabilities. This deprivation may be individual or collective."[17] It occurs when individuals or groups subjectively perceive themselves as unfairly disadvantaged in relation to

---

[11] Malecková, J. 2006. Terrorists and the societies from which they come. In *Tangled roots: Social and psychological factors in the genesis of terrorism*, ed. J. Victoroff, 35. NATO Security Through Science Series (Vol. 11). Oxford, UK: IOS Press.

[12] Ibid.

[13] Berrebi, C. 2003. *Evidence about the link between education, poverty and terrorism among Palestinians*. Princeton University Industrial Relations Section Working Paper No. 477. http://papers.ssrn.com /sol3/papers.cfm?abstract_id=487467.

[14] Segal, H. 1988. *Dear brothers: The West Bank Jewish underground*. Woodmere, NY: Beit-Shamai; Malecková, J. 2006. Terrorists and the societies from which they come. In *Tangled roots: Social and psychological factors in the genesis of terrorism*, ed. J. Victoroff, 36. NATO Security Through Science Series (Vol. 11). Oxford, UK: IOS Press.

[15] Atran, S. 2004. Mishandling suicide terrorism. *The Washington Quarterly* 27 (3): 67–90.

[16] Moghaddam, F. M. 2005. The staircase to terrorism: A psychological exploration. *American Psychologist* 60 (2): 162.

[17] Ted Robert Gurr cited in Hudson, R. A. 1999. *The sociology and psychology of terrorism: Who becomes a terrorist and why?* 162. A report prepared under an Interagency Agreement by the Federal Research Division, Library of Congress. http://www.loc.gov/rr/frd/pdf-files /Soc_Psych_of_Terrorism.pdf.

other reference groups, perceived as having similar attributes as their own, and that the individual/group are deserving of similar rewards as that reference group. In short, it is an indicator of how deprived one individual or a group feels in relation to another individual or group. The key here is the word "feel," as a person may not actually be deprived. What is crucial is that the individual perceives that he or she does not have something that they want, that another individual, who is in a comparable situation to their own, has. Furthermore, the individual must believe that they are entitled to the same thing.

In psychology, the use of relative deprivation is often associated with the frustration–aggression hypothesis. Scholars have stated that terrorists' behavior could be explained by the frustration–aggression hypothesis, which holds that every frustration an individual experiences leads that individual to engage in some type of aggression.[18] Others, however, have dismissed this hypothesis as being too simplistic and erroneous, as it holds that every act of aggression is always a consequence of a frustration experienced by an individual.[19]

In criminology, the use of relative deprivation is often conflated with anomie theory. Anomie refers to a state of "normlessness,"[20] in which the normal conditions of a society have been disrupted. Anomie theory posits that crime results from a disparity between culturally induced aspirations (e.g., the successful attainment of the American Dream) and the opportunities available to individuals to realize them.[21] Merton proposed several modes of adaptation to the strain[22]—in this case, the inability to achieve certain goals—and they were as follows: *conformity* (individuals accept their inability to achieve desired goals but pursue them anyway); *innovation* (pursue societal goals but use illegal means to achieve them); *ritualism* (no longer pursues societal goals but ardently adheres to legitimate means); *retreatism* (rejects both societal goals and the means to achieve them; stops being a productive member in society); and *rebellion* (rejects existing societal goals and the means to achieve them and develops new societal goals and new means to achieve them).

In an anomic society, all sectors of the society become fixated with the same goals that are often quite difficult for specific sectors of society to achieve (e.g., the poor or working class). These goals are viewed by all as an indicator of success. The sectors of society that have fewer resources and facilities expect to achieve the same goals as the more affluent sector. Accordingly, individuals in these sectors tend to resort to any means necessary to achieve these goals. In fact, an individual,

---

18 Dollard, J. et al. 1939. *Frustration and aggression*. New Haven, CT: Yale University Press.

19 Hudson, R. A. 1999. *The sociology and psychology of terrorism: Who becomes a terrorist and why?* 19. A report prepared under an Interagency Agreement by the Federal Research Division, Library of Congress. http://www.loc.gov/rr/frd/pdf-files/Soc_Psych_of_Terrorism.pdf.

20 The term was coined by Emile Durkheim; see Durkheim, E. 1947. *The division of labor in society*. Trans. G. Simpson. New York: Free Press.

21 Merton, R. 1938. Social structure and anomie. *American Sociological Review* 3 (5): 672–682.

22 Ibid.; Strain is defined as the "events or conditions that are disliked by individuals." Agnew, R. 2010. A general strain theory of terrorism. *Theoretical Criminology* 14 (2): 135.

if unable to achieve goals through legitimate means, is more likely to turn to alternative means to realize their societal and culturally induced aspirations. Their choice will not be guided by moralistic considerations when an anomic culture is prevalent. Instead, an individual will choose whichever is the most opportune and expedient way to achieve their goals, regardless of the legitimacy of the path taken to do so.

It is important to note that there are clear differences between relative deprivation theory and anomie theory; in particular, Merton's version of anomie involves an inability to realize culturally induced notions of success. It does not involve comparisons between groups but individuals measuring themselves against a general goal. The empirical implications of this difference in emphasis are significant: anomie theory would naturally predict the vast majority of crime to occur at the bottom of society among the lower classes, but relative deprivation theory does not necessarily have this overwhelming class focus. Utilizing the two theories together serves to provide a clearer picture of how social stresses and forces can be examined in conjunction with the subjective desires of individuals/groups in determining the origins of crime, even terrorism.

Some research in this area has partially supported the application of anomie theory to terrorism.[23] Others have illustrated the applicability and significance of relative deprivation theory to terrorism. For instance, Atran applied relative deprivation theory to suicide terrorism and observed that relative (and not absolute) deprivation was more significant in recruitment of suicide terrorists.[24] And yet, overall, studies have shown a weak link between absolute (and to a lesser extent relative) material deprivation and terrorism.[25] Indeed, history is replete with examples of individuals who have engaged in (or attempted to engage in) terrorist attacks in which material or relative deprivation did not play a role in their decisions to engage in terrorism. One such example was Nizar Trabelsi, who was a European soccer star before he traveled to Afghanistan and attended al-Qaeda training camps. Trabelsi was convicted in 2003 of planning to bomb a NATO base in Belgium.

Many believe that a better predictor of terrorism involves other forms of frustration beyond the inability of an individual to achieve their goals. In fact, many argue

---

[23] Ozgur, N. 2009. An application of anomie and strain theories to terrorism: Suicide attacks in Turkey. PhD diss., Virginia Commonwealth University; Koseli, M. 2006. Poverty, inequality and terrorism relationship in Turkey. PhD diss., 217, Wilder School of Government and Public Affairs, Commonwealth University, Richmond, VA.

[24] Atran, S. 2004. *Trends in suicide terrorism: Sense and nonsense.* World Federation of Scientists Permanent Monitoring Panel on Terrorism, Erice, Sicily. http://sitemaker.umich.edu/satran/files/atran-trends.pdf.

[25] For example, Smelser, N. J. 2007. *The faces of terrorism: Social and psychological dimensions.* Princeton, NJ: Princeton University Press; Merari, A. 2005. Social, organizational and psychological factors in suicide terrorism. In *Root causes of terrorism,* ed. T. Bjørgo. London: Routledge; De Coning, C. 2004. Poverty and terrorism: The root cause debate? *Conflict Trends* 3:20–29; Turk, A. 2004. Sociology of terrorism. *Annual Review of Sociology* 30:271–286; Atran, S. 2003. Genesis of suicide terrorism. *Science* 299(5612): 1538.

that individuals commit terrorist activities due to strain (and/or grievances).[26] They differ, however, in the types of strain that cause terrorism. Strain can include (apart from absolute and material deprivation) discrimination, denial of human rights, military occupation, harsh state oppression, and displacement or loss of one's home-land.[27] Strain can also refer to the problems associated with globalization. Consider non-Western countries. The spread of Western ideals and lifestyles in non-Western countries has had a significant impact in those areas.[28] Individuals residing in these territories react in one of two ways to the introduction of Western values and life-styles into their societies:[29] either (1) individuals in these countries will become anxious that their cultural traditions and values are being threatened by these newfound ideals. Frustrated by the perceived threat to their culture and collective identity, individuals may thus resort to violence in an attempt to preserve their own culture and traditions; or (2) individuals residing in these areas will embrace them and pursue the affluent lifestyle and freedoms, both political and social, associated with Western countries, such as the United States. If this occurs, however, frustration and anger may occur among individuals in these populations because of their inability to realize the idealistic lifestyle and/or their inability to have similar Western freedoms within their own countries. Strain, however, need not actually be experienced by the individual or group engaging in the terrorist attack. Individuals will engage in a terrorist attack if a group of "others" they identify with are experiencing strain. A case in point is ecoterrorists. These individuals engage in terrorist attacks as a direct response to harms done to other entities (e.g., animals).

Studies that have been conducted on the links between terrorism and strain have indicated mixed and weak support for any causal connections between the two.[30] The problem associated with strain theory is that it fails to explain why individuals turn to terrorism for only a specific and limited period of time. It also fails

---

26 For example, Callaway, R. L., and Harrelson-Stephens, J. 2006. Toward a theory of terrorism: Human security as a determinant of terrorism. *Studies in Conflict & Terrorism* 29 (7): 679–702; Piazza, J. A. 2006. Rooted in poverty? Terrorism, poor economic development, and social cleavages. *Terrorism and Political Violence* 18 (1): 159–177; Blazak, R. 2001. White boys to terrorist men. *American Behavioral Scientist* 44 (6): 982–1000; Gurr, T. R., and Moore, W. H. 1997. Ethnopolitical rebellion: A cross-sectional analysis of the 1980s with risk assessment for the 1990s. *American Journal of Political Science* 41 (4): 1079–1103.

27 Agnew, R. 2010. A general strain theory of terrorism. *Theoretical Criminology* 14 (2): 132–133.

28 Stevens, M. J. 2002. The unanticipated consequences of globalization: Contextualizing terrorism. In *The psychology of terrorism (Vol. III: Theoretical understandings and perspectives)*, ed. C. E. Stout, 31–56. Westport, CT: Praeger.

29 Moghaddam, F. M. 2005. The staircase to terrorism: A psychological exploration. *American Psychologist* 60 (2): 162.

30 Newman, E. 2006. Exploring the root causes of terrorism. *Studies in Conflict & Terrorism* 29 (8): 749–72; Robison, K. K., et al. 2006. Ideologies of violence: The social origins of Islamist and leftist transnational terrorism. *Social Forces* 84 (4): 2009–2026; De Coning, C. 2004. Poverty and terrorism: The root cause debate? *Conflict Trends* 3:20–29; Gurr, T. R., and Moore, W. H. 1997. Ethnopolitical rebellion: A cross-sectional analysis of the 1980s with risk assessment for the 1990s. *American Journal of Political Science* 41 (4): 1079–1103.

to explain why individuals, even though they are exposed to similar strain to that of terrorists, do not engage in terrorism.[31] The same holds true for material deprivation and relative deprivation. Indeed, theorists have argued that the inability of strain and material factors, such as poverty, to explain why individuals engage in terrorist activity highlights the central role of psychological factors in explaining terrorist acts.[32]

BECAUSE THEY SUFFER FROM A MENTAL DISORDER

Psychoanalytical theories and personality theories have been used to explain terrorism. Terrorism, here, is believed to be the manifestation of the psychic conflict between the id, ego, and superego within the terrorist. The primary unit of analyses for psychological theories is the individual. The major motivating element within an individual is personality. As such, it should be studied because terrorism is believed to be the result of the abnormal or dysfunctional mental processes within the individual's personality. Sigmund Freud developed an anatomy of the mind in order to understand how individuals deal with unconscious wishes. This search led him to the development of a structural view of personality. He viewed personality as consisting of three institutions or agencies, which were the *id, ego,* and *superego.* These institutions were said to have been closely linked to the three layers of consciousness.[33] The *id* is considered the unconscious layer. It is characterized by the mental processes outside an individual's awareness and seeks immediate gratification of needs. The *ego* is predominantly conscious, recognizes the need to delay gratification to achieve long-term goals, and creates strategies to maximize pleasure of activity and then minimize its pain. Lastly, the *superego* includes a combination of both unconscious and conscious processes and serves as the moral guide to right and wrong. Psychoanalytical theorists view the aggression exhibited by terrorists as the result of severe physical or emotional traumatization of the superego. From a psychoanalytical perspective,

> on the one side, the shamed part of the self is projected onto the target; it needs to be tortured and destroyed as a symbol of one's own image of weakness and victimhood. On the other side, a harsh superego—a punishing and absolving, absolute authority—is projected onto leaders, terrorist groups, and [in the case of religious terrorists] onto God.[34]

---

31 Victoroff, J. 2005. The mind of the terrorist: A review and critique of psychological approaches. *Journal of Conflict Resolution* 49 (1): 3–42; Newman, E. 2007. Weak states, state failure, and terrorism. *Terrorism and Political Violence* 19 (4): 463–488.

32 Moghaddan, F. M. 2005. The staircase to terrorism: A psychological exploration. *American Psychologist* 60 (2): 162.

33 Mischel, W. 1999. *Introduction to personality.* New York: Harcourt College, 39.

34 Wurmser, L. 2004. Psychoanalytical reflections on 9/11, terrorism, and genocidal prejudice: Roots and sequels. *Journal of the American Psychoanalytic Association* 52 (3): 924.

Terrorism can thus be understood as the externalization of the inner conflict of the superego of an individual (or individuals). Personality theorists provide similar causes for terrorism but believe that such behavior occurs due to elements of the personality and not subconscious factors. They believe that terrorists suffer from personality defects due to extremely negative childhood experiences, and consequently have a poor sense of self.[35] However, research has actually pointed to the lack of terrorist personality, especially one that could be used to explain all forms of terrorism and terrorists' motivations.

Self psychology might also explain why individuals engage in acts of terrorism. According to Kohut, in order to develop normally, an infant needs caring responses.[36] Failing to obtain such caring (e.g., in the form of maternal empathy) can lead to a narcissistic injury; that is, a damaged self-image, which inhibits the proper development of adult identity and morality. Likewise, Hubbard argued that terrorists are those who, in search of affiliation and meaning, have at an early stage of development suffered from parental rejection.[37] As a result of this rejection, the proper development of adult identity was impaired. Pearlstein sought to identify the factors that encouraged certain individuals to commit terrorist attacks.[38] He concluded that terrorists suffer from a "narcissistic injury," which causes them to engage in violence against themselves and others. This theory holds that individuals will seek to destroy the source of injury in what is known as narcissistic rage—the use of violence when the individual feels rejected, humiliated, or otherwise narcissistically injured. Essentially, this rage is directed against the damaged self and is projected onto the target of the terrorist as if it were the source of the intolerable feelings that the terrorist has of himself or herself.[39]

Terrorists are believed to have a damaged self-concept and rely on psychological defense mechanisms of "externalization" and "splitting," which are commonly attributed to individuals who are diagnosed with narcissistic and borderline personality disorders.[40] In fact, splitting is commonly used by individuals who suffered some form of psychological damage, such as narcissistic injury, during childhood.[41] Echoing

---

35 Post, J. 1984. Notes on a psychodynamic theory of terrorist behavior. *Terrorism: An International Journal* 7 (3): 241–256; Kaplan, A. 1981. The psychodynamics of terrorism. In *Behavioral and quantitative perspectives on terrorism*, eds. Y. Alexander and J. Gleason. New York: Pergamon; Ruby, C. L. 2002. Are terrorists mentally deranged? *Analyses of Social Issues and Public Policy* 2 (1): 18.

36 Kohut, H. 1978. *The search for the self*. New York: International Universities Press; Kohut, H. 1972. Thoughts on narcissism and narcissistic rage. *Psychoanalytic Study of the Child* 27:360–400.

37 Hubbard, D. G. 1971. *The skyjacker: His flights of fantasy*. New York: Macmillan.

38 Pearlstein, R. M. 1991. *The mind of a political terrorist*. Wilmington, DE: Scholarly Resources.

39 Crayton, J. W. 1983. Terrorism and the psychology of the self. In *Perspectives on terrorism*, eds. L. Z. Freedman and Y. Alexander, 33–41. Wilmington, DE: Scholarly Resources.

40 Post, J. M. 1984. Notes on a psychodynamic theory of terrorist behavior. *Terrorism: An International Journal* 7 (3): 242–256; Hudson, R. A. 1999. *The sociology and psychology of terrorism: Who becomes a terrorist and why?* 20. A report prepared under an Interagency Agreement by the Federal Research Division, Library of Congress. http://www.loc.gov/rr/frd/pdf-files/Soc_Psych_of_Terrorism.pdf.

41 Ibid.

Kohut, Post stated that "a salient feature of terrorists' psychology is projection, an infantile defense that assigns intolerable internal feelings to an external object when an individual [who] has grown up with a damaged self-concept idealizes the good self and splits out the bad self."[42] According to Kaplan, "terrorists will always find a 'reason' to commit violence, since violent behavior and association with like-minded individuals are the only things that will maintain the terrorist's self-esteem and sense of identity."[43] Likewise, other psychological theorists, such as Johnson and Feldman, Post, and Pearlstein, believe that terrorism offers a sense of identity and self-cohesion to the individual or individuals who have a fragile sense of self.[44]

Some psychological theorists and researchers hold that individuals engage in terrorism because they are insane or suffer from some form of mental disorder.[45] Insanity, here, is a legal definition, which indicates that a person did not know right from wrong when engaging in the terrorist act. A mental disorder can be defined as a clinical disease, illness, or disability of the mind. It impairs the normal psychological functioning of an individual. Two well-established classification systems for mental disorders exist: the Diagnostic and Statistical Manual of Mental Disorders (DSM) of the American Psychiatric Association and the International Classification of Diseases (ICD) of the World Health Organization (WHO). According to the classification system of the WHO, mental disorders refer to "the existence of a clinically recognizable set of symptoms or behavior associated in most cases with distress and with interference with personal functions."[46] Others consider terrorists as mentally disturbed individuals who have been brainwashed by the lies of their religious leaders.[47]

---

[42] Kohut, H. 1978. *The search for the self.* New York: International Universities Press; Kohut, H. 1972. Thoughts on narcissism and narcissistic rage. *Psychoanalytic Study of the Child* 27:360–400; Post, J. M. 1998. Terrorist psycho-logic: Terrorist behavior as a product of psychological forces. In *Origins of terrorism: Psychologies, ideologies, theologies, states of mind,* ed. W. Reich. Washington, DC: Woodrow Wilson Center; Post, J. M. 2004. *Leaders and their followers in a dangerous world: The psychology of political behavior.* Ithaca, NY: Cornell University Press.

[43] Kaplan, A. 1981. The psychodynamics of terrorism. In *Behavioral and quantitative perspectives on terrorism,* eds. Y. Alexander and J. Gleason, 35–50. New York: Pergamon; Ruby, C. L. 2002. Are terrorists mentally deranged? *Analyses of Social Issues and Public Policy* 2 (1): 17.

[44] Johnson, P. W., and Feldman, T. B. 1992. Personality types and terrorism: Self-psychology perspectives. *Forensic Reports* 5 (4): 293–303; Pearlstein, R. M. 1991. *The mind of the political terrorist.* Wilmington, DE: Scholarly Resources; Post, J. 1984. Notes on a psychodynamic theory of terrorist behavior. *Terrorism: An International Journal* 7 (3): 241–256; Post, J. 1986. Hostilité, conformité, fraternité: The group dynamics of terrorist behavior. *International Journal of Group Psychotherapy* 36 (2): 211–224; Post, J. 1987. "It's us against them": The group dynamics of political terrorism. *Terrorism* 10:23–35.

[45] For example, Cooper, H. A. 1976. The terrorist and the victim. *Victimology* 1:229–239.; Hacker, F. J. 1976. *Crusaders, criminals, crazies: terror and terrorism in our time.* New York: Norton; Taylor, M. 1988. *The terrorist.* London: Brassey's.

[46] World Health Organization. (n.d.).International Classification of Diseases, 11. http://www.who.int/classifications/icd/en/bluebook.pdf.

[47] Charny, I. W. 2007. *Fighting suicide bombing: A worldwide campaign for life.* London: Praeger Security International, 53.

Early studies of terrorists, such as Hubbard's 1971 study of hijackers, revealed that terrorists suffer from a mental disorder.[48] In his study of terrorists in the Red Army Faction, Wagenlehner concluded that these individuals had psychopathological disorders.[49] Some consider terrorists as sociopaths, psychopaths, or people with antisocial personality disorders.[50] An example of a terrorist with an antisocial personality disorder was Abu Musab al-Zarqawi, who was the head of al-Qaeda in Iraq (until his death in 2006).[51] Certain psychologists believe that terrorists suffer from personality disorders. In fact, Shaw, in his review of the limited existing psychiatric literature on terrorism, found that terrorists have been regularly diagnosed with narcissistic personality disorder and antisocial personality disorder.[52] Individuals with a narcissistic personality disorder are more prone to aggression and show arrogance, a lack of empathy, a sense of entitlement, and a tendency to exploit other individuals for their own selfish needs. In fact, the use of the psychological defense mechanisms of externalization and splitting is common among those diagnosed with narcissistic personality disorders.[53] Individuals with an antisocial personality disorder are also prone to aggression.[54] With this personality disorder, individuals tend to show a lack of remorse for their actions or the inability to understand or care about the effects of their behavior on other individuals.

Hewitt argued that although most terrorists are "normal," the rate of mental disorders is considerably higher in "lone wolves,"[55] who are individuals that engage in acts of violence independent of any leader, movement, or network of support (see Box 2-1). Spaaij's research supported Hewitt's observation. More specifically, having reviewed five cases of lone wolves, Spaaij found that four out of the five suffered from a mental disorder:[56] David Copeland (aka the London nailbomber), who engaged in terrorist attacks against the Asian, black, and gay communities in

---

[48] Hubbard, D. G. 1971. *The skyjacker: His flights of fantasy*. New York: Macmillan.

[49] Wagenlehner, G. 1978. Motivation for political terrorism in West Germany. In *International terrorism in the contemporary world*, ed. M. H. Livingston, 201. Westport, CT: Greenwood.

[50] Sageman, M. 2004. *Understanding terror networks*. Philadelphia: University of Pennsylvania Press, 81.

[51] Sageman, M. 2008. *Leaderless jihad: Terror networks in the twenty first century*. Philadelphia: University of Pennsylvania Press, 63.

[52] Shaw, E. D. 1986. Political terrorists: Dangers of diagnosis and an alternative to the psychopathology model. *International Journal of Law and Psychiatry* 8 (3): 359–368.

[53] Post, J. M. 1984. Notes on a psychodynamic theory of terrorist behavior. *Terrorism: An International Journal* 7 (3): 242–256; Hudson, R. A. 1999. *The sociology and psychology of terrorism: Who becomes a terrorist and why?* 20. A report prepared under an Interagency Agreement by the Federal Research Division, Library of Congress. http://www.loc.gov/rr/frd/pdf-files/Soc_Psych_of_Terrorism.pdf.

[54] According to the DSM, antisocial personality disorder was previously known as both a psychopathic and sociopathic personality disorder.

[55] Hewitt, C. 2002. *Understanding terrorism in America*. New York: Routledge, 80.

[56] It is important to note that the psychiatric assessments of these lone wolves have been contested. Spaaij, R. 2010. The enigma of lone wolf terrorism: An assessment. *Studies in Conflict & Terrorism* 33 (9): 862.

Box 2-1 Food for Thought: Who's Afraid of the "Lone Wolf"?

In Europe, individuals exist who operate as "lone wolves." These lone wolves, the so-called unaffiliated terrorists, lack formal ties with existing groups but fervently adhere to their ideologies. They are far more dangerous as they are almost impossible to identify, and thus more difficult to locate, track, and monitor.[1] This was the case in the Madrid, Spain, bombings on March 11, 2004, in which terrorists remotely detonated bombs on four commuter trains, killing 191 and injuring over 1,800. In fact, the Madrid bombings investigations revealed that the perpetrators were from a local sleeper cell who were inspired by, rather than directed by, al-Qaeda.[2] As Jorge Dezcallar (former head of CNL, Spanish security service) states, these terrorists are "almost impossible to detect."[3] The London bombings, which occurred on July 7, 2005, despite initial claims that they were directed under the leadership of Osama bin Laden, were actually perpetrated by a cell of radicalized young men who, inspired by al-Qaeda, decided to express their faith by engaging in these suicide attacks. It was argued that the investigations of the perpetrators of these bombings "forced counterterrorist chiefs to tear up their intelligence assessments of potential terrorists," because none of the individuals responsible for the attacks fit their existing threat profiles.[4]

Similar individuals have been found in the United States. On November 20, 2011, Jose Pimentel, a Dominican-born Muslim convert and Manhattan resident, was arrested by the NYPD for plotting to build and detonate bombs in New York City. Pimentel was a lone wolf and maintained a website (www.trueislam1.com), which contained bomb-making instructions taken from al-Qaeda's *Inspire* magazine. Unbeknownst to him, a person with whom he was in contact was an NYPD informant who recorded their conversations. This informant invited Pimentel to his apartment and videotaped him building a bomb. He is what has come to be known as a lone wolf. Lone wolves engage in acts of violence in support of a terrorist movement, group, or ideology. Like others before him, Pimentel was inspired by al-Qaeda's cause rather than directed by them. Another example involved Mohamed Osman Mohamud. On November 26, 2010, Mohamud, a 19-year-old Somalian immigrant, was arrested for attempting to detonate explosives in a van during a Christmas tree lighting ceremony at the Pioneer Courthouse Square in Portland, Oregon. A similar case occurred in 2007. Derrick Shareef, an American citizen and Muslim convert, was sentenced to prison for planning to set off explosives in the crowded Cherryvale Mall

---

[1] Leppard, D., and Winnett. R. 2005. Focus: Blair's extremism proposals attacked as the hunt continues for terror's new breed. *Sunday Times*, August 7, 2005. http://www.timesonline.co.uk /tol/news/uk/article552552.ece; Rai, M. 2006. *7/7: The London bombings, Islam, and the Iraq war*. London: Pluto, 156; Vidino, L. 2006. *Al-Qaeda in Europe: The new battleground of international jihad*. New York: Prometheus, 30.

[2] Sengupta, K. 2005. The police's nightmare: Home-grown terrorist. *The Independent*, July 13, 2005. http://news.independent.co.uk/uk/crime/article298802.ece; Rai, M. 2006. *7/7: The London bombings, Islam, and the Iraq war*. London: Pluto, 157.

[3] Ibid.

[4] O'Neill, S., and McGrory, D. 2005. Detectives draw up new brief in hunt for radicals. *The Times*, December 2005. http://www.timesonline.co.uk/tol/news/uk/article782897.ece; Rai, M. 2006. *7/7: The London bombings, Islam, and the Iraq war*. London: Pluto, 157.

(continues)

Box 2-1 Food for Thought: Who's Afraid of the "Lone Wolf"? (continued)

in Rockford, Illinois, during the Christmas season. Shareef, like Mohamud, was given dummy explosives by undercover FBI agents, who were posing as al-Qaeda supporters. In both cases, the suspects were arrested after they attempted to detonate the fake explosives. These lone wolves, or unaffiliated terrorists, lack ties with al-Qaeda and related Islamic terrorist groups but adhere to their ideology and harbor a deep hatred for the West. They are far more dangerous as they are almost impossible to identify, and thus more difficult to locate, track, and monitor. Is it even possible to counter this type of threat?

Britain, killing 3 and injuring 129; Theodore Kaczynski (aka the Unabomber), who engaged in a package and letter bombing campaign in the United States, which killed 3 and injured 23; and Franz Fuchs, who engaged in terrorist attacks in Austria that targeted immigrants, organizations, and individuals who he believed were friendly to foreigners, killing 4 and injuring 15. These individuals were diagnosed under the DSM as having a personality disorder, and Volkert van der Graaf (an animal rights activist in the Netherlands who shot and killed a Dutch politician, Pim Fortuyn, in Hilversum) was diagnosed with obsessive compulsive disorder. The fifth lone wolf evaluated, Yigal Amir, who shot and killed the Israeli Prime Minister Yitzhak Rabin in Tel Aviv in 1995, was found, according to a court-ordered psychiatric evaluation, to be neither mentally ill nor emotionally disturbed.[57] In 2008, in the United Kingdom, another terrorist attack was attempted by an individual who suffered from a mental disorder. In particular, Nicky Reilly, a Muslim convert inspired by al-Qaeda's cause (and not directed by them), who had Asperger's syndrome and was believed to also suffer from schizophrenia,[58] attempted to blow up a restaurant in Bristol.[59]

However, available evidence suggests little validity to the explanations of terrorism due to a high level of psychopathology among terrorists.[60] Indeed, many studies have shown the absence of major mental disorders among terrorists.[61] For instance, Heskin concluded that there was no psychological evidence that terrorists in Northern Ireland were psychopathic or otherwise mentally disturbed.[62] In addition, Ferracuti and Bruno concluded from their study of right-wing terrorists

---

[57] Ibid., p. 862.

[58] Asperger's syndrome is a developmental disorder that affects an individual's ability to, among other things, socialize and communicate effectively with others.

[59] Leppard, D., and Taher, A. 2008. MI5 fears jihadis will use mentally ill as suicide bombers. *Sunday Times*, May 25, 2008. http://www.timesonline.co.uk/tol/news/uk/article3999058.ece.

[60] Crenshaw, M. 1981. The causes of terrorism. *Comparative Politics* 13 (4): 379–399; Ruby, C. L. 2002. Are terrorists mentally deranged? *Analyses of Social Issues and Public Policy* 2 (1): 15–26.

[61] Sageman, M. 2004. *Understanding terror networks*. Philadelphia: University of Pennsylvania Press, 81.

[62] Heskin, K. 1984. The psychology of terrorism in Ireland. In *Terrorism in Ireland*, eds. Y. Alexander and A. O'Day. New York: St. Martin's.

in Italy that these individuals did not have a particular psychopathology that distinguished them from the rest of the population.[63] Moreover, psychiatric evaluations of 21 secular and 14 radical Islamic Middle Eastern terrorists revealed no DSM mental disorders.[64] Furthermore, uncontrolled empirical psychological studies of the Algerian Front de Liberation Nationale (FLN) and Hezbollah showed no DSM mental disorders.[65]

A main problem associated with psychological theories and perspectives is the lack of relevant data to support the existence of personality pathology among terrorists.[66] The beliefs that an abnormal terrorist personality exists and that psychological factors are the primary motivators of terrorism have been questioned by scholars on several occasions.[67] A review of the scientific literature suggests that terrorists are not dysfunctional or pathological.[68] For instance, Weatherston and Moran found no evidence to support the claim that there is a general connection between an individual's mental illness and his or her participation in terrorism.[69] In fact, the accepted view within the literature concerning a possible causal connection between mental disorders and terrorism is that there is little evidence that prior pathology causes individuals to engage in terrorist activities.[70] As Crenshaw concluded in her studies of terrorism, "the outstanding common characteristic of terrorists is their normality."[71]

---

[63] Ferracuti, F., and F. Bruno. 1981. Psychiatric aspects of terrorism in Italy. In *The mad, the bad and the different: Essays in honor of Simon Dinitz*, eds. I. L. Barak-Glantz and C. R. Huff. Lexington, MA: Lexington Books.

[64] Post, J. M., Sprinzak, E., and Denny, L. M. 2003. The terrorists in their own words: Interviews with thirty-five incarcerated Middle Eastern terrorists. *Terrorism and Political Violence* 15 (1): 171–84; Post, J. M., and Gold, S. N. 2002. The psychology of the terrorist: An interview with Jerrold M. Post. *Journal of Trauma Practice* 1 (3/4): 83–100.

[65] Merari, A. 1998. The readiness to kill and die: Suicidal terrorism in the Middle East. In *Origins of terrorism: Psychologies, ideologies, theologies, states of mind*, ed. W. Reich. Washington, DC: Woodrow Wilson Center Press.

[66] Sageman, M. 2004. *Understanding terror networks*. Philadelphia: University of Pennsylvania Press, 91.

[67] Crenshaw, M. 2000. The psychology of terrorism: An agenda for the 21st century. *Political Psychology* 21 (2): 405–420; Sageman, M. 2004. *Understanding terror networks*. Philadelphia: University of Pennsylvania Press; Merari, A., and Friedland, N. 1985. Social psychological aspects of political terrorism. In *Applied social psychology annual*, ed. S. Oskamp. Beverly Hills, CA: Sage.

[68] Ruby, C. L. 2002. Are terrorists mentally deranged? *Analyses of Social Issues and Public Policy* 2 (1): 15.

[69] Weatherston, D., and Moran, J. 2003. Terrorism and mental illness: Is there a relationship? *International Journal of Offender Therapy and Comparative Criminology* 47 (6): 707.

[70] Ginges, J. 1997. A psychological evaluation of different strategies for deterring terrorism. *Terrorism and Political Violence* 9 (1): 170–185; Shaw, E. D. 1986. Political terrorists: Dangers of diagnosis and an alternative to the psychopathology model. *International Journal of Law and Psychiatry* 8 (3): 359–368; Weatherston, D., and Moran, J. 2003. Terrorism and mental illness: Is there a relationship? *International Journal of Offender Therapy and Comparative Criminology* 47 (6): 699.

[71] Crenshaw, M. 1981. The causes of terrorism. *Comparative Politics* 13 (4): 379–399.

Individuals who subscribe to psychological perspectives of terrorism fail to realize that behavior is a product of not only individual (or internal) factors but also situational (or external) factors. The situational factors are the product of the environment of terrorists. In reality, like all behaviors (aberrant or otherwise), terrorism is too complex a phenomenon to be attributed to a single factor or even attributed to similar factors for all types of terrorist groups, terrorists, and their respective behaviors.

BECAUSE OF SOCIALIZATION

Socialization is the process of an individual's development whereby he or she learns the particular behaviors and skills accepted by society that are necessary for their successful functioning within that society. Socialization can result in both noncriminal and criminal behavior. On the one hand, certain social bonds can promote socialization and conformity of individuals to a society. These social bonds are[72] *attachment*, which relates to the individual's sensitivity to family, friends, community, and interest in others; *commitment*, which engages the individual's time, vigor, and effort spent in conforming to socially accepted customs of behavior (e.g., completing education); *involvement*, which includes being active in conventional activities (e.g., participating in civic affairs, becoming a member of a religious group and attending the services); and *belief*, which adheres to shared or communal morals and values such as being responsible and sensitive to the rights of others. These social bonds serve as barriers to an individual's involvement in criminal activity.

On the other hand, other studies have shown that individuals may engage in crimes, even terrorism, due to socialization. Indeed, existing literature shows that the attitudes, values, and beliefs individuals learn from the bonds formed with societal institutions (e.g., religious community and school) and individuals (e.g., family, teachers, peers, etc.) may lead them to engage in terrorist acts. Religious institutions (e.g., church, temple, and mosque) play a fundamental role in the socialization of youths. In fact, "religion is social, providing for the socialization of children into moral values; religion connects one to the community . . . Morality, meaning, and value through religion are reflected in one's daily life and through one's family and religious community."[73] Religious leaders see "themselves as teachers, and their followers usually attempt to shape the socialization of children through schooling, preaching, and religious services."[74] However, the messages portrayed by religious leaders may not always be those advocating for morality and peace. In the past, religious institutions have been found to promote terrorism. A case in point is the Finsbury Park mosque in London, which,

---

[72] Hirschi, T. 1969. *Causes of delinquency*. Berkeley and Los Angeles: University of California Press.

[73] French, R. 1999. From Yoder to Yoda: Models of traditional, modern, and postmodern religion in U.S. constitutional law. *Arizona Law Review* 41:49.

[74] Kiknadze, T. 2007. Terrorism as social reality. In *Understanding terrorism: Analysis of sociological and psychological aspects*, eds. S. Ozeren, I. D., Gunes, and D. M. Al-Badayneh, 60. NATO Science for Peace and Security Studies (Vol. 22). Oxford, UK: IOS Press.

according to British authorities, was used until 2003 to radicalize individuals and support members in engaging in terrorist activities.[75]

Another societal institution that plays a central role is schools. Because schools "transmit the values and attitudes of the society, they could play an important role in shaping attitudes about the rules of society, instilling the values of public duty, developing informal relations."[76] They affect youths' mental images or perceptions of themselves, their ideology, and their principles. A student may learn impressions of themselves that are injurious to their objectives or welfare. School constructions also outline peer relations that students have. These institutions encourage the development of ranked or hierarchical cliques and give emphasis to students being popular. However, in some countries, educational systems do not provide unifying, peaceful socialization; instead, these institutions send starkly different messages to different groups within it.[77] Schools may, thus, instead promote messages of hate and provide encouragement and justification to resorting to violence to resolve perceived conflicts.

Terrorists may also be influenced by others in their social circle to engage in attacks. The most important social groups that contribute to the socialization process are family and peers. Research exists that suggests that "individuals whose family members and friends are involved in terrorism are much more likely to be involved themselves."[78] The family plays a crucial role in shaping individuals' attitudes. It is also the principal setting in which social meanings are created. More specifically, "the family also shapes future social, cultural, political attitudes by locating the individual in the vast social world; establishing ethnic, linguistic, class, and religious ties, affirming cultural values, and directing occupational and economic aspirations."[79] Peers also influence individuals. In fact, "an individual may become interested in some processes or attend some meetings because close friends do so."[80] Research has shown that "where the individuals [became] active terrorists, the initial attraction [was] often made by a friend or group, rather than

---

[75] Mosque's Terrorist Roll Call. 2006. *Daily Mail*, February 7, 2006. http://www.dailymail.co.uk /news/article-376444/Mosques-terrorist-roll-call.html; Controversial Cleric of UK Mosque. 2003, April 1. *CNN World*. http://articles.cnn.com/2003-01-20/world/uk.hamzaprofile_1_finsbury-park -mosque-muslim-cleric-abu-hamza-london-mosque?_s=PM:WORLD.

[76] Kiknadze, T. 2007. Terrorism as social reality. In *Understanding terrorism: Analysis of sociological and psychological aspects*, eds. S. Ozeren, I. D. Gunes, and D. M. Al-Badayneh, 60. NATO Science for Peace and Security Studies (Vol. 22). Oxford, UK: IOS Press.

[77] Ibid.

[78] Sageman, M. 2004. *Understanding terror networks*. Philadelphia: University of Pennsylvania Press; Victoroff, J. 2005. The mind of the terrorist: A review and critique of psychological approaches. *Journal of Conflict Resolution* 49 (1): 3–42; Post, J. M. 2007. *The mind of the terrorist*. New York: Palgrave Macmillan; Smelser, N. J. 2007. *The faces of terrorism: Social and psychological dimensions*. Princeton, NJ: Princeton University Press; Abrahms, M. 2008. What terrorists really want. *International Security* 32 (4): 78–105.

[79] Kiknadze, T. 2007. Terrorism as social reality. In *Understanding terrorism: Analysis of sociological and psychological aspects*, eds. S. Ozeren, I. D. Gunes, and D. M. Al-Badayneh, 59–60. NATO Science for Peace and Security Studies (Vol. 22). Oxford, UK: IOS Press.

[80] Ibid., p. 61.

abstract ideology."[81] This was supported by other findings that similarly showed that decisions to join terrorist groups were rarely made individually; instead, outside influences played a role.[82] After becoming interested in the group and/ or attending certain meetings, an individual may modify "his or her interest and behavior to reflect those of the group in an effort to be accepted by members."[83]

Social process theories suggest that terroristic behavior is learned through social interaction. The socialization process that results from group membership is the primary way through which such learning occurs. Both psychology and criminology have played central roles in the development of social learning theory. Learning theories suggest that terrorism, like all other types of behavior, is learned. Individuals use the same process to learn behaviors, the rationalizations that accompany these behaviors, and the skills needed to carry out these behaviors, in both conventional and terrorist groups. Individuals who subscribe to this perspective emphasize the role of communication and socialization in acquiring learned patterns of terroristic behavior and the values supporting such behavior.

Social learning theory in these fields is generally associated with the work of Edwin Sutherland and Albert Bandura. According to Sutherland's differential association principle, individuals will be in a disposition to commit criminal behavior if they learn an excess of definitions favorable to the violation of law over definitions unfavorable to violation of law.[84] While Sutherland tried to show that criminal behavior is learned, Bandura attempted to explain how such behavior is learned. Bandura believed that aggression is a behavior that is learned by individuals through the process of behavioral modeling and imitation.[85] Individuals learn aggressive responses from observing others, either in person or through their environment and media. However, the effects of face-to-face or primary-group interactions are stronger than the media. With modeling, individuals learn by observing other individuals and repeating or mimicking their behaviors. Imitation involves

---

[81] Crenshaw, M. 1983. *Terrorism, legitimacy and power*. Middletown, CT: Wesleyan University Press; Ozer, M. 2007. The impact of group dynamics on terrorist decision making. In *Understanding terrorism: Analysis of sociological and psychological aspects*, eds. S. Ozeren, I. D. Gunes, and D. M. Al-Badayneh, 68. NATO Science for Peace and Security Studies (Vol. 22). Oxford, UK: IOS Press.

[82] This was found in the study of PKK members and Italian extremists. See Alkan, N. 2002. *Youth and terrorism*. Ankara, Turkey: EGM; and Potra, D. 2001. Terror against the state. In *The Blackwell companion to political sociology*, eds. K. Nash and A. Scott. Malden, MA: Blackwell, respectively. See also Ozer. M. 2007. The impact of group dynamics on terrorist decision making. In *Understanding terrorism: Analysis of sociological and psychological aspects*, eds. S. Ozeren, I. D. Gunes, and D. M. Al-Badayneh, 68. NATO Science for Peace and Security Studies (Vol. 22). Oxford, UK: IOS Press.

[83] Kiknadze, T. 2007. Terrorism as social reality. In *Understanding terrorism: Analysis of sociological and psychological aspects*, eds. S. Ozeren, I. D. Gunes, and D. M. Al-Badayneh, 61. NATO Science for Peace and Security Studies (Vol. 22). Oxford, UK: IOS Press.

[84] Sutherland, E. H. 1974. *Criminology*. Philadelphia: J.B. Lippincott, 75–76.

[85] Bandura, A. 1998. Mechanisms of moral disengagement. In. *Origins of terrorism: Psychologies, ideologies, theologies, states of mind*, ed. W. Reich. Washington, DC: Woodrow Wilson Center Press.

"committing [the] behavior modeled on, and following the observation of, similar behavior in others."[86]

Post held that group psychology could provide more insight into terrorism than individual psychology could.[87] Friendship and individuals' need to belong motivates them to join the terrorist group. For the individual, studies have shown that the group becomes a substitute family, in which the group leader (or leaders) becomes a substitute parent (or parents).[88] Membership in a terrorist group also offers individuals a well-defined role and purpose, and the opportunity for revenge for perceived or actual humiliation and deprivation.[89] Social psychological explanations of terrorism focus on group behavior and/or organizational processes such as conformity and disobedience of group members. Individual judgment and behavior is strongly influenced by group dynamics. Indeed, involvement in terrorist groups "may be further reinforced by powerful group dynamics such as groupthink, the subordination of the self before the group."[90] Here, "terrorists tend to submerge their own identities into the group, resulting in a kind of 'group mind' and group moral code that requires . . . obedience to the group."[91]

To be part of the group, total commitment to the cause is required. In essence, individuals are transformed into terrorists when they accept with blind, unquestioned faith the agenda (e.g., religious or political) of the group. To the religious terrorist group, acts take on a different meaning. Activities and behavior that might have been previously viewed as criminal are now labeled as necessary for religious warfare to obtain liberation from a foreign occupier. Individuals within the group have been promised an ultimate reward and believe that they have been chosen to carry out a fundamental task. This gives them a feeling of high importance. Pressures toward conformity and consensus are characteristics of terrorists groups. Some group forces include peer pressure, ideological indoctrination, and repetitive

---

86 Akers, R. 1998. *Social learning and social structure: A general theory of crime and deviance.* Boston: Northeastern University Press.

87 Post, J. 1987. "It's us against them": The group dynamics of political terrorism. *Terrorism* 10:23–35.

88 Hudson, R.A. 1999. *The sociology and psychology of terrorism: Who becomes a terrorist and why?* 35. A report prepared under an Interagency Agreement by the Federal Research Division, Library of Congress. http://www.loc.gov/rr/frd/pdf-files/Soc_Psych_of_Terrorism.pdf.

89 Hacker, F. J. 1983. Dialectic interrelationships of personal and political factors in terrorism. In *Perspectives on terrorism*, eds. L. Z. Freedman and Y. Alexander. Wilmington, DE: Scholarly Resources; Taylor, M., and Ryan., H. 1988. Fanaticism, political suicide and terrorism. *Terrorism* 11 (2): 91–111; Weinberg, L., and Eubank. W. L. 1987. Italian women terrorists. *Terrorism: An International Journal* 9 (3): 241–262; Stern, J. 1999. *The ultimate terrorists.* Cambridge, MA: Harvard University Press.

90 Hudson, R. A. 1999. *The sociology and psychology of terrorism: Who becomes a terrorist and why?* A report prepared under an Interagency Agreement by the Federal Research Division, Library of Congress. http://www.loc.gov/rr/frd/pdf-files/Soc_Psych_of_Terrorism.pdf.

91 Post, J. 1986. Hostilité, conformité, fraternité: The group dynamics of terrorist behavior. *International Journal of Group Psychotherapy* 36:211–224; Hudson, R. A. (1999). *The sociology and psychology of terrorism: Who becomes a terrorist and why?* 36. A report prepared under an Interagency Agreement by the Federal Research Division, Library of Congress. http://www.loc.gov/rr/frd/pdf-files/Soc_Psych_of_Terrorism.pdf.

training. Regardless of any individual predisposition to such behavior, group forces were found by scholars to influence the group's use of violence.[92]

Terrorists "immersion in secret, small-group activities leads to changes in perceptions among recruits: a legitimization of the terrorist organization and its goals, a belief that the ends justify the means, and a strengthening of a categorical us-versus-them view of the world."[93] Terrorist groups separate those in the in-group (i.e., those who are in the group; support the group; and hold the same ideals, values, and goals of the group) and those in the out-group (i.e., everyone else who is not part of the in-group). These in-group and out-group distinctions are especially prominent in collectivist cultures such as in the Middle East.[94] Collectivist cultures are "characterized by tight social networks in which people strongly distinguish between their own groups (in-groups, such as relatives, clans, and organizations) and other groups."[95] This social categorization is a hallmark of terrorist groups or organizations and individuals seeking to join them.[96] This categorization can lead to in-group favoritism and out-group discrimination.[97] In their study, Tajfel and Turner showed that the mere act of categorization of members as a group was sufficient to lead these individuals to display in-group favoritism.[98] Civilians here are also considered part of the out-group. As such, from the perspective of the terrorists within the group, "acts of violence against civilians are justified because civilians are part of the enemy, and only when civilians actively oppose the targeted 'evil forces' will they not be the enemy."[99]

---

[92] Crenshaw, M. 1992. How terrorists think: What psychology can contribute to understanding terrorism. In *Terrorism: Roots, impact, responses*, ed. L. Howard. New York: Praeger; Clayton, C. J., Barlow, S. H., and Ballif-Spanvill, B. 1998. Principles of group violence with a focus on terrorism. In *Collective violence* ed. H. V. Hall and L. C. Whitaker. Boca Raton, FL: CRC.

[93] Moghaddan, F. M. 2005. The staircase to terrorism: A psychological exploration. *American Psychologist* 60 (2): 161–169.

[94] Hofstede, G. H. 1991. *Cultures and organizations: Software of the mind*. New York: McGraw-Hill. Other societies such as the United States have been characterized as individualistic societies, which is a term used to refer to a "loosely knit social framework in society wherein individuals are supposed to take care of themselves and their immediate families only." Chanchani, S., and Theivanathampillai, P. (n.d.). *Typologies of culture,* 4. http://www.commerce.otago.ac.nz/acty /research/pdf/Typologies%20-%2026%20July%2002.pdf.

[95] Royer, S., and van der Velden, R. 2002, June 12. *Theories and concepts of internationalization and FDI topic: Culture's consequences: The Work of Geert Hofstede*, 8. http://wiwi.upb.de/bwl5 /lehre/SS02/ Seminar/Seminar%20FDI/Topic%2010%20Geert%20Hofstede.pdf.

[96] Pearlstein, R. M. 1991. *The mind of the political terrorist*. Wilmington, DE: Scholarly Resources; Taylor, M. 1988. *The terrorist*. London: Brassey's.

[97] Taylor, D. M., & Moghaddam, F. M. 1994. *Theories of intergroup relations: International social psychological perspectives*. Westport, CT: Praeger.

[98] Tajfel, H., and Turner, J. C. 1986. The social identity theory of inter-group behavior. In *Psychology of intergroup relations*, eds. S. Worchel and L. W. Austin. Chicago: Nelson-Hall.

[99] Moghaddan, F. M. 2005. The staircase to terrorism: A psychological exploration. *American Psychologist* 60 (2): 161–169.

Commonly, terrorism is viewed as a collective activity and as a result, academicians and researchers have focused analyses of terrorism on group dynamics and collective socialization. This group focus, however, does not provide sufficient explanation for a prominent threat of terrorism today, namely, that of lone wolves—homegrown terrorists. According to Crenshaw, acts of terrorism are not committed by individuals; instead, they are "are committed by groups who reach collective decisions based on commonly held beliefs, although the level of individual commitment to the group and its beliefs varies."[100] This, however, fails to take individual terrorists into consideration, that is, the process involved in the decision making of lone wolves. In addition, the decision making of the group depends on its structure. Groups that are decentralized can either make their decisions collectively or individually. The decision-making process depends on the group and its respective leader. Hierarchical structures, however, do not make their decisions collectively. Consider organized crime groups. These groups are often highly structured. For instance, in the Italian mafia, at the bottom of the hierarchy are soldiers, who report to lieutenants; lieutenants report to and receive orders from the underboss; the underboss reports directly to the boss; and finally, the boss, who is at the top of the hierarchy, always makes the decision for the group. Similar behavior is exhibited in certain terrorist groups. Prime examples of this include al-Qaeda leader Osama bin Laden (now deceased)[101] and the leader of Aum Shinrikyo, Shoko Asahar. These leaders were the sole decision makers for their groups.

If socialization, psychological factors, and absolute and relative material deprivation cannot provide adequate explanations as to why all forms of terrorists engage in terroristic acts, what can? Some theorists hold that terrorists engage in terrorism in response to opportunities that are present and their ability to follow through. In short, individuals engage in terrorism simply because they can.

BECAUSE THEY CAN

Many theorists have argued that criminal behavior is a product of rational thought and opportunity.[102] Rational choice theory is based on the economic model of crime. Becker's economic theory of crime holds that an individual will commit an offense if the expected utility (i.e., the likely gain in a particular activity) to him (or her)

---

100 Crenshaw, M. 1990. Questions to be answered, research to be done, knowledge to be applied. In *Origins of terrorism: Psychologies, ideologies, theologies, states of mind*, ed. W. Reich, 250. Cambridge, UK: Cambridge University Press.

101 However, Osama bin Laden's role in the attacks of al-Qaeda was more pronounced pre- and on 9/11.

102 Cornish, D. B., and R. V. Clarke, eds. 1986. *The reasoning criminal: Rational choice perspectives in offending*. New York: Springer; Clarke, R. V., and Felson, M. 1993. Introduction: Criminology, routine activity and rational choice. In *Routine activity and rational choice: Advances in criminological theory* (Vol. 5), eds. R. V. Clarke and M. Felson. New Brunswick, NJ: Transaction; Clarke, R. V., and Newman, G. R. 2006. *Outsmarting the terrorists*. London: Praeger Security International.

exceeds the utility he (or she) would get by using his (or her) time and resources on other activities.[103] Opponents of economic models of crime, which are predicated on rational behavior, claim that it is questionable whether it can explain a phenomenon largely viewed as irrational. An obvious problem is that some impulsive offenses and those committed under the influence of alcohol, drugs, or strong emotions may not easily be seen as the result of choices. While it is true that the economic model of crime does not fit the opportunistic and reckless nature of much crime and irrationality of offenders,[104] it can be used to explain terrorism.

Building on the economic analysis of criminal behavior, Clarke and Cornish conceptualize crime as the outcome of rational decisions. According to the rational choice perspective, offenders (or in this case, terrorists) weigh the costs and benefits of engaging in a particular activity. If the benefits of the action outweigh its costs, the terrorist will engage in that activity. Clarke and Cornish further noted that one of the assumptions of the rational choice perspective is that offenders engage in decision-making processes no matter how elementary and make a choice as to what activity to engage in.[105] For them, this process exhibits a measure of rationality, which may be constrained by other factors such as the limits of available information.[106] Terrorists are rational decision makers in the sense that they pursue identifiable goals. The assumption that terrorists are rational means that they are cognizant of the possible outcomes of a decision and that they choose the action that they believe will give them the highest expected utility. Terrorists calculate the anticipated benefits or utilities in engaging in their actions; that is, whether or not they can commit terrorist attacks more or less successfully.

According to Einstadter and Henry, "crime is not simply due to underlying motivations or predispositions, it also involves a concrete choice—or, in fact, a sequence of choices—that must be made if their motivations are to result in an actual criminal act."[107] Consider al-Qaeda. If it was just extreme religious ideology that motivated these terrorists, one would observe many more attacks than have occurred. There are many individuals worldwide who agree with the views

---

[103] Becker, G. S. 1968. Crime and punishment: An economic approach. *Journal of Political Economy* 76 (2): 176.

[104] De Haan, W., and Vos, J. 2003. A crying shame: The over-rationalized conception of man in the rational choice perspective. *Theoretical Criminology* 7 (1): 31; de Haan, W., and Loader, I. 2002. On the emotions of crime, punishment and social control. *Theoretical Criminology* 6 (3): 243–253.

[105] Clarke, R. V., and Felson, M. 1993. Introduction: Criminology, routine activity and rational choice. In *Routine activity and rational choice: Advances in criminological theory* (Vol. 5), eds. R. V. Clarke and M. Felson. New Brunswick, NJ: Transaction.

[106] Cornish, D. B., and Clarke, R. V. 2002. Crime as rational choice. In *Criminological theories: Bridging the past to the future*, ed. S. Cote, 291. London: Sage.

[107] Einstadter, W. and Henry, S. 1995. *Criminological theory: An analysis of its underlying assumptions* 2nd edition. Fort Worth, TX: Harcourt, Brace and Company; Lilly, J. R., Cullen, F. T., and Ball, R. A. 2002. *Criminological theory: Context and consequences*. London: Sage, 221.

of al-Qaeda yet who do not themselves become terrorists.[108] Loyalty to al-Qaeda's goals also plays a role in whether one decides to engage in terrorist activities or not. What serves as a limiting factor (on whether or not to employ such tactics) is terrorists' ability to achieve their objectives; that is, to what extent can they efficiently carry out an attack.

While terrorists' "acts might vary greatly in sophistication and the degree of planning and organization required," in all cases, terrorists seek "to maximize their benefits, while reducing the effort required and the risks of failure."[109] For members of al-Qaeda and affiliated groups, benefits may be considered rewards in heaven. That is, by engaging in this activity, terrorists believe they will "dwell amidst gardens and fountains and shall receive what their Lord will give them . . . for they have done good works."[110] These individuals believe that upon completion of their actions, they will receive "rewards of ecstasy in death and further rewards in eternity, such as seventy-two beautiful virgin maidens."[111] Terrorists may also consider as benefits the harm "to the society attacked—in terms of loss of life, destruction, disruption of commerce and heightened fear."[112]

From the perspective of religious terrorists, the costs of engaging in a terrorist attack are failing to conduct the attack, capture by authorities, and incapacitation. In addition, the benefits of engaging in a terrorist attack include (but are not limited to) causing death or serious bodily harm to the target, causing significant economic damage to the target, gaining attention to their cause, acquiring recruits, obtaining concessions from target governments, gaining honor and prestige among followers, obtaining support from the community, and even the death of the operative (due to perceived rewards in heaven). The latter is what makes individuals think that terrorists suffer from a mental disorder. The question asked by many is, how can one actually say that terrorists, especially those who choose death over life, are rational actors? When faced with the costs and benefits listed above, one could argue that a rational actor would most likely engage in terrorism because the benefits of committing a terrorist attack significantly outweigh the costs.

On numerous occasions, al-Qaeda has stated that terrorists are worth more dead than alive. In fact, suicide terrorism is considered the most cost-effective tactic. A case in point is when Ayman al-Zawahiri said, "the method of martyrdom operations [is] the most successful way of inflicting damage against the opponent

---

108 Cowen, T. 2006. Terrorism as theater: Analysis and policy implications. *Public Choice* 128 (1/2): 236.

109 Clarke, R. V., and Newman, G. R. 2006. *Outsmarting the terrorists*. London: Praeger Security International, 12.

110 *The Koran*, p. 367 (51:17) in Venkatraman, A. 2007. Religious basis for Islamic terrorism: The Quran and its interpretations. *Studies in Conflict and Terrorism* 30 (3): 232.

111 Pape, R. A. 2003. The strategic logic of suicide terrorism. *American Political Science Review* 97 (3): 344.

112 Clarke, R. V., and Newman, G. R. 2006. *Outsmarting the terrorists*. London: Praeger Security International, 12.

and least costly to the mujahideen in terms of casualties."[113] Therefore, for them, the cost of the death of suicide bombers is significantly outweighed by the benefits of engaging in this activity.

Contrary to the belief in the terrorist as irrational, their motivation, which can include extreme religious ideology and/or loyalty to a group or a group's cause, can be considered rational. These terrorists can be seen as acting rationally within the bounds of their own rationality according to their beliefs concerning the world around them. Irrational actors lack discipline. Their actions are characterized by spontaneity, lack of foresight, and lacking consideration for consequences. Terrorists do not fit this description. While emotions such as hatred and religious extremism do factor into the equation, despite claims to the contrary, these terrorists are rational. It takes discipline to coordinate and carry out attacks such as those on 9/11 and the bombings in Madrid and London. Their dedication, patience, and meticulous planning suggest rational decision making. Their actions are rational, not in the sense that emotions do not play into the decision-making process, but in that they weigh the costs and benefits of their alternatives before making a choice to orchestrate an attack.

Terrorism is a product of strategic choice, in which terrorists plan their attacks and make logical choices in order to be successful.[114] Therefore, while the terrorists appear irrational, the fact that attacks are conducted in accordance with specific objectives makes this act rational from the perspective of the terrorists. Terrorists should be considered as rational beings who take advantage of opportunities that present themselves to further their own ends. To be successful, a terrorist must have the means (capacity or capability), motivation, and opportunity to engage in an attack. By identifying and understanding the logic of terrorists' actions, policymakers can think of and devise ways to effectively counter them.

Researchers have applied these economic methods to analyze the measures that might work best to combat the threat of terrorism.[115] Situational crime prevention focuses on ways to reduce the opportunities for offending. Opportunities for terrorism can be reduced by increasing the effort involved; increasing the risks of failure; reducing the rewards of terrorism; and removing temptations, provocations, and excuses for terrorism.[116] Counterterrorism measures should make it more difficult for terrorists to achieve their objectives and thus increase the perceived costs. If the effort required to succeed in a task is raised high enough, the terrorists might give up on that task or take longer to execute their operations.

---

[113] Suicide terrorism: Martyrdom and murder. (2004, January 8). *The Economist*. http://www.economist.com/node/2329785; Clarke, R. V., and Newman, G. R. (2006). *Outsmarting the terrorists*. London: Praeger Security International, 55.

[114] Crenshaw, M. 1981. The causes of terrorism. *Comparative Politics* 13 (4): 379–399.

[115] Sandler, T., Enders, W., and Lapan, H. E. 1991. Economic analysis can help fight international terrorism. *Challenge* 34 (1): 11.

[116] Clarke, R. V., and Newman, G. R. 2006. *Outsmarting the terrorists*. London: Praeger Security International, 13.

Accordingly, an effective counterterrorism strategy should focus on ways to frustrate terrorists by making it more difficult and risky to commit terrorism and by reducing its rewards.

Rational choice theory can shed some light on the decision making of terrorists. The next section seeks to determine if terrorists share any common identifiable characteristics. If so, can a terrorist profile be created and used to identify terrorists?

TERRORIST PROFILE: WHAT DO TERRORISTS LOOK LIKE?

Attempts have been made to profile terrorists and identify common demographic and socioeconomic factors that are associated with terrorism.[117] Nevertheless, is it possible to build a profile of domestic and international terrorists based on information about the individual (e.g., gender, age, education, family status, criminal history, citizenship, ethnicity, and race)?[118]

Gender. There exists a common belief that all terrorist attacks are committed by males, with only a few exceptions. This, however, is not true. Many women have engaged in terrorist attacks either as part of a group or as a lone wolf inspired by a terrorist group's cause. Chechen terrorist groups regularly recruit women to engage in suicide attacks; these women have come to be known as the Black Widows. The Tamil Tigers are another group that actively seeks women recruits to engage in suicide terrorism. They are even said to have pioneered the use of women in suicide bombings.[119] An example of a woman lone wolf operative is Muriel Degauque, a Caucasian Muslim convert (from Christianity), who traveled to Iraq in November 2005 and detonated explosives on her person. Gender, therefore, is not a factor that can be used to profile terrorists; a member of a terrorist group or a lone wolf can be either a male or female.

The woman's role in terrorism depends on the group she is a part of, unless, of course, she engaged in the attack on her own accord and independent of any group. For example, in the Red Army Faction and the Red Brigades, women were not only operatives but also made up part of the groups' leadership (e.g., Gudrun Ensslin and Ulrike Meinhof for the RAF and Maria Curcio for the RB). In other groups, such as al-Qaeda, originally, women played only a supporting role. However, this has changed; more so since 9/11. Women have reportedly been used by al-Qaeda to train other women, run women's organizations and groups, and organize events, which constitute critical sources of al-Qaeda recruitment and fundraising

---

[117] Fields, R. M., Elbedour, S., & Hein, F. A. 2002. The Palestinian suicide bomber. In *The psychology of terrorism* (Vol. 2), ed. C. E. Stout. Westport, CT: Praeger; Ehrlich, P. R., & Liu, J. 2002. Some roots of terrorism. *Population and Environment* 24 (2): 183–191.

[118] Social status was also a factor. However, it is not included in the following sections as it was covered earlier in this chapter in the section on poverty and relative deprivation.

[119] Federal Bureau of Investigation. 2008, January 10. *Taming the Tamil Tigers: From here in the US.* http://www.fbi.gov/news/stories/2008/january/tamil_tigers011008.

for operations.[120] Jihad was predominantly what males in al-Qaeda engaged in. However, this too changed after 9/11. In early 2003, U.S. law enforcement officials learned that al-Qaeda planned to enlist women to engage in terrorist attacks to infuse an element of surprise into operations targeting the West. Moreover, in early 2004, European intelligence services stated that a monitored conversation between al-Qaeda terrorists revealed that there were other female operatives and recruits.[121]

The motivation for joining and playing a supporting or operational role in terrorism also differs between groups. Personal motives, including financial issues and the rape and/or murder of family members, are the most commonly cited reasons for engaging in terrorist attacks, especially suicide bombings.[122] For instance, many Black Widows revealed that they engaged in terrorist attacks to exact revenge for the deaths of their husbands who were killed by the Russian army.[123] Other than personal tragedies, relationships with males who are part of a terrorist group may also serve as a reason for women to join that group.[124] This was revealed as a reason for female terrorists joining the ETA.[125] Moreover, females have joined a terrorist group and/or engaged in terrorist attacks because of their belief in the group's cause.[126] Furthermore, social issues may also play a role. Specifically, in countries where gender inequality exists, interviews revealed that some Arab and Palestinian women in Israel participated as a way to accomplish this goal of

---

[120] Cunningham, K. J. 2007. Countering female terrorism. *Studies in Conflict and Terrorism* 30 (2): 121.

[121] Sciolino, E. 2004. Terror suspect in Italy linked to more plots. *New York Times*, June 11, 2004, p. A3; Nacos, B. L. 2005. The portrayal of female terrorists in the media: Similar framing patterns in the news coverage of women in politics and in terrorism. *Studies in Conflict and Terrorism* 28 (5): 447.

[122] Ozeren, S., and Gunes, I. D. 2007. Introduction: Sociological and psychological aspects of terrorism. In *Understanding terrorism: Analysis of sociological and psychological aspects*, eds. S. Ozeren, I. D. Gunes, and D. M. Al-Badayneh, 9. NATO Science for Peace and Security Studies (Vol. 22). Oxford, UK: IOS Press.

[123] Institute for National Security Studies (INSS). 2006, August. Black widows: The Chechen female suicide terrorists. *Jaffee Center for Strategic Studies, Tel Aviv University*. http://www .isn.ethz.ch/isn/Digital-Library/Publications/Detail/?ots591=0C54E3B3-1E9C-BE1E-2C24 -A6A8C7060233&lng=en&id=91164.

[124] Ozeren, S., and Gunes, I. D. 2007. Introduction: Sociological and psychological aspects of terrorism. In *Understanding terrorism: Analysis of sociological and psychological aspects*, eds. S. Ozeren, I. D. Gunes, and D. M. Al-Badayneh, 9. NATO Science for Peace and Security Studies (Vol. 22). Oxford, UK: IOS Press.

[125] MacDonald, E. 1992. *Shoot the women first*. New York: Random House.

[126] Galvin, D. M. 1983. The female terrorist: A socio-psychological perspective. *Behavioral Science and the Law* 1 (2): 19–32; Hudson, R. A. 1999. *The sociology and psychology of terrorism: Who becomes a terrorist and why?* 58–59. A report prepared under an Interagency Agreement by the Federal Research Division, Library of Congress. http://www.loc.gov/rr/frd /pdf-files/Soc_Psych_of_Terrorism.pdf.

attaining equality with men.[127] Consequently, the diversity of gender roles and motivations of women in terrorist groups calls into question the efficacy of using them as factors to predict potential terrorists.

Age. Studies have been conducted in an attempt to find an existing age profile for terrorists in order to determine which group in the population is most susceptible to terrorism. Russell and Bowman in their study of different terrorists around the world, found that the age range of active terrorists (not the leaders) were 22 to 25 years old, with the exception of Germans, Japanese, and Palestinians, whose age range was 20 to 25 years old.[128] Other studies revealed that active terrorists were younger and older than this age range. Many active members of the Tamil Tigers were 17 years old or younger. Niromi de Soyza was one such example. She joined the Tamil Tigers in 1987 at the age of 17 and became one of the first female soldiers in the group.[129] In addition, Hamas has been training teenagers as young as 14 at military camps in the Gaza Strip.[130] They have also been known to train children younger than 14 years old to use weapons against their perceived enemies and engage in suicide attacks. Likewise, the Palestinian Islamic Jihad has recruited children as young as 13 years of age to be suicide bombers and children as young as 11 to smuggle explosives and weapons.[131] In Iraq, children were recruited by al-Qaeda to engage in suicide terrorist attacks. In 2009, *The Times* of London reported that Special Forces Units in Iraq arrested four individuals under the age of 14 that made up a terrorist cell known as the "Birds of Paradise."[132]

By contrast, terrorists operating in the United States were found to represent a different age group. According to Smith, the average age of individuals at the time that they were indicted for their crimes was 39 for right-wing terrorists and 35 for left-wing terrorists.[133] Smith further noted that the members of the Armed Forces of Puerto Rican National Liberation (aka Fuerzas Armadas Liberacion Nacional

---

[127] Berko, A., Erez, E., and Globokar, J. L. 2010. Gender, crime and terrorism: The case of Arab/ Palestinian women in Israel. *British Journal of Criminology* 50 (4): 677–678.

[128] Russell, C. A., and Bowman, H. M. 1977. Profile of a terrorist. *Studies in Conflict and Terrorism* 1 (1): 17–34; Hudson, R. A. 1999. *The sociology and psychology of terrorism: Who becomes a terrorist and why?* 47. A report prepared under an Interagency Agreement by the Federal Research Division, Library of Congress. http://www.loc.gov/rr/frd/pdf-files/Soc_Psych _of_Terrorism.pdf.

[129] De Soyza, N. 2011. *Tamil Tigress: My story as a child soldier in Sri Lanka's bloody civil war.* Sydney, Australia: Allen & Unwin.

[130] Hamas Trains Teens at Military Camps in Gaza. 2009. *World Tribune*, August 5, 2009. http:// www.worldtribune.com/worldtribune/WTARC/2009/me_hamas0624_08_05.asp.

[131] Singer, P. W. 2005. The new children of terror. In *The making of a terrorist: Recruitment, training and root causes*, ed. J. J. F. Frost, 107. London: Praeger Security International.

[132] Hider, J. 2009. Al-Qaeda trained children "To be suicide bomb cell." *The Times* (London), April 21, 2009. http://www.timesonline.co.uk/tol/news/world/iraq/article6135887.ece.

[133] Smith, B. L. 1994. *Terrorism in America: Pipe bombs and pipe dreams.* New York: State University of New York Press, 48.

Puertorriqueña or FALN) and Los Macheteros who were indicted for terrorist activities were in their 30s.[134] Many domestic terrorist groups' leaders were also in their 30s, and some even in their 40s; examples include the leader of the Red Brigades, Renato Curcio, who was 35 at the time of his arrest in 1976, and Raúl Sendic, the leader of a Uruguay terrorist group known as Tupamaros, who was in his 40s when the terrorist group started operating.[135] The breadth of the age range of terrorists clearly shows that age is also not an effective predictor of terrorist behavior.

Education. Research on the education level of terrorists has also been conducted. The level of terrorists' education was found to differ between countries and terrorist groups. On the one side, research has shown that terrorists have little to no education.[136] In particular, the majority of the members in terrorist groups such as the Revolutionary Armed Forces of Colombia (Fuerzas Armadas Revolucionarias de Colombia or FARC), Shining Path, Tamil Tigers, Hamas, Hezbollah, and the PKK were poorly educated (if at all).[137] Ferracuti and Bruno also noted from their study of right-wing terrorists in Italy that these individuals were poorly educated.[138] The majority of right-wing terrorists in the United States were also found to be poorly educated; in fact, many of them were high-school dropouts.[139]

On the other side, existing research in this area shows that many terrorists have been educated in universities; the majority of whom have also received degrees from these institutions. In fact, left-wing terrorist groups in America were, overall, well-educated and professionally trained.[140] A case in point was Los Macheteros, in which many of the individuals indicted held university degrees and positions such as teachers and attorneys.[141] In addition, terrorists groups such as Aum Shinrikyo and 17 November had members who were well-educated. Moreover, research on terrorists operating in the West Bank and Gaza found that individuals who engaged in attacks against Israeli targets were more likely to be those with greater

---

[134] Ibid.

[135] Hudson, R.A. 1999. *The sociology and psychology of terrorism: Who becomes a terrorist and why?* A report prepared under an Interagency Agreement by the Federal Research Division, Library of Congress. http://www.loc.gov/rr/frd/pdf-files/Soc_Psych_of_Terrorism.pdf.

[136] Atran, S. 2003. Genesis of suicide terrorism. *Science* 299 (March 7): 153–1539.

[137] Hudson, R.A. 1999. *The sociology and psychology of terrorism: Who becomes a terrorist and why?* A report prepared under an Interagency Agreement by the Federal Research Division, Library of Congress. http://www.loc.gov/rr/frd/pdf-files/Soc_Psych_of_Terrorism.pdf.

[138] Ferracuti, F., and Bruno, F. 1981. Psychiatric aspects of terrorism in Italy. In *The mad, the bad and the different: Essays in honor of Simon Dinitz*, eds. I. L. Barak-Glantz and C. R. Huff. Lexington, MA: Lexington Books.

[139] Smith, B. L. 1994. *Terrorism in America: Pipe bombs and pipe dreams.* New York: State University of New York Press, 50.

[140] Ibid.

[141] Ibid.

years of education.[142] Furthermore, Sageman found that of the 172 al-Qaeda terrorists he studied, two-thirds of them had attended college.[143] In sum, research shows that individuals who engage in terrorist attacks can be either educated (on different levels) or noneducated. Accordingly, this factor is also not a very effective predictor of potential terrorists.

Family Status. In their study of different terrorists, Russell and Miller found that the majority of them were single.[144] Similarly, other studies showed that the individuals who were more likely to engage in terrorism were single males.[145] However, research has also shown that individuals who are married and have children are more likely to engage in terrorist attacks. For instance, Sageman found that three-quarters of the terrorists he studied (129 out of 172) were married and many of them had children.[146] Another study conducted on European jihadi terrorists found that among the 66 individuals for whom information was found, 39 were married or engaged at the time of their arrest, 8 had been divorced, 25 of them had children, and 22 were single.[147] Furthermore, many leaders of terrorist groups are married and have children. A case in point is Osama bin Laden. He had multiple wives and numerous children. For these reasons, this factor is also not a very effective indicator of potential terrorists.

Criminal History. Terrorist groups engage in serious criminal activity such as illicit firearms trafficking in pursuit of accomplishing their goals and funding their operations.[148] The investigation of the Madrid bombings revealed that the perpetrators of the attacks supported themselves by engaging in criminal activities. Consider once again Trabelsi (previously mentioned). He had engaged in drug dealing before becoming radicalized. Homegrown terrorists in the United States were also found to have criminal records. One such terrorist was James Cromitie,

---

[142] Krueger, A., and Malecková, J. 2002. *Education, poverty, political violence, and terrorism: Is there a causal connection?* National Bureau of Economic Research Working Paper No. 9074. http://papers.nber. org/ papers/W9074.

[143] Sageman, M. 2004. *Understanding terror networks.* Philadelphia: University of Pennsylvania Press.

[144] Russell, C. A., and Miller, B. H. 1983. Profile of a terrorist. In *Perspectives on terrorism*, eds. L. Z. Freedman and Y. Alexander. Wilmington, DE: Scholarly Resources.

[145] Abrahms, M. 2008. What terrorists really want. *International Security* 32 (4): 78–105; Smelser, N. J. 2007. *The faces of terrorism: Social and psychological dimensions.* Princeton, NJ: Princeton University Press; Merari, A. 2005. Social, organizational and psychological factors in suicide terrorism. In *Root causes of terrorism*, ed. T. Bjørgo. London: Routledge; Victoroff, J. 2005. The mind of the terrorist: A review and critique of psychological approaches. *Journal of Conflict Resolution* 49 (1): 3–42.

[146] Sageman, M. 2004. *Understanding terror networks.* Philadelphia: University of Pennsylvania Press.

[147] Bakker, E. 2006. Jihadi terrorists in Europe—Their characteristics and the circumstances in which they joined the jihad: An exploratory study, 40. *Netherlands Institute of International Relations-Clingendael.* http://www.clingendael.nl/publications/2006/20061200_cscp_csp_bakker.pdf.

[148] Makarenko, T. 2004. The crime–terror continuum: Tracing the interplay between transnational organized crime and terrorism. *Global Crime* 6 (1): 130.

the leader of a group of four (which included David Williams, Onta Williams, and Laguerre Payen), who sought to bomb military bases and synagogues in New York City. Cromitie had a criminal record and had served time in prison for selling drugs at a public school. Kevin Lamar James was another example. He was actually in prison when he started to convert fellow prisoners to Islam and recruited them to plan attacks against military installations and other targets in California. Literature also shows, however, that, overall, several groups and terrorists are law-abiding citizens—up until the point that they conspire to and subsequently engage in a terrorist attack (or attempt to commit an act of terrorism). In a study of 242 European jihadi terrorists, 58 had a prior criminal record.[149] The results indicate that the majority of individuals studied did not have a criminal record. Some homegrown terrorists in the United States were also found to have no prior criminal records. A case in point is Bryant Neal Vinas. In 2008, Vinas was charged with planning to attack a U.S. military base and providing information to al-Qaeda. Vinas had no connections to other terrorist groups and no prior criminal record.

Ethnicity, Race, Citizenship, and Religious Beliefs. For some terrorist groups, there is a single ethnicity: Shining Path members are Peruvian; FARC members are Colombian; Basque Fatherland and Liberty members are Basques; 17 November operatives were Greek; Red Brigades members were Italian; and Red Army Faction members were German (to name a few). Other terrorist groups are primarily composed of specific races. In the United States, left-wing terrorist groups consist primarily of minorities.[150] On the contrary, right-wing groups are largely made up of Caucasians (e.g., white supremacists).[151] The same could not be said for other groups, especially international terrorist groups. Those responsible for the bombings in London on July 7, 2005, consisted of three British citizens of Pakistani descent and a Jamaican (see Box 2-2). The failed attacks in London on July 21, 2005, were committed by East Africans.

The Madrid and London bombings, which together resulted in more than 250 deaths, demonstrated that Europe is facing a different type of threat from homegrown terrorists. While homegrown terrorism had occurred in the United States prior to 9/11—one example being Timothy McVeigh's bombing of the Alfred P. Murrah building in Oklahoma City in 1995—homegrown terrorism from al-Qaeda, extremist allies, and those inspired by al-Qaeda's cause has largely been attributed as a security issue prominent in Europe, which was revealed after the Madrid and London bombings. In particular, the Madrid bombings represented the first coordinated homegrown terrorist attack on European soil, whereas the London bombings represented the first suicide bombings from homegrown terrorists on European soil.

---

149 Bakker, E. 2006. Jihadi terrorists in Europe—Their characteristics and the circumstances in which they joined the jihad: An exploratory study, 40. *Netherlands Institute of International Relations-Clingendael.* http://www.clingendael.nl/publications/2006/20061200_cscp_csp_bakker.pdf.

150 Smith, B. L. 1994. *Terrorism in America: Pipe bombs and pipe dreams.* New York: State University of New York Press, 49.

151 Ibid.

Box 2-2   Who Were the London Bombers? Insights Into Their Profiles

On July 7, 2005, during morning rush hour in London, three suicide bombers (Shehzad Tanweer, Mohammad Sidique Khan, and Jermaine Lindsay) detonated bombs on their persons (less than one minute apart from each other) on three separate subway trains heading in different directions. Approximately one hour later, another suicide bomber (Hasib Hussain) detonated his explosive device on a bus. It was believed that mobile phones were used to set off these bombs. These terrorists were inspired by al-Qaeda's cause and not directed by them.

Demographic and socioeconomic information about these terrorists is included below.[1]

Shehzad Tanweer
- Second-generation British citizen
- Pakistani origin
- Played for a local cricket team
- Received a 2-year degree at Leeds Metropolitan University
- Left the university in 2003 before completing a 4-year degree
- Worked part-time at father's fish and chips store until November 2004
- Unemployed but supported by his family
- Still living with parents at the time of his death
- 22 years old when he died

Mohammad Siddique Khan
- Second-generation British citizen
- Pakistani origin
- Graduate of Leeds Metropolitan University
- Worked at a local primary school as a learning mentor, working with special needs children and those with language or behavioral problems
- Married in 2001
- Daughter born in May 2004
- 30 years old at the time of bombing

Hasib Hussain
- Second-generation British citizen
- Pakistani origin
- Very poor academic attendance and performance
- Stayed in college until the end of his course in June 2005
- Lived in deprived area but was not poor by the standards of the area
- Still living with parents at the time of his death
- 18 years old when he died

---

[1] The information on these terrorists was retrieved from the official report on the London bombings. See House of Commons. 2006, May 11. *Report of the official account of the bombings in London on 7th July 2005*. London: The Stationery Office. http://www.official-documents.gov.uk /document/hc0506/hc10/1087/1087.pdf.

(continues)

Box 2-2　Who Were the London Bombers? Insights Into Their Profiles (continued)

Jermaine Lindsay
- Born in Jamaica
- Moved to England with his mother
- Lindsay's mother converted to Islam in 2000. He converted almost immediately thereafter and took the name "Jamal"
- Around that time, in school, he began associating with troublemakers and was disciplined for handing out leaflets in support of al-Qaeda
- He married a white British convert to Islam (Samantha Lewthwaite)
- Had two children (a son, born April 11, 2004; a daughter, born July 22, 2005)
- He was unemployed at the time of the bombings
- He died at the age of 19

From what you know about the London bombers, can a single, common profile be developed of these terrorists?

However, recent FBI arrests have shed light on the existence of homegrown terrorists in the United States and the threat that they pose to the nation.

A review of the homegrown terrorists apprehended by agencies in Europe and the United States reveal that they have different profiles. Consider Daniel Patrick Boyd, a Caucasian U.S. citizen and homegrown terrorist, who was charged with providing material support to terrorists and conspiring to kill, kidnap, and injure individuals overseas on July 27, 2009. His sons also participated. Boyd was willing to send his children (Dylan and Zakariya, who were also charged with crimes) on suicide missions to Israel. In addition, Bryant Neal Vinas (previously mentioned) was a U.S. citizen with prior military service and as such, was able to travel freely outside the United States. Al-Qaeda has been trying to obtain such operatives and supporters because they could freely travel throughout the world on an American passport. One such case was Wadih el-Hage, a naturalized American citizen from Lebanon, who worked for al-Qaeda and was hired by Osama bin Laden himself primarily because of his citizenship.[152] Some of the homegrown terrorists arrested in the United States were not American citizens and were in the country illegally. In 2007, six foreign-born Muslims were arrested for planning to attack the military base in Fort Dix, New Jersey, and other military installations in New Jersey, Delaware, and Pennsylvania. Three of the men, Dritan Duka, Eljvir Duka, and Shain Duka, were in the United States illegally. The men had numerous traffic citations between them, which did not raise any red flags in their hometown.

Moreover, domestic and international terrorists and terrorist groups may or may not share a similar religious background. For those who subscribed to a religious ideology, 17 November members were Greek Orthodox. Likewise, members of the Provisional Irish Republican Army shared a similar religious background,

---

[152] Emerson, S. 2006. *Jihad incorporated: A guide to militant Islam*. New York: Prometheus, 32–33.

Catholicism. In addition, members of terrorist groups such as the Egyptian Islamic Jihad, the Islamic Movement of Uzbekistan, Ansar al-Islam (area of operation: Iraq), Al-Shabaab (area of operation: Somalia) and the Armed Islamic Group (area of operation: Algeria) were all Muslims. However, these distinctions are not so clear-cut in other terrorists and/or groups. In fact, Stanley Grant Phanor, one member of a group of homegrown terrorists inspired by al-Qaeda's cause that was convicted of planning to attack targets in the United States, such as the Sears Tower in Chicago and federal buildings in Florida, was a practicing Roman Catholic, not a Muslim. These converts are extremely valuable to the terrorist organizations because they do not fit law enforcement and intelligence agencies' traditional (albeit false) profile of an Islamic terrorist—male Arab Muslims between the ages of 17 and 40—and therefore, attract little attention by the authorities.

Smerconish argues that security efforts should target those "who look like terrorists."[153] But who looks like a terrorist? Intelligence shows that the domestic and international threat of terrorism includes terrorists of different profiles: homegrown; immigrants; and, for Islamic extremists, experienced jihadists and fresh converts. How can one determine what a terrorist looks like—that is, how can one create a terrorist profile—when individuals engaging in acts of terrorism include men, women, teenagers, rich, middle class, poor, educated, noneducated, immigrants, locals, individuals with prior criminal records, individuals with no criminal records, and individuals with no religious backgrounds or different religious backgrounds (e.g., Muslim, non-Muslim and Muslim converts)? Obviously, profiling in this case is impossible, because the description above could apply to the entire population. This, however, does not mean that all forms of profiling are futile. Other forms of profiling have fared better than this.[154] What is being argued here is that the profiling of terrorists based on demographic and socioeconomic factors is ineffective. What types of measures and policies would be effective? Prior to the analysis of counterterrorism, the factors that contribute to the sustainability of terrorist groups and terrorism must be examined.

HYPOTHETICAL SCENARIO

Shobbit Shabhara was born in the slums of Punjab, India. His parents moved to the United States when he was only 2 years old. Both parents, although educated, were unable to obtain work. As a result, his father started drinking heavily and eventually left his mother, who worked three jobs to be able to pay the rent. As such, from the age of 2 to 8 years old, Shabhara was largely left alone or in the care of neighbors. He hardly saw his mother, who died when he was 8 years old. He was subsequently placed in foster care. Throughout his adolescent years, he

---

[153] Smerconish, M. 2004. *Flying blind: How political correctness continues to compromise airline safety post 9/11*. Philadelphia: Running Press; Miniter, R. 2009. Profiling Arab Muslims is ineffective in fighting terror. In *Racial profiling: Opposing viewpoints series*, ed. D. E. Nelson, 124. New York: Greenhaven; Pipes, D. 2009. Profiling Arab Muslims is ineffective in fighting terror. In *Racial profiling: Opposing viewpoints series*, ed. D. E. Nelson. New York: Greenhaven.

[154] These other forms of profiling are explored later in the text.

engaged in petty theft. For one particular incident, he served a short sentence at a juvenile facility. As an adult, he was poor and unable to keep a job. Disillusioned with American society, he blamed the government for the way his life turned out and for the plight of his parents. He decided to engage in a terrorist attack to draw attention to his story. He believed that he would help effect change for future immigrants with his actions. On June 7, 2003, Shabhara began a 12-hour killing spree in lower Manhattan, targeting businessmen in Wall Street and government officials. Using a rifle and grenades, he killed 35 individuals and injured over 100 before being shot and killed by the police who responded to the scene.

1. Why did Shabhara turn to terrorism?
2. What can be done to try to prevent another attack like this?

CHAPTER SUMMARY

Various theories and hypotheses of terrorism were examined. Some theorists argue that individuals engage in terrorism because they are poor. Relative deprivation was also thought to cause individuals to engage in terrorist activity. Others focused on psychological studies to provide explanations for terrorist behavior. Socialization was also proposed as a possible explanation for terrorism. Opportunities to engage in terrorism and the ability of an individual to engage in such acts was also said to play a role. While numerous attempts have been made to profile terrorists, such attempts appear to be futile against homegrown terrorists apprehended after 9/11.

REVIEW QUESTIONS

1. Are terrorists poor?
2. Can relative deprivation explain why individuals engage in terrorist activity?
3. Do terrorists suffer from a mental disorder?
4. Individuals engage in terrorist activity due to socialization. Discuss.
5. Are terrorists rational?
6. Is there a terrorist profile?
7. Which, if any, theory best explains why individuals engage in terrorist behavior? Why do you think so?

chapter three

Factors Influencing the Sustainability of and Disengagement from Terrorism

Certain triggers have been identified that serve as catalysts for individuals in engaging in terrorist attacks. They are as follows: political (e.g., foreign occupier or conflict involving the ethnic or religious group a terrorist belongs to); economic (e.g., blocked mobility or loss of employment); social (e.g., real or perceived discrimination, alienation, or racism); and personal (e.g., the death of a loved one).[1] This chapter considers the factors that help sustain certain terrorist groups and the factors that led to the demise of other groups. To do so, it covers the religious, cultural, political, individual, social, and regional factors that influence terrorists. It also explores how these factors affect the trajectories of terrorist groups. It additionally examines factors that lead to an individual's disengagement with terrorist activities. The motivating questions for these analyses are: How and why do individuals leave terrorist groups? How do terrorist groups fail? Special attention will be paid to terrorist groups from Europe, Asia, and the Middle East.

---

[1] Silber, M. D., and Bhatt, A. 2007. Radicalization in the West: The homegrown threat. *New York City Police Department.* http://www.nyc.gov/html/nypd/downloads/pdf/public_information/NYPD _Report-Radicalization_in_the_West.pdf.

REALMS AFFECTING TERRORISM

Debates on counterterrorism measures and policies often ignore the characteristics that distinguish one terrorist group from another (like the Basque Fatherland and Liberty from al-Qaeda) and how these characteristics influence the effectiveness of government policies. Understanding the underlying factors that make the existence of terrorist attacks, such as the Madrid and London bombings, possible is paramount to building effective counterterrorism strategies. Pape argues that suicide terrorism depends on three components for its existence—the strategic, the social and the individual.[2] For him, suicide terrorism cannot be usefully examined unless all three factors are taken into account. Because this phenomenon occurs mainly as part of protracted campaigns that involve interactions among the terrorist organizations, local communities associated with terrorist organizations, and the individual suicide terrorists themselves, all three areas need to be examined.[3] Yet why does he apply this only to suicide attacks? What about other terrorist attacks such as the Madrid bombings, which did not involve suicide?[4] As will be shown below, terrorism (with few exceptions) depends on these factors, and a consideration of these issues can not only provide insight into the goals of domestic and international terrorists but also ways to effectively counter them.

Strategic

Terrorists pursue two types of goals: fundamental and instrumental. Fundamental goals consist of long-term objectives "such as the radical restructuring or replacement of the economic, political, social, and/or territorial status quo in a state or region."[5] A prime example of a group that follows these goals is the Islamic Jihad Union, which seeks to replace the existing rule in Uzbekistan with an Islamic state. Similarly, the Lashkar-e-Jhangvi aims to transform Pakistan into a Sunni Islamic state. Another fundamental goal is to cause the target government to change a policy. Examples of terrorists who pursue these objectives are special interest terrorists such as ecoterrorists and anti-abortion terrorists. A further fundamental goal involves the removal of occupying forces from the terrorists' homeland.

---

[2] Pape, R. A. 2005. *Dying to win: The strategic logic of suicide terrorism*. New York: Random House, 21.

[3] See ft 23 in ibid., p. 282.

[4] While several members involved in these bombings committed suicide, they only did so after the attacks, during the so-called Siege of Leganés. During this operation, in which the police had surrounded the apartment of these terrorists, after hours of fruitless negotiation, the Spanish police decided to storm the apartment, where "they tore down the front door and fired tear gas inside. It was a sign that the terrorists were expecting, and a few seconds later they detonated twenty kilograms of explosives, killing themselves and mortally injuring . . . an officer of the special forces." Vidino, L. 2006. *Al-Qaeda in Europe: The new battleground of international jihad*. New York: Prometheus, 305.

[5] Dutter, L. E., and Seliktar, O. 2007. To martyr or not to martyr: Jihad is the question, what policy is the answer? *Studies in Conflict and Terrorism* 30 (5): 431.

Examples of groups engaging in these activities are the Taliban and Hamas. These terrorists are often driven by political motivations of liberation from a perceived foreign occupier. Even suicide bombers "seek to achieve specific territorial goals, most often the withdrawal of the target state's military forces from what the terrorists see as national homeland."[6] Consider the Afghanistan war of 2001 and the Iraq war of 2003. Prior to these wars, al-Qaeda had not explicitly targeted Europe or its citizens, nor had any public statements been made by Osama bin Laden (or other members of al-Qaeda) of any grievances with Europe.[7] After European troops arrived and fought in these wars, al-Qaeda's stance toward Europe changed. From then on, Europe and its citizens were seen as legitimate targets of attacks. They were now targeted so European governments could be pressured to withdraw their troops and their support for these wars.

Instrumental (or operational) goals are "short-term, transient objectives, the achievement of which can be viewed as *logistical* successes . . . which terrorists *perceive* as relevant to the ultimate achievement of one or more fundamental goals" (emphasis in original).[8] Instrumental goals are pursued that fit with the group's fundamental objectives. From the perspective of the terrorists, therefore, these instrumental "attacks are designed to achieve specific political purposes: to coerce a target government to change policy, to mobilize additional recruits and financial support, or both."[9] The outcome of the Madrid bombings attests to this. The terrorists responsible for the Madrid bombings sought to influence the elections.[10] Indeed, Jamal Zougam (who was found guilty for his involvement in the bombings) verified this by asking, "Who won the election?" following his arrest on March 15, 2004. Believing that they were targeted because of their involvement in the Iraq war, Spaniards favored José Zapatero and his Socialist Party after the attack (before the attack, the Popular Party was ahead in the polls). Zapatero had promised to remove Spanish troops from Iraq.

The goals of terrorists vary; so too do the goals of suicide bombers. Not all suicide bombers engage in such attacks for religious reasons. A case in point is the Tamil Tigers. This group engages in suicide bombing to change existing government policies in their region and gain independence.[11] The majority of suicide cam-

6 Pape, R. A. 2003. The strategic logic of suicide terrorism. *American Political Science Review* 97 (3): 344.

7 Pape, R. A. 2005. *Dying to win: The strategic logic of suicide terrorism*. New York: Random House, 55.

8 Dutter, L. E., and Seliktar, O. 2007. To martyr or not to martyr: Jihad is the question, what policy is the answer? *Studies in Conflict and Terrorism* 30 (5): 431.

9 Pape, R. A. 2003. The strategic logic of suicide terrorism. *American Political Science Review* 97 (3): 344.

10 Indridason, I. H. 2008. Does terrorism influence domestic politics? Coalition formation and terrorist incidents. *Journal of Peace Research* 45 (2): 241–259.

11 Pape, R. A. 2005. *Dying to win: The strategic logic of suicide terrorism*. New York: Random House, 83–88; Fine, J. 2008. Contrasting secular and religious terrorism. *The Middle East Quarterly* XV (1). http://www.meforum.org/1826/contrasting-secular-and-religious-terrorism.

paigns were associated with terrorists seeking liberation from a foreign occupier and terrorists seeking to separate from an existing country and create their own independent state. The former includes the terrorist campaigns of the Palestinian Liberation Organization (PLO); the Abu Nidal Organization (ANO); the al-Aqsa Martyrs Brigades; the Palestinian Islamic Jihad (PIJ); the Palestine Liberation Front (PLF); the Popular Front for the Liberation of Palestine (PFLP); the Popular Front for the Liberation of Palestine-General Command (PFLP-GC); and Hamas against Israel; Hezbollah against Israel and the United States (at one point, this also included France); al-Qaeda against Israel, the United States, and its allies; the Taliban against the United States and its allies in Afghanistan; and Iraqi insurgents and terrorist groups against Israel, the United States, and its allies in Iraq. The latter includes the terrorist campaigns of the PKK against Turkey; the ETA against Spain; the Tamil Tigers against Sri Lanka; Kashmiri separatists against India; and Chechen separatists against Russia.

The goals that al-Qaeda terrorists pursue are both political and religious. On numerous occasions (both pre- and post-9/11), al-Qaeda operatives have cited political reasons for engaging in terrorism. Al-Qaeda commits violent acts against others to coerce them to behave or act according to the terrorist's interpretation of their religion.[12] Motivated by an ideology that inspires loyalty and facilitates action in accordance with the aims of al-Qaeda, they view terrorism and all forms of conventional and unconventional war as legitimate means of fighting a holy war (jihad).[13] They oppose "all nations and institutions that are not governed in a manner consistent with the group's particular extremist interpretation of Islam."[14] Thus, the terrorists' intent when engaging in violence is to kill for religious reasons or in the name of God. Nevertheless, ascribing al-Qaeda's strategic goals to religion alone would be inaccurate.

The Madrid and London bombings also fit with al-Qaeda's overall objectives. The Madrid bombers have been classified as part of a grassroots jihadist network (GJN). The assassination of Theo van Gogh was also said to have been orchestrated by such a group (the Hofstad group).[15] The GJN consists of individuals who operate within the country they reside in "and share the strategic objectives of the Global Jihad Movement (GJMV) but do not formally belong to the '[a]l Qaeda organization'

---

12 Al-Khattar, A. M. 2003. *Religion and terrorism: An interfaith perspective*. London: Praeger, 95.

13 Backes, U., and Jesse, E. 2002. Islamismus—Djihadismus—Totalitarismus—Extremismus. In *Extremismus and demokratie*, eds. U. Backes and E. Jesse, 18. Baden-Baden, Germany: Nomos; Stock, J., and Herz, A. 2007. The threat environment created by international terrorism from the German police perspective. *European Journal on Criminal Policy and Research* 13 (1/2): 89.

14 *United States v. Usama bin Laden et al.*, S (7) 98 Cr. 1023 (LBS), p. 34, http://www.fbi .gov/majcases/eastafrica/summary.htm; Alexander, Y., and Swetnam, M. S. 2001. *Usama bin Laden's al-Qaida: Profile of a terrorist network*. New York: Transnational, 1.

15 Vidino, L. 2006. *Al-Qaeda in Europe: The new battleground of international jihad*. New York: Prometheus, 347.

or other associated groups."[16] Their strategic objectives were identified by Sarhane Ben Abdelmajid Fakhet, the leader of the group that conducted the Madrid bombings, who explicitly stated in a suicide note that Spain's participation in the invasion of Iraq served as a justification for the terrorist attacks.[17] In particular, after several of the individuals responsible for the attacks committed suicide in their apartment, police found a tape on which the men "promised to continue their 'jihad until martyrdom'" if Spain did not "leave Muslim lands" and further stated that Spain was not safe and should "know that Bush and his administration will only bring destruction. We will kill you anywhere and in any manner."[18] Sarhane Ben Abdelmajid Fakhet also referred to a restoration of *Al Andalus* (i.e., Islamic rule over the Iberian Peninsula) as a reason for engaging in the Madrid bombings. Here, exacting revenge "for an event that has occurred 512 years before the Madrid bombing—the expulsion of Muslim rulers from Spain in 1492—and the obviously non-feasible purpose to restore the situation before this event serve[d] as a narrative to justify the killing of 191 victims and the wounding of over 1800 individuals."[19]

The perpetrators of the London bombings were essentially part of "an autonomous clique whose motivations, cohesiveness, and ideological grooming occurred in the absence of any organized network or formal entry into the jihad."[20] Their religious and political motivations were illustrated in one of the perpetrators' (Mohammad Sidique Khan) video statements. Like the propaganda videos by al-Qaeda operatives, the focus of Khan's video was on the "perceived injustices carried out by the West against Muslims justifying violence through his own . . . interpretation of Islam."[21] The London bombers' political motivation was made clear in Khan's video when he said,

> Your democratically elected governments continuously perpetuate atrocities against my people all over the world. And your support of them makes you directly responsible, just as I am directly responsible for protecting and avenging my Muslim brothers and sisters . . . Until we feel security, you will be our targets. And until you stop the bombing, gassing, imprisonment and torture of my people we will not stop this fight.[22]

---

16 Jordan, J., Mañas, F. M., and Horsburgh, N. 2008. Strengths and weaknesses of grassroot jihadist networks: The Madrid bombings. *Studies in Conflict and Terrorism* 31 (1): 17.

17 Schnellenbach, J. 2006. Appeasing nihilists? Some economic thoughts on reducing terrorist activity. *Public Choice* 129 (3): 303.

18 Vidino, L. 2006. *Al-Qaeda in Europe: The new battleground of international jihad.* New York: Prometheus, 305.

19 Schnellenbach, J. 2006. Appeasing nihilists? Some economic thoughts on reducing terrorist activity. *Public Choice* 129 (3): 303.

20 Kirby, A. 2007. The London bombers as "self-starters": A case study in indigenous radicalization and the emergence of autonomous cliques. *Studies in Conflict and Terrorism* 30 (5): 416.

21 See para. 39 in UK House of Commons. 2006, May 11. *Report of the official account of the bombings in London on 7th July 2005.* HC 1087. London: The Stationery Office. http://www.official-documents.gov.uk/document/hc0506/hc10/1087/1087.pdf.

22 Ibid.

While the London bombers, like the Madrid bombers, did act autonomously, their acts were very much in line with the organizational goals and visions of al-Qaeda. This vision concerns al-Qaeda's ability to effectively inspire "fellow Muslims in distant lands to embrace the jihad and rise up and challenge their apostate governments."[23] More specifically, al-Qaeda issued the following religious ruling (*fatwa*) on February 23, 1998, which included the following statement: "We—with God's help—call on every Muslim who believes in God and wishes to be rewarded to comply with God's order to kill the Americans and plunder their money wherever and whenever they find it."[24]

Terrorism is thus an integrated part of a strategy in which there are well-defined objectives. Most terrorists have a strategy. The tactical success of terrorist suicide attacks in the past demonstrated the value of these operations to would-be emulators.[25] There is evidence that shows that suicide terrorism works in extracting concessions from targeted governments. Perhaps the most commonly cited example illustrating the effectiveness of suicide terrorism is the American military's withdrawal from Lebanon after the suicide attacks of the terrorist group Hezbollah in 1983.[26] Other instances include a series of hijackings conducted by Palestinian terrorists (most of which were conducted by the Popular Front for the Liberation of Palestine) between 1968 and 1972, which resulted in the release of terrorists from prisons and, in the majority of instances, the freeing of the hijackers themselves.[27] Nations gave in to the terrorists' demands to spare the citizens of their own country from a retaliatory attack (or retaliatory attacks). Indeed, during the period of these hijackings, France, Germany, and Italy, among others, gave in to the demands of terrorists to prevent their own citizens from becoming targets of terrorism.[28] Examples abound of situations in which governments have met the demands of terrorists. States' failure to take an aggressive stance against

---

[23] See, more generally, Chapter 4 in Scheuer, M. 2003. *Through our enemies' eyes: Osama bin Laden, radical Islam and the future of America*. Washington DC: Brassey's, 61; Kirby, A. 2007. The London bombers as "self-starters": A case study in indigenous radicalization and the emergence of autonomous cliques. *Studies in Conflict and Terrorism* 30 (5): 426.

[24] Simon, S., and Martini, J. 2004/2005. Terrorism: Denying Al Qaeda its popular support. *Washington Quarterly* 28 (1): 131–145; Clarke, R. V., and Newman, G. R. 2006. *Outsmarting the terrorists*. London: Praeger Security International, 74.

[25] Hoffman, B., and McCormick, G. H. 2004. Terrorism, signaling, and suicide attack. *Studies in Conflict and Terrorism* 27 (4): 243–281.

[26] Clancey, P. 1983, December 20. Report of the DoD Commission on Beirut International Airport terrorist act, October 23, 1983. *HyperWar Foundation*. http://ibiblio.org/hyperwar/AMH/XX/MidEast/Lebanon-1982-1984/DOD-Report/index.html; Clarke, R. V., and Newman, G. R. 2006. Outsmarting the terrorists London: Praeger Security International, 56.

[27] Dershowitz, A. M. 2002. *Why terrorism works: Understanding the threat, responding to the challenge*. New Haven, CT: Yale University Press, 57–61.

[28] Dershowitz, A. M. 2002. *Why terrorism works: Understanding the threat, responding to the challenge*. New Haven, CT: Yale University Press, 99.

Box 3-1 Terrorist Attacks in Brief: The Case of Kabul, Afghanistan

Within 4 months, the Taliban struck several high-profile targets in Kabul, Afghanistan. The first one, which occurred in June 2011, involved a popular hotel among foreigners and government officials in Kabul, the Intercontinental Hotel. This hotel was attacked by nine Taliban militants. Ten civilians were killed along with the terrorists (some died from suicide attacks; others from security forces). These attacks illustrate the current vulnerability of hospitality security. The hotel was one of the most heavily secured locations in Kabul, and yet terrorists were able to attack. Two months later, in August 2011, Taliban suicide bombers attacked the British Council compound in Kabul, causing multiple deaths and injuries. The following month, in September 2011, the Taliban engaged in a coordinated attack against the U.S. Embassy, NATO headquarters, and other government buildings. It was estimated that 16 people (5 police officers and 11 Afghan civilians, including 6 children) were killed and over two dozen were injured.

terrorism in the past sent the message that "terrorism works."[29] This message, having been read loud and clear by future would-be emulators, has led to a significant increase in terrorist attacks, especially those involving suicide tactics, over the last 2 decades.[30]

By way of extension, this also implies that if terrorists were unsuccessful—their goals were not met and no concessions were obtained from the government—then the number of terrorist attacks and recruits would significantly decrease. Moreover, individuals will most likely desist from terrorism if their goals are achieved. Partial achievement of goals may also suffice for individuals and groups to desist from engaging in terrorism. Posed another way, removing the reason why terrorists engage in attacks often leads to the disbanding of the group and/or the decision of an individual to desist from terrorist activity. Consider, for example, the National Liberation Front (FLN). This group engaged in a violent terror campaign against French colonial rulers in Algeria. When an independent Algerian state was created, the group ceased their attacks.[31]

In general, terrorist attacks serve two purposes: to coerce opponents and to gain supporters. The latter constitutes the social logic of terrorism; without it, the terrorist organization would cease to exist.

---

[29] Dershowitz, A. M. 2002. *Why terrorism works: Understanding the threat, responding to the challenge*. New Haven, CT: Yale University Press.

[30] Pape, R. A. 2005. *Dying to win: The strategic logic of suicide terrorism*. New York: Random House, 22; Pape, R. A. 2003. The strategic logic of suicide terrorism. *American Political Science Review* 97 (3): 344.

[31] Henderson, H. 2001. *Global terrorism: The complete reference guide*. New York: Checkmark, 52.

Social

Terrorist groups can be put into one of five categories (which may or may not be mutually exclusive depending on the group): nationalist–separatist, left-wing, right-wing, special interest, and religious, according to the terrorists' primary motivations and ideologies.[32] The tactics of terrorists are more often than not shaped by their objectives and beliefs. For instance, terrorists who pursue ideologies of the creation of a Marxist state in their respective countries tend to target government and private industry officials (i.e., symbols of a capitalist state) and agents of the criminal justice system. An example of a group that targeted these individuals was the Red Brigades. Their kidnapping of a right-wing judge, Mario Sossi, and a politician, Aldo Moro, among others, attests to this. The Red Army Faction engaged in similar conduct with the kidnapping of a prominent German industrialist and president of the German Employer's Union, Hanns-Martin Schleyer.

In a comparable manner, terrorists who pursue ideologies of liberation or separation from a state tend to target domestic and international government officials and foreign residents. For example, the Provisional Irish Republican Army (PIRA) targeted British government officials, military, and police from Northern Ireland, and Northern Loyalist groups. The PIRA subsequently expanded its definition of legitimate targets. This was illustrated in the 1993 Warrington bombings. Here, two attacks took place: one at a gas storage depot in February and one on Bridge Street in March. The latter attack resulted in 2 deaths and more than 50 injuries.[33] In April 1993, the PIRA also conducted the Bishopsgate bombing. Here, a truck bomb was detonated in London's financial district, Bishopsgate, causing 1 death, 44 injuries, and approximately £1 billion in damage. When the PIRA diverted from its original targets and attacked these areas, public backlash occurred. Consequently, this group lost Irish supporters and operatives. This incident illustrates the importance of the social environment in helping sustain the group and, conversely, causing the demise of the group. While terrorism often commands broad social support within the national communities from which terrorists "recruit, because they are seen as pursuing legitimate rationalistic goals, especially liberation from foreign occupation,"[34] the opposite is also true. Specifically, if the terrorists' goals are no longer seen as legitimate and rational, then social support for terrorism (by new recruits or existing members in either an operational or supporting role) will, by consequence, decrease.

Necessary components of terrorism are a legitimizing ideology and a supportive and enabling community.[35] The role of the community in terrorism is critical as it provides or assists terrorists in finding resources for their group and missions such

---

[32] See the chapter on understanding terrorism.

[33] No deaths or injuries resulted from the gas storage depot as the bomb malfunctioned.

[34] Bloom, M. 2005. *Dying to kill: The allure of suicide terror*. New York: Columbia University Press, 22.

[35] Richardson, L. 2006. *What terrorists want*. New York: Random House, 106.

as funds, weapons, safe havens, recruits, and operatives (i.e., individuals willing to engage in either suicide or nonsuicide terrorist attacks). Without popular support, a terrorist group could not survive. For example, new recruits are needed to replace members of the group who are aging or have died; without these new recruits, eventually the group would cease to exist. To receive such support, the group must have engaged in a successful terrorist attack (i.e., one that fulfilled the terrorists' goal or goals), offer compensation to the community whenever required (i.e., in the event that an operative is killed, some economic support is provided to his or her family), and bestow an elevation of status to the individuals who engage in terrorist attacks and their families. In addition, the group must take special precautions to ensure that their attacks to do not target those who the community perceives as innocent. The terrorist group November 17 (17N) was popular among Greeks (at least in the beginning) because it took special precautions not to kill innocent bystanders (with some exceptions; for example, the failed bombing attempt at the Piraeus port in Athens, Greece, in June 2002). In addition, 17N targeted those considered wicked by the Greeks. One of their targets were prior officials from the Greek Junta, a dictatorship rule by the military in Greece between 1967 and 1974, which abolished civil rights; dissolved political parties; kept secret files on citizens; and exiled, imprisoned, killed, and tortured politicians and citizens for their political beliefs during its regime. On December 14, 1976, for instance, 17N assassinated an individual who served as a police captain during the military junta, Evangelos Mallios, who had been dishonorably discharged from the police force for allegedly torturing prisoners during the junta's rule.

Moreover, terrorist groups have to be careful about with whom they associate and form alliances. The consequences of obtaining support from and forming alliances with the wrong groups are evident in the case of the New World Liberation Front (NWLF), which was formed in San Francisco, California, in 1970.[36] This group linked itself to prison reform movements and allied itself with a group of militant ex-convicts known as the Tribal Thumbs.[37] As a result of this alliance, the public alienated and denounced the group. This, in consequence, led to the NWLF's demise.

For religious terrorism, especially Islamic extremism, the actions of the terrorist must be seen as justifiable by their community. For al-Qaeda, the actions of terrorists are legitimated through religious texts and individuals' interpretations of them. In order for al-Qaeda to succeed in accomplishing its objectives, its actions must be seen as legitimate. Terrorists often command broad social support within the communities from which they are recruited because they are seen as pursuing legitimate goals, such as liberation from a foreign occupier.[38] Yet, while the political goals are easily accepted, the tactics used by al-Qaeda can and have been called into question by members of the Islamic community.

---

[36] White, J. R. 2001. *Terrorism: An introduction.* Belmont, CA: Wadsworth Thomas Learning, 32.

[37] Ibid.

[38] Pape, R. A. 2005. *Dying to win: The strategic logic of suicide terrorism.* New York: Random House, 22.

Al-Qaeda justifies their actions through religious texts and their interpretations of them. Their use of violence derives from and is used to preserve extreme interpretations of the Koran.[39] These interpretations encourage them to muster "all the men and cavalry" at their "disposal [and] . . . strike terror into (the hearts of) the enemies."[40] They further serve as a justification for the use of violence and even suicide to the community and the individual. Religion is, therefore, used to further their political goals—to establish their legitimacy and incite the masses to follow their cause.

There exists a degree of ambiguity in the teachings of Islam. Terrorists exploit this, always finding excerpts in religious texts that legitimize the use of violence. While the Koran explicitly states that there will be no compulsion in religion, it also considers it a holy duty for followers to convert others to Islam. In principle, the Koran permits "the use of force as one means of spreading the Islamic faith, but only if strict rules are observed—for example, not attacking civilians and forewarning the enemy and thus forbids all forms of terror."[41] According to their religion, during warfare in defense of Islam (jihad), "Muslims soldiers must distinguish between combatants and non-combatants and make every effort to spare women and children."[42] The 9/11 attacks and the Madrid and London bombings did not conform to these criteria. Perhaps with the exception of some of the individuals who died in the Pentagon on 9/11, none of the casualties in these attacks were responsible for U.S. policy or the participation of Spain and the United Kingdom in the Afghanistan and Iraq wars (in 2001 and 2003, respectively).

The followers of Osama bin Laden reject the distinction between combatants and non-combatants.[43] Instead, they follow a binary logic to rationalize using violence, in which the

> unambiguous adaptation of Islamic principles to a political situation establishes a complete separation between "true believers," that is the Islamic fundamentalists, and the "enemy," defined as non-believers and those Muslims who are in any way connected to non-Islamic regimes.[44]

---

[39] Venkatraman, A. 2007. Religious basis for Islamic terrorism: The Quran and its interpretations. *Studies in Conflict and Terrorism* 30 (3): 231.

[40] Nazar, M. 1991. *Commandments by God in the Quran.* New York: The Message Publications, 733 (8:25); Venkatraman, A. 2007. Religious basis for Islamic terrorism: The Quran and its interpretations. *Studies in Conflict and Terrorism* 30 (3): 231.

[41] See ft 11 in Stock, J., and Herz, A. 2007. The threat environment created by international terrorism from the German police perspective. *European Journal on Criminal Policy and Research* 13 (1/2): 89.

[42] Mockaitis, T. R. 2007. *The "new" terrorism: Myths and reality.* London: Praeger Security International, 71–72.

[43] Ibid, p. 74.

[44] Hellmich, C., and Redig, A. J. 2007. The question is when: The ideology of al Qaeda and the reality of bioterrorism. *Studies in Conflict and Terrorism* 30 (5): 381.

The latter open-ended category is now considered as a legitimate target in the jihad.

Many spiritual leaders have sought to clarify what it means to "die by one's own hand." For example, a Hamas spiritual leader, Sheikh Ahmad Yasin, "declared that any suicide bomber who had received the blessing of a certified Muslim cleric should be considered a . . . martyr . . . who had fallen in the service of jihad rather than one who had committed suicide by personal intent."[45] Others, such as Sheikh Yusuf al-Qaradawi, an influential Sunni cleric based in Qatar, have affirmed Yasin's approach.[46] The classical (Islamist) jurists clearly distinguish between "facing certain death at the hands of the enemy and killing oneself by one's own hand."[47] Only the first is believed to lead to heaven. The morality of suicide attacks has been heavily debated among Islamists. Religious texts and their interpretations have served to provide different perspectives on similar events. As a result of varying religious interpretations of the Koran within Islamic communities, suicide bombings are viewed differently among the population. On the one hand, suicide bombers are celebrated as heroes and loyal sons (or daughters) of their religion.[48] These individuals command respect from the community, as do their surviving relatives. Here, suicide is redescribed as "honorable, pious, heroic, as self-sacrifice for a 'higher' cause."[49] Individuals' engagement in suicide bombings is viewed as a "noble sacrifice and martyrdom (*shahid*) in fulfillment of religious command and privilege to serve the true religion gloriously against the infidels (*jihad*)."[50] Indeed, Khosrokhavar, having engaged in a comparative analysis of martyrdom in Christianity, Islam, and Sikhism, found that it was mainly Islamic to sanction sacred death for the sake of the community (*umma*).[51] On the other hand, others consider suicide bombings as the act of cowards; evil deeds that deserve condemnation and not praise. For them, these acts not only violate the sanctity of human life but also violate Islamic prohibitions on the spilling of innocent blood.[52] Islam explicitly

---

[45] Tal, N. 2002, June. Suicide attacks: Israel and Islamic terrorism. *Strategic Assessment,* Jaffee Center for Strategic Studies, Tel Aviv University, 2; Fine, J. 2008. Contrasting secular and religious terrorism. *The Middle East Quarterly* XV (1). http://www.meforum.org/1826/contrasting-secular-and-religious-terrorism.

[46] Tal, ibid., p. 45; Fine, ibid.

[47] See ft 51 in Gambetta, D. 2005. Can we make sense of suicide missions? In *Making sense of suicide missions,* ed. D. Gambetta, 295. Oxford, UK: Oxford University Press.

[48] Charny, I. W. 2007. *Fighting suicide bombing: A worldwide campaign for life.* London: Praeger Security International, 45.

[49] Holmes, S. 2005. Al-Qaeda, September 11, 2001. In *Making sense of suicide missions,* ed. D. Gambetta, 137. Oxford, UK: Oxford University Press.

[50] Charny, I. W. 2007. *Fighting suicide bombing: A worldwide campaign for life.* London: Praeger Security International, 53.

[51] Khosrokhavar, F. 2005. *Suicide bombers: Allah's new martyrs.* Trans. D. Macey. London: Pluto, 149–153.

[52] Charny, I. W. 2007. *Fighting suicide bombing: A worldwide campaign for life.* London: Praeger Security International, 53.

condemns suicide bombings, because both suicide and the killing of innocent individuals are deemed a violation of Allah's will.[53]

Religious terrorists need to overcome that distinction in order to persuade their "supporters who consider suicide a sin that they are martyrs and not suicides."[54] A paramount preoccupation shared by individuals sacrificing their life for a cause is to make sure that the relevant others (here the Islamic community) do not think of them as being either mentally ill or sinful.[55] Unless their audience or target group is persuaded of this, one of the main purposes of suicide attacks—to encourage others to fight for the terrorists' cause and engage in similar activities—would be lost.[56] Just as they need to legitimize violent acts, they also need to convince others that they are martyrs and not just suicides. By socially legitimizing their acts, actions that should have been defined as suicide and murder are now being redefined as martyrdom and legitimate self-defense. With respect to suicide bombings, the Islamic communities' "admiration for suicide bombers is needed to establish martyrdom as a convincing reason for violence against civilians."[57] While it is unclear whether martyrdom motivates rather than consoles believers, its use seems to legitimate suicide for perpetrators, their families, and constituencies without whom al-Qaeda could not run suicide bombings.[58] Although al-Qaeda leaders go to great lengths to convince the public of the religious basis for killing innocent civilians and that suicide is an act of martyrdom, the terrorist who engages in these activities must also be convinced. The same holds true for other forms of terrorism. If the individual does not believe that their behavior is justified[59] and serves a specific purpose, he or she will not engage in terrorism.

Individual

Individuals, like communities, need to believe that the goals of the terrorist group are legitimate and the actions of the group are designed to achieve these objectives. Consider, once again, religious terrorism and, more specifically, Islamic extremists. For them, martyrdom provides a rationalizing narrative for the perpetrators of terrorism, their families, and constituencies, without which the groups or organizations that depend on popular support could not run their suicide operations.[60]

---

53 Ibid., p. 45.

54 Gambetta, D. 2005. Can we make sense of suicide missions? In *Making sense of suicide missions*, ed. D. Gambetta, 295. Oxford, UK: Oxford University Press.

55 Ibid.

56 Ibid.

57 Pape, R. A. 2005. *Dying to win: The strategic logic of suicide terrorism.* New York: Random House, 21.

58 Gambetta, D. 2005. Can we make sense of suicide missions? In *Making sense of suicide missions*, ed. D. Gambetta, 293. Oxford, UK: Oxford University Press.

59 The meaning of this is explored in the next section.

60 Gambetta, D. 2005. Can we make sense of suicide missions? In *Making sense of suicide missions*, ed. D. Gambetta, 293. Oxford, UK: Oxford University Press.

Often ignored is the fact that terrorists need to justify their actions and to reassure themselves that they are acting in an honorable way for a cause. Terrorists seek to find some kind of justification for their violence, killing of non-combatants, and, in the case of suicide bombers, taking their own lives in order to perceive their actions as sound. They seek to justify their immoral actions through neutralization techniques.

Sykes and Matza's theory of neutralization attempts to explain how reprehensible actions are justified by those who perpetrate them.[61] This theory suggests that juvenile delinquents try to justify their behavior in order to alleviate guilt. These techniques also serve to motivate offenders by providing them with justifications for violating social norms. Neutralization techniques have been used outside Sykes and Matza's analysis of juvenile delinquents to include other acts of violence, even terrorism.[62] Five neutralization techniques were identified by Sykes and Matza: denial of responsibility, denial of injury, denial of the victim, condemnation of condemners, and the appeal to higher loyalties. Certain techniques are better adapted to particular acts than to others. Three techniques—the appeal to higher loyalties, denial of the victim, and the condemnation of condemners—will be explored below.

With the first technique, appeal to higher loyalties, it is important to note that deviation from norms may occur not because they are "rejected but because other norms, held to be more pressing or involving a higher loyalty, are accorded precedence."[63] Specifically, "internal and external social controls may be neutralized by sacrificing the demands of the larger society for the demands of a smaller group to which the delinquent belongs."[64] Through this technique, another necessary component of terrorist operations (especially suicide operations) is revealed: disaffected individuals.[65] Here, an important distinction needs to be made. These disaffected individuals are those who are disillusioned by mainstream society. The London bombers are one such example. Islam offers a sense of community to these disaffected individuals by providing them with a sense of belonging and a purpose. Terrorists' groups also provide them with a sense of belonging. In fact, in Sageman's (2004) study of the biographies of 171 jihadists, he found that the growing bonds and social ties within these groups were important factors that eventually turned these groups into terrorist cells.[66]

---

61 Sykes, G., and Matza, D. 1957. Techniques of neutralization: A theory of delinquency. *American Sociological Review* 22 (6): 664–670.

62 Young, J. 2007. *The vertigo of late modernity*. London: Sage; Al-Khattar, A. M. 2003. *Religion and terrorism: An interfaith perspective*. London: Praeger.

63 Sykes, G., and Matza, D. 1957. Techniques of neutralization: A theory of delinquency. *American Sociological Review* 22 (6): 669.

64 Ibid.

65 Richardson, L. 2006. *What terrorists want*. New York: Random House, 106.

66 Sageman, M. 2004. *Understanding terror networks*. Philadelphia: University of Pennsylvania Press, cited in Schnellenbach, J. 2006. Appeasing nihilists? Some economic thoughts on reducing terrorist activity. *Public Choice* 129 (3): 304.

Al-Qaeda terrorists' primary loyalty is to their religion and their Islamic community. For them, their religion is the only acceptable moral system, and through it, terrorist acts are justified.[67] These terrorists also claim altruistic goals that go beyond personal interests.[68] Altruistic motives are those whose acts of extreme self-sacrifice are believed to best further the interests of the group.[69] The London bombers fit the paradigm of altruistic suicide, in which high levels of group integration and respect for Islamic community values led them to commit suicide out of a sense of duty.[70] Often, individuals engage in suicide bombings to help family members in the hope that the group will provide economic assistance to their families once they have completed their missions. Others commit suicide bombings for their communities. According to Durkheim, the more an individual values his or her community, the more likely he or she will kill himself or herself for the sake of the community, because he or she believes it is their duty to do so.[71] The homicidal dimension of the terrorist act makes individuals "overlook an important cause leading to it—that many suicide terrorists are killing themselves to advance what they see as the common good."[72] Terrorists' altruistic motives are significant in the individual logic of terrorism (especially suicide terrorists) because self-sacrificial acts, like martyrdom, propagate terrorism. The portrayal of suicide bombers as martyrs serves to encourage others to follow suit, although such recruits are not limited to those who engage in suicide tactics.

With the second neutralization technique, denial of the victim, "the moral indignation of self and others may be neutralized by an insistence that the injury is not wrong in light of the circumstances."[73] To be precise, "the injury, it may be claimed, is not a real injury; rather, it is a form of rightful retaliation or punishment."[74] This point is extremely important because while the discussion of terrorism focuses on innocent civilians, they do not exist in the terrorist's mindset.[75] For terrorists, if one is not supporting them, then one is against them—there is no middle

---

[67] Al-Khattar, A. M. 2003. *Religion and terrorism: An interfaith perspective*. London: Praeger, 92.

[68] Ibid., p. 88.

[69] Gambetta, D. 2005. Can we make sense of suicide missions? In *Making sense of suicide missions*, ed. D. Gambetta, 270. Oxford, UK: Oxford University Press.

[70] Altruistic suicide was one of the forms of suicide identified in Emile Durkheim's famous study on 19th-century suicides. Spaulding, J. A., and Simson, G. 1951. *Suicide: A study in sociology*. Trans. E. Durkheim. New York: Free Press, 219; Pape, R. A. 2005. *Dying to win: The strategic logic of suicide terrorism*. New York: Random House, 23.

[71] Durkheim, E. 1951. *Suicide: A study in sociology*. Trans. J. A. Spaulding and G. Simson. New York: Free Press, 219.

[72] Pape, R. A. 2005. *Dying to win: The strategic logic of suicide terrorism*. New York: Random House, 180.

[73] Sykes, G., and Matza, D. 1957. Techniques of neutralization: A theory of delinquency. *American Sociological Review* 22 (6): 668.

[74] Ibid.

[75] German, M. 2007. *Thinking like a terrorist: Insights from a former FBI undercover agent*. Washington, DC: Potomac, 101.

ground. Once again, consider Mohammad Sidique Khan's (a London bomber) video statement, which stressed that civilians' support of their governments makes them directly responsible for the attacks. Terrorists also "deflect blame for specific incidents by pointing to the larger culpability of the other side."[76] This is similar to Bandura's analysis of the technique of attributing blame to the victim in order to avoid self-sanction.[77] Here, perpetrators view themselves as victims who were provoked. As such, the actual victims of the crime (or in this case, terrorist attack) are blamed and viewed as bringing this action upon themselves.

With the third technique, condemnation of the condemners, "justification at this point is based on the argument that whoever condemns a violent act, especially the victim, is worse than the offenders and therefore is a worthy target."[78] According to Sykes and Matza, with this technique, individuals shift the focus of their attention from their own deviant acts to the motives and behavior of those who disapprove of their violations.[79] Each side sees the other as the true wrongdoer, who performs reprehensible acts that need to be condemned; whether it is the terrorists that claim these "others" are infidels or "others" who claim that these terrorists are "evil beings" worthy of condemnation. To justify their behavior, terrorists are better able to inflict mass casualties when they do not consider the targets (i.e., the victims) as human beings.[80] While terrorists may acknowledge that they are engaging in violence or committing illegal acts, they will claim that the "others," those who condemn them, are actually engaging in even worse activities.[81]

DESISTANCE FROM TERRORISM

With terrorists, as with ordinary criminals, neutralization techniques do not serve to suppress or eliminate their feelings, but to justify their behavior by rationalizing their actions. The behavior of terrorists differs according to their role. Some individuals may choose to take an operational role (e.g., conduct a terrorist attack), while others may instead decide to take on a supporting role (e.g., providing safe havens for terrorists or donating funds to terrorist groups). A person's decision to engage (or disengage) from terrorism is influenced by psychological traits, political and/or religious motives, and interactions with their environment. The decision to disengage from terrorism may be voluntary or involuntary. Voluntary decisions may be the

---

[76] Mockaitis, T. R. 2007. *The "new" terrorism: Myths and reality*. London: Praeger Security International, 15.

[77] Bandura, A. 1999. Moral disengagement in the perpetration of inhumanities. *Journal of Personality and Social Psychology Review* 3 (3): 193.

[78] Al-Khattar, A. M. 2003. *Religion and terrorism: An interfaith perspective*. London: Praeger, 88.

[79] Sykes, G., and Matza, D. 1957. Techniques of neutralization: A theory of delinquency. *American Sociological Review* 22 (6): 668.

[80] Bandura, A., Barbaranelli, C., Caprara, G., and Pastorelli, C. 1996. Mechanisms of moral disengagement in the exercise of moral agency. *Journal of Personality and Social Psychology* 71 (2): 364–374.

[81] Al-Khattar, A. M. 2003. *Religion and terrorism: An interfaith perspective*. London: Praeger, 92.

result of an assessment of alternative options. For example, the available amnesty from the government may be seen by terrorists as a legitimate reason to disengage from future terrorist attacks. A case in point was the Islamic Salvation Front (FIS), a fundamentalist party in Algeria that ended its conflict with the government in June 1999 with the signing of an amnesty agreement.[82] Even policies that allowed terrorists to obtain reduced sentences or other concessions from the government assisted in individuals' long-term disengagement from terrorism. A case in point is the effect on the Red Brigades of Italy's "carrot and stick" provisions in Law 191 and the Cossiga Law. For instance, in 1980, General Carlo Alberto Dalla Chiesa captured Patrizio Peci, the leader of the Red Brigades column in Turin. He offered Peci a softer punishment in exchange for information that led to the arrest of Mario Moretti and other members of the leadership of the Red Brigades. Similar effects occurred with the use of this system on other operatives of the Red Brigades. Ultimately, this led to the demise of this terrorist group. By contrast, an involuntary decision to leave the terrorist group or disengage in terrorist attacks includes being forced out of the group by a leader, member, or members; incapacitated by criminal justice agents; or killed by members of the group, law enforcement agencies, or others.

Terrorist groups can be classified into two types: recidivists, those who repeatedly engage in terrorist attacks throughout their lifetime; and one-hit wonders, those who engage in a single attack and either are killed in the process or desist from future terrorist activity.[83] Disengagement from terrorist activities means one of two things: First, the individuals desist from all forms of activities associated with terrorism. Second, an individual disengages from a specific role—operations goal (e.g., executing a terrorist attack)—within a terrorist group or, for a terrorist who is not officially part of the terrorist group, he or she desists from executing terrorist attacks. However, these individuals do not desist from terrorism entirely. Instead, they take on a different role within the group or organization, such as a supporting role (raises funds, provides weapons, etc.). Those not part of the group may provide support to existing organizations. Disengagement from terrorism does not necessarily imply that an individual's view of terrorism changes. They may still view terrorism as a legitimate form of retaliation in certain circumstances; the only difference is that they have desisted from engaging in such practices. To change views on terrorism, deradicalization is required, wherein a fundamental change occurs in the individual's understanding of the legitimacy of terrorism. Conversely, "disengagement refers to a behavioral change, such as leaving a group or changing one's role within it. It does not necessitate a change in values or ideals, but requires relinquishing the objective of achieving change through violence."[84]

---

[82] Henderson, H. 2001. *Global terrorism: The complete reference guide.* New York: Checkmark, 52.

[83] Blomberg, S. B., Engel, R. C., and Sawyer, R. 2010. On the duration and sustainability of transnational terrorist organizations. *Journal of Conflict Resolution* 54 (2): 303–330.

[84] Fink, N. C., and Hearne, E. B. 2008, October. Beyond terrorism: Deradicalization and disengagement from violent extremism, i. *International Peace Institute Publications.* http://www.ipinst.org/media/pdf/publications/beter.pdf.

When individuals leave or disengage from the terrorist group, reasons that are often cited are disillusionment and revulsion with the tactics or goals being pursued by the group and social tensions within the group (i.e., when the group engages in activities perceived as illegitimate by a member or supporter of the group).[85] For instance, individuals will leave the group if they believe the acts of the group are unjustified. A case in point is Nasir Abas, a prior member of Jemaah Islamiya and its predecessor groups for more than 18 years.[86] According to Abas, he distanced himself and eventually left the group in the aftermath of a series of church bombings conducted by Jemaah Islamiya that killed 19, because such practices were against the teachings of the Prophet.[87] Likewise, a prior member of the Provisional Irish Republican Army, Sean O'Callaghan, expressed revulsion when "a colleague commented on the death of a policewoman from a bomb explosion, 'I hope she's pregnant and we get two for the price of one.'"[88] Generally, individuals will continue to support or engage in terrorism as long as they believe that the goals they are pursuing are legitimate.

For groups, there exists another factor that affects the sustainability of the group—the loss of the leader. History has shown that the loss of a terrorist group leader (by capture or killing) has often led to the demise of the group. For example, in France, the Action Directe, which was motivated by a Marxist ideology, essentially dwindled after many of its key leaders were arrested.[89] Similarly in Spain, law enforcement agencies' arrest of GRAPO's leadership led to the subsequent demise of the group.[90] The Lorenzo Zelaya Popular Revolutionary Forces (FRP-LZ), a Honduran Marxist–Leninist group that sought to overthrow the Honduran government, disbanded after their leader, Efrain Duarte Salgado, was arrested.[91] In the United States, similar occurrences were observed with the arrest of the Black Liberation Army leaders[92] and with the Order, a violent right-wing (white supremacist) group, when the arrest of its major players essentially destroyed the group.[93] Furthermore, with the death of Jemaah Islamiya's ideological leader, Osama bin Laden, the capture of their core leadership based in the Philippines

---

85 Bjørgo, T., and Horgan, J. eds. 2008. *Leaving terrorism behind: Individual and collective disengagement*. New York: Routledge.

86 Ripley, A. 2008, March 13. Reverse radicalism. *Time Magazine*. http://www.time.com/time/specials/2007/article/0,28804,1720049_1720050_1722062,00.html.

87 Ibid.

88 Horgan, J. 2005. Psychological factors related to disengaging from terrorism: Some preliminary assumptions and assertions. In *A future for the young: Options for helping Middle Eastern youth escape the trap of radicalization*, ed. C. Benard. RAND's Initiative on Middle East Youth Working Paper Series. Santa Monica, CA: RAND. http://www.rand.org/pubs/working_papers/2006/RAND_WR354.pdf.

89 Henderson, H. 2001. *Global terrorism: The complete reference guide*. New York: Checkmark, 39

90 Ibid., p. 40.

91 Ibid., p. 61.

92 Ibid., p. 65.

93 Ibid., pp. 66–67.

(including Umar Patek), and the disruption of their tactical alliances with al-Qaeda, scholars and practitioners have predicted the demise of this group.[94]

Terrorist groups have ended due to the group's participation in the political process and negotiations with the government.[95] A prime example was the Provisional Irish Republican Army. After negotiations, the Good Friday Agreement was signed in Belfast on April 10, 1998. Under this agreement, among other things, Sinn Fein (the political party of the IRA) would have an active role in the political process (i.e., it received a seat in the Northern Ireland Council). Comparably, the Movement of April 19 (M-19), a Colombian terrorist group seeking to overthrow the government and end U.S. imperialism, began to function as a regular political party after signing several peace accords with the government.[96]

THE MAINTENANCE OF TERRORISM

Terrorist groups have ended due to other of factors as well. Research has shown that regional, socioeconomic, and political factors affect the survival of terrorist organizations.[97] Regional factors, however, do not play as prominent a role for terrorists, such as the homegrown terrorists in the United States and Europe who are inspired by al-Qaeda's cause rather than directed by them.[98] In the case of such terrorists, geographic location is unimportant. They do not need to travel overseas to obtain training. Instead, the Internet has helped sustain them; the same holds true for terrorist groups. In fact, the Internet provides opportunities for terrorists to communicate relatively undetected; to spread propaganda; and to plot, fund, and coordinate attacks. Al-Qaeda has been known to make use of the opportunities afforded to them by communications media. The manner in which such exploitation occurs is explored below.

First, and most importantly, modern electronic media provide the opportunity for terrorists to communicate undetected. Terrorists use phone communications when public meetings become too risky. Members of al-Qaeda have been known to use different types of secret communication when they are under physical

---

[94] Zenn, J. 2011. Demise of Philippines' Abu Sayyaf terrorist group begins in Abbottabad. *Terrorism Monitor* (May 27). http://www.jamestown.org/programs/gta/single/?tx_ttnews [tt_news]=37979&cHash=e6dd052c2d186b30065466a7e52dc5cc.

[95] Alterman, J. B., Simon, S., Crenshaw, M., and Wilkinson, P. 1999. *How terrorism ends.* Special Report No. 48. Washington, DC: United States Institute for Peace. http://kms1.isn.ethz .ch/serviceengine/Files/ISN/39859/ipublicationdocument_singledocument/9300e093-30a8-4893 -be61-b110a20fe47f/en/1999_may_sr48.pdf.

[96] Henderson, H. 2001. *Global terrorism: The complete reference guide.* New York: Checkmark, 61.

[97] Rapoport, D. 1992. Terrorism. In *Encyclopaedia of government and politics*, eds. M. Hawkeworth and M. Kogan, Vol. 2, 1061–1082. London: Routledge; Blomberg, S. B., Engel, R. C., and Sawyer, R. 2010. On the duration and sustainability of transnational terrorist organizations. *Journal of Conflict Resolution* 54 (2): 327.

[98] Examples of these homegrown terrorists were discussed in the section on perspectives on terrorism.

Box 3-2 Food for Thought—Al-Qaeda's Version of Cosmopolitan Magazine: The New Wave in the Recruitment and Radicalization of Muslim Women?

Al-Qaeda's media committee, which is tasked with publicizing al-Qaeda's religious rulings and spreading propaganda to Muslims worldwide, has developed a new method with which to recruit and radicalize individuals. In 2010, they created an English-language magazine known as *Inspire*. This magazine was designed to recruit Muslims in the West to engage in acts of terrorism. In 2011, another magazine was created. The focus for this magazine, however, was Muslim women. To produce more women extremists for its cause, al-Qaeda has launched its own version of an American women's magazine (such as *Cosmopolitan*), known as *Al-Shamikha* (i.e., *The Majestic Woman*). Similarly to the American magazine, it offers women information about health concerns and advice on skin care and marriage (although in this case, it contains information about marrying a mujahideen). In contrast to existing women's magazines, *Al-Shamikha* also informs women on how to obtain and operate lethal weapons and create explosives. It additionally encourages martyrdom and includes interviews with the wives of martyrs, praising their husbands for their actions. Has al-Qaeda found the key to tapping into a largely untapped market? If so, to what effect?

surveillance. Furthermore, terrorists have relied on e-mails and instant messaging for the receipt of operational instructions when face-to-face or even phone contact proved too risky.[99]

Second, the Internet provides the opportunity to spread propaganda. Military materials have been (and continue to be) posted online by supporters of al-Qaeda. These include Arabic translations of Western materials and al-Qaeda virtual magazines, such as *Sawt al Jihad* (The Voice of the Jihad), *Al Battar* (al-Qaeda's military manual),[100] and *Al Khansaa* (al-Qaeda's women's magazine).[101] Several websites have been identified by U.S. authorities that feature international news on al-Qaeda and fatwas (decisions on applying Muslim law).[102] One website has been repeatedly cited by U.S. officials as al-Qaeda's personal library because it houses 3,000 books and articles on their strategies and ideology.[103] Furthermore,

---

[99] Gruen, M. 2006. Terrorist indoctrination and radicalization on the Internet. In *Terrorism and counterterrorism*, eds. R. D. Howard and R. L. Sawyer. Dubuque, IA: McGraw-Hill.

[100] Paz, R. ed. 2004. Who wants to email al Qaeda? Project for the research of Islamist movements (PRISM). *Global Research in International Affairs (GLORIA) Center, Occasional papers* 2 (2): 1–3. http://www.e-prism.org/images/PRISM_no_2_vol_2_-_Who_Wants_to_Email_Al-Qaeda.pdf.

[101] Usher, S. 2004, August 24. "Jihad" Magazine for women on web. *BBC News.* http://news .bbc.co.uk/2/hi/middle_east/3594982.stm; Emerson, S. 2006. *Jihad incorporated: A guide to militant Islam.* New York: Prometheus, 472.

[102] See, for example, alneda.com; Thomas, T. L. 2003. Al Qaeda and the Internet: The danger of "cyberplanning." *Parameters* 23 (1): 113.

[103] http://tawhed.ws.

the perpetrators of the Madrid bombings had downloaded more than 50 electronic books by jihadi authors onto their computers.[104]

The Internet is also used as a tool for psychological warfare. Since 9/11, terrorists have disseminated graphic images of violence on the Internet in order to encourage sympathizers to engage in acts of aggression.[105] Al-Qaeda also exploits the media as a means of waging psychological warfare by disseminating the ideology of violent international jihad through "audio and video messages to Arab broadcasting stations and through the Internet with ever-increasing frequency."[106] The frequent posting on their websites of the number of attacks they have committed is not only used to laud their own accomplishments and boast about their capabilities but also to inspire sympathetic Web surfers.[107] The Internet thus provides a means for terrorists to find and connect with one another, justify and intensify their anger, and mobilize resources to arrange, direct, and subsequently execute attacks. Recruiters have been known to frequent chat rooms and cyber cafés in search of potential adherents and prospective terrorists. By providing individuals with the ability to transmit propaganda to anyone in the digital world (and allow these individuals access to it), the Internet has become a powerful recruitment tool for terrorists.[108]

Furthermore, the Internet provides them with the opportunity to plan and organize attacks, such as the opportunity to research possible types of attacks; the opportunity to obtain material for weapons; the opportunity to receive training (for example, online through videos); and to finance terrorism. Various electronic journals (e.g., *Mu'askar al-Battar*) and manuals (e.g., the *Anarchist Cookbook* and the *Terrorist Handbook*) are available online, providing logistical information on targets and offering instructions on everything from bomb making, construction of crude chemical weapons, and sniper training to guidelines for establishing secret training camps and safe houses.[109] For example, a pro–al-Qaeda website offers its viewers courses on how to prepare explosives.[110] Terrorists, such as the London bombers, had documents and manuals downloaded on their computers, which contained information on how to construct bombs.[111] The Internet has also been (and

---

104 Felter, J. H. 2007, May 3. The Internet: A portal to violent extremism. *Statement Before the Committee on Homeland Security and Governmental Affairs*, United States Senate, First Session, 110th Congress, p. 4. http://www.investigativeproject.org/documents/testimony/224.pdf.

105 Emerson, S. 2006. *Jihad incorporated: A guide to militant Islam*. New York: Prometheus, 470.

106 Stock, J., and Herz, A. 2007. The threat environment created by international terrorism from the German police perspective. *European Journal on Criminal Policy and Research* 13 (1/2): 90.

107 Emerson, S. 2006. *Jihad incorporated: A guide to militant Islam*. New York: Prometheus, 467.

108 Anti-Defamation League. 2002. Jihad online: Islamic terrorists and the Internet, 3. http://www.adl.org/internet/jihad_online.pdf.

109 See, more generally, Lia, B. 2005. *Globalisation and the future of terrorism: Patterns and redictions*. New York: Routledge.

110 See http://al3dad.jeeran.com; Lia, ibid., p. 176.

111 UK House of Commons. 2006, May 11. *Report of the official account of the bombings in London on 7th July 2005*. HC 1087. London: The Stationery Office. http://www.official-documents.gov.uk/document/hc0506/hc10/1087/1087.pdf.

is being) used by terrorists for training purposes. For instance, one website, which is mostly in Arabic, provides video and audio clips that include "detailed advice on physical training, surveillance of targets, and various operational tactics."[112] Scheuer argued that the perpetrators of the London bombings "may well have profited from the urban-warfare training al-Qaeda has made readily available on the Internet."[113] What is apparent is that terrorists and their supporters are

> building a massive and dynamic online library of training materials . . . covering such varied subjects as how to mix ricin poison, how to make a bomb from commercial chemicals, how to pose as a fisherman and sneak through Syria into Iraq, how to shoot at a U.S. soldier, and how to navigate by the stars while running through a night-shrouded desert.[114]

Finally, terrorists use the Internet to finance their activities. They have been known to raise funds on the Internet by making pleas, often in multiple languages, for donations on websites, chat rooms, and through targeted electronic mailing services. Several ways have been identified by intelligence authorities as to how terrorists raise funds on the Internet, such as soliciting funds from charities (and sometimes posing as charities, by, for example, creating a fake website with pictures of starving children); by pretending to need money for the clothing, food, shelter, and education of a population; organizing and implementing fundraising activities; and supporting their operations by perpetrating online crimes such as identity theft or fraud (for example, al-Qaeda has been known to steal credit card numbers and use them in online stores to buy supplies for jihadists).[115] Chechen terrorists have publicized the numbers of bank accounts to which sympathizers can contribute. Homegrown terrorists such as Jermaine Lindsay (one of the London bombers) engaged in legitimate online selling and trading to fund the cell's operations.[116] He was later found to have traded perfumes for materials that were used in making the bombs for the attacks on London—materials, which, if tracked by authorities, would not have aroused suspicion.

Accordingly, terrorists do not need to be in close proximity to each other in regions where training facilities and/or other operatives exist for the group to survive. It is becoming increasingly clear that terrorists take advantage of the

---

112 www.tajdeed.net; Emerson, S. 2006. *Jihad incorporated: A guide to militant Islam*. New York: Prometheus, 471.

113 Scheuer, M. 2005, August 5. *Assessing London and Sharm al-Sheikh: The role of Internet intelligence and urban warfare training*. http://jamestown.org/terrorism/news/articlephp?articleid =2369764.

114 Coll, S., and Glasser, S. B. 2007. Terrorists turn to the Web as base of operations. *Washington Post*, August 7, 2007. http://www.washingtonpost.com/wp-dyn/content/article/2005/08/05 /AR2005080501138_pf.html.

115 Hinnen, T. M. 2004. The cyber-front in the war on terrorism: Curbing terrorist use of the Internet. *The Columbia Science and Technology Law Review* 5:9.

116 UK House of Commons. 2006, May 11. *Report of the official account of the bombings in London on 7th July 2005*. HC 1087. London: The Stationery Office. http://www.official -documents.gov.uk/document/hc0506/hc10/1087/1087.pdf.

opportunities afforded to them by these media, especially the Internet, to communicate undetected, conduct campaigns to gain sympathy for their cause, to train and recruit adherents, to raise funds, and to prepare and organize attacks.

DIRECTIONS FOR COUNTERTERRORISM

Most research shows that the "reasons for becoming a terrorist, staying a terrorist, and then disengaging from terrorism were often different and context-specific."[117] As there is no single factor that can predict terrorism, no single terrorist profile, no single terrorist personality or mindset that fits all forms of domestic and international terrorism, there is also no single pattern to the sustainability of and disengagement from terrorism. However, this chapter showed that despite the differences between forms of terrorism and its sustainability, counterterrorism can learn from the three realms that effect the survival of terrorism. More specifically, the strategic realm illustrates that an effective counterterrorism strategy would deal with the goals of terrorism. If the goals of the terrorist group are no longer valid or cease to exist, so too does the group's justification for continuation and engagement in terrorism. Nevertheless, it is important to note that when some groups have ended under these circumstances, others were created in their place. For instance, when the PIRA supported the peace process and disarmed, two splinter groups of dissidents (those against the peace process) formed the Real IRA (RIRA) and the Continuity IRA (CIRA), which are still active today. The social and individual realms also offer insights into counterterrorism. To deal with these areas, governments should look into soft approaches to terrorism, such as rehabilitation programs, signing peace accords, and engaging in negotiations with terrorists. Studies have also shown that the detection, capture, punishment, and incapacitation of terrorists, especially when they are leaders, may precipitate the demise of the group or organization. Accordingly, an effective counterterrorism strategy must also include such measures.

HYPOTHETICAL SCENARIO

A new terrorist group has formed in the United States known as the American Jihad. This group seeks to create an Islamic state in America and vehemently opposes the wars in Iraq (now officially over) and Afghanistan. Members of the group have repeatedly informed the United States that it will continue to bomb the country's government buildings and citizens until America removes its troops from

---

[117] Horgan, J. 2005. Psychological factors related to disengaging from terrorism: Some preliminary assumptions and assertions. In *A future for the young: Options for helping Middle Eastern youth escape the trap of radicalization*, ed. C. Benard. RAND's Initiative on Middle East Youth Working Paper Series. Santa Monica, CA: RAND. http://www.rand.org/pubs/working_papers/2006/RAND_WR354.pdf; Fink, N. C., and Hearne, E. B. 2008, October. Beyond terrorism: Deradicalization and disengagement from violent extremism. international peace institute publications, 3. http://www.ipinst.org/media/pdf/publications/beter.pdf.

the Middle East. This group has engaged in many successful attacks, many of them suicide bombings. The last attack killed over 100 women and children.

As a counterterrorism official, what measures would you recommend to cause the individuals in the group to desist from terrorism?

CHAPTER SUMMARY

Terrorism primarily depends on three components for its existence: the strategic, the social, and the individual. These factors can help explain the sustainability of terrorist groups and the propensity of individuals to engage in terrorism. By way of extension, these same factors could also explain why some terrorist groups fail and why individuals decide to disengage in terrorist activity. Technology has additionally played a role in not only sustaining terrorist groups, but also in enabling terrorists to recruit new followers; surreptitiously communicate; spread propaganda; and plan, fund, and organize terrorist attacks.

REVIEW QUESTIONS

1. What types of strategic goals do terrorists pursue?
2. What role does the community play in sustaining a terrorist group?
3. How does a terrorist justify his or her behavior? Why is such a justification important?
4. Post 9/11, it is becoming increasingly difficult for terrorists to attend training camps. How has this impacted their ability to plan and engage in terrorist attacks?
5. Terrorists' charities and fundraising organizations are being monitored by law enforcement agencies. How are terrorists currently funding their operations?
6. Provide an example of a group that is no longer in existence. What led to the group's demise?
7. How can the information included in this chapter be used to develop more effective counterterrorism measures?

part *two*

Driving Forces Behind Counterterrorism Policies

Terrorism is a complex phenomenon for governments and policymakers; so too are the measures with which to combat this threat, namely, counterterrorism. Counterterrorism can be divided according to policy and tactics. Counterterrorism policy consists of a general plan of action, in that counterterrorism practices or tactics essentially boil down to the specific actions taken by law enforcement and intelligence agencies. Here, counterterrorism involves the proactive and reactive deployment of intelligence and security assets to deal with terrorism. Before analyzing counterterrorism measures and policies, it is important to understand the driving forces behind them. These forces can both shed light on the current state of counterterrorism and provide explanations as to why certain counterterrorism policies and measures represent a remarkable shift in perspectives, especially concerning their legitimacy for use in combating terrorism.

The objectives of this part are threefold. First, it seeks to determine how much of a threat terrorism is (Chapter 4). It also examines the factors that influence the public's and governments' perception of the risk of terrorism. Second, it investigates the types of measures governments around the globe have implemented in the aftermath of terrorist attacks (Chapter 5). It further considers the types of measures required to deal with the threat of terrorism post-9/11. Third, it explores the affect of these measures on citizens and noncitizens alike (Chapter 6). In particular, it analyzes the legal, social, and political consequences of counterterrorism policies and measures implemented in the war on terrorism. This chapter also explores the justifications governments offer for the implementation and use of specific counterterrorism measures.

chapter four

Terrorists Here, Terrorists There, Terrorists Everywhere: Assessing the Risk of Terrorism

This chapter considers the nature, extent, and risk of terrorism and the threat posed by terrorists and terrorist groups. It also explores the factors that influence the public's perception of terrorism and violent extremism. It additionally examines if these views differ according to terrorist group. Moreover, it looks at whether some groups more than others in the target society perceive terrorists favorably and why. Furthermore, it investigates the cognitive factors that influence individuals' and governments' perception of the risk of terrorism. By looking at how individuals perceive threats to personal safety, one can find explanations for public support or tolerance of measures that erode individual human rights.

THE THREAT OF TERRORISM: AN EVALUATION

Terrorist threats are evaluated in terms of risk. Risk concerns the calculation of the magnitude of harm (its adverse impact) and the likelihood of harm (its probability of occurring).[1] The reach, nature, and extent of this risk are pervasive, with

---

[1] Harvard Law Review Association. 2002. Responding to terrorism: Crime, punishment, and war. *Harvard Law Review* 115 (2): 1230; see also, more generally, Lupton, D. 1999. *Risk*. London: Routledge.

Table 4-1 Terrorist Attacks in Iraq Between January 1, 2004–December 31, 2010

Group Type	Attacks	Deaths
Islamic Extremist (Shia)	431	1,002
Islamic Extremist (Sunni)	3,107	15,763
Islamic Extremist (Unknown)	41	68
Secular/Political/Anarchist	11	182
Tribal/Clan/Ethnic	1	0
Unknown	21,923	33,240
Total	25,514	50,255

Source: Data obtained from the Worldwide Incidents Tracking System of the National Counterterrorism Center.

many countries threatened by international and domestic terrorism. The threat of terrorism, however, is country-specific. Indeed, certain areas around the world are more prone to terrorist attacks than others. A case in point is Iraq. Following Operation Iraqi Freedom, Iraq was subjected to 25,514 terrorist attacks between January 1, 2004, and December 31, 2010, which resulted in 50,255 deaths and 112,080 wounded (see Table 4-1). Many of these attacks were conducted by individuals who did not claim responsibility for them. Nevertheless, of the remaining attacks, Islamic extremists executed the majority (3,579), which claimed 16,833 lives and wounded 40,940 individuals.

By contrast, other countries such as the Seychelles are less prone to terrorist attacks. Between January 1, 2004, and December 31, 2010, one terrorist attack occurred in the country from an unknown source, which resulted in no injuries or deaths. It is important to note that in some countries, there are even regional differences in the threat of terrorism. For example, the domestic threat of terrorism in Spain is concentrated in its northeastern region, as history shows that Euskadi ta Askatasuna (ETA) focuses its attacks on government targets in that area.

The risk of terrorism, however, is calculated based on more than just its impact (deaths and injuries). The risk of a terrorist threat is also based on its probability of occurring. And yet, even if the likelihood of a terrorist attack is minimal, the risk of terrorism may still be high if the magnitude of devastation it may cause is significant. Terrorism risk assessments are accomplished using a variety of subjective and objective measures. Various tools have been created in an attempt to objectively measure risk. One such tool is the Terrorism Risk Index (created by Maplecroft, a global risks advisory firm), which used data from June 2009 to June 2010 from the Worldwide Incidents Tracking System of the National Counterterrorism Center to assess the risk of terrorism in 196 countries. The calculations of the Terrorism Risk Index (TRI) are based on frequency, intensity, and historical factors. The first factor, frequency, constitutes the incidence of attacks within the country over a specific period of time. The second factor, intensity, looks at both the lethality of the attack (those resulting in deaths or intended to result in deaths) and the number of attacks deliberately designed to inflict mass casualities. Small-scale attacks that typically do not kill or are not meant to kill individuals will not score high here. Instead, those attacks that are designed to kill as many as possible receive a high score. The third and final factor considered by the index is the history of terrorist activity in the country. This is determined by the past experiences the country has had with terrorism, including any longstanding terrorist groups operating in it (e.g., Spain has had an active terrorist group, ETA, since 1959). The TRI classified several countries as being under the extreme risk of terrorism. The top 10 are Somalia, Pakistan, Iraq, Afghanistan, Palestinian Occupied Territories, Colombia, Thailand, the Philippines, Yemen, and Russia (see Table 4-2).

While the number of attacks and deaths in Somalia seems, upon initial inspection, to pale in comparison to those of Pakistan, Iraq, and Afghanistan, this is not the case. According to the TRI report, Somalia has the highest number of deaths from terrorism per population, and the fatalities per terrorist attack far surpassed those in Iraq and Afghanistan. It is also at the top of the index due to al-Qaeda's alliance with the al-Shabaab militant group within its territory.[2]

Table 4-2 Terrorist Attacks Between June 2009–June 2010

Country	Attacks	Deaths	Injured
Somalia	569	1,460	3,428
Pakistan	1,661	2,789	6,154
Iraq	2,734	4,033	16,585
Afghanistan	2,818	3,311	5,128
Palestinian Occupied Territories (Gaza Strip & West Bank)	275	30	261
Colombia	307	263	501
Thailand	566	410	1,054
Philippines	301	349	385
Yemen	116	124	116
Russia	454	429	1,254

Source: Data obtained from the Worldwide Incidents Tracking System of the National Counterterrorism Center.

---

2 Al-Shabaab is an Islamic extremist organization with links to al-Qaeda, which operates in Somalia and primarily targets Somalia's transitional government and its Ethiopian supporters. Hanson, S. 2011, August 10. Al-Shabaab. *Council on Foreign Relations.* http://www.cfr.org /somalia/al-shabaab/p18650.

Box 4-1   Terrorism in Brief: Coordinated Suicide Bombings in Morocco

In May 2003, a total of 12 suicide bombers engaged in a coordinated attack against a Jewish Community Center, the Belgian consulate, the Hotel Farah, and the Casa De España social club in Casablanca, resulting in 45 deaths (bombers included). In 2007, in March and April, a series of suicide bombings occurred in Casablanca. The first attack occurred on March 11, 2007, at an Internet café. Two suicide bombers entered the café and tried to log on to an extremist website. Upon realizing what they were trying to do, the owner told them not to log on to the website. When the individuals refused, the owner locked the door and threatened to notify the police. One of the terrorists was carrying a bomb and detonated it, killing himself and injuring four others (owner included). In April 2007, three suicide bombers detonated explosives in the Hay Farah district of Casablanca. The same month in Casablanca, a suicide bombing occurred beside the U.S. Consulate. In April 2011, another terrorist attack occurred; a bomb exploded in a crowded café in Marrakesh, Morocco, killing 15 people and injuring 19. According to the U.S. Department of State, due to these attacks and current intelligence showing that terrorists will continue to carry out attacks in Morocco, the threat of terrorism against U.S. interests and citizens in Morocco remains high.[1]

[1] U.S. Department of State. 2011. Morocco: Country specific information. *Travel.State.Gov.* http://www.travel.state.gov/travel/cis_pa_tw/cis/cis_975.html.

The report further indicates that the majority of Western countries are not classified or even considered as being at extreme risk of terrorism. A few European countries are the exception. One such example is Greece. Even though the attacks were largely not intended to be fatal, it was classified as high risk because of the total number of attacks (156) by left-wing groups and the massive disruption that the attacks caused. For instance, on September 2, 2009, explosives in a van detonated outside of the Athens Stock Exchange. Other attacks that occurred during this period include (but are not limited to) a bomb that exploded in a courthouse in Thessaloniki (January 9, 2010), a bomb exploding in the Greek Parliament in Athens (May 14, 2010), and a parcel bomb that was sent to the Ministry for Public Order in Greece, which resulted in the death of a police officer (June 24, 2010).

By contrast, the United States, United Kingdom, and France were placed in the medium-risk category. Other countries, such as Canada, were placed in the low-risk category. Their placement in these categories is not surprising as, among other things, the total number of attacks and resultant deaths within these countries are quite low (see Table 4-3). Despite the low number of attacks, on the whole, citizens of these countries believe that a terrorist attack is imminent.[3] An online Angus Reid Public Opinion poll conducted in November 2010 revealed that 3 in 5

---

[3] The public's opinion of terrorism could be analyzed on both the individual level, which can be obtained by surveys, and state level, which examines terrorism from the lens of existing weak state institutions or political oppression. The focus of this analysis is on the individual level.

Table 4-3   Terrorist Attacks Between June 1, 2009–June 31, 2010

Country	Group Type	Attacks	Deaths	Injured
United States	Environmental/ Anti-Globalization	2	0	0
	Islamic Extremist (Sunni)	3	13	44
	Islamic Extremist (Unknown)	1	1	1
	Neonazi/Fascists/White Supremacists	1	1	0
	Secular/Political/Anarchist	1	0	0
	Total	8	15	45
United Kingdom	Christian Extremist	1	1	0
	Islamic Extremist (Sunni)	1	0	1
	Secular/Political/Anarchist	24	1	11
	Unknown	1	0	3
France	Islamic Extremist (Unknown)	1	0	1
	Secular/Political/Anarchist	19	1	6
	Unknown	6	0	0
Canada	Secular/Political/Anarchist	2	0	0
	Unknown	3	0	0

Source: Data obtained from the Worldwide Incidents Tracking System of the National Counterterrorism Center.

Americans (59%) and 4 in 5 Britons (74%) believe that a terrorist attack is "very likely" or "moderately likely" to happen in their country in the next year.[4] The poll further showed that 38% of Canadians surveyed believed that their country will likely be a victim of a terrorist attack in the future.

While terrorism still exists and terrorist attacks continue to be conducted, the type of terrorists engaging in such acts are not primarily Islamic extremists. Secular/political/anarchist terrorist groups are more likely to commit attacks in these countries. This is also evident in Table 4-4, which depicts the total number of attacks by group type in the United States, United Kingdom, France, and Canada between January 1, 2004, and January 1, 2011.

Terrorist attacks by Islamic extremists are extremely rare events. However, even though the probability of an attack from them is minute, individuals may subjectively consider the risk as great because the consequences are usually extremely severe. Consider the United Kingdom, wherein the Worldwide Incidents Tracking System database revealed that between January 1, 2004, and June 1, 2011, a total of 111 terrorist attacks were conducted by secular/political/anarchist groups, which resulted in 7 deaths and 189 people injured. On July 7, 2005, in a single

[4] Angus Reid. 2010, November 11. *Three-in-four Britons foresee a terrorist attack in the next year.* http://www.visioncritical.com/wp-content/uploads/2010/11/2010.11.11_Terrorism.pdf.

Table 4-4 Terrorist Attacks Between January 2004–January 2011

Country	Group Type	Attacks	Deaths	Injured
United States	Environmental/ Anti-Globalization	8	0	4
	Islamic Extremist (Sunni)	3	13	44
	Islamic Extremist (Unknown)	2	1	10
	Neonazi/Fascists/White Supremacists	1	1	0
	Secular/Political/Anarchist	12	1	0
	Unknown	6	0	0
	Total	**32**	**16**	**58**
United Kingdom	Christian Extremist	1	1	0
	Islamic Extremist (Sunni)	4	52	703
	Islamic Extremist (Unknown)	1	0	0
	Secular/Political/Anarchist	111	7	189
	Unknown	75	53	790
	Total	**192**	**112**	**1,682**
France	Islamic Extremist (Unknown)	2	0	11
	Secular/Political/Anarchist	179	3	28
	Unknown	129	4	7
	Total	**310**	**7**	**46**
Canada	Secular/Political/Anarchist	6	0	0
	Unknown	5	0	1
	Total	**11**	**0**	**1**

Source: Data obtained from the Worldwide Incidents Tracking System of the National Counterterrorism Center.

coordinated suicide bombing of London's public transportation system, 52 individuals were killed and over 700 were injured.

In addition, although the probability of an attack by Islamic extremists is low in these countries, their public expressed significant concerns over Islamic extremism. For example, in France, 66% of individuals surveyed (634 of 960) believed that international terrorism was a major threat to their country.[5] Another survey, conducted by the Pew Research Center's Global Attitudes Project, revealed that individuals residing in the United States, Great Britain, France, and Canada were concerned about Islamic extremism in their countries (see Table 4-5).[6]

[5] Angus Reid. 2008, July 24. Global terrorism is main enemy for French. *Global Monitor.* http://www.angus-reid.com/polls/32985/global_terrorism_is_main_enemy_for_french/.

[6] Pew Research Center. 2005, July 14. Islamic extremism: Common concern for Muslim and Western publics. *Pew Global Attitudes Project.* http://pewglobal.org/2005/07/14/islamic-extremism-common-concern-for-muslim-and-western-publics/.

Table 4-5 Concern About Islamic Extremism Within Their Country

Country	Very Concerned	Somewhat Concerned
United States	31	39
Great Britain	34	36
France	32	41
Canada	22	34

Source: Data obtained from Pew Research Center's Global Attitudes Project.

As the above table shows, 71% of those surveyed in France, 70% of those surveyed in the United States and Great Britain, and 56% of those surveyed in Canada expressed worry about Islamic extremism within their countries. This survey also revealed that 78% of those surveyed in Germany, which was classified as being under a low risk of terrorism by the TRI, were concerned about Islamic extremism in their country. In particular, 35% and 43% were very and somewhat concerned, respectively, with this threat in Germany. Even though the risk of terrorism in these areas is low and the likelihood of occurrance much less, individuals still believe that the risk is great. Why is this the case?

RISK PERCEPTION, PUBLIC SUPPORT, AND COUNTERTERRORISM

Risk perception is country-specific. Certain governments perceive the risk of terrorism as great, and the citizens of their countries do too. This risk perception is informed by prior terrorist attacks in their country; the existence of domestic and homegrown terrorists within their borders; and the tactics, targets, and goals of terrorists in their countries (including those terrorists who are outside of the country's borders but plan attacks in them). In some countries, however, terrorists are viewed favorably. A survey conducted by Pew Research Center between March 21, 2011, and April 26, 2011, revealed that 73% of Palestinians had a favorable view of Fatah, a Palestinian nationalist group that operates in Israel, the West Bank, and Gaza.[7] From the same sample surveyed, 61% viewed Hezbollah favorably. From the 61% that viewed Fatah favorably, 74% of them were from the West Bank and 39% were from Gaza. Such favoritism may exist due to the welfare functions that certain terrorist groups perform (e.g., Hamas and Hezbollah) and in so doing, gain support from communities.

Even some groups more than others in the target society perceive terrorists favorably. A prime example of this is Lebanon, where approximately 71% of Shia Muslims surveyed expressed a positive view of Hamas.[8] Those who agree with

---

[7] Pew Research Center. 2011, May 17. Arab spring fails to improve U.S. image: Obama's challenge in the Muslim world. *Global Attitudes Project.* http://pewglobal.org/2011/05/17/arab-spring-fails-to-improve-us-image/5/.

[8] Ibid.

terrorists' goals are also more likely to perceive terrorists favorably and not as a threat. Indeed, in a survey conducted by Pew Research Center's Global Attitudes between March 21 and April 26, 2011, some 68% of Palestinian Muslims believed that "suicide attacks in defense of Islam can often or sometimes be justified, a level of support essentially unchanged from 2007."[9] Specifically, approximately 7 in 10 Palestinian Muslims (68%) of those surveyed believed that "suicide bombing and other forms of violence against civilian targets can often or sometimes be justified in order to protect Islam from its enemies." This view was largely held by those surveyed in both the West Bank (66%) and Gaza (70%).[10]

Accordingly, the country in which a person resides, as well as the group to which a person belongs within a society, can influence an individual's perception of the risk of terrorism. In addition, the way in which a person perceives terrorism influences whether or not someone will support either terrorists or counterterrorists. Public support is also dependent upon other factors, including the actions a government takes to combat terrorism. What is usually observed after a terrorist attack is a show of force—a battery of counterterrorism measures. These measures act as evidence that the government is doing something to combat terrorism instead of idly sitting by waiting for another attack to occur. From the point of view of governments, laws often create "the favorable impression that certain misconduct has been taken seriously and dealt with appropriately."[11] Governments seek to provide something that is considered relatively short in supply in the aftermath of attacks, namely, security. Security, here, refers to the mechanisms, such as counterterrorism measures, to provide protection for citizens.[12] The provision of security and the maintenance of law and order are often cited by governments as the reasons for taking expansive measures to protect citizens from the threat of terrorism. It has to be recognized that counterterrorism "legislation can be justified because of the way terrorists operate, which makes them hard to catch and convict, because of the risks that they pose to society, and because it is important to be able to pre-empt, as well as to deter, terrorism."[13] Nonetheless, counterterrorism measures require broad public support. The public needs to approve of policies in order for them to be effective. If the public does not support these measures, governments' use of them will foster distrust and in consequence, the population subjected to them will be more inclined to resist them, thus making them less effective.[14]

Rational-choice economic models portray individuals as rational actors who process information and are capable of making informed predictions about the

---

9 Ibid.

10 Ibid.

11 Ashworth, A. 2000. Is criminal law a lost cause? *Law Quarterly Review* 116:225.

12 Schneier, B. 2006. *Beyond fear: Thinking sensibly about security in an uncertain world.* New York: Springer, 13.

13 Cohen, S. A. 2004. Policing security: The divide between crime and terror. *National Journal of Constitutional Law* 15:443–444.

14 Ibid., p. 444.

probability of future events. However, other perspectives challenge that an individual's risk perception is simply a product of objective information. There are certain personal (e.g., demographics), structural (e.g., experience with terrorism) and situational factors, such as expected loss, catastrophic potential, and beliefs in cause, that can influence the public's perception of terrorism. Risk perception involves a subjective judgment, anticipating the likelihood and consequences of a future event. This subjective assessment is derived from psychological uncertainty and is based on an individual's mental attitude and state of mind. As such, in reality, risk perception is flawed or distorted; often the result of misinformation. This form of risk perception may adversely impact a government's ability to counter it.

According to economic theory of regulation, the demand for government action corresponds to the perceived risk to be regulated.[15] Given that governments do not always know (and often express that they do not know) when and where the next terrorist attack will take place (or at what magnitude and under what circumstances), the scope of the perceived risk of terrorism from both the public's and government's perspective is enormous. Typically, the public's perception of risk is considered politically more important than mathematical reality because the public seeks laws in areas such as environmental protection and national security on the basis of their judgments about the probabilities associated with certain threats (perception of risk), like pollution or terrorism.[16] It bears on the demand for (and hence also the supply) of regulation. It is, therefore, important to look at the underlying mechanisms involved in risk perception because they can explain how public attention and support may be directed in favor of certain issues but not others. In what follows, special attention will be paid not only to governments' presentation of the threat of terrorism post-9/11 (especially homegrown terrorism) but also the public's perception of this threat.

THE ROLE OF HEURISTICS: BELIEVING THAT TERRORISTS ARE ALL AROUND US

Post-9/11, governments worldwide and the media presented terrorism as a threat posed by individuals who could be anyone and strike anywhere. In response to this threat, measures were quickly implemented without considerable analyses of their economic and social impact or debate as to their ability to deal with the threat that politically justified their implementation.[17] To combat this threat, measures requiring the mass registration and surveillance of citizens were implemented.[18]

---

15 Harvard Law Review Association. 2002. Responding to terrorism: Crime, punishment, and war. *Harvard Law Review* 115 (2): 1229.

16 Bannister, F. 2005. The panoptic state: Privacy, surveillance and the balance of risk. *Information Polity* 10 (1/2): 72; Jolls, C., Sunstein, C. R., and Thaler, R. 1998. A behavioral approach to law and economics. *Stanford Law Review* 50:1518.

17 The implications of the speedy implementation of measures are explored in the section on the war on terrorism and the impact on counterterrorism policy.

18 Mass surveillance and mass registration measures implemented post-9/11 are examined elsewhere.

For example, this occurred in the European Union in the aftermath of the Madrid and London bombings. When mass surveillance and mass registration measures were being negotiated in the European Union, there were many debates in Member States' newspapers, on the Internet, and among institutions of Member States (such as parliaments, human rights organizations, telecommunications and Internet service providers, academic conferences, etc.). Shortly after they were adopted by European Community institutions, debates on these measures largely subsided. For the most part, only human rights organizations, academic conferences, and the like discussed mass surveillance and mass registration measures. Public opposition to such measures were largely absent in the EU. One known case of resistance to these measures involved a protest in Germany. In particular, one of the largest street protests occurred on September 22, 2007, in which more than 15,000 marched in Berlin under the slogan "Liberty Instead of Fear—Stop the Surveillance Mania!" calling for the rejection of pervasive surveillance measures.[19] These numbers, however, pale in comparison to the total number of EU citizens, approximately 460 million, the vast majority of whom remained silent on the issue. Normally, these measures would provoke public resistance. However, this did not occur. What role did the public's assessment of the risk of terrorism play?

Cognitive psychologists and policy researchers have investigated the underlying mechanisms that govern risk perception.[20] Research has shown that psychological reactions to terrorism play a fundamental role in understanding public support of counterterrorism measures.[21] As terrorism threatens greater harm and poses a greater perceived risk, the public demands increased government action. Thus, by looking at how individuals perceive threats to personal safety, one can find explanations for governments' introduction of expansive counterterrorism measures and the public's support of them. Framing this study requires a two-pronged analysis. First, it assesses the actual risk of terrorism and the public's and government's perception of this risk. To do so, it considers certain heuristics (or rules of thumb) individuals rely on, such as the availability heuristic, probability neglect, and prospect theory, when thinking about risks. Second, it explores how this perception influences individuals' tolerance or support for measures that restrict their human rights.

Availability Heuristic

Individuals' calculations of probabilities are beset with cognitive fallacies.[22] One of the most common fallacies or source of bias is known as the availability heu-

---

[19] Digital Civil Rights in Europe. 2007, September 26. Largest anti-surveillance street protest in Germany for 20 years. *EDRI*. http://www.edri.org/edrigram/number5.18/liberty-instead-of-fear.

[20] Slovic, P. 1987. Perception of risk. *Science* 236:280–285; Kasperson, R. E., Renn, O., Slovic, P., Brown, H. S., Emel, J., Goble, R., Kasperson, J. X., and Ratick, S. 2000. The social amplification of risk: A conceptual framework. In *The perception of risk*, ed. P. Slovic, 233. London: Earthscan.

[21] Huddy, L., Feldman, S., Taber, C. and Lahav, G. 2005. Threat, anxiety, and support of anti-terrorism policies. *American Journal of Political Science* 49 (3): 593.

[22] Harvard Law Review Association. 2002. Responding to terrorism: Crime, punishment, and war. *Harvard Law Review* 115 (2): 1230.

ristic. The availability heuristic makes "some risks seem especially likely to come to fruition whether or not they actually [will]."[23] Individuals employ the availability heuristic whenever they estimate the frequency or probability of an event by the ease with which those instances could be brought to mind.[24]

The introduction of laws to counter terrorist threats can in themselves promote availability. That is, if a measure responds to the problems associated with terrorism, individuals may come to see those problems as readily available.[25] Consider, for example, antisocial behavior. When it was introduced into the law and order discourse of the UK government, it "acquired a burgeoning life of its own in the public arena assisted by an increased volume of legislation."[26] Specifically, the UK government made a small problem larger by making antisocial behavior into a major policy and as a result, making more people aware of it in their surroundings.[27]

Even discussions of low-probability threats may increase the judged (or perceived) probability of that threat regardless of what the evidence indicates.[28] For the public, the media constitutes a primary source of information concerning social problems and political discourse on how to deal with terrorist threats.[29] Thus, it plays an important role in shaping the public's perception of risk. With news media, individuals are much more likely to believe the depiction of crime presented to them.[30] Studies have shown that the media's emphasis on certain crimes leads the public to believe that such crimes are most likely to be committed. For example, Singer and Endreny noted how the reporting of a single terrorist incident involving U.S. citizens in Greece led to a major decline in the numbers of U.S. citizens prepared to travel to Europe.[31]

---

[23] Sunstein, C. R. 2005. *Laws of fear: Beyond the precautionary principle.* Cambridge, UK: Cambridge University Press, 35.

[24] See Tversky, A., and Kahneman, D. 1982. Availability: A heuristic for judging frequency and probability. In *Judgment under uncertainty: Heuristics and biases,* eds. D. Kahneman, P. Slovic, and A. Tversky, 163–164. Cambridge, UK: Cambridge University Press; Slovic, P., Fischhoff, B., and Lichtenstein, S. 2000. Rating the risks. In *The perception of risk,* ed. P. Slovic, 105. London: Earthscan.

[25] Parallels drawn with Sunstein's example of climate change, see Sunstein, C. R. 2006. The availability heuristic, intuitive cost-benefit analysis, and climate change. *Climatic Change* 77:206.

[26] Burney, E. 2005. *Making bad people behave: Anti-social behaviour, politics, and policy.* Devon, UK: Willan, 3.

[27] Tonry, M. 2004. *Punishment and politics.* Cullompton, UK: Willan, 57.

[28] Slovic, P., Fischhoff, B., and Lichtenstein, S. 2000. Rating the risks. In *The perception of risk,* ed. P. Slovic, 107. London: Earthscan.

[29] Crelinsten, R. D. 2002. Analysing terrorism and counter-terrorism: A communication model. *Terrorism and Political Violence* 14 (2): 100.

[30] Callanan, V. J. 2005. *Feeding the fear of crime: Crime-related media and support for three strikes.* New York: LFB Scholarly, 61.

[31] Singer, E., and Endreny, P. 1993. *Reporting on risk: How the mass media portrays accidents, diseases, disasters and other hazards.* New York: Russell Sage Foundation, 1–2; Furedi, F. 1997. *Culture of fear: Risk-taking and the morality of low expectation.* London: Cassell, 51.

Availability is also affected by the frequency of the occurrence of events. In the weeks following the attacks on 9/11 and the Madrid and London bombings, the mass media focused its attention almost exclusively on the threat of terrorism and the governments' responses to it, reinforcing the availability of the attacks themselves.[32] In addition, on an almost daily basis, the media shows

> a plethora of vehicle-borne or person-borne (suicide) attacks in Iraq, Afghanistan and elsewhere, targeting crowded public places such as markets, schools, hotels and hospitals, as well as sites of symbolic and iconic value such as religious and tourist locations. These are just the type of attack that is feared might be emulated in a western city.[33]

Politicians also focus on the vulnerabilities of their countries to terrorist attacks by highlighting weaknesses in porous national borders and critical infrastructure (including public works, communications, air traffic control, public surface transport, and emergency systems). Politicians and the media refer to these bombings and vulnerabilities on countless occasions as a way of emphasizing "the reality of seemingly distant threats and the need to incur significant costs to counteract them."[34] However, repeated stories direct public attention toward particular risk problems, thus making the public familiar with them.[35] Familiarity affects how individuals think because it can affect the availability of instances.[36] Accordingly, individuals consider an event likely to happen because it is easy to recall. A risk that is familiar (available) will be seen as more serious than one that is less familiar.

Salience can further affect how individuals think about risks. For example, the impact of seeing a house burning down either in person or on the television is probably greater on individuals' perception of risk than reading about a fire in a local newspaper.[37] Availability, which is produced by "a particularly vivid case or new finding that receives considerable media attention," plays a major role in the public's perception of that risk.[38] Rare but high-consequence events, such as 9/11 and the

---

[32] Kuran, T., and Sunstein, C. R. 1999. Availability cascades and risk regulation. *Stanford Law Review* 51 (4): 685; Harvard Law Review Association. 2002. Responding to terrorism: Crime, punishment, and war. *Harvard Law Review* 115 (2): 1231.

[33] Coaffee, J. 2009. Protecting the urban: The dangers of planning for terrorism. *Theory, Culture & Society* 26 (7/8): 346.

[34] Sunstein, C. R. 2006. The availability heuristic, intuitive cost-benefit analysis, and climate change. *Climatic Change* 77:206.

[35] Kasperson, R. E., et al. 2000. The social amplification of risk: A conceptual framework. In *The perception of risk*, ed. P. Slovic, 241. London: Earthscan.

[36] Sunstein, C. R. 2005. *Laws of fear: Beyond the precautionary principle.* Cambridge, UK: Cambridge University Press, 37.

[37] Tversky, A., and Kahneman, D. 1982. Judgments under uncertainty. In *Judgment under uncertainty: Heuristics and biases*, eds. D. Kahneman, P. Slovic, and A. Tversky, 11. Cambridge, UK: Cambridge University Press; Sunstein, C. R. 2006. The availability heuristic, intuitive cost-benefit analysis, and climate change. *Climatic Change* 77:198.

[38] Loewenstein, G., and Mather, J. 1990. Dynamic processes in risk perception. *Journal of Risk and Uncertainty* 3:155; Sunstein, C. R. 2005. *Laws of fear: Beyond the precautionary principle.* Cambridge, UK: Cambridge University Press, 38.

Madrid and London bombings, tend to be more vividly remembered, thus making individuals more likely to overestimate these risks. Accordingly, the more visible or salient the event is, the easier it is to recall and overestimate its likelihood.

The availability heuristic can, therefore, produce an inaccurate assessment of probability.[39] By focusing on one or two incidents, the public's perception of the risk of these incidents is likely to be substantially exaggerated as a result of increased publicity. The mass media covers risks selectively according to how rare or dramatic they are (because such risks are newsworthy). This disproportionate coverage can explain why individuals downplay common and often more serious risks such as smoking, suicide, heart disease, etc. while perceiving uncommon risks such as terrorism as great. Research has shown that levels of individuals' perceived risks were "linked to willingness to support aggressive anti-terrorist policies."[40]

Probability Neglect

If one or more incidents are both salient and emotionally gripping, individuals tend not to think about probability at all.[41] Specifically, when strong emotions are involved, individuals tend to focus on the badness of the outcome (e.g., a terrorist attack), "rather than on the probability that the outcome will occur."[42] This is known as probability neglect. Consider the following: in a U.S. public opinion poll, individuals were asked if they were more, less, or not willing to fly on airplanes, go into skyscrapers and travel overseas, as a result of the terrorist attacks on September 11, 2001.[43] The results indicate that the vast majority of Americans surveyed were "not willing" or "less willing" to fly on airplanes, go into skyscrapers, and travel overseas in the aftermath of 9/11 (see Table 4-6). In particular, 96–99% of those surveyed were "not willing" or "less willing" to fly on airplanes, 94–98% were "not willing" or "less willing" to go into skyscrapers, and 95–97% were "not willing" or "less willing" to travel overseas.

It is argued that even the word "terrorism" evokes images of disaster, thus making individuals focus on the outcome and not the likelihood of it occurring.[44] In fact, governments often express uncertainty concerning if, when, and under what conditions a terrorist attack will occur. The fact that those in charge of pro-

---

[39] Sunstein, ibid., p. 39.

[40] Huddy, L., Feldman, S., Taber, C., and Lahav, G. 2005. Threat, anxiety, and support of anti-terrorism policies. *American Journal of Political Science* 49 (3): 593–608; Jenkin, C. M. 2006. Risk perception and terrorism: Applying the psychometric paradigm. *Homeland Security Affairs* 2 (2): 3.

[41] Sunstein, C. R. 2005. *Laws of fear: Beyond the precautionary principle*. Cambridge, UK: Cambridge University Press, 206.

[42] Sunstein, C. R. 2003. Terrorism and probability neglect. *Journal of Risk and Uncertainty* 26 (2): 121.

[43] Gallup. 2011. *Terrorism in the United States.* http://www.gallup.com/poll/4909/Terrorism-United-States.aspx.

[44] Sunstein, C. R. 2005. *Laws of fear: Beyond the precautionary principle*. Cambridge, UK: Cambridge University Press, 40.

Table 4-6 Poll on Terrorism

Action	Date of Poll	Not willing %	Less willing %	More willing %	No opinion
Fly on Airplanes	Aug 18–20, 2006	30	67	1	2
	Sep 2–4, 2002	33	65	1	1
	May 28–29, 2002	27	69	1	3
	Mar 8–9, 2002	33	64	1	2
	Sep 14–15, 2001	43	56	< 0.5%	1
Go into Skyscrapers	Aug 18–20, 2006	22	72	2	4
	Sep 2–4, 2002	30	67	1	2
	May 28–29, 2002	27	68	1	4
	Mar 8–9, 2002	27	70	1	2
	Sep 14–15, 2001	35	63	< 0.5%	2
Travel Overseas	Aug 18–20, 2006	47	50	1	3
	Sep 2–4, 2002	47	50	*	3
	May 28–29, 2002	43	52	1	4
	Mar 8–9, 2002	45	52	1	2
	Sep 14–15, 2001	48	48	1	3

Source: Gallup Poll on Terrorism in the United States.

viding security for the public express uncertainty with their ability to do so can increase the public's perception of the perceived threat. Due to probability neglect, it is not difficult for governments to trigger public fear.[45] Governments' promotion and use of the public's beliefs and assumptions about risk and fear in order to achieve certain goals are features of the politics of fear.[46] The foundation of the politics of fear is the belief that citizens are all actual or potential victims in need of protection by the state from the source of the fear.[47] A major source of fear is terrorism. The use of fear to control behavior has been recognized as a political tool, in which fear turns the public into the vulnerable—the easily led. Accordingly, the language used—the rhetoric strategy—to communicate to the masses can be used to invest fear or unease in a policy issue.

---

[45] Ibid., pp. 124–125.

[46] Altheide, D. L. 2006. *Terrorism and the politics of fear*. Lanham, MD: Alta Mira; Altheide, D. L. 2006. The mass media, crime, and terrorism. *Journal of International Criminal Justice* 4 (5): 982.

[47] Garland, D. 2001. *The culture of control: Crime and social order in contemporary society*. Chicago: University of Chicago Press, 11; Altheide, D. L. 2006. The mass media, crime, and terrorism. *Journal of International Criminal Justice* 4 (5): 993.

Consider the counterterrorism measures introduced in Germany in response to 9/11. They were implemented to allay the anxieties and fear felt by both the public and the government and its agencies. Germans not only feared becoming victims of terrorist attacks themselves, but were also afraid of providing a safe harbor for terrorists to plan and instigate attacks from German soil (as was found to have happened for the 9/11 attacks).[48] Therefore, by focusing on the dynamics of fear, the public and governments' overreaction to risks to national security can be explained. The more powerful the enemy, the greater the fear, and thus, the more imperative it appears for governments to act.

The impact of terrorism can be determined by the media's portrayal of the threat.[49] Through media such as television, the "effects of terrorism extend well beyond its immediate victims and physical destruction" including a broader target population.[50] Through the process of risk amplification, which increases public fear of risks, the adverse consequences of a dramatic, horrific event (like the Madrid and London bombings) can extend beyond the direct damages to victims (loss of life or limb) and property. Indeed, fear, crime, terrorism, and victimization are (or can be) experienced vicariously through the mass media by the public.[51] The psychological effect that terrorist attacks have on individuals far removed from the incident itself is known as the multiplier effect.[52]

The medium through which the psychological effects (evoking a sense of horror, fear, indignity, and vulnerability in individuals removed from the incident) of terrorism are transmitted is typically a news source, such as television.[53] Once this information is retrieved, individuals communicate their fear and concern to one another; the widespread fact of fear and concern then increases media attention and the cycle continues until individuals move on to other risks that the media present to them.[54] Consider the Columbine shootings in Colorado. The media saturation of rare school shootings further reinforces beliefs in a "widespread 'pattern

---

[48] Stafferling, C. J. M. 2006. Terror and law: German responses to 9/11. *Journal of International Criminal Justice* 4 (5): 1153.

[49] Falkenrath, R. 2001. Analytic models and policy prescription: Understanding recent innovation in US counterterrorism. *Studies in Conflict and Terrorism* 24 (3): 171.

[50] See, for example, Crenshaw, M. 1986. The psychology of political terrorism. In *Political psychology*, ed. M. G. Hermann. San Francisco: Jossey-Bass; Long, D. E. 1990. *The anatomy of terrorism*. New York: Free Press; Wardlaw, G. 1982. *Political terrorism*. Cambridge, UK: Cambridge University Press; Huddy, L., Feldman, S., Taber, C., and Lahav, G. 2005. Threat, anxiety, and support of anti-terrorism policies. *American Journal of Political Science* 49 (3): 593.

[51] Altheide, D. L. 2006. Terrorism and the politics of fear. *Cultural Studies ↔ Critical Methodologies* 6 (4): 419.

[52] Falkenrath, R. 2001. Analytic models and policy prescription: Understanding recent innovation in US Counterterrorism. *Studies in Conflict and Terrorism* 24 (3): 171.

[53] Ibid.

[54] Sunstein, C. R. 2006. The availability heuristic, intuitive cost-benefit analysis, and climate change. *Climatic Change* 77:203.

of violence' until the epidemic is taken as truth and fear sets in."[55] Another example was given by Furedi, who argued that highly publicized child murders, such as the killing of the toddler James Bulger by two other children in England, helped shape the impression that these tragedies "could happen to every child."[56] The disappearance of Madeleine McCain on May 3, 2007, from Prais Da Luz, Portugal while on vacation with her parents is another example. High volumes of information can thus mobilize latent fears about a particular risk and enlarge the extent to which particular failures or consequences of events can be imagined.[57] The nature of these events engenders public outrage and a call for action (in terms of legislation) on the part of the government.

Media attention to terrorism is also believed to encourage future terrorist incidents. This is known as the contagion hypothesis. This theory suggests that the media can provoke terrorism, provide lessons on how to engage in terrorist attacks, and spread terrorism from place to place around the globe.[58] What can also occur from widespread and repeated coverage of terrorism and the response of governments to terrorism is what Wilkins termed "deviancy amplification."[59] Deviancy amplification describes how the media and law enforcement agencies (even the government) can create, with their actions, an increase in deviance (or in this case, terrorism). As reactions by governments become more severe toward terrorists, terrorist attacks become more prominent and ruthless in response. As such, any overreaction by governments to terrorist attacks may also increase the likelihood of terrorist attacks in the near future. This overreaction may also serve to advance terrorists goals.[60]

To maximize the impact of their attacks, terrorists carry them out in a bold, unexpected, and even bizarre manner in order to create the impression that anything is possible.[61] Consider the threat of homegrown terrorism. As Furedi stressed, a threat that can be found anywhere in a community acquires a "ubiquitous and menacing character. Its very proximity to people's everyday lives serves as a reminder

---

[55] Monahan, T. 2006. The surveillance curriculum: Risk management and social control in the neoliberal school. In *Surveillance and security: Technological politics and power in everyday life*, ed. T. Monahan, 116. New York: Routledge.

[56] Furedi, F. 1997. *Culture of fear: Risk-taking and the morality of low expectation*. London: Cassell, 24, 109–110.

[57] Kasperson, R. E. et al. 2000. The social amplification of risk: A conceptual framework. In *The perception of risk*, ed. P. Slovic, 241–242. London: Earthscan.

[58] Tan, Z. C. W. 1989. The role of media in insurgent terrorism: Issues and perspectives. *International Communication Gazette* 44 (3): 204.

[59] See Wilkins, L. T. 1967. *Social policy, action, and research: Studies in social deviance*. London: Tavistock.

[60] How this occurs is explored in the section on media and the Internet.

[61] Homer-Dixon, T. 2002. The rise of complex terrorism. *Foreign Policy* (January 1): 58.

Box 4-2   Food for Thought—Airport Security: Is the Real Threat Before Boarding?

On December 27, 1985, terrorists associated with the Abu Nidal group[1] engaged in simultaneous terrorist attacks on the Leonardo da Vinci airport in Rome and the Schwechat airport in Vienna. The four terrorists in Rome threw hand grenades and opened fire on passengers who were waiting to check in for flights to the United States and Israel. Around the same time, in Vienna, three terrorists threw hand grenades and opened fire on passengers seeking to travel to Israel. In these attacks, 16 people were killed (including three terrorists) and approximately 100 were injured before police and security personnel disarmed the terrorists.

1. What is being done at airports to protect passengers while they are checking in and before they enter passenger terminals?
2. Are existing security measures, if any, able to deal with this type of threat?

---

[1] A splinter terrorist group from the Palestine Liberation Organization that seeks to liberate Palestine and destroy Israel.

that the enemy is at home."[62] By stressing the existence of an omnipresent enemy within the community with nothing to fear and nothing to lose, governments and the media are making matters worse by creating the impression that there is no defense against this kind of threat, thus causing widespread panic and fear.

By labeling terrorists as "evil," "irrational," "extremists," or "fanatics," attention is diverted away from the fact that these individuals employ violence and even engage in suicide tactics to achieve specific political goals.[63] Terrorist attacks are aimed at convincing governments and their citizens that they can strike anywhere at any time. In reality, this is not the case. Terrorists have political objectives and are, despite popular beliefs, restrained by them. Were such terrorists less bound by these goals, one would expect to see more of these attacks. For instance, for some attacks that have deviated from al-Qaeda's long-term objectives, leaders of the movement such as Abu Bakr Naji (a well-known al-Qaeda propagandist and jihadi leader) have expressed their concerns. They believe that overzealous new recruits may jeopardize the movement if these recruits' actions and their implications are not fully considered before a decision is made to attack a particular target.[64]

---

[62] Furedi, F. 2007. *Invitation to terror: The expanding empire of the unknown.* New York: Continuum, 95.

[63] For more information see Sprinzak, E. 2000. Rational fanatics. *Foreign Policy* (September 1): 73.

[64] See more generally the concerns expressed by Naji, A. B. 2006, May 23. The management of savagery: The most critical stage through which the Umma must pass, 17–19. Trans. W. F. McCants; Naji, A. B. 2004. *The management of barbarism,* 7–8. http://ctc.usma.edu/publications/pdf/Management_of_ Savagery.pdf.

Probability neglect has several implications for law and policy, particularly in the context of counterterrorism. If probabilities are neglected, especially when emotions are engaged, then excessive public concern will be given to specific low-probability risks.[65] Probability neglect also leads individuals "to focus on the worst case, even if it is highly improbable."[66] This helps explain excessive reactions to low-probability risks of harm. When probability neglect is at work, the public's attention is focused on the bad outcome itself, and they are inattentive to the fact that it is unlikely to occur. If probability neglect characterizes individual judgment under particular circumstances, governments and law enforcement agencies are likely to be neglecting probability under those same circumstances. If the public shows unusually strong reactions to low-probability harms, a democratic government is likely to act accordingly.

In the context of terrorism, especially after 9/11, it seems that governments respond to probability neglect (whether it is their own, the public's, or a combination of both), resulting in regulation that might be unjustified or even counterproductive. Hörnqvist suggests that a security perspective overrules mere law, especially when instances threaten social order,[67] as is the case with terrorism. The key word is *perceived*. The perception that matters the most is that of the public. If they perceive the threat as it is presented to them by the government and the media, then these individuals will accept the government's measures. As Bannister argued, "irrational fear, especially on a mass scale, can lead to all sorts of undesirable outcomes, not least a public willingness to cede important freedoms and civil rights in response to what may be an imagined, or even a manufactured, myth of danger."[68] In line with this argument, neuroscience reveals that emotions motivate individuals to act and cause individuals "to prioritize security over other values."[69]

The public's perception of the risk of terrorism can produce effects such as increased anxiety, and government and law enforcement's response to these perceived threats, such as increased surveillance, can act to amplify these public reactions. Heightened anxiety about the threat of terrorism may partly explain the tolerance (lack of dissent) or public support for the expansion of surveillance powers. The psychological effects of anxiety are politically important because they lead to an overestimation of risk and risk-averse behavior.[70] Therefore, terrorism

---

[65] Sunstein, C. R. 2005. *Laws of fear: Beyond the precautionary principle*. Cambridge, UK: Cambridge University Press, 39–40.

[66] Ibid., p. 35.

[67] Hornqvist, M. 2004. The birth of public order policy. *Race and Class* 46 (1): 30–52; Altheide, D. L. 2006. Terrorism and the politics of fear. *Cultural Studies ↔ Critical Methodologies* 6 (4): 418.

[68] Bannister, F. 2005. The panoptic state: Privacy, surveillance and the balance of risk. *Information Polity* 10 (1/2): 72.

[69] Kaufman, S. J. 2006. Symbolic politics or rational choice? Testing theories of extreme ethnic violence. *International Security* 30 (4): 51.

[70] Lerner, J. S., and Keltner, D. 2001. Fear, anger and risk. *Journal of Personality of Social Psychology* 81 (1): 146–159; Huddy, L., Feldman, S., Taber, C., and Lahav, G. 2005. Threat, anxiety, and support of anti-terrorism policies. *American Journal of Political Science* 49 (3): 593.

can lead to public demand for legal interventions that might not reduce the risks at stake and might even make the situation worse.[71]

Prospect Theory

Prospect theory is used to accentuate a number of anomalies in individuals' reactions to risks.[72] This theory emphasizes the public's aversion to significant harms that have a low probability of occurring (if government follows the judgment of its citizens, then it will be risk averse as well).[73] Prospect theory predicts an overreaction to small probabilities of catastrophic outcomes. That is, it suggests that individuals will seek regulation to prevent harms that are grave but that are highly unlikely to occur. For example, individuals typically overestimate the danger of air travel and underestimate the danger of automobile racing and bungee jumping. Therefore, by focusing on these aspects of the theory, it may be possible to understand certain forms of risk regulation that show an exaggerated response to low-probability harms.[74] Although this theory can be taken as a form of probability neglect, it "does not set out any special role for emotions . . . and it does not predict that people will react in any special way to emotionally gripping risks" (unlike probability neglect).[75] While availability or vividness biases may be one explanation for why individuals overestimate low-probability events and underestimate high-probability events, in prospect theory, "it is proposed that over weighting of low probability events occurs regardless."[76]

One way overestimation is explained is through individuals' loss aversion (an aspect of prospect theory)—their dislike of losses from the status quo.[77] Specifically, individuals are "far more willing to tolerate familiar risks than unfamiliar ones, even if they are statistically equivalent."[78] Research has shown that

[71] This is especially likely when governments overreact, as this reaction is in line with the terrorists' objectives.

[72] Kahneman, D., and Tversky, A. 1979. Prospect theory: An analysis of decision under risk. *Econometrica* 47 (2): 263–291; see also Sunstein, C. R. 2002. Probability neglect: Emotions, worst cases, and law. *The Yale Law Journal* 112 (1): 61–107.

[73] Sunstein, C. R. 2005. *Laws of fear: Beyond the precautionary principle.* Cambridge, UK: Cambridge University Press, 26.

[74] Noll, R., and Krier, J. 1990. Some implications of cognitive psychology for risk regulation. *Journal of Legal Studies* 19 (2): 749–760.

[75] Sunstein, C. R. 2003. Terrorism and probability neglect. *Journal of Risk and Uncertainty* 26 (2): 123.

[76] Jackson, J., Allum, N., and Gaskell, G. 2004, June 4. Perceptions of risk in cyberspace. *Cyber Trust and Crime Prevention Project, London School of Economics*, 5. http://www.berr.gov .uk/files/file15284.pdf.

[77] Sunstein, C. R. 2005. *Laws of fear: Beyond the precautionary principle.* Cambridge, UK: Cambridge University Press, 35.

[78] See Slovic, P., Fischhoff, B., and Lichtenstein, S. 2000. Facts and fears: Understanding perceived risk. In *The perception of risk*, ed. P. Slovic, 137–143. London: Earthscan; Sunstein, C. R. 2005. *Laws of fear: Beyond the precautionary principle.* Cambridge, UK: Cambridge University Press, 43.

the number of individuals who have died from worldwide terrorism is not much greater than the number of individuals who have drowned in their bathtubs in the United States.[79] Moreover, since 2001, "fewer people have been killed in America by international terrorism than have drowned in toilets or have died from bee stings."[80] When loss aversion is at work, individuals fear the former risk more than the latter even though they are (approximately) statistically equivalent. Consider another example: a comparison between air and automobile travel. Traffic accidents (familiar risk) represent a much greater risk than terrorism (unfamiliar risk). In order to put things into perspective, the following examples were used by Adams: the total death toll in the Madrid bombings (191 people) represents approximately the number of individuals killed in Spain about every 12 or 13 days in traffic accidents; whereas the total death toll in the London bombings is approximately equivalent to six days of traffic fatalities in the UK, where on average 9 individuals die and over 800 are injured daily.[81] In the United States alone, the number of motor vehicle deaths (36,284) in 2009 was more than double the number of those killed worldwide by terrorists in that year (15,310).[82] During that period, the total number of deaths in the United States from terrorist attacks was 16.[83] While the risk of death is greater when travelling by automobile, far more individuals are afraid of terrorist attacks than driving or being driven in automobiles. Individuals, therefore, show a disproportionate fear of risks that are unfamiliar.

Research has shown that individuals desire a sense of control in the face of uncertainty and danger.[84] Because of this, individuals tend to show disproportionate fear of risks that are involuntary or hard to control. Adams argued that individuals react strongly to terrorist attacks because harm is intentional and not accidental.[85] For example, individuals are less likely to tolerate malignly imposed risks,

---

[79] Mueller, J. 2005. Simplicity and spook: Terrorism and the dynamics of threat exaggeration. *International Studies Perspectives* 6 (2): 220.

[80] Mueller, J. 2006. *Overblown: How politicians and the terrorism industry inflate national security threat and why we believe them.* New York: Free Press; Furedi, F. 2007. *Invitation to terror: The expanding empire of the unknown.* New York: Continuum, 158.

[81] Adams, J. 2005. What kills you matters, not numbers. *The Social Affairs Unit,* 1. http://www.socialaffairsunit.org.uk/blog/archives/000512.php; see also Litman, T. 2005, December 2. Terrorism, transit, and public safety: Evaluating the risks. *Victoria Transport Policy Institute,* 6. http://www.vtpi.org/transitrisk.pdf.

[82] Center for Disease Control and Prevention. 2011. Deaths: Preliminary data for 2009. *National Vital Statistics Report* 59 (March 16): 42.

[83] This information was retrieved from the Worldwide Incidents Tracking System of the National Counterterrorism Center.

[84] Brown, J. D., and Siegel, J. M. 1988. Attributions for negative life events and depression: The role of perceived control. *Journal of Personality and Social Psychology* 54 (2): 316–322; Woods, J. 2007. What we talk about when we talk about terrorism: Elite press coverage of terrorism risk from 1997 to 2005. *The Harvard International Journal of Press/Politics* 12 (3): 5.

[85] Adams, J. 2005. What kills you matters, not numbers. *The Social Affairs Unit,* 4. http://www.socialaffairsunit.org.uk/blog/archives/000512.php.

which include crimes such as mugging, rape, and murder.[86] The same could be said about terrorism. By contrast, individuals are more tolerant of voluntary risks such as smoking or engaging in extreme sports such as mountain climbing. Individuals are also more tolerant of risks they can control such as driving their own vehicles. Accordingly, individuals are less tolerant of risks they cannot control such as using public transport systems. That is, while individuals may voluntarily board airplanes, "buses and trains, the popular reaction to crashes in which passengers are passive victims, suggests that the public demand a higher standard of safety in circumstances in which people voluntarily hand over control of their safety to pilots, or to a bus or train driver."[87] Public transport, however, is safer than automobile travel. A study conducted by Sivak and Flannagan showed that if one were to calculate the probability of an American being killed in one non-stop airline flight, it "is about one in 13 million (even taking the September 11 crashes into account), while to reach that same level of risk when driving on America's safest roads, rural interstate highways, one would have to travel a mere 11.2 miles."[88] While the risk of death is greater when travelling by automobile, far more individuals are afraid of flying than driving or being driven in an automobile.[89] Despite the Madrid and London bombings, public transport is still an extremely safe form of travel.[90] Specifically, studies have shown that the "traffic fatality rate per passenger-kilometer is less than one-tenth that of automobile travel."[91]

Sunstein claims that if loss aversion is at work, governments will focus heavily on the losses introduced by a particular risk and downplay the benefits foregone as a result of implementing measures to deal with that risk.[92] Public fear might produce unjustified intrusions on human rights resulting from individuals' use of the three underlying sources of error mentioned above (availability heuristic, probability neglect, and prospect theory) in their assessment of risk. If individuals are more fearful than they ought to be, they will seek or tolerate incursions into their human rights that could not have been justified if fear were not disproportionate.[93] The public place their trust in governments to protect them from current terrorist threats and possible future attacks. Individuals may even complacently give up their liberties

---

[86] Ibid.; see also, more generally, Adams, J. 1999. *Risk*. London: UCL.

[87] Adams, J. 2005. ibid., p. 3.

[88] Sivak, M., and Flannagan, M. J. 2003. Flying and driving after the September 11 attacks. *American Scientist* 91 (1): 6–9; Mueller, J. 2005. Simplicity and spook: Terrorism and the dynamics of threat exaggeration. *International Studies Perspectives* 6 (2): 222–223.

[89] Bannister, F. 2005. The panoptic state: Privacy, surveillance and the balance of risk. *Information Polity* 10 (1/2): 73.

[90] Litman, T. 2005, December 2. Terrorism, transit, and public safety: Evaluating the risks. *Victoria Transport Policy Institute*, 2. http://www.vtpi.org/transitrisk.pdf.

[91] Ibid.

[92] Sunstein, C. R. 2005. *Laws of fear: Beyond the precautionary principle*. Cambridge, UK: Cambridge University Press, 42.

[93] Ibid., p. 206.

to governments, believing that they will be made safer as a result.[94] By focusing on the evil and spectacle of terrorism, a danger arises "of distorting rational analysis not only about the probability of terrorism,[95] but also about the best way to prevent it and limit its harms."[96]

HYPOTHETICAL SCENARIO

Intelligence was received that Ayman al-Zawahiri had ordered an attack to take place on the 10th anniversary of 9/11 in New York City. He had ordered three men to carry out the attack, which allegedly included the use of car bombs. Three men were caught in Canada. It is unclear whether these individuals were the ones recruited by al-Zawahiri. What if the attack had occurred in New York City? In 2010, Maplecroft, through its risk assessment tool, the Terrorism Risk Index, gave the United States a medium risk rating.

1. Would an attack, such as the one mentioned above, affect the risk rating of the United States? If so, in what way?

CHAPTER SUMMARY

Many countries are threatened by international and domestic terrorism. This risk of terrorism depends on the country and the terrorists operating within its borders and/or against it. Statistics show that the probability of a terrorist attack occurring is quite low. However, the impact of a terrorist attack is significant. It is the extent of the impact of a terrorist attack that causes the risk of terrorism to be considered high. Individuals, when thinking about risks, tend to rely on certain heuristics; namely, the availability heuristic, probability neglect, and prospect theory. These heuristics govern how individuals view and assess risk. A terrorist attack, its presentation by the media, and the actions of the government in response to it, can also significantly influence the public and their views of the threat of terrorism.

---

94 Romero, A. 2003. Living in fear: How the U.S. government's war on terror impacts American lives. In *Lost liberties: Ashcroft and the assault on personal freedom*, ed. C. Brown. New York: New Press; Bloss, W. 2007. Escalating U.S. police surveillance after 9/11: An examination of causes and effects. *Surveillance and Society* 4 (3): 223.

95 Sunstein, C. R. 2005. *Laws of fear: Beyond the precautionary principle.* Cambridge, UK: Cambridge University Press; Ramraj, V. V. 2005. Terrorism, risk perception and judicial review. In *Global anti-terrorism law and policy*, eds. V. V. Ramraj, M. Hor, and K. Roach, 107. Cambridge, UK: Cambridge University Press.

96 Sunstein, C. R. 2003. Terrorism and probability neglect. *Journal of Risk and Uncertainty* 26 (2/3): 121–136; Roach, K. 2006. Must we trade rights for security? The choice between smart, harsh, or proportionate security strategies in Canada and Britain. *Cardozo Law Review* 27 (5): 2167.

REVIEW QUESTIONS

1. What is risk?
2. How is the risk of terrorism determined?
3. What are cognitive heuristics?
4. What role does the government play in the public's perception of risk?
5. What role does the media play in the public's perception of risk?
6. What are the differences between probability neglect and prospect theory?
7. Why do individuals tend to overreact and overestimate low-probability risks?

chapter five

The Era of Uncertainty and Precaution

This chapter explores the raison d'être behind worldwide policies aimed at combating terrorism. This chapter contends that the driving force behind worldwide policies aimed at combating the uncertain threat of post-9/11 terrorism is the precautionary principle. According to this principle, lack of knowledge (or certainty) is not a reason for inaction. Within this section, the notion of preemption is also analyzed in order to determine what type of measures are required to counter the terrorist threat and which preemptive measures are being used around the globe.

FOR AN UNCERTAIN FUTURE, USE PRECAUTION

In a catchphrase: Better safe than sorry.
—CASS SUNSTEIN[1]

Risk assessments take into consideration both the likelihood of the threat and the seriousness of the attack if realized. The likelihood of falling victim to a terrorist attack is minute. In fact, research has shown that one is more likely to die from a traffic accident than from a terrorist attack.[2] The current risk of terrorism is great,

---

[1] Sunstein, C. R. 2005. *Laws of fear: Beyond the precautionary principle.* Cambridge, UK: Cambridge University Press, 13.

[2] See, for example, Mueller, J. 2005. Simplicity and spook: Terrorism and the dynamics of threat exaggeration. *International Studies Perspectives* 6(2):220.

not because of the likelihood of its occurrence, but because of the magnitude of devastation. The attacks on and after 9/11 were of a different quantitative and qualitative nature than those of the past. In quantitative terms, before al-Qaeda, only 14 terrorist attacks had killed more than 100 people at once in the entire 20th century.[3] Those killed on 9/11 numbered approximately the entire population of civilians and combatants killed in Northern Ireland since 1969 (approximately 3,500).[4] Terrorism post-9/11 is also qualitatively different because it is perpetrated by stateless enemies without any territory or population to defend. Consequently, the reach of the threat has no boundaries, and, as a result, the targeting of these enemies poses unique challenges for governments. Intelligence shows that al-Qaeda consists of nomadic and amorphous networks characterized by the diffusion of its groups; as such, it challenges the abilities of governments to infiltrate the networks and to track these terrorists.[5] Post 9/11, the threat of al-Qaeda and affiliates is also not limited to a particular state or country, but is in fact global.

Al-Qaeda's motivation and capacity to inflict mass casualties constitutes another difference. The attacks on and after 9/11 also demonstrated how the tactics used by terrorists are changing: women and teenagers now participate in operations.[6] Women and teenagers are used to infuse an element of surprise in attacks because they are not considered as likely al-Qaeda operatives by authorities. As a result, they are highly effective in achieving al-Qaeda's objectives. The change in al-Qaeda's tactics can also be found in their preference for unconventional weapons (e.g., using planes as missiles, amassing chemical and biological weapons). Al-Qaeda manuals have also been found with formulas and step-by-step instructions on how to create biological and chemical weapons.[7] Intelligence also showed that al-Qaeda had

> completed plans and obtained the materials required to manufacture two biolog-ical toxins—botulinum and salmonella—and the chemical poison cyanide. They are also close to a feasible production plan for anthrax, a far more lethal weapon, which kills 90 percent of untreated victims if spread by inhalation and as many as 75 percent of those treated when the first symptoms become evident.[8]

---

3 Jenkins, B. 2001. The organization of men: Anatomy of a terrorist attack. In *How did this happen? Terrorism and the new war*, eds. J. F. Hoge Jr. and G. Rose, 5. New York: Harper Collins.

4 Gunaratna, R. 2006. The al-Qaeda threat and the international response. In *Terrorism: Critical concepts in political science, Vol. IV: The fourth or religious wave*, ed. D. C. Rapoport, 317. London: Routledge.

5 Whine, M. 2001. The new terrorism. *Stephen Roth Institute, Tel Aviv University*. http://www .tau.ac.il/Anti-Semitism/asw2000-1/whine.htm.

6 See Chapter 1, Vidino, L. 2006. *Al-Qaeda in Europe: The new battleground of international jihad*. New York: Prometheus.

7 Boettcher, M. 2001. Evidence suggests al-Qaeda pursuit of biological, chemical weapons. *CNN* November 14, 2001. http://archives.cnn.com/2001/WORLD/asiapcf/central/11/14/chemical.bio /index.html.

8 Gellman, B. 2003. Al Qaeda near biological, chemical arms production. *The Washington Post*, March 23, 2003. http://www.washingtonpost.com/wp-dyn/content/article/2006/06/09 /AR2006060900918.html.

In August 2002, CNN revealed that it had received several videotapes in Afghanistan, one of which contained experiments that al-Qaeda operatives conducted with chemical agents on dogs.[9] In addition, Abu Mohammed al-Ablaj, who was believed to be a trainer of al-Qaeda operatives, had stated that al-Qaeda was planning to use sarin gas and poison the drinking water in cities in the United States and other Western nations.[10] On the use of weapons of mass destruction, al-Qaeda spokesperson Suleiman Abu Gheith posted the following on al-Qaeda's website:[11] "It is our right to fight them with chemical and biological weapons, so as to afflict them with the fatal maladies that have afflicted the Muslims because of the [Americans'] chemical and biological weapons."[12] In May 2003, a fatwa (a religious ruling) that justified the use of weapons of mass destruction asserted, "[i]f the Muslims could defeat the infidels only by using these kinds of weapons, it is allowed to use them even if they kill them all, and destroy their crops and cattle."[13] However, it is important to note that even during war, Muslims are prohibited from destroying crops, trees, and livestock, as it is strictly prohibited by Islamic religion. Anticipating that this would be a restraining factor for some operatives in engaging in chemical and biological terrorist attacks, al-Qaeda issued the above religious ruling to overcome this.

This change in the choice of weapons also demonstrates how al-Qaeda is seeking to maximize the infliction of damage caused by their attacks by killing as many innocent civilians as possible. The unprecedented scale of casualties and devastation that resulted from the most significant terror operation in history,[14] namely, 9/11, attests to this. Accordingly, the hallmark of this form of terrorism is that it "poses a greater threat to a more diverse array of targets" because it is less discriminating toward its targets, more likely to target innocent civilians, and has

---

[9] Robertson, N. 2002. Disturbing scenes of death show capability with chemical gas. *CNN.* http://articles.cnn.com/2002-08-19/us/terror.tape.chemical_1_chemical-weapons-nerve-agent-al-qaeda-tapes?_s=PM:US; Pita, R. 2007. Assessing al-Qaeda's chemical threat. *International Journal of Intelligence and CounterIntelligence* 20(3): 483.

[10] Pita, ibid., p. 495.

[11] The website it was published on was www.alneda.com.

[12] The Middle East Media Research Institute (MEMRI). 2002, June 12. "Why we fight America": Al-Qa'ida spokesman explains 11 September and declares intentions to kill 4 million Americans with weapons of mass destruction. *The Jihad and Terrorism Threat Monitor.* http://www.memrijttm.org/ content/en/report.htm?report=678; Pita, R. (2007). Assessing al-Qaeda's chemical threat. *International Journal of Intelligence and CounterIntelligence* 20(3): 495.

[13] Paz, R. 2005, September 12. Global jihad and WMD: Between martyrdom and mass destruction. *Hudson Institute, Center on Islam, Democracy, and the Future of the Muslim World.* http://www.currenttrends.org/research/detail/global-jihad-and-wmd.

[14] The attacks on 9/11 consisted of carefully synchronized multiple suicides that caused more deaths than those at Pearl Harbor. The next nine most deadly terrorist attacks each involved a few hundred, whereas 3,212 lost their lives on 9/11. See Ericson, R. V., and Doyle, A. 2004. Catastrophic risk, insurance, and terrorism. *Economy and Society* 33(2): 142.

the ability to strike from remote distances without warning.[15] It is this factor that makes this form of terrorism stand out in its destructiveness.

Lord Butler, in his report on intelligence and terrorism (the Butler Report), noted that in the aftermath of 9/11, Osama Bin Laden's belief in the legitimacy of using weapons of mass destruction, combined with the prominence of suicide attacks, transformed the calculus of the threat.[16] According to the Butler Report, the reason for this transformation was the desire of these terrorists to cause devastation and casualties on a massive scale, "undeterred by the fear of alienating the public from their own supporters" (which had been noted by the Joint Intelligence Committee as a constraining factor in their tactics and choice of targets in the early 1990s) or by considerations of their own personal survival. These factors significantly inflated the risk of terrorism while simultaneously making the risk assessment of the certainty and imminence of the threat based on these factors (e.g., willingness to die for their cause, access and motivation to use biological weapons) considerably more difficult. Conceptualizing the current threat of international terrorism in terms of risk, however, asserts the calculability of future harms and thus the plausibility of assessing the likelihood and degree of the threat posed. What happens when such calculations and assessments are impossible?

When risk fails to address the threat involved, the logic of precautionary action in the face of uncertainty takes over.[17] The uncertainty that surrounds terrorism, its perpetrators, and their future plans has been the cause of great concern for governments worldwide. The incalculability of the nature, probability, scope, and potential targets of terrorists in the aftermath of 9/11 have shifted policy focus in combating this threat from sole reliance on risk assessment to the inclusion, and now prominence, of precautionary measures in the face of uncertainty. The logic of precautionary measures in response to uncertainty is derived from the precautionary principle. The precautionary principle figures prominently in many international instruments, such as Principle 15 of the 1992 Rio Declaration at the United National Conference on Environment and Development (UNCED); Article 2(2)(a) of the 1992 Convention for the Protection of the Marine Environment of the North-East Atlantic; Article 3(3) of the 1992 United Nations Framework Convention on Climate Change; and Article 4(3)(f) of the Bamako Convention on the Ban of the Import into Africa and the Control of Transboundary Movement and Management of Hazardous Wastes within Africa. This principle emerged from the German notion of *Vorsorgeprinzip* (foresight principle) during the drafting of

---

15 Burnett, J. and Whyte, D. 2005. Embedded expertise and the new terrorism. *Journal for Crime, Conflict and the Media* 1 (4): 5.

16 Gunaratna, R. 2006. The al-Qaeda threat and the international response. In *Terrorism: Critical concepts in political science, Vol. IV: The fourth or religious wave*, ed. D. C. Rapoport, 480–481. London: Routledge.

17 O'Malley, P. 2004. *Risk, uncertainty and government*. London: Glasshouse, 23.

air pollution legislation in Germany in the early 1970s.[18] It embodies the notions of prospective planning to avoid environmental damage, early detection of harms through comprehensive research, and taking actions to forestall potential harms in advance of conclusive scientific evidence.[19] This principle, introduced into European law by the Treaty on European Union 1992, requires that when there is a threat of serious harm, "lack of full scientific certainty" should not be used as a reason for inaction.[20] The precautionary principle targets situations in which there is both scientific uncertainty and the possibility of serious and irreversible damage. Such a situation is exemplified by the current threat of terrorism posed by al-Qaeda.

Precautionary logic drives counterterrorism policies. When there are threats or potential threats of irreversible grave harm, lack of full certainty should not be used as a reason for rejecting or postponing the implementation of measures. In fact, the precautionary principle denies authorities the ability to idly stand by and do nothing in situations of threatened but unpredictable grave harms.[21] According to international law,

> wherever, on the basis of the best information available, there are reasonable grounds for concern that serious and/or irreversible harm . . . may be caused, . . . proportional action to prevent and/or abate this harm must be taken, including in the face of scientific uncertainty regarding the cause, extent and/or probability of the potential harm.[22]

The key word here is proportional. Proportionality requires that the course of action chosen corresponds to the size (likelihood and magnitude) of the risk involved. Cost-benefit analysis is considered as a particular expression of proportionality.[23] Counterterrorism measures are burdensome and costly. A question rarely asked by policymakers in this field is whether counterterrorism spending is proportionate to the threat of terrorism. Cost-benefit analysis is required in order to ensure that a form of worst-case thinking is not at work when developing and implementing precautionary measures in response to the current threat of terrorism. This threat "so panics those who are confronted with it that they respond immediately to avert it, without consideration of whether even more fearful consequences will accrue

---

18   See Boehmer-Christiansen, S. 1994. The precautionary principle in Germany: Enabling government. In *Interpreting the precautionary principle*, eds. T. O'Riordan and J. Cameron, 31. London: Earthscan.

19   Ibid.; Harding, R., and Fisher, E. 1999. Introducing the precautionary principle. In *Perspectives on the Precautionary Principle*, eds. R. Harding and E. Fisher, 4. Sydney, Australia: Federation Press.

20   Harding and Fisher, ibid.

21   Dershowitz, A. M. 2006. *Preemption: A knife that cuts both ways.* New York: W. W. Norton.

22   Trouwborst, A. 2006. *Precautionary rights and duties of states.* Leiden, the Netherlands: Martinus Nijhoff, 159.

23   Case T-13/99 *Pfizer Animal Health SA v. Council of the European Union* [2002] ECR II-3305.

thereby."[24] Such worst-case thinking, however, can exact a high social (e.g., deprivation of human rights) and economic price from society.

Preemption similarly deals with situations of uncertainty by licensing action to be taken against threatened and unpredictable harms.[25] Two forms of preemption are explored below: preemptive war and preemptive measures with which to combat terrorism.

PREEMPTIVE WAR

The United States' responses in the war on terrorism attest to the application of the precautionary principle. For example, in the United States, the Bush Administration's strategy (National Security Strategy 2002) for the war on terrorism called for precautionary responses against potential enemies (e.g., rogue states) with uncertain capabilities and targets, even before the threat of attack was imminent.[26] The precautionary principle constitutes a driving force behind preemption. Preemption is an aspect of a country's legitimate self-defense authority. Proponents of preemption defend it by claiming that it is a necessary response to terrorists (who cannot be deterred), rogue states, and the proliferation of weapons of mass destruction.[27] By contrast, opponents of preemption contend that a country that uses it exacerbates distrust among its allies and encourages other states (rogue states included) to take similar actions.[28]

Preemption has a long history in international law. In fact, "international law recognized that nations need not suffer an attack before they can lawfully take action to defend themselves against forces that present an imminent danger of attack."[29] After World War I and World War II, laws were created to prohibit countries' use of force. In particular, Article 2(4) of the UN Charter holds that "all Members shall refrain in their international relations from the threat or use of force against the territorial integrity or political independence of any state, or in any other manner inconsistent with the Purposes of the United Nations." There

---

24 Waldron, J. 2004. Terrorism and the uses of terror. *Journal of Ethics* 8(1): 15.

25 Dershowitz, A. M. 2006. *Preemption: A knife that cuts both ways.* New York: W. W. Norton.

26 Stern, J., and Wiener, J. B. 2006. Precaution against terrorism. *Journal of Risk Research* 4 (June 9): 393.

27 See, for example, Lieber, R. J. 2005. *The American era: Power and strategy for the 21st century.* New York: Cambridge University Press; Kaufman, R. G. 2007. *In defense of the Bush doctrine.* Lexington: University Press of Kentucky; Renshon, S. A. 2007. The Bush doctrine considered. In *Understanding the Bush doctrine: Psychology and strategy in an age of terrorism,* eds. S. A. Renshon and P. Suedfeld. New York: Routledge.

28 See, for example, Jervis, R. 2003. Understanding the Bush doctrine. *Political Science Quarterly* 118:365–358; Rhodes, E. 2003. The imperial logic of Bush's liberal agenda. *Survival* 45(1): 131–154; Eland, I. 2002. The empire strikes out: The "new imperialism" and its fatal flaws. *Policy Analysis* 459:1–27. http://www.cato.org/pubs/pas/pa-459es.html.

29 Bush, G. W. 2002, September. The national security strategy of the United States. *Office of the President of the United States.* Washington, DC: White House, 15. http://usiraq.procon.org /sourcefiles/National%20Security%20Strategy.pdf

are only two exceptions to this prohibition: individual and collective self-defense against an armed attack. Specifically, according to Article 51 of the UN Charter,

> [n]othing in the present Charter shall impair the inherent right of individual or collective self-defense if an armed attack occurs against a Member of the United Nations, until the Security Council has taken measures necessary to maintain international peace and security. Measures taken by Members in the exercise of this right of self-defense shall be immediately reported to the Security Council and shall not in any way affect the authority and responsibility of the Security Council under the present Charter to take at any time such action as it deems necessary in order to maintain or restore international peace and security.

Self-defense is justified when an attack is underway or has already occurred. According to *Nicaragua v. United States* (Nicaragua case),[30] the International Court of Justice (otherwise known as World Court), which is the primary judicial organ of the United Nations, stated that only acts grave enough to be considered as an armed act could trigger the right to individual or collective self-defense. The use of force is also authorized if there is clear and convincing evidence that the enemy (the target of the force) is planning another attack. However, this defensive attack must be necessary, proportionate, and must be carried out within a reasonable period of time following the initial attack by the enemy.

The United States has used preemptive force to prevent potential (and not actual) armed attacks in the future. The first time the United States used preemptive force against a terrorist organization was in response to the 1998 Kenya and Tanzania bombings.

> On August 5, 1998, an Arab-language newspaper in London published a letter from the International Islamic Front for Jihad, in which it threatened retaliation against the U.S. for the Albanian operation—in a "language they will understand." Two days later, the U.S. Embassies in Kenya and Tanzania were bombed.[31]

Specifically, on August 7, 1998, al-Qaeda operatives launched coordinated terrorist attacks in Africa, which resulted in 213 deaths. Here, two U.S. embassies were targeted: one in Nairobi, Kenya, and the other in Dar es Salaam, Tanzania. Out of the 213 deaths, 23 were U.S. citizens (12 killed in Kenya and 11 in Tanzania) and over 5,000 people were injured in both bombings.

Communication intelligence established the location of al-Qaeda training camps in Afghanistan. On August 20, 1998, the United States fired missiles at these locations in retaliation for the al-Qaeda bombings of the embassies in Kenya and Tanzania.[32] A facility in Sudan, which was suspected of manufacturing precursors

---

30 [1986] ICJ 14.

31 Mayer, J. 2005. Outsourcing torture: The secret history of America's "extraordinary rendition" program. *The New Yorker*, February 14, 2005, p. 106.

32 Maddrell, P. 2009. Failing intelligence: U.S. intelligence in the age of transnational threats. *International Journal of Intelligence and Counterintelligence* 22(2): 211.

for chemical weapons (i.e., a critical nerve gas component), was destroyed as well.[33] This facility was targeted even though it did not pose an imminent threat.

What was so significant about this preemptive strike? According to a U.S. Congressional report on the Kenya and Tanzania bombings, this was the first time the United States

> launched such a strike within the territory of a state which presumably is not con-
> clusively, actively and directly to blame for the action triggering retaliation . . . .
> launched military strikes at multiple terrorist targets within the territory of more
> than one foreign nation . . . [and] . . . attacked a target where the avowed goal
> was not to attack a single individual terrorist but an organizational infrastructure
> instead.[34]

This technique was lauded as providing disincentives for other would-be terrorists, disrupting sources of funding, weapons, and safe havens for terrorists, and limiting their ability to operate.[35] Nevertheless, this approach may have a negative impact as well. According to the Congressional report, such preemptive tactics

> undermine . . . the rule of law, violating the sovereignty of nations with whom
> we are not at war; . . . could increase, rather than decrease, incidents of terrorism
> at least in the short run; . . . may be characterized as anti-Islamic; and . . . may
> radicalize some elements of populations and aid terrorist recruitment.[36]

The Clinton Administration claimed that their preemptive response was a legitimate form of self-defense pursuant to Article 51 of the UN Charter.[37] To justify its response to the Kenya and Tanzania bombings, the Clinton Administration also invoked Section 324(4) of the Antiterrorism and Effective Death Penalty Act of 1996, which holds that the "President should use all necessary means, including covert action and military force, to disrupt, dismantle, and destroy international infrastructure used by international terrorists, including overseas terrorist training facilities and safehavens."[38] This belief was also evident in the Bush Administration's 2002 National Security Strategy. Former U.S. Secretary of Defense Donald Rumsfeld stated during an interview,

> I will say this, there is no question but that the United States of America has
> every right, as every country does, of self-defense, and the problem with ter-
> rorism is that there is no way to defend against the terrorists at every place and
> every time against every conceivable technique. Therefore, the only way to deal

---

33 Dagne, T. 2002, January 17. Africa and the war on terrorism. *CRS Report for Congress*, 1. http://fpc.state.gov/documents/organization/7959.pdf; Perl, R. F. 1998. Terrorism: U.S. response to bombings in Kenya and Tanzania: A new policy direction? *CRS Report for Congress* 98-733 F, p. 1. http://www.policyarchive.org/handle/10207/bitstreams/674.pdf.

34 Perl, ibid., p. 3.

35 Ibid.

36 Ibid., p. 4.

37 Ibid., p. 6.

38 Ibid.

with the terrorist network is to take the battle to them. That is in fact what we're doing. That is in effect self-defense of a preemptive nature.[39]

Post 9/11, the United Nations Security Council passed two resolutions (Resolution 1368 and 1373) in 2001, which stated that countries have the right to self-defensive action in response to the September 11 attacks and terrorism. The U.S. Congress engaged in similar conduct by issuing a joint declaration authorizing the President to

> use all necessary and appropriate force against those nations, organizations, or persons he determines planned, authorized, committed, or aided the terrorist attacks that occurred on September 11, 2001, or harbored such organizations or persons, in order to prevent any future acts of international terrorism against the United States by such nations, organizations or persons.[40]

This right to use self-defense was reiterated in the 2002 U.S. National Security Strategy:

> The United States has long maintained the option of preemptive actions to counter a sufficient threat to our national security. The greater the threat, the greater is the risk of inaction—and the more compelling the case for taking anticipatory action to defend ourselves, even if uncertainty remains as to the time and place of the enemy's attack. To forestall or prevent such hostile acts by our adversaries, the United States will, if necessary, act preemptively.[41]

The United States initiated an armed attack against Afghanistan, after the attacks on September 11, 2001, on the basis of evidence that indicated that future attacks were imminent. To justify this armed attack, evidence was provided that showed that 9/11 was just one of a series of attacks against the United States over the years by Osama bin Laden. Specifically, bin Laden had been tied to the 1993 World Trade Center attack, the 1993 attack on U.S. soldiers in Somalia, the 1998 U.S. embassy bombings in Kenya and Tanzania, the attack on the USS Cole in 2000 (see Box 5-1), and of course, the attacks on September 11, 2001.[42]

For preemption to be justified, nonmilitary tactics must be pursued before choosing to engage in the use of force against a country. This was evident in Operation Enduring Freedom—the Afghanistan War. Before the Afghanistan War, it was requested of the Taliban, on two separate occasions, to turn over those responsible

39 Rumsfeld, D. H. 2001, October 28. News transcript: Secretary Rumsfeld remarks at stakeout outside ABC TV. *U.S. Depatment of Defense.* http://www.defense.gov/transcripts/transcript.aspx ?transcriptid=2225.

40 107th Congress. *Authorization for use of military force.* Public Law 107-40 [S.J. Res. 23] (September 18, 2001).

41 Bush Administration. 2002. *National security strategy.* http://georgewbush-whitehouse.archives .gov/nsc/nss/2002/nss5.html.

42 UK Prime Minister's Office. 2003, May 15. September 11 attacks—Culpability document. *The National Archives.* http://webarchive.nationalarchives.gov.uk/+/number10.gov.uk/archive /2003/05/september-11-attacks-culpability-document-3682.

Box 5-1   Terrorist Attack In Brief: The USS Cole Bombing

On October 29, 2000, in Aden, Yemen, two al-Qaeda suicide bombers detonated explosives from a motorboat after reaching their target, the naval destroyer USS Cole. This bombing resulted in the deaths of 17 sailors, 39 injured, and extensive damage to the ship. This was a new tactic used by al-Qaeda, who had, prior to this incident, used truck bombs for major targets. It is important to note that Aden was a relatively new port for refueling by the U.S. Navy. Prior to January 1999, the port used was Djibouti in the Horn of Africa. Why did the port for refueling change? In 1998, there was severe turmoil in the Horn of Africa, the Kenya and Tanzania bombings occurred, an internal war started in Sudan, there was instability in Somalia, and the war between Ethiopia and Eritrea was still going strong.[1] No threat information existed or had been received by intelligence agencies that Aden was a high-risk port or that an attack was imminent. As the Commander in Chief of the U.S. Central Command, General Tommy Franks, stated before the United States Senate Armed Services Committee "had such warning been received, action would have been taken by the operating forces in response to the warning."[2]

---

[1] Perl, R., and O'Rourke, R. 2001, January 30. Terrorist attack on USS Cole: Background and issues for congress. *CRS Report for Congress*, 5. http://fl1.findlaw.com/news.findlaw.com/cnn /docs/crs/coleterrattck13001.pdf.

[2] Franks, T. R. 2000, October 25. *Statement made by General Tommy R. Franks, Commander in Chief, US Central Command, before United States Senate Armed Services Committee*, 12. http:// armed-services.senate.gov/statemnt/2000/001025tf.pdf.

for the 9/11 attacks in order to avoid preemptive action by the United States. On each occasion, it flatly refused to provide the United States with the al-Qaeda operatives. This was not the first time that such a request had been made of the Taliban. In the aftermath of the Kenya and Tanzania bombings, the UN Security Council in Resolution 1267 condemned the attacks by Osama bin Laden and demanded that the Taliban surrender bin Laden without further delay. In its resolution, the Security Council further deplored "the fact that the Taliban continues to provide safe haven to Usama bin Laden and to allow him and others associated with him to operate a network of terrorist training camps from Taliban-controlled territory and to use Afghanistan as a base from which to sponsor international terrorist operations." The Taliban regime had responded that no evidence existed against Osama bin Laden; as such, neither bin Laden nor his network would be expelled.[43]

While support existed for the use of force against Afghanistan, it largely dwindled after such force was used against terrorists and states outside of Afghanistan. In fact, the Iraq war that followed was significantly different. Iraq was invaded not in response to an imminent threat, but to a probable threat. The United States

---

[43] UK Prime Minister's Office. 2003, May 15. September 11 Attacks – Culpability document. *The National Archives*. http://webarchive.nationalarchives.gov.uk/+/number10.gov.uk/archive/2003 /05/september-11-attacks-culpability-document-3682.

argued that it had the right to self-defense against Iraq due to its possession of (or intent to possess) WMDs, its refusal to decommission these weapons, and its links to international terrorists (e.g., al-Qaeda) that have in the past targeted the United States and had plans to attack the United States in the future.[44] To justify its use of preemption against Iraq, the Bush Administration stated that "deterrence based only upon the threat of retaliation is less likely to work against leaders of rogue states more willing to take risks, gambling with the lives of their people, and the wealth of their nations."[45] Additionally, the Bush Administration noted:

> Today, our enemies see weapons of mass destruction as weapons of choice. For rogue states these weapons are tools of intimidation and military aggression against their neighbors . . . Traditional concepts of deterrence will not work against a terrorist enemy whose avowed tactics are wanton destruction and the targeting of innocents; whose so-called soldiers seek martyrdom in death and whose most potent protection is statelessness. The overlap between states that sponsor terror and those that pursue WMD compels us to action.[46]

Iraq was prohibited by the UN Security Council from developing nuclear weapons in the aftermath of the Persian Gulf War of 1990–1991. On February 5, 2003, U.S. Secretary of State Colin Powell presented the UN Security Council "with evidence the United States maintained irrefutably and undeniably demonstrated Iraqi noncompliance with Resolution 1441; in particular, Secretary Powell alleged Iraq concealed WMD from inspectors and that a large [al-]Qaeda cell was active in Iraq and working together with Baghdad."[47] Even if Iraq had violated its disarmament requirement, the mere possession of such material is not considered an "armed attack" to justify the use of force against this country, at least not according to the jurisprudence of the International Criminal Court.[48] Other countries have engaged in similar preemptive attacks. A case in point is Israel, which had engaged in a preemptive attack against Iraq in 1981. In particular, Israel fired at an Iraqi nuclear reactor in Ostrik to prevent Iraq from developing nuclear weapons. This action was condemned by the UN Security Council under Resolution 487 (1981).

---

44 Drumbl, M. A. 2003. Self-defense and the use of force: Breaking the rules, making the rules, or both? *International Studies Perspectives* 4(4): 411.

45 Bush Administration. 2002. *National Security Strategy.* http://georgewbush-whitehouse .archives.gov/nsc/nss/2002/nss5.html.

46 Ibid.

47 Knowlton, B. 2003. Speech seen as strong but unlikely to sway skeptic. *New York Times*, February 5, 2003. http://www.nytimes.com/2003/02/05/international/06REACT.html; Tyler, P. E. 2003. Intelligence break led U.S. to tie envoy killing to Iraqi Qaeda cell. *New York Times*, February 6, 2003. http://www.nytimes.com/2003/02/06/world/threats-responses-terror-network -intelligence-break-led-us-tie-envoy-killing.html; Drumbl, M. A. 2003. Self-defense and the use of force: Breaking the rules, making the rules, or both? *International Studies Perspectives* 4(4): 416.

48 See the advisory opinion of the International Court of Justice, Legality of the Threat or Use of Nuclear Weapons, on July 8, 1996.

To justify America's plan to engage in a preemptive war against Iraq, former U.S. Secretary of Defense Colin Powell presented evidence that Saddam Hussein had biological and chemical weapons in the past, and noted that no confirmation (in the form of evidence) existed on how and if he had destroyed his stockpile.[49] He further noted that Saddam Hussein had used WMDs in the past, citing his use of mustard and nerve gas against the Kurds in 1988, which led to the death of 5,000 men, women, and children.[50] However, conclusive evidence of WMDs in Iraq was not found. In fact, in October 2002, the National Intelligence Council, in its report, the "National Intelligence Estimate on Iraq's Continuing Programs for Weapons of Mass Destruction," erroneously concluded that Iraq had inventories of weapons of mass destruction.[51] Indeed, according to a report by Charles Duelfer, who was chosen by the Bush Administration to investigate Iraq's weapons program, Saddam Hussein did not have the capability to develop WMDs and considered Iran and Israel more of a threat than it did the United States.[52] Moreover, solid evidence that Saddam Hussein was supporting al-Qaeda and plotting with them to attack America was also not presented.

Nevertheless, Iraq was invaded by the United States (and the United Kingdom) without the authorization of the UN Security Council. This was confirmed when the former United Nations Secretary General Kofi Annan stated that the U.S.-led war in Iraq was not in conformity with the UN Charter and thus illegal.[53] Theorists argue that for a "just war" to be legitimate, countries must show that they have *jus ad bellum* (the right to go to war) and *jus in bello* (the right conduct during the war).[54] In the case of the Iraq war, *jus ad bellum* was not established according to international law. If convincing evidence had existed that Iraq had been involved in the past in terrorist attacks against the United States and was planning to engage in future attacks,[55] the UN Security Council would have authorized the use of force, according to Annan.[56]

---

[49]   Powell, C. 2003. Full text of Powell speech [Pt I]. *BBC News*, February 5, 2003. http://news.bbc.co.uk/2/hi/middle_east/2729525.stm.

[50]   Powell, C. 2003. Full text of Powell speech [Pt II]. *BBC News*, February 5, 2003. http://news.bbc.co.uk/2/hi/middle_east/2730855.stm.

[51]   Best Jr., R. A. 2008. What the intelligence community got right about Iraq. *Intelligence and National Security* 23(3): 289.

[52]   Duelfer, C. A. 2004. Comprehensive revised report with addendums on Iraq's weapons of mass destruction (Duelfer Report). *U.S. Government Printing Office*, 31, 34. http://permanent.access.gpo.gov/ DuelferRpt/ Volume_1.pdf.

[53]   MacAskill, E., and Borger, J. 2004. Iraq war was illegal and breached UN charter, says Annan. *The Guardian*, September 16, 2004. http://www.guardian.co.uk/world/2004/sep/16/iraq.iraq.

[54]   Asad, T. 2010. Thinking about terrorism and just war. *Cambridge Review of International Affairs* 23(1): 3–24.

[55]   Credible evidence of this had not been found. MacEachin, D. 2004. National Commission on Terrorists Attacks upon the United States. *Twelfth Public Hearing, NTSB Conference Center*. http://www.9-11commission.gov/archive/hearing12/9-11Commission_Hearing_2004-06-16.htm.

[56]   MacAskill, E., and Borger, J. 2004. Iraq war was illegal and breached UN charter, says Annan. *The Guardian*, September 16, 2004. http://www.guardian.co.uk/world/2004/sep/16/iraq.iraq.

Furthermore, on March 7, 2003, Hans Blix, the head of the UN Monitoring, Verification and Inspection Commission (UNMOVIC) from March 2000 until June 2003, reported that Iraq had begun cooperating more with the weapons regime. The "majority of the Security Council believed that the practice of containment by inspections was working and that lethal force was not necessary."[57] This, of course, meant that there was no need for an armed attack against Iraq. Nonetheless, on March 20, 2003, in a

> follow-up letter to the Security Council reporting on the use of force against Iraq, the United States argued that the 1991 ceasefire with Iraq had been removed owing to Iraq's material breach of the weapons decommissioning resolutions, thereby reviving the authorization to use force against Iraq as set out in Resolution 678.[58]

This letter further noted that with the war in Iraq "the United States was acting in its own defense and in the collective defense of the international community from the threat posed by Iraq."[59] The opportunity to manage the risk posed by Saddam Hussein and his regime through containment by the international community was, therefore, bypassed in favor of a preemptive response seeking regime change in Iraq (Operation Iraqi Freedom).

Usually, the country seeking to engage in preemptive attacks has the burden of proof to show that an armed attack against them is imminent. Sufficient evidence was not presented to show that an attack on the United States was imminent. Therefore, with the war on Iraq, the United States extended the meaning of preemptive war to include armed action against probable and not imminent attacks. The operating principle or standard of action provided by former U.S. Vice

---

Box 5-2 Food for Thought: Taking a Leaf Out of the Playbook of the United States: Preemptive Self-Defense For All?

One of the reasons why the United States engaged in the war in Iraq was that Saddam Hussein allegedly had in his possession WMDs and posed a threat to the United States. Credible intelligence on plans of Iraq to attack the United States with these weapons was not presented. The UN Security Council also had not approved the war. What does this mean for other states?

Worldwide, there are feuding countries that have a long history of seeking to cause harm to each other. In some cases, the countries even possess weapons of mass destruction. To each other, these countries pose a possible future threat. Imagine that certain feuding countries, such as Pakistan, India, North Korea, and South Korea decide to go to war. Specifically, Pakistan decides to attack India and North Korea decides to attack South Korea. Could these countries justify their use of force by citing the U.S.-led Iraq war?

---

57 Drumbl, M. A. 2003. Self-defense and the use of force: Breaking the rules, making the rules, or both? *International Studies Perspectives* 4(4): 416.

58 Ibid.

59 Ibid.

President Dick Cheney, known as the "One Percent Doctrine" (or Cheney Doctrine), demonstrates this by stating that "if there was even a one percent chance of terrorists getting a weapon of mass destruction—and there has been a small probability of such an occurrence for some time—the United States must now act as if it were a certainty."[60] The One Percent Doctrine represents a more extreme version of the precautionary principle, known as the ultraconservative precautionary principle. The application of this version of the principle is triggered in the most minimal way possible (for example, a 1% chance of terrorists obtaining a weapon of mass destruction), "whilst the response is conceived of in the most robust way possible" by taking action as if the danger is certain.[61] Therefore, even though there is a lack of certainty and a minimal probability of an attack, the potential severity of the attacks is deemed to be sufficient to trigger preemptive action. The types of preemptive actions taken in response to the uncertainty surrounding terrorism will be explored in the next section.

PREEMPTIVE RESPONSES TO THE UNKNOWN

The counterterrorism measures implemented in the aftermath of 9/11 attest to the application of the precautionary principle. Given the nature of this threat and the goals of these terrorists, states' sole reliance on exacting retribution by capturing and pursuing individuals who have already perpetrated the crime is inappropriate because of the possibility of severe and irreversible damage that may result from the attack. The current threat of terrorism also poses unique challenges to existing measures and policies, such as those based on deterrence. A measure or policy aimed at deterrence would prevent individuals from engaging in crime by impacting their rational decision-making processes, which, according to rational choice theory,[62] involves criminals weighing the costs of committing a crime (e.g., the risk of apprehension) against the benefits (e.g., monetary gains). According to this theory, the offender goes through a series of rational decisions and makes a choice (even if done in a split second) that the benefits outweigh the costs, and then commits the crime. If crime is a rational choice, then increasing the certainty and even the severity of punishment for a particular crime should shift the cost-benefit balance away from the criminal behavior.[63]

Examples of such measures are those aimed at situational terrorism prevention, which focus on ways to reduce the opportunities for terrorism. Counterterrorism measures should make it more difficult for terrorists to achieve their

---

[60] Suskind, R. 2006. *The one percent doctrine: Deep inside America's pursuit of its enemies since 9/11*. London: Simon and Schuster, 62.

[61] See ft. 12 in Gardiner, S. M. 2006. A core precautionary principle. *The Journal of Political Philosophy* 14(1): 37.

[62] Cornish, D. B., and Clarke, R. V. eds. 1986. *The reasoning criminal: Rational choice perspectives in offending*. New York: Springer.

[63] Bachman, R., and Schutt, R. K. 2003. *The practice of research in criminology and criminal justice*, 2nd ed. London: Pine Forge, 35.

objectives and thus increase the perceived costs of so doing. If the effort required to succeed in a task is raised high enough, the terrorists might give up on that task or take longer to execute their operations. Reducing the opportunities for terrorism is an essential task of counterterrorism, one that is easily overlooked. Nevertheless, a consequence of implementing these types of countermeasures is the displacement of terrorist attacks to more vulnerable targets and countries.

Former U.S. President George W. Bush's National Security Strategy states that "traditional concepts of deterrence will not work against a terrorist enemy."[64] While deterrent policies may have proved useful and sufficient in the Cold War, this may not be the case with current terrorists (al-Qaeda and affiliates), state-less enemies without territory or population to defend, who pursue nonnegotiable objectives.[65] In fact, it could be argued that al-Qaeda and related Islamic terrorists cannot be deterred by conventional punishment. Consider the application of the rational decision-making processes underlying deterrent policies to these terrorists. Even if the cost of committing a terrorist act is indefinite imprisonment or even execution by the state, if the individual is a suicide bomber, the benefits, purely from the religious perspective of the terrorist, consist of eternity in paradise. Thus, the prospect of punishment such as death is, for the terrorists, a cost that is more than outweighed by the benefits.

Dershowitz argues that while there are no morally acceptable ways of deterring terrorists who are willing to die for their cause, there are morally unacceptable tactics, such as the killing of innocent relatives of these suicide bombers, which may deter some such suicide terrorists.[66] Aside from the moral issues raised and the inappropriateness of these measures for democracies, killing these terrorists, either publicly as a form of deterrence (as Israel does when it executes members of terrorist groups) or in combat, through military intervention, will not mitigate the terrorist threat. In fact, attacking these terrorist groups is like cutting one of the heads of the Hydra: more heads will grow in the place of the one that was cut off. Indeed, terrorists, especially al-Qaeda, "have a very high capacity for replenishing human losses."[67] Also, al-Qaeda's use of diffuse, linear organizations to implement multiple and often uncoordinated attacks against military forces has raised serious

---

64 Bush Administration. 2002, September. *The national security strategy of the United States of America*. Washington, DC:US Government Printing Office, 15; Davis, P. K., and Jenkins, B. M. 2002. *Deterrence and influence in counterterrorism: A component in the war on al-Qaeda*. Santa Monica: CA: RAND.

65 As such, no peace talks are conceivable. Al-Qaeda and followers have made this clear in public statements in the media. The *9/11 Commission report* also noted that individuals who are fully committed to Osama bin Laden's version of Islam "are impervious to persuasion." See Kean, T. H., and Hamilton, L. H. 2004. *The 9/11 Commission report: Final report of the national commission on terrorist attacks upon the United States*. New York: W.W. Norton, 375.

66 Although he also added that democracies should not employ these tactics. Dershowitz, A. M. 2006. *Preemption: A knife that cuts both ways*. New York: W. W. Norton, 8 and ft. 18, 278.

67 Gunaratna, R. 2005. Al-Qaeda in Europe: Today's battlefield. In *Al-Qaeda now: Understanding today's terrorists*, ed. K. J. Greenberg, 43. Cambridge, UK: Cambridge University Press.

concerns about the military's ability to fight such adversaries.[68] In addition, the U.S. military's attacks and presence in the Persian Gulf illustrate how deterrent strategies such as their military intervention made matters worse by increasing support for and recruitment to al-Qaeda rather than minimizing or preventing it.[69]

Moreover, the U.S. response to terrorism, which primarily focuses on targeting operational terrorist cells (i.e., those planning and preparing attacks), also demonstrated how by attacking only operational cells, the terrorist organization can never be destroyed.[70] This is illustrated in Donald Rumsfeld's (former U.S. Defense Secretary) reflection on the progress of the war on terrorism: "Are we capturing, killing, or deterring and dissuading more terrorists everyday than the madrassas and the radical clerics are recruiting, training and deploying against the U.S.?"[71] If one continues to target only the operational infrastructure of al-Qaeda, then the likely outcome is that the organization will survive as a result of the existing support networks, which means the fight against terrorism will continue, without progress, indefinitely.[72] The investigations of 9/11 revealed that not only were there al-Qaeda operational cells in the United States and Europe but also a significant number of al-Qaeda support cells, which make up terrorist networks that are both affiliated and unaffiliated with al-Qaeda. Moreover, the attacks on Madrid and London brought home the lesson that attention needed to be paid to these support networks, which had received relatively less consideration than operational networks after 9/11. Thus, sole reliance on conventional methods of deterrence (military presence, capture, indefinite imprisonment, injury, or death) will not offer the United States or Europe protection against these terrorists. Indeed, this position has been supported by many terrorism scholars and analysts who believe that deterrence strategies alone cannot effectively counter the current threat of terrorism.[73]

---

[68] Jones, S. G. 2007. Fighting networked terrorist groups: Lessons from Israel. *Studies in Conflict and Terrorism* 30(4): 281–282.

[69] Pape, R. A. 2006. The strategic logic of terrorism. In *Terrorism: Critical concepts in political science, Vol. IV: The fourth or religious wave*, ed. D. C. Rapoport, 173. London: Routledge; Similarly, UK Chief of General Staff, Sir Richard Dannatt, stated that UK armed forces' presence in Iraq undoubtedly exacerbates the difficulties they, along with the rest of the world, are experiencing with these terrorists. General seeks UK Iraq withdrawal. 2006. *BBC*, October 13, 2006. http://news.bbc.co.uk/2/hi/uk_news/6046332.stm.

[70] Gunaratna, R. 2005. Al-Qaeda in Europe: Today's battlefield. In *Al-Qaeda now: Understanding today's terrorists*, ed. K. J Greenberg, 43.Cambridge, UK: Cambridge University Press.

[71] Rumsfeld's war-on-terror memo. 2003. *USA Today*, October 16, 2003, p. 1. http://www.usatoday.com/news/washington/executive/rumsfeld-memo.htm; Kean, T. H., and Hamilton, L. H. 2004. *The 9/11 Commission report: Final report of the National Commission on Terrorist Attacks upon the United States*. New York: W.W. Norton, 374–375.

[72] Gunaratna, R. 2005, Al-Qaeda in Europe: Today's battlefield. In *Al-Qaeda now: Understanding today's terrorists*, ed. K. J. Greenberg, 45. Cambridge, UK: Cambridge University Press.

[73] See, for example, Betts, R. K. 2002. The soft underbelly of American primacy: Tactical advantages of terror. In *September 11, terrorist attacks, and U.S. foreign policy*, ed. J. C. Demetrios, 46. New York: Academy of Political Science.

The metric of success in the global war on terrorism is defined by law enforcement and intelligence agencies' ability to prevent, preempt, and deter attacks.[74] Given the devastation caused by terrorist attacks and the unique problems they pose for regular passive policies of deterrence,[75] nations worldwide have taken a more active response to countering terrorism, such as preemptive strikes and covert actions. In the face of death and/or serious bodily harm, conventional punishment often occurs too late. Counterterrorism is thus becoming less about reacting to terrorism than addressing the conditions that make it possible and forestalling individuals from actually engaging in such attacks. In this sense, counterterrorism seeks to reduce opportunities for terrorism, harden existing targets, and increase surveillance before an attack will occur.

The impact of 9/11, the Madrid and London bombings, and the continuous threat of catastrophic risk have significantly increased the pressure on states to think and act preemptively. Preemption "seeks to intervene when the risk of harm is no more than an unspecified threat or propensity as yet uncertain and beyond view."[76] Preemptive measures are justified on the assumption that if states wait until the harm is realized, it will significantly increase the risks.[77] While intelligence agencies had been tracking the activities of Osama bin Laden (at least up until his death) and his "World Islamic Front for Jihad against the Jews and Crusaders" long before 9/11, the terrorist threats that nations are faced with today go beyond al-Qaeda or any single terrorist group.[78] Consequently, the enemies that nations are faced with today have uncertain capacities and intentions, which makes the forecasting of new and emerging trends in terrorism extremely difficult.

As a result, preemptive measures are taken in order to prevent and forestall rather than permit the devastating consequences that can come from attacks such as those of 9/11 and even the Madrid and London bombings (on a lesser scale). The power behind the preemption doctrine is a formidable one; the nexus of new threats—terrorism, weapons of mass destruction—mandate, if not require, a new response.[79] In light of the current threat of terrorism, preemption of future terrorist attacks is taking precedence over responding to the attacks after they have occurred. The question that follows is, what types of new, preemptive responses are required?

---

74 Hoffman, B. 2003. Al Qaeda, trends in terrorism, and future potentialities: An assessment. *Studies in Conflict and Terrorism* 26(6): 438.

75 Such as technology-based barriers (i.e., metal detectors), target hardening, instituting stricter laws, and so on.

76 Zedner, L. 2007. Seeking security by eroding rights: The side-stepping of due process. In *Security and human rights*, ed. B. Goold and L. Lazarus, 259. Oxford, UK: Hart.

77 Crawford, N. C. 2005. The justifications of pre-emption and preventive war doctrines. In *Just war theory: A reappraisal*, ed. M. Evans, 25. Edinburgh: Edinburgh University Press.

78 Cragin, K., and Daly, S. A. 2004. *The dynamic terrorist threat: An assessment of group motivations and capabilities in a changing world*. Santa Monica, CA: RAND, 85.

79 Blinken, A. J. 2003/2004. From preemption to engagement. *Survival* 45(4): 34.

The Response to the Al-Qaeda Virus

Investigations of 9/11 and those that occurred for attempted and realized terrorist attacks after it, revealed that not only were there al-Qaeda operational cells in Europe and the United States (among other countries) but also a significant number of al-Qaeda support cells, which make up terrorist networks that are both affiliated and unaffiliated with al-Qaeda. The attacks on Madrid and London brought home the lesson that attention needed to be paid to these support networks, which had received relatively less consideration than operational networks after 9/11. In considering the best response to the threat of terrorism, states have thus recognized that they need to move beyond focusing on operational networks of al-Qaeda to also targeting support networks. Indeed, in Europe and the United States, the number of support networks (which includes homegrown terrorists, al-Qaeda affiliates, and terrorists inspired by al-Qaeda) far exceeds the number of operational networks. Support networks, despite the lack of attention they have received, are extremely dangerous because like computer viruses, they can mutate; in this case, into operational cells and thus carry out attacks. Unfortunately, as with computer viruses, there is currently no consensus as to which measures are likely to counter this threat effectively.

Nevertheless, there are key identifiable elements in the measures used to tackle computer viruses that could be applied to preemptive measures aimed at dealing with support networks. Some of the most prominent identifiable elements include detection, containment, and starving[80] of a computer virus.[81] Measures aimed at facilitating the first and primary element, detection, are critical when faced with the support networks of al-Qaeda. This occurs because the "detectable" networks are usually those that are operational. It is argued that by painstakingly detecting al-Qaeda's worldwide infrastructure and human network, it can be dismantled and its leadership can be neutralized.[82] Here, governments' seek pre-crime prediction, which "relies on intelligence, frequently linked to surveillance, based on the suspicion that an event may occur some time in the future."[83] This form of prospective detection seeks to prevent something (such as terrorism) from occurring in the future by finding these individuals before they commit a serious crime. Indeed,

---

[80] We can starve computer viruses out by developing computer environments in such a way as to "provide no nutrients for viruses to develop: make it so it will take a virus developer extreme pain in terms of complexity to handle, to achieve little gain in terms of virus survival." See Rideau, F. R. 2002. *Design ideas for a future computer virus . . . and for a future security architecture.* http://fare.tunes.org/articles/virus_design.html.

[81] Nachenberg, C. 1997. Computer virus—Coevolution: The battle to conquer computer viruses is far from won, but new and improved antidotes are controlling the field. *Communications of the ACM* 40(1): 51.

[82] Gunaratna, R. 2006. The al-Qaeda threat and the international response. In *Terrorism: Critical concepts in political science, Vol. IV: The fourth or religious wave,* ed. D. C. Rapoport, 299. London: Routledge.

[83] McCulloch, J., and Carlton, B. 2006. Preempting justice: Suppressing of financing of terrorism and the "War on Terror." *Current Issues in Criminal Justice* 17(3): 404.

current efforts in the EU and the United States to combat terrorism are focused on enabling the early detection of terrorist threats by collecting, processing, and storing information about all citizens.

The second element, containment, helps keep a computer virus from spreading. However, given the nature of al-Qaeda, capturing and incapacitating members of detected support networks (as well as operational networks) are not enough. Al-Qaeda's ideology also needs to be quashed. Both of these are required in order to keep the al-Qaeda virus (both organization and ideology) from spreading. Furthermore, governments can "starve" terrorists out by making it extremely difficult to plan, plot, and carry out their attacks, and also by finding ways to gain public support for Western democracies' cause on the war on terrorism. The latter is critical because it undermines support for these terrorists groups, thus preventing further recruitment by al-Qaeda and support for their cause.[84] Interestingly, these elements are identified in the European Union's Plan of Action to Combat Terrorism, which among other objectives calls for maximizing the capacity within EU bodies and member states to detect, investigate, and prosecute terrorists and to prevent terrorist attacks, thus reducing the access of terrorists to financial resources and addressing the factors that contribute to the support for, and recruitment into, terrorism.[85] Likewise, the UN Action to Counter Terrorism seeks to address the conditions that are conducive to terrorism and to prevent and combat terrorism. Moreover, UN Security Resolution 1368 (2001) and UN Security Resolution 1373 (2001) stressed the need for more measures with which states can prevent and suppress the financing and preparation of terrorism.

Other countries and organizations have followed suit. A case in point is the African Union.[86] In 2004, in the Declaration of the Second High-Level Intergovernmental meeting on the Prevention and Combating of Terrorism in Africa, member states who were part of the African Union were urged to sign, ratify, or accede to the 1999 Organization of African Unity Convention on the Prevention and Combating of Terrorism.[87] According to Article 4(2) of this convention, African states are required to "prevent their territories from being used as a base for the planning, organization or execution of terrorist acts or for the participation or collaboration in these acts in any form whatsoever" and to "develop and strengthen methods of monitoring and detecting plans or activities aimed at the illegal cross-border transportation, importation, export, stockpiling and use of

---

84 Jones, S. G. 2007. Fighting networked terrorist groups: Lessons from Israel. *Studies in Conflict and terrorism* 30(4): 297.

85 European Council. 2004, March 25. *Declaration on combating terrorism.* 9, 14–17. http://www.consilium.europa.eu/uedocs/cmsUpload/DECL-25.3.pdf.

86 Previously known as the Organization of African Unity. The list of members of the African Union is available on their website at http://www.africa-union.org/root/au/memberstates/map.htm.

87 African Union. 2004. October 13–14. Declaration of the second High-Level Intergovernmental Meeting on the Prevention and Combating of Terrorism in Africa, Algiers, Algeria. http://www.africa-union.org/Terrorism/DECLARATION%20Algiers% 20REV.pdf.

arms, ammunition and explosives and other materials and means of committing terrorist acts."[88] The ASEAN Convention on Counter Terrorism is another example.[89] Article VI of this convention requires parties to take the necessary steps to prevent the commission of terrorist acts; prevent those who plot, support, and/or engage in terrorist acts from doing so within their territories; prevent and suppress the financing of terrorism; and prevent the movement of terrorists or terrorist groups by using effective border controls. Similar measures were proposed in the 2002 Inter-American Convention Against Terrorism and the 2004 Convention Against Terrorism by the Cooperation Council for the Arab States of the Gulf.[90]

A further similarity between al-Qaeda and computer viruses is their capacity to evolve. If the threat of terrorism governments are faced with is constantly changing, then thinking about how to counter this threat must also evolve.[91] In the aftermath of the Madrid and London bombings, both the European Council's Declaration on Combating Terrorism and the Council of the European Union's Declaration on the EU Response to the London bombings[92] reflects this change and evolution in views on how to combat the threat. In these declarations, the measures proposed are aimed at facilitating the mass surveillance of movement (e.g. PNR and biometric IDs) and communications (creation of measures to facilitate the wide retention of communications data) of European citizens, which were, prior to these attacks, considered indefensible. Comparable measures were implemented in the aftermath of 9/11 in the United States. To prevent future acts of terrorism against the United States and its allies, the USA Patriot Acts were passed: the USA Patriot Act of 2001 and the USA Patriot Act Improvement and Reauthorization Act of 2005. These acts, among other things, were passed to increase the powers of agents of the criminal justice system, facilitate information sharing and cooperation among government agencies, provide investigators with enhanced surveillance and wiretapping capabilities, and increase the penalties for those who commit terrorist acts or who assist or harbor terrorists. These new and more expansive preemptive policies are aimed at disrupting support and operational networks within

---

[88] Organization of African Unity. 1999. Organization of African Unity Convention on the Prevention and Combating of Terrorism, Algiers, Algeria. https://www.unodc.org/tldb/pdf/conv_oau_1999.pdf.

[89] ASEAN stands for Association of Southeast Asian Nations and includes the following countries, Vietnam, Cambodia, Singapore, Thailand, Indonesia, Malaysia, Burma, Brunei, the Philippines, and the Lao People's Democratic Republic.

[90] For further information on these and other international instruments on combating terrorism, see United Nations Office of Drugs and Crime (UNDOC). 2011. *(Inter-)regional action against terrorism*. https://www.unodc.org/tldb/en/regional_instruments.html.

[91] B. Hoffman. 2005. Al-Qaeda: Then and now. In *Al-Qaeda Now: Understanding today's terrorists*, ed. K. J.Greenberg, 9. Cambridge, UK: Cambridge University Press.

[92] European Council. 2004, March 25. *Declaration on combating terrorism*. http://www.consilium.europa.eu/uedocs/cmsUpload/DECL-25.3.pdf; Council of the European Union. 2005, July 13. *Declaration on the EU Response to the London bombing*. http://www.libertysecurity.org/IMG/pdf/JHA_Council_13_ July_2005.pdf.

Europe and the United States by detecting, investigating, pursuing, and facilitating the subsequent prosecution of terrorists.

HYPOTHETICAL SCENARIO

A rogue country has developed a strain of the variola virus (smallpox) for use as a biological weapon. This country is hostile toward the European Union and the United States. Credible intelligence exists that this country has facilities in place to create these weapons and that they are planning to launch attacks against the EU and the United States. The United Nations passed a resolution calling for this country to cease and desist in its creation of these weapons. However, the country has failed to do so.

What should the international community do next? Please explain why you think this is the case in your response and ensure that the steps that you recommend are legally justified.

CHAPTER SUMMARY

Countries and individuals tend to err on the side of caution against potential catastrophic risks such as terrorism. Precautionary logic drives counterterrorism strategies, policies, and measures. A driving force behind preemption is the precautionary principle. Usually, preemption is advocated when deterrence cannot work. Two preemptive actions were explored in this chapter: war and counterterrorism measures. Preemptive war is considered a form of legitimate self-defense if the threat of an armed attack is imminent. This threat must be credible and based on solid evidence. The preemptive response used, however, must be proportional to the threat. To engage in a preemptive attack, the UN Security Council must be informed prior to engaging in the act and must approve it. With respect to counterterrorism, when there are threats or potential threats of irreversible grave harm, lack of full certainty should not be used as a reason for rejecting or postponing the implementation of measures to combat those threats. Many of the measures implemented after 9/11 seek to prevent and forestall rather than permit terrorist attacks to occur and respond to them after the fact.

REVIEW QUESTIONS

1. What role does uncertainty play in counterterrorism?
2. What is the relevance of the precautionary principle to counterterrorism?
3. When do states have *jus ad bellum*?
4. Was the Afghanistan war justified? Why or why not?
5. Was the Iraq war justified? Why or why not?
6. Is deterrence a lost cause after 9/11?
7. What preemptive responses have been taken in response to current threats of terrorism?

chapter six

War on Terrorism: Impact on Counterterrorism Policy

We have met the enemy, and he is us.
—Pogo

In the aftermath of 9/11, the United States declared a war on terrorism. The war on terrorism, however, is not a war in the traditional sense. In fact, the war on terrorism operates outside of existing principles of warfare, running contrary to many widespread beliefs on wars and laws of wars. Wars were originally conceived as being waged against nation-states by nation-states. For instance, Article 2 of the Third Geneva Convention of 1949 noted that this instrument applied "to all cases of declared war or of any other armed conflict which may arise between two or more of the High Contracting Parties, even if the state of war is not recognized by one of them."[1] The war on terrorism differs from this notion as it is not waged against states. It is primarily waged against nonstate actors with no specific homeland to defend (with few exceptions). Existing laws of war, however, were not envisioned as applying to a conflict between a state and a nonstate actor or group.

The 9/11 Commission sought to clarify which terrorists the war on terrorism was aimed at. According to the 9/11 Commission report, "the enemy is not just 'terrorism,' some generic evil . . . the catastrophic threat at this moment in history is more specific. It is the threat posed by Islamist terrorism—especially the

---

[1] *Convention (III) Relative to the Treatment of Prisoners of War.* (Geneva, August 12, 1949).

al-Qaeda network, its affiliates, and its ideology."[2] The 2006 National Strategy for Combating Terrorism sought to clarify the target by noting that

> the principal terrorist enemy confronting the United States is a transnational movement of extremist organizations, networks, and individuals—and their state and non-state supporters—which have in common that they exploit Islam and use terrorism for ideological ends.

These definitions do not include those terrorists who have no connection to Islamic extremism but still pose a threat to countries worldwide. Nevertheless, the target of the war is not the only issue that arises with the war on terrorism.

The concept of war has been attributed to other threats to nations. Some examples include the war on poverty, the war against crime, and the war on drugs. These were not actual wars but metaphorical wars. Indeed, a major criticism levied against the use of the phrase "war on terrorism" is that it "is not an accurate description of the conflict and can be very misleading. Terrorism is not an enemy, it is a method employed by an enemy."[3] Yet the war on terrorism both encompasses actual wars and declares a metaphorical war against terrorism. Specifically, two wars, Operation Enduring Freedom (Afghanistan war) and Operation Iraqi Freedom (Iraq war), have been waged under the banner of the "war on terrorism." In addition, the war reference is misleading as it suggests that successful military operations serve as an indicator of a successful counterterrorism strategy.[4] The UK Foreign Secretary, David Miliband, echoed this statement by declaring that the "war on terrorism 'implied a belief that the correct response to the terrorist threat was primarily a military one—to track down and kill a hard core of extremists.'"[5] Yet, as will be seen later in the text, this tactic will not defeat terrorism and may, in fact, propagate it. Furthermore, and most important, the characterization of the response to terrorists as a war on terrorism has licensed governmental use of extraordinary powers usually reserved for situations that threaten the life a nation.

This chapter covers the consequences of the war on terrorism. This analysis is motivated by the following questions: What impact does the phrasing of the fight against terrorism as a war have on counterterrorism policy? What measures are considered justified in the war on terrorism? The following sections seek to answer these questions by looking at the speed with which counterterrorism legislation was introduced, the presentation of the terrorist threat as an emergency,

---

2 National Commission on Terrorist Attacks. 2004. *The 9/11 Commission report: Final report of the National Commission on Terrorist Attacks upon the United States*, 362. http://www .9-11commission.gov/report/911Report.pdf.

3 Addicott, J. F. 2008. The war on terror—War on metaphor. *International Institute for Counterterrorism*. http://www.ict.org.il/Articles/tabid/66/Articlsid/474/currentpage/1/Default.aspx.

4 Haque, A. A. 2007. Torture, terror, and the inversion of moral principle. *New Criminal Law Review* 10 (4): 613.

5 Borger, J. 2009. War on terrorism a mistake, says British prime minister. *The Sydney Morning Herald*, January 16, 2009. http://www.smh.com.au/news/world/war-on-terrorism-a-mistake-says -british-minister/2009/01/15/1231608886374.html.

and the rhetoric and the reference to the responses of the terrorist threat as a war on terrorism.

THE NEED FOR SPEED: TERRORISM AS AN EMERGENCY

Historically and presently, counterterrorism legislation has emerged as a "legislative response to violence and is generally characterized by emergency provisions which herald extensions of police powers, a curtailment of civil liberties and an ideological assertion of state power."[6] Countries worldwide have recognized the threat posed by terrorism and, as a result, have enacted various measures to combat this threat. These countries, which have predominantly dissimilar political and legal systems, have approached the threat of terrorism in various ways. A common characteristic of many counterterrorism measures is the speed with which they are passed following terrorist attacks. In the United Kingdom, legislation has been rushed through Parliament following terrorist attacks. For example, the 1974 Prevention of Terrorism (Temporary Provisions) Act was debated for a mere 17 hours before it was approved.[7] This act was implemented in response to the Provisional Irish Republican Army's extensive bombing campaign in the 1970s. Among the bombings that occurred during that time were

- *M62 coach bombing.* On February 4, 1974, an explosive device was detonated on a coach carrying approximately 50 people from Manchester, England, along the M62 motorway to an army base in Catterick, North Yorkshire. In this attack, 12 people were killed, including 8 off-duty soldiers and 2 young children.
- *Guildford pub bombings.* On October 5, 1974, bombs were detonated in two pubs, the Horse and Groom and the Seven Stars, in Guildford, England. The bombings resulted in 5 deaths and 65 injuries.
- *Birmingham pub bombings.* On November 21, 1974, bombs were detonated in two central pubs, the Mulberry Bush and the Tavern in the Town, killing 21 people and injuring 182.

The Prevention of Terrorism Act of 1974 was enacted on November 29, 1974, only 8 days after the Birmingham pub bombings. Among other things, this law prohibited individuals from attending a meeting (of more than 2 people) that was designed to support the PIRA. Additionally, and more controversially, if a person was carrying or wearing any items that caused reasonable suspicion that the person was a member of a terrorist group, they could be given a fine or imprisoned. This was not the only piece of legislation that was implemented in England with remarkable speed after terrorist attacks. A case in point is the Criminal Justice

---

6 Green, P. 1988. *The prevention of terrorism and its legislative process.* Institute of Criminal Justice, Occasional Paper No. 3. Southampton, UK: University of Southampton Press.

7 Thomas, P. 2002. Legislative responses to terrorism. *The Guardian.* http://www.guardian.co .uk/world/2002/sep/11/september11.usa11.

Act (Terrorism and Conspiracy) Act of 1998. This act was rushed through Parliament 27 hours after the Omagh bombing in Northern Ireland, where the Real Irish Republican Army (Real IRA), a splinter terrorist group from the PIRA, executed an attack that killed 29 individuals and injured 220.[8]

In other countries, similar occurrences have been observed. In the United States, on October 26, 2001, just six weeks after 9/11, Congress passed the broadest anticrime act in American history, the USA Patriot Act. According to the ACLU,

> [t]he Senate version of the Patriot Act, which closely resembled the legislation requested by Attorney General John Ashcroft, was sent straight to the floor with no discussion, debate, or hearings. Many Senators complained that they had little chance to read it, much less analyze it, before having to vote. In the House, hearings were held, and a carefully constructed compromise bill emerged from the Judiciary Committee. But then, with no debate or consultation with rank-and-file members, the House leadership threw out the compromise bill and replaced it with legislation that mirrored the Senate version. Neither discussion nor amendments were permitted, and once again members barely had time to read the thick bill before they were forced to cast an up-or-down vote on it.[9]

Despite these occurrences, the bill, in both the Senate and House of Representatives, was passed almost unanimously.

In Europe, the Data Retention Directive (Directive 2006/24/EC), which requires the mass retention of communications data on all European citizens was also rushed through. Usually, the adoption of a measure—from the European Commission draft proposal to the final vote—takes approximately one year.[10] The adoption of the Directive was passed with indecent haste. The Commission submitted a legislative proposal to the European Parliament and Council on the 21st of September 2005. The vote on the Directive was scheduled for December 15, 2005. This afforded European Community institutions less than 3 months to meet the December deadline. The speeding up of the legislative processes, however, leaves little room for democratic scrutiny and deliberation of the measure, often leading to the implementation of draconian measures.

The increasing speed of legislative decision making is also attributed to the presentation of the threat of terrorism as an emergency. Specifically, in the aftermath of both the Madrid and London bombings, European Community institutions stressed the urgency of the situation and the need to immediately implement

---

8 Thomas, P. A. 2002/2003. A view from abroad. *Boston Review* 27 (December/January): 2. http://bostonreview.net/BR27.6/thomas.html; Timeline: Omagh bombing. 2009. *The Guardian*, June 8, 2009. http://www.guardian.co.uk/uk/2002/jul/26/northernireland.

9 American Civil Liberties Union. 2010, December 10. *Surveillance under the USA Patriot Act.* http://www.aclu.org/ national-security/surveillance-under-usa-patriot-act.

10 Digital Rights Ireland. 2005, December 15. *Data Retention Directive passed.* http://www .digital rights.ie/2005/12/15/data-retention-directive-passed/.

measures such as those on mandatory data retention.[11] Security responses, especially after dramatic events such as the Madrid bombings, often articulate a need for swift and decisive countermeasures.[12] The Declaration on Combating Terrorism, which was introduced 2 weeks after the Madrid bombings, attests to this.[13]

Presenting these events as emergencies or crises put pressure on institutions to speed up the decision-making process. Can the threat of terrorism be described as an emergency necessitating such a response? According to Gross, an emergency, which comprises a sudden, urgent, and usually unforeseen event that poses a fundamental threat and requires immediate action, is "inherently linked to concepts of 'normalcy' in the sense that the former is considered to be outside the ordinary course of events or anticipated actions."[14] The events of September 11, 2001, were considered an emergency. This emergency or unanticipated event was characterized by Taleb as a "Black Swan."[15] The term Black Swan has been used by Taleb to define any event that occurred outside of the realm of expectations.

What is the relevance of the term Black Swan? According to Taleb, prior to the discovery of black swans in Australia, all swans were assumed to be white. This notion held true as long as white swans were the only ones found in the discovered world. Once a black swan was discovered, the perceptions of what swans were had to change and did change. This one black swan was all that was needed to invalidate "a general statement derived from millennia of confirmatory sightings of millions of white swans."[16] This is similar to 9/11. This one event was all that was needed to change the perceptions of what terrorism was and what terrorists can do. What other terrorist attacks are Black Swans? Can any of the successful attacks perpetrated post-9/11 be considered Black Swans?

Consider the Madrid and London bombings. In order to determine whether the Madrid and London bombings were Black Swans, they must meet three criteria posed by Taleb. First, the event must be an "outlier," since "it lies outside the realm of regular expectations, because nothing in the past can convincingly point to its possibility."[17] Both the Madrid and London bombings were outliers. In particular, the Madrid bombings represented the first coordinated homegrown terrorist attack

---

11 For Madrid, see European Council. 2004, March 25. *Declaration on combating terrorism*, 2–3. http://www.consilium.europa.eu/uedocs/cmsUpload/DECL-25.3.pdf; For London, see Council of the European Union. 2005, July 13. *Declaration on the EU response to the London bombing*, 6. http://www.libertysecurity.org/IMG/pdf/JHA_Council_13_July_2005.pdf.

12 Huysmans, J. 2004. Minding exceptions: The politics of insecurity and liberal democracy. *Contemporary Political Theory* 3:332.

13 European Council. 2004, March 25. Declaration on combating terrorism, 3–8. http://www.consilium.europa.eu/uedocs/cmsUpload/DECL-25.3.pdf.

14 Gross, O. 2003. Chaos and rules: Should responses to violent crises always be constitutional. *The Yale Law Journal* 112:1070–1071.

15 Taleb, N. N. 2007. *The Black Swan: The impact of the highly improbable*. London: Penguin, xvii.

16 Ibid., p. xvii.

17 Ibid.

on European soil, which was perpetrated by Islamic extremists affiliated with al-Qaeda; whereas, the London bombings represented the first homegrown suicide bombings on European soil from terrorists inspired by al-Qaeda's cause. Second, the event must carry with it a severe impact. This was evident in both bombings, which resulted in more than 250 deaths combined and thousands injured, not to mention the disruption of commerce, damage to the transportation industry, and heightened fear among the public. For the third criteria, Taleb argues that "in spite of its outlier status, human nature makes us connect explanations for its occurrence after the fact, making it explainable and predictable."[18] Such explanations and predictions were plentiful following both the Madrid and London bombings. Specifically, after the attacks, it was argued that the involvement of Spain and the United Kingdom in the Afghanistan (2001) and Iraq (2003) wars made them terrorist targets. As such, an attack should have been expected. What few had anticipated, however, was that the attacks would have been implemented by their own countrymen.[19] As Taleb argues, if a terrorist attack (the event in its entirety) had been anticipated (which was not the case for the terrorist attacks on Madrid and London), then measures would have been implemented in order to ensure it would not take place. That is, had it been predictable, it would not have occurred.

Accordingly, the Madrid and London bombings meet Taleb's three criteria and as such, can be characterized as Black Swans. However, while these attacks were Black Swans and "exceptional" in their nature, the threat of terrorism is not. Specifically, the low predictability and devastating impact of these Black Swans deflects attention from an important truth about them: that they are low-probability events. The threat of terrorism encompasses events like 9/11 and the Madrid and London bombings, thus making it seem as if the threat itself is exceptional when in fact it is not. The threat of terrorism is not exceptional because it has become an integral facet in citizens' daily lives. As Gross observes, "for normalcy to be 'normal,' it has to be the general rule, the ordinary state of affairs, whereas emergency must constitute no more than an exception to the rule."[20] Currently, the threat of terrorism has indeed become part of the normal state of affairs. As such, it cannot be described as exceptional or an emergency. The same could be said about the war on terrorism.

The United States did declare a state of emergency in the immediate aftermath of the terrorist attacks on September 11, 2001, and used emergency powers to respond to these attacks. The United States is no longer in a state of emergency even though the war on terrorism is still ongoing. The nature of the war on terrorism would make any claims of a state of emergency, if they existed, extremely difficult because of the irreconcilable nature of this war with the term "emergency." As Gross argues, the concept of an emergency "must be informed by notions of

---

18 Ibid., pp. xvii–xviii.

19 Gove, M. 2006. *Celsius 7/7*. London: Phoenix.

20 Gross, O. 2003. Chaos and rules: Should responses to violent crises always be constitutional. *The Yale Law Journal* 112(5):1071.

Box 6-1   The Non–Black Swan: The 1993 WTC Attacks Had Been Predicted

On February 26, 1993, Ramzi Yousef and Eyad Ismoil drove a truck laden with explosives (composed of urea nitrate, which is a homemade fertilizer-based explosive) to the World Trade Center and parked it underneath the North Tower. The perpetrators responsible for the attack believed that the explosion from the truck bomb would be sufficient to take down both towers (i.e., by toppling one tower into the other). This, however, did not occur. Nevertheless, the building sustained significant damage; 6 deaths and over 1,000 injuries resulted.

A civil lawsuit was filed against the Port Authority of New York and New Jersey (hereafter Port Authority).[1] This lawsuit referred to documents that showed that several security assessments had revealed that the World Trade Center was vulnerable to a terrorist attack. In fact, one report included a hypothetical scenario that resembled the actual 1993 attack. Specifically, the Office of Special Planning (OSP) prepared a report on the security risks of the World Trade Center, which included the following possible scenario that was eerily similar to what actually occurred:

> A time bomb-laden vehicle could be driven into the WTC and parked in the public parking area. The driver could then exit via elevator into the WTC and proceed with his business unnoticed. At a predetermined time, the bomb could be exploded in the basement. The amount of explosives used will determine the severity of damage to that area.[2]

This was considered as a likely occurrence due to the 1983 Beirut, Lebanon, bombings that consisted of a similar tactic. Specifically, on April 18, 1983, the U.S. Embassy in Beirut was destroyed by a suicide car-bombing perpetrated by Hezbollah, resulting in 49 deaths and 120 injuries. That same year in Beirut, on October 23, 1983, a coordinated truck-bombing against U.S. and French barracks was carried out by Hezbollah, which killed 241 U.S. Marines and 58 French troops.

In the 1980s, the Port Authority had commissioned other individuals and organizations to conduct security assessments of the World Trade Center. Before the OSP issued its report in July 1985, the Port Authority hired Charles Schnabolk (an outside consultant) to assess the threat of terrorism to the WTC. His report indicated that terrorist attacks in the form of bombings to the World Trade Center were probable and that the parking lot of the building was extremely vulnerable. According to Schnabolk, "with little effort terrorists could create havoc without being seriously deterred by the current security measures."[3] Schnabolk recommended that the following measures be implemented immediately: the improvement of existing surveillance in the parking lot and the screening of all incoming vehicles for explosives.[4]

In November 1985, the OSP report noted that the WTC's "parking for 2,000 vehicles in the underground areas presents an enormous opportunity, at present, for terrorists to park an explosives filled vehicle that could affect vulnerable areas."[5] The

---

[1] *Nash v. Port Authority of New York and New Jersey* 856 N.Y.S.2d 583 (2008).

[2] *Nash v. Port Authority of New York and New Jersey*, 51 A.D.3d 337, 341 (2008).

[3] Ibid., p. 340.

[4] Ibid., pp. 340–341.

[5] Ibid., p. 341.

(continues)

Box 6-1 The Non–Black Swan: The 1993 WTC Attacks Had Been Predicted (continued)

OSP recommended that all public parking in the WTC be eliminated.[6] Realizing this recommendation was not viable, the OSP proposed that at the very least, the parking lot entrances needed to be staffed and vehicles subjected to random searches.[7] In 1986, a report from an outside consulting firm, Science Applications International Corporation, revealed similar vulnerabilities and made similar recommendations (e.g., eliminating public parking and instituting vehicle searches). The Port Authority dismissed the recommendations from the reports by claiming that they were inconvenient and would result in an unacceptable revenue loss.[8]

In its defense, the Port Authority claimed that since an attack had not previously occurred on the WTC, it had no duty to prevent against such an attack. The Port Authority further claimed that

> even if the garage bombing was foreseeable, it was under no legally enforceable
> obligation to take any of the recommended precautions against its occurrence. This
> general claim of nonliability is specifically premised upon defendant's contentions
> that, in making decisions respecting the security of its premises, it was acting in a
> governmental capacity and enjoyed consequent immunity.[9]

This argument was dismissed by the court, which held that the evidence overwhelmingly supported the view that had the Port Authority taken into account the recommendations in these reports and enforced them to fulfill its duty to reasonably secure its premises, the harm and damage sustained during the 1993 WTC attacks would have been prevented.

This was not the only time that catastrophic harm had been predicted. A case in point was Hurricane Katrina. In 2004, emergency officials from 50 emergency management organizations (parish, state, federal, and volunteer) participated in a 5-day exercise in Baton Rouge, Louisiana. The scenario these agencies participated in involved a Category 3 hurricane, "Hurricane Pam." This exercise revealed the catastrophic consequences of such a hurricane hitting New Orleans. This exercise focused on the response to the catastrophe after the fact. It did not involve any recommendations on how to mitigate the harm if such a risk came to fruition. It did, however, include recommendations to improve the preparedness of agencies in dealing with a disaster of this magnitude. Some of the recommendations included building approximately 1,000 shelters, identifying lead and support agencies for search and rescue, transportation plans for stranded residents, and ways to resupply hospitals in the aftermath of the disaster.[10] These tasks were not implemented prior to Hurricane Katrina in 2005. The effect of this is well-known as the lack of preparation in the relief effort in response to this disaster has been widely criticized.

---

[6] Ibid.

[7] Ibid., pp. 341–342.

[8] Ibid., p. 342.

[9] Ibid., p. 343.

[10] FEMA. 2004, July 23. *Hurricane Pam exercise concludes.* http://www.fema.gov/news/news release.fema?id=13051.

temporal duration and exceptional danger."[21] While there is no doubting that 9/11 and the attacks on Madrid and London were extraordinary crises, there is "no reason to believe that the threat of terrorism will recede any time soon."[22] Therefore, the ongoing war on terrorism blurs the distinction between normalcy (the normal state of affairs) and emergency in the face of a war that is sustained indefinitely against a succession of terrorist cells or rogue states lacking territories and borders. Because no one knows when the war on terrorism will be over, it cannot reasonably be described as an emergency.

Due to the presentation of this threat as an emergency, the legislative decision-making process was sped up, thus not allowing sufficient time for deliberation and contest on the content of counterterrorism measures. In what follows, how the threat of terrorism was communicated to the public is explored.

COUNTERTERRORIST RHETORIC: COMMUNICATING THE THREAT TO THE PUBLIC

While rhetoric has become known as the voice of democracy, the earliest rhetorical texts consisted of speeches in homicide trials, whose proceedings were largely dictated by laws (Draco's homicide laws in ancient Greece) predating democratic rule.[23] Socrates defined rhetoric as an "art of persuasion"; that is, the art of going to any and every length (πάντα λέγειν), such as deceptions, lies, force, and so on, to achieve persuasion.[24] Rhetoric is used to both persuade an audience that the issue raised is paramount and then to convince them to take their side.[25] Reflective strategy is a type of rhetoric in which government officials use discourse first to assert their legitimacy and then press for action.[26] One way legitimacy is established is by using the distinction between "us" (friend) and "them" (enemy) in political discourse. The calls for unity, the existence of a collective "we" or "us," not only mobilize the masses in support of political power to combat "them," but also serves to justify or legitimate this power in spite of the means (the measures) used by authorities to achieve the end (combating the threat). This bipolar view of the world divides individuals (and even nations) into those who are with and those who are against terrorists. The government (the counterterrorist in this case) uses this bipolar discourse to vehemently oppose the terrorist, who is presented as inhumane and barbaric.[27] The calls

---

21 Gross, O. 2006. What "emergency" regime? *Constellations* 13 (1): 74.

22 Schulhofer, S. J. 2002. *The enemy within: Intelligence gathering, law enforcement and civil liberties in the wake of September 11*. New York: Century Foundation, 68.

23 For more information, see Carawan, E. 1998. *Rhetoric and the law of Draco*. Oxford, UK: Clarendon, 1.

24 Πλάτων (Plato), Πολιτεία (*The Republic*) (360 BC), 494e4 in Too, Y. L. 1995. *The rhetoric of identity in Isocrates: Text, power, pedagogy*. Cambridge, UK: Cambridge University Press, 2–3.

25 Carawan, E. 1998. *Rhetoric and the law of Draco*. Oxford UK: Clarendon, 5.

26 Leeway, R. W. 1991. *The rhetoric of terrorism and counterterrorism*. New York: Greenwood, 72, 75.

27 Ibid., p. 72.

Box 6-2   Food for Thought—On Winning the War on Terrorism: Is There an End in Sight?

According to the 2006 National Security Strategy of the Bush Administration, "in the long run, winning the War on Terror means winning the battle of ideas, for it is ideas that can turn the disenchanted into murderers willing to kill innocent victims . . . Winning the War on Terror [also] requires winning the battles in Afghanistan and Iraq."[1] The Bush Administration had additionally claimed that the war would not stop until it was won. Yet neither the Bush Administration nor the current Obama Administration has been able to clearly define the enemy, the locus of the conflict, and how victory in this war will be achieved. In addition, those detained pursuant to the war on terrorism are placed in Guantanamo Bay. Normally, those imprisoned during a war are released when the war is over.

1. What does this mean for Guantanamo Bay detainees?
2. Can this war be won?
3. What barriers exist to winning this war?
4. Can these barriers be overcome?

---

[1]   Bush Administration. 2006, March. The national security strategy. *White House.* http://georgewbush-whitehouse.archives.gov/nsc/nss/2006/sectionIII.html.

---

for unity and action against the "others" may therefore serve as a means to suppress dissent and reduce the scope for democratic debate.

Rhetoric is further used to present terrorist attacks as those threatening national survival, requiring a war to be waged against the nation's enemies. The terminology of warfare, such as the war on terrorism, gives the impression that we are "on our way towards a state of emergency, where our normal moral perceptions of right and wrong, good and evil, are set aside in favor of a kind of emergency morality, a war ethic."[28] For Schmitt, enemies are politically significant because they create an emergency, which requires exceptional political action to assure the survival of the nation.[29] By presenting the terrorist threat this way, as endangering the life of a nation, more restrictions of individuals' human rights are tolerated.

Nevertheless, aside from speeding up the legislative decision-making process, the presentation of the threat of terrorism as an emergency has other implications in terms of the reach and scope of measures and their acceptance by the public. In response to the terrorist attacks on 9/11, Madrid and London, the United States and

---

[28]   Halvorsen, V. 1998. Straffeprosess, moral og utradisjonelle etterforskningsmetoder. *Nytt Norsk Tidskrift* 4: 344 in Flyghed, J. 2002. Normalising the exceptional: The case of political violence. *Policing and Society* 13 (1) 24.

[29]   Schmitt, C. 1985. *Political theology*. Trans. G. Schwab. Cambridge, MA: MIT Press; Huysmans, J. 2006. *The politics of insecurity: Fear, migration and asylum in the EU*. New York: Routledge, 133.

the European Union enacted what Ignatieff calls piecemeal emergency legislation.[30] That is, while no general "state of emergency" was declared in the United States and the European Union, countries have implemented a series of counterterrorism measures that suspend portions of the law on individuals suspected of terrorism. For example, prisoners in Guantanamo Bay for terrorism-related offenses were (and some still are) denied due process. However, these measures are also being used on individuals who are not suspected of terrorism. These counterterrorism measures seek to normalize the emergency, wherein the rule of law is relaxed (though usually not completely), and there is no clearly defined threat.[31] Consequently, even piecemeal emergency legislation can significantly damage the rule of law.[32]

Security powers resulting from counterterrorism measures are best understood as extraordinary powers. Whether or not such powers can be circumscribed in law has been an issue that has been debated. Schmitt believed that provisions in constitutions for emergency powers were futile because they fail to anticipate novel crises. That is, he believed that an emergency cannot be circumscribed in law nor made to conform to the normal legal order because no legal order can reasonably foresee all potential crises and as such, no existing law can constrain which measures may be required in an emergency.[33] While Schmitt was correct to argue that existing norms cannot foresee all potential crises that may necessitate an exception, he was incorrect in his assertion that this exception could not be anticipated procedurally.[34] Specifically, even if the actual content of the emergencies could not be predicted, it is still possible to predict that these emergencies may occur and to establish procedures for them.[35] The provisions in constitutions and the derogation clauses in human rights instruments obviously attest to this. A case in point is Russia. Article 56 of the Russian Constitution allows

> individual restrictions of rights and liberties with identification of the extent and of their duration . . . [These restrictions] may be instituted in conformity with the federal constitutional law under conditions of the state of emergency in order to ensure the safety of citizens and protection of the constitutional system.[36]

---

30 Ignatieff, M. 2005. *The lesser evil: Political ethics in the age of terror*. Edinburgh, Scotland: Edinburgh University Press, 26.

31 Dyzenhaus, D. 2001. The permanence of the temporary: Can emergency powers be normalized? In *The security of freedom: Essays on Canada's anti-terrorism bill*, eds. R. J. Daniels, P. Macklem, and K. Roach, 28–29. Toronto, Canada: University of Toronto Press.

32 Ignatieff, M. 2005. *The lesser evil: Political ethics in the age of terror*. Edinburgh, Scotland: Edinburgh University Press, 31.

33 Schmitt, C. 1985. *Political theology*. Trans. G. Schwab. Cambridge, MA: MIT Press, 6.

34 Scheuerman, W. E. 2006. Survey article: Emergency powers and the rule of law after 9/11. *The Journal of Political Philosophy* 14 (1): 62; Zuckerman, I. 2006. One law for war and peace? Judicial review and emergency powers between the norm and the exception. *Constellations* 13 (4): 526.

35 Zuckerman, ibid.

36 According to Article 56(3) of the Russian Constitution, certain rights, however, are excluded from restriction: Articles 20, 21, 23(1), 24, 28, 34(1), 40(1), and 46–54.

The notion of a state of emergency or state of exception also exists in many European constitutions[37] and affords these states with emergency powers necessary to deal with potential crises. The European Convention on Human Rights also affords member states emergency powers during a "time of war or other public emergency threatening the life of the nation" under Article 15 of the convention (the explicit provision for derogation), by allowing them to derogate from certain rights (except Article 2—excluding death that results from lawful acts of war—Article 3, 4.1, and 7) for the period of the emergency. The existence of these clauses generally represents the consensus that it is inevitable for governments to resort to exceptional measures in times of emergency. Despite the existence of these provisions, no state in Europe, except the United Kingdom, relied on Article 15 derogations to justify the implementation of their counterterrorism measures in the aftermath of 9/11. Nonetheless, member states (and even the European Union) have resorted to using emergency powers (e.g., indefinite detention) even though they have not officially declared that they are in a state of emergency.

These powers, however, should be constrained by the rule of law. They should also be exercised in accordance with human rights instruments. By contrast, Schmitt believed that legal restraints on emergency powers are inappropriate for exceptional circumstances because the situation may necessitate the need to resort to the use of absolute power, thus surrendering the legal restraints on its exercise.[38] In light of this, what occurs, according to Agamben, is a suspension of the legal "order that is in force in order to guarantee its existence" (i.e., the "state of exception" suspends the law in order to defend it).[39] Therefore, as Schmitt argued, an effective response to the emergency must be "outside the rule of law," and thus, "cannot be limited by the rule of law,"[40] because the emergency precludes the possibility that emergency powers can be "regulated, controlled, and ultimately subjected to democratic standards of legitimacy."[41] Accordingly, in order for a democratic society to effectively deal with an emergency, he believed

[37] See, for example, the Estonian Constitution, 1991, Articles 129–131 and the Constitution of the Republic of Serbia, 1995, Articles 67 and 89; Ignatieff, M. 2005. *The lesser evil: Political ethics in the age of terror*. Edinburgh, Scotland: Edinburgh University Press, 31.

[38] Schmitt, C. 1985. *Political theology*. Trans. G. Schwab,. Cambridge, MA: MIT Press, 6; Scheuerman, W. E. 2006. Survey article: Emergency powers and the rule of law After 9/11. *The Journal of Political Philosophy* 14 (1): 67.

[39] Agamben, G. 2005. *State of exception*. Trans. K. Attell. Chicago: University of Chicago Press, 31.

[40] Schmitt, C. 1985. *Political theology*. Trans. G. Schwab,. Cambridge, MA: MIT Press, cited in Dyzenhaus, D. 2001. The permanence of the temporary: Can emergency powers be normalized? In *The security of freedom: Essays on Canada's anti-terrorism bill*, eds. R. J. Daniels, P. Macklem, and K. Roach, 22. Toronto, Canada: University of Toronto Press.

[41] Schmitt, C. 1985. *Political theology*. Trans. G. Schwab,. Cambridge, MA: MIT Press, cited in Zuckerman, I. 2006. One law for war and peace? Judicial review and emergency powers between the norm and the exception. *Constellations* 13 (4): 62.

that they must give up their fundamental commitments to human rights and the rule of law.[42] The pressing question is whether this sacrifice is really necessary.

SECURITY VS. HUMAN RIGHTS: TRADE-OFFS, BALANCES, OR NONE OF THE ABOVE?

Human rights are indivisible; freedom and security are not alternatives: they go hand in hand, one enabling the other.
    —MEP GRAHAM WATSON (*EUROPEAN PARLIAMENT DEBATE*, SEPTEMBER 7, 2005)

A state that abandons its commitments to human rights and "has security as its only task and source of legitimacy is a fragile organism; it can always be provoked by terrorism to turn itself terroristic."[43] Accordingly, both security and human rights are of fundamental importance. Their relative importance, however, "changes from time to time and from situation to situation"; the greater the threat posed to the nation's safety, the stronger the grounds for seeking to repress that activity even at some cost to civil liberties.[44] The war on terrorism, which has served as a platform for governments to launch a series of counterterrorism measures aimed at strengthening security while in so doing restricting human rights, demonstrates this. Consider, for example, the creation of communications, DNA, and fingerprint databases in the EU. These measures would have been almost unthinkable before the war on terrorism. Yet, as a result of this war, they are now all considered legitimate responses to combat terrorism.

A specific pragmatic objection to expansive counterterrorism measures implemented during the war on terrorism is that the liberties sacrificed in order to meet the present threat are not likely to be regained easily. History shows that such measures often become permanent, and the restraints on civil liberties that result from these measures do too. In fact, it is not uncommon to find measures that were initially enacted as temporary provisions to counter terrorism subsequently enacted as permanent legislation.[45] For example, the Northern Ireland (Emergency Provisions) Act of 1973, which empowered the government to detain

---

42 Schmitt, C. 1985. *Political theology.* Trans. G. Schwab,. Cambridge, MA: MIT Press, cited in Dyzenhaus, D. 2001. The permanence of the temporary: Can emergency powers be normalized? In *The security of freedom: Essays on Canada's anti-terrorism bill*, eds. R. J. Daniels, P. Macklem, and K. Roach, 22. Toronto, Canada: University of Toronto Press.

43 Agamben, G. 2001. On security and terror. Trans. S. Zehle. *Frankfurter Allgemeine Zeitung*, September 20, 2001. http://www.egs.edu/faculty/giorgio-agamben/articles/on-security -and-terror/

44 Posner, R. 2001. Security versus civil liberties. *The Atlantic Monthly*, December 2001. http:// www.theatlantic.com/past/docs/issues/2001/12/posner.htm.

45 Matassa M., and Newburn, T. 2003. Policing and terrorism. In *Handbook of policing*, ed. T. Newburn, 476. Devon, UK: Willan; Thomas, P. A. 1995. Identity cards. *Modern Law Review* 58 (5), 703–704.

those suspected of terrorism for 72 hours based on subjective suspicion, was supposed to be a temporary measure to deal with the Provisional Irish Republican Army. However, it lasted 26 years until the Terrorism Act of 2000 was instated. In addition, in the United Kingdom, the Prevention of Terrorism (Temporary Provisions) Acts became permanent with the passage of the Prevention of Terrorism Act of 1989.[46] Likewise, the Criminal Evidence Order (Northern Ireland) of 1988 limited the right to silence[47] of suspected terrorists; this was justified at the time by the government's claim that the lack of cooperation of suspected terrorists was hampering counterterrorism efforts.[48] In 1994, the British Parliament approved the Criminal Justice and Public Order Act, which incorporated the limitations on the right to silence for suspected terrorists set out in the 1988 order into ordinary criminal justice legislation.

Consider s. 34 of the Criminal Justice and Public Order Act of 1994, which put pressure on suspects not to exercise their right to silence because it permitted "courts to draw adverse inferences from a suspect's refusal to answer questions."[49] The limitations to the right to silence, which were set by this act, were now applied to all suspects (not just those suspected of terrorism). As Ignatieff observes, this illustrates that the ambit of such measures "has a way of spreading: measures introduced to stop terrorists are then used . . . to catch criminals and other types of offenders."[50] This phenomenon is known as the "risk of mission (or function) creep," in which measures justified in the name of the war on terrorism and used to combat terrorism will subsequently be used for a wider set of applications, including ordinary criminal justice purposes.[51] For example, in the United Kingdom, the Regulation of Investigatory Powers Act of 2000, initially intended for use in the fight against crime and terrorism, has been used for minor offenses such as to detect neighborhood nuisance and to check whether or not individuals lied on a school education form by declaring that their child lived within a school's catchment area. Concerning the transposition of the EU Data Retention Directive into national law, stored electronic

---

46 Gross, O. 2001. Cutting down trees: Law-making under the shadow of great calamities. In *The security of freedom: Essays on Canada's anti-terrorism bill*, eds. R. J. Daniels, P. Macklem, and K. Roach, 48. Toronto, Canada: University of Toronto Press.

47 The Strasbourg Court recognized the privilege against self-incrimination and the right to silence as being implicit in the right to a fair trial, which is guaranteed under Article 6(1) of Convention. Ashworth, A., and Redmayne, M. 2005. *The criminal process*, 3rd ed.. Oxford, UK: Oxford University Press, 35.

48 Zedner, L. 2005. Securing liberty in the face of terror: Reflections from criminal justice. *Journal of Law and Society* 32 (4): 515.

49 Reiner, R. 2000. *The politics of the police*, 3rd ed. Oxford, UK: Oxford University Press, 167.

50 Ignatieff, M. 2005. *The lesser evil: Political ethics in the age of terror*. Edinburgh, Scotland: Edinburgh University Press, 30.

51 Cole, D., and Dempsey, J. X. 2006. *Terrorism and the constitution: Sacrificing civil liberties in the name of national security*. New York: New Press, 229.

communications information, originally introduced for use in terrorism investigations, is now being sought by associations of copyrights holders to identify infringements in Spain.[52]

The broad scope of the powers afforded to governments to deal with situations such as 9/11 and the Madrid and London bombings, however, are linked to the belief that the adopted measures do "not affect ordinary law which applies to ordinary decent folk, i.e., to ourselves" and are instead "directed against a clear enemy of 'others' namely the terrorists."[53] Dworkin asserts that "the trade-off is not between *our* liberty and *our* security in times of threat, but between *our* security and *their* liberty"; by "their," Dworkin means "the freedoms of small suspect groups, like adult male Muslims."[54] For instance, many of the restrictions on liberty resulting from U.S. authorities' responses to the 9/11 attacks were limited to noncitizens, such as the indefinite detention of terrorist suspects and enemy combatants in Guantanamo Bay.[55] The U.S. Justice Department's actions post-9/11, in which they detained hundreds of persons based on little more than the fact that they were Arab or Muslim noncitizens, clearly demonstrates this.[56] Yet what happens when citizens of a nation or member state are responsible for terrorist attacks? Consider the United Kingdom, where the attacks in London on July 7, 2005, were perpetrated by its own citizens. After these bombings, Britain acknowledged that it had allowed the al-Qaeda Hydra to grow inside its own society relatively undetected.[57] The recognition of the existence of homegrown terrorists led to the rapid revision of the assumption that terrorists affiliated with al-Qaeda and those inspired by al-Qaeda's cause were noncitizens. Accordingly, this distinction is not limited to citizens and noncitizens but is more generally applicable to the distinction between *us* (ordinary, law-abiding citizens) and a clearly defined set of others, *them* (such as terrorists).

---

52 Opinion of AG Kokott on July 18, 2007, on Case C-275/06 *Productores de Música de España (Promusicae) v. Telefónica de España SAU* [2007] ECDR CN1, para. 1; See also Case C-275/06 *Productores de Música de España (Promusicae) v. Telefónica de España SAU* (ECJ 8 March 2008, OJ C64/9).

53 Gross, O. 2001. Cutting down trees: Law-making under the shadow of great calamities. In *The security of freedom: Essays on Canada's anti-terrorism bill*, eds. R. J. Daniels, P. Macklem, and K. Roach, 44. Toronto, Canada: University of Toronto Press.

54 Dworkin, R. 2002. The threat to patriotism. In *Understanding September 11*, eds. C. Calhoun, P. Price, and A. Timmer. New York: New Press; Ignatieff, M. 2005. *The lesser evil: Political ethics in the age of terror*. Edinburgh, Scotland: Edinburgh University Press, 32.

55 Sunstein, C. R. 2005. *Laws of fear: Beyond the precautionary principle*. Cambridge, UK: Cambridge University Press, 216.

56 Cole, D. 2002. Enemy aliens. *Stanford Law Review* 54 (5): 985; See also Cole, D. 2003. *Enemy aliens: Double standards and constitutional freedoms in the war on terrorism*. New York: New Press.

57 After 7/7, British officials estimated that there were approximately 16,000 British Muslims either actively engaged in or in support of al-Qaeda's cause. See Phillips, M. 2006. *Londonistan: How Britain is creating a terror state within*. London: Gibson Square, 8–9.

The measures governments implement against *them* are accepted on the assumption that they do not and will not apply to *us*. That is, by selectively targeting a clearly defined set of others, these measures assure citizens that their own civil liberties are not in jeopardy. The limited target of such measures also makes them easier for the majority to accept because they are not sacrificing their own civil liberties.[58] The distinction between *us* and *them* also results in a greater willingness to afford governments the use of exceptionally broad powers in the face of crises. As Gross argues, the "clearer distinction between *us* and *them* and the greater the threat *they* pose to *us*" (emphasis added), the greater the scope of the powers assumed by the government and tolerated by the public.[59] The abridgments of *their* rights are justified, therefore, when the threat of terrorism appears to endanger *our* security.[60]

And yet, as Cole observes, the argument that only the rights of *others* are targeted, and as such, *we* "need not worry, is in an important sense illusory," for what governments do to *others* "today provides a precedent for what can and will be done to" *us* tomorrow.[61] In time, those who were previously part of the *us* group may find themselves in the *them* group once boundaries are redefined.[62] Consider, for example, the United States:

> When the President introduced the concept of military justice with his military tribunal order in November, . . . he reassured Americans that it would not apply to them but only to noncitizens. Yet now the administration has crossed that line and asserted the same authority with respect to the two US citizens, [Yaser Esam] Hamdi and [José] Padilla, that it asserts with respect to the foreign citizens held at Guantanamo.[63]

The trade-off is, therefore, in contrast to what Dworkin and others say,[64] between our civil liberties and our security in the face of the current threat.

---

58 Cole, D. 2002. Enemy aliens. *Stanford Law Review* 54 (5):1003.

59 Gross, O. 2003. Chaos and rules: Should responses to violent crises always be constitutional. *The Yale Law Journal* 112:1037.

60 Ignatieff, M. 2005. *The lesser evil: Political ethics in the age of terror.* Edinburgh, Scotland: Edinburgh University Press, 32.

61 Cole, D. 2002/2003. Their liberties, our security. *Boston Review* 27 (December/January): 11. http://bostonreview.net/BR27.6/cole.html.

62 Gross, O. 2002/2003. Misguided response. *Boston Review* 27 (December/January): 3. http://bostonreview.net/BR27.6/gross.html.

63 Cole, D. 2002/2003. Their liberties, our security. *Boston Review* 27 (December/January): 12. http://bostonreview.net/BR27.6/cole.html.

64 Dworkin, R. 2002. The threat to patriotism. In *Understanding September 11*, eds. C. Calhoun, P. Price, and A. Timmer. New York: New Press; Cole, D. 2002. Enemy aliens. *Stanford Law Review* 54 (5): 985; Cole, D. 2002/2003. Their liberties, our security. *Boston Review* 27 (December/January). http://bostonreview.net/BR27.6/cole.html; Gross, O. 2002/2003. Misguided response *Boston Review* 27 (December/January). http://bostonreview.net/BR27.6/gross.html; Tribe, L. H. 2002/2003. Liberty for all: A response to David Cole's "their liberties, our security." *Boston Review* 27 (December/January). http://bostonreview.net/BR27.6/tribe.html.

In times of threat and fear, governments tend to take actions that sacrifice human rights. This occurs because it is believed that in order to increase one good (security), another good (rights) must be given up. Here, it is assumed that if "we decide to hold on to these rights and to our democratic traditions more generally, then our collective security may suffer."[65] What is evidently problematic is the belief that rights must be traded off (or even sacrificed) for security and the lack of concern that restrictions or derogation of specific rights is occurring. The European Convention on Human Rights (1950) specifies conditions that allow for derogation of certain rights. In particular, the convention explicitly states the conditions under which a state can interfere with qualified rights.[66] For instance, there is a provision within the very phrasing of the right to privacy, Article 8(2), that allows for certain restrictions by public authorities (in the interests of national security, public safety, or the economic well-being of the country, for the prevention of disorder or crime, for the protection of health or morals, or for the protection of the rights and freedom of others), when such restrictions are compatible with the right to respect for private life, the home, and correspondence. These exceptions "were intended to provide a sufficient balance between the requirements of individual privacy and the needs of law enforcement and state security."[67] Balancing, here, does not presuppose a zero-sum equilibrium, but "at least a reasonable and genuine link between the aim invoked and the measures interfering with private life for the aim to be regarded as legitimate."[68] The measures taken "must be absolutely necessary, . . . and they may be taken only if and to the extent that exercise of the right in question is calculated to prevent public authorities from protecting these interests."[69]

However, a problem arises when individuals view security and human rights in terms of "trade-offs" or "balances," because they fail to understand security and its relation with these rights. Security should be seen as a means of maintaining citizens' "way of life,"[70] which encompasses the respect for human rights. The

---

65   Valverde, M. 2001. Governing security, governing through security. In *The security of freedom: Essays on Canada's anti-terrorism bill*, eds. R. J. Daniels, P. Macklem, and K. Roach, 83. Toronto, Canada: University of Toronto Press.

66   Qualified rights include the right to respect for private life (Article 8), the right to freedom of thought and religion (Article 9), the right to freedom of expression (Article 10), and the right to freedom of assembly and association (Article 11).

67   Rowland, D. 2003, April. *Privacy, data retention and terrorism*, 28th BILETA Conference: Controlling Information in the Online Environment, London. http://www.bileta.ac.uk/Document%20Library/1/Privacy,%20Data%20Retention%20and%20Terrorism.pdf.

68   *Rotaru v. Romania.* 2000 8 BHRC 449 in concurring opinion of Judge Wildhaber.

69   Velu, J. 1973. The European Convention on Human Rights and the Right to Respect for Private Life, the Home and Communications. In *Privacy and human rights*, ed. A. H. Robertson, 72. Manchester, UK: Manchester University Press.

70   Here, "way of life" refers to the institutional and cultural traditions and values of a democratic society (e.g., respect for the rule of law). Kleinig, J. 2007, January 17. *Liberty and security in an era of terrorism*, 7. Paper presented in the Oxford Criminology Seminar Series 2006/07, Center for Criminology, University of Oxford, UK.

problem, therefore, is that instead of seeing security as it is with respect to human rights (i.e., mutually dependent), security and human rights are considered mutually exclusive.[71] Human rights and security are mutually dependent because if one is not secure and lives in fear, one is not free. If one is not free, then, one cannot live one's life with dignity (the right to shape one's life as best as one can within the limits of law by, for example, developing one's own relationships, associations, thoughts free from oppression; making one's own decisions; having a voice in public affairs etc.).[72] Thus, to effect their security, in accordance with social contract theory,[73] individuals choose to enter into civil society, characterized by institutions (such as those identified by Locke: legislative, judicial, and executive) "that are designed to secure for its members conditions that will enable the exercise of their rights."[74] Security, in this sense, can and should be seen as the very means by which we enjoy our civil liberties. Given that security is the very means by which citizens enjoy human rights, the means used to counter the threat must also respect rights and abide by the rule of law.

DEALING WITH THE "EMERGENCY": A BETTER APPROACH

Schmitt was wrong in assuming that democracies cannot respond to emergencies unless they abandon the rule of law and their commitments to fundamental human rights. In both the Declaration on Combating Terrorism and the Council Declaration on the EU Response to the London Bombing, it was argued that acts of terrorism are attacks against the founding principles of the European Union. Among such principles is respect for the rule of law and human rights. However, the institutions that made these declarations also advocated for the creation and implementation of measures that neither accord with the rule of law nor respect human rights. If the EU abandons the rule of law and human rights, it "sacrifices the very aim of its existence to the means which it adopts to preserve this."[75] Such an occurrence can never be justified.

---

71 Zedner, L. 2005. Securing liberty in the face of terror: Reflections from criminal justice. *Journal of Law and Society* 32 (4): 533; Waldron, J. 2003. Security and liberty: The image of balance. *The Journal of Political Philosophy* 11 (2): 191–210.

72 Ignatieff, M. 2005. *The lesser evil: Political ethics in the age of terror.* Edinburgh, Scotland: Edinburgh University Press, 5.

73 Social contract theory constitutes "the belief that political structures and the legitimacy of the state derive from an (explicit or implicit) agreement by individual human beings to surrender (some or all of) their private rights in order to secure the protection and stability of an effective social organization or government. Kemerling, G. n.d. *Philosophy pages: Dictionary.* http://www .philosophypages.com/dy/s7.htm.

74 Kleinig, J. 2007, January 17. *Liberty and security in an era of terrorism,* 5. Paper presented in the Oxford Criminology Seminar Series 2006/07, Center for Criminology, University of Oxford, UK.

75 Fontana, B. trans and ed. (1988). *Constant: Political writings.* Cambridge, UK: Cambridge University Press; Zuckerman, I. 2006. One law for war and peace? Judicial review and emergency powers between the norm and the exception. *Constellations* 13 (4): 524.

One way this could be prevented is by allowing governments, when faced with an emergency, to resort to emergency powers that are limited in "time, space, and object."[76] That is, states' powers should be based on facts that justify the claim that there is an emergency and constrained by both the time limits of the emergency (since the time limit of the war on terrorism is unknown, sunset clauses and periodic reviews should be included in the measures) and limits on the specific means that may be used to respond to the emergency.[77] The South African Constitution has such limits; specifically, in the strict supermajoritarian requirements in its emergency power regime. It also requires that after 21 days of declaring an emergency, an extension of the emergency authority be approved by 60% of the National Assembly.

Additionally, the state of emergency cannot last more than 3 months. Flyghed provided a good illustrative example of why this is needed.[78] In Sweden, a law was passed in 1952 to deal with an exceptional circumstance (espionage).[79] As an exceptional measure, it would apply for only one year at a time, then Parliament would determine each year whether or not to extend the life of the measure. Despite the 1-year time limit safeguard, this measure has been in force for approximately 50 years. Another example involves Egypt, which has been in a "state of emergency" almost without interruption since the Six Day War in 1967. Egypt's Emergency Law of 1958 extended police powers, suspended some constitutional rights, held individuals for months without being charged for a crime, authorized censorship, and restricted nongovernmental political activity (e.g., political protests).[80] Egypt is currently working on ending the state of emergency. This, in fact, was a key demand of the protestors who ousted President Hosni Mubarak in February 2011.

Consider also the use of exceptional clause 2.2 of the Schengen Convention by EU Member States to reinstate border checks post-9/11. Such border checks can be reinstated only in exceptional circumstances. As Apap and Carrera argued,

> even though this provision must be used exclusively under the exceptional circumstances of an emergency and for a limited period of time, looking at the

---

[76] See ft 3, p. 64 in Bigo, D. 2006. Security, exception, ban and surveillance. In *Theorizing surveillance: The panopticon and beyond*, ed. D. Lyon. Collompton, UK: Willan.

[77] Dyzenhaus, D. 2001. The permanence of the temporary: Can emergency powers be normalized? In *The security of freedom: Essays on Canada's anti-terrorism bill*, eds. R. J. Daniels, P. Macklem, and K. Roach, 27. Toronto, Canada: University of Toronto Press.

[78] Flyghed, J. 2002. Normalising the exceptional: The case of political violence. *Policing and Society* 13 (1): 33.

[79] Svenska författningssamling (SFS) (Swedish Code of Statutes) 1952:58.

[80] Law No. 162 of 1958, which was renewed by temporary resolution no. 560/1981 for one year. It has since been periodically renewed up until 2011. See Amnesty International. 2011. Time for justice: Egypt's corrosive system of detention. http://www.amnesty.org/en/library/asset/MDE12/029/2011/en/3c835ce6-8d5e-4103-9d7b-6bc75202b31c/mde120292011en.pdf.

states' practices, however, their use of the provision has not been so exceptional, but rather a common practice.[81]

Emergency powers should be used to deal with the consequences of major terrorist attacks, only after a state of emergency is declared, in order to react to some exigent circumstance; however, such powers should expire or cease to be operational after the emergency has passed.[82] Most importantly, what should not occur is what happened in Sweden: an emergency measure introduced to deal with a very specific situation should not later be expanded and made a permanent part of the ordinary criminal justice system.

By presenting the threat of terrorism as an emergency, legal restraints on counterterrorism measures are being relaxed. The use of the war rhetoric, and the consideration of terrorism as "exceptional" (when in fact, it is not), has put governments under pressure by speeding up decisions. The speeding up of decisions, coupled with the calls for unity, may therefore serve as a means to suppress dissent and reduce the scope of democratic debate when expansive counterterrorism measures are introduced to combat this so-called exceptional threat.

Sunstein argues that as the magnitude of the terrorist threat increases, governments' arguments for intruding on human rights also increases.[83] Especially if the risk is great (whether real or perceived), governments might, for example, allow law enforcement and intelligence agencies to engage in practices that would not have been permitted under normal circumstances. Since misjudgement of risk frequently leads to poor decision-making, the public can easily be swayed into thinking that expansive measures that curb civil liberties will automatically work. With daily reminders of terrorism through the media (especially online news) and governments' repetition and emphasis on the gravity of the threat, the fear of terrorism is not expected to diminish anytime soon. As Schneier argues, when individuals do not understand risk, they make bad security trade-offs.[84] Is this prevalent among counterterrorism measures? The next section of the text seeks to determine just that by examining several global counterterrorism measures and policies, with three main objectives: First, to explore various coercive and noncoercive measures used against domestic and international terrorists. Second, to establish the efficacy of these measures in dealing with the types of terrorists that legally and politically justified their implementation. Third, to consider whether such measures and policies could be used to deal with the threat of terrorism post-9/11; namely, against

---

81   Apap, J., and Carrera, S. 2003, November. *Maintaining security within borders: Towards a permanent state of emergency in the EU?* CEPS Policy Brief 41, p. 3.

82   Heymann, P. B. 2002. Civil liberties and human rights in the aftermath of September 11. *Harvard Journal of Law and Public Policy* 25 (2): 451; Cohen, S. A. 2004. Policing Security: The Divide Between Crime and Terror. *National Journal of Constitutional Law* 15(3): 448.

83   Sunstein, C. R. 2005. *Laws of fear: Beyond the precautionary principle.* Cambridge, UK: Cambridge University Press, 217.

84   Schneier, B. 2006. *Beyond fear: Thinking sensibly about security in an uncertain world.* New York: Springer, 31.

individuals who support terrorism and/or engage in terrorist attacks because they are inspired by al-Qaeda's cause rather than directed by or linked to them.

HYPOTHETICAL SCENARIO

On October 1, 2011, U.S. homegrown terrorists inspired by al-Qaeda engaged in coordinated attacks on vehicles on the Brooklyn, Ed Koch Queensboro, and George Washington bridges in New York City. These individuals attacked their targets using automatic weapons and improvised explosive devices. The perpetrators were killed by law enforcement agents who responded to the scene. These attacks resulted in 100 deaths (excluding the perpetrators) and over 1,000 injured.

1. Would this attack be considered as a Black Swan? Why do you think so?
2. If the same attack had occurred in Israel, would it be considered as a Black Swan? Why or why not?
3. How would the U.S. government respond to such an attack?

CHAPTER SUMMARY

The war on terrorism does not fit with existing notions of warfare. While this war has targeted states and nonstate actors, the actual targets of the war on terrorism have not been defined. No one knows how long this "war" will last. In fact, this is one of the major criticisms leveled at the war on terrorism. By describing a nation's approach to combating terrorism as a war, several adverse legal and political changes arise as a result. The rhetoric and the reference to the responses of the terrorist threat as a war on terrorism, the speeding up of the process by which counterterrorism legislation is introduced, and the presentation of terrorist threat as an emergency have resulted in extraordinary governmental powers and restrictions on civil liberties for citizens and noncitizens alike, regardless of their links with terrorism.

REVIEW QUESTIONS

1. What are the consequences of calling the current effort to combat terrorism a war?
2. When can a country declare a state of emergency?
3. Is the war on terrorism an emergency?
4. Which terrorist attacks were Black Swans? Why do you think so?
5. What role does rhetoric play in counterterrorism?
6. What is the relationship between civil liberties and security?
7. How can an emergency be better regulated?

part three

Counterterrorism: Evaluating What Works and What Doesn't Work in the Discipline

This section examines existing measures taken by governments, international organizations, law enforcement and intelligence agencies. To be effective, counterterrorism strategies, measures, and policies must efficiently deal with the threat. Some countries have long-established counterterrorism statutes with which to deal with terrorism. Certain countries, such as Northern Ireland, South Africa, and Israel, have experienced terrorism for decades. Current counterterrorism measures draw on legislation from regions that have developed and employed protracted campaigns over extended periods of time against terrorists. Examples of these regions are Israel, Sri Lanka, Italy, Northern Ireland, and Spain. Some strategies have effectively eradicated the specific terrorist groups in their countries. However, other counterterrorism campaigns have been ineffective, calling into question the legitimacy of relying on these countries for guidance. Furthermore, the fact that both international and domestic terrorism persists today illustrates the magnitude of the problem and the intricacy of its resolution. Different terrorists and terrorist groups respond to different measures. Indeed, some tactics and policies are more effective than others, depending on the terrorist or terrorist group targeted. Thus, the creation of a successful "one size fits all" counterterrorism tactic or policy is unfeasible. However, this does not preclude the ability to create a counterterrorism strategy consisting of effective measures that should be maintained and used wherever appropriate.

chapter seven

Panopticism: Intelligence Gathering, Surveillance, and Registration

Philip Heymann predicted that the fear of terrorism will change societies by creating an "intelligence state," in which intelligence agencies are not limited in gathering private information, have no burden of establishing the need for such information beyond a reasonable doubt, and can engage in illegal activities secretly and thus without political accountability.[1] A characteristic of such a state would be that vast quantities of information concerning citizens' private data and wholly innocent activities would be collected by intelligence agencies in order to increase the stock of analyzable information in the hope that such information "may" tie into something else in the future. The society described above is not a fictitious scenario but an imminent reality in countries around the globe, especially the United States and member states in the European Union. This chapter first examines intelligence agencies' knowledge of the threat of terrorism. It then explores how the intelligence state has been made possible by countries' intelligence-gathering, surveillance, and registration measures. This chapter subsequently looks at whether some groups are more likely than others to be countered by these measures and why this is the case. Finally, it investigates the efficacy of these measures in combating terrorism.

---

[1] Heymann, P. B. 2003. *Terrorism, freedom, and security: Winning without a war.* Cambridge, MA: MIT Press, 135–138.

INTELLIGENCE AGENCIES AND THE THREAT OF TERRORISM: WHAT DO THEY KNOW?

There are known knowns, there are things we know we know. We also know there are known unknowns; that is to say, we know there are some things we do not know. But there are also unknown unknowns—the ones we don't know we don't know.
— DONALD RUMSFELD (U.S. DEPARTMENT OF DEFENSE NEWS BRIEFING, 2002)

The "known knowns" of which Rumsfeld spoke of are those aspects of the threat that agencies already know. Intelligence agencies and law enforcement officials might know the identities of gang members, drug lords, or organized crime groups, thus making them "knowable." This knowledge places these agencies in a good position to implement sensible and proportionate countermeasures against the threats posed by these groups. Even such terrorist groups as the Red Army Faction and November 17 had identifiable hierarchies and leaders, thus making the identities and inner workings of this form of threat "knowable" to the appropriate agencies. The same could be said about al-Qaeda, which prior to 9/11 had an identifiable command and control structure. This structure included a consultation council (majilis al shura) that considered, discussed, and approved major actions or policies such as the issuance of a religious ruling (fatwa); a religious committee that deliberated on religious rulings; a military committee, which reviewed and approved military matters (e.g., the planning and execution of an attack); a business committee, which oversaw al-Qaeda's business and financial affairs; and a media committee, whose activities included the printing and circulation of information.[2] However, the extent to which al-Qaeda's centralized element still exists and functions post-9/11 is heavily debated.[3] Dishman argued that after 9/11, al-Qaeda was forced to decentralize because it lost an overwhelming majority of its leadership, which comprised the heart of al-Qaeda's command center.[4] Today, al-Qaeda is viewed more as a "network of networks," which are flexible, adaptable, decentralized, diversified, and transnational.[5] Knowledge of the members and

---

2 Statements made by prosecution witness Jamal al-Fadl (a former member of al-Qaeda, who later defected and became an informant for the United States) under oath in the Southern District Court of New York on February 6, 2001, cited in Alexander, Y., and Swetnam, M. S. 2001. *Usama bin Laden's al-Qaida: Profile of a terrorist network.* New York: Transnational, 3.

3 Some argue that al-Qaeda no longer has an identifiable hierarchy, see e.g., Burnett, J., and Whyte, D. 2005. Embedded expertise and the new terrorism. *Journal for Crime, Conflict and the Media* 1 (4): 4; whereas others argue that it does, see e.g., Gunaratna, R. 2002. *Inside Al Qaeda.* New York: Berkeley, 78 and Hoffman, B. 2007. Review Article: What went wrong. *Studies in Conflict and Terrorism* 30 (1): 93.

4 Dishman, C. 2005. The leaderless nexus: When crime and terror converge. *Studies in Conflict and Terrorism* 28 (3): 243.

5 Whitaker, R. 2003. After 9/11: A surveillance state? In *Lost liberties: Ashcroft and the assault on personal freedom*, ed. C. Brown, 52. New York: New Press.

leaders of al-Qaeda also helped intelligence agencies track and incapacitate them.[6] A case in point is Osama bin Laden (see Box 7-1).

Box 7-1   Food for Thought—The Death of Osama bin Laden: Is this the Beginning of the End of Al-Qaeda?

In the past, Pakistan has harbored Taliban and al-Qaeda operatives and provided them with a safe haven in their country.[1] Paul Maddrell noted in 2009 that intelligence agencies believed that Osama bin Laden was hiding in the region.[2] It turns out that they were right. What led intelligence agencies to finding him? One of bin Laden's close associates, Abu Ahmed al-Kuwaiti. Intelligence agencies first turned their attention toward al-Kuwaiti after he engaged in a telephone conversation with an individual that the United States had placed under wiretap surveillance. During the conversation, al-Kuwaiti informed his friend that he was back with the people with whom he was before. Intelligence agencies believed that this meant that he was with al-Qaeda leadership and maybe even bin Laden. His movements were subsequently tracked using a combination of human and technology intelligence resources. This monitoring led U.S. intelligence agencies to the compound in Abbottabad, Pakistan. This compound had no phone lines, 12- to 18-foot walls, and was eight times the size of other homes within the area.[3]

Satellite imaging was critical at this point. It was used not only to study the compound but also to try to determine whether someone the intelligence agencies had dubbed "the pacer" (because he would stroll in the courtyard for 1 to 2 hours each day) was in fact Osama bin Laden. While the available technology never obtained a clear view of the individual's face, the National Geospatial-Intelligence Agency analyzed the satellite imagery and determined that the person's height was between 5 feet 8 and 6 feet 8.[4] Osama bin Laden was 6 feet 4. Even though bin Laden's presence could not be verified with certainty, President Barack Obama authorized U.S. Navy Seals to raid the compound in Abbottabad. This raid occurred without notifying Pakistani authorities, as it was believed that the integrity of the mission would be

---

[1] Maddrell, P. 2009. Failing intelligence: U.S. intelligence in the age of transnational threats. *International Journal of Intelligence and Counterintelligence* 22 (2): 209.

[2] Ibid.

[3] Ross, B., Cole, M., and Patel, A. 2011, May 2. Osama bin Laden: Navy Seals operation details of raid that killed 9/11 al Qaeda leader. ABC News. http://abcnews.go.com/Blotter/khalid-sheikh-muhammad-capture-osama-bin-laden-courier/story?id=13506413.

[4] Woodward, B. 2011. Death of Osama bin Laden: Phone call pointed U.S. to compound—and to "The Pacer." *Washington Post*, May 6, 2011. http://www.washingtonpost.com/world/national-security/death-of-osama-bin-laden-phone-call-pointed-us-to-compound-and-to-the-pacer/2011/05/06/AFnSVaCG_story.html.

(continues)

---

6 For example, some known members of al-Qaeda include Jamal Ahmed al-Fadl, Ayman al-Zawahiri (co-founder of al-Qaeda), and Mohammed Al-Saafani (prime suspect in the USS Cole bombing). See Alexander, Y., and Swetnam, M. S. 2001. *Usama bin Laden's al-Qaida: Profile of a terrorist network*. New York: Transnational, 6–19.

Box 7-1   Food for Thought—The Death of Osama bin Laden: Is this the Beginning of the End of Al-Qaeda? (continued)

jeopardized.[5] On May 1, 2011, President Obama informed the media in a televised address that Osama bin Laden was shot and killed during the raid.

In the aftermath of bin Laden's death, his second in command, Ayman al-Zawahiri, was appointed as the new head of al-Qaeda.

1. What was achieved with the death of Osama bin Laden?
2. How and to what extent has his death affected al-Qaeda?
3. What does this mean for the war on terrorism?
4. What, if any, type of retaliation should the United States expect from al-Qaeda operatives and supporters? If retaliation is expected, how has the United States prepared for this?

---

[5] Schmidle, N. 2011. Getting Bin Laden: What happened that night at Abbottabad. *The New Yorker*, August 8, 2011. http://www.newyorker.com/reporting/2011/08/08/110808fa_fact _schmidle?currentPage =all.

On the other hand, intelligence agencies are aware of the fact that there are certain aspects of a threat that are unknown to them (known unknowns). A case in point is the use of weapons of mass destruction (WMDs) by al-Qaeda. While the use of WMDs by terrorists does not constitute a trend,[7] the fact that al-Qaeda appears to be seeking to maximize the devastation they cause and has declared its intent to procure and use these types of weapons provides intelligence agencies with reasonable expectation that it is likely to occur in the future.[8] Specifically, "al-Qaeda and the Taliban have . . . obtained information about how to manufacture nuclear, chemical, and biological weapons from . . . Pakistani nuclear scientists."[9] In addition, the Butler Report stated that credible intelligence exists that reveals that al-Qaeda has a significant interest in obtaining toxic materials and the capability and intent to use weapons-grade nuclear material.[10] As Tucker argues, to pose a real threat of toxic terror (or threat of weapons of mass destruction), a group must have both the capability and motivation to acquire and use such weapons (nuclear, chemical, or biological).[11] Because the Butler Report shows that

---

[7] With the exception of the sarin gas attack on the Tokyo subway in March 1995 (killed 12; injured over 1,000) and the anthrax letters sent in the aftermath of 9/11 to several news media offices and two senators, Senate Judiciary Committee Chairman Patrick Leahy and Senate Majority Leader Tom Daschle, in the U.S. (killed 5; made 17 ill).

[8] Duyvesteyn, I. 2004. How new is the new terrorism? *Studies in Conflict and Terrorism* 27 (5): 448.

[9] Maddrell, P. 2009. Failing intelligence: U.S. intelligence in the age of transnational threats. *International Journal of Intelligence and Counterintelligence* 22 (2): 209–210.

[10] Butler Report. 2006. The nature and use of intelligence and terrorism. In *Terrorism: Critical concepts in political science (Vol. IV: The fourth or religious wave)*, ed. D. C. Rapoport, 480. London: Routledge.

[11] Tucker, J. B. 2000. Introduction. In *Toxic terror: Assessing terrorist use of chemical and biological weapons*, ed. J. B. Tucker, 9. Cambridge, MA: MIT Press.

al-Qaeda has both the capability and willingness to use these weapons, there exists a real threat of toxic terror (or WMD terror). The "unknown" in this situation is when and how the terrorist attack will occur in the future.

By contrast, the last category, "unknown unknowns," is one of the identifying characteristics of the current threat of terrorism, which makes security against this threat an overwhelming task. When faced with this type of threat, agencies find it extremely difficult to identify and implement appropriate measures to counter it. In this category, "unknown unknowns" are threats that "we don't even know that we don't know." For instance, old or new technologies can be used in surprising ways, new twists can be put on old ideas, and new attacks can occur that agencies have never thought of.[12] The attacks on the World Trade Center and the Pentagon on 9/11, in which terrorists used planes loaded with jet fuel as missiles, are a prime example of this type of threat. Another example was the coordinated suicide attacks on July 7, 2005, in London. Specifically, Shehzad Tanweer, Mohammad Sidique Khan, Hasib Hussain, and Jermaine Lindsay engaged in multiple coordinated terrorist attacks on London's transportation system. These terrorists were inspired by al-Qaeda's cause and not directed by them.

The current threat of terrorism is implicit in the category of "unknown unknowns" because it even includes "enemies we don't know yet are enemies."[13] Al-Qaeda is a global organization with a network of cells, including preparatory and sleeper cells in over 60 countries, and collaborators and supporters among all the main extreme Islamic groups in the world.[14] Their long-term goals include infiltrating and assimilating in society, and as such, they could be anyone and could be anywhere.[15] This becomes evident when reviewing the following names: Pierre Robert, Christian Gancarski, Thomas Fisher, Steven Smyrek, David Courtailler, Lionel Dumont, Willie Virgile Brigitte, and David Sinclair. While these are not the types of names that governments, intelligence officers, and law enforcement agencies expect to see when reviewing a list of individuals charged with participation in al-Qaeda,[16] these individuals, in fact, make up a part of the extremely varied community formed by al-Qaeda in Europe.[17] These individuals are all Europeans who converted to Islam. The same holds true when reviewing the names of some of the homegrown terrorists detected and captured in the United States for attempting to engage in terrorist attacks both domestically and abroad because they were

---

12 Schneier, B. 2006. *Beyond fear: Thinking sensibly about security in an uncertain world*. New York: Springer, 273.

13 Ibid.

14 Wilkinson, P. 2002. The war without frontiers. *Scotland On Sunday*, September 8, 2002. http://www.martinfrost.ws/htmlfiles/without_frontiers.html.

15 Cragin, K., and Daly, S. A. 2004. *The dynamic terrorist threat: An assessment of group motivations and capabilities in a changing world*. Santa Monica, CA: RAND, 85.

16 Their assumptions are based on authorities' erroneous belief that terrorists affiliated with al-Qaeda fit a profile, such as Arab male Muslim, age 18–40 years old.

17 See Chapter 1, Vidino, L. 2006. *Al-Qaeda in Europe: The new battleground of international jihad*. New York: Prometheus, 23–62.

inspired by al-Qaeda's cause rather than directed by them: Daniel Boyd, David Williams, Kevin Lamar James, Stanley Grant Phanor, and Colleen LaRose. Such individuals are plentiful in Europe and the United States and are extremely valuable to terrorist organizations because they do not fit the traditional profile of a terrorist and therefore attract little attention by the authorities.[18] These individuals are just the type of people who make up the category of the "unknown unknowns."

This form of terrorism extends beyond traditional al-Qaeda members to include terrorists of different profiles (homegrown or immigrants, experienced jihadis, and fresh converts from different religions or with no prior religious background), whose nature is elusive.[19] This, combined with their swelling numbers, "make[s] the work of . . . intelligence [and law enforcement] agencies a true nightmare."[20] To assist intelligence and law enforcement agencies, measures are required that can find these individuals among the population.

MAKING THE "UNKNOWN UNKNOWNS" KNOWN: THE CREATION OF THE INTELLIGENCE STATE

After 9/11, governments worldwide called for the pervasive collection of data as a means with which to find terrorists and prevent them from engaging in terrorist attacks before they occur. Intelligence is collected to "identify the leaders, members, bank accounts and other financial hiding places, sources of money, sanctuaries, weapons caches, facilities, allies, and places of recruitment of terrorist organizations so that all can be eliminated."[21] It is most often obtained using covert activities such as IMINT (imagery intelligence), SIGINT (signal intelligence) and HUMINT (human intelligence). IMINT has been used to provide early warning of threats and conflicts (e.g., the photo imaging satellite, French Helios-1A, launched in 1995, was capable of this) and to provide a visual image for a forthcoming target of a covert operations (e.g., satellite images were used to determine the layout of the compound Osama bin Laden was residing in). SIGINT is designed to detect transmissions from radar, communications, and broadcast systems and involves measures such as visual surveillance and wiretaps. By contrast, HUMINT is not technology oriented. Instead, it encompasses the attainment of intelligence via informers and infiltration of terrorist groups.

The task that intelligence agencies are faced with is how to make the terrorist threat known. According to Burnett and Whyte, one method is by targeting individuals and/or groups that are tangentially associated with terrorists by extending the powers of intelligence and police agencies against Muslims, asylum seekers,

---

18　Ibid., p. 28.

19　Ibid., p. 24.

20　Ibid.

21　Maddrell, P. 2009. Failing intelligence: U.S. intelligence in the age of transnational threats. *International Journal of Intelligence and Counterintelligence* 22 (2): 203.

and protestors.[22] The current extension of police and intelligence agencies' powers through surveillance technologies clearly illustrates this. As of August 2007, the United States has been issuing e-passports, which contain an RFID (Radio Frequency Identification) chip with the passport information inside and a digital photo that enables biometric comparison through the use of facial recognition software. In fact, the standardized photo image, which is compatible with the International Civil Aviation Organization (ICAO) 9303 biometric data interchange formats, has been presented as enabling "law enforcement agencies to use facial recognition technology to help apprehend" terrorists. Facial recognition software targets individuals who are already in a database as the result of specific prior conduct or allegations.[23] Technology that is using this software is being used, among other places in the world, by UK law enforcement agencies "who deploy cameras to scan certain public places to compare faces with those of known wanted criminals." [24] Such technology is also being used at airports. An example of this is Keflavik International Airport in Iceland, where facial recognition biometrics were installed in its "closed circuit TV infrastructure linked to a database of criminals and potential terrorists compiled by the European Union."[25] The International Criminal Police Organization (Interpol) has also expressed its interest in expanding its role to include the mass screening of passengers moving around the world by creating a huge biometric facial scan database of international travelers so they can cross-check everyone against a database of terror suspects, international criminals, and fugitives.[26]

Another example, the U.S. National Security Entry-Exit Registration System (NSEERS), which was implemented because the terrorists responsible for 9/11 had entered the United States with valid temporary visas, was promoted as preventing future terrorist attacks and enhancing border security by documenting and monitoring visitors to the United States.[27] This program "captures and archives biographic data and images of the faces and fingerprints of select foreign nationals

22 Burnett, J., and Whyte, D. 2005. Embedded expertise and the new terrorism. *Journal for Crime, Conflict and the Media* 1 (4): 7.

23 Dershowitz, A. M. 2002. *Shouting fire: Civil liberties in a turbulent age,* 1st ed. London: Brown, 479. In Israel's Ben Gurion airport, passengers are invited to submit to biometric screening for convenience, specifically, they can submit biometric data in order to avoid long queues. See Atkinson, R. D. 2001, September. How technology can help make air travel safe again. *Progressive Policy Institute Policy Report,* 6–7. http://www.ndol.org/documents/Airport_Security_092501.pdf.

24 See Atkinson, ibid., p. 6.

25 Ibid.

26 Watson, S. 2008, October 20. *Interpol details plans for global biometric facial scan database.* http://www.infowars.com/interpoldetails-plans-for-global-biometric-facial-scan-database/.

27 NSEERS required both general registration, which included the collection of biometric data, fingerprints, and photographs of individuals, and special registration for selected nationals, which required individuals to provide more detailed biographic information, reporting to INS upon arrival to the United States, and 30 days after arrival, and re-registering annually. Finn, J. 2005. Potential threats and potential criminals: Data collection in the national security entry-exit registration system. In *Global policing and surveillance: Borders, security, identity,* eds. E. Zureik and M. B. Salter, 139–141. Devon, UK: Willan.

visiting or residing in the United States on temporary visas."[28] The selectivity of NSEERS is not only overtly discriminatory but also contributes to the construction and reinforcement of race-based suspicion.[29] The U.S. Visitor and Immigrant Status Indicator Technology (US-VISIT) program was created in 2004 to succeed NSEERS. Unlike NSEERS, US-VISIT required the collection of data on all foreigners entering or leaving the country (not just those of current or even previous suspect states).

The Personal Identification Secure Comparison and Evaluation System (PISCES) is another such program. PISCES is a "terrorism interdiction system," which "matches passengers inbound for the United States [from airports in high-risk countries] against facial images, fingerprints and biographical information" of known terrorists and affiliates.[30] Some of the countries that have PISCES include Iraq, Pakistan, Algeria, Afghanistan, the Philippines, Tunisia, Yemen, and Morocco. Pakistan, however, is seeking to replace PISCES with their own software, the Integrated Border Management System (IBMS). This software allegedly allows the integration of biometric data and provides visa-issuing authorities with access to the information in the database, features that PISCES was said to be missing.[31]

Other international programs of particular note are those of the Philippines and Japan. The Philippines has a program in place, the Philippine Biometrics Initiative (PBI), which collects fingerprints, photographs, and other information on suspected terrorists and provides this data to the appropriate Philippine authorities. This information is also made available to U.S. authorities.[32] In Japan, fingerprinting and facial image technologies are used in airports to identify suspicious travelers. In addition, Japan has a Biometric Immigration Control System, which, from November 2007 to October 2009, "denied entry to 1,465 foreign nationals who attempted to enter Japan using forged or altered passports or re-enter after being previously deported from Japan."[33]

In Europe, the Council of Europe's Convention on Cybercrime contains provisions for the collection of communications data. Among its various provisions,

---

[28] See ibid., pp. 139, 152–153.

[29] Finn, J. 2005. Potential threats and potential criminals: Data collection in the national security entry-exit registration system. In *Global policing and surveillance: Borders, security, identity*, eds. E. Zureik and M. B. Salter, 139. Devon, UK: Willan.

[30] Madsen, W. 2002, March. The business of the watchers: Privacy protections recede as the purveyors of digital security technologies capitalize on September 11. *Multinational Monitor* 23 (3). http://multinationalmonitor.org/mm2002/02march/march02corp3.html.

[31] Imtiaz, S. 2011. Pakistan to replace "insecure" US border watch software. *Tribune*, June 8, 2011. http://tribune.com.pk/story/184568/pakistan-to-replace-insecure-us-border-watch-software/.

[32] U.S. Department of State. 2010, August. Country reports on terrorism 2009, 55. *Office of the Coordinator for Counterterrorism*. http://www.state.gov/documents/organization/141114.pdf.

[33] Ibid., p. 45.

this convention includes procedures for the preservation of computer-stored data and electronic communications data (or traffic data, which consists of data about a communication). Data preservation, which is based on targeted surveillance, provides "authorities with the power to order the logging and disclosure of traffic data in regards to . . . communications" on a case-by-case basis.[34] The Cybercrime Convention allows law enforcement agencies to request data to be preserved upon notice for certain periods of time (the "fastfreeze—quick thaw" model). Under this model, service providers are to store the data quickly upon request by law enforcement authorities. This model provides only for individual secure storage of data, which is subsequently quickly released to the authorities upon receipt, for example, of a court order. These technologies narrow the focus so as to target specific individuals and not intrude wholesale on the entire population. Accordingly, the common characteristics of these counterterrorism policies are their "selectivity" and "targeting" of specific individuals.

Despite the claims of many authors[35] that counterterrorism measures are inherently selective, several current measures illustrate a new, emerging trend, one that does not focus on the targeting of suspected terrorists. The technologies used, such as iris scans, biometrics, and DNA, "rely heavily on the use of searchable databases, with the aim of anticipating, pre-empting, and preventing acts of terrorism by isolating in advance potential perpetrators."[36] The measures using these technologies are not targeting specific suspect groups but are instead searching for targets. What is emerging in the war on terrorism is a risk-based approach focusing on the collection and analysis of data in order to determine suspicious activity. Consider measures aimed at combating terrorism financing. They represent "a marked break with earlier regimes of money laundering regulation, which focused on tracing criminal money— associated with narcotics or political corruption—after the crime."[37] Financial data nowadays is collected and analyzed using software in order "to identify suspicious

---

[34] Breyer, P. 2005, May 11. Telecommunications data retention and human rights: The compatibility of blanket traffic data retention with the ECHR. *European Law Journal* 3:373.

[35] See, for example, Sunstein, C. R. 2005. *Laws of fear: Beyond the precautionary principle.* New York: Cambridge University Press; Whitaker, R. 2006. A Faustian bargain? America and the dream of total information awareness. In *New politics of surveillance and visibility*, eds. K. D. Haggerty and R. V. Ericson, 141–170. Toronto, Canada: University of Toronto Press; Dworkin, R. 2002. The threat to patriotism. In *Understanding September 11*, eds. C. Calhoun, P. Price, and A. Timmer, 273–285. New York: New Press; Ignatieff, M. 2005. *The lesser evil: Political ethics in the age of terror.* Edinburgh, Scotland: Edinburgh University Press, 32.

[36] Lyon, D. 2003. Surveillance after September 11, 2001. In *The intensification of surveillance: Crime, terrorism and warfare in the information age*, eds. K. Ball and F. Webster, 18. London: Pluto.

[37] de Goede, M. 2004, September 9–11. *The risk of terrorist financing: Politics and prediction in the war on terrorist finance.* Constructing World Orders Conference Standing Group on International Relations Transnational Politics of Risk Panel (Den Haag). http://www.sgir.org/conference2004 /papers/de%20Goede%20-%20The%20Risk%20of%20Terrorist%20Financing.pdf.

transactions that may indicate terrorist behavior."[38] Accordingly, individuals are profiled based on their transactions. Suspicious activity includes individuals without regular income and expenditure wire transferring money internationally.[39] Consequently, some of the individuals who may be considered as potential suspects are immigrants, students, and the unemployed.[40]

Techniques of governance in the war on terrorism "rely heavily on sophisticated computer technology and complex mathematical modelling to mine data and single out suspicious behavior."[41] Data-mining tools are used to "identify patterns of behavior that are supposedly indicative of terrorist activity, in order to assess the level of risk that individuals pose to the state."[42] Some measures in the counterterrorism arsenal that use these tools involve the prescreening of passengers by the Transportation Security Administration under the direction of the Intelligence Reform Terrorism Prevention Act of 2004, the 9/11 Commission recommendations, and the 9/11 Commission Act 2007. A program used to screen passengers was the U.S. Terrorism Information Awareness (TIA) project. This project was designed to sift through electronic trails—airline and parking tickets, credit card receipts, e-mails, and telephone calls—created by terrorist suspects.[43] Computer Assisted Passenger Prescreening System (CAPPS II) is another program developed to analyze data from government and commercial databases and classify passengers according to their level of risk (e.g., acceptable, unacceptable, or unknown risk). This information would then be used to determine the level of security screening each passenger should receive. Other programs created in the United States such as the Multistate Anti-Terrorism Information Exchange (MATRIX) targeted specific individuals who fit an existing risk profile determined by sophisticated data-mining tools.[44]

The funding for TIA, CAPPS II, and MATRIX has been withdrawn. Currently, the program that is operational is Secure Flight, which seeks to identify whether passenger names match any of those listed on the terror watch list, which has come to be known as the "no-fly" list. Faisal Shahzad, who was responsible for the failed attempt to bomb Times Square in New York City in May 2010, boarded a plane of Emirates Airline that was headed to Dubai 6 hours after his name was added

---

38 Amoore, L., and deGoede, M. 2005. Governance, risk, and dataveillance in the war on terror. *Crime, Law and Social Change* 43 (2/3): 152.

39 Ibid., p. 154.

40 Ibid.

41 Ibid., p. 151.

42 International Campaign Against Mass Surveillance (ICAMS). 2005, April. *The emergence of a global infrastructure for mass registration and surveillance*, 20. http://www.i-cams.org/ICAMS1 .pdf.

43 Ball, K., and Webster, F. 2003. The intensification of surveillance. In *The intensification of surveillance: Crime, terrorism and warfare in the information age*, eds. K. Ball and F. Webster, 3. London: Pluto.

44 The MATRIX program was removed in March 2005 because one of the data-mining tools used focused on, among other things, age, gender, and ethnicity.

to the no-fly list. He almost escaped because existing policy allowed airlines 24 hours within which to check the no-fly list after it has been updated. As a result of the Shahzad incident, airlines are now required to check the no-fly list for updates every 2 hours.

The purpose of Secure Flight is to prevent suspected terrorists from boarding planes.[45] It also requires airlines to submit passenger information to the Department of Homeland Security for flights to, from, and within the United States. Passenger information must also be submitted for the planes that fly over the United States. This program checks "passenger information against a consolidated Federal watch list maintained by the Terrorist Screening Center."[46] Australia has a similar program in place, Advanced Passenger Processing (APP), which focuses on incoming international flights and matches "passenger information against preexisting travel alert lists."[47]

There is an important difference here to be noted: this type of surveillance does not monitor a particular person who certain law enforcement authorities think is suspicious, it monitors everyone. This is similar to the U.S. National Security Agency's (eavesdropping) model,[48] which was applied to the communications of all Americans. Here, agencies eavesdropped on every phone call, thus making this measure a form of wholesale surveillance. This becomes evident when reviewing a series of measures that were introduced in the United States and the EU to prevent and combat terrorism, but which contributed to the creation of an intense system of mass registration, identification, and surveillance of individuals and their movements. Specifically, after 9/11, the Enhanced Border Security Visa Entry Act of 2002 mandated that all individuals entering the United States had to eventually use passports, visas, and other travel documents with biometric identifiers[49] that were recognized by national and international standards. Subsequently, the Real ID Act of 2005 was passed, which required biometrics for state driver's licenses and ID cards. Under Section 202(b)(5) of this act, each card (either driver's license or ID) must contain a digital photograph of the person. The digital image of the card or license holder has also been mandated by Section 7214 of the Intelligence Reform and Terrorism Prevention Act of 2004. Moreover, the Department of Homeland

---

[45] The systems in place to prescreen passengers with terror watch lists have failed in the past. A case in point is Yusuf Islam (formerly Cat Stevens), who in 2004 had boarded a United Airlines flight from London to Washington. The TSA had failed to prevent him from boarding the aircraft despite the fact that his name was on a "no fly" list. When authorities became aware that he was on the flight, they diverted the plane to Bangor, Maine, where security officials questioned him and had him subsequently deported back to the United Kingdom.

[46] Office of the Inspector General. 2005, August. *Review of the terrorist screening center's efforts to support the secure flight program.* http://www.usdoj.gov/oig/reports/FBI/a0534/chapter1.htm.

[47] Koc-Menard, S. 2006. Australia's intelligence and passenger assessment programs. *International Journal of Intelligence and Counterintelligence* 19 (2): 219.

[48] All citizens were randomly spied on without the need for probable cause or a search warrant. Its legitimacy has been severely criticized by both the public and politicians alike.

[49] Examples of biometrics include fingerprints and retinal scans.

Security, whose primary responsibility is to prevent terrorist attacks within the United States and reduce U.S. vulnerability to terrorism (see Title I Section 101 of the Homeland Security Act of 2002), issued a Notice of Proposed Rulemaking that required the photos on state driver's licenses and IDs to be, similar to e-passports, compatible with the ICAO 9303 biometric data interchange formats. The EU has similar biometric passports, although they have not been fully implemented.[50] In Canada, biometric passports have been issued with a plan to have all Canadians have them by the end of 2011.[51] These passports include date of birth, place of birth, physical characteristics, and a photo.

Some countries have biometric national IDs cards or will have them in a few years (e.g., Morocco and Belgium). In 2009, the Israeli parliament passed a biometrics bill that seeks to create a biometric database containing fingerprints and facial images.[52] This information will also be stored on chips within Israel's national IDs and passports. Pakistan, Yemen, and Indonesia, among others, have similar databases in place. Another database that stores biometric data is Eurodac, which contains the fingerprints of all applicants for asylum in the EU and all of the illegal immigrants found in the European Union. The Visa Information System (VIS), another example, is a database that holds visa application information and biometrics of third-party-country nationals who need a visa to enter the Schengen area. The US-VISIT system converges integrated databases with biometric identifiers (such as electronic fingerprints, iris scans, and facial recognition) and uses them as a source of identification and prediction.[53] Moreover, the Prüm Treaty called for police and security agencies shared access to an unprecedented range of personal information, such as fingerprints, DNA records, and vehicle details. The Prüm Treaty was created in order to improve access to and the exchange of information, especially in the fight against terrorism. Furthermore, the Hague Programme, which also foresaw ambitious measures concerning exchange of information in the fight against terrorism, created an EU-wide right of use of data by removing national borders from the principle of data collection, storage, and use.[54] This program also adopted the "principle of availability," which meant that an information network would be realized in which data held by national law enforcement

50   Commission (EC) Proposal for a Council Regulation on standards for security features and biometrics in EU citizens' passports' COM (2004) 116 final (February 18, 2004).

51   Saint-Cyr, Y. 2010, June 6. E-passport a privacy concern. *Innovya—Traceless biometrics technology*. http://innovya.com/tag/rfid-enabled-passports/.

52   U.S. Department of State. 2010, August. Country reports on terrorism 2009, 125. *Office of the Coordinator for Counterterrorism*. http://www.state.gov/documents/organization/141114.pdf.

53   Amoore, L., and deGoede, M. 2005. Governance, risk, and dataveillance in the war on terror. *Crime, Law and Social Change* 43 (2/3): 163.

54   Balzacq, T., Bigo, D., Carrera, S., and Guild, E. 2006, January. *Security and the two-level game: The Treaty of Prüm, the EU and the management of threats*. CEPS Working Document No. 234, p. 2.

agencies in all European Union member states was made available to other agencies, thus allowing for the exchange of such information across national borders.[55]

In international borders, what is occurring is what van der Ploeg terms the "informatization of borders," in which information systems at the border can be linked to a host of other databases containing personal information.[56] Border surveillance technologies may attach an individual into already existing group profiles, which decrease the freedom of movement and dignified treatment of individuals. For example, border surveillance technologies may classify an individual as a "high-risk" or "suspect" if he or she is registered in US-VISIT, Eurodac, or VIS, a look-alike of someone on a watch list, or a citizen from a refugee-generating State.[57] Other biometric measures are also used. Specifically, at Israel's Ben Gurion Airport, passengers are invited to submit to biometric screening for convenience; that is, individuals submit biometric data in order to avoid long queues.[58] Here, likewise to the border surveillance technologies mentioned above, biometrics become vital in identifying undesirable populations and sorting masses between those who are desirable (low risk) from those who are undesirable (high risk).[59] Biometrics also speed up the movement of frequent travelers and low-risk populations through programs at borders, airports, and other transport agencies (e.g., US-VISIT). The belief is that this biometric data has the ability to secure identity. The accuracy of this belief, however, has been questioned.

Biometric solutions are proposed because, as proponents argue, "our bodies, or rather the information extracted from our bodies, are unique tokens of identification" and as such, almost impossible to forge.[60] It is also very difficult, if not impossible, for an individual to disassociate oneself from one's biometric, in the sense that they are their biometric.[61] Accordingly, biometric technologies are represented as "infallible and unchallengeable verifiers of the truth about a person."[62]

---

[55] Hustinx, P. J. 2006, May 12. *A framework in development: Third pillar and data protection.* Speech of European Data Protection Supervisor at Warsaw, p. 4. http://www.edps.europa.eu/publications/speeches/06-05-12_article_Warsaw_third_pillar_EN.pdf.

[56] van der Ploeg, I. 2006. Borderline identities: The enrollment of bodies in technological reconstruction of borders. In *Surveillance and security: Technological politics and power in everyday life*, ed. T. Monahan, 191. New York: Routledge.

[57] Ibid., p. 193.

[58] See Atkinson, R. D. 2001, September. *How technology can help make air travel safe again.* Progressive Policy Institute Policy Report, 6–7. http://www.ndol.org/documents/Airport_Security _092501.pdf.

[59] Aas, K. F. 2006. "The body does not lie": Identity, risk and trust in technoculture. *Crime Media Culture* 2 (2): 146.

[60] Ibid., p. 145.

[61] van der Ploeg, I. 2002. Biometrics and the body and information: Normative issues of the socio-technical coding of the body. In *Surveillance as social sorting*, ed. D. Lyon. London: Routledge, cited in Introna, L. D., and Wood, D. 2004. Picturing algorithmic surveillance: The politics of facial recognition systems. *Surveillance and Society* 2 (2/3): 177–178.

[62] Amoore, L., and deGoede, M. 2005. Governance, risk, and dataveillance in the war on terror. *Crime, Law and Social Change* 43 (2/3): 165.

However, these technologies are open to inaccuracy. For instance, certain diseases, such as cysts in the eye, can significantly alter biometric characteristics. Furthermore, biometrics can also be temporarily or permanently altered by a physical injury. Specifically, a cut, burn, or scar on fingertips can significantly alter fingerprints. Thus, it may result in the failure to accurately identify an individual. This individual may, in consequence, be denied a service to which he or she is entitled or access to some place to which he or she has authorization to enter.

Another measure that seeks to prevent and combat terrorism by, for example, stopping terrorists before they board the aircraft, is the agreement that the United States signed with the European Union to have Passenger Name Record (PNR) data, which includes contact information, billing information, the travel agency where the ticket was purchased, and any available Advance Passenger Information (API), such as nationality and date of birth,[63] collected by air carriers, processed, and transferred to the Department of Homeland Security. The EU has similar agreements with Canada[64] and Australia.[65] Other countries such as Saudi Arabia, Japan, Singapore, South Korea, South Africa, and New Zealand have enacted relevant PNR legislation and/or are currently using PNR without having signed any formal agreements. By contrast, Mexico has an API System (APIS) instead of a PNR system. APIS supports "targeting efforts, increased information sharing, and enhanced intelligence capabilities in connection with efforts to identify aliens who may raise terrorism concerns at ports of entry."[66]

Unlike API, with PNR data, risk assessment of passengers can be conducted and "unknown" persons can be identified (i.e., individuals that might potentially be of interest to agencies and who were, up until the assessment, unsuspected).[67] This data can also be matched "against other PNR for the identification of associates of suspects, for example by finding who travels together."[68] In fact, PNR

---

63 See API Directive, Directive 2004/82/EC on the obligation of carriers to communicate passenger data [2004] OJ L 261.

64 Commission (EC). 2005, May 19. *Proposal for a Council Directive on the Conclusion of an Agreement between the European Community and the Government of Canada on the Processing of Advance Passenger information (API)/Passenger Name Record (PNR) Data.* COM(2005) 200 final. http://www.statewatch.org/news/2005/may/eu-canada-pnr-agreement.pdf.

65 Council of the European Union. 2008, June 10. *Agreement between the European Union and Australia on the processing and transfer of European Union-sourced passenger name record (PNR) data by air carriers to the Australian Customs Service.* (Brussels, 9946/08). http://www.statewatch.org/news/2008/jun/eu-australia-pnr-agreement-2008.pdf; Commission (EC). 2010, September 21. *On the global approach to transfers of Passenger Name Record (PNR) data to third countries.* COM(2010) 492 final, p. 2. http://www.statewatch.org/news/2010/sep/eu-com-pnr-global-approach-com-492-10.pdf.

66 U.S. Department of State. 2010, August. Country reports on terrorism 2009, 182. *Office of the Coordinator for Counterterrorism.* http://www.state.gov/documents/organization/141114.pdf.

67 Commission (EC). 2010, September 21. On the global approach to transfers of Passenger Name Record (PNR) data to third countries. COM(2010) 492 final, p. 4. http://www.statewatch.org/news/2010/sep/eu-com-pnr-global-approach-com-492-10.pdf.

68 Ibid.

data can be used "for trend analysis and creation of fact-based travel and general behavior patterns, which can then be used in real time."[69]

Another measure implemented in the European Union around the same time as PNR was the Data Retention Directive (Directive 2006/24/EC),[70] which was originally proposed in 2004 (yet passed in 2006) and permitted the wide retention of communications data. The Data Retention Directive mandates the blanket retention of data on all EU citizens (for a period of no greater than 2 years), which can reveal "who everyone talks to (by e-mail and phone), where everyone goes (mobile phone location coordinates), and what everyone reads online (websites browsed)."[71] Through communications data, intelligence and law enforcement agencies can "identify suspects, examine their contacts, establish relationships between conspirators, and place them in a specific location at a certain time."[72] This measure is in fact considered one of the most important and most controversial measures proposed by the EU and its Member States in order to facilitate the tracking and prosecution of terrorists and to improve the coordination of availability of information and cooperation between those involved in fighting terrorism. Indeed, top on the list of the European Union's counterterrorism plan was mandatory data retention. Both the Declaration on Combating Terrorism and the Declaration on the EU Response to the London Bombings called for the expedient creation and implementation of measures on data retention as part of their plan to combat terrorism in the EU.[73] When data retention was debated in the European Parliament, Charles Clarke (the then President-in-Office during the UK Presidency of the Council) argued that of all the measures introduced in the EU counterterrorism strategy, which included those aimed at developing programs to protect critical infrastructure against terrorist attacks and adopting a strategy to address radicalization and terrorist recruitment, he attached the greatest importance to achieving common standards for the retention of data.[74] This measure aims at harmonizing and making compulsory the *a priori* retention of traffic (data about the communication), location (data concerning the locations from which a particular

69 Ibid.

70 Council Directive (EC) 2006/24 of 15 March 2006 on the retention of data generated or processed in connection with the provision of publicly available electronic communications services or of public communications networks and amending Directive 2002/58/EC [2006] OJ L105/54.

71 Bowden, C. 2002. Closed circuit television for inside your head: Blanket traffic data retention and the emergency anti-terrorism legislation. *Computer and Telecommunications Law Review* 8 (2): 21.

72 UK Home Office. 2003, March. *Consultation paper on a Code of Practice for Voluntary Retention of Communications Data*, p. 7. http://www2.poptel.org.uk/statewatch/news/2003/mar/atcs.pdf.

73 European Council. 2004, March 25. *Declaration on combating terrorism.* http://www.consilium.europa.eu/uedocs/cmsUpload/DECL-25.3.pdf; Council of the European Union. 2005, July 13. *Declaration on the EU response to the London bombing.* http://www.libertysecurity.org/IMG/pdf/JHA_Council_13_July_2005.pdf.

74 European Parliament. 2005, December 13. *Data retention.* [Debate].

communication was made), and other related data (data that is necessary to identify a subscriber or registered user) of individuals in order to make sure that it is available to authorities.[75]

The above measures illustrate how such technologies of surveillance are being used to create an "intelligence state" by significantly increasing the quantity of analyzable information for subsequent use by authorities. The implementation of these measures also demonstrates how such technologies of surveillance are being indiscriminately applied against the entire population, regardless of their links with terrorism. The aspiration of achieving total surveillance is apparent in the measures mentioned above. It has to be noticed that measures requiring the collection of passenger information, biometric data, and telecommunications and electronic communications data on all EU citizens reveal that the state (member state governments and their agencies) is the primary agent of surveillance. These measures seek to create an environment in which information on every citizen can be stored, analyzed, monitored, made available, and shared with law enforcement and intelligence agencies. Citizens can be registered, their movements can be tracked, and their telecommunications and electronic communications can be monitored. When viewed together, these measures illustrate how governments are increasingly seeking universal surveillance of their citizens. The question that follows is: How do these measures aid authorities in making the uncertain threat of terrorism knowable?

To make a terrorist threat known, actionable intelligence on terrorists is sought by using information retrieved from measures of mass surveillance such as IDs, licenses, and passports with biometric identifiers (e.g., digital image and fingerprints) and the databases created by the them, programs that screen all travelers (e.g., Secure Flight), and monitor all visitors to the United States and other noncitizens (e.g., US-VISIT). It is in response to the threat of the "unknown unknowns" that governments seek to "gain access to a seamless web of information on citizens and non-citizens drawing on all potential sources."[76] The belief is that "the more information available . . . the greater the likelihood there is of constructing accurate high risk categories and thus actionable profiles of potential terrorists."[77] This belief is based on the premise that we first need all information in order to filter through it and find the profiles of terrorists. Once these profiles have been

---

[75]   See Articles 1–5, Council Directive (EC) 2006/24 of March 15, 2006, on the retention of data generated or processed in connection with the provision of publicly available electronic communications services or of public communications networks and amending Directive 2002/58/EC [2006] OJ L105/54; See Rowland, D. 2003, April. *Privacy, data retention and terrorism.* 8th BILETA conference: Controlling Information in the Online Environment, London, p. 2. http://www.bileta.ac.uk/Document%20Library/1/Privacy,%20Data%20Retention%20and%20Terrorism.pdf.

[76]   Whitaker, R. 2006. A Faustian bargain? America and the dream of total information awareness. In *New politics of surveillance and visibility*, eds. K. D. Haggerty and R. V. Ericson, 147. Toronto, Canada: University of Toronto Press.

[77]   Ibid.

determined, a target population is then created. Since there are enemies "we don't even know yet are enemies," the counterterrorism measures employed cannot be selective, for we may not know (some of) the targets. Due to the existence of these enemies and the fact that terrorists can effectively infiltrate and assimilate into society, all are considered risks. As such, surveillance of the entire population pervades on the basis that no one can be trusted.[78] If all are considered risks, then the surveillance of the entire population seeks to create a situation in which everything can be seen. If everything can be seen, "then, goes the reasoning, everything may be controlled" and if surveillance can be thorough enough, then terrorist attacks "can be anticipated and appropriate action taken to remove (or at least) mitigate them."[79] As Jacques Ellul had "once commented, 'to be sure of apprehending criminals, it is necessary that *everyone* be supervised.'"[80]

The logic behind these measures is that if all individuals are registered and their identities verified and movements tracked, then the veritable terrorist can be detected. Proponents of this logic argue that these measures can deter terrorists by making it difficult for them to travel to and operate in the United States and other locations worldwide. Taking into consideration the analysis of the current threat of terrorism, are these mass surveillance measures designed in such a way as to effectively counter or at least mitigate the threat? If so, which ones?

THINKING LIKE A TERRORIST: EXPLORING THE EFFICACY OF MEASURES

Biometric identifiers have been included in IDs and driver's licenses because it is believed that they make it more difficult for terrorists to obtain these sources of identification.[81] ID cards and licenses with biometric identifiers can be issued if a document such as a birth certificate is shown. This document, however, can be easily faked. For example, intelligence has shown that terrorists have obtained genuine passports by using a falsified personal identity and fraudulent supporting documents.[82] The risks associated with biometric ID cards and passports have also been highlighted. In 2008, the Chaos Computer Club (a group of German hackers) published a fingerprint of the German Minister for the Interior, Wolfgang Schäuble

---

78 Walker, C. 2005. Prisoners of "war all the time." *European Human Rights Law Review* 11:50.

79 Ball, K., and Webster, F. 2003. The intensification of surveillance. In *The intensification of surveillance: Crime, terrorism and warfare in the information age*, eds. K. Ball and F. Webster, 4. London: Pluto.

80 Ellul, J. 1964. *The technological society*. New York: Knopf, 100, cited in Yesil, B. 2006. Watching ourselves: Video surveillance, urban space, and self-responsibilization. *Cultural Studies* 20 (4): 409.

81 Thiessen, P. R. 2008. Silicon Flatirons writing competition: The real ID act and biometric technology: A nightmare for citizens and the states that have to implement it. *Journal on Telecommunications and High Technology Law* 6:483.

82 Rudner, M. 2008. Misuse of passports: Identity fraud, the propensity to travel, and international terrorism. *Studies in Conflict and Terrorism* 31 (2): 103.

(a known supporter of the collection and use of biometrics to prevent terrorism), in order to prove that the biometric authentication introduced in German passports and national identity cards poses great risks to security.[83] Additionally, the same year, a computer researcher at the University of Amsterdam was able to clone the chips of two British passports (one of which contained the picture of Osama bin Laden) and pass these cloned chips as genuine through the passport reader; in so doing, also raising concerns about the security of the proposed national ID card scheme in the United Kingdom, which used the same biometric technology.[84] As Schneier pointed out, the method used on the European Union passports and IDs would work on any country's e-passport (and now most probably ID scheme) because all of them adhere to the same ICAO standard.[85] These technologies also deflect attention away from terrorists who possess valid IDs and are not in the databases or terrorist watch lists.

When thinking about how to prevent terrorism effectively, it is vital to focus on the specific forms of terrorism (such as those revealed by 9/11 and the Madrid and London bombings) that measures are designed to defend against. One of the main goals of terrorists is to remain hidden, to conceal their identities and activities. For example, to avoid detection, Osama bin Laden and his associates' resided in a compound with no phone line or Internet access. Mobile phones were also not used. As such, phone calls were never made or received in the compound. To make a phone call, individuals in the compound (e.g., Abu Ahmad al-Kuwaiti) would drive a significant distance away from the compound (approximately 90 minutes) to place a call or even put the battery in their mobile phone.[86] They also burned the trash instead of allowing it to be collected from the compound. Additionally, the al-Qaeda-inspired terrorist cells in the United States and EU revealed that these groups were small, secretive, and suspicious toward outsiders. A case in point was the London bombers. They did not have any criminal records, nor did they engage in illicit activities to warrant the attention of the authorities. As such, they became "known" to authorities only after they executed their coordinated suicide bombings on the London transport system. Lone wolves are also extremely difficult to detect without credible intelligence. The success of these terrorists relies upon them not being known to authorities. Because terrorists seek to maintain the secrecy of their operations, it is highly doubtful that a measure that explicitly states that individuals' identities and their movements will be subject to mass surveillance will be

83 Digital Civil Rights in Europe (EDRI). 2009, January 28. Privacy in Germany 2008: A new fundamental right, a privacy mass movement. *EDRI-gram 7.2.* http://www.edri.org/edri-gram /number7.2/germany-2008-surveillance-fundamental-right.

84 Digital Civil Rights in Europe (EDRI). 2008, August 27. Cloning e-Passports. *EDRI-gram* 6.16. http://www.edri.org/edrigram/number6.16/clone-epassports.

85 Schneier, B. 2006, August 3. Hackers clone RFID passports. *Schneier on Security Blog.* http:// www.schneier.com/blog/archives/2006/08/hackers clone r.html.

86 Woodward, B. 2011. Death of Osama bin Laden: Phone call pointed U.S. to compound— and to "The Pacer." *Washington Post,* May 6, 2011. http://www.washingtonpost.com/world /national-security/death-of-osama-bin-laden-phone-call-pointed-us-to-compound-and-to-the -pacer/2011/05/06/AFnSVaCG_story.html.

effective in combating this threat. By substitution or adaptation, terrorists will find other means to prepare, organize, and subsequently carry out their attacks.

Terrorists "switch to other activities . . . or initiate a new type of activity against which the defender has taken few, if any, deterrent or preventive steps."[87] More recent studies have found evidence of substitution effects, which occur in response to government implementation of counterterrorism measures.[88] Consider how substitution works with respect to terrorists' responses to government profiling of their organization and members. For example, in the past, terrorists have sought to foil profiling efforts by shaving their beards or even dying their hair blond.[89] Current terrorists blend in to the society they live in, thus making them very difficult to detect. Many terrorists can adopt (or have adopted) "several behaviors typical of Western street culture, such as dressing like rappers, smoking marijuana and drinking alcohol, yet watching jihadi videos and having pictures of Osama bin Laden on the display of their cell phones."[90] In response to profiling, terrorists may recruit individuals from nonprofiled groups, which will subsequently expand the overall pool of available potential terrorists.[91] The problem associated with this process is illustrated as follows: with the London bombers,

> you have three British citizens of Pakistani descent. You have Germaine Lindsay, who is Jamaican. You have the next crew, on July 21st, who are East African. You have a Chechen woman in Moscow in early 2004 who blows herself up in the subway station. So whom do you profile?[92]

The response of governments was to implement mass surveillance instead of targeted in order to supposedly overcome this. However, because terrorists have begun recruiting from outside their profile, what is to say that they will not find ways to avoid being detected by mass surveillance measures?

---

87   Dutter, L. E., and Seliktar, O. 2007. To martyr or not to martyr: Jihad is the question, what policy is the answer? *Studies in Conflict and Terrorism* 30 (5):431.

88   Enders W., and Sandler, T. 2005. After 9/11: Is it all different now? *Journal of Conflict Resolution* 49 (2): 259–277; Enders W., and Sandler, T. 2004. An economic perspective on transnational terrorism. *European Journal of Political Economy* 20 (2): 301–316; Dutter, L. E. and Seliktar, O. 2007. To Martyr or Not to Martyr: Jihad is the Question, What Policy is the Answer? *Studies in Conflict and Terrorism* 30(5): 431.

89   Tucker, J. B. 2003, March. Strategies for countering terrorism: Lessons from the Israeli experience. *Journal of Homeland Security.* http://coincentral.wordpress.com/2008/06/04 /strategies-for-countering-terrorism-lessons-from-the-israeli-experience/; Harcourt, B. E. 2007. Muslim profiles post-9/11: Is racial profiling an effective counter–terrorist measure and does it violate the right to be free from discrimination? In *Security and human rights*, eds. B. Goold and L. Lazarus, 86–87. Oxford, UK: Hart.

90   Vidino, L. 2007. Current trends in jihadi networks in Europe. *Terrorism Monitor* 5 (20): 9.

91   Harcourt, B. E. 2007. Muslim profiles post-9/11: Is racial profiling an effective counter-terrorist measure and does it violate the right to be free from discrimination? In *Security and Human Rights*, eds. B. Goold and L. Lazarus, 80. Oxford, UK: Hart.

92   Gladwell, M. 2006. Troublemakers: What pit bulls can teach us about profiling. *The New Yorker*, February 6, 2006, p. 2. http://www.newyorker.com/archive/2006/02/06/060206fa_fact.

Terrorists also learn to adapt to new counterterrorism measures. Adaptation refers to a longer-term process whereby the offender population, which is "constantly on the lookout for new crime opportunities, subsequently discovers weaknesses in the defensive measures or is presented with some new technology that could defeat the measures, and is then able to begin committing the crimes again."[93] Consider the foiled terrorist plot in the summer of 2006 in London, which intended to blow up the planes of three major U.S. airlines (United, American, and Continental) over the UK and the United States.[94] Post-9/11, some of the airport security measures implemented included a general prohibition on passengers from carrying pocket knives, box-cutters (directly after 9/11), and cigarette lighters (after Richard Reid, the "shoe bomber") on board aircrafts. The terrorist plot of August 2006 included a tactic that was not covered by measures implemented post-9/11, carrying explosives in a liquid form onto planes. Terrorists such as the perpetrators of 9/11 and the Madrid bombings are learning, growing organisms that understand that the mastery of "technologies that make them successful will allow them to self-perpetuate themselves as well as defeat the intelligence being gathered by the very governments hunting them."[95] Even if the current counterterrorism measures effectively prevent terrorist attacks, in time, terrorists will find a way to circumvent these initially successful measures.

Some unanticipated consequences of implementing countermeasures are the displacement of terrorists' activities. The crime displacement hypothesis holds that when faced with reduced opportunities, offenders will "displace their attention to some other time, place or target; will change their methods; or might even begin to commit some other form of crime."[96] For example, a study conducted by Cauley and Im found that while the installation of greater airport security measures in 1973 was followed by a reduction in aircraft hijackings, there was a corresponding increase in non-skyjacking terrorist incidents.[97] It has to be noticed that the majority of counterterrorism measures, which focus on airline travel, increase the risk that terrorists will attack less protected targets (e.g., shopping malls) and means of transport (e.g., subway). In fact, Derrick Shareef planned to bomb the

---

93 Clarke, R. V., and Newman, G. R. 2006. *Outsmarting the terrorists*. London: Praeger Security International, 40.

94 Oliver, M., and Batty, D. 2006. "Mass murder terror plot" uncovered. *The Guardian*, August 10, 2006. http://www.guardian.co.uk/world/2006/aug/10/terrorism.politics.

95 Colarik, A. M. 2006. *Cyber terrorism: Political and economic implications*. London: Idea Group, 9.

96 Clarke, R. V., and Newman, G. R. 2006. *Outsmarting the terrorists*. London: Praeger Security International, 37.

97 Cauley, J., and Im, W. I. 1988. Intervention policy analysis of skyjackings and other terrorist incidents. *American Economic Review* 78:27–31. Several extensive quantitative studies have found similar results: Enders, W., and Sandler, T. 1993. The effectiveness of antiterrorism policies: A vectorautoregression-intervention analysis. *American Political Science Review* 87:829–844; Enders, W., and Sandler, T. 2000. Is transnational terrorism becoming more threatening? A Timeseries investigation. *Journal of Conflict Resolution* 44:307–332; Enders, W., and Sandler, T. 2002. Patterns of transnational terrorism, 1970–1999: Alternative Timeseries estimates. *International Studies Quarterly* 46:145–165; Dutter, L. E., and Seliktar, O. 2007. To martyr or not to martyr: Jihad is the question, what policy is the answer? *Studies in Conflict and Terrorism* 30 (5): 437.

Cherryvale Mall in Illinois during the Christmas season and Bryant Neal Vinas had informed U.S. officials that he had provided al-Qaeda with information about the New York transit system and that al-Qaeda planned to blow up a Long Island Rail Road commuter train in New York's Penn station. While counterterrorism measures may give the government a temporary advantage, terrorists tend to find ways to circumvent or counter them. When faced with such measures, terrorists become more skilled, and their actions become much more sophisticated in formulating new counter responses in order to achieve their objectives. As Marx argued, while "the nature of the game may be altered . . . the game does not stop."[98]

Everything in terrorists' actions—their changes in offender profile, offense profile, targets, and tactics—illustrates their main priority of remaining invisible. To effectively combat terrorism, one must innovate faster than terrorists "and must be smarter in thinking ahead and making counter-moves—especially those that take offenders time, effort and expense to combat."[99] Terrorists constantly seek new opportunities. As such, the United States needs to "develop a capacity to anticipate the features of products, targets, weapons, and other systems that provide new opportunities to terrorists."[100] Counterterrorism measures need to take this into consideration and anticipate that terrorists will adapt their practices so as to avoid detection by authorities.

Sophisticated techniques are used by terrorists in order to avoid detection. Specifically, Marx identified several behavioral techniques used by individuals to subvert surveillance.[101] One such technique is avoidance. Avoidance moves are passive and do not attempt to directly engage or tamper with surveillance.[102] With this technique, individuals' actions are displaced to "times, places and means in which the identified surveillance is presumed to be absent."[103] Consider al-Qaeda's use of the Internet to spread propaganda. Video messages from Abu Musab al-Zarqawi (a known al-Qaeda leader who died in June 2006) were spreading like a virus on the Internet in 2005. Websites and message boards were used to distribute these videos. While different websites simultaneously uploaded these videos, they were subsequently removed from them after a short period of time and placed on other ones for further distribution. These websites were frequently updated and propaganda removed and switched to different online

---

98 Marx, G. T. 1981. Ironies of social control: Authorities as contributors to deviance through escalation, nonenforcement and covert facilitation. *Social Problems* 28 (3): 226.

99 Ekblom, P. 2005. How to police the future: Scanning for scientific and technological innovations which generate potential threats and opportunities in crime, policing, and crime reduction. In *Crime science: New approaches to preventing and detecting crime*, eds. M. J. Smith and N. Tilley, 32. Devon, UK: Willan.

100 Clarke, R. V., and Newman, G. R. 2006. *Outsmarting the terrorists*. London: Praeger Security International, 206.

101 Marx, G. T. 2003. A tack in the shoe: Neutralizing and resisting the new surveillance. *Journal of Social Issues* 59 (2): 369–390.

102 Ibid., p. 375.

103 Ibid.

locations in order to avoid detection. This made it extremely difficult for authorities to track who was uploading these videos and from where. Other avoidance techniques may also be employed by terrorists. The European Council recognized the possibility that the retention of traffic data may not help law enforcement agencies because offenders can easily circumvent them by using "alternative ways to access the internet, such as internet-cafes or libraries."[104] Terrorists can easily avoid detection by using passports and IDs—altered or counterfeited and obtained by sympathizers—if required to provide identification to use these services.[105] Moreover, terrorists can easily prevent their data from being traced through simple practical means such as using prepaid (or stolen) mobile phones (the method used by the Madrid bombers), acquiring phone cards from outside the country they are in and switching them regularly, using different mobile telephones from foreign suppliers, and using public telephone boxes.

Consider another avoidance technique used by an organized crime group, the Sicilian Mafia, which uses small slips of paper (either tiny handwritten or typewritten notes), known as *pizzini*, for high-level communications. It is the preferred way of communication to avoid fax or phone taps. Perhaps terrorists will mimic the Sicilian Mafia and resort to using *pizzini* as a means of communication between them in order to avoid the surveillance of their telecommunications and electronic communications, or future technology may afford them with other means for communicating undetected. They may even resort to using ordinary mail. Numerous online and print manuals have been published by al-Qaeda on how to mail letters and items in order avoid detection by authorities.[106]

Explicit instructions exist on how members of al-Qaeda should communicate with each other in order to avoid detection. Indeed, terrorists are taught how to use the Internet to send messages and how to encrypt those communications in order to avoid detection by authorities and make sure that their messages are read only by the intended recipients. With easily available spoofing (electronic concealment of Internet addresses) techniques, terrorists can send encrypted e-mail from hidden locations on the Internet to and from each other undetected.[107]

They can also avoid detection by changing their IP or e-mail addresses. Consider the IP address, which is a unique identifier assigned to a computer by service

---

104 Commission (EC). 2005, September 21. *Annex to the Proposal for a Directive of the European Parliament and of the Council on the retention of data processed in connection with the provision of public electronic communication services and amending Directive 2002/58/EC.* Staff Working Document Extended Impact Assessment COM(2005) 438 final, p. 17. http://ec.europa. eu/justice_home/ doc_centre/police/doc/sec_2005_1131_en.pdf.

105 For more information on how such tactics are being used by terrorists, see Rudner, M. 2008. Misuse of passports: Identity fraud, the propensity to travel, and international terrorism. *Studies in Conflict and Terrorism* 31 (2): 95–110.

106 Gunaratna, R. 2002. *Inside al-Qaeda: Global network of terror.* London: Hurst and Company, 81.

107 See Carter, P. 2003, March 12. *Al Qaeda and the advent of multinational terrorism: Why material support prosecutions are key in the war on terrorism.* http://writ.news.findlaw.com /student/20030312_carter.html.

providers when it connects to the Internet. Whenever users request a website, connect to another site, or chat online, their IP address is sent. Without this address, the computer on the other end of the communications would not know where to send the reply. IP addresses are used to identify users and can be used by authorities to trace the origin of a message or website. However, it is common for terrorists to use fake identification when registering with service providers. The Internet also provides several applications by which users can conceal themselves and their transactions. A user can register for a website without identifying himself or herself by first visiting a site called an anonymizer, which replaces the user's IP address with another IP address that cannot be traced back to the user.[108] While the investigations of authorities can determine that a message was sent from (or that a website was registered from) an anonymizer, they will be unable to identify the individual who visited the anonymizer.[109] Accordingly, IP addresses may not always be traced back to the user.

Terrorists have also created innovative techniques to protect their secure communications. For example, they have been known to send fake streams of e-mail spam to disguise a single targeted message.[110] Al-Qaeda has also reportedly used a technique known as an electronic or virtual "dead drop" to communicate.[111] This technique involves opening up an account, creating a message, saving this message as a draft, and then transmitting the account user name and password to the intended recipient (or recipients). The receiver of this information then logs onto the account and reads the message that was saved as a draft. This technique was used by the perpetrators of the Madrid bombings. They communicated with other members of their cell by saving messages for one another in preselected e-mail accounts.[112] By using this technique, terrorists avoid having their e-mails intercepted by eavesdroppers. Intelligence also reveals that al-Qaeda operatives and supporters use steganography to send messages to each other online. This technique was reportedly used by al-Qaeda operatives who plotted to blow up the U.S. Embassy in Paris, France, in 2001. With steganography, only those individuals with the appropriate software can see the hidden messages.

The extent to which terrorists have used these advanced techniques to avoid surveillance remains unclear. Some analysts argue that terrorist tactics do not need to be so sophisticated in their use of computer technology, when coded language

---

108 Hinnen, T. M. 2003/2004. The cyber-front in the war on terrorism: Curbing terrorist use of the Internet. *The Columbia Science and Technology Law Review* 5:11.

109 Ibid.

110 Thomas, T. L. 2003. Al Qaeda and the Internet: The danger of "cyberplanning". *Parameters* 33 (Spring): 115.

111 Coll, S., and Glasser, S. B. 2005. Terrorists turn to the Web as base of operations. *Washington Post*, August 7, 2005, p. A01. http://www.washingtonpost.com/wp-dyn/content/article/2005/08/05/AR2005080501138_pf.html.

112 McLean, R. 2006. Madrid suspects tied to e-mail ruse. *International Herald Tribune*, April 28, 2006. http://www.iht.com/articles/2006/04/27/news/spain.php.

sent in plain text messages or placing advertisements on websites would suffice.[113] Currently, there is concern among intelligence agencies that because terrorists are now well aware of the NSA's interception capabilities that communications intelligence will contain misinformation.[114]

What is also questionable is whether the requests made by law enforcement and intelligence authorities to extract information from these databases can be provided in a timely manner. The sheer volume of the data that is generated by these measures may overburden law enforcement and intelligence agencies' efforts by burying them in an avalanche of information. Detecting terrorists through retained data "requires the manipulation of massive databases of individual transactions and histories in order to look for the veritable needle in a haystack."[115] The total volume of data makes it extremely difficult to track and trace any specific type of information. Therefore, the vast amount of information might not be useful because it cannot be efficiently translated or analyzed. Indeed, the 9/11 Commission report drew attention to the inability of intelligence agencies in the United States to effectively process and use the intelligence that they already have.[116] For instance, even with sophisticated data-mining techniques and Internet surveillance systems such as Carnivore, it is argued that there is little hope of sorting and sifting through the voluminous numbers of e-mails sent everyday in order to find a few notes sent by terrorists.[117] The overabundance of information can actually impede law enforcement and intelligence agencies in finding terrorists.

Intelligence agencies are preoccupied with the quantity rather than the quality of finished intelligence without full cognizance of the amorphous network of adversaries and the need for a review of finished intelligence.[118] However, in order to be useful, intelligence requires effective collection, processing, and analyzing of information. The most damaging of failures in the intelligence process is the inability to make use of the available data and give adequate warning to prevent an attack from occurring. This occurred on 9/11. It is important to note that the lack of available information was not the reason for the intelligence failure of 9/11; the

---

[113] Costigan, S. S. 2007. Terrorists and the Internet: Crashing or cashing in? In *Terrornomics*, eds. S. S. Costigan and D. Gold, 119. Aldershot, UK: Ashgate.

[114] Maddrell, P. 2009. Failing intelligence: U.S. intelligence in the age of transnational threats. *International Journal of Intelligence and Counterintelligence* 22 (2): 214.

[115] Looking in the Wrong Places: Financing Terrorism. 2005, October 22. *The Economist* 377 (8449): 73–75; Clarke, R. V., and Newman, G. R. 2006. *Outsmarting the terrorists*. London: Praeger Security International, 204.

[116] Kean, T. H., and Hamilton, L. H. 2004. *The 9/11 Commission report: Final report of the National Commission on Terrorist Attacks upon the United States*. New York: W.W. Norton, 417. http://govinfo.library.unt.edu/911/report/911Report.pdf.

[117] Carter, P. 2003, March 12. *Al Qaeda and the advent of multinational terrorism: Why material support prosecutions are key in the war on terrorism.* http://writ.news.findlaw.com/student /20030312_carter.html.

[118] Tyakoff, A. 2009. Counter terrorism and systems dynamics: Modeling organizational learning in post modern terrorist groups. In *Terrorism and global insecurity: A multidisciplinary perspective*, ed. K. Alexander, 179–192. Chicago: Linton Atlantic.

lack of sharing information between agencies and the connecting of the dots from available intelligence were. For example, "when an FBI agent in Phoenix reported that suspected radical Islamists were applying for flying lessons at a particular flight school in Arizona, his report languished within the Bureau because it tallied with no agreed warning indicator."[119] This intelligence failure was noted in the 9/11 Commission report. After 9/11, intelligence agencies worldwide understood that knowledge sharing was required both within and across domestic and foreign intelligence agencies.[120]

In the wake of the attacks on September 11, 2001, the Homeland Security Act of 2002 was established. This act called for the creation of the Department of Homeland Security (DHS), a new Cabinet-level federal unit whose primary mission is to protect the United States by coordinating intelligence efforts and communication with law enforcement. The DHS aims to prevent, deter, protect against, and respond to threats to the United States by creating better transportation security systems, strengthening border security, reforming immigration processes, increasing overall preparedness, and enhancing information sharing about terrorist activities.[121]

CONCLUDING THOUGHTS ON THE INTELLIGENCE STATE

While intelligence gathering, mass surveillance, and mass registration measures have assisted in the detection and capture of known terrorists, the extent to which it can make "unknown unknowns" known has yet to be determined. Although proponents of mass surveillance and registration (biometric IDs, licenses and passports, PNR data transfers, the Secure Flight program, and US-VISIT, to name a few) argue that these measures make it difficult for terrorists to insert operatives into the countries; recent arrests in the United States and Europe indicate that this is not the case. As a matter of fact, a current main security issue is not preventing terrorists from entering countries, but that many terrorists are already there (i.e., homegrown terrorists).

Consider the homegrown terrorists arrested in the United States. Most of them were law-abiding citizens with valid driver's licenses and passports. Even those who had committed crimes in the past operated under the radar of law enforcement and intelligence agencies and had not done anything out of the ordinary to warrant their attention up until the point at which they conspired to engage in terrorist activities. Even with biometrically enhanced IDs, licenses, and passports, as well as Secure Flight and PNR programs, these individuals would not have been detected by these agencies.

Mass surveillance measures provide a detailed roadmap for terrorists on how to avoid detection. Terrorists are known for researching information on

---

[119] Maddrell, P. 2009. Failing intelligence: U.S. intelligence in the age of transnational threats. *International Journal of Intelligence and Counterintelligence* 22 (2): 213.

[120] Lahneman, W. J. 2004. Knowledge-sharing in the intelligence community after 9/11. *International Journal of Intelligence and Counterintelligence* 17 (4): 629.

[121] Federal Bureau of Investigation. 2005. Terrorism 2002–2005. *U.S. Department of Justice.* http://www.fbi.gov/stats-services/publications/terrorism-2002-2005/terror02_05.pdf.

Box 7-2 Pakistan and al-Qaeda: The Relationship

Prior to locating Osama bin Laden, the belief was that al-Qaeda operatives, including bin Laden, were hiding in caves in Afghanistan. Many operatives, however, were in Pakistan. For example, the following operatives were apprehended in Pakistan: Abu Zubaydah, who the CIA believed was the third or fourth in command in al-Qaeda, operated training camps, and was involved in every major terrorist operation carried out by al-Qaeda, was captured in 2002 in Faisalabad;[1] Ramzi bin al-Shibh, who was believed to have played a central role in the attacks on 9/11, was arrested in Karachi in 2002;[2] Khalid Sheikh Mohammad, who was the mastermind of the 9/11 attacks, was arrested in Rawalpindi in 2003;[3] Abu Faraj al-Libbi, who was considered to be third in command, was arrested in 2005 in Peshawar;[4] and Umar Patek, a deputy commander of Jemaah Islamiyah (al-Qaeda's Southeast Asian affiliate group), was also found in Pakistan. Patek was responsible for the Bali bombings in 2002, which were conducted against two nightclubs that were very popular among Australian tourists, Paddy's Pub and the Sari Club, and were located opposite one another. The first bomb detonated in Paddy's Pub by a suicide bomber wearing a vest with explosives. Survivors of the bomb frantically exited Paddy's Pub only to encounter a second bomb that had been placed in a vehicle parked in front of the Sari Club. This bomb was triggered by a mobile phone 15 seconds after the initial blast. The total death toll for these bombings was 202. The CIA tipped off Pakistani authorities as to Patek's whereabouts in their country. He was subsequently arrested in Abbottabad in January 2011. Interestingly, this was the same area where Osama bin Laden had been residing. Nevertheless, intelligence agencies have not revealed whether or not Patek met with or had plans to meet with Osama bin Laden.

---

[1] Abu Zubaydah. 2009. *New York Times*, April 20, 2009. http://topics.nytimes.com/topics /reference/timestopics/people/z/abu_zubaydah/index.html.

[2] Ramzi bin al-Shibh. 2010. *New York Times*, August 18, 2010. http://topics.nytimes.com/top /reference/timestopics/people/b/ramzi_bin_alshibh/index.html?scp=1&sq=%95%09Ramzi%20 bin-al%20Shibh &st=cse.

[3] McCarthy, R., and Burke, J. 2003. Top 9/11 suspect seized in Pakistan. *The Guardian*, March 2, 2003. http://www.guardian.co.uk/world/2003/mar/02/alqaida.terrorism.

[4] Abu Faraj al-Libbi. 2011. *New York Times*, May 2, 2011. http://topics.nytimes.com/top/reference /timestopics/people/l/abu_faraj_al_libbi/index.html?scp=1-spot&sq=Abu%20Faraj%20 al-Libbi&st=cse.

---

the West in order to determine their vulnerabilities. Accordingly, it is questionable whether measures that openly declare their intentions while revealing their vulnerabilities can be effective against this type of threat. Effective measures in combating terrorism require a level of secrecy. In fact, secrecy of operations was key to arresting the homegrown terrorists in the United States. This secrecy involved the use of undercover agents and informants, each of which will be explored later in the text.

HYPOTHETICAL SCENARIO

Adam Smith, a 25-year-old U.S. homegrown terrorist, wants to engage in a terrorist attack to avenge the death of Osama bin Laden. He has no ties with al-Qaeda or any other Islamic terrorist group. Adam recently applied for and received a passport. He will use this passport to travel to London via a flight out of JFK. He is planning to blow up the airplane midflight with explosives he has smuggled aboard.

Adam has no job or criminal record. He lives with his parents, who support him. Given that he has no income of his own, he bought his airline ticket with a credit card that he stole from his father. When he arrives at the airport, would any of the existing surveillance measures covered in this chapter flag him as a potential terrorist? Why or why not?

CHAPTER SUMMARY

One obvious way in which agencies seek to make such a threat known is the gathering of intelligence on terrorist suspects and/or groups. Intelligence gathering with surveillance and registration measures have always been considered vital to the counterterrorism arsenal. These measures seek to prospectively identify travelers, citizens, and noncitizens who pose threats to security. The current threat of terrorism has provided the political justification for measures of mass registration and surveillance. These measures illustrate the accumulation of individuals' personal data from biometric information, passenger details, and travel information. All are to be used for the prevention and combating of terrorism. It is apparent that such measures seek to create an environment in which information on every individual can be stored, analyzed, monitored, made available, and shared with security, law enforcement and intelligence agencies. With these measures, individuals can be registered and their movements can be tracked. When viewed together, these measures illustrate how governments are increasingly seeking the total surveillance of citizens and noncitizens alike. Counterterrorism measures need to take this into consideration and anticipate that terrorists will adapt their practices so as to avoid detection by authorities. To be effective, they require a certain degree of secrecy to prevent terrorists from being able to counter them.

REVIEW QUESTIONS

1. What is the significance of the intelligence state?
2. How is intelligence primarily obtained?
3. How did intelligence agencies fail on 9/11?
4. Evaluate the technological measures implemented post 9/11. How effective are they?
5. What are the "unknown unknowns?"

6. What types of measures have been implemented in response to the "unknown unknowns?"
7. In what ways does the knowledge of the terrorist threat dictate the counter-measures used to combat it?
8. Are any of the measures covered in this chapter designed to deal with homegrown terrorists? Why or why not?

chapter eight

Police Tactics: The Good, the Bad, and the Ugly

This chapter examines the global police tactics used to combat terrorism pre- and post-9/11. Special emphasis will be placed on interrogations, torture (especially the "ticking time bomb" hypothesis), warrantless house searches, and the use of undercover agents and informants. What impact did (or does) the use of these tactics on terrorists have on their respective countries? What can we learn from the use of these measures? Are these measures legally justified? How might the use of these measures affect the government's ability to prosecute terrorists? Are they effective counterterrorism measures? Should these measures be used to deal with the terrorist threat that the United States is faced with today?

GLOBAL POLICING OF TERRORISM

Law enforcement and intelligence agencies' objectives have merged in the aftermath of 9/11. Like intelligence agencies, law enforcement authorities seek to gather and analyze information on those planning terrorist attacks. Accordingly, the boundaries between law enforcement and intelligence agencies have begun to blur in response to the post-9/11 terrorist threat. Today, law enforcement agencies are responsible for detecting terrorists and preventing, investigating, and responding to their attacks. International, federal, state, and local law enforcement agencies now play an important role in counterterrorism. Of particular importance to this analysis are the International Criminal Police Organization (Interpol), European Police (Europol), and national law enforcement agencies, such as those in the United Kingdom, United States, and Israel.

Interpol

Interpol facilitates cross-border cooperation, support, and assistance among law enforcement agencies in 188 member countries, within the boundaries of national laws and the Universal Declaration of Human Rights. As part of its services, Interpol provides a global communication system (I-24/7), which enables law enforcement agencies in countries to request, submit, and access data instantly in a secure environment.[1] Additionally, it provides law enforcement agencies with immediate and direct access to various databases that hold information about known criminals, terrorists, fingerprints, DNA profiles, stolen vehicles, stolen art, and stolen or lost travel documents (to name a few).[2]

Interpol's policies concerning terrorism also include international coordination of investigations on websites for terrorism-related purposes. One of Interpol's most important functions is the sharing of member countries' crime-related information using notices. The types of notices that can be issued are as follows:[3] *red notice*, which seeks the arrest or provisional arrest of wanted individuals for the purpose of extradition; *yellow notice*, which assists in locating missing persons and individuals who cannot identify themselves; *blue notice*, which collects additional data about an individual's identity or activities relating to a crime; *black notice*, which seeks information on unidentified bodies; *green notice*, which provides warnings and intelligence on those who have committed crimes and are likely to commit the same crimes in other countries; *orange notice*, which warns the police, government agencies, and international organizations of possible threats from disguised weapons, parcel bombs, and other dangerous material; and *purple notice*, which provides data about the modi operandi, tactics, and hiding places of criminals. After 9/11, blue notices were issued for the 19 hijackers responsible for 9/11, and red notices were issued for terrorists connected to these attacks and certain high-level al-Qaeda operatives.[4] Moreover, in 2002, the Interpol Terrorism Watch List became operational and currently provides law enforcement agencies with information on fugitive and suspected terrorists who have been subjected to red, blue, and other notices.[5] Furthermore, to combat terrorism more effectively, Interpol maintains liaisons with other international organizations that combat terrorism, including an agreement with Europol to cooperate in the policing of

---

[1] Interpol. 2010. *Secure global police communications services.* http://www.interpol.int/Public /ICPO/corefunctions/securecom.asp.

[2] Interpol. 2010. *Operational data services and databases for police.* http://www.interpol.int /Public/ICPO/corefunctions/databases.asp.

[3] Interpol. 2010. *Interpol notices & diffusion.* http://www.interpol.int/Public/Notices/default.asp.

[4] Deflem, M. 2006. Global rule of law or global rule of law enforcement? International police cooperation and counter-terrorism. *The Annals of the American Academy of Political and Social Science* 603:245, 247.

[5] Deflem, M. 2010. *The policing of terrorism: Organizational and global perspectives.* New York: Routledge, 117.

terrorism and an agreement with the Arab Interior Minister's Council to facilitate the exchange of information with Arab law enforcement agencies.[6]

Europol

By contrast to Interpol's global approach to counterterrorism, Europol's contribution to counterterrorism is more focused and specifically geared toward Europe's issues and concerns about terrorism, especially Islamic extremism. Europol was established by the Treaty on European Union (Maastricht Treaty) of 1992. It facilitates the exchange of data between law enforcement, customs, and security agencies. It primarily seeks to disrupt criminal and terrorist networks and assist EU states in their investigations of terrorists and the measures they use to combat these threats.[7] Unlike Interpol, Europol does not have the power to conduct investigations nor is it authorized to arrest suspected criminals.

Europol's 24/7 operational service center coordinates cross-border investigations. According to Europol's website, this system coordinates about 12,000 of these investigations each year.[8] In addition, Europol cooperates with other agencies such as the Counter Terrorism Group (CTG), which was formed after 9/11 by the heads of the police and intelligence services in the European Union.[9] Despite this, oftentimes Europol has difficulty completing its mandate as national intelligence and law enforcement agencies frequently fail or are unwilling to share information. Consequently, this usually prevents Europol from completing its objectives efficiently and effectively. The European Union has recognized this deficiency and stated that in order to provide "citizens with a high level of safety within an area of freedom, security and justice," a common action among EU member states is required in the field of police cooperation. The cooperation sought is "between police forces, customs authorities and other competent authorities in the Member States, both directly and through . . . Europol."[10]

National Law Enforcement Agencies

National law enforcement agencies play a fundamental role in counterterrorism. Some agencies have significant experience in the detection and investigation of terrorists, especially those countries that have domestic terrorist groups. A case in point is Israel, where the police are involved before a terrorist attack has taken

---

6 Deflem, M. 2007. International police cooperation against terrorism: Interpol and Europol in comparison. In *Understanding and responding to terrorism*, eds. H. Durmaz, B. Sevinc, A. S. Yayla, and S. Ekici, 20. Amsterdam: IOS.

7 Europol. 2011. *Protecting Europe.* https://www.europol.europa.eu/content/page/protecting -europe-21.

8 See https://www.europol.europa.eu/.

9 Deflem, M. 2007. International police cooperation against terrorism: Interpol and Europol in comparison. In *Understanding and responding to terrorism*, eds. H. Durmaz, B. Sevinc, A. S. Yayla, and S. Ekici, 22. Amsterdam: IOS.

10 See Article 29 of the Treaty on European Union, as amended by the Treaty of Amsterdam and the Treaty of Nice.

place, once an attack is underway, and after it has occurred. Before an attack, law enforcement agencies focus on the early prevention, interdiction, and treatment of sources of terrorism.[11] Early prevention is achieved through the gathering and analysis of intelligence. This intelligence is used to detect terrorists and potential plots. Special operations police units are also trained in rapidly entering towns and villages where terrorist activities are being planned. For instance, as part of Israel's interdiction efforts, special police units, along with the Army and the Shabak (Israel Security Agency), engaged in raids in the West Bank in places where explosives and other terrorist devices were manufactured.[12] During these raids, they would confiscate and destroy the items they discovered and bring in suspects found in these areas for questioning.

Additionally, police are responsible for educating and training the public in recognizing suspicious terrorist activity and the ways to report such suspicious behavior. Other countries have engaged in promoting terrorism awareness. For instance, the United Kingdom developed information packets and websites to raise public awareness of terrorism, made reporting mechanisms available online through the media and in public transportation systems via intercom announcements and posters, and created public–private partnerships to discuss potential threats and appropriate measures with which to respond to these threats. The United States has also engaged in similar activities.

Moreover, in Israel, once an attack has been initiated, the police immediately block roadways in the target area (if known), conduct intensive searches of suspected terrorists and locations where terrorists or explosive devices are believed to be, and fortify security at potential targets.[13] Basically, situational terrorism prevention measures are implemented. These measures seek to slow down the perpetrators and make it more difficult for them to engage in a terrorist attack, thus increasing the chances of authorities intercepting them before they execute an attack.[14]

Finally, in the aftermath of an attack, the police are responsible for coordinating emergency services in the area and restoring the site.[15] Principally, after an attack has occurred, the police, often the first responders to the scene, are responsible for controlling the damage. Basically, they are responsible for all of the activities that take place until the scene has been secured. Upon arriving at the scene, all nonessential personnel are removed and the boundaries of the scene are set; then

---

[11] Weisburd, D., Jonathan, T., and Perry, S. 2009. The Israel model of policing terrorism. *Criminal Justice and Behavior* 36 (12): 1265.

[12] Ibid., p. 1266.

[13] Perlinger, A., Hasisi, B., and Pedahzur, A. 2009. Policing terrorism in Israel. *Criminal Justice and Behavior* 36 (12): 1281.

[14] Weisburd, D., Jonathan, T., and Perry, S. 2009. The Israel model of policing terrorism. *Criminal Justice and Behavior* 36 (12): 1267.

[15] Perlinger, A., Hasisi, B., and Pedahzur, A. 2009. Policing terrorism in Israel. *Criminal Justice and Behavior* 36 (12): 1281.

Box 8-1   Food for Thought: Mass Surveillance in New York City

New York City has decided to take a leaf out of London's counterterrorism playbook. The Lower Manhattan Security Initiative, a mass surveillance initiative consisting of a network of surveillance cameras; license plate readers; and chemical, biological, and radiological weapons sensors protecting high-profile buildings, institutions, bridges, and infrastructure in lower Manhattan, mirrors London's "Ring of Steel." The "Ring of Steel," which also includes concrete barriers, roadblocks, and checkpoints, was initially developed to deal with the domestic terrorist group, the Provisional Irish Republican Army (PIRA). Since then, it has helped combat international and home-grown terrorists (e.g., al-Qaeda and its allies). A case in point involves the perpetrators of the bombings of the London mass transit system on July 7, 2005. The network of surveillance cameras deployed in London not only helped identify them, but also helped track the suspects of the subsequent failed attempt to bomb the transit system on July 21, 2005. The Lower Manhattan Security Initiative was expanded to include midtown, which covers the streets between 30th and 60th and includes now landmarks such as the United Nations and the Empire State Building. Recent reports in the United Kingdom show that the 2 million closed-circuit televisions (CCTVs) in London have been largely ineffective as crime prevention tools. In August 2009, a senior Scotland Yard officer, Detective Chief Inspector Mick Neville, stated that fewer than one crime is solved per 1,000 surveillance cameras in London.[1] The crime most often solved through the use of CCTV is vehicle theft. Why were these figures so dismal? And what does this mean for the crime (and terrorism) fighting effectiveness of these measures in Manhattan?

_____

[1] Hope, C. 2009. 1,000 CCTV cameras to solve just one crime, Met police admits. Telegraph, August 25, 2009. http://www.telegraph.co.uk/news/uknews/crime/6082530/1000-CCTV-cameras -to-solve-just-one-crime-Met-Police-admits.html.

a single path of entry and exit is established to protect the scene and preserve the evidence. The personal information (e.g., name, phone number, work and home address) of all of those who enter and exit the scene are then recorded. In the case of a bombing, management of the scene involves the creation of an inner perimeter (e.g., where the device detonated and within range of the blast that occurred) and an outer perimeter (e.g., the area beyond the limits of the blast). The bomb squad should be the only people who enter the inner perimeter until it has been cleared for any other explosive devices that may have been planted by the terrorists. After the inner perimeter has been cleared for explosives, emergency service personnel and forensic investigators may enter the area to tend to any victims and collect physical evidence, respectively. Evidence found at the scene may be able to provide information about the perpetrators. After evidence is collected, the police seek to restore the site by clearing the scene. According to Weisburd, Jonathan, and Perry, in Israel,

> all [of] these activities are expected to be accomplished in no more than 4 hours.
> The police view timing as being critical, not only to prevent contamination of

evidence but also . . . to enable the public to continue with its daily routine as quickly as possible. The rapid cleanup of the site is expected to minimize the ongoing effect of the attack and the related psychological distress of the public.[16]

Furthermore, the Israeli police and the media work together to keep the public informed during and after a terrorist attack. The public is also informed of any roads, facilities, or public places that have been closed and any alternate routes that have been assigned for safer travel.

In England, special powers of arrest, detection, and search were given to law enforcement agencies to deal with the Provisional Irish Republican Army. Specifically, Section 11 of the Northern Ireland (Emergency Provisions) Act of 1978 provided a police officer with the ability to arrest anyone he suspected of being a terrorist. This act also provided police with the ability to engage in warrantless searches if they suspected someone of terrorism. In particular, Section 16 of the Northern Ireland (Emergency Provisions) Act of 1978 provided that a police officer may enter and search any premise where the person to be arrested is or in any place the police officer suspects the person to be. Spain provided law enforcement agencies with similar expansive powers in response to the ETA's bombings in the Spanish cities of Bilbao, Vitoria, and Santander and its attempt to derail a train carrying civil war veterans in 1961. Like the British police, the Spanish authorities were afforded sweeping powers of arrest, detention, and search.

The level of police focus on counterterrorism depends on the risk of terrorism in their country, city, or state; the size of the agency; and its capabilities (e.g., available staff and financial resources). Law enforcement agencies in areas with a low risk of terrorism and that have limited staff and economic resources are more likely to limit their efforts to increase terrorism awareness and engage in counterterrorism training. Conversely, law enforcement agencies with the necessary resources and that face a high risk of attack are more likely to considerably restructure their day-to-day operations to include counterterrorism practices.

Unlike in Israel and the United Kingdom, police officers in the United States did not have significant experience with terrorism. After 9/11, this changed and U.S. law enforcement agencies were given a larger role in counterterrorism. Given that terrorism is not a traditional problem for law enforcement agencies in the United States, it may seem that police are poorly prepared to effectively deal with various terrorist threats. However, the community policing effort has helped train police to effectively address the underlying social problems that engender crime. Additionally, local law enforcement officers are now trained and continue to participate in training throughout their careers to address and be prepared for terrorism and terrorism-related criminal activity. Officers must make risk assessments of the potential damage that terrorists pose to their community. These assessments focus on critical infrastructure and likely targets, a sense of how critical the threat is, the vulnerability of the community to a terrorist attack, a calculation of casualties and

---

16 Weisburd, D., Jonathan, T., and Perry, S. 2009. The Israel model of policing terrorism. *Criminal Justice and Behavior* 36 (12): 1269.

Box 8-2   Evading Checkpoints: The Case of the Hamas

Between 2000 and 2008, approximately 12,000 mortars and rockets were fired at Israeli targets; 3,000 of these were used in 2008 alone.[1] Israel responded by engaging in Operation Cast Lead, which involved a 3-week airstrike and ground operations in the Gaza Strip. Intelligence gathered during Operation Cast Lead revealed that the Hamas had created underground tunnels under the Sinai–Gaza border in order to smuggle weapons, explosives, and ammunition.[2] The openings of these tunnels were hidden and oftentimes these tunnels led to houses, factories, greenhouses, and mosques where weapons and explosives were stored. Intelligence further revealed that weapons and explosives were stored in schools and hospitals as well.

Prior to their use of rockets and mortars, Hamas suicide bombers or active shooters would have to enter Israel in order to bomb its facilities and people. In addition, Hamas operatives would have to get past border security agents at checkpoints. The underground tunnels and the availability of rockets and mortars changed this. Consequently, the Hamas do not have to enter Israel to attack it with explosive devices, and its operatives can travel from the Gaza Strip to Egypt using the underground tunnels, thus avoiding Israeli security agents and checkpoints.

[1] State of Israel. 2009, July. The operation in Gaza: 27 December 2008–18 January 2009. *Israel Ministry of Foreign Affairs.* http://www.mfa.gov.il/NR/rdonlyres/E89E699D-A435-491B-B2D0 -017675DAFEF7 /0/GazaOperationwLinks.pdf.

[2] Weiner, J. R., and Bell, A. 2009. The Gaza war of 2009: Applying humanitarian law to Israel and Hamas. *San Diego International Law Journal* 11:31.

other risks, and a counterterrorism response.[17] Consider the building of the One World Trade Center in New York as a replacement for the World Trade Center and a tribute to the victims of 9/11. The New York City Police Department called attention to the fact that the original design was vulnerable to attack from a truck bomb on the West Side Highway and as a result, the blueprints were modified to prevent such an attack.[18]

Within the Department of Justice, the Office of Community Oriented Policing Services (COPS) provides law enforcement and communities with resources that enable them to respond to terrorism threats in several important ways. COPS uses technological advancements to gather and use intelligence effectively, increases communication between police and other public agencies, works with federal agencies and local victims agencies to assist victims of terrorism, and seeks to improve intelligence collection and processing.[19] Law enforcement agencies are also

[17] Leson, J. 2005. Assessing and managing the terrorism threat: New realities. Washington, DC: U.S. Department of Justice.

[18] Winner, L. 2006. Technology studies for terrorists: A short course. In *Surveillance and security: Technological politics and power in everyday life,* ed. T. Monahan, 286. New York: Routledge.

[19] Chapman, R., Baker, S., Bezdikian, V., Cammarata, P., Cohen, D., Leach, N., Schapiro, A., Scheider, M., Varano, M., and Boba, R. 2002. Local law enforcement responds to terrorism: Lessons in prevention and preparedness. Washington, DC: U.S. Department of Justice; Thatcher, D. 2005. The local role in homeland security. *Law and Society Review* 39 (3): 635–676.

working to respond to the needs of victims of terrorism through the government-sponsored Terrorism and International Victims Unit (TIVU). This organization develops programs to help victims of terrorism, mass violence, and other transnational crimes by providing medical assistance, financial aid, and legal guidance.

Members of "local" law enforcement are no longer doing their job only at the local level. Increasingly, law enforcement agencies have established regional mutual aid agreements under which multiple criminal justice agencies are contracted to respond to specific problems, such as terrorism. Mutual aid agreements have also facilitated information sharing between neighboring and regional criminal justice agencies.[20] Overall, the importance and growing role of law enforcement in counterterrorism has been referred to as a new paradigm or era in American policing.[21]

Two tactics used by law enforcement agencies—infiltration and interrogation—are critical to the detection, prevention, investigation, and prosecution of terrorists. Each of these are explored in further detail in the following sections.

THE ART OF INFILTRATION: INFORMANTS, SUPERGRASSES, AND UNDERCOVER AGENTS

To infiltrate terrorist groups, law enforcement agencies use undercover agents, agent provocateurs, and informants. Undercover agents are trained to behave and think like a terrorist in order to gain access to the terrorist organization. Agent provocateurs are individuals who find themselves in a position to commit criminal activities to gain further access within a terrorist group or organization. An agent provocateur can be a police officer or an individual who is employed by law enforcement or other federal agencies to work undercover in order to entice or provoke a person to engage in an illegal activity. Agent provocateurs often encourage the activities of a terrorist, terrorist groups, or terrorist organizations; this activity may or may not be authorized by the police. Like undercover agents, informants are used to provide law enforcement agencies with insight into actions of terrorists and their groups. Informants are also placed in key areas to alert authorities to an operative of a terrorist group or anyone requesting access to someone from whom they could purchase explosive devices. Even though infiltrating terrorist groups is time-consuming and risky, it produces valuable intelligence on the operatives and inner workings of an organization.

Informants can access information that is not easily available using other forms of intelligence gathering. Sometimes the individuals used as informants do not have a prior connection to the group. Instead, they are recruited by police for the purpose of joining a group and providing information on it. Nonetheless, informants are usually those who are or were part of the terrorist organization, close

---

[20] Lynn, P. 2005. Mutual aid: Multijurisdictional partnerships for meeting regional threats. Washington, DC: U.S. Department of Justice.

[21] Ortiz, C., Hendricks, N., & Sugie, N. 2007. Policing terrorism: The response of local police agencies to homeland security concerns. *Criminal Justice Studies* 20 (2): 91–109.

to it, or in a position that enabled them to easily penetrate the group. Police also rely on outsiders for information, that is, those not linked to the terrorist group or organization in any way. Such outsiders include members of the public, bystanders who witnessed an event, and victims of the terrorist group; basically, a person not associated with the group who may have observed terrorist activity.

Pre-9/11, law enforcement agencies concentrated their counterterrorism efforts on the infiltration of domestic terrorist groups. For instance, to combat terrorism, Israel established a network of informers that supplied Israeli security services with information on Palestinian terrorist cells and their activities.[22] Another example involved Italy. General Carlo Alberto Dalla Chiesa, the head of the anti-terror group at the time, successfully infiltrated the Red Brigades with informants and undercover agents. Similarly, law enforcement efforts focused on the recruitment and insertion of informants and undercover agents in the Provisional Irish Republican Army. As a result of these efforts, informants and undercover agents successfully infiltrated all levels of the PIRA.

The PIRA, however, did not stand idly by against this tactic. They educated members and the community on tactics employed by recruiters. The PIRA also took steps to ensure that the information leaked to police and other security services was of little use to these agencies. Additionally, they aggressively sought informants within their ranks. Police handling of informants thus proved quite complicated. Indeed, authorities found it extremely difficult to communicate with informants for fear of arousing suspicion. The PIRA used many techniques to find informants in their ranks. In at least one instance, the PIRA organized the hijacking of a postal van. They subsequently reviewed the contents of the mail to see if the British government was issuing checks to any individual.[23] When the PIRA found an informant, they engaged in punishment beatings. Women who were believed to be informants were most likely exiled. Moreover, amnesty was offered to some informers who, for whatever reason, sought to terminate their association with security services. In particular, in January 1982, the PIRA announced amnesty for all individuals who were working or had worked as an informant for security services. The amnesty period lasted only 2 weeks. Once the period expired, the PIRA threatened to take (and eventually took) repressive action against known informants. Furthermore, the PIRA was known to execute informants. It is estimated that the PIRA murdered about 71 suspected informants.[24] Other terrorist groups also murdered any suspected informants in their group. For instance, an informant was murdered when Action Directe, a terrorist group in France, discovered that this individual had been providing information about the group to the state

---

[22] The elaborate network of informants collapsed during the First Intifada. Eventually, Israel reorganized its network of informants.

[23] Ilardi, G. J. 2009. Irish Republican Army counterintelligence. *International Journal of Intelligence and Counterintelligence* 23 (1): 18.

[24] Sarma, K. 2005. Informers and the battle against republican terrorism: A review of 30 years of conflict. *Police Practice and Research* 6 (2): 167.

security agency (Renseignements Généraux).[25] Likewise, during the First Intifada, hundreds of informants were killed by Palestinian terrorists.

Certain informants who provided testimony in Northern Ireland and Britain were known as "supergrasses." A supergrass is "someone who has participated in a number of criminal enterprises, who not only gives information to the police about them, but also agrees to give evidence in court against a significant number of persons alleged to be his accomplices in crime."[26] An accomplice can provide information on a crime by testifying in court. The purpose of such testimony is often to implicate others and provide information about a terrorist organization. The testimony of a supergrass is beneficial to the investigation and prosecution of terrorists in several ways. First, they provide insight into the inner workings of a terrorist organization. Second, key members of the group can be identified from the testimony of supergrass operatives. Third, they enable witnesses who were otherwise too frightened to testify for fear of retaliation to come forward. Fourth, supergrasses help create an atmosphere of distrust within the terrorist group, which can, in turn, disrupt its operations. This also became evident in other cases in which informants and undercover agents had successfully infiltrated terrorist groups. An example of this is the Ku Klux Klan, which was infiltrated by male and female informants and undercover officers. This infiltration eroded group trust as many rival KKK factions accused each others' leaders of being informants for the FBI.

The testimony of a supergrass may also have adverse consequences for the investigation and prosecution of terrorism-related cases. Supergrasses are often offered immunity from prosecution for confessed crimes, reduced prison sentences, and witness protection services (i.e., new identities, new lives). There are inherent dangers associated with this process, as police often determine the punishment for an individual, a task which usually belongs to the courts. Also, immunity becomes particularly problematic when those granted immunity for crimes they committed have engaged in more serious crimes than those they implicate. It may further result in a loss of public confidence in the fair administration of justice, especially if violent terrorists are provided immunity only for the sake putting one or more other terrorists in prison.[27] Such loss of confidence may also result in miscarriages of justice—individuals wrongfully imprisoned for terrorism-related offenses.

Besides Northern Ireland and Britain, other EU countries provide terrorists with a way out of the group or organization they belonged to. In particular, laws were implemented in Europe that enabled terrorists to turn state's evidence in return for a significant reduction in prison sentence. For example, former Red

---

[25] The Renseignements Généraux is formally known as the Direction Centrale des Renseignements Généraux (Central Directorate of General Intelligence). Reinares, F. 1998. Democratic regimes, international security policy and the threat of terrorism. *Australian Journal of Politics and History* 44 (3): 368.

[26] Bonner, D. 1987. Combating terrorism: Supergrass trials in Northern Ireland. *Modern Law Review* 51 (1): 23.

[27] Of course, there are arguments in favor of this, especially if those individuals are likely to engage in terrorist attacks.

Army Faction members became a *staatzeuge* (state witness) in return for lenient sentences.[28] In fact, the four founding members of the RAF (Andreas Baader, Ulrike Meinhof, Gudrun Ensslin, and Jan Karl Raspe) were convicted primarily on the testimony of Gerhard Müller, who had turned state's evidence.[29] Pursuant to Article 57 of the German Penal Code, convicted terrorists who renounced terrorism could have their sentences reduced, suspended, or deferred. Likewise, in Italy, Section 625 of *Legge Cossiga* of 1979 and Section 304 of *Legge Sui Pentiti* of 1982 awarded a substantial reduction in penalties if terrorists agreed to collaborate with police and judicial authorities.[30] In addition, to combat terrorism, the "carrot and stick" provisions of *Legge Cossiga* and *Legge Sui Pentiti* were used, and the *pentiti* ("penitence") system was established, in which terrorists were offered softer punishment in exchange for information that subsequently led to the arrest of other individuals within their group. Unlike the U.S. system, Italy did not offer protection to those who cooperated with authorities under the *pentiti* system. Regardless, the *pentiti* system had encouraged many terrorists to collaborate with authorities. Similarly, Israel employed the carrot–stick approach to recruit rank-and-file members of terrorist groups, creating an elaborate intelligence network.

There are, however, significant dangers to using evidence from accomplices, informants, and supergrasses. Informants and supergrasses who have been discovered by the terrorist groups may be used by the terrorists to provide law enforcement authorities with disinformation. Controversially, money may also be provided to informants and supergrasses. The amount involved and the reasons for the payments have always been a matter of dispute. Paid informants may invent information to justify or enhance their incomes from law enforcement agencies. Israel provides payments for some informants but not for others. Specifically, Israel distinguishes between Israeli Jews, who are called "spies," and Palestinians, who are called "collaborators."[31] Spies are entitled to remuneration; so too are their family members if the spy is murdered. The same cannot be said about Palestinians.[32] Israel thus treats its informants differently. This practice, however, is counterproductive, as it discourages Palestinians from assisting the government and as such, hinders recruitment efforts for new informants.

In Israel, after the First Intifada, informants were primarily recruited from prison populations. These individuals were offered a reduction in sentence. A

---

28 Greer, S. 1995. Towards a sociological model of the police informant. *British Journal of Sociology* 46 (3): 523.

29 Ibid.

30 Das, D. K. 1990. Impact of antiterrorist measures on democratic law enforcement: The Italian experience. *Terrorism* 13 (2): 96.

31 Cohen, H., and Dudai, R. 2005. Human rights dilemmas in using informers to combat terrorism: The Israeli-Palestinian case. *Terrorism and Political Violence* 17 (1/2): 239.

32 See, for example, de Quetteville, H. 2005. Israel abandons refugees from "village of traitors." *The Telegraph*, October 16, 2005. http://www.telegraph.co.uk/news/worldnews/middleeast/israel/1500772/Israel-abandons-refugees-from-village-of-traitors.html.

problem arises with using prisoners as they may agree to provide information to authorities in exchange for the reduction of their sentence, with no intention of actually providing authorities with any valuable information about the terrorist group and its plans. The accomplice, informant, or supergrass may be dishonest and/or seeking revenge against another individual. If a police officer unknowingly obtains false information from an informant and uses that information to arrest a suspect, the court will usually uphold the police officer's actions—although this will not occur if the information a police officer used was from an informant who frequently provides law enforcement agencies with false information. Usually, to be admissible in court, accomplice evidence needs to be corroborated with other evidence (e.g., physical evidence and other witness testimony), and yet such corroborative evidence does not always exist. In fact, oftentimes the trial judge must rely solely on the accomplice's statement to make a decision. Prior to 1977, individuals could be prosecuted solely on the testimony of a supergrass. This, however, changed in the aftermath of *R v. Turner*,[33] which examined the reliability of supergrass testimony. In 1977, the Director of Public Prosecution in Britain responded that no further prosecution can be brought when the sole evidence against the defendant is provided by a supergrass.[34]

Terrorist groups have also planted informants into police, security, and other government agencies. For example, the PIRA had spies in the police and government who would provide them with information.[35] This tactic is not unique to the PIRA. For instance, a lieutenant colonel in the Israel Defense Force, Omar El-Heyb, was caught spying for Hezbollah.[36] Furthermore, terrorist groups have taken measures to prevent infiltration by authorities. Specifically, to avoid such detection and infiltration, the PIRA created an almost autonomous section based in Britain (known as the England Department) that was decentralized and made up of multiple cells of operatives (with 4 operatives to each cell). The England Department consisted of a sophisticated and extremely secure network of operatives. The cells that were placed in England effectively assimilated into society. Informers could not easily infiltrate these cells. If they did, they would not be able to compromise other cells as the members' identities were closely guarded. Indeed, the members of one cell did not know the identities of members of the other cells. In the same way, the decentralized nature of al-Qaeda post-9/11 poses problems for police infiltration. Even if a cell is infiltrated, terrorists of one cell often do not know the identity of terrorists in another cell. Accordingly, infiltrating such groups provides little intelligence on the organization as a whole. What it can do is reveal

---

[33] (1975) 61 CR. App. R. 67.

[34] Ingoldsby, C. 1999. Supergrass testimony and reasonable doubt: An examination of DPP v. Ward. *Trinity College Law Review* II, 38.

[35] IRA Sleepers in Top Positions. 2005. *BBC News*, December 30, 2005. http://news.bbc.co.uk / 2/hi/uk_news/northern_ireland/4546628.stm.

[36] Bennet, J. 2002. Israeli Bedouin colonel is formally charged with spying. *The New York Times*, October 25, 2002. http://www.nytimes.com/2002/10/25/international/middleeast/25MIDE.html.

the identities of all of the members in the cell and help prevent that particular cell from engaging in terrorist attacks.

To try to overcome this barrier to infiltrating the PIRA, British authorities encouraged undercover agents and informants to seek intelligence officer positions to gain information on the identities of the operatives of cells in the England Department. Even though this method proved successful for British authorities, this technique would not be effective against the current threat of homegrown terrorism. This threat includes operatives that are inspired by al-Qaeda's cause but have no direct ties with them. The possibility of their identities being known by al-Qaeda central is very unlikely.

HUMINT Works

Human intelligence (HUMINT) yields the best intelligence on terrorist organizations and terrorists' operations. According to Tenet, the intelligence obtained from arrested al-Qaeda leaders has provided enormous insight into al-Qaeda's strategy, motivation, thinking, and operatives; more than that which had been obtained from other forms of intelligence, such as COMINT and IMINT.[37] Much of the existing intelligence on al-Qaeda has primarily been retrieved from arrested al-Qaeda members, especially leading figures such as Khalid Sheikh Muhammad and Abu Zubaydah.[38] Informants, undercover agents, and agent provocateurs have also provided intelligence on terrorists. Using these individuals, federal, and local authorities had infiltrated these homegrown terrorist groups by leading these groups to believe that these agents belonged to al-Qaeda or to other extremist organizations that are allies of al-Qaeda.

Given that there is no accurate, single terrorist profile for agencies to target in their investigations, law enforcement agencies focus on the environment in which terrorists operate. Agencies know that homegrown terrorists often do not have any connections or associations with other terrorists or terrorist organizations. Accordingly, most homegrown terrorists actively seek weapons and explosive devices from criminal elements, with the exception of those who create their own bombs from materials they purchase online or in stores that do not draw the unwanted attention of authorities (e.g., the London bombers).[39] Realizing this, authorities have placed undercover agents posing as weapons dealers, explosive dealers, and even al-Qaeda operatives. These agents also exist online in forums frequented by al-Qaeda operatives and supporters.

---

[37] Tenet, G. 2007. *At the center of the storm: My years at the CIA.* London: Harper Press, 256; Maddrell, P. 2009. Failing intelligence in the age of transnational threats. *International Journal of Intelligence and Counterintelligence* 22 (2): 211.

[38] Tenet, ibid., pp. 250–257; Maddrell, ibid., p. 212.

[39] Those who create their own devices without any training or experience run the risk that their devices will fail. This was the case with several terrorists, including the Faisal Shahzad (the device he planted in Times Square failed) and the July 21 London bombers, whose devices failed to detonate on London's transport system.

Such individuals have provided significant insight into homegrown terror-ists. In fact, the detection of the homegrown terrorists in the United States has been largely based on human intelligence. One such case involved the homegrown terrorist cell known as Miami 7 (Patrick Abraham, Burson Augustin, Rotschild Augustine, Narseal Batiste, Naudimar Herrera, Lyglenson Lemorin, and Stanley Grant Phanor), who were suspected of plotting to blow up the Sears Towers in Chicago, the Miami FBI building, and other targets.[40] An FBI informant had infil-trated the group by posing as an al-Qaeda operative. Batiste, the leader of the cell, had requested $50,000 from the person posing as an al-Qaeda operative and boasted that the attack would be "as good or greater than 9/11."[41] Undercover FBI agents posing al-Qaeda operatives and supporters have also foiled other terrorism plots in the United States. Derrick Shareef, who attempted to bomb the Cher-ryvale Mall in Chicago during the Christmas season in 2007, and Mohamed Osman Mohamud, who was planning to detonate explosives in a van during a Christmas tree lighting ceremony in Portland, Oregon, were given fake explosives by indi-viduals they believed were associated with al-Qaeda. In both instances, these indi-viduals were arrested after they attempted to detonate the explosives.

ELICITING INFORMATION AND CONFESSIONS: INTERROGATION AND TORTURE

The interrogation of suspects plays a critical role in the investigation and pros-ecution of terrorists. Suspected terrorists are interrogated in order to obtain confessions and information about the group they are affiliated with, associates, financiers, and planned attacks. Interrogation rooms lack windows, contain only a table and a few chairs, and are purposely free from extraneous sounds. Often, the temperature within these rooms is high in order to make the suspect uncom-fortable. Obtaining confessions from terrorist groups is frequently an extremely difficult task as the majority of the members have been trained in ways to resist interrogation techniques. For example, the Green Book of the Provisional Irish Republican Army includes a detailed analysis of interrogation techniques and ways to overcome them. It particularly notes that British authorities used sleep depriva-tion, denied suspects the use of bathroom facilities, and would interrogate suspects for extended period of times without a break.[42] The length of an interrogation can determine the outcome. Interrogations that occur for extended periods of time cause stress and fatigue in the subject and may result in the suspect providing a false confession for the sole purpose of ending the process. Research has shown

---

40 Pincus, W. 2006. FBI role in terror probe questioned. *The Washington Post*, September 2, 2006. http://www.washingtonpost.com/wp-dyn/content/article/2006/09/01/AR2006090101764_pdf.html.

41 Thompson, P., and Baxter, S. 2006. Bizarre cult of Sears Tower "plotter." *The Sunday Times*, June 25, 2006. http://www.timesonline.co.uk/tol/news/world/article679075.ece.

42 Interestingly, these were the same methods the PIRA used to interrogate suspected informants and undercover agents.

that the average length of interrogations that produce false confessions was 16.3 hours.[43] According to Davis and O'Donahue, the exhaustion brought about by lengthy interrogations "may lead to greater interrogative suggestibility via deficits in speed of thinking, concentration, motivation, confidence, ability to control attention, and ability to ignore irrelevant or misleading information."[44] The Green Book provides operatives with information on interrogation practices so they can prepare for such an occurrence should they be captured by law enforcement agencies. If captured, the Green Book instructs, operatives are not to say anything to authorities, as the purpose of the interrogation is to obtain a confession.

Extreme methods of police interrogation are also used to elicit information and confessions. Some such methods include coercion, abuse, and torture. Coercion exploits the target's rational responses and seeks to influence them. This tactic may include the use of verbal threats. By contrast, torture consists of "the intentional infliction of extreme physical pain or psychological distress on a person, for such ends as inducing the betrayal of some cause or intimate, intimidating actual or potential opponents, or as an exercise of dominance or sadism simply for its own sake."[45] The essential elements of torture are pain, fear, and uncertainty.[46] For an action to be considered torture, a "deliberate infliction of great pain or some other intensely distressing affective state (fear, shame, disgust, and so forth) on an unwilling person" is required.[47] With torture, agencies seek to inflict or threaten pain so as to make the target of the torture provide information and/or a confession. In addition, to fit the criteria of torture, an individual must not be able to morally and/or legally resist his or her tormentor. Up until a Supreme Court ruling in 1999, the use of torture to elicit a confession during an investigation was sanctioned by the Israeli judiciary.[48]

There is currently no clear agreement in academic literature, legislation, and jurisdiction on the distinction "between torture, coercion, and manipulation, or whether such techniques as sleep and sensory deprivation, isolation, or prolonged questioning should count as forms of torture."[49] A common form of torture involves making the target an active participant in his or her own abuse. Consider Abu Ghraib prison, wherein detainees "were made to masturbate in front of jeering captors."[50]

---

[43] Drizin, S. A., and Leo, R. A. 2004. The problem of false confessions in the post-DNA world. *North Carolina Law Review* 82:949.

[44] Davis, D., and O'Donahue, W. 2003. The road to perdition: Extreme influence tactics in the interrogation room. In *Handbook of forensic psychology*, ed. W. O'Donahue, 957. New York: Basic.

[45] Sussman, D. 2005. What's wrong with torture? *Philosophy & Public Affairs* 33 (1): 2.

[46] Ibid., p. 10.

[47] Ibid., p. 5.

[48] Addicott, J. F. 2009, May 13. What went wrong: Torture and the office of legal counsel in the Bush Administration. *United States Senate Committee on the Judiciary*. http://www.judiciary. senate.gov/hearings/testimony.cfm?id=e655f9e2809e5476862f735da14945e6&wit_id=e655f9e2 809e5476862f735da14945e6-1-5.

[49] Sussman, D. 2005. What's wrong with torture? *Philosophy & Public Affairs* 33 (1): 1.

[50] Ibid., p. 22.

Torture also involves having "victims . . . stand, or maintain contorted postures ('stress positions') for prolonged periods of time."[51] Additionally, torture tactics include physical torture (e.g., beatings, kicking, punching, burning by cigarette, and twisting of limbs), psychological torture (e.g., verbal threats, sleep deprivation, poor food quality, and continuous noise) and humiliation.[52] The same methods have been considered as "torture lite" by different countries and organizations. Specifically, certain "journalists, military intelligence personnel, and academics . . . distinguish between two kinds of torture: *torture*, which is violent, . . . cruel and brutal, and *torture lite*, which refers to interrogation methods that are, it is claimed, more restrained and less severe than real torture."[53] Torture lite includes

> a range of techniques that, unlike more traditional forms of torture, do not physically mutilate the victim's body. Such techniques commonly include extended sleep deprivation, forced standing (also known as stress positions), isolation, manipulation of heat and cold, noise bombardment, personal humiliation, and mock execution.[54]

Torture lite has also been described as "enhanced interrogation techniques," though the latter includes tactics that would not fit the description of torture lite. Some forms of enhanced interrogation techniques include[55]

- *Attention Grab.* During the interview, the interrogator grabs the suspect by the front of the shirt and shakes them.
- *Attention Slap.* During the interview, the interrogator uses an open hand slap on the suspect's face to cause him or her pain and trigger fear.
- *Belly Slap.* During the interview, the interrogator uses an open hand slap on the suspect's belly, which is aimed to cause significant pain but no external injuries. Punches are not authorized as medical personnel have warned that internal injury could occur.
- *Long Time Standing.* Interrogators force detainees to stand while handcuffed and shackled to the floor for more than 40 hours. The exhaustion and sleep deprivation that results from the use of this technique is said to yield confessions; however, authentic confessions are not often (if at all) achieved.
- *Cold Cell.* Detainees are left to stand naked in a cell whose temperature is about 50 degrees Fahrenheit. Periodically, the detainee is doused with cold water.

---

[51] Ibid.

[52] Sinn Fein/Irish Republican Army. 1979. *Green Book*. Belfast, Ireland.

[53] Wolfendale, J. 2009. The myth of "torture lite." *Ethics and International Affairs* 23 (1): 47.

[54] Ibid., pp. 47–48.

[55] Ross, B., and Esposito, R. 2005, November 18. CIA's harsh interrogation techniques described. http://abcnews.go.com/Blotter/Investigation/story?id=1322866.

- *Waterboarding.* Detainees are immobilized and water is poured over their face while lying down, simulating drowning. Khalid Sheikh Mohammed was subjected to this technique.

The International Committee of the Red Cross (ICRC) reported that using the following methods of coercion in a routine and systematic way to extract information from a suspect was tantamount to torture:[56] suffocation by water; hoodings, which were sometimes implemented in conjunction with beatings and/or exposure to loud noise and music; slapping, punching, kicking, and beatings with hard objects; handcuffing naked prisoners to bars in dark and completely bare cells; exposure to cold temperature in cells and interrogation rooms; confinement in a box to severely restrict movement; sleep deprivation; restriction and deprivation of food; and threats of ill-treatment and reprisals against families. The courts, however, have yet to find that the treatment of suspected terrorists during interrogations amounted to torture. Consider the treatment of Provisional Irish Republican Army sympathizers by British police and security services. The European Court of Human Rights (Strasbourg Court) held that the actions of British police and security services toward PIRA sympathizers did not amount to torture.[57] The Strasbourg Court did, however, rule that these individuals were subjected to inhumane and degrading treatment.[58] The jurisprudence of the Strasbourg Court reveals that the difference between "torture" and "inhumane and degrading treatment" is the amount of suffering and pain experienced, where as torture comprises the deliberate infliction of inhumane treatment that causes severe and cruel pain and suffering.

All of the above tactics have been used by democratic countries such as the United States. Specifically, suspected terrorists were subjected to "water-boarding, false burial, 'Palestinian hanging' (where the prisoner is suspended by his arms, manacled behind his back), being left naked in a cold cell and doused with cold water, and being made to stand forty hours while shackled to a cell floor."[59] In 2004, a U.S. Army report noted 94 cases of confirmed or possible detainee abuse in Iraq.[60] Similarly, in 2006, "an Army spokesman reported more than 600 accusations of detainee abuse in Iraq and Afghanistan since October 2001 and disciplinary actions against 251 soldiers."[61] Memoranda of the Department of Defense and the policies of Donald Rumsfeld justified the use of aggressive interrogative techniques against suspected terrorists by vehemently claiming that these tactics

---

[56] International Committee of the Red Cross. 2007, February 14. *Report on the treatment of fourteen "high value detainees" in CIA Custody*, 7–8. http://www.nybooks.com/media/doc/2010/04/22/icrc-report.pdf.

[57] *Ireland v. The United Kingdom* (App. No. 5310/71) (1978) 2 EHRR.

[58] Ibid.

[59] Kutz, C. 2007. Torture, necessity and existential politics. *California Law Review* 95 (1): 235–236.

[60] White, J., and Higham, S. 2004. Army calls abuses "aberrations." *The Washington Post*, July 23, 2004. http://www.washingtonpost.com/wp-dyn/articles/A7124-2004Jul22.html.

[61] Dycus, S., Berney, A. L., Banks, W. C., and Raven-Hansen, P. 2007. *National security law*. New York: Aspen, 763.

do not constitute torture. Available reports also refer to the treatment of detainees as abuse and not torture.

This distinction was made because torture violates domestic and international law. Specifically, according to Article 1 of the UN Convention Against Torture and Other Cruel, Inhuman or Degrading Treatment or Punishment, torture refers to

> any act by which severe pain or suffering, whether physical or mental, is intentionally inflicted on a person for such purposes as obtaining from him or a third person information or a confession, punishing him for an act he or a third person has committed or is suspected of having committed, or intimidating or coercing him or a third person, or for any reason based on discrimination of any kind, when such pain or suffering is inflicted by or at the instigation of or with the consent or acquiescence of a public official or other person acting in an official capacity. It does not include pain or suffering arising only from, inherent in, or incidental to lawful sanctions.

Article 2(2) of this convention further states that "no exceptional circumstances whatsoever, whether a state of war or a threat of war, internal political instability or any other public emergency, may be invoked as a justification of torture." Torture is also prohibited in human rights instruments. Article 5 of the Universal Declaration on Human Rights, Article 7 of the International Covenant on Civil and Political Rights, Article 3 of the European Convention on Human Rights, and Article 5(2) of the American Convention on Human Rights state that "no one shall be subjected to torture or to inhuman or degrading treatment or punishment." In a time of war, human rights conventions allow for the derogation of certain rights. However, the right to be free from torture and inhumane and degrading treatment is an absolute right; it is nonderogable, even in a time of war. Similar to the UN Convention on Torture, this is explicitly stated in other human rights instruments. A case in point is Article 15(2) of the European Convention on Human Rights, which states that even during a time of war or other crisis threatening the life of the nation no derogation of Article 3 shall be made.

To avoid violating the law by torturing prisoners themselves, some countries have opted to torture terrorists through the practice of extraordinary rendition. Here, suspected terrorists are sent to countries whose security services are known to engage in torture. The most common destinations for detainees to be extradited are Egypt, Jordan, Syria, and Morocco.[62] Egypt's notorious secret police, *Mukhabarat*, even had a reputation for their brutality. For instance, principal methods of the torture used in Egypt "included victims being: stripped and blindfolded; suspended from a ceiling or doorframe with feet just touching the floor; beaten with fists, whips, metal rods, or other objects; subjected to electrical shocks; and doused with cold water."[63] Examples of suspected terrorists extradited to these countries

---

[62] Mayer, J. 2005. Outsourcing torture: The secret history of America's "extraordinary rendition" program. *The New Yorker*, February 14, 2005, p. 106.

[63] U.S. Department of State. 2004, February 2004. 2003 country reports on human rights practices: Egypt. *Bureau of Democracy, Human Rights, and Labor.* http://www.state.gov/g/drl/rls/hrrpt /2003/27926.htm.

abound. Consider Maher Arar, a Canadian engineer who was born in Syria. He was detained on his way to Canada upon returning from a vacation with this his family to Tunisia. While detained, American authorities questioned him about his possible links with terrorist suspects. He was subsequently flown to Jordan and driven to Syria. During his interrogation, he was beaten and detained in a basement cell with no windows for approximately a year. What led to his capture, interrogation, torture, and detention was his association with someone who authorities believed was associated with al-Qaeda.

Others argue for the use of torture because they believe it works in obtaining valuable information and eliciting confessions for illicit activities. Following the death of Osama bin Laden in May 2011, many reports surfaced that the vital piece of intelligence that led authorities to his hideout (i.e., the name of his courier) was obtained from authorities' use of torture on Khalid Sheikh Mohammed, who was waterboarded 183 times.[64] This, however, is incorrect. Khalid Sheikh Mohammed did not ever reveal such information while being tortured. He revealed this information only after a significant period of time had passed from the final time he was tortured.

The use of torture is considered a choice between two evils. Here, torture can be justified if it is the only way to prevent a greater evil from occurring to others. The ticking time bomb hypothesis is brought forward as the primary justification for torture. Specifically, the ticking time bomb hypothesis involves the following scenario: a government has detained an individual who has knowledge of an imminent terrorist attack—for example, a bomb that will go off in the next couple of hours in a major city in the United States. The ticking time bomb hypothesis depicts the threat as being so extensively severe, if materialized, that failing to do something is completely unacceptable. Moreover, agencies know (not suspect) that the person in custody knows the location of the bomb. This type of situation, however, does not reflect reality. Many of the individuals who are detained may or may not be terrorists and may or may not know about a planned terrorist attack. Basically, in situations in which torture is used, the torturer does not know with certainty that the subject of the torture has the information that is sought. Accordingly, in cases in which the target of the torture is innocent and/or does not have the information sought, the only way that the torture will stop is to provide the torturer with the information or confession that is sought. Individuals who are tortured tend to tell the torturer whatever they believe the torturer wants to hear. In so doing, they falsely incriminate themselves of whatever the torturer is accusing them of.

In reality, torture is a notoriously unreliable method of gaining intelligence, and it is counterproductive as it undermines respect for authority. As a matter of fact, the use of torture led to false information that was later used to justify the war in Iraq. The person tortured in this instance was Ibn al-Sheikh al-Libi. He was subjected to extraordinary rendition and sent to Egypt. According to reports, he was waterboarded and forced to remain standing overnight in a cold cell while

---

64 Shane, S., and Savage, C. 2011. Bin Laden raid revives debate on value of torture. *New York Times*. http://www.nytimes.com/2011/05/04/us/politics/04torture.html?_r=1.

being repeatedly doused with icy water.[65] Specifically, Ibn al-Sheikh al-Libi had informed interrogators that Saddam Hussein was training al-Qaeda members to use chemical weapons. This information was then used to legitimate the preemptive war against Iraq.

To date, no evidence exists that information obtained from interrogations that involve torture is reliable.[66] In addition, in summarizing existing research on torture survivors, Basoglu concluded that torture "generates intense hatred and desire for vengeance against the perpetrators, radicalizing even ordinary people with no strong political views."[67] Survivors of torture have also stated that they would have said anything to have the torture end.[68] In his interviews with the International Committee of the Red Cross, Khalid Sheikh Mohammed stated that

> [d]uring the harshest period of my interrogation . . . I gave a lot of false information in order to satisfy what I believed the interrogators wished to hear in order to make the ill-treatment stop. . . . I'm sure that the false information I was forced to invent . . . wasted a lot of their time and led to several false red-alerts being placed in the U.S.[69]

Information and evidence obtained through torture can significantly hamper an investigation, as it is excluded from criminal courts during prosecution. In the U.S. court system, all evidence obtained would be excluded based on the fruit of the poisonous tree doctrine[70] if it is proven that the confession from torture was the only reason that the evidence was obtained. Accordingly, torture undermines efforts to incarcerate terrorists by way of the criminal justice system. Nevertheless, alternative approaches have been taken to deal with terrorism, such as preventive detention.

History has shown that interrogators' use of coercion, abuse, and torture to elicit confessions and obtain information have resulted in significant miscarriages of justice. Consider the Guildford Four, Maguire Seven, and Birmingham Six. In these cases, British law enforcement agencies were willing to employ whatever

---

65 Malinowski, T. 2008. Restoring moral authority: Ending torture, secret detention, and the prison at Guantanamo Bay. *The ANNALS of the American Academy of Political and Social Science* 618:152.

66 Costanzo, M., Gerrity, E., and Lykes, M. 2007. Psychologists and the use of terror in interrogations. *Analyses of Social Issues and Public Policy* 7:7–20.

67 Basoglu, M. 2009. A multivariate contextual analysis of torture and cruel, inhuman, and degrading treatments: Implications for an evidence-based definition of torture. *American Journal of Orthopsychiatry* 79:142.

68 McCoy, A. 2006. *A question of torture: CIA interrogation, from the cold war to the war on terror.* New York: Metropolitan /Henry Holt.

69 Danner, M. 2009, April 9. US torture: Voice from the Black Sites. *New York Review of Books.* http://www.nybooks.com/articles/archives/2009/apr/09/us-torture-voices-from-the-black-sites /?pagination=false&printpage=true.

70 The U.S. Supreme Court created the fruit of the poisonous tree doctrine in *Silverthorne Lumber Co. v. United States* 251 US 385 (1920).

tactic was believed necessary to obtain confessions.[71] These tactics were made possible by the Prevention of Terrorism Act of 1974, which provided police with expansive powers.

The Guilford Four (Paul Michael Hill, Gerard "Gerry" Conlon, Patrick "Paddy" Armstrong, and Carole Richardson) were convicted of bombing two Guildford pubs, which were popular with British Army personnel. The bombings, which occurred in October 1974, resulted in 5 deaths and 65 wounded. During the interrogation of the Guildford Four, police used coercive tactics to obtain confessions from them such as intimidation, threats of causing harm to family members, and torture. The Prevention of Terrorism Act of 1974 enabled these individuals to be held without charge for up to a week. By the end of the week, and after being continuously subjected to these coercive tactics, all had confessed to committing these bombings. However, there was no real evidence that these individuals were members of the Provisional Irish Republican Army or that they had conducted these attacks. Despite this, they were all sentenced to life imprisonment. In addition, Gerry Conlon and Paul Hill had alibis to account for their whereabouts during the bombings. However, the prosecutor purposely hid these alibis from the defense. In 1989, after several appeals, their convictions were reversed and the Guildford Four were freed.

During the investigations of the Guildford Four bombings, police raided Anne Maguire's home in London on December 3, 1974, and found nitroglycerine. Subsequently, the Maguire Seven (Anne Maguire, Patrick Maguire, Patrick Maguire Jr., Vincent Maguire, Sean Smyth, Patrick O'Neill, and Patrick "Guiseppe" Conlon) were convicted of handling explosives that were allegedly being provided to the Provisional Irish Republican Army. The sentences they received ranged from 5 to 14 years imprisonment. Guiseppe Conlon, the father of Gerry Conlon of the Guildford Four, died in prison while serving his sentence. In 1991, the prison sentences of the Maguire Seven were quashed after it was revealed that the London Metropolitan police had beaten some of the defendants into confessing and withheld vital information that would have cleared them from the charges.

The Birmingham pub bombings occurred on November 21, 1974. Explosive devices were detonated in two central pubs of Birmingham, England, killing 21 individuals and injuring 182. The Birmingham Six (Hugh Callaghan, Patrick Joseph Hill, Gerard Hunter, Richard McIlkenny, William Power, and John Walker) were accused of carrying out the attack. During interrogations, they were threatened, beaten, tortured, and subjected to mock executions by the police. After approximately 16 years of imprisonment, their sentences were quashed when evidence surfaced that their written confessions were altered by the police and that the forensic evidence presented in court, which the prosecution stated proved without a shadow of a doubt that the defendants handled explosives, was inaccurate.[72] The

---

71 Lutz, B. J., Ulmschneider, G. W., and Lutz, J. M. 2002. The trial of the Guildford Four: Government error or government persecution. *Terrorism and Political Violence* 14 (4): 123.

72 1991: Birmingham Six Freed After 16 Years. 1991. *BBC News*, March 14, 1991. http://news .bbc.co.uk/onthisday/hi/dates/stories/march/14/newsid_2543000/2543613.stm.

cases of the Guildford Four, Maguire Seven, and Birmingham Six clearly indicate the problems associated with using torture and any means that authorities deem necessary to elicit a confession. These cases show the miscarriages of justice that can occur when using these tactics.

Despite the lack of evidence that torture produces quality intelligence, arguments have been brought forward calling for the legalization of torture.[73] Other scholars are against torture on moral grounds but believe that an absolute ban on torture is unachievable. Specifically, such individuals believe that there should be an absolute ban on torture while allowing for *ex post facto* ratification in emergency situations. Cases in point are Richard Posner and Oren Gross, who believe that torture can be justified in exceptional circumstances.[74] Here, torture could not be used unless judicial and executive officers believe that compelling evidence exists as to its necessity. Alan Dershowitz believed that the problem with torture was not that it was being used but that it was currently being employed without accountability and oversight.[75] To remedy this situation, he proposed that a judicial torture warrant should be available. Posner, however, argued that the warrant may not bring more accountability and transparency to the process. In particular, individuals seeking the warrant may embellish the truth, and judges may not want to place themselves in the position of allowing a catastrophic attack to occur (at least in the eyes of the public) because they did not approve a torture warrant.

While the use of torture and coercive tactics has no proven effectiveness, other measures have succeeded in eliciting valuable intelligence and truthful confessions. Indeed, softer interrogation approaches such as developing rapport with suspected terrorists have been effective in past terrorism cases. The FBI interrogation guidelines call for the use of rapport building and actually forbid the use of torture.[76] After 9/11, authorities dismissed this approach as being too time-consuming, stressing the need to obtain intelligence as quickly as possible due to the nature and prevalence of the threat. In light of this, other measures were sought, regardless of their limited reliability.

Nonetheless, the good practices of policing are those that should be followed by countries worldwide in the fight against terrorism. In the face of the current threat posed by al-Qaeda and those inspired by them, the United States should train its undercover agents in the Arabic language and culture. More emphasis should be placed on the use and training of agents as undercover operatives to

---

[73] Lewis, A. 2004. Making torture legal. *The New York Review of Books*, June 15, 2004, pp. 4–8 cited in Sussman, D. 2005. What's wrong with torture? *Philosophy & Public Affairs* 33 (1): 2.

[74] Posner, R. A. 2006. Torture, terrorism, and interrogation. In *Torture: A collection*, ed. S. Levinson. Oxford, UK: Oxford University Press; Gross, O. 2006. The prohibition on torture and the limits of the law. In *Torture: A collection*, ed. S. Levinson. Oxford, UK: Oxford University Press.

[75] Dershowtiz, A. M. 2002. *Why terrorism works: Understanding the threat, responding to the challenge.* New Haven, CT: Yale University Press.

[76] Sevastopulo, D. 2008. FBI concerns on prisoner abuse "ignored." *Financial Times*, May 20, 2008. http://www.ft.com/cms/s/0/0cd821a8-26ba-11dd-9c95-000077b07658.html#axzz1X2sYUB12.

not only infiltrate the groups and cells located within the United States but also to place them in strategic areas where weapons and explosive materials and devices are sold for terrorists' use. Special attention should also be paid online as the investigations of several terrorist attacks (executed and prevented) revealed that the perpetrators used the Internet to communicate with al-Qaeda operatives and supporters in order to gain information on how to create explosives and conduct a terrorist attack. These tactics should be used because not only are they in accordance with domestic and international laws, but they also work. These methods have been used to successfully detect, prevent, investigate, and prosecute terrorists both within and outside the United States. The tactics that should be avoided are improper interrogation techniques and torture, which are illegal and often lead to misleading information. Indeed, extreme methods of police interrogation tend to elicit false confessions from suspected terrorists. To be effective, interrogations need to be geared toward eliciting the truth rather than securing a confession. If, as governments claim, time is of the essence in terrorism-related investigations, then authorities should not waste their time and resources on tactics that have, more often than not, proven ineffective.

HYPOTHETICAL SCENARIO

On February 3, 2012, at Rockefeller Center in New York City, five female suicide bombers detonated explosives in their backpacks. The attack killed 50 individuals and injured over 100. The police were the first responders to the scene.

1. What are the responsibilities of the police?
2. What can be done to minimize the impact of the attack?

CHAPTER SUMMARY

Counterterrorism has become an integral part of policing. For some countries, this shift occurred prior to 9/11, due to the domestic terrorist groups within their borders. For others, like the United States, law enforcement authorities played a more prominent role in counterterrorism after the attacks on September 11, 2001.

Human intelligence programs were predominately used by police to recruit informants and infiltrate terrorist organizations. Undercover agents, agent provocateurs, and supergrasses were also used to gain insight into the identities of terrorists and the inner workings of terrorist organizations. However, the testimony of informants and supergrasses may not be reliable.

Police have interrogated suspects to obtain information and elicit confessions. Even though it is illegal, torture has been used during interrogations. To engage in such tactics, governments have claimed that their activities do not amount to torture. In addition, to avoid being accused of torturing suspected terrorists, countries have engaged in extraordinary rendition practices. Nevertheless, human rights conventions on torture can be violated not only when a country engages in torture but also when that country deports terrorist suspects to third-party countries that are known to engage in torture. Regardless, extraordinary rendition became a common practice after 9/11, as many terrorist suspects were sent to countries that were well known for engaging in torture.

The information that is obtained through torture and aggressive interrogation techniques cannot be trusted. Individuals subjected to these methods fabricate information in an effort to stop the pain inflicted upon them. Intelligence obtained from such tactics also unnecessarily wastes governments' time and resources. Instead, counterterrorism efforts should focus on tactics that have successfully worked in the past, such as interrogation practices that focus on rapport building; the placement of informants in key areas to detect terrorist activity; and the utilization of trained undercover agents to infiltrate terrorist networks.

REVIEW QUESTIONS

1. What role do police officers have in counterterrorism?
2. If a terrorist attack occurs, what tasks are the police responsible for?
3. What are the differences between agent provocateurs, informants, and supergrasses?
4. What problems arise when relying on an informant's testimony to prosecute a suspected terrorist?
5. Why are interrogations important in counterterrorism?
6. Is torture justified?
7. Is the information obtained by torture reliable? Why or why not?

chapter nine

Preventive Detention: Lock Them Up and Throw Away the Key

This chapter examines the widespread use of preventive detention as a method of dealing with terrorists. The particular emphasis of this chapter will be on the countries using this tactic and the groups on which they used this counterterrorism tactic. Guantanamo Bay and its legitimacy will also be explored. The main motivating questions of this chapter are: Is preventive detention anathema to the rule of law? What can we learn from the historical use of this tactic in various countries around the world? What are the repercussions of using this tactic against terrorists? Is preventive detention an effective measure?

INCAPACITATION: A FORM OF COUNTERTERRORISM

Incapacitating terrorists allows governments to take them out of circulation. Essentially, it reduces the effects of terrorism in society not by altering either the terrorists or the environment but by rearranging the distribution of terrorists in society. This, in consequence, protects society from these terrorists. In some cases, during such incapacitation, rehabilitation efforts occur, which have been promoted by countries that implement it as an effective counterterrorism measure that reduces terrorists' long-term capacity to engage in terrorist attacks.

Incapacitation is a form of punishment. Usually, offenders are incapacitated after they have been convicted of a crime. There are, however, certain exceptions to this. The jurisprudence of U.S. courts reveals that detention prior to trial or without trial should be carefully limited.[1] Accordingly, preventive detention is authorized only in the narrowest of circumstances in which procedural safeguards are in place to ensure that such a measure is absolutely necessary. Public interest arguments are often promoted to justify the use of preventive detention. The government can detain a person prior to conviction if he or she is considered a flight risk and/or a danger to others. Also, a person who is mentally unstable can be detained if he or she presents a danger to the public. In addition, a juvenile who poses a danger to the community can be detained until trial. Moreover, a government may detain an alien they deem to be potentially dangerous while deportation proceedings are pending. Furthermore, in times of war or insurrection, governments can detain individuals believed to be dangerous to society.

An exception to incapacitation postconviction is pre-charge detention. Pre-charge detention differs according to the offense one is suspected of having committed. For terrorists, the maximum period of detention before charge varies from country to country. Consider the United Kingdom, where the procedures for the arrest and detention of terrorist suspects are included in Section 41 and Schedule 8 of the Terrorism Act of 2000. Pursuant to this act, the maximum period of detention for terrorist suspects is 28 days. The length of pre-charge detention has been justified on the grounds that post-arrest evidence gathering in connection with the terrorism offense usually takes a considerable amount of time and resources.[2]

Nevertheless, the 28-day period given has rarely been used by authorities. According to UK Home Office minister Hazel Blears, between January 20, 2004 and September 4, 2005, a total of 357 people were arrested under the Terrorism Act of 2000, of whom 36 had been held for more than seven days.[3] Even though a 14-day period for detaining suspects without charge was in effect at the time, 321 (out of 357) suspects were charged in less than eight days. Therefore, as Home Office ministers argued, the "full 14-day detention period under the Criminal Justice Act 2003, which came into force on 20 January 2004, is rarely used."[4] In spite of these figures, the period of pre-charge detention was extended from 14 days to 28 days under the Terrorism Act of 2006. This act initially sought to extend

---

[1] *United States v. Salerno et al*, 481 U.S. 739, 755 (1987); *United States v. Melendez-Carrion*, 790 F.2d 984, 1000-1001(2d Cir. 1986).

[2] UK Home Office. 2011, January. *Review of counter-terrorism and security powers: Review findings and recommendations*, 7–8. http://www.homeoffice.gov.uk/publications/counter-terrorism /review-of-ct-security-powers/review-findings-and-rec?view=Binary.

[3] These statistics were provided to the Home Office by the police. Hansard HC vol 437 col 501W (October 12, 2005). http://www.publications.parliament.uk/pa/cm200506/cmhansrd/vo051012 /text/51012w07. htm#51012w07.html_spnew1.

[4] Peck, M. 2005, October 20. The Terrorism Bill 2005–2006. *HC Library Research Paper* 05/66, 39. http://www.parliament.uk/commons/lib/research/rp2005/rp05-066.pdf.

pre-charge detention for up to 90 days, but a last minute compromise was made that restricted detention to 28 days.[5] To date, only

> 11 individuals have been held for over 14 days pre-charge detention—nine were arrested in Operation Overt (the so-called "transatlantic airline plot" in 2006), one in . . . a Manchester-based arrest in 2006 . . . and one in Operation Seagram (the London Haymarket and Glasgow airport attacks in 2007). Six of these 11 people were held for the maximum 27–28 days: three were charged, three [were] released without charge.[6]

Given that for the majority of the detainees the full 14-day detention period was not used, the extension of pre-charge detention from 14 to 28 days seems to exceed that which is ordinarily useful for law enforcement purposes. Other countries, however, do not have such an extensive period of pre-charge detention (see Table 9-1).

In addition, in some countries, terrorists are treated differently than ordinary criminals. A case in point is France, wherein suspected terrorists in custody are allowed to contact a lawyer only after 48 hours. In some cases, an extension may be given to the police to prevent the suspect's access to a lawyer for 72 hours. The attorney is not provided with the case file prior to the meeting and is allowed to meet with the detainee for only 30 minutes. In contrast, for the majority of detainees suspected of crimes other than terrorism in France, access to a lawyer is given to the suspect upon request.

Another exception to incapacitation after conviction is preventive detention. Incapacitation and preventive detention similarly seek to protect the public from offenders and prevent future offending behavior. However, there are stark differences between them, not in terms of their purpose, but in terms of the circumstances in which they are used. Preventive detention occurs before someone has been charged and/or convicted of a crime. It constitutes "a deprivation of liberty that is based on a prediction of harmful conduct which is not time-limited by culpability or other considerations."[7] Here, individuals are detained because they are suspected of having committed a crime or are suspected of seeking to commit a crime sometime in the future. On the surface, this seems like a desirable approach to dealing with terrorists, especially because it seeks to preempt a terrorist attack by preventing it from taking place rather than responding to it after the fact. However, as this chapter will show, this process is fraught with accountability and transparency issues. In the post-9/11 world, an inclination to jettison human rights has been observed; the most prevalent measure with which to do so has been the

---

[5] Smith, A. 2007. Balancing liberty and security? A legal analysis of United Kingdom anti-terrorist legislation. *European Journal of Criminal Policy Research* 13 (1/2): 78.

[6] UK Home Office. 2011, January. *Review of counter-terrorism and security powers: Review findings and recommendations*, 8. http://www.homeoffice.gov.uk/publications/counter-terrorism/review-of-ct-security-powers/review-findings-and-rec?view=Binary.

[7] Slobogin, C. 2003. A jurisprudence of dangerousness. *Northwestern University Law Review*. 98(1): 2.

Table 9-1 Pre-Charge Detention for Terrorists: A Comparison Between Certain Countries

Country	Pre-Charge Detention (Maximum)
United States	2 days*
Canada	1 day
South Africa	2 days
United Kingdom	28 days
Ireland	7 days**
France	6 days
Germany	2 days
Italy	4 days
Spain	5 days
Denmark	3 days
Norway	3 days
Sweden	4 days
Russia	5 days
Turkey	7 days
Australia	1 day***
New Zealand	2 days

*An exception to this are individuals suspected of terrorism that have been detained pursuant to executive war powers and immigration law and are dealt with outside of the criminal justice system in the United States.

**Usually, for terrorism cases the maximum is 3 days; however, if gangland-type of activity is involved, the period of pre-charge detention can be extended to 7 days.

***Australia allows for 14-days of preventive detention for terrorist suspects; yet, this differs from pre-charge detention because during preventive detention a suspect cannot be questioned.

liberal use of preventive, indefinite detention on those suspected (and not convicted) of terrorism.

THE LEGALITY OF PREVENTIVE DETENTION

The prohibition of indefinite or arbitrary detention exists in international human rights instruments. For example, it is explicitly included in Article 9 of the Universal Declaration of Human Rights[8] and Article 7(3) of the American Convention on Human Rights.[9] In addition, it is included in Article 147 of the Geneva Convention, which holds that the "willful deprivation of the rights of [a] fair and regular trial" are a grave breach of the convention, and Article 9(1) of the International Covenant on Civil and Political Rights (ICCPR), which states: "Everyone has the

---

[8] Article 9 of the Universal Declaration of Human Rights states that "no one shall be subjected to arbitrary arrest, detention or exile."

[9] Article 7(3) of the American Convention on Human Rights states that "no one shall be subject to arbitrary arrest or imprisonment."

Box 9-1 Terror Interrupted: Foiled Plots in the United Kingdom

Operation Overt

In the summer of 2006 in London, authorities foiled a terrorist plot to blow up the planes of three major U.S. airlines (United, American, and Continental) over the UK and the United States.[1] The individuals implicated in this plot were UK citizens: Abdullah Ahmed Ali, Assad Sarwar, Tanvir Hussain, Umar Islam, Arafat Waheed Khan, Waheed Zaman, and Ibrahim Savant. Upon arrest and search of their property, multiple martyrdom videos were found with the perpetrators depicted in them. These individuals were under surveillance by the police and MI5 for approximately 1 year. The terrorists' conversations were recorded. During these conversations, these terrorists discussed how to smuggle bomb components onto an airplane and the potential use of babies to smuggle liquid explosives onto the plane via their bottles so as to avoid attention by authorities. Terrorists were to carry explosive ingredients disguised as beverages and detonators made out of common electronic devices such as mobile phones and music players. Authorities believed that they were planning to smuggle chemicals on board that could combine into an explosive mixture but that are innocuous if carried separately.

Operation Seagram

Operation Seagram involved a wide-ranging international investigation into the 2007 Glasgow and London car bombs. In Glasgow, Kafeel Ahmed (driver) and Bilal Abdulla (passenger) crashed their vehicle into the international airport's Terminal 1 with the intention of causing an explosion.[2] Instead of an explosion, a fire ensued. The last terrorist attack to have taken place in Scotland prior to this event was the Lockerbie bombing in 1988, in which Pan Am Flight 103 crashed following the detonation by terrorists of an onboard bomb while the aircraft was in flight.

In London, two car bombs were discovered 1 day prior to the Glasgow terrorist attack in the Haymarket area of London. These bombs were isolated and defused before they could be detonated. It was believed that Ahmed and Abdulla assembled these car bombs as well. Ahmed was severely burned and eventually died from the injuries he sustained in the Glasgow attack; Abdulla was tried and convicted of conspiracy to commit murder, receiving a 32-year prison sentence.

---

[1] Oliver, M., and Batty, D. 2006. Mass murder terror plot uncovered. *The Guardian*, August 10, 2006. http://www.guardian.co.uk/world/2006/aug/10/terrorism.politics.

[2] Leppard, D. et al. 2007. Biting back at terror suspects. *The Sunday Times*, July 8, 2007. http://www.timesonline.co.uk/tol/news/uk/crime/article2042409.ece.

right to liberty and security of person. No one shall be subjected to arbitrary arrest or detention. No one shall be deprived of his liberty except on such grounds and in accordance with such procedure as are established by law."

Those indefinitely detained have been denied the normal legal processes available to those suspected of crimes, such as the right to be informed of the evidence against them, the right to a speedy and public trial, and the right to an attorney. These rights, however, are included in constitutions, resolutions, and international human rights instruments. For instance, the Body of Principles for the Protection of All Persons under Any Form of Detention or Imprisonment, which was adopted by United Nations General Assembly Resolution 43/173 (December 9, 1988), provides that all detained persons are entitled to legal counsel (Principle 18). This right was reiterated in the UN Standard Minimum Rules for the Treatment of Prisoners, which claimed that legal counsel should be ensured to untried prisoners.[10] Most human rights instruments also require the prompt notification of an individual of the charges against him or her and that the individual be promptly brought before a judge.[11] This right is also included in Principle 10 of the UN General Assembly's Body of Principles for the Protection of All Persons under Any Form of Detention or Imprisonment.[12] In practice, however, the majority of countries have derogated from these instruments.

Countries can derogate from this right during an emergency that threatens the life of a nation. For example, Article 4(1) of the ICCPR holds that:

> In time of public emergency which threatens the life of the nation and the existence of which is officially proclaimed, the States Parties to the present Covenant may take measures derogating from their obligations under the present Covenant to the extent strictly required by the exigencies of the situation, provided that such measures are not inconsistent with their other obligations under international law and do not involve discrimination solely on the ground of race, colour, sex, language, religion or social origin.

To derogate from human rights instruments, certain steps must be taken. For instance, Article 4(3) of the ICCPR states that:

> Any State Party to the present Covenant availing itself of the right of derogation shall immediately inform the other States Parties to the present Covenant, through the intermediary of the Secretary-General of the United Nations, of the provisions from which it has derogated and of the reasons by which it was actuated. A further communication shall be made, through the same intermediary, on the date on which it terminates such derogation.

And yet, few countries that are signatories to human rights instruments have taken advantage of the provisions included within them that allow such derogation. Nevertheless, such derogations are not a new phenomenon; they have been used by countries worldwide both pre- and post-9/11.

---

[10] These standards were adopted by the First United Nations Congress on the Prevention of Crime and the Treatment of Offenders, which was held at Geneva in 1955. These standards were subsequently approved by the Economic and Social Council in the following Resolutions: 663 C (XXIV) of July 31, 1957 and 2076 (LXII) of May, 13 1977. It is available at http://www2.ohchr.org/english/law/treatmentprisoners.htm.

[11] See, for example, Article 9(2) and 9(3) of the ICCPR, Articles 5(2) and 5(3), European Convention on Human Rights and Article 10, Universal Declaration of Human Rights.

[12] UN General Assembly. 1988, December 9. *Body of principles for the protection of all persons under any form of detention or imprisonment* (A/RES/43/173). http://www.unhcr.org/refworld/docid/3b00f219c. html.

PREVENTIVE DETENTION: THEN

The term preventive detention has been used interchangeably with administrative detention, internment, indefinite detention, and arbitrary detention. Internment has been the term of choice to describe the detention of enemies during war or insurgencies. In the past, internment was often used by countries and deemed as a necessary measure during war or other situations that threatened the life of the nation. For example, internment was used by the United States during the Civil War and World War II. During World War II, in the wake of Japan's attack on Pearl Harbor, the President issued Executive Order 9066 (February 19, 1942), which authorized the Secretary of War to prescribe military areas from which any or all persons can be excluded. As a result, over 100,000 Japanese civilians, which included citizens and permanent resident aliens, were relocated from the West Coast and detained in housing known as "War Relocation Camps."[13] The Japanese internment officially ended in January 1945.

In times of war, nations such as the United States have had and used virtually unchecked executive power to detain individuals believed to be hostile to the nation. Indeed, the Supreme Court has approved nearly unrestrained executive power to detain enemy aliens during war.[14] The same holds true for Britain. During both World Wars, such unrestricted executive power was also observed with the enactment of Regulations 14B and 18B. Regulation 14B allowed the Home Secretary to imprison any individual who he believed threatened public security. Likewise, Regulation 18B gave the Home Secretary the power to detain a person to prevent actions detrimental to public safety and national defense. For both World Wars, Britain used the Isle of Man for the internment of enemy aliens.

Internment has also been used against terrorists. Here, individuals have been detained to prevent them from possibly committing crimes, such as terrorism, in the future. Britain used internment to deal with the Provisional Irish Republican Army. In 1970, terrorism violence had significantly intensified:

> The number of explosions recorded by the police jumped dramatically from a total of 8 in 1969 to 155 in 1970 . . . Between January and July 1971, the violence intensified, being marked by a dramatic upsurge in terrorist activity by the [P]IRA. Police statistics record[ed] a total of 304 explosions, including 94 for the one month of July.[15]

On August 9, 1971, the Prime Minister of Northern Ireland, Brian Faulkner, used the Civil Authorities (Special Powers) Act of 1922 to authorize the British Army and Royal Ulster Constabulary to engage in internment without trial of suspected terrorists.[16] By the time internment ended in 1975, approximately 2,000

---

13 National Park Service. 2007, January 8. *Personal justice denied: Report of the Commission on Wartime Relocation and Internment of Civilians.* http://www.nps.gov/history/history/online _books/personal_justice_denied/index.htm.

14 *Ludecke v. Watkins*, 335 U.S. 160 (1948).

15 *Ireland v. United Kingdom* (App No 5310/71) [1978] ECHR 1.

16 This was known as Operation Demetrius.

Irish Catholics had been detained in prison camps. This counterterrorism measure taken by Britain actually worked to the advantage of the Provisional Irish Republican Army because it increased recruitment and support for their group. This was largely attributed to the fact that many of those placed in internment were not actually members or associates of the PIRA. Accordingly, those who viewed the actions of Britain as unjust were more likely to sympathize with and advocate for the PIRA's cause. As such, the use of this measure by the British was soon found to be counterproductive and even beneficial to the PIRA's cause. In fact, the British Prime Minister, Edward Heath, later admitted that internment was a mistake and had provided the Provisional Irish Republican Army with "a way to recruit from amongst people who had been interned, and . . . proved impossible to stop."[17] A former British Intelligence officer, Frank Steele, who had served in Northern Ireland during internment also noted that this measure "barely damaged the [P]IRA's command structure and led to a flood of recruits, money and weapons."[18]

Israel has also engaged in such detention for suspected terrorists and those hostile to Israel. During the Palestinian uprising from 1987 to 1993 (the First Intifada) against Israel's occupation of Palestinian Territories, Israel detained thousands of Palestinians without charge or trial (some for months, others for years). This detention was pursuant to the powers afforded to a country during a declared state of emergency, which Israel has been in since 1948. In Israel, the legal basis for preventive detention is found in the Defense (Emergency) Regulations Act of 1945 and the Emergency Powers (Detention) Law of 1979. According to the Israeli Supreme Court, administrative detention (i.e., preventive detention) in Israel is lawful as long as the evidence that indicates that the suspect is involved in a plan for a future act of terrorism is timely, reliable, and credible.[19] Israel can issue a detention order pursuant to these laws, which authorizes the detention of an individual for up to 6 months; however, this detention can be renewed indefinitely. Other countries have comparable provisions. For instance, in Sri Lanka, a suspect can initially be detained for up to 72 hours. However, pursuant to the Prevention of Terrorism Act of 1979, the Defense Minister can issue an administrative order allowing the detention of an individual for up to 18 months without charge or trial.[20] In Italy, Sec. 625 of the 1979 Law (*Legge Cossiga*) made preventive detention for up to 12 years legal.

---

[17] Malinowski, T. 2009, June 10. The legal, moral, and national security consequences of "prolonged detention": Testimony of Tom Malinowski for the Senate Judiciary Subcommittee on the Constitution. *Human Rights Watch*. http://www.hrw.org/en/news/2009/06/10/legal-moral -and-national-security-consequences-prolonged-detention.

[18] Ibid.

[19] Criminal Appeal 6659/06, *Anonymous v. The State of Israel*, P.D. 54(1) 721 (2008) (Hebrew). The decision is available in English at: http://elyon1.court.gov.il/files_eng/06/590 /066/n04/06066590.n04.htm

[20] This act is still in effect, although it was temporarily suspended during the 2002 Ceasefire Agreement between Sri Lanka and the Tamil Tigers.

Not all forms of preventive detention are indefinite in nature. Other countries have exercised greater restraint with preventive detention. For instance, in the Philippines, preventive detention is allowed for only a limited period. Beyond that, the detention becomes illegal, and those responsible for the extension of the detention outside of the legal limits can be held liable under existing laws. The vast majority of nations, however, did not exercise this form of restraint post-9/11.

PREVENTIVE DETENTION: NOW

Predicting future acts of terrorism is no easy task; nor is predicting the future dangerousness of suspected terrorists. Future dangerousness is an inherently uncertain, subjective phenomenon. In fact, it is virtually impossible to accurately predict whether or not a particular suspected terrorist in detention will be a future threat to society. Yet in spite of this, countries worldwide have treated such assessments as an objective reality. Indeed, thousands of individuals are being detained around the world on mere suspicion of engaging in terrorism-related activities. In addition, many of these countries have domestic laws legitimizing the use of prolonged preventive detention without charge or trial.[21] Particular emphasis will be placed on the forms of preventive detention implemented in Malaysia, the United Kingdom, Australia, Sri Lanka, Saudi Arabia, Israel, and the United States.

Malaysia. This country not only has a law authorizing preventive detention but also liberally places suspected terrorists in prolonged confinement. As of December 2008, Malaysia had not prosecuted any of its detained terrorists. Instead, it used the Internal Security Act (ISA) of 1960 to detain terrorist suspects without bringing them to trial.[22] In 2009, it was reported that Malaysia used the ISA more cautiously and released 39 of its detainees.[23] Singapore similarly has an act with the same title, which allows the government to detain individuals without trial under specific, defined circumstances. The ISA system has been described as purely preventive.[24]

United Kingdom. In the United Kingdom, the Anti-Terrorism, Crime and Security Act of 2001 allowed for the removal or indefinite detention of foreign nationals who were suspected of terrorist activity. This practice of indefinite detention of foreign nationals suspected of terrorism, however, was found be unlawful.[25] In the wake of this finding by the House of Lords, the Control Order was introduced in Britain against those suspected of involvement in terrorism. A

---

[21] Some countries include Israel, Malaysia, Singapore, Sri Lanka, Bangladesh, Nigeria, Tanzania, and Pakistan.

[22] U.S. Department of State. 2009, April 30. Country reports on terrorism 2008. *Office of the Coordinator for Counterterrorism.* http://www.state.gov/s/ct/rls/crt/2008/122433.htm.

[23] U.S. Department of State. 2010, August. Country reports on terrorism 2009. *Office of the Coordinator for Counterterrorism*, 51. http://www.state.gov/documents/organization/141114.pdf.

[24] Human Rights Watch. 2005, September 26. *Detention without trial.* http://www.hrw.org/en /node /11608/section/2.

[25] The so-called "Belmarsh case." *A v. SSHD* [2004] UKHL 56.

Control Order is a civil preventative order that imposes "one or more obligations upon an individual which are designed to prevent, restrict or disrupt his or her involvement in terrorism-related activity."[26] Breach of this civil order carries with it a criminal penalty. Indeed, if such an order is violated, a person may receive up to 5 years of imprisonment.[27] With Control Orders, the UK Home Secretary has the power to impose serious restrictions on fundamental rights—right to privacy and freedom of movement, association, and expression—on those suspected of involvement in terrorism.[28] Specifically, the Home Secretary can impose house arrest, extensive curfews, restrictions on access (e.g., computers and/or communications equipment) and contact with personal associates, electronic tagging, and reporting requirements. Pursuant to the Prevention of Terrorism Act of 2005, an individual subjected to a Control Order "is not allowed to know about the evidence discussed in closed hearings or to give directions to the special advocate appointed by the court to defend his interests."[29] The Control Order, thus, affords the state the ability to impose restrictions on an individual suspected of terrorism without exposing intelligence to public scrutiny, which normally occurs if the person was prosecuted (see Box 9-2).

Australia. Like the United Kingdom, Australia has adopted preventive detention policies for terrorists. In addition, the UK Control Order has since been copied in Australia, where the Anti-Terrorism Act (No. 2) of 2005 authorized the use of Control Orders against individuals suspected of terrorism for the purpose of preventing them from engaging in terrorism-related activities. Australia has also introduced Preventive Detention Orders (PDOs) and Prohibited Contact Orders (PCOs) for terrorists. Pursuant to Section 105 of the Australian Criminal Code Act of 1995, PDOs can be issued by senior members of the Australian Federal Police against an individual suspected of terrorism in order to prevent an imminent attack or to preserve evidence that relates to a terrorist attack. There are, however, time restrictions to their use. An initial PDO can be used to detain a suspected terrorist for up to 24 hours. Subsequently, a continued PDO may be issued to extend the suspect's detention to a maximum of 48 hours. Another measure that can be used against suspected terrorists is the PCO. Senior members of the Australian Federal Police (or a current or ex-judicial officer) can issue a PCO that prohibits a person from contacting the individuals named in the order while he or she remains under preventive detention.[30]

---

[26] See the UK Home Office website http://security.homeoffice.gov.uk/counter-terrorism-strategy/legislation/pta/.

[27] See Section 9(4)(a) of the Prevention of Terrorism Act of 2005.

[28] Human Rights Watch. 2009, March 2. *UK: "Control orders" for terrorist suspects violate rights.* http://www.hrw.org/news/2009/03/01/uk-control-orders-terrorism-suspects-violate-rights.

[29] Ibid.

[30] Sections 105.14A, 105.15(1), 105.15(4), and 105.16(1) of the Australian Criminal Code Act of 1995.

Box 9-2   Food for Thought—Control Orders: A Violation of the Rule of Law?

The determination of whether or not a measure abides by the rule of law depends on its procedural and substantive conceptions. Legal positivists and natural law theorists disagree on their conceptions of the rule of law. Legal positivists (notably H. L. A. Hart), who hold a procedural view of the rule of law, believe that the question of what a law is should (and must) be kept separate from questions of what the law should be.[1] Legal positivism is a doctrine about the nature of law, wherein "the legal validity of a rule or decision depends on its sources (... where it has come from, and how, and when), rather than its merits (... whether or not it is a good rule or decision)."[2] As such, positivism does not view the actual content of the law itself or the necessary qualities of law, of "good" law (e.g., that it be respectful of rights), of the legal system, or of adjudication, as part of the determination as to whether or not a particular measure abides by the rule of law.[3] Instead, the rule of law is considered as "just one of the virtues by which a legal system may be judged and by which it is to be judged. It is not to be confused with democracy, justice, equality (before the law or otherwise), human rights of any kind or respect for persons or for the dignity of man."[4] However, this does not mean that those who subscribe to this view are not concerned with the content of the law. For them, the content of the law, "is a matter of substantive justice," where "substantive justice is an independent ideal, in no sense part of the ideal of the rule of law."[5] Thus, issues concerning the legality of a measure should be separated from the issues surrounding the determination of the actual content of the law in question.

The determination of whether a measure abides by the rule of law, according to this conception, requires the examination of the legal and procedural propriety of the law. Consider the Prevention of Terrorism Act of 2005 in the United Kingdom, in respect of which the government abided by the procedures for enacting this law (readings of the bill in Parliament and the passing of this bill through all of the appropriate channels of the legislative process). Accordingly, from a procedural perspective, this particular measure abides by the rule of law.

However, a substantive view of the rule of law would render a different result. Classical natural law theorists (most famously St. Thomas Aquinas), who hold a

---

[1] Hart, H. L. A. 1961. *The concept of law.* Oxford, UK: Clarendon.

[2] Dickson, J. 2007, January. Legal positivism: Laws and legal systems. In *Jurisprudence: A guide through the subject,* eds. J. Dickson et al., 4. University of Oxford, Faculty of Law. http://denning.law .ox.ac.uk/jurisprudence/guide.pdf.

[3] Craig, P. 1997. Formal and substantive conceptions of the rule of law: An analytical framework. *Public Law* (Autumn): 467; Jowell, J. 2004. The rule of law's long arm: Uncommunicated decisions. *Public Law* (Summer): 246.

[4] Raz, J. 1979. *The authority of law: Essays on law and morality.* Oxford, UK: Oxford University Press, 211.

[5] Dworkin, R. 1985. *A matter of principle.* Cambridge, MA: Harvard University Press, 11.

(continues)

Box 9-2　Food for Thought—Control Orders: A Violation of the Rule of Law? (continued)

substantive view of the rule of law, are identified with the motto "lex injusta non est lex" (an unjust law is not a law), "which appears to be a claim about the validity of laws."[6] Natural law theorists believe that it is impossible to talk about a "bad" (or "unjust" law). If a law is not a "good" law (a "just" law), then it is not law. By contrast, contemporary natural law theorists (notably John Finnis) believe that it is possible for a law to be unjust and still be a law. For them, moral reasons exist "for obeying even an unjust law: for example, if the law is part of a generally just legal system, and public disobedience of the law might undermine the system, there is a moral reason for at least minimal public compliance with the unjust law."[7] This conception goes beyond procedural propriety by stating that the laws themselves must be in substance in accordance with the rule of law. Therefore, the actual content of the law and whether or not it is a good law or a bad law is examined when determining whether or not a measure abides by the rule of law.[8] In contrast to the procedural perspective, this view does not distinguish between the notion of the rule of law and substantive justice.

Consider again the example of the Prevention of Terrorism Act of 2005, in respect of which the British government abided by the procedures for enacting the laws (passing the bill through all of the appropriate channels). Although from a procedural perspective this measure abides by the rule of law, from a substantive view this is not the case. Specifically, this act gives the UK Home Secretary the power to issue control orders (which range from restrictions on communications to house arrest) that severely restrict the liberty of individuals suspected of terrorism without any need for a trial prior to their imposition.[9] Ironically, in the case that led to the setting up of control orders, A and Others v. Secretary of State for the Home Department,[10] the House of Lords held that indefinite detention of foreign nationals suspected of terrorism was unlawful. As Lord Nicholls stated, "indefinite imprisonment without charge or trial is anathema in any country which observes the rule of law. It deprives the detained person of the protection a criminal trial is intended to afford."[11] While control orders replaced indefinite imprisonment, their severe restrictions on liberty amount almost to house arrest. The rule of law requires adherence to due process rights, including the right to a fair trial, "the presumption of innocence,

---

[6] Lamond, G. 2007, January. The natural law tradition. In *Jurisprudence: A guide through the subject*, eds. J. Dickson et al., 4. University of Oxford, Faculty of Law. http://denning.law.ox.ac.uk/jurisprudence/guide.pdf.

[7] Bix, B. 1996. *Jurisprudence: Theory and context*. London: Sweet and Maxwell, 73.

[8] Craig, P. 1997. Formal and substantive conceptions of the rule of law: An analytical framework. *Public Law*, 467.

[9] See ft. 79 in Zedner, L. 2005. Securing liberty in the face of terror: Reflections from criminal justice. *Journal of Law and Society* 32 (4): 523.

[10] *A and others v. Secretary of State for the Home Department* and *X and others v. Secretary of State for the Home Department* [2004] UKHL 56.

[11] Ibid., (opinions delivered on December 16, 2004, House of Lords Session 2004–2005), para. 74, p. 47. http://www.publications.parliament.uk/pa/ld200405/ldjudgmt/jd041216/a&others.pdf.

> **Box 9-2 Food for Thought—Control Orders: A Violation of the Rule of Law? (continued)**
>
> the prohibition on retrospective penalties and the guarantee of judicial impartiality and independence."[12] By failing to provide for a trial prior to the imposition of these orders, individuals' due process rights are considerably undermined. In so doing, it can be argued that these control orders violate the rule of law.
>
> 1. What other counterterrorism measures implemented in the war on terrorism violate the rule of law from a procedural perspective? From a substantive perspective?
>
> ----
>
> [12] Foster, S. 2003. *Human rights and civil liberties.* London: Longman, 13.

Sri Lanka. Sri Lanka has also engaged in preventive detention post-9/11. In fact, Human Rights Watch has charged Sri Lanka with violating the human rights of Tamil detainees by denying them the right to be informed of the charges against them, the right to legal counsel, and the right to trial.[31] In Sri Lanka, those illegally detained have numbered approximately 300,000.[32] Pursuant to the 2005 Emergency Regulations, suspected Tamil Tigers, or individuals connected to them in some way, who surrendered to the government were detained in a Protective Accommodation and Rehabilitation Center for up to 1 year (with the possibility of extension to 2 years). The courts have no authority to release detainees. Before individuals were placed in a detention center, they were screened by the government in military-run campuses known as "welfare centers." To determine whether or not individuals were affiliated with the Tamil Tigers, authorities relied on allegations made by individuals and paramilitary groups within the camps. The International Commission of Jurists contended that this screening and detention process lacks credibility, accountability, and transparency.[33] Instances of prisoner mistreatment have also been recorded. Over the years, Amnesty International, Human Rights Watch, and the Asian Human Rights Commission have reported instances of Sinhalese soldiers raping Tamil women and girls upon arrest or during detention.[34]

----

[31] Human Rights Watch. 2010, January 27. *Sri Lanka: President's new term time for accountability: UN Secretary-General should work for independent international investigation.* http://www.hrw.org/news/2010/01/27/sri-lanka-president-s-new-term-time-accountability.

[32] Human Rights Watch. 2009, June 11. *Sri Lanka: End illegal detention of displaced population.* http://www.hrw.org/en/news/2009/06/11/sri-lanka-end-illegal-detention-displaced-population.

[33] Immigration and Refugee Board of Canada. 2011, February 21. Sri Lanka: Treatment of suspected Liberation Tigers of Tamil Eelam (LTTE) members or supporters, including information about how many are in detention; whether the government continues to screen Tamils in an attempt to identify LTTE suspects (January 2010–21 January 2011). *United Nations High Commissioner for Refugees (UNHCR).* http://www.unhcr.org/ refworld/docid/4e43b8b32.html.

[34] Ibid.

Saudi Arabia. The UN Working Group on Arbitrary Detention has condemned the use of arbitrary and long-term administrative detention in Saudi Arabia,[35] which has certain laws in place that govern individual detention. According to Article 116 of the Law of Criminal Procedure, an individual must be promptly notified of the reasons for his detention. Additionally, Article 34 of the Law of Criminal Procedure stipulates that a detained individual must be informed of his charges within 48 hours of his arrest. Moreover, pursuant to Article 34 of the Law of Criminal Procedure, the detainee must also be brought to trial within 6 months of arrest or alternatively, if this does not occur, the person must be released. Despite the existence of this article, several cases have gone to the Saudi Board of Grievances for unlawful detention. Human Rights Watch provided several examples in a report on the counterterrorism practices of Saudi Arabia.[36] For instance, Tamir Muhammad al-Matrudi's son Imad was being detained without charge or trial since June 7, 2004, in the prison belonging to the General Directorate for Investigations (*mabahith*). Tamir successfully sued the *mabahith* to release his son, and the Saudi Board of Grievances ordered his release. However, in May 2009, Tamir contacted Human Rights Watch to complain that his son had yet to be released. A similar case involved Majid al-Husaini, whose father sought assistance from the Human Rights Watch because a ruling by the Saudi Board of Grievances was not being upheld by the *mabahith*.

Israel. The UN Working Group on Arbitrary Detention has also condemned the use of arbitrary and long-term administrative detention in Israel.[37] Preventive detention practices in Israel have also been condemned by human rights organizations. Specifically, in 2002, Israel introduced the Imprisonment of Illegal Combatants Law, which calls for measures that bear a striking resemblance to the United States' use of indefinite detention. Pursuant to this law, individuals can be detained based on suspicion that they are seeking to directly or indirectly attack Israel. The Chief of General Staff of the Israel Defense Forces issues the detention orders. In addition, this law criminalizes association with anyone engaged in hostile activity toward Israel. The law was upheld by Israel's Supreme Court by claiming that its infringement of detainee's rights was justified as it applied only to acts of terrorism against Israel. According to this law, detainees are considered a security risk and can be detained without charge or trial until the hostilities end. Given that Israel

---

35 The UN Working Group on Arbitrary Detention has further condemned the use of arbitrary and long-term administrative detention in several countries, including (but not limited to) Iraq, Iran, Israel, Egypt, Lebanon, Yemen, India, Pakistan, Singapore, China, Peru, Venezuela, and Colombia. See UN General Assembly. 2011, January 19. Report of the working group on arbitrary detention. *Human Rights Council, Sixteenth Session.* http://www2.ohchr.org/english/bodies/hrcouncil /docs/16session/A-HRC-16-47.pdf.

36 See Human Rights Watch. 2009, August 10. *Human rights and Saudi Arabia's counterterrorism response.* http://www.hrw.org/en/node/84893/section/5.

37 UN General Assembly. 2011, January 19. Report of the working group on arbitrary detention. *Human Rights Council, Sixteenth Session.* http://www2.ohchr.org/english/bodies/hrcouncil /16session/A-HRC-16-47.pdf.

has been in a state of emergency since 1948, the prospect of nearing a conclusion to the hostilities seems very unlikely.

United States. In the months following 9/11, the U.S. Department of Justice secretly arrested and detained more than 1,200 foreign nationals based on little more than the fact that they were Arab or Muslim noncitizens.[38] Many of these individuals were deported, and only a few have been charged with terrorism-related offenses. A report by the Office of the Inspector General revealed that the Department of Justice implemented a policy of "indiscriminate and haphazard" detention of noncitizens.[39] According to the American Civil Liberties Union, "these detentions entailed the round-up of hundreds of primarily Arab, Muslim, and South Asian men, often without any information linking them to terrorism, and subjecting them to series of special measures that violated their basic rights, such as prolonged detention without charge . . . [and] interference with the right to counsel."[40]

More than 5,000 suspected terrorists were arrested in the aftermath of 9/11. Out of all of these suspects, sufficient evidence to bring formal charges against them existed for only three of these individuals.[41] Moreover, suspected terrorists captured in the aftermath of 9/11 either overseas or in the United States were placed predominantly in Camp Delta in Guantanamo Bay, Cuba.

Guantanamo Bay: The Legal Black Hole

President George W. Bush signed an executive order, Military Order of November 13, 2001, on the Detention, Treatment, and Trial of Certain Non-Citizens in the War Against Terrorism. This order called for the military detention and trial by military commissions for noncitizens whom the President designated as being involved in international terrorism, such as al-Qaeda operatives. In particular, this order provided the Secretary of Defense with the power to detain individuals, either in the United States or abroad, and initiate charges against them in a military tribunal. The decisions of a military tribunal cannot be appealed.

The Bush administration alternatively used the words *enemy combatant* and *illegal combatant* to refer to members of al-Qaeda, the Taliban, and other terrorists

---

38 Parker, A., and Fellner, J. 2004, January. Above the law: Executive power after September 11 in the United States. *Human Rights Watch, World Report 2004*. http://www.globalissues.org/article /460/executive-power-after-9-11-in-the-united-states.

39 Office of the Inspector General. 2003. The September 11 detainees: A review of the treatment of aliens held on immigration charges in connection with the investigation of the September 11 attacks, 70. *Department of Justice*. http://www.justice.gov/oig/special/0306/full.pdf.

40 American Civil Liberties Union. 2005. *Coalition letter urging the senate to closely examine nominee Michael Chertoff's record*. http://www.aclu.org/national-security/coalition-letter-urging -senate-closely-examine-nominee-michael-chertoffs-record.

41 Scarry, E. 2005, March 31. Five errors in the reasoning of Alan Dershowitz. *The Commission on Intelligence Capacities of the United States on Weapons of Mass Destruction*, Washington, DC; Constanzo, M. A., and Gerrity, E. 2009. The effects and effectiveness of using torture as an interrogation device: Using research to inform the policy debate. *Social Issues and Policy Review* 3 (1): 184.

who were being indefinitely detained by the military in Guantanamo Bay. These terms have also been used to refer to individuals who do not qualify for prisoner of war status under the Geneva Conventions. Essentially, what this means is that these individuals are not entitled to the protections afforded by the Geneva Conventions of 1949 and their Protocols, which are reserved for lawful combatants. Similar to the indefinite detention practices of the United States, Israel's Imprisonment of Illegal Combatants Law of 2002 applies only to individuals who do not qualify as prisoners of war under the Geneva Convention. Accordingly, just like the United States, this form of detention is used only against enemy combatants. Pakistan has also followed suit. In fact, suspected terrorists are being indefinitely detained by the Pakistani military. In 2010, it was claimed that these individuals had been detained for approximately 1 year and had not been allowed to contact lawyers, family members, and human rights organizations.[42] Pakistani officials argue that this is done because the ordinary criminal justice system is incapable of and cannot be trusted to handle these suspected terrorists.[43] This is the same argument that has been brought forth by other countries, including the United States, although in the United States it is less an issue of trust and more an issue of the inability to effectively prosecute terrorists based on greater defendant protections and heightened evidentiary standards in civilian courts.

Against these claims lies successful convictions and incapacitation of terrorists around the world. Indeed, even the United States has convicted al-Qaeda terrorists in civilian courts and is currently housing terrorists in its maximum security prisons. A case in point is Zacarias Moussaoui (conspirator of 9/11). Others housed within American prisons are the convicted terrorists who conspired with Osama bin Laden in the 1998 U.S. Embassy bombings in Kenya and Tanzania (Mohamed Rashed Daoud al-Owhali, Khalfan Khamis, Mohammed Saddiq Odeh, and Wadih el-Hage)[44] and those who were convicted for their role in the 1993 WTC bombing (Mahmud Abouhalima, Ahmed Ajaj, Nidal Ayyad, Clement Rodney Hampton-El, Eyad Ismail, El Sayyid Nosair, Mohammed A. Salameh, and Ramzi Yousef). Moreover, John Walker Lindh, an American citizen who was caught in Afghanistan while fighting U.S. forces, was charged in a federal district court and pled guilty to violating 50 U.S.C. § 1705(b) by supplying services to the Taliban and violating 18 U.S.C. § 844(h)(2) for carrying an explosive during the commission of a felony. He was sentenced to 20 years imprisonment for the commission of these crimes. Furthermore, Ahmed Ghailani, a Guantanamo Bay detainee, was

---

[42] Witte, G., and DeYoung, K. 2010. Pakistan holding thousands in indefinite detention, officials say. *Washington Post*, April 22, 2010. http://www.washingtonpost.com/wp-dyn/content/article /2010/04/ 21/AR 2010042102658.html.

[43] Ibid.

[44] Weiser, B. 2001. A nation challenged: The embassy plot. *The New York Times*, December 25, 2001. http://www.nytimes.com/2001/12/25/nyregion/a-nation-challenged-the-embassy-plot-prison -switch-for-terrorist s-in-bombings.html.

successfully tried in a U.S. civilian court.[45] In November 2010, he was convicted of a single count of conspiracy to destroy government buildings and property. The other 280 charges against him were dropped. Yet, despite this occurrence, he still received the maximum penalty: life imprisonment without the possibility of parole.

The Supreme Court has played a contentious role in the war on terrorism, especially in regard to the detention of enemy combatants (members of al-Qaeda and the Taliban) by U.S. authorities in Guantanamo Bay. According to the doctrine established by President George W. Bush, enemy combatants are not afforded rights reserved for members of official state militaries or criminal defendants. Indeed, the designation of Guantanamo Bay detainees as enemy or illegal combatants has severe repercussions. By designating certain individuals as enemy combatants, they are subjected to special detention rules. Specifically, these individuals are not afforded the right to counsel, and their detention is subjected to limited judicial review (if any). In addition, protections against unreliable evidence are relaxed, and secret evidence can be used against detainees. This was observed in the case Ali Saleh Kahlah al-Marri. On June 23, 2003, President Bush declared al-Marri, a suspected member of al-Qaeda, an enemy combatant. Al-Marri, a Qatari nationalist, was arrested as a material witness in the FBI's investigation of the 9/11 attacks. He had come to America to pursue a degree in computer science from Bradley University. In July 2004, his lawyers filed a request for habeus corpus. The U.S. government opposed it and submitted a declaration, classified as "secret," which was prepared by Jeffrey Rapp, the Director of the Joint Intelligence Task Force for Combating Terrorism at the Defense Intelligence Agency. The evidence against al-Marri was largely hearsay. Normally, hearsay evidence is inadmissible; however, it was not in al-Marri's case because of *Hamdi v. Rumsfeld*.[46] In this case, the court ruled that hearsay evidence was admissible because Yaser Esam Hamdi was an enemy combatant.

Additionally, evidence is often withheld from enemy combatants and the detainee is usually unable to cross-examine witnesses. The latter restriction violates the right of a defendant to confront the witnesses against him (known as the Confrontation Clause) included within the Sixth Amendment to the U.S. Constitution, which states that:

> In all criminal prosecutions, the accused shall enjoy the right to a speedy and public trial, by an impartial jury of the State and district wherein the crime shall have been committed, which district shall have been previously ascertained by law, and to be informed of the nature and cause of the accusation; to be confronted with the witnesses against him; to have compulsory process for obtaining witnesses in his favor, and to have the Assistance of Counsel for his defence.

---

[45] Freedom House. 2011, August 17. *Freedom in the world 2011—United States of America.* http://www.unhcr.org/refworld/docid/4e4bb0f636.html.

[46] 542 U.S. 507 (2004).

In *Crawford v. Washington*,[36] the court explicitly stated that the framers of the U.S. Constitution "would not have allowed admission of testimonial statements of a witness who did not appear at trial unless he was unavailable to testify, and the defendant had had a prior opportunity for cross-examination."[37] This court further noted that the ultimate goal of the Confrontation Clause of the Sixth Amendment

> is to ensure reliability of evidence, but it is a procedural rather than a substantive guarantee. It commands, not that evidence be reliable, but that reliability be assessed in a particular manner: by testing in the crucible of cross-examination . . . Dispensing with confrontation because testimony is obviously reliable is akin to dispensing with jury trial because a defendant is obviously guilty. This is not what the Sixth Amendment prescribes.[38]

Accordingly, by preventing detainees from confronting witnesses against them, they become unable to test the reliability of the evidence presented against them.

The United States has been severely criticized by human rights organizations for using the term enemy combatants to circumvent the U.S. criminal justice system and side-step due process for detainees.[47] *In re Guantanamo Detainee Cases*,[48] the court held that detainees deserve the due process rights of the Fifth Amendment to the U.S. Constitution, which holds that:

> No person shall be held to answer for a capital, or otherwise infamous crime, unless on a presentment or indictment of a Grand Jury, except in cases arising in the land or naval forces, or in the Militia, when in actual service in time of War or public danger; nor shall any person be subject for the same offence to be twice put in jeopardy of life or limb; nor shall be compelled in any criminal case to be a witness against himself, nor be deprived of life, liberty, or property, without due process of law; nor shall private property be taken for public use, without just compensation.

The restrictions to due process and trial rights are predominantly aimed at enemy aliens. Two detainees who were U.S. citizens served as exceptions: Yaser Hamdi, who was caught in the battlefield in Afghanistan fighting against U.S. forces in the Fall of 2001, and José Padilla, who was detained as he entered Chicago's O'Hare Airport in May 2002 for his alleged participation in a plot to engage in a radiological bomb attack.

President Bush declared Hamdi and Padilla enemy combatants, a term previously used only for foreigners. Citing *Ex parte Quinn*[49] as an authority, these two U.S. citizens were placed in military detention at Guantanamo Bay and, like other detainees in the facility, were denied habeas corpus, a safeguard that protects an individual from arbitrary detention by mandating that a detainee has access to a lawyer and will be brought to court to determine the legality of their detention. The

---

[47] See, for example, Human Rights Watch. 2002, June 11. *U.S. circumvents court with enemy combatant tag.* http://www.hrw.org/en/news/2002/06/11/us-circumvents-courts-enemy-combatant-tag.

[48] 355 F. Supp 2d 443 (D.D.C. 2005).

[49] 317 U.S. 1, 25 (1942).

government argued that Hamdi and Padilla did not have the right to an attorney because they had not been charged with a crime. In *Hamdi v. Rumsfeld*[50] and *Rumsfeld v. Padilla*,[51] the government argued that the Non-Detention Act of 1971 did not apply to Hamdi and Padilla because it referred only to detentions made by the Attorney General and not those made by the President or military authorities.[52] Under this act, which is codified in 18 U.S.C. § 4001(a), only Congressional authority can authorize the detention of suspected subversives without the normal constitutional protections usually afforded with this process. The courts, however, did not agree. In *Hamdi*, the court held that while governments could detain illegal combatants, detainees with U.S. citizenship had the right to challenge their detention. After the Supreme Court ruling in *Hamdi*, he was subsequently released to Saudi Arabia in 2004. For Padilla's case, a federal judge ruled that he had the right to a lawyer and had the right to challenge his detention.[53] In 2008, Padilla was tried by a U.S. civilian court and convicted of conspiracy to commit murder, kidnap, and maim people in a foreign country.[54] He was sentenced to 17 years and 4 months imprisonment.

In *Rasul v. Bush*,[55] the Supreme Court held that U.S. courts have the authority to determine whether detainees are being wrongfully held in Guantanamo Bay. Accordingly, detainees have the right to challenge the legality of their detention in the courts of the District of Columbia. The Detainee Treatment Act of 2005 was passed after the ruling in *Rasul* and held that federal courts did not have jurisdiction to hear Guantanamo Bay detainees' challenges to their detention. However, on June 29, 2006, the Supreme Court held that terrorist suspects detained in Guantanamo Bay must receive due process provisions consistent with the military system and international standards or be released from military custody. In *Hamdan v. Rumsfeld*,[56] in a 5 to 3 decision, the Supreme Court held that it had jurisdiction to rule on the matter and that the federal government did not have authority to set up these particular special military commissions, which were ruled illegal under both the Uniform Code of Military Justice and the Geneva Convention. In addition, Salim Ahmed Hamdan was charged with conspiracy to commit terrorism. The Supreme Court held in *Hamdan* that conspiracy is not traditionally tried as a war crime. The decision was an affront to the Bush administration's plan to

---

[50] 542 U.S. 507 (2004).

[51] 542 U.S. 426 (2004).

[52] Elsea, J. K. 2004, March 15. Detention of American citizens as enemy combatants. *CRS Report for Congress*, 3. http://www.fas.org/irp/crs/RL31724.pdf.

[53] Weiser, B. 2002. Threats and responses: The courts; Judge says man can meet with lawyer to challenge detention as enemy plotter. *New York Times*, December 5, 2002. http://www.nytimes.com/2002/12/05/us/threats-responses-courts-judge-says-man-can-meet-with-lawyer-challenge-detention.html.

[54] Jose Padilla. 2009. *New York Times*, March 6, 2009. http://topics.nytimes.com/top/reference/timestopics/people/p/jose_padilla/index.html.

[55] 542 U.S. 466 (2004).

[56] 548 U.S. 557 (2006).

try terrorists as enemy combatants in military tribunals, which do not give defendants the same rights as prisoners of war under the Geneva Convention. The Bush administration was sharply critical of the decision.

Although the ruling dealt a blow to the Bush administration's efforts in the war on terrorism, the Supreme Court did not categorically prohibit military commissions. In a concurring opinion with the majority, Justice Stephen Breyer wrote, "Congress has denied the President the legislative authority to create military commissions of the kind at issue here. Nothing prevents the President from returning to Congress to seek the authority he believes necessary." In contrast, Justice Antonin Scalia forcefully criticized the Supreme Court and its decision. Fundamentally, he argued that no court had jurisdiction to hear court requests of a detainee from Guantanamo Bay. In Justice Scalia's words,

> [o]n December 30, 2005, Congress enacted the Detainee Treatment Act (DTA). It unambiguously provides that, as of that date, "no court, justice, or judge" shall have jurisdiction to consider the habeas application of a Guantanamo Bay detainee. Notwithstanding this plain directive, the Court today concludes that, on what it calls the statute's *most natural* reading, *every* "court, justice, or judge" before whom such a habeas application was pending on December 30 had jurisdiction to hear, consider, and render judgment on it. This conclusion is patently erroneous. And even if it were not, the jurisdiction supposedly retained should, in an exercise of sound equitable discretion, not be exercised (emphasis in original).

In response to the *Hamdan* ruling, the Military Commissions Act of 2006 was established by Congress. This act stipulated that the President has the power to indefinitely detain anyone—citizen and noncitizen alike—whom he has deemed as having provided material support to anti-U.S. hostilities. This process, however, is particularly problematic because it can be abused, as trials are conducted in secret and the executive has exclusive power over detainees without the usual checks and balances in place.

The Military Commissions Act, thus, created a new system of military commissions that could try citizens and noncitizens suspected of involvement in terrorist activity. These military commissions differ from those struck down by *Hamdan* because they allow defendants to appeal their convictions to a civilian appellate court. Those detainees who are brought before the U.S. Military Commissions can choose only attorneys who have been approved by the executive. These military commissions also have lax rules concerning hearsay evidence (i.e., they allow it if it is deemed reliable), allow evidence obtained through coercive interrogation and/ or torture to be introduced if it was obtained prior to the passage of the Detainee Treatment Act of 2005, limit the discovery rights of detainees by preventing disclosure of classified sources and methods of interrogation from the defense, and the defense does not have access to all exculpatory evidence (i.e., if it is classified). The latter is particularly troublesome as it illustrates that there is no requirement to inform the defense of this exculpatory evidence allowing for potential miscarriages of justice to occur in the future. The Military Commissions Act further prohibited

Guantanamo Bay detainees from filing for habeas corpus in U.S. courts in order to challenge the legality of their detention. It further noted that Guantanamo Bay detainees were unlawful enemy combatants, which precluded them from invoking Geneva Convention rights. Moreover, this act codified offenses that could be tried in military commissions and included conspiracy and providing material support for terrorism in the list of crimes.

The habeas corpus restriction in this act was struck down by the ruling in *Boumediene v. Bush*,[57] in which the court ruled that Guantanamo Bay detainees must be allowed to challenge their detention in federal courts through the writ of habeas corpus. In this case, the court still avoided making a decision on whether the President had the authority to detain prisoners at Guantanamo Bay. It is clear that the controversy surrounding counterterrorism measures is fiercely debated, even among Supreme Court Justices.

The Obama administration officially abandoned the term *enemy combatant* and pledged to shut down Guantanamo Bay within a year of the President's inauguration. Yet, as of April 2012, this facility has not closed. Indeed, many prisoners still remain in the facility. The Obama administration has sought to try some of the detainees in U.S. courts. However, the relocation of Guantanamo Bay detainees to prison facilities in the United States and their trials in criminal court has received significant congressional and public opposition.[58]

Some detainees are awaiting trial in federal courts, while others are scheduled to be brought before revamped military commissions. Other detainees are scheduled to be released and/or transferred to other countries. However, there are also detainees who cannot be tried and must be held in Guantanamo Bay.[59] These detainees are an obstacle to the closing of the facility. So too are detainees who are authorized to be released but have nowhere to go. Particularly problematic are detainees whose home countries have refused to take them or who cannot be sent to their home countries for fear of harsh treatment and punishment. Many of these detainees have also been refused by third countries. A prime example of this was seen in the 17 Uighur men (members of a minority Turkic diaspora in China) who have been detained in Guantanamo Bay for approximately seven years.[60] As early as 2003, the U.S. government admitted that these individuals were not enemy combatants. However, they have yet to be released because if sent to China they would likely face the persecution and torture that other members of their group have experienced. The United States also refused to grant them asylum in their

57 553 U.S. 723 (2008).

58 Freedom House. 2011, August 17. *Freedom in the world 2011—United States of America.* http://www.unhcr.org/refworld/docid/4e4bb0f636.html.

59 Finn, P. 2009. Obama endorses indefinite detention without trial for some now at Guantanamo. *Washington Post*, May 22, 2009. http://www.washingtonpost.com/wp-dyn/content/article/2009/05 /21/AR2009052104045.html.

60 Brennan Center of Justice. 2009, December 11. *Kiyemba v. Obama* (Amicus Brief): Court Cases. *New York University School of Law.* http://www.brennancenter.org/content/resource/kiyemba _v_bush/.

own country and have yet to find another country that will accept this group. As of 2009, Albania, Bermuda, and Palau have offered to take some of the 17 Uighur men into their country.

Guantanamo Bay and the labeling of its detainees as enemy combatants has not only served as a source of contention among the international community but has also produced serious consequences for the fight against terrorism in the United States. Terrorists have used both of these points to show the injustices that the United States has perpetrated and continues to perpetrate against Muslims. Guantanamo Bay and the label of enemy combatants has also served as a recruitment tool for al-Qaeda and affiliates. Many of the terrorists captured after 9/11 have made reference to the detainees in Guantanamo Bay and other military prison facilities (e.g., Abu Ghraib) in their martyrdom videos as reasons for engaging in jihad. Nowhere is this more prevalent than among the homegrown terrorists captured in the United States and Europe who are inspired by al-Qaeda's cause. Moreover, several instances have been reported of individuals who were detained by the U.S. government in Guantanamo Bay having, upon release, joined a terrorist group and/or engaged in terrorism-related activities.[61] For those unjustly detained in Guantanamo Bay, a similar situation has been observed. Militant detainees have also used Guantanamo Bay as a recruiting ground. Just as internment in Northern Ireland had increased PIRA recruitment both with detainees who had no prior terrorism connection and with supporters who believed that the response of Britain was unjust, so too has the indefinite detention of Guantanamo Bay detainees bred more terrorists and provided terrorist groups and organizations with a justification for targeting the United States.

The mistreatment of detainees in Guantanamo Bay and other U.S.-controlled prisons has also served as a recruiting tool for terrorists and provided terrorists with a reason to promote attacks on the United States. In 2002, the media reported that interrogators seeking actionable intelligence forced "detainees to stand or kneel for hours in black hoods or spray painted goggles, bombard[ed] the detainees with lights 24 hours a day, with[held] painkillers from wounded detainees, confin[ed] them in tiny rooms or [bound] them in painful positions, subject[ed] them to loud noises, and depriv[ed] them of sleep."[62] A case in point was Omar Khadr, who was captured while fighting U.S. forces in Afghanistan. He was shot three times but survived after having sustained not only wounds in his chest, but also shrapnel in his head. Videotaped interrogations from Guantanamo Bay were posted on the Internet. These tapes provided insight into the interrogations that occurred within this detention center. While being interrogated, Khadr's demeanor often changed

---

61　Entous, A., and Stewart, P. 2010. U.S. believes 1 in 5 ex-detainees joining militants. *Reuters.* http://www.reuters.com/article/2010/01/06/us-yemen-guantanamo-usa-idUSTRE6044MI20100106.

62　Priest, D., and Gellman, B. 2002. U.S. decries abuse but defends interrogations. *Washington Post,* December 26, 2002, p. A1, cited in Dycus, S., Banks, W. C., and Raven-Hansen, P. 2007. *Counterterrorism Law.* New York: Wolters Kluwer, 401.

from indifference to grief-filled rants of despair.[63] A reporter for the *New York Times* revealed the contents of a secret government report, which stated that to make Khadr "more amenable and willing to" speak with interrogators, they moved him to a new cell every 3 hours during his hours of sleep for 3 weeks to deny him uninterrupted sleep.[64]

The mistreatment of detainees in U.S. military prisons in Afghanistan, Iraq, and Guantanamo Bay has been widely depicted in international media. The now notorious images of American military engaged in the torture of Abu Ghraib detainees attests to this. These images showed detainees simulating sexual acts, being piled on top of one another naked, and standing while hooded with wires connected to their genitals and fingertips.[65] Nine American soldiers were charged and found guilty for their treatment of detainees. The charges against the soldiers included cruelty, assault, indecent acts, and maltreatment of detainees.[66] The investigation into what happened in Abu Ghraib revealed that there was a shortage of trained interrogators and as a result, military personnel who lacked this training were called to fill in. Even though some of the individuals who engaged in this abuse were tried and convicted, this incident had significant adverse consequences. After the release of the photos of prisoner mistreatment in Abu Ghraib, the violence against U.S. soldiers in Iraq increased.[67] A young Iraqi man stated that violence was inevitable, as

> [i]t is a shame for foreigners to put a bag over their heads, to make a man lie on the ground with your shoe on his neck . . . This is a great shame for the whole tribe. It is the duty of that man, and of our tribe, to get revenge on that soldier—to kill that man. Their duty is to attack them, to wash the shame. The shame is a stain, a dirty thing—they have to wash it. We cannot sleep until we have revenge.[68]

The images of detainees being beaten and sexually humiliated by U.S. soldiers thus became a recruiting tool for Iraqi insurgents.

---

[63] Austen, I. 2008. Blurry peek at questioning of a Guantanamo inmate. *New York Times*, July 16, 2008. http://www.nytimes.com/2008/07/16/world/16khadr.html.

[64] Austen, I. 2008. Citing new report, lawyers for Canadian detainee denounce abuse. *New York Times*, July 11, 2008. http://www.nytimes.com/2008/07/11/world/americas/11khadr.html?scp=1&sq=omar+khadr+torture&st=nyt.

[65] Hannah, M. 2006. Torture and the ticking bomb: The war on terrorism as a geographical imagination of power/knowledge. *Annals of the Association of American Geographers* 96 (3): 622.

[66] Risen, J. 2004. The struggle for Iraq: Treatment of prisoners. *The New York Times*, April 29, 2004. http://www.nytimes.com/2004/04/29/world/struggle-for-iraq-treatment-prisoners-gi-s-are-accused-abusing-iraqi-captives.html.

[67] New Abu Ghraib Images Broadcast. 2006. *BBC News*, February 15 2006. http://news.bbc.co.uk/2/hi/middle_east/4715540.stm.

[68] Danner, M. 2005. Torture and truth: America, Abu Ghraib, and the war on terror. *New York Review of Books*, March 4, 2005, p. 12. http://www.nybooks.com/articles/17150.

Despite criticisms from human rights organizations and its conflict with existing laws, indefinite detention of suspected terrorists is still in effect in the United States and other countries around the globe. In fact, at the end of 2011, President Obama signed the National Defense Authorization Bill, which includes provisions that authorize the indefinite military detention of Americans. In signing this bill (now a law), the President expressed serious reservations about specific provisions that regulate the interrogation, detention, and prosecution of suspected terrorists.[69] The President also declared that his administration would not detain Americans without trial.

While this law may be effective in preventing terrorists from engaging in future crimes by incapacitating them, it is only so if those detained are actually terrorists. With the existing practice of relaxed rules of evidence, the inability to test the reliability of information presented against the detainee, the lack of transparency in proceedings, and diminished due process and trial rights, one cannot be sure beyond a reasonable doubt (as most criminal trials require) that those detained are actually terrorists. In addition, some detainees are in Guantanamo Bay not because they have actually committed a crime, but because they pose the risk to a target society or the international community at-large that they might commit a crime sometime in the future. Even if it is in principle justifiable to attempt to incapacitate risky individuals in order to enhance security, the use of indefinite detention as a means to prevent someone from potentially committing a crime is indefensible. As a preemptive measure, indefinite detention legitimates the substantial curtailment of human rights, such as liberty, at earlier points in time than those of the ordinary criminal justice process, before the requirement of *mens rea* ("guilty mind"), much less *actus reus* ("guilty actions"), have been established.

HYPOTHETICAL SCENARIO

Legislation has been introduced in the United States that authorizes the use of Control Orders for terrorists. You have been hired to conduct an impact assessment of their use.

1. What legal issues arise from their implementation?
2. How effective would these Control Orders be against suspected terrorists?

CHAPTER SUMMARY

Terrorists are incapacitated as a form of punishment and to protect society from possible attacks. Preventive detention has been used to deal with enemies during ongoing wars and domestic and international terrorists. The practices of pre-charge detention among countries has varied; so too has the practice of indefinite detention, which is not in accordance with human rights instruments. The only

---

[69] McAuliff, G. 2011, December 31. Obama signs defense bill despite "serious reservations." *Huffington Post*. http://www.huffingtonpost.com/2011/12/31/obama-defense-bill_n_1177836.html.

exception to this is its use during an emergency that threatens the life of the nation. However, to be authorized to derogate from certain rights during an emergency, the country must officially declare the emergency and follow the appropriate procedures stipulated in conventions for derogating from these human rights. Some countries have created alternative methods with which to deal with terrorism, such as Control Orders, Preventive Detention Orders, and Prohibited Contact Orders. Others have created separate facilities and processes outside of the ordinary criminal justice system with which to deal with terrorists. Guantanamo Bay is the most prominent and controversial system of indefinite detention of suspected terrorists. Since the inception of detention in Guantanamo Bay, various laws and court rulings have altered the way it operates and how detainees are treated. Enemy combatants are not afforded the protections of the Geneva Convention and have restricted due process and trial rights. Detainees are not notified of their crimes, provided counsel, or allowed habeas corpus or other forms of judicial review of the reasons for their incarceration. While the Obama administration has removed the designation of detainees as enemy combatants, prisoners are still housed within Guantanamo Bay, and the fate of many of them remains uncertain even today.

REVIEW QUESTIONS

1. Are preventive detention and indefinite detention synonymous?
2. How prevalent is the practice of indefinite detention?
3. Is preventive detention lawful?
4. What lessons can be learned from the use of preventive detention in the past?
5. How have the uses of preventive detention changed post-9/11?
6. What are the consequences of labeling a detainee as an enemy combatant?
7. What type of prisoner can be held in Guantanamo Bay?
8. Can Guantanamo Bay be shut down?

chapter ten

Punishing Terrorists: Unjustifiably Harsh?

He who fights with monsters might take care lest he thereby become a monster.
—FRIEDRICH NIETZSCHE (*BEYOND GOOD AND EVIL*, APHORISM 146)

Even though the use of preemptive tactics has significantly increased in counterterrorism, this by no means implies that the use of tactics that deal with terrorist attacks after they have occurred have decreased. Punishment of terrorists still plays a prominent role in counterterrorism. To be justified, punishment must serve a purpose. In this chapter, the retributive and deterrence goals of punishment are explored. The retributive perspective is essentially retrospective. This perspective can be traced back to Immanuel Kant, who believed that people who commit "wrongs" deserved to be punished, and in so doing, society was paying them back—exacting retribution—for their wrongs. The purpose of this form of punishment is to allocate moral blame for the crime. It thus solely focuses on past actions of an offender. The future conduct of an offender is of no concern here in deciding the type and amount of punishment for that offender.

While retribution is inherently retrospective, deterrence is prospective. Deterrence policies are premised on the belief that criminals fear sanctions. If the certainty and severity of punishments increases, then deterrence theory holds that individuals will desist from crime. For example, deterrence occurs when an individual wants to engage in terrorism, realizes that his or her actions may involve incarceration or capital punishment, and as a result, changes his or her mind and decides instead to adhere to the law. There are two types of deterrence: general and specific. General deterrence holds that individuals will engage in unlawful activity if they do not fear that they will be punished or apprehended; whereas, specific deterrence holds that punishment should be severe enough to ensure that criminals do not repeat terrorist actions.

This chapter covers the harsh approaches to terrorism. Specifically, it examines certain forms of individual and collective punishment that countries around the globe have used to deal with domestic and international terrorists such as targeted killings, life imprisonment, capital punishment, public beheadings/executions, house demolitions, and sanctions. Which of these have proven to be effective counterterrorism measures? What was (is) the impact of these measures on society? Which ones, if any, should be used to deal with the homegrown terrorists in the United States?

INDIVIDUAL PUNISHMENT

Individual punishment is exacted solely on those who are deemed to be terrorists or responsible in some way for a terrorist attack. Three types of individual punishment are explored here: targeted killings, life imprisonment, and the death penalty.

Targeted Killing

Unlike other counterterrorism tactics, targeted killing is not designed to detect, capture, or incapacitate a target. Instead, it seeks to eliminate a target. Specifically, targeted killing involves a deliberate government decision to order the death of a designated enemy. It often occurs in retaliation to an attack in order to prevent and deter such acts from occurring in the future. Targeted killings are not a new phenomenon. Many countries have used such tactics, including the United States. For example, in 1986, President Ronald Reagan ordered Operation El Dorado Canyon, which consisted of an air strike on the home residence of the Libyan ruler Muammar Qaddafi (now deceased).[1] The operation was unsuccessful as Qaddafi was not in the compound at the time of the attack. Yet leaders of countries have not been the only targets of such tactics.

Terrorists are often the targets of these ordered killings. Usually, key operatives are targeted to disrupt terrorist organizations. An example of this involved Qaed Salim Sinan al-Harithi, who was targeted because of his role in the planning of the bombings of the USS Cole. On November 4, 2002, a CIA-controlled Predator unmanned aerial vehicle fired a missile at a vehicle carrying al-Harithi and five others in Yemen. All of the occupants of the vehicle were killed. On May 7, 2005, another alleged senior member of al-Qaeda, Haitham al-Yemeni, was killed in Pakistan by a missile fired by a Predator drone.[2] This was not the

---

[1] Blum, G., and Heymann, P. B. 2010. *Laws, outlaws, and terrorists*. Cambridge, MA: MIT Press, 73.

[2] Amnesty International. 2005, May 18. United States of America: An extrajudicial execution by the CIA? http://www.amnesty.org/en/library/asset/AMR51/079/2005/en/bcffa8d8-d4ea-11dd-8a23 -d58a49c0d652/amr510792005en.html.

first time that the United States had engaged in a targeted killing operation in Pakistan. In addition, a targeted killing operation was launched against Ayman al-Zawahiri, but instead of killing al-Zawahiri, eighteen innocent civilians were killed.[3] Another targeted killing occurred in January 2007, in which an Air Force AC-130 Spectre gunship was used to target suspected al-Qaeda terrorists in Somalia. According to the Chairman of the U.S. Joint Chiefs of Staff at the time, General Peter Pace, the strike in Somalia was executed pursuant to the authority given to the military after 9/11 by the government "to hunt and kill terrorism suspects around the globe."[4]

A more recent example of targeted killing involved Anwar al-Awlaki, a U.S. citizen who was affiliated with al-Qaeda in the Arabian Peninsula (AQAP). Al-Awlaki, along with Samir Khan, was killed in a U.S.-ordered missile strike by Predator drones in Yemen on September 30, 2011. Al-Awlaki was considered a prominent spiritual ideologue for English-speaking jihadists in the West, frequently posting publications and lectures online. Certain homegrown terrorist plots uncovered in the United States were said to be influenced by al-Awlaki's teachings. Among them was the November 2009 shooting at Fort Hood and the attempted Christmas 2009 suicide bombing on a plane. In the first incident, Nidal Malik Hassan, a U.S. Army officer stationed at Fort Hood, was inspired by al-Awlaki to engage in the attack and not directed by him. During his attack at Fort Hood, Hassan shot and killed 13 individuals and wounded 30. The second incident involved Umar Farouk Abdulmutallab, who, claiming to have been directed by al-Awlaki to engage in the attack, attempted to ignite the liquid explosives in his underpants while on board Northwest Flight 253 over Detroit. However, he failed due to the intervention of a vigilant passenger. The targeted killings of Anwar Al-Awlaki and Samir Khan are believed to have been detrimental to al-Qaeda. Al-Awlaki and Khan targeted Muslims in the United States and Europe as recruits. One of Al-Awlaki's sermons was viewed over 40,000 times on YouTube.[5] With his fluency in English and media production experience, Khan, a U.S. citizen and editor-in-chief of the English-language *Inspire* magazine, might not be easily replaced by AQAP.

Targeted killing operations have successfully killed a number of senior al-Qaeda members, including Mohammed Atef, who was the chief of al-Qaeda military operations. However, such targeted killings were not limited to al-Qaeda members and affiliates. Terrorists have been frequent targets for assassination or targeted killings, especially by Israel's secret service, the Mossad. For instance, in retaliation for the massacre of the Israeli Olympic athletes in Munich in 1972, Israel

---

3 Blum, G., and Heymann, P. B. 2010. *Laws, outlaws, and terrorists.* Cambridge, MA: MIT Press, 74.

4 Mazzetti, M. 2007. Pentagon sees move in Somalia as blueprint. *New York Times,* January 13, 2007. http://www.nytimes.com/2007/01/13/world/africa/13proxy.html.

5 Michaels, J. 2011. Death of Al-Qaeda cleric puts wrench in propaganda machine. *USA Today,* October 2, 2011. http://www.usatoday.com/news/world/story/2011-10-02/al-qaeda-propaganda /50637286/1.

authorized the assassination of officials of Black September, the Palestinian para-military group held responsible for the attack. Israel has also engaged in targeted killings against other "targets, including Egyptian intelligence officers involved in orchestrating infiltrations into Israel in the 1950s, German scientists developing missiles for . . . Egypt in the 1960s, . . . and prominent leaders of Palestinian and Lebanese terrorist networks, such as the Secretary-General of Hezbollah in 1992."[6] Another country that has engaged in targeted killings is Russia. Consider their targeted killing of leaders of terrorist groups. Chechen leaders whom Russia has targeted and killed include, among many others, Ibn Khattab, a Chechen terrorist leader who was believed to have died from poisoning in 2002; Abu Walid, who was suspected of having taken over for Khattab after his death; and Shamil Basayev, who was believed to have been responsible for the 2002 Dubrovka theater siege and the Beslan school shootings.[7]

Justifying Its Use

Targeted killings could be justified by a state invoking a legitimate right to self-defense. According to international law, in order to use force against another state, a country must ensure that its actions do not violate Article 2(4) of the UN Charter, which holds that "[a]ll members shall refrain in their international relations from the threat or use of force against the territorial integrity or political independence of any state, or in any other manner inconsistent with the Purposes of the United Nations." Two exceptions to this are military actions authorized by the United Nations and a state's right to self-defense. Article 51 of the UN Charter explicitly states that:

> Nothing in the present Charter shall impair the inherent right of individual or collective self-defence if an armed attack occurs against a Member of the United Nations, until the Security Council has taken measures necessary to maintain inter-national peace and security. Measures taken by Members in the exercise of this right of self-defence shall be immediately reported to the Security Council and shall not in any way affect the authority and responsibility of the Security Council under the present Charter to take at any time such action as it deems necessary in order to maintain or restore international peace and security.

Nevertheless, a person should be targeted only if he or she presents a serious security risk based on available evidence and/or reliable, corroborated intelligence information that clearly implicates him or her. Targeted killing is unjustified against an individual with only minor involvement in terrorist activity and whose actions do not endanger public safety. This tactic can be used only against

---

6 Blum, G., and Heymann, P. B. 2010. *Laws, outlaws, and terrorists.* Cambridge, MA: MIT Press, 74–75.

7 Scher, G. 2009, December 8. Chechen jihad: An analytical overview. *International Institute for Counter-Terrorism.* http://www.ict.org.il/Articles/tabid/66/Articlsid/743/currentpage/1/Default .aspx.

individuals who, directly or indirectly, participate in terrorism in a manner equivalent to armed conflict.[8]

Gross noted that even if "a peaceful resolution with a terrorist group is often impossible and that there is no way to extradite terrorists, a state should nevertheless refrain from engaging in targeted killing as a form of self-defense except as a last resort."[9] Indeed, failure to do so, according to Amnesty International, amounts to extrajudicial killing. Amnesty International stated that extrajudicial killings involve the unlawful and deliberate killing of an individual by order of the government, even though other viable options exist to deal with the terrorist, such as arrest and incapacitation. Consider, once again, the case of Haitham al-Yemeni. Human rights organizations, such as Amnesty International, believe that the United States and Pakistan should have sought to arrest al-Yemeni rather than decide to kill him.[10] International law dictates that lethal force should be used only as a last resort. Failure to explore other options before deciding to execute a target amounts to extrajudicial killing, which is illegal.[11] Extrajudicial killings are always unlawful. As such, wars, threats of war, internal political instability, or others forms of public emergency may not be invoked as a justification for their use.[12] However, according to the Obama administration, targeted killing operations and the use of lethal force against particular individuals does not constitute unlawful extrajudicial killing when a state is engaged in an armed conflict and legitimate self-defense.[13]

To be lawful, such an action must be future oriented, seeking to protect the security of the state, and not limited to merely punishing past transgressions.[14] In addition, as Dinstein argues, Article 51 is purposely restrictive and confines self-defense to responses to an armed attack.[15] Likewise, Sofaer stated that Article 51

---

[8] Guiora, A. 2005. "Terrorism on trial": Targeted killing as active self-defense. *Case Western Reserve Journal of International Law* 37:332.

[9] Gross, E. 2001. Thwarting terrorist acts by attacking the perpetrators or their commanders as an act of self-defense: Human rights versus the state's duty to protect its citizens. *Temple International and Comparative Law Journal* 15:228–229 cited in Wachtel, H. A. 2005. Targeting Osama Bin Laden: Examining the legality of assassination as a tool of U.S. foreign policy. *Duke Law Journal* 55:677.

[10] Amnesty International. 2005, May 18. United States of America: An extrajudicial execution by the CIA? http://www.amnesty.org/en/library/asset/AMR51/079/2005/en/ bcffa8d8-d4ea-11dd-8a23 -d58a49c0d652/amr510792005en.html.

[11] Ibid.

[12] Ibid.

[13] Bowcott, O. 2011. Osama bin Laden: US responds to questions about killing's legality. *The Guardian*, May 3, 2011. http://www.guardian.co.uk/world/2011/may/03/osama-bin-laden-killing -legality.

[14] Dinstein, Y. 1994. *War, aggression and self-defense*, 2nd ed. Cambridge, UK: Cambridge University Press, 183–185; Kendall, J. N. 2002. Israeli counter-terrorism: "Targeted killings" under international law. *North Carolina Law Review* 80:1083; Bowett, D. 2002. Reprisals involving recourse to armed force. *American Journal of International Law* 66:3.

[15] Ibid., Dinstein, Y. 1994, pp. 183-185.

restricts the use of force to be applied only in response to an armed attack against a state's territories.[16] It is argued that what the United States has engaged in post-9/11 is what Schachter has termed "defensive retaliation,"[17] which may be considered a justified action when a state has good reason to expect a series of attacks from the target. The United States was entitled to engage in defensive retaliation against Osama bin Laden to defend against continuing terrorist threats. In the past, the United States has been subjected to a series of attacks orchestrated by bin Laden, including the attack on the World Trade Center in 1993, the 1993 attack on U.S. soldiers in Somalia, the 1998 U.S. Embassy bombings in Kenya and Tanzania, and 9/11. Due to these "armed conflicts," the United States could invoke Article 51 of the UN Charter to counter this threat. It is argued that targeted killings are not a form of punishment. According to Schachter, this retaliation serves as a deterrent. This, however, does not preclude the use of this action for both retaliatory and deterrent purposes. If this action was solely implemented for the purpose of revenge or retaliation, then it would not be defensive. Such an action would amount to extrajudicial killing, which is used to kill enemies of the state, not for operational or self-defense purposes but to punish any opponents of the state.[18]

To engage in targeted killings in other nations, the permission of the government of the country that the target is in must be obtained. It has been reported that for the targeted killings in Pakistan, Yemen, and Somalia, among others, the United States had obtained permission from the countries prior to engaging in those killings.[19] Yet there are instances in which permission has not been obtained prior to executing armed attacks within a country's territory. A case in point is the operation to capture Osama bin Laden. Here, Pakistani authorities were not contacted for fear that someone would warn bin Laden of the imminent raid. Even though bin Laden was killed in the raid, U.S. authorities have stated that their operation was not a targeted killing. However, U.S. Special Forces were authorized to shoot to kill. Nonetheless, if this was a targeted killing, this action might be justified on the grounds that sometimes apprehension of a terrorist could not be a viable option considering the enormous risks involved in detention. Accordingly, if capture poses a great risk to the United States (or any other country for that matter), at least more so than the risk involved in engaging in a targeted killing of an individual, then targeted killing might be considered as a feasible alternative for terrorists who pose an imminent threat to the country in question.

---

16 Sofaer, A. D. 1989. The sixth annual Waldemar A. Solf lecture in international law: Terrorism, the law, and the national defense. *Military Law Review* 126:93.

17 Schachter, O. 1984. The right of states to use armed force. *Michigan Law Review* 82:1638.

18 Guiora, A. 2005. "Terrorism on trial": Targeted killing as active self-defense. *Case Western Reserve Journal of International Law* 37:330.

19 Cullen, P. M. 2007, March 30. The role of targeted killing in the campaign against terrorism. *US Army War College, Strategy Research Project.* http://www.dtic.mil/cgi-bin/GetTRDoc ?AD=ADA471529& Location=U2&doc=GetTRDoc.pdf.

Benefits of Its Use

Targeted killing is promoted as preventing significant losses of life that would have resulted if the terrorists were able to execute attacks. Others promote this method as being "a preferable option to bombing or large-scale military sweeps that do far more harm to genuine noncombatants."[20] Indeed, as Guiora argues, if conducted properly, targeted killings can minimize the number of innocent civilians lost during the conflict between the government and the terrorists.[21] Civilian casualties should be avoided. However, the Israel Defense Forces have reported that this is not simple, as their targets have been known to hide in civilian homes and other densely populated areas.[22] According to the Israeli human rights group, B'Tselem, between September 2000 and December 2006, a total of 339 Palestinians were killed, of which 210 were subjects of targeted killings and 129 were civilian bystanders.[23] In Israel, the Supreme Court has noted that after every targeted killing, an investigation is required to ensure that it was lawfully implemented.[24] In Israel, such targeted killings are authorized by the legislature and the judiciary only as a last resort when all other attempts to capture the terrorist alive have been exhausted by authorities.[25]

Proponents of targeted killing believe that killing individuals vital to the organization can prevent it from effectively operating. Additionally, having a targeted killing policy in place is thought to make high-level operatives in a terrorist organization flee and be on the run. Even the idea that these operatives may be targeted was said to be enough to affect the operations of the organization. Israel's policy of targeted killing has been lauded as crippling its Arab adversaries' capabilities.[26]

---

[20] David, S. R. 2003. Reply to Yael Stein: If not combatants, certainly not civilians. *Ethics and International Affairs* 17:139.

[21] Guiora, A. 2005. "Terrorism on trial": Targeted killing as active self-defense. *Case Western Reserve Journal of International Law* 37:325.

[22] Israel Ministry of Foreign Affairs. 2002, August 5. *Answers to frequently asked questions: Palestinian violence and terrorism: The international war against terrorism: What was Operation Defensive Shield?* http://www.mfa.gov.il/MFA/MFAArchive/2000_2009/2002/8/Answers+to+Frequently+Asked+Questions-+Palestinian.htm; Gorelick, B. A. 2003. The Israeli response to Palestinian breach of the Oslo Agreements. *New England Journal of International and Comparative Law* 9:669.

[23] B'Tselem. 2006, December 13. *High court of justice imposes limitations on Israel's target killing policy.* http://www.btselem.org/firearms/20061219_targeted_killing_ruling.

[24] On December 11, 2005, the Israeli Supreme Court ruled on the legality of targeted killings in the Palestinian Territories in *The Public Committee Against Torture in Israel v. The Government of Israel.* http://elyon1.court.gov.il/ files_ENG/02/690/007/a34/02007690.a34.htm.

[25] Gross, E. 2002. Terrorism and the law: Democracy in the war against terrorism—The Israeli experience. *Loyola of Los Angeles Law Review* 35:1194; Gorelick, B. A. 2003. The Israeli response to Palestinian breach of the Oslo Agreements. *New England Journal of International and Comparative Law* 9:669.

[26] See David, S. R. 2002, September. Fatal choices: Israel's policy of target killing. *Mideast Security and Policy Studies* 51. *The Begin-Sadat Center for Strategic Studies, Bar-Ilan University,* 6. http://www.biu.ac.il/SOC/besa/david.pdf.

However, no concrete evidence exists that targeted killings are effective in crippling terrorist organizations.[27]

Adverse Consequences

Targeted killings could also have severe adverse consequences. Relations between countries may be affected by them, especially when a country has not given permission for such an action within its own borders. The strained relationship between Pakistan and the United States since the killing of Osama bin Laden attests to this. The international community has also been vocal about its disapproval of targeted killings. For example, the United States, Australia, the European Union, Russia, and the league of Arab States have expressed condemnation of Israel's use of targeted killings.[28] A specific pragmatic objection to targeted killing is the reaction of not only the international community but also those who are targeted. This is evident in the strained relations between Israelis and Palestinians. Those who argue against the use of targeted killings have stated that this tactic actually increases the number of Israelis killed. Specifically, in response to this tactic, terrorists engage in retaliatory strikes. David provided four instances in which aggressive retaliatory strikes soon followed targeted killings.[29] The first involved the targeted killing of Yehiya Ayash in January 1996. In response to his death, four retaliatory suicide bombings were conducted, which resulted in the deaths of 50 Israelis. The second incident involved the killing of the leader of the Popular Front for the Liberation of Palestine (PFLP), Mustafa Zibri, 2 months after which the PFLP killed Israeli cabinet minister Rehavam Ze'evi. The third incident concerned the 2002 targeted killing of Tanzim[30] leader Raed al-Karmi. A wave of suicide bombings occurred following this incident, resulting in numerous deaths. The fourth incident involved the 2002 targeted killing of Hamas leader Sheik Salah Shehada. This incident derailed the ongoing peace negotiations between Israel and Palestinian leaders. Indeed, former UN Secretary General Kofi Annan had repeatedly urged Israel to end the use of this tactic because it not only violates international law but also undermines any efforts that are currently being made toward achieving peace in the Middle East.[31]

---

27 Ibid., p. 8.

28 Keinon, H., Zacharia, J., and Lahoud, L. 2001. UN, US: Stop targeted killings. *Jerusalem Post*, July 6, 2001, p. A1; David, S. R. 2002, September. Fatal choices: Israel's policy of target killing. *Mideast Security and Policy Studies* 51. *The Begin-Sadat Center for Strategic Studies, Bar-Ilan University*, 10. http://www.biu.ac.il/SOC/besa/david.pdf; Rantissi Killing: World Reaction. 2004. *BBC News*, April 18, 2004. http://news.bbc.co.uk/2/hi/middle_east/3635907.stm.

29 David, S. R. 2002, September. Fatal choices: Israel's policy of target killing. *Mideast Security and Policy Studies* 51. *The Begin-Sadat Center for Strategic Studies, Bar-Ilan University*, 9. http://www.biu.ac.il/SOC/besa/david.pdf.

30 Tanzim is a nationalist/separatist terrorist group that operates in Israel, the West Bank, and the Gaza Strip.

31 David, S. R. 2002, September. Fatal choices: Israel's policy of target killing. *Mideast Security and Policy Studies* 51. *The Begin-Sadat Center for Strategic Studies, Bar-Ilan University*, 10. http://www.biu.ac.il/SOC/besa/david.pdf.

Another major criticism of targeted killing concerns the fact that those subjected to it are "not afforded a hearing or granted the right to appeal the decision."[32] In addition, if governments have de facto power to kill terrorists, there is no verifiable obligation for them to demonstrate that the individual targeted was indeed a terrorist and that all other measures were exhausted before engaging in this act.[33] Another argument against targeted killing is the intelligence that will be lost by killing an operative. Moreover, the killing of a leader of a terrorist group may backfire, resulting not only in increased publicity and sympathy for the group's cause but also the creation of a martyr, which can attract new recruits, providing them with justification for engaging in terrorist attacks.

Targeted killings may serve only as a temporary victory, as terrorists have many individuals to replace those who are killed. Even though the loss of those in leadership positions may temporarily adversely impact the organization, eventually these positions are filled and operations will resume. A case in point is the replacement of Osama bin Laden. Soon after his demise, his role was assumed by Ayman al-Zawahiri. If al-Zawahiri is killed, there are others who can take his place. Nevertheless, the killing of a terrorist group's leadership may indeed have significant unintended consequences. When a leader is subjected to targeted killing, his or her replacement may be even more brutal than his or her predecessor. In other instances, as a result of the death of leadership, the group may adapt and become a more effective decentralized organization that is harder to destroy. This became evident in the aftermath of the destruction of the majority of al-Qaeda's leadership post-9/11. Consequently, al-Qaeda was forced to decentralize. This decentralization poses significant problems in determining the number of operatives associated with the organization and the leadership of these smaller groups that were created that make up the current threat of al-Qaeda. The nature of the threat of the al-Qaeda brand of terrorism today makes possible the existence of a terrorist group without its "head." A hierarchical leadership is no longer required to sustain a terrorist organization. This is demonstrated by the decentralized nature of al-Qaeda and the ability and willingness of individuals to engage in terrorist attacks independent of any direction or guidance from leadership. A case in point is the lone wolf terrorist. Accordingly, targeted killings can make a bad situation worse. Arresting the leader of a terrorist group is far more effective in damaging the group than targeted killing. Apart from the arrest of a leader, the treatment of the leader while in the custody of authorities is also critical. The leader must be treated humanely, so his arrest does not serve as a platform for recruitment for the terrorist organization. This, however, is not enough. A terrorist leader must also be prevented from communicating with the group while in prison. Consider the case of West Germany, wherein the government passed the Kontaktsperregesetz (Law

---

[32] Guiora, A. 2005. "Terrorism on trial": Targeted killing as active self-defense. *Case Western Reserve Journal of International Law* 37:330.

[33] Anderson, K. 2009. Targeted killing in U.S. counterterrorism strategy and law. In *Legislating the war on terror: An agenda for reform*, ed. B.Wittes, 362. Washington, DC: Brookings Institution.

Banning Contacts) in 1977, which was a direct response to the Red Army Faction's kidnapping of Hanns-Martin Schleyer, a prominent German industrialist and president of the German Employer's Union. Schleyer did not survive the abduction. German authorities suspected that incarcerated RAF leaders not only initiated the kidnapping but also directed the kidnappers from within prison. This law was passed to prevent such activities from occurring in the future by providing a legal basis with which to cut off the contact of RAF members with the outside world while they were awaiting trial.

Just Deserts for Terrorists: A Case for Life Imprisonment or Capital Punishment?

Another method of punishing terrorists is the death penalty. Capital punishment involves the implementation of a death sentence and the eventual execution of a prisoner. This form of punishment is exacted as a form of retribution. The notion of retribution derives from the following Biblical reference concerning compensation for harms done: "Wherever hurt is done, you shall give life for life, eye for eye, tooth for tooth, hand for hand, foot for foot, burn for burn, bruise for bruise, wound for wound."[34] From a retributionist point of view, therefore, a person who murders another must receive the punishment of death. As Immanuel Kant noted,

> [i]f . . . he has committed a murder, he must die. In this case, there is no substitute that will satisfy the requirements of legal justice. There is no sameness of kind between death and remaining alive even under the most miserable conditions, and consequently there is also no equality between the crime and the retribution unless the criminal is judicially condemned and put to death.[35]

Many countries see capital punishment as a fitting punishment for terrorists. For example, in India, a death sentence was upheld for Mohd Arif, a member of Lashkar-e-Taiba (a Pakistani-based Islamic terrorist organization that is linked to al-Qaeda), for his role in the 2000 Red Fort attack in Delhi, India, in which three people were killed (2 Army *jawans* and 1 civilian).[36] The death penalty is also implemented because it is believed to deter terrorism. However, this assertion has not been empirically proven.[37] After the 1993 WTC attack, legislation was introduced in the United States—the Federal Death Penalty Act of 1994—to expand the use of the death

---

34 Exodus 21:23–25.

35 Murphy, J. G. 1979. Cruel and unusual punishments. In *Retribution, Justice and Therapy*, 22. Dordrecht, The Netherlands: D. Reidel.

36 Supreme Court upholds death penalty for LeT terrorist in Red Fort attack. 2011. *India: Daily News and Analysis*, August 10, 2011. http://www.dnaindia.com/india/report_supreme-court -upholds-death-penalty-for-let-terrorist-in-red-fort-attack_1574446.

37 Chapter 8, Hood, R. 2002. *The death penalty: A worldwide perspective*. Oxford, UK: Oxford University Press; Sunstein, C. R., and Vermuele, A. 2005. Is capital punishment morally required? The relevance of life-life tradeoffs. *Stanford Law Review* 58:703–750; Radelet, M. L., and Akers, R. L. 1996. Deterrence and the death penalty: The views of the experts. *Journal of Criminal Law and Criminology* 87 (1): 1–16; and Erlich, I. 1975. The deterrent effect of capital punishment: A question of life and death. *The American Economic Review* 65 (3): 397–417.

penalty to include terrorism. Regardless of the new law providing capital punishment for terrorism cases, Timothy McVeigh was not deterred and bombed the Alfred P. Murrah FBI building in Oklahoma in 1995.

According to Amnesty International, 96 countries have abolished the death penalty.[38] Other countries retain the death penalty for ordinary crimes but have not executed any person in over 10 years. These countries are considered as abolitionists because even though they have the death penalty, they are not using it as a form of punishment.[39] Of the remaining countries that administer capital punishment, 9 of them have abolished the death penalty only for ordinary crimes. Specifically, the laws of these "countries . . . provide for the death penalty only for exceptional crimes such as crimes under military law or crimes committed in exceptional circumstances."[40] Retentionist countries have and use the death penalty for ordinary crimes.[41]

Countries that have the death penalty execute prisoners by lethal injection, firing squad, electrocution, gas chamber, and hanging. Only Saudi Arabia uses public beheadings as a form of capital punishment. Beheadings are a form of *Qisas*—Islamic law punishments. Crimes for which public beheadings have been

---

[38] Albania, Andorra, Angola, Argentina, Armenia, Australia, Austria, Azerbaijan, Belgium, Bhutan, Bosnia-Herzegovina, Bulgaria, Burundi, Cambodia, Canada, Cape Verde, Colombia, Cook Islands, Costa Rica, Cote D'Ivoire, Croatia, Cyprus, Czech Republic, Denmark, Djibouti, Dominican Republic, Ecuador, Estonia, Finland, France, Gabon, Georgia, Germany, Greece, Guinea-Bissau, Haiti, Holy See, Honduras, Hungary, Iceland, Ireland, Italy, Kiribati, Kyrgyzstan, Liechtenstein, Lithuania, Luxembourg, Macedonia, Malta, Marshall Islands, Mauritius, Mexico, Micronesia, Moldova, Monaco, Montenegro, Mozambique, Namibia, Nepal, Netherlands, New Zealand, Nicaragua, Niue, Norway, Palau, Panama, Paraguay, Philippines, Poland, Portugal, Romania, Rwanda, Samoa, San Marino, Sao Tome And Principe, Senegal, Serbia (including Kosovo), Seychelles, Slovakia, Slovenia, Solomon Islands, South Africa, Spain, Sweden, Switzerland, Timor-Leste, Togo, Turkey, Turkmenistan, Tuvalu, Ukraine, United Kingdom, Uruguay, Uzbekistan, Vanuatu, and Venezuela. Amnesty International. 2011. *Abolitionist and retentionist countries*. http://www.amnesty.org/en/death-penalty/abolitionist -and-retentionist-countries.

[39] Algeria, Benin, Brunei, Burkina Faso, Cameroon, Central African Republic, Congo (Republic of), Eritrea, Gambia, Ghana, Grenada, Kenya, Laos, Liberia, Madagascar, Malawi, Maldives, Mali, Mauritania, Morocco, Myanmar, Nauru, Niger, Papua New Guinea, Russian Federation, South Korea, Sri Lanka, Suriname, Swaziland, Tajikistan, Tanzania, Tonga, Tunisia, and Zambia. Amnesty International. 2011. *Abolitionist and retentionist countries*. http://www.amnesty.org/en/death -penalty/abolitionist-and-retentionist-countries.

[40] Bolivia, Brazil, Chile, El Salvador, Fiji, Israel, Kazakstan, Latvia, and Peru. Amnesty International. 2011. *Abolitionist and retentionist countries*. http://www.amnesty.org/en/death-penalty /abolitionist-and-retentionist-countries.

[41] Afghanistan, Antigua and Barbuda, Bahamas, Bahrain, Bangladesh, Barbados, Belarus, Belize, Botswana, Chad, China, Comoros, Democratic Republic of Congo, Cuba, Dominica, Egypt, Equatorial Guinea, Ethiopia, Guatemala, Guinea, Guyana, India, Indonesia, Iran, Iraq, Jamaica, Japan, Jordan, Kuwait, Lebanon, Lesotho, Libya, Malaysia, Mongolia, Nigeria, North Korea, Oman, Pakistan, Palestinian Authority, Qatar, Saint Kitts and Nevis, Saint Lucia, Saint Vincent and the Grenadines, Saudi Arabia, Sierra Leone, Singapore, Somalia, Sudan, Syria, Taiwan, Thailand, Trinidad and Tobago, Uganda, United Arab Emirates, United States of America, Vietnam, Yemen, and Zimbabwe. Amnesty International. 2011. *Abolitionist and retentionist countries*. http://www .amnesty.org/en/death-penalty/abolitionist-and-retentionist-countries.

sanctioned include murder, rape, armed robbery, and drug trafficking. People have been executed in Saudi Arabia for homosexuality as well. Beheadings are extremely gruesome; with this form of execution, blood spurts from the severed carotid artery and the jugular veins of the neck after decapitation. The executions occur on the Sabbath (Friday) after the afternoon prayers. These executions are administered in the public square. Before the execution, the person to be beheaded is tranquilized and then brought out and made to kneel on a blue plastic tarp. After the person's name and crime is read before the witnesses (i.e., the crowd in the public square), the executioner beheads the individual. Following the execution, newspapers in Saudi Arabia are required to make an announcement with information about the crime and the court ruling.[42] In 2005, three male terrorists were beheaded in al-Jawf, Saudi Arabia.[43] Their bodies and severed heads were displayed on poles in a public square in front of a mosque. The exact number of beheadings that occurred between 1990 to 2010 are unknown. However, it was estimated that during this time, approximately 1,360 individuals were beheaded. Specifically, the available estimates for each year are as follows:[44] 750 beheadings occurred from 1990 to 2001; 47 in 2002; 53 in 2003; 36 in 2004; 83 in 2005; 38 in 2006; 158 in 2007; 102 in 2008; 67 in 2009; and 26 in 2010.

The justification for public beheadings has been heavily debated, even among Saudi nationals and religious imams. A big source of contention is the government-sanctioned beheadings of juveniles. The UN Convention on the Rights of the Child prohibits the execution of a juvenile. Specifically, the government cannot impose a death sentence on a person under the age of 18 who committed a crime. Saudi Arabia is a signatory to this convention and thus is required to comply with it. However, the juvenile offenders on death row indicate otherwise. Additionally, cases of juvenile offenders who were executed after Saudi Arabia became a signatory clearly show that this country is not in compliance with the convention. A case in point was the execution Moeid bin Hussein Hakami, who was only 16 at the time of his execution and had been given a death sentence for the murder he committed at the age of 13.[45]

According to U.S. Supreme Court Justice Potter Stewart in *Gregg v. Georgia*,[46] "capital punishment is an expression of society's moral outrage at particularly

---

[42] Saloom, R. 2005. Is beheading permissible under Islamic law? Comparing terrorist jihad and the Saudi Arabian death penalty. *UCLA Journal of International Law and Foreign Affairs* 10:246.

[43] Saudi Authorities Execute Three Convicted Terrorists. 2005. *USA Today*, April 3, 2005. http://www.usatoday.com/news/world/2005-04-03-saudi-beheadings_x.htm.

[44] Amnesty International. 2009, May 12. *Juveniles among five men beheaded in Saudi Arabia.* http://www.amnesty.org/en/news-and-updates/news/juveniles-among-five-men-beheaded-saudi-arabia-20090512; Saudi Arabia's Beheading Culture. 2009. *CBS New*, February 11, 2009. http:// www.cbsnews. com/stories/2004/06/25/world/main626196.shtml.

[45] Amnesty International. 2008. *Affront to justice: Death penalty in Saudi Arabia.* http://www .amnesty.org/en/library/asset/MDE23/027/2008/en/dc425c41-8bb9-11dd-8e5e-43ea85d15a69/ mde230272008en .pdf.

[46] *Gregg v. Georgia*, 428 U.S. 153 (1976) (para 18).

Box 10-1   Food for Thought—Beheadings as a Terrorist Tactic: What Are the Implications?

Terrorists also capture and behead individuals in the Middle East, Africa, and Asia. A case in point is Daniel Pearl, who was the South Asia Bureau Chief of the *Wall Street Journal* in Mumbai, India. In 2002, Pearl was kidnapped while investigating alleged connections between a radical Pakistani cleric and Richard Reid (the infamous shoe bomber). Pearl was set up by al-Qaeda to think that he would interview the cleric. On February 1, 2002, Daniel Pearl was beheaded by al-Qaeda terrorists in Pakistan. The video of his beheading was played worldwide. Ahmed Omar Saeed Sheikh was implicated and sentenced to death for the kidnapping and murder. The mastermind of 9/11, Khalid Sheikh Mohammed, recently claimed that he beheaded Daniel Pearl.

Instances of terrorists' beheading captured individuals abound. In 2004, Al-Qaeda in the Arabian Peninsula decapitated American engineer Paul Johnson, Jr. in Saudi Arabia after officials in the country did not meet the demands of the terrorists (i.e., releasing their imprisoned terrorist allies).[1] The same year in Iraq, Nicholas Berg, an American businessman, and Kim Sun-il, a South Korean translator for a U.S. military supplier, were beheaded by al-Qaeda-linked terrorists.[2] Additionally, in that year in Iraq, three other men, Jack Hensley, Eugene Armstrong, and Kenneth Bigley, who were working on reconstruction projects for Gulf Supplies and Commercial Services, were kidnapped and subsequently beheaded by terrorists.[3]

These beheadings were videotaped, photographed, and posted on the Internet or sent to news stations to ensure broadcast worldwide.

1. What purposes do beheadings serve? That is, why do terrorists record beheadings (e.g., videotape and photograph) and seek to broadcast them to the wider public?
2. What are the repercussions of such broadcasting?

---

[1] Saudi Arabia's Beheading Culture. 2009. *CBS News*, February 11, 2009. http://www.cbsnews.com/stories/2004/06/25/world/main626196.shtml.

[2] Ibid.

[3] Body of Slain American Hostage Found. 2004. *CNN*, September 22, 2004. http://articles.cnn.com/2004-09-22/world/iraq.beheading_1_eugene-jack-armstrong-al-zarqawi-hensley-and-bigley?_s=PM:WORLD.

offensive conduct. This function may be unappealing to many, but it is essential in an ordered society that asks its citizens to rely on legal processes rather than self-help to vindicate their wrongs." Justice Stewart further noted that "when people begin to believe that organized society is unwilling or unable to impose upon criminal offenders the punishment they 'deserve,' then there are sown the seeds of anarchy—of self-help, vigilante justice, and lynch law."[47] As such, capital

---

[47] *Furman v. Georgia, supra,* 408 U.S. 153 at 308, 92 S. Ct., at 2761 (Stewart, J., concurring)] (para 18).

punishment is implemented, as it is believed to give terrorists or other murderers their "just deserts."[48] But is capital punishment really what terrorists deserve?

To be considered punishment, it must actually impose a hardship on the terrorist. The desire of Islamic terrorists is to achieve martyrdom. Accordingly, death is sought by this type of terrorist. In light of this, a more fitting form of punishment would actually be life imprisonment. In this way, martyrdom is not achieved. Even suicide in prison would not achieve martyrdom for Islamic terrorists, as, in this case, suicide is not considered martyrdom. Other types of terrorists have also sought to martyr themselves for their cause. Therefore, to be effective, a counterterrorism policy should avoid making martyrs of terrorists.

Capital punishment enhances terrorists' goals by turning those executed into martyrs, inviting retaliatory strikes by supporters or other members of the terrorist group, increasing recruitment to the group and/or its cause, and enhancing the objectives of a group. Moreover, killing these terrorists, either publicly with beheadings or other forms of capital punishment, will not mitigate the terrorist threat. There are many more recruits willing and able to take the place of the operatives who are killed. A cost that terrorists seek to avoid is incapacitation. This prevents them from being able to achieve their goals, one of which is martyrdom. Accordingly, the threat of incarceration may serve as a deterrent. However, the punishment must be severe enough to warrant the attention of a perpetrator, and the offender must be certain that he or she will be punished.

COLLECTIVE PUNISHMENT

Other than punishing an individual terrorist, some countries engaged in collective punishment, which seeks to punish others for the acts of terrorists and terrorist groups. Collective punishment is used as a way to indirectly impact a terrorist's behavior. It can effectively deter wrongdoing only if those punished are in a position to monitor and control the terrorist's behavior. This form of punishment seeks not only to reveal the terrorist's identity to others but also to deter future acts of terrorism. Three types of collective punishment are explored here: house demolitions, border closing and blockades, and sanctions.

House Demolition

One form of collective punishment is house demolition. This technique is implemented by Israel against suspected Palestinian terrorists. Domestic law in Israel enables military commanders to order the demolition of a home and confiscate the land if an explosive device has been detonated on the property or if it belongs to a suspected terrorist. The families of Palestinians known or suspected of engaging in terrorism-related activity against Israeli soldiers and civilians have also had their

---

[48] Von Hirsch defines just deserts as follows: "The offender may justly be subjected to certain deprivations because he deserves it; and he deserves it because he has engaged in wrongful conduct—conduct that does or threatens injury and that is prohibited by law." von Hirsch, A. 1976. *Doing justice: The choice of punishments.* New York: Hill and Wang, 51.

homes demolished.[49] In particular, in Israel, Regulation 119(1) of the Defense Regulations of 1945 holds that

> A military commander may by order direct the forfeiture to the Government of Palestine of any house, structure or land from in which he has reason to suspect that any firearm has been illegally discharged, or any bomb, grenade or explosive or incendiary article illegally thrown detonated, exploded or otherwise discharged or of any house, structure or land situated in any area, town, village, quarter or street the inhabitants or some of the inhabitants of which he is satisfied have committed, or attempted to commit, or abetted the commission of, or been accessories after the fact to the commission of, any offence against these Regulations involving violence or intimidation or any Military Court offence, and when any house, structure or land is forfeited as aforesaid, the Military commander may destroy the house or the structure or anything in or on the house, the structure or the land.

Since 2001, the Israeli army has destroyed approximately 500 homes.[50] These homes are often destroyed by detonating explosives, resulting in damage to other neighboring homes as well. According to Israeli authorities, these demolitions are not meant to punish terrorists for their actions. Instead, they are used to deter other Palestinians from engaging in terrorist attacks. In fact, the Israeli Supreme Court had stated that the only legitimate purpose for house demolition is deterrence.[51] In *Sabich v. Military Commander of Judea and Samaria Region*,[52] the Israeli Court noted that house demolitions "may have influence even on terrorists who are willing to sacrifice their lives in suicide attacks." Additionally, the policy on house demolition "may deter those persons actually contemplating terrorist acts as well as those who might harbor terrorists or encourage such acts."[53]

The demolition of houses of known or suspected terrorists is considered collective punishment. Article 33 of the Geneva Convention defines collective punishment as punishment for an offense that he or she has not personally committed. This article further prohibits pillage, reprisals against protected persons and their property, collective penalties, and measures of intimidation or terrorism. Likewise, other instruments that prohibit collective punishment include the Hague Convention of 1899. In particular, Article 50 of the Hague Convention, holds that "no general penalty, pecuniary or otherwise, can be inflicted on the population on

---

[49] A3. Amnesty International, Report on House Demolition and Destruction of Land and Property in Israel and the Occupied Territories, Executive Summary, London, 18 May 2004 (excerpts). 2004. *Journal of Palestine Studies* 33 (4): 176.

[50] Ibid., p. 177.

[51] Zemach, A. 2004. The limits of international criminal law: House demolitions in an occupied territory. *Connecticut Journal of International Law* 20:69.

[52] 50(1) P.D. at 358–359

[53] Reicin, C. V. 1987. Preventative detention, curfews, demolition of houses and deportations: An analysis of measures employed by Israel in the administered territories. *Cardozo Law Review* 8:547; Gorelick, B. A. 2003. The Israeli response to Palestinian breach of the Oslo Agreements. *New England Journal of International and Comparative Law* 9:674.

account of the acts of individuals for which it cannot be regarded as collectively responsible." The national laws of many countries also specifically prohibit collective punishment.

The demolition of houses is also explicitly prohibited under international law. Article 53 of the Geneva Convention states that "[a]ny destruction by the Occupying Power of real or personal property belonging individually or collectively to private persons, or to the State, or to other public authorities, or to social or cooperative organizations, is prohibited, except where such destruction is rendered absolutely necessary by military operations." Similarly, Article 23(g) of the Hague Convention holds that it is prohibited "to destroy or seize the enemy's property, unless such destruction or seizure be imperatively demanded by the necessities of war." Despite the fact that it conflicts with international law, the Israeli High Court has ruled in favor of house demolitions. Indeed, the court has stated that domestic laws such as Regulation 119 take precedent over international treaties and conventions.[54]

Closed Borders and Blockades

History has shown that the use of blockades as a military tactic can have a devastating affect on its target. In 404 BC, Sparta's blockade of Athens caused its population to starve, which forced Athens to surrender. This tactic is also used to combat terrorism in order to obtain a similar effect—to have terrorists desist from their activities and surrender. Israel often engages in this counterterrorism tactic. It has closed borders and created blockades in Palestinian Occupied Territories. Another example is the blockade implemented against Hamas in the Gaza Strip to hold them accountable for the rocket attacks launched from the Gaza Strip. The blockade had a severe adverse impact on the economy and population in Gaza. All exports from Gaza were blocked. In addition, Israel restricted "the entry of food, medical supplies, educational equipment and building materials" into the Gaza Strip.[55] Basically, imports were severely limited; only a few humanitarian goods and foodstuffs were allowed. In 2007, some "75% of Gaza's factories . . . closed because they [were] not allowed to import raw material or export finished products, forcing thousands of families to rely on food aid to survive."[56] Many households experienced water and food shortages. The denial of basic goods and necessities led to multiple deaths of those requiring medical treatment.[57]

---

[54] Grebinar, J. 2003. Responding to terrorism: How must a democracy do it? *Fordham Urban Law Journal* 1 (31): 261.

[55] Amnesty International. 2010, January 18. *Gaza: Blockade "suffocating" daily life—New Report.* http://www.amnesty.org.uk/news_details.asp?NewsID=18574.

[56] Urquhart, C. 2007. Blockade helps Gaza militants, says report. *The Guardian*, July 5, 2007. http://www.guardian.co.uk/world/2007/jul/06/israel.

[57] Amnesty International. 2011. *Israel and the occupied Palestinian territories.* http://www.amnesty.org/en/region/israel-occupied-territories/report-2009.

Box 10-2   A Different Form of Counterterrorism

In Israel, the amendment to the Citizenship Law of 1952 and Entry to Israel Law of 1952 are also used as counterterrorism measures. These laws restrict Palestinians' ability to receive citizenship based on family unification. The restrictions are placed on men between the ages of 18 and 35 and women between the ages of 18 and 25. These laws were premised on the belief that a Palestinian terrorist would marry an Israeli woman (or a Palestinian woman would marry an Israeli man) in order to obtain citizenship and gain access to Israeli territories. This contention, however, has not been supported by evidence.

This blockade not only failed to hold Hamas responsible and accountable for the attack on Israel but also strengthened their movement. Moreover, those impacted were civilians, as Hamas increased mortar attacks after the blockade instead of decreasing them. During Israel's Operation Cast Lead, large-scale destruction of homes and other property occurred in the Gaza Strip, the West Bank, and a Bedouin village in the south of Israel. In these zones, severe restrictions were placed on the population, which caused humanitarian hardship and placed the entire population in these areas virtually under imprisonment.[58] Other Palestinian Occupied Territories were subjected to similar measures. For instance, "in the West Bank the movement of Palestinians was severely curtailed by some 600 Israeli checkpoints and barriers, and by the 700 km fence/wall which the Israeli army continued to build mostly inside the West Bank."[59]

The use of blockades has been condemned by the international community, as some countries that have implemented them have prevented humanitarian aid from reaching targeted countries. This occurred with Israel's blockade of Occupied Palestinian Territories. In 2007, Sari Bashi, the director of Gisha, an Israeli human rights organization, stated, "Israel is attempting to achieve political objectives by exerting pressure on 1.4 million women, men and children, whose suffering is supposed to bring about the change it wants—toppling Hamas control in Gaza."[60] Bashi further noted that "in reality, a policy of collective punishment is being imposed upon 1.4 million people, in violation of international humanitarian law and contradictory to Israel's interest. Destroying Gaza's economy only exacerbates dependence on extreme elements."[61]

The UN Fact Finding Mission on the Gaza Conflict was tasked with investigating Israeli operations in Gaza before, during, and after Operation Cast Lead. On September 29, 2009, a report by Justice Richard Goldstone (the Goldstone

---

[58] Ibid.

[59] Ibid.

[60] Urquhart, C. 2007. Blockade helps Gaza militants, says report. *The Guardian*, July 5, 2007. http://www.guardian.co.uk/world/2007/jul/06/israel.

[61] Ibid.

Report) was presented to the UN Human Rights Council in Geneva. The Goldstone Report claimed that members of the Israel Defense Forces "were responsible for [the] deliberate targeting of civilians, for the destruction of critical infrastructure in Gaza, and for using weapons such as white phosphorous in highly populated areas, all of which it deemed to be violations of international humanitarian law."[62] Israel denied the claims that were made in the report. In another UN report, which concerned Israel's naval blockade of the Gaza Strip, the Palmer Commission noted that "Israel faces a real threat to its security from militant groups in Gaza . . . The naval blockade was imposed as a legitimate security measure in order to prevent weapons from entering Gaza by sea and its implementation complied with the requirements of international law."[63] In 2011, a United Nations panel reporting to the UN Human Rights Council rejected the conclusion of the Palmer report, saying "the blockade had subjected Gazans to collective punishment in 'flagrant contravention of international human rights and humanitarian law' . . . The four-year blockade deprived 1.6 million Palestinians living in the enclave of fundamental rights."[64]

Sanctions

A further form of punishment is sanctions, which some believe to be the appropriate response to terrorist behavior. Sanctions are imposed on the population of a third-party country in response to the actions or policies of its leader or in retaliation for acts of terrorism. Indeed, a principal tool for dealing with international terrorism is sanctions. Diplomatic and economic sanctions are usually implemented in response to terrorism. Diplomatic sanctions usually involve reducing or expelling "diplomatic staff of the respective country in or from their national territory and/or reduc[ing] or withdraw[ing] their own diplomatic staff from that country."[65] Economic sanctions are the focus of this section.

Comprehensive economic sanctions are a form of collective punishment. In order to change the behavior of the state, its citizens are targeted. However, those who are subjected to these measures are largely those who have not engaged in the illicit behavior allegedly warranting the sanction. Such actions indiscriminately punish a population for the behavior of its leadership or working group (or groups) operating within its territories. The logic behind the measures is that "the imposition of economic coercion will exercise sufficient 'bite' that citizens in the target country will exert political pressure to force either a change in the behavior of the

---

[62] U.S. Department of State. 2010, March 11. 2009 human rights report: Israel and the occupied territories. *Country Reports on Human Rights Practices*. http://www.state.gov/g/drl/rls/hrrpt /2009/nea/ 136070.htm.

[63] Keinon, H. 2011. Palmer report: Gaza blockade legal, IDF force excessive. *Jerusalem Post*, September 1, 2011.http://www.jpost.com/DiplomacyAndPolitics/Article.aspx?id=236369.

[64] Nebehay, S. 2011. U.N. experts say Israel's blockade of Gaza illegal. *Reuters*, September 13, 2011. http://www.reuters.com/article/2011/09/13/us-un-gaza-rights-idUSTRE78C59R20110913.

[65] Heupel, M. 2007. The security council's approach to terrorism. *Security Dialogue* 38 (4): 482.

authorities or their removal altogether."[66] By contrast, some scholars believe that sanctions may have an adverse affect as they tend to induce moral outrage (both by those they are imposed on and members of the international community) and send the message that the target population's well-being is of no concern to the state imposing the sanction.[67] Moreover, at times, sanctions may increase the solidarity of the terrorist group targeted and provide them with many more recruits from the general population who were subjected to the sanction through no fault of their own. The reaction, however, depends on the severity of the sanction. It is important to note that sanctions are not effective by themselves in achieving the aims of the organization imposing them; other measures are required.

In 1997, the Foreign Terrorist Organizations Sanctions Regulations was published, which criminalized providing support or resources to foreign terrorist organizations designated by the Secretary of State. The U.S. Department of Treasury has several economic sanction programs currently in effect. The organizations that are designated as supporting or engaging in terrorism pursuant to Executive Orders 13224 and 12947 are either terrorist groups that support their activities through fundraising or charities that raise funds for terrorist organizations. After President George W. Bush issued Executive Order 13224, investigations revealed that terrorists used charitable organizations and donors both within and outside the United States to fund and support their activities.

Post-9/11, the United States implemented numerous sanctions against companies and charities for supporting terrorism. One such example involved the Al-Haramain Islamic Foundation. Americans were prohibited by the government from donating to or engaging in business with the Al-Haramain Islamic Foundation.[68] The Obama administration recently added to the list the Falah-e-Insaniat Foundation, a Pakistani charity that was found to be affiliated with Lashkar-e-Taiba.[69] A further example of this involved the largest Islamic charity in America, the Holy Land Foundation for Relief and Development. An investigation by the FBI revealed that Hamas used this charity to raise funds for its operations. Consequently, pursuant to Executive Order 12334, the assets of the Holy Land Foundation for Relief and Development were frozen. Charities are not the only fronts used to fund terrorist activity. Terrorist organizations also create businesses and corporations to transfer illicit funds. The businesses and corporations are then used to raise funds or transfer money for terrorist activities.

---

66 Weiss, T. et al. eds. 1997. *Economic gain and civilian pain: Humanitarian impacts of economic sanctions.* New York: Rowman & Littlefield.

67 DeNardo, J. 1985. *Power in numbers: The political strategy of protest and rebellion.* Princeton, NJ: Princeton University Press; Bueno de Mesquita, E., and Dickson, E. S. 2007. The propaganda of the deed: Terrorism, counterterrorism, and mobilization. *American Journal of Political Science* 51 (2): 364–381.

68 U.S. moves against Saudi-based charity. 2008. *MSNBC*, June 19, 2008. http://www.msnbc.msn.com/id/25268064/ns/world_news-terrorism/t/us-moves-against-saudi-based-charity/.

69 Baker, S. 2010. U.S. hits Pakistani charity with terror sanctions. *The Blaze*, November 26, 2010. http://www.theblaze.com/stories/u-s-hits-pakistani-charity-with-terror-sanctions/.

The U.S. Department of Treasury has also lifted sanctions from companies and charities since 9/11. Specifically, the China Great Wall Industry Corporation was "accused of providing material support to Iran's missile program. The firm's U.S. subsidiary, G.W. Aerospace, had been designated because of its relationship to China Great Wall."[70] The Department of Treasury lifted its sanctions after a rigorous and thorough compliance program was implemented to prevent any further dealings with Iran.

All individuals in the United States, including charities, are prohibited from dealing with individuals and organizations designated as associated with terrorism under these Executive Orders. An exception to this rule exists: the Department of Treasury's Office of Foreign Assets Control (OFAC) may authorize an individual or company to engage in business with a designated person, organization, or country. OFAC is also responsible for administering economic and trade sanctions against target countries. After an individual or entity is designated a target, it is the responsibility of the OFAC to block the assets of the designee. The designation is made known on its Specially Designated Nationals (SDNs) lists, (on which individuals or entities are labeled as Specially Designated Global Terrorists [SDGTs]), the Federal Register, and OFAC's website (although only to inform the public of a SDGT addition to the SDN list). OFAC's SDN list includes individuals and organizations with whom U.S. persons and companies are prohibited from contracting for services or conducting transactions.[71] The U.S. Department of State claims that upon designation, any and all transactions and dealings with the designee from persons within the United States are strictly prohibited.

According to the U.S. Department of State, these designations are also believed to:[72]

- Deter donations or contributions to designated individuals or entities;
- Heighten public awareness and knowledge of individuals or entities linked to terrorism;
- Promote due diligence of other governments and private sector entities to avoid associations with designees;
- Disrupt terrorist networks, thereby cutting off access to resources;
- Encourage designated entities to desist from terrorism.

Measures have also been implemented in the United States that block the assets of illegal money remitters. Both the USA Patriot Act of 2001 and the USA Patriot Act Improvement and Reauthorization Act of 2005 target the financial backing of terrorist groups in several ways: by holding U.S. banks accountable for their dealings

---

[70] U.S. moves against Saudi-based charity. 2008. *MSNBC*, June 19, 2008. http://www.msnbc.msn .com/id/25268064/ns/world_news-terrorism/t/us-moves-against-saudi-based-charity/.

[71] For the most recent SDN List, see http://www.treasury.gov/ofac/downloads/t11sdn.pdf.

[72] U.S. Department of State. 2001, September 23. Executive Order 13224. *Office of the Coordinator for Counterterrorism.* http://www.state.gov/s/ct/rls/other/des/122570.htm.

with foreign banks, by strengthening laws on money laundering as they relate to terrorist financing, and by creating asset forfeiture laws in matters involving the funding of terrorist activities. Pursuant to the USA Patriot Act 2001, to be lawful, money remitters were required to register as a money service business. This registration subjected them to terrorist finance and money laundering regulations. It further required money remitters to report suspicious activities and keep accurate records of all financial transactions and customer information.

To avoid detection, terrorists are believed to have used the hawala banking system, which involves the transfer of money without actually moving it and bypasses regulations for money remitters.[73] How does it work?

> Upon customer request, a U.S.-based hawaladar—a hawala operator—will call, fax, or email their hawaladar associate in [a Middle Eastern, African, South Asian or other country that uses such a system], for example, with the specifics of the transaction (i.e., amount and password only—no names are used). This hawaladar in [the target country where the money will be transferred to] will then pay the requested amount out of his/her own funds, and in local currency, upon receiving the agreed upon password from the recipient. The only paper trail might be a notation, often encoded or in a little-known dialect . . . , of the debt obligation in internal books. The funds are distributed, often delivered right to the door of the intended recipient, . . . without receipts or paperwork.[74]

Accordingly, hawala systems operate outside of formal financial institutions. This money transfer is based entirely on the honor system; as such, no promissory instruments are exchanged.

Sanctions have been placed on specific terrorists. For instance, on August 16, 2011, the U.S. Department of Treasury placed sanctions on three senior members of Jemaah Islamiya—Umar Patek, Abdul Rahim Ba'asyir, and Muhammad Jibril Abdul Rahman.[75] Sanctions have also been implemented against those countries that harbor and/or sponsor terrorists. According to the U.S. Department of State, if the United States designates a specific country as a sponsor of international terrorism, the following sanctions are usually imposed:[76] a ban on arms-related sales and exports, rigid controls over goods and services that could significantly enhance terrorist's capabilities or the state's ability to support terrorism, and a prohibition on the provision of economic assistance to this country. Other miscella-

---

73 McCulloch, J., and Pickering, S. 2005. Suppressing the financing of terrorism: Proliferating state crime, eroding censure and extending neo-colonialism. *British Journal of Criminology* 45 (4): 470–486.

74 Bowers, C. B. 2009. Hawala, money laundering, and terrorism finance: Micro-lending as an end to illicit remittance. *Denver Journal of International Law and Policy* 37:379–380.

75 U.S. Department of Treasury. 2011, August 16. *Treasury sanctions three senior members of the Jemaah Islamiya terrorist network.* http://www.treasury.gov/press-center/press-releases/Pages /tg1276.aspx.

76 U.S. Department of State. 2001, April 30. *Overview of state-sponsored terrorism.* http://www .state.gov/s/ct/rls/crt/2000/2441.htm.

neous restrictions imposed seek to punish those not directly involved in sponsoring terrorism. In particular, the United States has denied companies and individuals tax credits for any income they may have earned in a country that has been designated as sponsoring terrorism. In addition, America can prohibit an individual from engaging in a financial transaction with a terrorist state. Normally, sanctions include the banning of the import of goods to or any export of goods from the countries in question except for supplies that are strictly needed for medical purposes and, in humanitarian circumstances, foodstuffs.

Articles 8, 17, and 20 in 1947 Rio Treaty permit the Organization of American States (OAS) to impose sanctions on a third party. Another organization with the power to impose sanctions according to its treaty is the European Union. Sanctions have also been taken on an international level. After the bombings of the embassies in Kenya and Tanzania, the United Nations called on the Taliban to refrain from supporting Osama bin Laden and providing a safe haven for him and his followers. The Taliban refused. Accordingly, the UN Security Council compelled all Member States to implement comprehensive sanctions against the Taliban in 1999.[77] In 2000, the UN Security Council mandated that each Member State: desist from providing military assistance and training to Afghanistan; implement an arms embargo against the territory controlled by the Taliban; freeze the financial assets of the Taliban, Osama bin Laden, and his associates; and prevent the importation of acetic anhydride, a substance that was used by the Taliban to transform opium into heroin.[78]

Moreover, internationally, nongovernmental organizations (NGOs) have been designated by the 1267 Sanctions Committee to shut down international charities that fund operations for terrorists and terrorist organizations. The United Nations

> created a sanctions committee that maintains a list of individuals and entities belonging or related to the Taliban, Osama bin Laden and Al Qaeda. The resolution obliges all states to freeze the assets, prevent the entry into or the transit through their territories, and prevent the direct or indirect supply, sale and transfer of arms and military equipment with regard to the individuals and entities on the list.[79]

It has further declared that "acts, methods, and practices of terrorism are contrary to the purposes and principles of the United Nations and that knowingly financing, planning and inciting terrorist acts are also contrary to the purposes and principles of the United Nations."[80] The resolution calls on Member States to "prevent and suppress the financing of terrorist acts" and "refrain from providing

---

[77] UN Security Council Resolution 1267 (1999).
[78] UN Security Council Resolution 1333 (2000).
[79] UN Security Resolution 1267 (1999).
[80] UN Security Resolution 1373 (9/28/01).

any form of support, active or passive, to entities or persons involved in terrorist acts."[81] Countries

> are obliged to criminalize terrorist activity and financing, freeze terrorist-related funds and assets, deny safe haven to those who 'finance, plan, support, or commit terrorist acts, or provide safe havens,' prevent the movement of terrorists or terrorist groups, cooperate with other governments and the international community on the anti-terrorism front, and become parties to all terrorism-related conventions and protocols.[82]

These terrorist financing prohibitions, however, refer only to the Taliban, Osama bin Laden, and al-Qaeda-affiliated organizations, which are designated under Resolution 1267. It thus does not criminalize the financing or the creation of safe havens for other terrorist and terrorist groups.

When a state responds aggressively to terrorism, it will gain a reputation for punishing terrorists and in so doing, it is believed, will deter others from engaging in such acts. While such an assertion has not been tested, many states adhere to it. Consider an Islamic terrorist. The killing of an Islamic extremist as a form of punishment does not have a deterrent effect. In fact, the opposite tends to occur, as it mobilizes supporters to target the government that punished the individual. Indeed, coercive tactics such as targeted killings, house demolition, blockades, sanctions, public beheadings, and other forms of capital punishment are said to increase opposition to the government implementing it instead of decreasing it. As Waldron notes, "of course, this is not a reason for *not* punishing the perpetrators of murderous attacks, but the reasons for punishing [should instead be for] reasons of justice, not security (via general deterrence)."[83] Punishment, if rendered, must be necessary and in accordance with domestic and international laws. Most importantly, in order for an act to be considered punishment, it must actually impose a hardship on the perpetrator. The choice of appropriate punishment will ultimately depend on the perpetrator.

HYPOTHETICAL SCENARIO: WHAT MIGHT HAVE HAPPENED IF OSAMA BIN LADEN WAS CAPTURED INSTEAD OF KILLED?

Imagine that U.S. Special Forces had captured Osama bin Laden during their raid on his compound in Abbottabad, Pakistan. He is currently being held at Guantanamo Bay.

1. What security risks would arise from his detention?
2. How might his followers react to his capture and detention?
3. In hindsight, was capture and detention instead of killing a better option?

---

[81] Ibid.

[82] Anti-Defamation League. 2004, October. *Multilateral responses to terrorism: The United Nations.* http://www.adl.org/Terror/tu/tu_38_04_09.asp.

[83] Waldron, J. 2003. Security and liberty: The image of balance. *The Journal of Political Philosophy* 11 (2): 191.

CHAPTER SUMMARY

Targeted killing involves the intentional killing of an individual or individuals with a government's approval. Countries have authorized targeted killings in the past and continue to do so today. Targeted killings often occur in retaliation to a terrorist attack in order to prevent and deter further acts of terrorism. Such killings can be justified to preempt actions that could pose severe security risks to a country. Additionally, they may be justified if the arrest and detention of an individual exposes the country to serious harms. Post-9/11, targeted killings have been used multiple times against targets in Afghanistan, Iraq, Pakistan, and Yemen.

Human rights organizations have argued that many of the U.S. targeted killings of terrorists, post-9/11, constituted extrajudicial killings and thus were in violation of international law. Even though targeted killing has been referred to as extrajudicial killing, it differs from it in several respects. Targeted killing is authorized when incapacitation of terrorists through arrest is operationally impossible. By contrast, extrajudicial killing occurs when other options such as arrest are feasible yet not pursued by the authorizing government before deciding to kill the target. Targeted killings could also have severe adverse consequences.

Capital punishment has also been used to punish terrorists. However, it is clearly counterproductive as a counterterrorism measure, as it makes martyrs of terrorists and in so doing, enhances the objectives of these terrorists. Moreover, if a decision is made to execute a terrorist, supporters may retaliate by kidnapping citizens or government officials of the target country and refuse to release them unless the terrorist is freed.

Furthermore, collective punishment has also been used to combat terrorism. As punishment, Israel demolishes the homes of suspected terrorists and/or their families. Nevertheless, this form of punishment is prohibited by international law. Blockades and sanctions are also imposed against states within which terrorists operate to discourage the perpetrators and others from engaging in terrorism and/or supporting it. Sanctions are also imposed on individuals, companies, and other entities that support terrorism.

REVIEW QUESTIONS

1. What is the difference between an extrajudicial killing and a targeted killing?
2. Under what circumstances may a targeted killing be justified?
3. Should a terrorist be given capital punishment or life imprisonment?
4. Are house demolitions in accordance with international law?
5. What are the implications of a blockade?
6. What types of sanctions have been implemented against terrorists?
7. How effective is collective punishment as a counterterrorism practice?

chapter eleven

Rehab for Terrorists

Governments have realized the importance of noncoercive measures in the fight against terrorism. This chapter covers these "soft approaches" to terrorism. More specifically, it explores a tactic for dealing with terrorists that moves beyond the common forms of punishment, namely, rehabilitation. Rehabilitation can be thought of as a means of restoring terrorists to good citizenship through programs of training, treatment, and counseling. This form of "punishment" seeks to deal with the consequences of a crime. It is also forward looking, seeking to prevent terrorism from occurring in the future. Incapacitating terrorists merely serves as a temporary fix if the sentence imposed is one in which the terrorists may be released back into society. What happens when terrorists are released? What will prevent them from reengaging in terrorist attacks?

Proponents argue that rehabilitation may be the answer. In particular, these individuals assume that terrorism always has causes that are discoverable and open to treatment, and that if terrorists are not treated, they will become worse. This form of punishment seeks to change those aspects of the terrorist's traits, personality, views, and lifestyle that predisposed them to terrorism and to develop the skills, obtain the knowledge, and have available the opportunities to enable them to desist from engaging in terrorism. Rehabilitation programs seek to show individuals that terrorism is immoral and unjustifiable. To rehabilitate an individual, knowledge of the type of terrorism an individual is engaged in[1] and what motivates individuals to join and desist from terrorism is required.[2]

---

[1] See the chapter in this text on the introduction to terrorism.

[2] See the chapters in this text on perspectives on terrorism and factors influencing the sustainability of and disengagement from terrorism.

Before evaluating the rehabilitation programs that have been implemented around the globe to combat terrorism, this chapter explores the role of prisons in the radicalization and recruitment of terrorists. It then examines the types of terrorists currently housed within certain prisons in Europe, the United States, the Middle East, and Asia, and how these terrorists affect prison infrastructure, management of inmates, and staffing of prisons. This chapter then considers the factors in prison that are conducive to terrorism. Finally, this chapter highlights existing rehabilitation programs and their efficacy in preventing future acts of terrorism from participants in the program.

PRISONS MATTER: INCUBATORS FOR TERRORISM?

Prisons play a prominent role in terrorist recruitment and radicalization. Recruitment refers to the solicitation of individuals to engage in terrorists acts or other terrorism-related activity, whereas radicalization refers to the process whereby individuals adapt extremist views, including the belief that the use of violence to achieve goals is justified for political and/or religious purposes. Examples abound of individuals who were recruited and radicalized while serving sentences in prisons for crimes other than terrorism. A review of post-9/11 homegrown terrorists in the United States revealed that some had criminal records and were radicalized in prison. Indeed, studies have shown that U.S. prisons provide an ideal breeding ground for radicalizing men and women.[3] A case in point was Michael Finton, a U.S. citizen and homegrown terrorist from Illinois, who converted to a radical form of Islam while serving his sentence in prison for another crime. In 2009, he tried to blow up a federal courthouse and was sentenced to 28 years in prison. Another example was James Cromitie, the leader of a group of four (which included David Williams, Onta Williams, and Laguerre Payen), who sought to bomb military bases and synagogues in New York City in 2008.[4] Cromitie had a criminal record and had served time in prison for selling drugs at a public school. It was in prison that he was radicalized. A further well-known example is Kevin Lamar James, who is believed to be the founder of a terrorist group in prison known as Jam'yyat Al-Islam Al-Saheeh. James, a U.S. citizen, converted fellow prisoners to Islam while serving his sentence and recruited them to plan attacks against military installations and other targets in California.[5]

---

[3] Cilluffo F., et al. 2006. Out of the shadows: Getting ahead of prisoner radicalization. *A special report by the George Washington University Homeland Security Policy Institute and the University of Virginia Critical Incident Analysis Group.* http://community.nicic.gov/blogs/corrections_headlines /archive/2006/09/19/Getting -Ahead-of-Prisoner-Radicalization.aspx.

[4] Wakin, D. J. 2009, May 23. *Imams reject talk that Islam radicalizes inmates.* http://www .nytimes.com/2009/05/24/nyregion/24convert.html?n=Top/Reference/Times%20Topics/People /C/Cromitie,%20James.

[5] Van Duyn, D. 2006, September 19. *Congressional testimony: Statement of the FBI Deputy Assistant Director of the Counterterrorism Division before the Senate Committee on Homeland Security and Governmental Affairs and Related Agencies.* http://www.fbi.gov/congress/congress06 /vanduyn091906.htm; Transnational terrorism, security and the rule of law. 2008, November 17. *Radicalization, recruitment and the EU counter-terrorism strategy,* 28. http://www .transnationalterrorism.eu/tekst/publications/WP4%20Del%207.pdf.

> **Box 11-1 Terrorist Attack in Brief: The Failed Bombings in London on July 21, 2005**
>
> After the London bombings on July 7, 2005, on July 21, 2005, four African immigrants, Muktar Said Ibrahim, Ramzi Mohammed, Hussain Osman, and Yassin Omar, sought to re-create the event by engaging in suicide bombings against London's transport systems. Like the 7/7 bombers, these individuals targeted three subway trains and one bus. However, the explosives in their backpacks failed to detonate. All four of the bombers were sentenced to life in prison in 2007.

Likewise, British authorities believe that their own correctional institutions have served as an area for terrorist recruitment and radicalization. In particular, Mukta Said Ibrahim, one of the perpetrators of the attempted bombings on July 21, 2005 (see Box 11-1), was considered to have been radicalized in Britain while incarcerated at either Huntercombe or Feltham Young Offenders Institution.[6] Richard Reid, who notoriously tried to light explosives in his shoe (hence, his nickname "the Shoe Bomber") while on board an international flight traveling from Paris to Miami, was also an inmate at Feltham Young Offenders Institution and was similarly suspected of being radicalized in this institution.[7]

The European Union Counter-Terrorism Strategy, which is in line with counterterrorism strategies of the United Nations and countries worldwide, seeks to prevent individuals "from turning to terrorism by tackling the factors or root causes which can lead to radicalization and recruitment, in Europe and internationally."[8] To do so, authorities must be able to identify and disrupt such behaviors by focusing on the conditions that are conducive to terrorism. Building upon the EU Counter-Terrorism Strategy, the Strategy for Combating Radicalization and Recruitment to Terrorism called for Member States of the European Union to identify places where radicalization may occur and implement policies to prevent the radicalization and recruitment of individuals. Prisons were identified by Member States as a main place of recruitment and radicalization.[9] As such, Member States implemented measures at correctional facilities requiring the "collection of information, enhanced prisoner management, the presence of qualified mainstream religious

---

6 Pantucci, R. 2008, March 24. Britain's prisoner dilemma: Issues and concerns in Islamic radicalization. *Terrorism Monitor* 6 (6). http://www.jamestown.org/single/?no_cache=1&tx_ttnews %5Btt_news%5 D=4806.

7 Doward, J. 2007. Extremists train young convicts for terror plots. *The Guardian*, July 15, 2007. http://www.guardian.co.uk/uk/2007/jul/15/ukcrime.prisonsandprobation.

8 Council of the European Union. 2005, November 30. *The European Union counter-terrorism strategy.* http://register.consilium.eu.int/pdf/en/05/st14/st14469-re04.en05.pdf.

9 Other areas in which radicalization takes place is the Internet, community, and educational and religious institutions.

teachers in prisons, and training of penitentiary staff to recognize and address radicalization."[10]

These strategies are specifically designed to deal with the greatest security threat to Europe: al-Qaeda, affiliates, and individuals inspired by al-Qaeda's cause. Europe has played a central role in al-Qaeda's operations because over the past 20 years, it has become a major base of operations for al-Qaeda and related Islamic terrorist groups.[11] If one were to trace back and review the attacks carried out by al-Qaeda before 9/11, one would find that almost every attack had some link with Europe.[12] For example, in the weeks following the attacks: law enforcement authorities in various EU Member States (France, Germany, and Spain, to name a few) "flushed out dozens of suspected terrorists linked to Osama bin Laden"; two Member States, Germany and Spain, were identified as key logistical and planning bases for the attacks; and numerous individuals suspected of their involvement in 9/11 were arrested in France, Germany, Belgium, Spain, Italy, and the United Kingdom.[13] Furthermore, the investigations of 9/11 revealed that not only were there al-Qaeda operational cells in Europe but also a significant number of al-Qaeda support cells, which make up terrorist networks that are both affiliated and unaffiliated with al-Qaeda. By focusing on these individuals, the EU strategy, however, is limited. It is designed to deal with specific types of terrorists—Islamic extremists (e.g., al-Qaeda members, supporters, and those inspired by their cause)—and in so doing, excludes all other forms of terrorism. Nevertheless, other measures have been implemented in prisons in European and other countries to prevent the radicalization and recruitment of inmates, the creation of terrorist groups, and the planning and execution of attacks within and outside prisons. These measures have taken into account different types of terrorism and include adjusting prison regimes to deal with existing terrorist threats and addressing factors that are conducive to various forms of terrorism within prisons.

Prison Regimes

There are two main factors that affect the prison regime of terrorists: the number of terrorists and the type of terrorism. In terms of the number of terrorists, a correctional facility that houses 100 terrorists will operate differently than one that houses fewer than 10. A study published in 2010 showed that the Netherlands held

---

[10] EU Counter-Terrorism Coordinator. 2007, November 23. The EU strategy for combating radicalization and recruitment – Implementation report. *Council of the European Union*, 4. http://register.consilium.europa.eu/pdf/en/07/st15/st15443.en07.pdf.

[11] Vidino, L. 2006. *Al-Qaeda in Europe: The new battleground of international jihad.* New York: Prometheus, 16.

[12] For example, in 1992, one of the planners (Ahmed Ajaj) of the 1993 bombings of the World Trade Center landed at JFK Airport in New York with a fake Swedish passport. See ibid., pp. 16–17.

[13] Gallis, P. 2002, October 17. European counterterrorist efforts: Political will and diverse responses in the first year after September 11. *CRS Report for Congress*, 60. http://digital.library.unt.edu/govdocs/crs//data/2002/upl-meta-crs-7032/RL31612_2002Oct17.pdf?PHPSESSID=62dbcfafd074d37d493f 462fd480e3a6.

5 terrorists in its penitentiary system.[14] Due to the limited number of terrorists, these individuals were housed in a separate terrorism wing within one of its prisons.[15] In the United Kingdom, prisons (e.g., HMP Belmarsh) have a high-security unit within which to house high-risk offenders such as terrorists. This unit holds a total of 48 prisoners and is composed of 4 wings, each of which has 12 single occupancy cells.[16] As such, this facility and others like it are not designed to handle the ever-increasing number of individuals convicted of terrorism-related offenses. For larger numbers of individuals convicted of terrorism-related offenses, such as 100, different approaches have been taken. Either all terrorists have been placed in a single facility (e.g., Guantanamo Bay) or they have been dispersed among the country's prisons. Generally, the primary emphasis of countries seeking to house terrorists in correctional facilities is security and containment, and as a result, many countries tend to disperse terrorist prisoners among correctional institutions to prevent a high concentration of them in a single facility, which is a security risk. Detention facilities housing terrorists and insurgents have been the frequent target of armed assaults by militants in an attempt to free the prisoners, some of which have been successful. For instance, "in March 2007 a large group of militants purportedly from al-Qaeda in Iraq, assaulted a jail in Mosul, Iraq and freed 140 prisoners, most of whom were insurgents."[17] Dispersal of terrorists among correctional facilities also prevents a group of prisoners from rallying to escape. For example, in July 2005 a group of detainees "managed to escape from the Coalition detention facility in Bagram, Afghanistan."[18] Having recognized these risks, the United Kingdom, France, and Spain, among other countries, disperse terrorists to different high-security prisons within their countries.[19]

---

[14] Neumann, P. R. 2010. Prisons and terrorism: Radicalisation and de-radicalisation in 15 countries. *The International Center for the Study of Radicalisation and Political Violence*, 17. http://icsr.info /publications/papers/1277699166PrisonsandTerrorismRadicalisationandDeradicalisationin15 Countries.pdf.

[15] Ibid., p. 18.

[16] HM Chief Inspector of Prisons. 2003, May 26–June 4. *Report on a full announced inspection of HM Prison Belmarsh*. London: HM Chief Inspector of Prisons, 37. http://inspectorates. homeoffice.gov.uk/ hmiprisons/inspect_reports/hmp-yoiinspections; Hannah, G., Clutterbuck, L., and Rubin, J. 2008. Radicalization and rehabilitation. Understanding the challenge of extremists and radicalized prisoners. *RAND Corporation*, 46. http://www.rand.org/content/dam/rand/pubs /technical_reports/2008/RAND_TR571.pdf.

[17] Qaeda-led Militants Storm Iraq Jail, Free 140. 2007. *Reuters*, March 6, 2007. http://www. reuters.com/ article/2007/03/06/idUSIBO665135; Hannah, G., Clutterbuck, L., and Rubin, J. 2008. Radicalization and rehabilitation. Understanding the challenge of extremists and radicalized prisoners. *RAND Corporation*, 45. http://www.rand.org/content/dam/rand/pubs/technical_reports /2008/RAND_TR571.pdf.

[18] Hannah et al., 2008, ibid., p. 46.

[19] Neumann, P. R. 2010. Prisons and terrorism: Radicalisation and de-radicalisation in 15 countries. *The International Center for the Study of Radicalisation and Political Violence*, 18. http://icsr.info /publications/papers/1277699166PrisonsandTerrorismRadicalisationandDeradicalisationin15 Countries.pdf.

Several types of terrorists can be housed within a country's correctional facilities. Certain prisons, such as those in France and Spain, have several hundred suspected terrorists of different types within their prison populations. Religious terrorists (Islamic extremists) and separatist terrorists (the Basque Fatherland and Liberty or ETA) are held in Spanish prisons; whereas, religious terrorists and terrorists from the National Liberation Front of Corsica (*Fronte di Liberazione Naziunale Corsu* or FLNC), a group seeking to separate from France and create an independent state on the island of Corsica, make up part of the prison population in France. In the United States, religious and right-wing extremists represent the terrorist population. Special-interest terrorists, such as anti-abortion extremists and ecoterrorists, also exist among the prison population. Depending on the types of terrorism within the prison population, correctional institutions have to decide where and how to house terrorists in their facilities to prevent terrorists from plotting attacks, spreading propaganda, and recruiting and radicalizing members from the general prison population. Countries are faced with a dilemma of whether or not to segregate terrorists or allow them to mix freely with other prisoners. These methods, however, are not without criticism. Each has resulted in some form of public backlash and has served as a source of protest for prisoners. Whatever prison regime for terrorists is chosen, it must be informed by the motivation and behaviors of the terrorists within its facilities.

Placing Terrorists in the General Population. There are certain benefits to placing terrorists among the general population. Here, terrorists are treated no differently than other inmates. This is also the image projected to the outside world—terrorists do not receive treatment that is preferential or inferior and are subjected to the same rules and regulations as other inmates.

The dispersal and placement of terrorists within the general population has also been heralded as preventing these groups from organizing and plotting attacks. Yet this is not entirely true. These terrorists can find like-minded individuals among inmates and subsequently engage in self-segregation from the general population in order to plot terrorist activities free from interference by authorities and other inmates. Indeed, prisoners have been known to cohabitate with individuals of the same beliefs in order to obtain solidarity and avoid conflict with individuals of different beliefs. This form of segregation, however, can be problematic as it often leads to the spreading of radical ideologies, the plotting of escapes, and the planning of attacks inside and outside of the prisons.

The dispersal and placement of terrorists also provides terrorists with access to new potential recruits. Indeed, if a terrorist is allowed to freely interact with the general population, they may recruit others to their organization. For instance, in the United States, Richard Butler, the founder of Aryan nations, a white supremacist Christian identity group,[20] was known for reaching out to fellow inmates and

---

[20] Christian identity is a racist and anti-Semitic religious ideology that holds that its members are the descendants of the "Lost Tribes" of Ancient Israel.

recruiting them to his cause.[21] Similar situations have been observed with Islamic extremists. Chaplains had informed U.S. authorities that the terrorists from the 1993 World Trade Center bombing, while placed among the general population, had radicalized other inmates by teaching them that engaging in acts of terrorism was an integral part of Islam.[22] Also, in an interview with the Islamic magazine *Nida'ul Islam*, Abu Muhammad al-Maqdisi, an extremely important jihadist ideologue, revealed that he sought to convert individual inmates while serving his sentence. In fact, many prisoners affiliated with al-Qaeda believe it is their duty to convert others to their faith and spread their ideology (*dawa*). These individuals will exploit any and every opportunity to convert other offenders to their own extremist interpretation of Islam and make them into supporters of al-Qaeda's cause. Accordingly, for such terrorists who seek to recruit and radicalize other inmates, separation from the general population would be a more appropriate option.

Separating Terrorists from the General Population. Some countries have opted to house terrorists in a separate area of prison facilities or in a facility that holds only terrorists. In the past, terrorists have been separated from the general population because it was believed that the former might exert a subversive influence on the latter. This option was said to work best with terrorists who have no formal ties to a group or are in a group in which leaders and followers have no direct contact with each other and members act of their own volition. In a prison, these terrorists are, therefore, unlikely to know one another. As such, placing these terrorists within the same facility is unlikely to result in the creation of a command and control structure. Most countries see the value in this and have opted to segregate terrorists from the general prison population.

By contrast, members of a cohesive and hierarchical terrorist group are more likely to know one another if imprisoned in the same facility and are more likely to try to re-create the group's command and control structure within the prison they are housed. Indeed, when such terrorists are segregated, they are able to maintain organizational hierarchy among those placed in the cells and perfect their operational skills. The goals of these types of terrorists, therefore, are not to recruit or radicalize others in prison but to re-create command and control structures. Nationalist and separatist terrorists fall within this category. Prime examples of this are the Provisional Irish Republican Army (PIRA) and the ETA.

In Northern Ireland, PIRA prisoners did not want to influence, recruit, or even associate with the general prison population. Instead, they wanted to distance themselves from other inmates. This occurred because PIRA inmates were initially granted political (prisoner of war) status and as such, they were accorded more privileges than the general population. Accordingly, authorities were not concerned

21 Anti-Defamation League. 2002. *Dangerous convictions: An introduction to extremist activities in prisons*, 23. http://www.adl.org/learn/Ext_Terr/dangerous_convictions.pdf.

22 Prisons Breeding Ground For Terror. 2004. *The Washington Times*, May 5, 2004. http://www.washingtontimes.com/news/2004/may/5/20040505-111705-4604r/.

that the PIRA would seek to gain more followers from inside the prison. Instead, they were concerned that they would re-create their command and control structure in prison and conspire to engage in attacks upon release, inside the prison, or plan attacks for others to commit outside of the prison. The same concern existed in Spain for ETA prisoners, who were known to exercise control over other imprisoned members of the group and their families.[23] Realizing this, authorities spread ETA terrorists among different prisons in the country to prevent them from re-creating their command and control structure.[24] The ETA protested this separation. Nevertheless, their attempts to gain sympathy for their cause in order to force Spain to transfer them to Basque prisons were unsuccessful.

Separation of terrorists from the general population is a viable option for those seeking to recruit and radicalize other inmates. As illustrated above, some terrorists, however, do not seek to do this. Accordingly, for these types of terrorists, dispersal would be more appropriate as it would help prevent the formation of groups with strong command and control structures within a single prison. Many countries have opted to not only separate prisoners from the general population by placing them in a few locations but also to isolate them from each other. Concentrating prisoners is beneficial from a resource perspective because intelligence-gathering capabilities, specialized personnel (e.g., linguists), staff training, and so on are needed in only a few locations.[25] Understanding the benefits in concentrating and limiting terrorist offenders to only a few prisons, the U.S. Federal Bureau of Prisons has plans to "consolidate all international terrorist inmates in approximately six institutions for enhanced management and monitoring. The approximately 146 international terrorist inmates will be re-classified under a new classification system as to their security designations and the resulting information will be used to determine where to house the inmates."[26] However, this set-up is not without its flaws. Isolating prisoners is a security risk and has been the source of much protest worldwide.

Countries such as Saudi Arabia have created special incarceration facilities that separate terrorists from other criminals and even place them into individual cells.[27] The same holds true in the United States, where several convicted terrorists

23 Hannah, G., Clutterbuck, L., and Rubin, J. 2008. Radicalization and rehabilitation. Understanding the challenge of extremists and radicalized prisoners. *RAND Corporation*, 23. http://www.rand.org/content/ dam/rand/pubs/technical_reports/2008/RAND_TR571.pdf.

24 Neumann, P. R. 2010. Prisons and terrorism: Radicalisation and de-radicalisation in 15 countries. *The International Center for the Study of Radicalisation and Political Violence*, 18. http://icsr.info /publications/papers/1277699166PrisonsandTerrorismRadicalisationandDeradicalisationin15 Countries.pdf.

25 Hannah et al., 2008, above n 23, p. xi.

26 U.S. Department of Justice, Office of the Inspector General, 2006, September. The Federal Bureau of Prison's monitoring of mail for high-risk inmates, 50. http://www.justice.gov/oig/reports /BOP /e0609/final.pdf.

27 Counterterrorism Implementation Task Force. 2007. *First report of the working group on radicalization and extremism that lead to terrorism: Inventory of state programmes*, 9. http:// www.un.org/terrorism /pdfs/radicalization.pdf.

such as Richard Reid and Ramzi Yousef, one of the individuals who planned the 1993 World Trade Center bombing, were removed from the general prison population and are currently in the supermax facility in Florence, Colorado, known as ADX Florence. Other notorious prisoners in ADX Florence include Abdul Hakim Murad, convicted for his involvement in a 1995 plot by al-Qaeda to blow up 12 planes (11 of which were bound for the United States) in a 48-hour period; Wadih el-Hage, a conspirator in the 1998 U.S. Embassy bombings; Zacarias Moussaoui, a conspirator in the 9/11 attacks; and Eric Robert Rudolph, a terrorist associated with the Christian identity movement, who is well-known for his 1996 bombing in Atlanta during the Summer Olympics. Other nonreligious terrorists in the facility include Terry Nichols, a co-conspirator in the Oklahoma City bombings, and Theodore Kaczynski, the Unabomber, who was responsible for a mail-bombing spree that spanned approximately 20 years.

The high-security section of the ADX Florence prison in which these terrorists are housed is known as "Bombers Row."[28] Eric Robert Rudolph contacted a reporter from *Time* magazine and informed her that within this section of the prison, individuals are isolated in single-occupant cells for 23 out of 24 hours a day.[29] Inmates are housed in this manner to ensure that they do not have the opportunity to radicalize and recruit other inmates. However, even in such a set-up, radicalization and recruitment is possible. Rudolph informed the reporter that the cells in this area are not soundproof, so individuals can communicate through the vents and walls. In fact, Rudolph reported that he often overheard the Arabic (see Box 11-2) and English conversations of other prisoners.[30] In view of that, terrorists may be able to radicalize and recruit others as they can freely communicate with one another through their cells.

Porous Prison Security: Conducive to Terrorism

Poor prison security has resulted in followers or fellow terrorists liberating incarcerated terrorists from prison. This was the case with the Red Brigades, when one of the founders, Renato Curcio, was liberated from prison by his wife and three other members of the Red Brigades in 1975.[31] Poor security can also result in terrorists planning attacks from within prison walls. In Spain, adherents to an Islamic sect in prison known as Takfir wa al-Hijra were actively involved in planning several significant terrorist attack plots.[32] Despite the best efforts in prisons, terrorists have managed to communicate with followers and the public, incite others to engage in terrorism, recruit other inmates, and plan operations from behind prison walls.

---

28 Vollers, M. 2006. Inside bomber row. *Time Magazine*, November 5, 2006. http://www.time.com/time/magazine/article/0,9171,1555145,00.html.

29 Ibid.

30 Ibid.

31 He was, however, later rearrested by authorities.

32 Mili, H. 2006, June 29. Jihad without rules: The evolution of al-Takfir wa al-Hijra. *Terrorism Monitor* 4 (13). Washington, DC: Jamestown Foundation.

Box 11-2   Language, Prison Staff, and Terrorists: The Case for Arabic?

Terrorists have conversed in different languages in prisons to surreptitiously communicate their extremist beliefs and plot attacks and escapes. The Provisional Irish Republican Army would converse in Gaelic to avoid prison staff and other prisoners from being privy to their communications. Arabic has also been the language of choice (for those who can speak it) among jihadist prisoners worldwide. In fact, the Federal Bureau of Investigation has claimed that just like right-wing terrorists used ancient scripts as code to communicate with one another, Muslim extremists in U.S. prisons use the Arabic language and script as codes to communicate and smuggle radical Islamic materials inside and outside of the prison undetected by authorities.[1]

1. Should prison staff be required to know Arabic (both oral and written profi-
   ciency) in facilities that house Islamic extremists? Why or why not?
2. What are the barriers, if any, to its implementation?

---

[1] Criminal Investigative Division. 2006, July 20. Gangs use ciphers and secret codes to communicate. *Federal Bureau of Investigation Intelligence Bulletin* (Unclassified); Cilluffo F., et al. 2006. Out of the shadows: Getting ahead of prisoner radicalization. *A special report by the George Washington University Homeland Security Policy Institute and the University of Virginia Critical Incident Analysis Group*, 6. http://com munity.nicic.gov/blogs/corrections_headlines/archive/2006/09/19/Getting -Ahead-of-Prisoner-Radicalization.aspx.

Within prisons, three factors are conducive to terrorism: untrained staff and/ or a short supply of staff, the mistreatment of prisoners, and the lack of legitimate and qualified chaplains.

Staffing. Overcrowding of prisons has also resulted in prison staff focusing almost all of their resources on maintaining law and order within the prisons. This emphasis of resources in this area leaves little to no resources to investigate allegations of radicalization within their prisons. In California, officials have reported that "every investigation into radical groups in their prisons uncovers new leads, but they simply do not have enough investigators to follow every case of radicalization."[33] The overcrowding and the understaffing of prisons has also amplified the conditions that are conducive to radicalization. Specifically, with a shortage of staff, prisoners are often able to illicitly spread propaganda, incite others to engage in terrorism, plan terrorist attacks, and recruit other inmates to their cause. The consequences of having insufficient staff to run facilities that house high-security risk inmates was illustrated in the report published by the U.S. Department of Justice, Office of the Inspector General. Among the security issues noted in the report were that the federal prison reviewed did not adequately screen inmates' mail and phone calls and did not have the personnel required to translate foreign-language mail to support

---

[33] Cilluffo F., et al. 2006. Out of the shadows: Getting ahead of prisoner radicalization. *A special report by the George Washington University Homeland Security Policy Institute and the University of Virginia Critical Incident Analysis Group*, 5. http://community.nicic.gov/blogs/corrections _headlines/archive/2006/09/19/Getting-Ahead-of-Prisoner-Radicalization.aspx.

the screening needs of the prison.[34] Consider ADX Florence, where an estimated 90 unscreened letters were sent by imprisoned terrorists between 2002 and 2004, the majority of which reached Islamic extremists.[35]

Reviews of high-security prisons have also found that the staff working in these facilities were improperly trained. A case in point is Britain's high-security prison that houses terrorists. An inspection found that staff working in critical areas of the prison did not have the requisite training needed for these positions.[36] Staff in these facilities must be trained on how to diminish the distribution of propaganda. Many inmates try to promote their cause outside prison walls and rally support for themselves. While in prison in the United States, Rod Coronado wrote for a magazine known as *No Compromise*, which supports the Animal Liberation Front.[37] What is particularly disturbing is that such writings urge individuals to take radical actions, both inside and outside prisons. For instance, Craig Marshall informed readers of *Earth First!* that "writing letters to fallen comrades raises the spirits of those of us who are incarcerated, but when someone picks up a bomb, instead of a pen, is when my spirits really soar."[38] A further example involved David Lane, a founding member of the Order, who remained active while imprisoned and frequently wrote in extremist publications (either existing ones or ones that he developed). In fact, Lane developed the *14 Word Press* from behind prison walls and often wrote pieces for a newsletter published by the press, *Focus Fourteen*.[39]

Staff must also be able to prevent recruitment to terrorism. Recruiters freely seek new members among the prison population and are able to communicate extremist political and religious views to fellow prisoners without fear of negative consequences. Accordingly, correctional facilities should provide better training of staff in order to detect recruiters in prison. One way in which terrorists attempt to recruit others is by passing out fringe publications promoting their cause. An example of such a prison publication was *The Way* by the Aryan Nation.[40] Prison staff must additionally be trained to identify radicalization among prisoners. Realizing this, countries such as Austria, Germany, and France have received financial awards from the European Commission for projects aimed at enhancing "the capacity of prison staff to recognize and address radicalization within penitentiary

---

[34] U.S. Department of Justice, Office of the Inspector General, 2006, September. The Federal Bureau of Prison's monitoring of mail for high-risk inmates, ii–ix. http://www.justice.gov/oig/reports /BOP/ e0609/final.pdf

[35] Ibid., p. i.

[36] Moyes, S. 2008. Belmarsh prison in south east London fails security review. *The Mirror*, June 2, 2008. http://www.mirror.co.uk/news/top-stories/2008/02/06/belmarsh-prison-in-south-east -london-fails-security-review-115875-20310554/.

[37] Anti-Defamation League. 2002. Dangerous convictions: An introduction to extremist activities in prisons, 25. http://www.adl.org/learn/Ext_Terr/dangerous_convictions.pdf.

[38] Ibid.

[39] Ibid., p. 28.

[40] Ibid., p. 24.

institutions."[41] In addition, Dutch authorities have concentrated convicted jihadists into detention centers in which prison staff are specially trained to detect signs of radicalization among prisoners.[42] Moreover, the National Offender Management Service (NOMS) in the United Kingdom was tasked with implementing screening tools for materials entering and exiting the prisons and providing prison staff with guidance on how to identify radicalized prisoners, prevent recruitment, and identify suitable interventions in the event that either should arise.[43] Furthermore, in the United States, the Federal Bureau of Prisons activated the Counter-Terrorism Unit (CTU) in 2006 "to assist in identifying inmates involved in terrorist activities; coordinate translation services; monitor/analyze terrorist inmate communications; [and] develop and provide relevant training" to existing prison staff.[44]

To prevent such radicalization, prisons need to free themselves from literature containing terrorist propaganda. Restrictions on acceptable literature and screening of material both entering and exiting the prisons have been employed. In the United States, to deal with the proliferation of radical religious material and publications within prisons, the Federal Bureau of Prisons has developed a more comprehensive system of monitoring this literature. Internet use has been restricted as well. However, some individuals have learned to bypass such restrictions. From HMP Belmarsh prison in London, Abu Qatada published *fatwas* on the Internet, calling for a holy war and the killing of moderate Muslims.[45] In Belmarsh, another prisoner developed a website from his laptop in his cell encouraging others to engage in terrorist attacks.[46] Recent news reports in the United Kingdom claim that some al-Qaeda top members are smuggling propaganda inside and outside of high-security prisons. Chayme Hamza, the daughter-in-law of Abu Hamza, was arrested under the UK Prison Act of 1952 (which criminalizes the possession of a prohibited item in prisons) for attempting to smuggle a mobile phone SIM card into Belmarsh, where

---

[41] EU Counter-Terrorism Coordinator. 2007, November 23. The EU strategy for combating radicalisation and recruitment – Implementation report. *Council of the European Union*, 4. http://register.consilium.europa.eu/pdf/en/07/st15/st15443.en07.pdf.

[42] Ongering, L. 2007, June 27. Home-grown terrorism and radicalization in The Netherlands: Experiences, explanations and approaches. *Testimony to the Deputy National Coordinator for Counterterrorism, US Senate Homeland Security and Governmental Affairs Committee.* http://hsgac.senate.gov/_files/062707Ongering.pdf; Hannah, G., Clutterbuck, L., and Rubin, J. 2008. Radicalization and rehabilitation. Understanding the challenge of extremists and radicalized prisoners. *RAND Corporation*, 51. http://www.rand.org/content/dam/rand/pubs/technical_reports/2008/RAND_TR571.pdf.

[43] UK Home Office. 2011, July. *CONTEST: The United Kingdom strategy for countering terrorism*, 70. http://www.homeoffice.gov.uk/publications/counter-terrorism/counter-terrorism-strategy/strategy-contest?view=Binary.

[44] U.S. Department of Justice, Federal Bureau of Prisons. 2010. *The bureau celebrates 80th anniversary.* http://www.bop.gov/about/history/first_years.jsp.

[45] Leppard, D. 2009. Terrorists smuggle fatwas out of secure prisons. *The Sunday Times*, November 15, 2009. http://www.timesonline.co.uk/tol/news/uk/article6917296.ece.

[46] Doward, J. 2007. Extremists train young convicts for terror plots. *The Guardian*, July 15, 2007. http://www.guardian.co.uk/uk/2007/jul/15/ukcrime.prisonsandprobation.

Abu Hamza was being held.[47] Her husband, Mohamed Kamel Mostafa, Abu Hamza's son, was arrested the next day over the same incident.

Treatment. Terrorists may become radicalized due to abuse and/or neglect in prisons. In fact, Atwan claims that Sayid Qutb,[48] an influential propagandist of Islamic extremist groups, may have been radicalized because of his torture and mistreatment while imprisoned in Egypt.[49] In Egyptian prisons, Ayman al-Zawahiri was said to have transformed from a moderate militant to a radical extremist and recruited others to his cause.[50] In addition, terrorist prisoners may seek to mobilize supporters for their cause by highlighting real or exaggerated injustices and grievances experienced within prisons. Reporting on real, fictitious, or exaggerated conditions of prisoners, jihadist magazines (e.g., *Al-Fursan* and *Sada al-Jihad*) and websites serve as a way to gain sympathy for their cause and turn individuals against the terrorist's target (even its own citizens).[51]

Allegations of torture, discrimination, and other forms of mistreatment or rights violations have occurred that have resulted in protests (both by prisoners and the public). Consider the PIRA. In March of 1976, British authorities revoked their prisoner of war status, causing PIRA prisoners to protest en masse. Among the most well-known methods of their protest were the hunger strikes from March to October 1981 in the H-Blocks of Long Kesh (HM Prison Maze). In this prison, the hunger strike claimed the lives of Bobby Sands, Frances Hughes, Raymond McCreesh, Patsy O'Mara, Joe McDonnell, Martin Hurson, Kevin Lynch, Kiernan Doherty, Thomas McIlwee, and Mickey Devine. This hunger strike galvanized not only Irish national support but also support from other publics worldwide. Hunger strikes have been used in the past by not only the PIRA but also by the Red Army Faction in West Germany, Kurdish separatists in Turkey, Palestinian prisoners in Israeli prisons, Guantanamo Bay detainees, and inmates in U.S. prisons in order to gain attention for their cause.[52] For example, when RAF

---

[47] Abu Hamza is currently awaiting extradition to the United States. His extradition, however, is pending because he appealed his extradition. His case is now at the European Court of Human Rights, which requested a report from the United States detailing the length of his sentence and the conditions of the prison he will be sent to; namely, the supermax prison in Florence, Colorado; Abu Hamza's Daughter-in-law Arrested Trying to Smuggle SIM Card into Belmarsh Prison Under her Burka. 2010. *Daily Mail Reporter*, December 22, 2010. http://www.dailymail.co.uk/news/article-1340735 /Abu-Hamzas-daughter-law-arrested-trying-smuggle-sim-card-Belmarsh-Prison-burka.html.

[48] Qutb produced influential works for Islamic extremists while serving a prison sentence from 1954 onwards for his alleged participation in an assassination attempt against the then Egyptian President Nasser.

[49] Atwan, A. B. 2006. *The secret history of Al-Qaeda*. London: Saqi, 72.

[50] Stracke, N. 2007. Arab prisons: A place for dialogue and reform. *Perspectives on Terrorism* 1 (4): 7. http://www.terrorismanalysts.com/pt/index.php/pot/article/view/15/33.

[51] Qa'id, S. H. 2005, November. Haqiqat Ma Yajri Wara' al-Qudban fi Sujoun al-American. *Sada al-Jihad*, 26.

[52] Hannah, G., Clutterbuck, L., and Rubin, J. 2008. Radicalization and rehabilitation. Understanding the challenge of extremists and radicalized prisoners. *RAND Corporation*, 44. http://www.rand.org/content/ dam/rand/pubs/technical_reports/2008/RAND_TR571.pdf.

members were placed in solitary confinement in prison, they went on a hunger strike to protest this occurrence. This hunger strike helped the RAF to gain some public support for their cause, especially among the younger population.[53] Additionally, Guantanamo Bay prisoners went on a hunger strike purportedly for reasons that included mistreatment during interrogation and as a means to protest their innocence.[54] These protests have helped terrorist groups, for some of them have gained sympathy, recruits, and supporters for their cause. Prison staff must ensure that terrorists are treated fairly in prison. The verified instances of staff mistreatment of prisoners in Guantanamo Bay and the Abu Ghraib prison and the backlash that ensued shows the consequences of failing to do so.

Chaplains. The shortage of qualified chaplains in prison is said to contribute to radicalization and recruitment in prisons.[55] The lack of chaplains has played a role in radicalization because it has afforded terrorists with the opportunity to preach their own extremist interpretation of religion to any prisoner who is willing to listen. For example, Abu Hamza preached radical sermons to followers from his cell in HMP Belmarsh prison.[56] The radicalization of Muslims within prisons has also been said to be attributed to the lack of personnel with a comprehensive understanding of Islam. Studies have shown that "Muslims with little knowledge of Islam are likely to attach great value to the words of imams on religious matters. Such attributed authority makes prison imams particularly influential when it comes to incubating and spreading radical attitudes through prisons."[57]

Many local, state, and federal facilities in the United States do not have trained Muslim chaplains; accordingly, volunteers and contractors are often used in these facilities instead. Volunteers and contractors are not required to have formal

---

[53] "A survey carried out in July 1971 by the Institut Allensbach showed that 20% of Germans under the age of 30 felt some degree of sympathy for the actions of the RAF, which, incidentally, had not yet been very violent until that point." Neve, R., Vervoorn, L. Leeuw, F., and Bogaerts, S. 2006. *First inventory of policy on counterterrorism*, 13. http://transcrime.cs.unitn.it/tc/fso/Altre%20pubblicazioni/First%20inventory%20of%20policy%20 20on%20counterterrorism%20-%20italian%20contribution%20to%20NCBT.pdf.

[54] Guantanamo Inmates Declare Hunger Strike. 2005. *MSNBC News*, July 21, 2005. http://www.msnbc.msn.com/id/8657690/ns/us_news-security/.

[55] Van Duyn, D. 2006, September 19. *Congressional testimony: Statement of the FBI Deputy Assistant Director, of the Counterterrorism Division before the Senate Committee on Homeland Security and Governmental Affairs and related agencies.* http://www.fbi.gov/congress/congress06/vanduyn091906.htm; Transnational terrorism, security and the rule of law. 2008, November 17. *Radicalization, recruitment and the EU counter-terrorism strategy*, 28. http://www.transnationalterrorism.eu/tekst/publications/WP4%20Del% 207.pdf.

[56] Leppard, D. 2009. Terrorists smuggle fatwas out of secure prisons. *The Sunday Times*, November 15, 2009. http://www.timesonline.co.uk/tol/news/uk/article6917296.ece.

[57] Olsen, J. 2008, January. Radikalisering i Danske fængsler – Hvad sker der, og hvad kan der gøres?" (Radicalization in Danish prisons: What happens and what can be done?). *DIIS-Brief*, Copenhagen: Danish Institute for International Studies; Transnational terrorism, security and the rule of law. 2008, November 17. *Radicalization, recruitment and the EU counter-terrorism strategy*, 28. http://www.transnationalterrorism.eu/tekst/publications/WP4%20Del%207.pdf.

religious education.[58] The lack of formal religious education of individuals who provide religious sermons in prisons serve as a reason for inmates to gravitate toward other inmates expressing radical views. To fill this void of chaplains, terrorists have often taken on the role of mentor and spiritual advisor for inmates. A case in point was Abu Doha, one of al-Qaeda's main recruiters, who took courses in Belmarsh prison that enabled him to mentor other inmates.[59]

Similarly, in the United States, white supremacist groups have served as spiritual advisors for other inmates. For instance, an Order member, Richard Kemp, became a spiritual leader, enabling him to spread messages of hate and white supremacy to other inmates.[60] Indeed, there are some groups within prisons that use religion as a venue through which to express their radical beliefs. For example, it is claimed that white supremacists claim adherance to religious sects in order to allow them to circumvent certain prison regulations and promote their racist ideologies.[61] Examples of groups in prison that align themselves with Christian identity ideology to do just that include (but are not limited to) Posse Comitatus, Aryan Nations, and the Order.

The absence of monitoring of religious services has been said to not only be advantageous to those seeking to radicalize individuals but could serve as an important forum to facilitate the spreading of extremist materials within prisons. Knox reported that a survey of 193 wardens of state correctional facilities in the United States "showed that only half of religious services were physically supervised and just over half used any sort of audio or video monitoring capabilities."[62] To address this situation in the United States, the Federal Bureau of Prisons has "mandated the constant supervision of inmate-led groups, and is requiring that the provision of Islamic teachings and study-guides must be prepared by Islamic

---

58 Cilluffo F., et al. 2006. Out of the shadows: Getting ahead of prisoner radicalization. *A special report by the George Washington University Homeland Security Policy Institute and the University of Virginia Critical Incident Analysis Group*, 5–6. http://community.nicic.gov/blogs/corrections _headlines/archive/2006/09/19/ Getting -Ahead-of-Prisoner-Radicalization.aspx.

59 Leppard, D. 2009. Terrorists smuggle fatwas out of secure prisons. *The Sunday Times*, November 15. http://www.timesonline.co.uk/tol/news/uk/article6917296.ece.

60 Anti-Defamation League. 2002. Dangerous convictions: An introduction to extremist activities in prisons, 31. http://www.adl.org/learn/Ext_Terr/dangerous_convictions.pdf.

61 Ibid., p. 23.

62 Knox, G. W. 2005. *The problem of gangs and security threat groups in American prisons today: Recent research, findings from the 2004 Prison Gang survey*. National Gang Crime Research Center; Cilluffo F., et al. 2006. Out of the shadows: Getting ahead of prisoner radicalization. *A special report by the George Washington University Homeland Security Policy Institute and the University of Virginia Critical Incident Analysis Group*, 5. http://community.nicic.gov/blogs /corrections_headlines/archive/2006/09/19/Getting-Ahead-of-Prisoner-Radicalization.aspx; U.S. Department of Justice, Office of the Inspector General, 2006, September. *The Federal Bureau of Prison's monitoring of mail for high-risk inmates*, 17. http://www.justice.gov/oig /reports/BOP/e0609/final.pdf.

chaplains who are full-time [prison] staff."[63] Additionally, the Federal Bureau of Prisons has taken steps to help ensure that those providing religious services at prisons are qualified to do so.[64] These individuals are now subjected to more rigorous background checks before being hired to provide such services (i.e., have the necessary academic training and education). The United States is not alone in this endeavor. Other countries have developed or are developing special prisoner programs (Algeria, Austria, Belgium, Canada, France, Germany, Malaysia, the Netherlands, Saudi Arabia, Singapore, United Kingdom, and Slovenia) to prevent their prisons from becoming breeding grounds for terrorists and terrorism recruitment centers.[65] The programs also involve mandating that all prisons have appropriately trained staff and qualified chaplains working in their facilities.

While most imprisoned terrorists seek to propagate terrorism, there also exist terrorists who want to renounce violence and desist from future terrorist activity. For those individuals, countries have created rehabilitation and disengagement programs in prisons around the globe. Accordingly, even though prisons have served as breeding grounds for terrorism, the same places have also been used as venues to promote the positive transformation of prisoners.

REALISTIC GOALS FOR COUNTERTERRORISM STRATEGIES: DISENGAGEMENT OR DERADICALIZATION?

Disengagement refers to the processes whereby an individual or group desists from terrorist activity. Disengagement with terrorism may occur individually or collectively. Collective disengagement from terrorist activity has happened in the past, though it is a rare occurrence. This process usually occurs in groups in which there is an authoritarian leader and a hierarchical command and control structure.[66] The Provisional Irish Republican Army is a case in point. Another example involved the Egyptian Islamic Group (IG), whose leaders decided on their own initiative to collectively disengage from terrorism while in prison. Their decision was the result of a combination of factors, such as the potential for defeat and possible war (e.g., like that experienced by Algeria).[67] These factors led to a revision of the legitimacy

---

[63] U.S. Department of Justice. 2006, September 5. Department of Justice anti-terrorism efforts since Sept. 11, 2001. *Department of Justice fact sheet.* http://www.usdoj.gov/opa/pr/2006/September/06 _opa_590.html; Cilluffo F., et al. 2006. Out of the shadows: Getting ahead of prisoner radicalization. *A special report by the George Washington University Homeland Security Policy Institute and the University of Virginia Critical Incident Analysis Group,* 14. http://community.nicic.gov/blogs/corrections _headlines/archive/2006/09/19/Getting-Ahead-of-Prisoner-Radicalization.aspx.

[64] Cilluffo F. , et al., 2006. Ibid, p. 12.

[65] Counterterrorism Implementation Task Force. 2007. *First report of the working group on radicalization and extremism that lead to terrorism: Inventory of state programmes,* 9. http:// www.un.org/terrorism/pdfs/radicalization.pdf.

[66] Neumann, P. R. 2010. Prisons and terrorism: Radicalisation and de-radicalisation in 15 countries. *The International Center for the Study of Radicalisation and Political Violence,* 18. http://icsr.info /publications/papers/1277699166PrisonsandTerrorismRadicalisationandDeradicalisationin15 Countries.pdf.

[67] Ibid., p. 42.

of the group's use of violence to achieve its goals. In Colombia, the United Self-Defense Forces of Colombia (Autodefensas Unidas de Colombia or AUC) opted for the demobilization of its members but not necessarily psychological disengagement from terrorism.[68]

Some policies were created in Europe with the intention of reintegrating terrorist prisoners back into society. One such policy was created in Spain to deal with the ETA, known as reinsertion. With this policy, prisoners were offered early release only if they renounced violence, severed all ties with the terrorist organization, acknowledged the harm and suffering they caused, and declared that they would respect the law.[69] Pursuant to this policy, they were required to sign a legal document that included these conditions along with a statement that the terrorist acknowledges that if he or she does not abide by these conditions, they would be reimprisoned. Another such program was created in Italy to deal with the Red Brigades. This program was implemented pursuant to the 1987 dissociation law. Under this law, terrorist prisoners were required to confess to all crimes (terrorism or other crimes) committed (regardless of whether or not they had been convicted of these crimes), denounce terrorism, and sever all ties with the Red Brigades. In exchange for these agreements, these individuals were sent to less-restricted prisons and allowed to work outside of the prison while they were serving their sentence in order to begin to lay the foundations for their reintegration into society after their release.[70] At the time of the implementation of this program, the Red Brigades terror campaign was subsiding. However, this does not imply that in order for such programs to be effective, the groups must be in a similar state as that of the Red Brigades. In fact, the ETA's reintegration program was effective despite being implemented during a period in which the ETA was actively involved in a terror campaign against Spain. This approach is promising, as it shows that such a program can be used for one of the greatest international threats today: namely, al-Qaeda and those inspired by this group. In fact, programs do exist in the Middle East, Africa, Asia, and Europe that focus on these terrorists.

How does a terrorist enter these programs? To take part in the above programs, terrorists must first make the decision to disengage from terrorism. These programs were not designed to change individuals' attitudes about terrorism; they just provided them with an alternative option should they choose to abandon terrorism, leave their terrorist group, or otherwise desist from terrorist activity. Essentially, it provides terrorists with a way out. Other programs have sought to

---

[68] Fink, N. C., and Hearne, E. B. 2008, October. Beyond terrorism: Deradicalization and disengagement from violent extremism. *International Peace Institute Publications*, 12. http://www.ipinst.org/media/pdf/publications/beter.pdf.

[69] Silke, A. 2011. Disengagement or deradicalization: A look at prison programs for jailed terrorists. *The Sentinel*, January 1, 2011. *Center for Combating Terrorism*. http://www.ctc.usma.edu/posts/disengagement-or-deradicalization-a-look-at-prison-programs-for-jailed-terrorists; Heiberg, M. 2007. ETA: Euskadi 'ta Askatasuna. In *Terror, insurgencies and states: Breaking the cycle of protracted conflict*, eds. M. Heiberg, B. O'Leary, and J. Tirman. Philadelphia: University of Pennsylvania Press.

[70] Silke, 2011. Ibid.

do the opposite: to change the mindset and beliefs of the terrorists, that is, to show them that terrorism is morally (or in other cases, religiously) unjustified. These rehabilitation programs are explored below.

EXISTING REHABILITATION PROGRAMS: A REVIEW

Rehabilitation programs have to be oriented toward a certain type of terrorist. A different program will work for left-wing terrorists than would for religious terrorists. Programs to deradicalize terrorists exist in many countries. Deradicalization is a process by which an individual or group renounces violence, disengages from radical behavior, and alters their views about the morality and legitimacy of engaging in violence to adhere to their goals. Deradicalization programs refer to the programs "that are generally directed against individuals who have become radical with the aim of reintegrating them into society or at least dissuading them from violence."[71] Even the types of terrorists that programs have sought to deradicalize have varied. Which types of terrorists could benefit from rehabilitation programs? Most programs have focused on religious terrorism. As noted earlier, programs to deradicalize those linked to al-Qaeda, including both those who are actual members of al-Qaeda and those who are merely inspired by al-Qaeda, have been established in multiple countries with the intention of reforming these terrorists. To a lesser extent, countries have also focused on right-wing terrorists. For example, in Germany, programs exist in which ex-Nazis campaign against Nazism.[72] For nationalist/separatist terrorists, rehabilitation programs do not seem well-suited due to the group's ideology and goals. Instead, opening up lines of communication with the target government, engaging in negotiations, seeking cease-fire and amnesty agreements (wherever desirable), and providing the group with a role in the political process,[73] are more appropriate counterterrorism strategies for these terrorists. Additionally, such groups (e.g., ETA), along with left-wing terrorists (e.g., Red Brigades), have been better suited for the disengagement programs mentioned above. Therefore, to be effective, a counterterrorism strategy must be tailored toward dealing with specific terrorists or terrorist groups. Such strategies must take into account the individual's and/or group's ideology and goals.

Several studies have been commissioned by governments concerning radicalization in prisons and ways to the deradicalize terrorists. Deradicalization and disengagement programs in the Middle East, Africa, and Asia seek to create healthy and stable social environments for prisoners free from radical influences. Particular

---

71 Horgan, J. 2008. Deradicalisation or disengagement? *Perspectives on Terrorism* 2 (4). http://www.terrorismanalysts.com/pt/index.php/pot/article/view/32/html; Counterterrorism Implementation Task Force. 2008. *First report of the working group on radicalization and extremism that lead to terrorism: Inventory of state programmes*, 6. http://www.un.org/terrorism/pdfs/radicalization.pdf.

72 EXIT-Deutschland BfV (Aussteigerprogram für Rechtsextremisten vom Bundesamt für Vergassungsschutz).

73 These processes will be explored in further detail in a section on making peace with terrorists.

emphasis will be placed on those created in Yemen, Saudi Arabia, Egypt, Singapore, the United States, and the United Kingdom.

Yemen. The prisons in Yemen are understaffed and suffer from poorly trained guards and mistreatment of prisoners. To make matters worse, the prisons are significantly overcrowded and terrorists are mixed in with the general population. As such, these prisons are fertile grounds for those seeking to recruit and radicalize members of the general prison population. In an attempt to address the radicalization and recruitment of individuals to terrorism, Yemen developed a rehabilitation program: the Committee for Dialogue, an initiative based on religious reeducation. In this program, Islamic clerics engage in dialogue with participants to challenge the religious basis of terrorist ideologies in an effort to correct the detainees' distorted beliefs.[74] Yemen's program addresses critical issues in the jihad, such as the true concept of jihad in Islam, the significance of adherence to Islamic law, and the importance of understanding the true rules involved in declaring someone an unbeliever *(takfir)*.[75] Basically, such a program seeks to persuade religious terrorists of the error of their ways and promote an understanding of Islam that considers violent extremism as religiously unjustified.

However, Yemen's detention facilities and rehabilitation programs for terrorists leave much to be desired. Among other things, Yemen lacks a secure facility within which to house prior Guantanamo Bay detainees and a system for monitoring them upon release.[76] Nonetheless, the monitoring of prisoners upon their release is essential. As a report by the Homeland Security Policy Institute and the Critical Incident Analysis Group noted, "upon release from prison, the inability to track inmates coupled with lack of social support to reintegrate them into the community gives rise to a vulnerable moment in which they may be recruited by radical groups, posing as social support organizations that are more interested in their own extremist agendas than in the welfare of released prisoners."[77] In particular, after being released, inmates are vulnerable to reoffending, as they often have little if any financial, family, and emotional support. For those who draw financial support from well-off terrorist groups, these government programs offer little to no incentive, as they are more likely to provide less financial support than

---

[74] Taarnby, M. 2005. Yemen's committee for dialogue: The relativity of a counter terrorism success. In *A future for the young: Options for helping Middle Eastern youth escape the trap of radicalization*, ed. C. Benard. RAND Working Paper, WR-354. Washington, DC: RAND National Security Research Division; Horgan, J. 2008. Deradicalisation or disengagement? *Perspectives on Terrorism* 2 (4). http://www. terrorismanalysts.com/pt/index.php/pot/article/view/32/html.

[75] Stracke, N. 2007. Arab prisons: A place for dialogue and reform. *Perspectives on Terrorism* 1 (4): 10. http://www.terrorismanalysts.com/pt/index.php/pot/article/view/15/33.

[76] U.S. Department of State. 2010, August. Country reports on terrorism 2009. *Office of the Coordinator for Counterterrorism*, 147. http://www.state.gov/documents/organization/141114.pdf.

[77] Cilluffo F., et al. 2006. Out of the shadows: Getting ahead of prisoner radicalization. *A special report by the George Washington University Homeland Security Policy Institute and the University of Virginia Critical Incident Analysis Group*, v. http://community.nicic.gov/blogs/corrections_headlines/archive/2006/09/19/ Getting-Ahead-of-Prisoner-Radicalization.aspx.

the terrorist would have received from the terrorist group. Newly released inmates must distance themselves from radicalized communities, groups, and other individuals. When family and friends are radicalized, additional problems arise.

Programs that do not monitor prisoners after completion result in high rates of recidivism. Upon completion of Yemen's program, some of its graduates were later found to be fighting in Iraq.[78] Politicians, academicians, and researchers have also claimed that this occurrence may be attributed to the fact that Yemen's rehabilitation program was not accompanied by a reintegration program. Even though religious reeducation is indeed an important step in terrorist rehabilitation, an effective program cannot be based on this alone. The case of Yemen clearly illustrates this.

Saudi Arabia. An integral part of a counterterrorism strategy is quashing terrorists' ideologies. Understanding this, the Kingdom of Saudi Arabia has decided to "fight thoughts with thoughts."[79] According to a Saudi Arabian Ministry of Interior study, individuals taking part in the program were misguided and had fallen victim to the extremists' "cause by exposure to video, film, and other material that urged them to 'sympathize' with people in Afghanistan and Iraq."[80] Indeed, most programs aimed at dealing with religious terrorism share a common notion that terrorists are victims "whose religious ideas are based on misinformation and a lack of proper knowledge about Islam, making re-education and reform both necessary and possible."[81] The programs in Saudi Arabia, Singapore, and the Philippines are largely based on this notion. Essentially, in so doing, these schemes seek to deprogram individuals of their extremist views of Islam. This "has led to some participants actually breaking down in tears as they realize they have violated their religion's principles through committing violent acts."[82]

Like the governments in Yemen, Singapore, and the Philippines, the Saudi Arabian government believes that the main reason for terrorism is the ignorance

---

78 Johnsen, G. D. 2006, February 23. Yemen's passive role in the war on terrorism. *Terrorism Monitor* 4 (4). Washington, DC: Jamestown Foundation; Hannah, G., Clutterbuck, L., and Rubin, J. 2008. Radicalization and rehabilitation. Understanding the challenge of extremists and radicalized prisoners. *RAND Corporation,* 37. http://www.rand.org/content/dam/rand/pubs/technical_reports/2008/RAND_TR571.pdf.

79 Zoepf, K. 2008. Deprogramming jihadists. *The New York Times,* November 9, 2008. http://www.nytimes.com/2008/11/09/magazine/09jihadis-t.html.

80 U.S. Department of State. 2009, April 30. Country reports on terrorism 2008. *Office of the Coordinator for Counterterrorism.* http://www.state.gov/s/ct/rls/crt/2008/122433.htm.

81 Neumann, P. R. 2010. Prisons and terrorism: Radicalisation and de-radicalisation in 15 countries. *The International Center for the Study of Radicalisation and Political Violence,* 51. http://icsr.info/publications/papers/1277699166PrisonsandTerrorismRadicalisationandDeradicalisationin15Countries.pdf.

82 Bennett, D. 2008. How to defuse a human bomb. *The Boston Globe,* April 13, 2008. http://www.boston.com/bostonglobe/ideas/articles/2008/04/13/how_to_defuse_a_human_bomb/; Fink, N. C., and Hearne, E. B. 2008, October. Beyond terrorism: Deradicalization and disengagement from violent extremism. *International Peace Institute Publications,* 6. http://www.ipinst.org/media/pdf/publications/beter.pdf.

about the true nature of the religion of Islam. It has delivered its programs accordingly. In Saudi Arabia, existing programs are designed to deradicalize terrorists—to turn them away from terrorism. Its rehabilitation program, Al-Munasaha, involves scholars, intellectuals, and psychologists with the goal of helping terrorists overcome their extremist views. The Al-Munasaha program

> as well as sister programs in the United Kingdom, France, the Netherlands, Iraq, Yemen, Malaysia, Singapore, Thailand and Indonesia mainly target individual militants as opposed to organizations. When such programs succeed, the end result is usually individual de-radicalization as opposed to collective abandonment of political violence by a jihadist movement. [83]

This program initially targeted only those who had not physically committed a terrorist attack; that is, it was applied only to those who indicated a willingness and motivation to do so. The Saudi program later included repatriated Guantanamo Bay detainees and Saudi militants returning from Iraq in its programs, treating them at a separate Center for Counseling and Advice.[84] The inclusion of repatriated Guantanamo Bay detainees in these programs is vital because the Department of Defense has reported

> that at least seventy-four Guantanamo detainees—one in five of those freed—returned to terrorist activity after release. This includes at least eleven graduates of the Saudi program, one of whom fled to Yemen after release and became deputy commander of al-Qaeda in the Arabian Peninsula, an al-Qaeda affiliate linked to two recent incidents in the United States.[85]

Along with a rehabilitation program, the Saudi Arabian government has counter-radicalization programs within its prison designed to stop terrorists from recruiting from within the prison and for countering terrorist's ideology. In addition, they also have parallel programs in place that seek to reintegrate them back into society. Following a prisoner's commitment to disengage from terrorism and then completion of a rehabilitation program, upon release a prisoner participates in Saudi Arabia's *al Ria'ya* (Care) program, which is specially designed to house prisoners in the immediate aftermath of their release and provide them with "psychological counseling, religious education and promotes debate and dialogue between them and the organizers of the program."[86] This program includes "periodical 'check-ups' with members of the security services, . . . social and economic assistance for former prisoners and their families, help with finding wives, jobs and even

---

[83] Ashour, O. 2009. De-radicalizing jihadists may just work. *Alarabiya News*, September 20, 2009. http://www.alarabiya.net/views/2009/09/20/85514.html.

[84] Poges, M. 2010, January 22. The Saudi deradicalization experiment. *Council on Foreign Relations*. http://www.cfr.org/ terrorism/saudi-deradicalization-experiment/p21292.

[85] Ibid.

[86] UN Counter-Terrorism Implementation Task Force. 2008. *First report of the working group on radicalization and extremism that lead to terrorism: Inventory of state programmes*, 18. http://www.un.org/terrorism/pdfs/radicalization.pdf.

start-up funds for budding entrepreneurs."[87] The government assists ailing relatives and/or provides financial support to the terrorist's spouse and children to show detainees that they are not the enemy.[88] In addition, Saudi Arabia and other countries worldwide have realized that rehabilitation and reintegration programs should also foster social responsibility among prisoners serving time for terrorism-related offenses by mandating that they take part in "job training and education schemes, which are meant to provide the basis for a meaningful and socially secure existence."[89] Individuals in Saudi Arabia's aftercare program are further required to attend regular meetings with religious clerics, "whose continued association with the former prisoners [has been found to ease] their transition from prison to society and allows them to carry on a social relationship which is likely to have been critical in their transformation."[90] Accordingly, the program is comprehensive, affecting almost every aspect of the prisoner's life.

The rehabilitation and reintegration program of the Kingdom of Saudi Arabia is more intricate than any other program worldwide. Saudi Arabia has boasted that many terrorists who completed the rehabilitation and aftercare programs have been successfully reintegrated back into society. The Saudi Arabian program, however, has seen its share of failures. Specifically, two Saudi citizens and former Guantanamo Bay detainees, Mohammed al-Harbi and Said Ali al-Shihri, successfully completed the program, but were subsequently rearrested for engaging in terrorist activity. In fact, both appeared in propaganda videos for al-Qaeda in the Arabia Peninsula announcing its formation in Yemen.[91] Moreover, a former graduate of the program and member of al-Qaeda, Jaber Al-Fayfi, contacted "the Prince Muhammad bin Naif Counseling and Care Center, where the Munasaha program takes place" to surrender and asked for his return to the country.[92] Some view this as a success for the program. Specifically, a spokesperson for the Interior Ministry, Mansour Al-Turki, stated that the fact that these individuals are returning even after straying to their old ways showed a "rising level of awareness and understanding of the deceptive methods employed by al-Qaeda vis-à-vis its operatives."[93] Others, however,

---

[87] Neumann, P. R. 2010. Prisons and terrorism: Radicalisation and de-radicalisation in 15 countries. *The International Center for the Study of Radicalisation and Political Violence*, 55. http://icsr.info /publications/papers/1277699166PrisonsandTerrorismRadicalisationandDeradicalisationin15 Countries.pdf.

[88] Stracke, N. 2007. Arab prisons: A place for dialogue and reform. *Perspectives on Terrorism* 1 (4). http://www.terrorismanalysts.com/pt/index.php/pot/article/view/15/33.

[89] Neumann, P. R. 2010. Prisons and terrorism: Radicalisation and de-radicalisation in 15 countries. *The International Center for the Study of Radicalisation and Political Violence*, 51. http://icsr.info /publications/papers/1277699166PrisonsandTerrorismRadicalisationandDeradicalisationin15 Countries.pdf.

[90] Ibid., p. 55.

[91] U.S. Department of State. 2009, April 30. Country reports on terrorism 2008. *Office of the Coordinator for Counterterrorism*, 142. http://www.state.gov/s/ct/rls/crt/2008/122433.htm.

[92] Saudi Columnists: The Government Program to Rehabilitate Extremists is a Failure. 2010, November. *The Middle East Media Research Institute*, 1. http://europenews.dk/ en/node/36947.

[93] Ibid.

criticized Saudi Arabia as showing extreme leniency toward terrorists who are not serious about disengaging from terrorism in the long term.[94] Approximate recidivist rates are available for the graduates of the Saudi Arabian program. These rates indicated that an estimated 25% of Guantanamo Bay detainees will reoffend, whereas, for all other participants in the program, reoffending rates were estimated at 10%.[95] The Saudi Arabian government continues to adjust its program in response to failures in order to minimize the return of its graduates to terrorism and other forms of violence.

Egypt. Like Saudi Arabia and Yemen, the Egyptian rehabilitation program focuses on the religious reeducation of terrorists. In fact, in Egypt, clerics go to prisons and counsel the prisoners. Egypt has a rehabilitation program in place in which prisoners who wanted to participate were separated from those who rejected the program. The prisoners who refused to participate in the program were sent to other Egyptian prisons.

Egypt differs from other programs, as within its prisons, collective disengagement and deradicalization from terrorism occurred. Of course, this was not attributed to any particular action of the government. Instead, it was the terrorist group that decided to do this, without the help of any existing programs. In particular, when the leaders of al-Jama'a al-Islamiya, which at the time was one of the largest and most violent extremist Islamic terrorist groups in Egypt, were imprisoned, they collectively renounced violence. The leaders also criticized al-Qaeda's ideology and tactics and offered a new, alternative interpretation of jihadist principles; one in which violence was justified only if used in self-defense (although this term is also subject to interpretation). The leaders of this group have authored approximately 25 volumes supporting the group's newfound nonviolent ideology with rational and religious arguments.[96] The majority of the terrorists within this group desisted from terrorist activity. A decade later, another Egyptian group, al-Jihad al-Islamiya, followed in the footsteps of al-Jama'a al-Islamiya by renouncing violence and disengaging from terrorist activity. This group's denouncement of violence was particularly important as its former leader was Ayman al-Zawahiri, the current leader of al-Qaeda. Like al-Jama'a al-Islamiya, this group reviewed its ideology and tactics and then collectively disengaged from terrorism.

This occurrence shows that a terrorist group's decision to end violence can have a profound impact on others who engage in violence. Indeed, deradicalized terrorist groups "often interact with violent ones and in some cases the former influences the latter, a sort of domino effect demonstrated in the" *al-Jama'a al-Islamiya* and *al-Jihad al-Islamiya* cases in Egypt, the Islamic Salvation Army (AIS) and factions from the Armed Islamic Group (GIA), the Salafist Group for

---

[94] Ibid.

[95] U.S. Department of State. 2009, April 30. Country reports on terrorism 2008. *Office of the Coordinator for Counterterrorism*, 142. http://www.state.gov/s/ct/rls/crt/2008/122433.htm.

[96] Ashour, O. 2009. De-radicalizing jihadists may just work. *Alarabiya News*, September 20, 2009. http://www.alarabiya.net/views/2009/09/20/85514.html.

Preaching and Combat (GSPC) "and other militias in Algeria and de-radicalized Islamist figures and individual suspects in Saudi Arabia." [97]

Egypt soon realized the importance of using the collective disengagement of these terrorist groups as an example for other prisoners. In fact, the Egyptian government and other governments worldwide have used respected clerics and former combatants who have renounced terrorism in an attempt to reverse violent radical teachings. Individuals who have left their terrorist past behind them are used by countries with rehabilitation programs to serve as examples for terrorists in prisons and as individuals who could relate to the prisoners' current situation. The most ideal individuals are those who served as leaders in terrorist groups, leading propagandists, or other individuals whom terrorists admire, respect, and consider as role models. Upon release from prison, al-Jama'a al-Islamiya leaders toured prison facilities in Egypt; first, holding discussions with middle-ranking commanders and then engaging in dialogue with the group's foot soldiers to provide religious reeducation to prisoners.[98]

Other Middle Eastern and African Countries. Jordan has a rehabilitation program as well. Specifically, Jordan's Public Security Directorate (PSD) is a program that is designed to convince terrorists, through dialogue with jurists and professors of Islamic law, to revise their extremist views and in so doing, limit the dangerous influence that such individuals may have on others in the prison population.[99] Jordan also has a classification system that allows for the identification and segregation of terrorists within prisons.[100] Similarly, Kuwait has a treatment facility, the al-Salam Center, modeled after the rehabilitation center in the Kingdom of Saudi Arabia. This rehabilitation center includes prior Kuwaiti detainees from the Guantanamo Bay Detention Center. This center is housed within a secured area inside "Kuwait's Central Prison and is governed by a board of government officials, medical experts, and a religious scholar."[101] Likewise, Libya has a rehabilitation and reintegration program in place. Its neighbor, Tunisia, however, does not have such programs. Morocco, like Libya and the countries mentioned above, provides for the reeducation and social reintegration of terrorist prisoners back into society.[102]

Singapore. Singapore requires a similar form of rehabilitation to those mentioned above. Members of Jemaah Islamiya and the Moro Islamic Liberation Front (MILF), an Islamic terrorist group located in the southern Philippines, were

---

[97] Ibid.

[98] Neumann, P. R. 2010. Prisons and terrorism: Radicalisation and de-radicalisation in 15 countries. *The International Center for the Study of Radicalisation and Political Violence*, 42. http://icsr.info/publications/papers/1277699166PrisonsandTerrorismRadicalisationandDeradicalisationin15 Countries.pdf.

[99] U.S. Department of State. 2009, April 30. Country reports on terrorism 2008. *Office of the Coordinator for Counterterrorism*. http://www.state.gov/s/ct/rls/crt/2008/122433.htm.

[100] U.S. Department of State. 2010, August. Country reports on terrorism 2009. *Office of the Coordinator for Counterterrorism*, 128. http://www.state.gov/documents/organization/141114.pdf.

[101] Ibid., p. 135.

[102] U.S. Department of State. 2009, April 30. Country reports on terrorism 2008. *Office of the Coordinator for Counterterrorism*. http://www.state.gov/s/ct/rls/crt/2008/122433.htm.

required to undergo religious counseling while detained in prisons.[103] Here, a program was developed to counter the group's radical ideologies to prevent its spread in Singapore's Muslim community. The core mission of Singapore's rehabilitation program, which is led by clerics, is the religious reeducation of terrorists.[104] The program in Singapore was modeled after Saudi Arabia's rehabilitation program.

In Singapore's program, certain common factors were mentioned by participants as reasons for their disengagement from terrorism, such as "familial influences, frustration at lack of progress achieved through violence, trauma after attacks, disillusionment with leadership, and so forth."[105] This program also offers religious counseling and education to prior detainees long after they are released from prison, as officials strongly believe that radical ideologies cannot be eradicated by short-term counseling.[106] Beyond the rehabilitation program, Singapore assists the families of detainees by offering them financial assistance, educational opportunities, and counseling. This support is also provided by Saudi Arabia. Both of these countries understand that if the government fails to provide for them "then it is possible that extremist elements will move in to provide" it instead.[107] Authorities in Singapore have reported that detainees responded positively to their rehabilitation programs; however, the recidivism rates of detainees who were subsequently released are currently unknown.

Singapore further created the Religious Rehabilitative Group (RRG) to deal with its imprisoned terrorists in order to "study the Jemaah Islamiya's ideology, offer expert opinion in understanding Jemaah Islamiya's interpretation of Islam, produce necessary counter-ideological materials and to conduct public education for the Muslim community on religious extremism."[108] Problems arose when prisoners were

---

103 Ibid.

104 Neumann, P. R. 2010. Prisons and terrorism: Radicalisation and de-radicalisation in 15 countries. *The International Center for the Study of Radicalisation and Political Violence*, 51. http://icsr.info /publications/papers/1277699166PrisonsandTerrorismRadicalisationandDeradicalisationin15 Countries.pdf.

105 Fink, N. C., and Hearne, E. B. 2008, October. Beyond terrorism: Deradicalization and disengagement from violent extremism. *International Peace Institute Publications*, 10. http:// www.ipinst.org/publication/all-publications/detail/24-beyond-terrorism-deradicalization-and -disengagement-from-violent-extrem ism.html.

106 From the Singaporean response to the February 18 CTITF letter. Received on March, 27 2008; UN Counter-Terrorism Implementation Task Force. 2008. *First report of the working group on radicalization and extremism that lead to terrorism: Inventory of state programmes*, 18. http:// www.un.org/terrorism /pdfs/radicalization.pdf.

107 Boueck, C. 2007, August 16. Extremist re-education and rehabilitation in Saudi Arabia. *Terrorism Monitor* 5 (16): 3. Washington, DC: Jamestown Foundation; Hannah, G., Clutterbuck, L., and Rubin, J. 2008. Radicalization and rehabilitation. Understanding the challenge of extremists and radicalized prisoners. *RAND Corporation*, 36. http://www.rand.org/content/dam/rand/pubs /technical_reports/2008/RAND_ TR571.pdf.

108 Hassan, M., and K. G. Pereire. 2006. An ideological response to combating terrorism—The Singapore perspective. *Small Wars and Insurgencies* 17 (4): 461; Hannah, G., Clutterbuck, L., and Rubin, J. 2008. Radicalization and rehabilitation. Understanding the challenge of extremists and radicalized prisoners. *RAND Corporation*, 36. http://www.rand.org/content/dam/rand/pubs /technical_reports/2008/RAND _TR571.pdf.

due to be released back to their families and communities that were still radical. This significantly increases the likelihood that the individual will reengage in terrorism. These issues arose with Jemaah Islamiya terrorists, whose members are primarily individuals with family or marital ties to one another. Accordingly, if one member desists from terrorism and leaves the group, his or her family often still remain as members of the group. When families and communities foster rather than inhibit the radicalization process, the relocation of family and participants should be considered. Depending on the number of terrorist participants, the cost of doing so may be prohibitive. Implementing soft approaches to terrorism is generally costly; as such, in developing countries with scarce resources, such a counterterrorism strategy is not a viable option, unless it is financially backed by another country.

Other Asian Countries. The Philippines has a rehabilitation program that is modeled after the one in Singapore. Malaysia has a similar program as well. In 2005, Malaysian authorities held Jemaah Islamiya and Darul Islam (a religious terrorist group that seeks to create an Islamic state in Indonesia) terrorists within their prisons. Some were undertaking rehabilitation programs while subjected to preventive detention pursuant to the Internal Security Act. Indonesia has a rehabilitation program as well. The Indonesian program brings reformed terrorists to speak with its detainees. One such high-profile individual who desisted from terrorism is Nasir Abas, who visits terrorists in prisons in Indonesia and persuades them to cooperate with authorities.[109] Abas himself had cooperated with criminal justice agents to help them capture, prosecute, and convict members of Jemaah Islamiya who plotted the Bali bombings. He also published a book in 2005 in which he argued against killing civilians and spoke critically of Jemaah Islamiya.[110]

The Indonesian rehabilitation program is different from those in Saudi Arabia, Singapore, and other countries mentioned above, as it is run by the police. In 2010, the capture of Abdullah Sonata, a former graduate of the program, resulted in the Minister of Justice and Human Rights, Patrialis Akbar, claiming that the Indonesian rehabilitation program was a failure. Sonata was not the only graduate to have returned to terrorism. Bagus Budi Pranoto, a bomb maker, participated in the deradicalization program while serving his sentence for his role in the 2004 Australian Embassy bombing in Jakarta. After his release, he assisted other terrorists in the attacks on the JW Marriott and Ritz-Carlton hotels in Jakarta.[111]

United States. Noticing the benefits of such programs, the United States has also created a similar program in Iraq aimed at reforming Islamic extremists in U.S. administered prisons and detention centers where Iraqis are imprisoned or

---

109 Ripley, A. 2008. Reverse radicalization. *Time Magazine*, March 13, 2008. http://www.time.com /time/specials/2007/article/0,28804,1720049_1720050_1722062,00.html.

110 Ibid.

111 Rayda, N. 2010. Terrorist 'rehab' a failure: Minister. *Jakarta Globe*, June 26, 2010. http:// www.thejakartaglobe.com/home/terrorist-rehab-a-failure-minister/382698.

detained for terrorism or terrorism-related activities.[112] In particular, the United States has created a program to deradicalize and rehabilitate detainees at Camp Cropper and Camp Bucca in Iraq. According to Fink and Hearne, this program

> is geared towards training suspected insurgents in different occupational skills (e.g., farming, carpentry, art) while simultaneously fostering religious discussion and paying participants for their work. Consequently, participants have an alternative source of income and social support to the extremist groups to which they might otherwise have turned. Additionally, the program encourages the involvement of families through visits and facilitates educational opportunities. The hefty price tag of this program is $1 billion for one year.[113]

As they further noted, winning the "hearts and minds" of terrorist operatives and supporters is vital to an effective counterterrorism strategy and as such, countries "may feel that these costs are far outweighed by the costs of inaction or neglect, and vital to countering the adverse effects of negative publicity, for example[,] following incidents of detainee maltreatment at Abu Ghraib and Guantanamo Bay."[114]

United Kingdom. The UK Home Office reported that other than structural (e.g., social, economic equality) and motivational factors (e.g., discrimination, whether real or perceived), environmental factors played a prominent role in radicalization and recruitment. One such place where radicalization and recruitment takes place in the United Kingdom is in its prisons. Accordingly, the United Kingdom implemented programs (which are currently in operation) both inside prisons and for prisoners upon their release, which deal with radicalization and recruitment to terrorism. These programs increase an individual's chances of becoming successfully rehabilitated and reintegrated back into society. To increase the success rate of deradicalization and disengagement programs, certain community groups have been "given active roles in the implementation of prisoners' probationary regimes. In addition to providing vocational training and, in some cases, academic education, these groups take an active interest in shaping former prisoners' social environments and attitudes, including—when necessary—psychological counseling and the discussion of theological and political issues."[115]

---

112 Stracke, N. 2007. Arab prisons: A place for dialogue and reform. *Perspectives on Terrorism* 1 (4). http://www.terrorismanalysts.com/pt/index.php/pot/article/view/15/33.

113 Miller, J. 2008. Anti-Jihad U. *City Journal*, May 2, 2008. www.city-journal.org/2008/eon 0502jm.html; Fink, N. C., and Hearne, E. B. 2008, October. Beyond terrorism: Deradicalization and disengagement from violent extremism. *International Peace Institute Publications*, 13. http://www .ipinst.org/publication/all-publications/detail/24-beyond-terrorism-deradicalization-and -disengagement-from-violent-extrem ism.html.

114 Fink and Hearne, 2008. Ibid..

115 Neumann, P. R. 2010. Prisons and terrorism: Radicalisation and de-radicalisation in 15 countries. *The International Center for the Study of Radicalisation and Political Violence*, 21. http://icsr.info /publications/papers/1277699166PrisonsandTerrorismRadicalisationandDeradicalisationin15 Countries.pdf.

Other countries have developed or are developing special prisoner programs (Algeria, Austria, Belgium, Canada, France, Germany, the Netherlands, and Slovenia) to prevent their prisons from becoming breeding grounds for terrorists and terrorism recruitment centers.[116] Additionally, countries such as Sweden, Colombia, Canada, Austria, France, and the Netherlands (to name a few) have designed programs to prepare violent extremists for reintegration into society. For example, in Sweden, a program exists that supports individuals who would like to desist from terrorism. Bjørgo noted that some prisoner programs focus exclusively on the reduction of the number of active participants in terrorism as seen in programs such as the Child Combatant Program of the Colombian Ministry of Interior and the Reincorporation Program of the Colombian Ministry of Justice. Here, a precondition for the release of prisoners is a shift in attitude and behavior away from terrorism.[117]

Almost all of the terrorist radicalization and disengagement programs have experienced some degree of failure. Accordingly, the efficacy of deradicalization programs has been called into question. Silke argued that the reoffending of terrorist prisoners was low to begin with. He used data from the United Kingdom, which showed that of the 196 convictions for terrorist-related offenses, the majority of "which were connected to al-Qaeda-related extremism,"[118] none of these individuals "have been re-arrested or convicted for subsequent involvement in terrorist activity (or apparently any other illegal activity)."[119] Some believe that it makes little sense to have disengagement programs without deradicalization schemes because an individual, after taking part in a disengagement program, would return to their community with extremist religious beliefs still in tow. However, as Silke noted, certain terrorist groups desisted without participation in a deradicalization program. Examples of such groups include the Red Brigades, PIRA, and ETA.

Despite such questioning, the efficacy of these programs has not been measured by any comprehensive, quantitative empirical studies. This is in large part due to the fact that the metrics of success for these programs are extremely difficult

---

116 Counterterrorism Implementation Task Force. 2007. *First report of the working group on radicalization and extremism that lead to terrorism: Inventory of state programmes*, 9. http://www.un.org/terrorism/pdfs/radicalization.pdf.

117 Bjorgo, T. 2005. Reducing recruitment and promoting disengagement from extremist groups: The case of racist sub-cultures. In *A future for the young: Options for helping Middle Eastern youth escape the trap of radicalization*, ed. C. Benard. RAND Working Paper, WR-354. Washington, DC: RAND National Security Research Division; Horgan, J. 2008. Deradicalization or disengagement? A process in need of clarity and a counterterrorism initiative in need of evaluation. *Perspectives on Terrorism*, 4 (2). http://www.terrorismanalysts.com/pt/index.php/pot/article/view/32/html.

118 Silke, A. 2010. Terrorists and extremists in prison: Psychological issues in management and reform. In *The psychology of counter-terrorism*, ed. A. Silke. London: Routledge; Silke, A. 2011, January 1. Disengagement or deradicalization: A look at prison programs for jailed terrorists. *Combating Terrorism Center*. http://www.ctc.usma.edu/posts/disengagement-or-deradicalization-a-look-at-prison-programs-for-jailed-terrorists.

119 Silke, 2011. Ibid.

to define, as countries markedly differ in terms of their program objectives and the benchmarks against which program outcomes are measured. Further complicating matters is the variation in the type and number of terrorists housed within correctional facilities, which also affects the comparison between prison regimes across the globe. What's more, comparisons of these programs are nearly impossible because they are run differently among various countries, and each country (among other things) differs according to the operation of the programs and the eligibility requirements for entering them.

Counterterrorism strategies have focused on preventing terrorism and the pathways that lead to terrorism. To do so, the institutions where radicalization takes place must be targeted along with the individuals who are vulnerable to radicalization. Soft approaches such as disengagement, deradicalization, and reintegration programs are required to in order to accomplish this. These soft approaches also serve another purpose: they remove two justifications for terrorism—the apathy of government and excessive force. These programs should be included not in lieu of existing detection and prevention policies but to complement existing strategies. The value of these programs must be understood as widespread support is needed—financially, socially, and politically—for these programs to succeed and survive. Indeed, counterterrorism strategies such as these are costly, however, with the increase in the number of incarcerated terrorists, past cases of terrorists radicalized in prisons, and evidence of prisons increasingly serving as recruiting and radicalization grounds, funding provided in this area is money well-spent. Cutting off new recruits can eventually lead to a terrorist group's demise.

Dealing with the environmental factors that influence individuals in participating in terrorist activities is one important step in achieving this. Having recognized this, the European Union, the United States, and other countries in Asia, Africa, and the Middle East have implemented measures to this effect. It is clear that more research in this area is required in order to determine the efficacy of these programs. However, until such research is conducted, improving prison conditions, separating terrorists, providing rehabilitation programs, training staff, and screening chaplain services is a step in the right direction.

Is rehabilitation the key to an effective long-term counterterrorism strategy? This analysis has shown that rehabilitation programs may not be *the key* in counterterrorism strategies, but they are *a key* component of worldwide counterterrorism strategies if such policies and tactics are indeed aimed at eradicating sources of terrorism. These programs show promise and are in line with and included in the European Union, United Nations, United States, and other nations' counterterrorism strategies targeting the radicalization and recruitment of terrorists. Yet prisons are not the only places where radicalization and recruitment occurs. Terrorist ideology is spread via other forums, among the most prominent of which are the media and the Internet, each of which are explored later in the text.

HYPOTHETICAL SCENARIO

The U.S. government has decided to implement a rehabilitation program similar to that of Saudi Arabia. It has hired as special advisors some of the Saudi Arabian officials who created and oversee the program in their own country.

1. What are the pros and cons of implementing a rehabilitation program in the United States that resembles the one currently running in Saudi Arabia?
2. Are there obstacles to implementing this program? If so, how might they be overcome?
3. Would you make any changes to the Saudi Arabian rehabilitation program? If so, which ones?

CHAPTER SUMMARY

Prisons have become terrorist recruitment centers and breeding grounds for violent extremism. Prison security has contributed to this problem. Countries worldwide have different types of terrorists, such as right-wing, left-wing, religious, nationalist–separatist, and special interest terrorists, housed within their prison population. The number and forms of terrorism within prisons affects the regime. Governments have chosen between a few existing options on how to incarcerate terrorists. Unfortunately, as research has shown, whatever choice they make carries with it certain negative consequences. To address terrorist recruitment and radicalization in prisons, security measures are implemented to reduce the factors that are conducive to their occurrence. Recently, prisons have adopted a new role—as a place for rehabilitation and reform. Rehabilitation programs are an integral part of the counterterrorism strategies of several countries worldwide seeking to combat terrorist radicalization. Reintegration programs have also been adopted by certain countries to both assist the terrorist in transitioning back into society and minimize the likelihood of recidivism.

REVIEW QUESTIONS

1. To what extent does radicalization exist in prisons?
2. What can be done to improve security in prisons?
3. What factors are conducive to radicalization and recruitment in prisons?
4. Are current efforts in prisons sufficient to combat radicalization?
5. Which is more more preferable, disengagement programs or deradicalization programs? Why?
6. How have rehabilitation programs fared?
7. Which, if any, country's rehabilitation program has been the most successful? Why do you think so?
8. Should rehabilitation programs be included in every country's counterterrorism strategy? Why or why not?

chapter twelve

The Media and the Internet: Insights Into Quashing Terrorist Ideology

There are many forums within which terrorists' ideology spreads. One of them, namely, prisons, has been covered elsewhere. Intelligence has revealed that other prominent venues for spreading terrorists' ideology include mosques, youth clubs, and community centers. In these institutions, like-minded persons congregate, discuss extremist ideologies, and become radicalized. The terrorist plots in the aftermath of 9/11 demonstrate this. In Australia, authorities uncovered a planned terrorist attack on Melbourne and Sydney (Operation Pendennis). Investigations revealed that the plotters of the attack were radicalized in the Brunswick mosque. Likewise, during the investigations of the Madrid bombings, authorities discovered that the terrorists were radicalized in the Islamic Cultural Center (*Centro Cultural Islamico*; a.k.a. M-30 mosque). Similarly, in England, a report by the New York City Police Department revealed that "Beeston's extremist mosque and surrounding community, including youth clubs, gyms, and Islamic bookshop served as the 'extremist incubators'" for the London bombers.[1] Moreover, in the United States, several intercepted terrorist plots revealed terrorists' radicalization in the abovementioned institutions and support for terrorism by these institutions. A case

---

[1] Silber, M. D., and Bhatt, A. 2007. Radicalization in the West: The homegrown threat. *New York City Police Department Intelligence Division*, 33. http://www.nypdshield.org/public/Site Files/documents/NYPD_Report-Radicalization_in_the_West.pdf.

in point is the Portland Seven, who in October 2002 were arrested in Oregon by the FBI for attempting to aid and join al-Qaeda forces in Afghanistan. The operatives were found to have attended the Islamic Center of Portland (*Masjid as-Saber*), which was known for spreading extremist ideologies. A further example involved the Dar Al Hijrah Islamic Center in Falls Church, Virginia. The leadership of this center has been linked with Islamic terrorists groups such as Hamas and the Muslim Brotherhood.[2] In addition to mosques, community centers, and youth clubs, the media serves as recruitment and radicalization tools for terrorists.

To combat radicalization, rehabilitation programs have been implemented.[3] Apart from this, another soft approach than can be used to combat terrorist radicalization and recruitment involves targeting terrorists' ideology using noncoercive measures such as counterpropaganda and counternarratives. This chapter looks at the soft-power strategy of creating effective counternarrative or stories to win the information war on terrorism. First, it explores the relationship between the media and terrorism by addressing the complex interaction among policymakers, media, terrorists, and the public in the multinodal flow of information. It then examines the factors that shape the reporting of terrorism. A primary emphasis of this chapter is on the role played by the media in accomplishing the terrorists' agenda and the possible ways that the media can avoid this without curtailing the entrenched right to have a free press. The chapter then evaluates the counterpropaganda campaigns used by various countries against their domestic terrorist groups. Finally, it explores the feasibility of the United States engaging in a counterpropaganda campaign and its efficacy against al-Qaeda terrorists and their affiliates.

MEDIA AND TERRORISM: A TOXIC RELATIONSHIP?

> *Terrorism is a creature of the media.*
> —ROBERT A. FRIEDLANDER[4]

Primarily, terrorists rely on the media to portray their cause favorably and to have their activities covered in such a way as to damage their target(s). Their interactions with the media are principally aimed at garnering attention, recognition, and legitimacy.[5] Prior to the Internet, terrorists relied on television news to cover their attacks and broadcast their messages. In addition to television, other media such as magazines, newspapers, pamphlets, posters, and other print materials were the only available tools with which to disseminate information. With the advent of

---

[2] Emerson, S. 2006. *Jihad incorporated: A guide to militant Islam in the US*. New York: Prometheus, 442.

[3] See the chapter on rehab for terrorists in this text for more information on rehabilitation.

[4] Friedlander, R. A. (1982). Iran: The Hostage Seizure, the Media, and International Law. In *Terrorism: The Media and the Law*, ed., A. H. Miller, 58. Dobbs Ferry, New York: Transnational.

[5] Alexander, Y., Carlton, D., and Wilkinson, P. eds. 1979. *Terrorism: Theory and practice*. Boulder, CO: Westview, 162.

the Internet, this soon changed. Terrorists became less dependent on television news and print materials. Nowadays, terrorists freely spread propaganda online via videos, websites, online magazines, online publications, and so on. Indeed, the Internet serves as an enabler to terrorism, as it provides access to a wide range of information on weapons, targets, and potential vulnerabilities. It also serves as an incubator for terrorism with its websites, chat rooms, bulletin boards, social networking sites, and peer-to-peer networks. The online environment also serves as a virtual meeting place for individuals to discuss extremist ideologies.

Additionally, spiritual leaders can be contacted online. Leading propagandists are also available to assist in organizing, controlling, and motivating individuals to support and/or engage in terrorism. Undeniably, these individuals provide new recruits or existing supporters with the justifications to engage in terrorist attacks, especially suicide bombings. Furthermore, the Internet provides a forum for individuals to obtain access to extremists' propaganda. Consider Farooque Ahmed, a homegrown terrorist born in Ashburn, Virginia, who was charged on October 27, 2010, with planning to attack targets in and around Washington, DC. How was he caught? Ahmed shared his plan with "al-Qaeda operatives" who were actually undercover FBI agents. What is particularly troubling about Ahmed is that he had no formal ties to al-Qaeda and received no formal terrorist training abroad. How then did such an individual become radicalized? Intelligence has shown that homegrown terrorists receive training materials, review al-Qaeda propaganda, and watch sermons of extremist clerics via the Internet. Despite their increasing use of the Internet, terrorists and terrorist groups still rely, to a certain extent, on television news for coverage of their attacks and for the communication of threats and demands.

Many theorists have sought to explain the relationship between the media and terrorism. According to Wilkinson, terrorism "by its very nature is a psychological weapon which depends upon communicating a threat to a wider society. This, in essence, is why terrorism and the media enjoy a symbiotic relationship."[6] This was echoed by Jenkins, who claimed that "terrorists want a lot of people watching and a lot of people listening. . . . Terrorists choreograph incidents to achieve maximum publicity, and in that sense, terrorism is theater."[7] This was evident with Black September. Indeed, the value of the media was made clear by this terrorist organization when they stated that they had planned the attacks on Israeli athletes during the 1972 Munich Olympic Games because they

> knew that the people in England and America would switch their television sets from any program about the plight of the Palestinians if there was a sporting event on another channel. So we decided to use their Olympics, the most sacred

[6] Wilkinson, P. 2001. *Terrorism versus democracy*. London: Frank Cass, 177.

[7] Jenkins, B. M. 1985. Will Terrorists Go Nuclear? *Orbis: A Journal of World Affairs* 29 (3): 507–515; Hickey, N. 1976. Terrorism and television. *TV Guide*, July 31–August 6, 1976, p. 4; Tan, Z. C. W. 1988. Media publicity and insurgent terrorism: A twenty-year balance sheet. *International Communication Gazette* 42 (1): 4–5.

ceremony of this religion, to make the world pay attention to us. . . . From Munich onwards, nobody could ignore the Palestinians or their cause.[8]

As Bell stated, terrorists "understand . . . prime time, the need to escalate [their] deeds, to manipulate the media, to reach the masses."[9] In fact, publicity is everything for terrorists.[10] Terrorist attacks are designed to elicit a specific response from civilians, the government, followers, and other members of the terrorist group. If an act of terrorism is not seen or acknowledged by anyone, then it serves no purpose. A terrorist group would not be able to sustain itself without the media because it not only helps bring attention to the terrorists' cause but also assists them in gaining new followers and recruits.

The media actually helps terrorists' causes by providing information detrimental to the West, portraying Western countries as unable to defend their territories and populations, and promoting terrorists' objectives. Basically, by announcing the actions of terrorists, the mass media serves as instruments of terrorist propaganda. However, the media have a responsibility to mitigate their role in propagating terrorism. In fact, the media has a very important role in counterterrorism as its broadcasts can affect viewers.[11] The overall consensus among theorists and researchers is that the media is a powerful propaganda tool that is capable of shaping the attitudes of the public.[12] Indeed, in consonance with this line of reasoning, researchers have found that the mass media can have a dangerous impact on the psychological well-being of the public.[13] In fact, in her study, Slone found that media portrayal of terrorism provoked anxiety in some individual viewers.[14] During times of terror, the media should aggressively still rumors and speculations to lessen the anxiety of the public. This is particularly important because in times

---

[8] Dobson, C., and Paine, R. 1977. *The Carlos complex: A pattern of violence*. London: Hodder and Stoughton, 15; Weimann, G. 2008. The psychology of mass-mediated terrorism. *American Behavioral Scientist* 52 (1): 70.

[9] Bell, J. B. 1978. *A time of terror: How democratic societies respond to revolutionary violence*. New York: Basic, 54.

[10] Laqueur stated that "the media are the terrorists' best friend. The terrorist's act by itself is nothing; publicity is all." Laqueur, W. 1976, March. The futility of terrorism. *Harper's* 252 (1510): 104.

[11] Studies exist that support and refute this hypothesis. Studies that reject it include: Curran, J., Gurevitch, M., and Woollacott, J. 1982. The study of the media: Theoretical approaches. In *Culture, society and the media*, eds. M. Gurevitch, T. Bennett, J. Curran, and J. Woollacott. London: Routledge; Studies that support it include Herman, E. S., and Chomsky, N. 1988. *Manufacturing consent: The political economy of the mass media*. New York: Pantheon; Lee, M. A. 1990. *Unreliable sources: A guide to detecting bias in mass media*. New York: Carol; Slone, M. 2000. Responses to media coverage of terrorism. *Journal of Conflict Resolution* 44 (4): 508–522; Tan, Z. C. W. 1988. Media publicity and insurgent terrorism: A twenty-year balance sheet. *International Communication Gazette* 42 (1): 3–32.

[12] Herman and Chomsky, ibid.; Lee, , ibid.

[13] Bandura, A. 1986. *Social foundations of thought and action: A social cognitive theory*. Englewood Cliffs, NJ: Prentice Hall; Slone, M. 2000. Responses to media coverage of terrorism. *Journal of Conflict Resolution* 44 (4): 515.

[14] Slone, ibid.

of uncertainty, it is highly likely that individuals become more dependent on the media as a source of information.[15]

FREEDOM OF SPEECH AND REPORTING OF TERRORISM

In light of the relationship between terrorism and the media and the public's increased dependency on the media during times of uncertainty, measures have been taken to stifle terrorists' increased use and manipulation of communications media by "limiting terrorists' access to the conventional mass media . . . and minimizing . . . terrorists' capacity for manipulating the media."[16] One way this has been done is by "reducing and censoring news coverage of terrorist acts and their perpetrators."[17] Many theorists have agreed with this perspective. As Young proposed, the media should be given certain directions by authorities because media coverage is conducive to terrorist activity.[18] History is replete with instances in which countries have requested (and in some cases, mandated) that television media not publicize the messages of terrorists. For example, "Condoleezza Rice and other officials from the U.S. Administration asked major American television stations, just after 9/11, to stop airing bin Laden messages, because they may incite violence against Americans, or even contain secret messages for sleeper cells."[19] In addition, successful actions have been taken against broadcasts inciting violence and promoting terrorism. The banning by the United States, Australia, France, Spain, and the Netherlands (to name a few) of the satellite broadcast of al-Manar, a television station in Lebanon that is affiliated with Hezbollah, attests to this.[20] Even so, while it is relatively easy to ban satellite broadcasts, the same cannot be said about Internet websites. Additionally, while satellite broadcasts like al-Manar can be banned, they can still be easily accessed online.

In general, governments want the media to cover events in a manner that promotes the government's agenda. Initially, this is what U.S. news media did post-9/11. Consider the study conducted by Jasperson and El-Kikhia concerning

---

15 Tan, Z. C. W. 1989. The role of media in insurgent terrorism: Issues and perspectives. *International Communication Gazette* 44 (3):193.

16 Weimann, G. 2008. The psychology of mass-mediated terrorism. *American Behavioral* Scientist 52 (1): 70.

17 Ibid.

18 Tan, Z. C. W. 1988. Media publicity and insurgent terrorism: A twenty-year balance sheet. *International Communication Gazette* 42 (1): 4.

19 Transnational Terrorism, Security and the Rule of Law. 2008, July 23. *Terrorism and the media*, 46. http://www.transnationalterrorism.eu/tekst/publications/WP4%20Del%206.pdf.

20 EU Rapid. 2005, March 17. *EU rules and principles on hate broadcasts: Frequently asked questions (Memo/05/98)*. http://europa.eu/rapid/pressReleasesAction.do?reference=MEMO/05 /98&format=HTML&aged=1&language=EN&guiLanguage=en; Transnational Terrorism, Security and the Rule of Law. 2008, July 23. *Terrorism and the media*, 58. http://www.transnationalterrorism .eu/tekst/publications/WP4%20Del%206.pdf.

the coverage of the Afghanistan war by CNN and Al-Jazeera.[21] This study revealed that CNN's coverage of the war reinforced the positions of the administration of the United States and contained patriotic messages. By contrast, Al-Jazeera focused on alternative policies that could be implemented instead of a war and the death toll of the war. The latter is particularly important when emphasis is placed on the number of Muslim deaths, as this serves as a source of discontent throughout the Middle East.[22]

Censorship has been advocated as a way to stifle terrorists' ideology. The censorship of the media in terms of their coverage of terrorism, however, is objectionable because it opens up the door for the use of censorship for other security threats in the future. Moreover, public perception of information censorship may lead to mistrust of the media and the government. Despite these criticisms, censorship is advocated as an effective tool to combat terrorism. The argument is that if the media does not cover terrorism, then it will disappear.[23] Yet this belief fails to account for the Internet. Even if all television news media were to agree to not cover terrorism, terrorist attacks would still be covered online by private websites and social networking sites such as Twitter, Facebook, and MySpace. Specifically, the Internet bypasses any attempts for censorship. Consider that China has attempted to censor the Internet, managing to block many prodemocracy websites from its citizens, yet it is unable to block all websites, chat rooms, and other forums on the Internet from their use by Chinese dissidents.

The same issues arise when trying to promote self-restraint among news media in publicizing terrorism-related activities. Here, the Internet also serves as a barrier to effective enforcement of a blanket policy (official and unofficial) of noncoverage of terrorism. In addition, this perspective fails to account for the cases in which the media has been forced to publicize certain measures and events. In particular, there have been instances in which the media did not want to cover an event but was forced to do so in order to prevent the deaths of others. A prime example of this involved the hijacking of a TWA airplane in 1976, in which "Croatian hijackers . . . demanded that flyers be dropped over several large cities, and that . . . high ranking newspapers such as *The New York Times* and *The Washington Post* print statements made by the terrorists. The newspapers agreed and the statements were printed."[24] This, however, by no means constitutes a trend. In

21 Papacharissi, Z., and de Fatima Oliveira, M. 2008. News frames terrorism: A comparative analysis of frames employed in terrorism coverage in U.S. and U.K. newspapers. *The International Journal of Press/Politics* 13 (1): 58.

22 Ibid.

23 Transnational Terrorism, Security and the Rule of Law. 2008, July 23. *Terrorism and the media*, 45. http://www.transnationalterrorism.eu/tekst/publications/WP4%20 Del%206.pdf.

24 Pitt, D. E. 1987. Hijacker of '76 T.W.A. flight burrows out of federal prison. *The New York Times*, April 18, 1987. http://www.nytimes.com/1987/04/18/nyregion/hijacker-of-76-twa-flight-burrows-out-of-federal-prison.html; Transnational Terrorism, Security and the Rule of Law. 2008, July 23. *Terrorism and the media*, 9. http://www.transnationalterrorism.eu/tekst/publications/WP4%20 Del%206.pdf.

the majority of cases, the media willingly cover these events and publicize terrorists' messages. This occurs because the news media want to be the first to cover a story, make the story as timely and dramatic as possible, and protect a society's right to know.[25] Nevertheless, the pursuit of these objectives has been criticized.

The media has frequently been criticized for interfering with the work of law enforcement agencies and jeopardizing the successful outcome of incidents.[26] Such conflict with the media and law enforcement agencies does not exist in every country. A case in point is Israel, where the police and the media understand the importance and benefits of joint counterterrorism actions, working together to release only specific information about a terrorist attack. Usually, the media warns the public to be alert and stay away from crowded places.[27] Such a relationship should also be sought in other countries. A better working relationship between the media and governments is required. They do not need to work against each other; doing so is counterproductive. This is especially true with regard to counterterrorism. To promote better working relationships, discussions should be opened between the news media and government representatives. In this way, both parties can build relationships and come to an agreement on best practices in counterterrorism without compromising the missions of their organizations.

Another criticism leveled against the media is that they have released information that governments claim to be detrimental to counterterrorism efforts. Government officials, law enforcement agencies, academicians, and policymakers have criticized U.S. news media for releasing too much information, especially the type of information that some perceive as constituting state secrets. For instance, according to the U.S. government, *The New York Times* released critical data on how terrorist financing was revealed, thereafter severely hindering authorities' abilities in this area. In particular, in 2006, *The New York Times* published an article detailing a U.S. Department of Treasury's program, the Terrorist Financing Tracking Program (TFTP), which tracked terrorists' financing via SWIFT.[28] The TFTP had been successfully used in the past to find al-Qaeda operatives. For instance, this program led U.S. authorities to Riduan Isamuddin (a.k.a. Hambali), who ordered the Bali bombings. *The New York Times* claimed that the public had the right to know about the program.[29] Another argument brought forward

---

25 Perl, R. F. 1997, October 22. Terrorism, the media, and the government: Perspectives, trends and options for policymakers. *Congressional Research Service*. http://www.fas.org/irp/crs/crs-terror.htm.

26 Alexander, Y. 1978. Terrorism, the media and the police. *Journal of International Affairs* 32 (1): 112–113; Tan, Z. C. W. 1989. The role of media in insurgent terrorism: Issues and perspectives. *International Communication Gazette* 44 (3): 202–203.

27 Weisburd, D., Jonathan, T., and Perry, S. 2009. The Israeli model for policing terrorism: Goals, strategies, and open questions. *Criminal Justice and Behavior* 36 (12): 1268.

28 Lichtblau, E., and Risen, J. 2006. Bank data is sifted by U.S. in secret to block terror. *New York Times*, June 23, 2006. http://www.nytimes.com/2006/06/23/washington/23intel.html.

29 Hume, B., Baier, B., and Angle J. 2007, June 27. Political headlines: New York Times reports financial surveillance program. *Center for National Policy*. http://www.centerfornationalpolicy.org/index.php?ht=display/ContentDetails/i/428.

justifying the publication of this information was that the SWIFT program was covered by other newspapers in the past (e.g., *The Washington Post* and *The Baltimore Sun*). However, these newspapers did not cover SWIFT to the extent and detail that *The New York Times* did. Echoing this, former U.S. Department of Treasury Secretary John Snow stated that instead of merely stating that terrorists' finances were tracked via SWIFT, they revealed the exact means of doing so.[30] Indeed, critics of this publication argued that *The New York Times* should have been prosecuted for publishing this information pursuant to the Espionage Act of 1917. Even the Public Editor of *The New York Times*, Byron Calame, later stated, on October 22, 2006, that the publication concerning the TFTP was unjustified. Specifically, he argued that the TFTP was secret and should have remained so because the program was legal and there was no evidence that it had been abused by the government in any way.[31] In spite of this, there were no repercussions for the printing of this "state secret" by *The New York Times*.

Other than the Espionage Act of 1917, other U.S. laws exist that criminalize the publication of specific information. For example, the Atomic Energy Act of 1954 criminalizes the publication of the designs of nuclear weapons. In addition, the COMINT Act of 1950 criminalizes the publication of classified information pertaining to cryptography or code breaking. Another example is the Intelligence Identity Protection Act of 1982, which made it a crime to publish the names of undercover Central Intelligence Agency (CIA) officers and other intelligence officers of the United States. Curiously, there have not been any successful prosecutions of journalists under the Espionage Act and the laws mentioned above, only their sources. Additionally, these laws are in obvious tension with the First Amendment, which states, in part, that "Congress shall make no law . . . abridging the freedom of speech, or of the press." Despite this, no court has struck down these laws.

Beyond the United States, the European Convention on Human Rights (ECHR) requires European journalists not only to obey ordinary criminal law but also to act "in good faith in order to provide accurate and reliable information in accordance with the ethics of journalism."[32] Theoretically, a government can restrict the media's coverage of terrorist-related incidents if they can prove the effects of such coverage are so grave that they endanger public safety and/or national security. More specifically, according to Article 10 of the ECHR, "[e]veryone has the right to freedom of expression. This right shall include freedom to hold opinions and to receive and impart information and ideas without interference by public authority and regardless of frontiers. This article shall not prevent states from requiring the

[30] Hunt, T. 2006. Bush slams leak of terror financing info. *FoxNews*, June 26, 2006. http://www.foxnews.com/wires/2006Jun26/0,4670,BushTerroristFinancing,00.html.

[31] Calame, B. 2006. Baking data: A mea culpa. *New York Times*, October 22, 2006. http://www.nytimes.com/2006/10/22/opinion/22pubed.html?pagewanted=2&_r=2.

[32] *Bergens Tidende and others v. Norway* (App no 26132/95) (2001) 31 EHRR 16, para. 53; Transnational Terrorism, Security and the Rule of Law. 2008, July 23. *Terrorism and the media*, 52–53. http://www.transnationalterrorism.eu/tekst/publications/WP4%20Del%206.pdf.

licensing of broadcasting, television or cinema enterprises." Article 10 is a qualified right because it is subject to the limitations set out in Article 10(2), which are as follows:

> The exercise of these freedoms, since it carries with it duties and responsibilities, may be subject to such formalities, conditions, restrictions or penalties as are prescribed by law and are necessary in a democratic society, in the interests of national security, territorial integrity or public safety, for the prevention of disorder or crime, for the protection of health or morals, for the protection of the reputation or the rights of others, for preventing the disclosure of information received in confidence, or for maintaining the authority and impartiality of the judiciary.

Countries within Europe also have national measures to prevent the publication of information that can endanger public safety and impede counterterrorism efforts. For instance, in the United Kingdom, injunctions can be used to prevent the publication of material that is confidential or contains state secrets. However, this is only an effective remedy if the government has been informed of the prospect of publication of this information well in advance. The problem, however, is that in reality it is often too late for governments to do anything about the publication of information that can place the public in danger and hinder counterterrorism efforts. This is true because remedies for such an incident usually exist only after the fact. Actually, "there are very few legal opportunities for governments to restrict the media in their terrorism related broadcasts."[33]

It is essential to remember that freedom of the press and freedom of expression/speech are not absolute rights. They are qualified rights, as Article 10(2) of the ECHR shows. This is also evident in other human rights instruments.[34] Accordingly, such rights can be subjected to restrictions as long as the curtailment is for a legitimate reason, in accordance with the law, and necessary in a democratic society. No entity can be above the law. The press needs to be vulnerable to prosecution when it violates the laws governing secrecy. It is therefore imperative that criminal justice agents take a more proactive approach in prosecuting individuals who violate these laws. To improve the working relationship between the media, government, and law enforcement agencies, the media should be educated on the importance of their role in counterterrorism. This can be accomplished through conferences involving prominent government officials, law enforcement agencies, and the media.

NARRATIVES AND PROPAGANDA

Propaganda is a tool of manipulation. Particularly, it distorts reality to manipulate individuals. The importance of propaganda in influencing the population has also been noted by Carlos Marighella. In his manual, the *Urban Guerrilla*, he noted that:

---

[33] Transnational Terrorism, Security and the Rule of Law. 2008, July 23. *Terrorism and the media*, 53. http://www.transnationalterrorism.eu/tekst/publications/WP4%20Del%206.pdf.

[34] See, for example, Article 19 of the International Covenant on Civil and Political Rights and Article 19 of the Universal Declaration of Human Rights.

Box 12-1 Food for Thought—The 2002 Media Disclosure of the Forth-coming U.S. War in Iraq: Does the Public Have the Right to Know?

On July 5, 2002, *The New York Times* published an article that detailed the plans of President Bush to invade Iraq. In particular, the article revealed that there existed

> an American military planning document call[ing] for air, land and sea-based forces to attack Iraq from three directions—the north, south and west—in a campaign to topple President Saddam Hussein . . . Special operations forces or covert C.I.A. operatives would strike at depots or laboratories storing or manufacturing Iraq's suspected weapons of mass destruction and the missiles to launch them.[1]

The article further described some of the contents of a highly classified document, titled "CentCom Courses of Action." *The New York Times* later defended the publication arguing that they did so because the Bush administration had declared that they had no intentions to invade Iraq. During a debate titled "Freedom of the Press Does Extend to State Secrets" at Intelligence Squared in NYC, David Sanger, *The New York Times* Chief Washington Correspondent, stated that the "*New York Times* served an enormously important public interest there by making it clear to the public that no matter what government officials were saying in public to them, in fact they had a plan . . . to invade a foreign country."[2] In the aftermath of the publication of this article, many officials in the Bush administration called for the prosecution of *The New York Times*. No prosecution, however, was ever brought against the newspaper.

1. Was *The New York Times* justified in publishing this information?
2. Can the media be prosecuted for such a leak?
3. Should it be prosecuted for releasing this information? Why or why not?

---

[1] Schmitt, E. 2002. U.S. plan for Iraq is said to include attack on 3 sides. *New York Times*, July 5, 2002. http://www.nytimes.com/2002/07/05/world/us-plan-for-iraq-is-said-to-include-attack-on-3-sides.html?scp=1&sq=july%202002%20iraq%20invasion&st=cse.

[2] Intelligence Squared US. 2011, June 8. *Freedom of the press does extend to state secrets*. http://intelligencesquaredus.org/index.php/past-debates/.

With the existence of clandestine propaganda and agitational material, the inventive spirit of the urban guerrilla expands and creates catapults, artifacts, mortars and other instruments with which to distribute the anti-government propaganda at a distance. Tape recordings, the occupation of radio stations, the use of loudspeakers, graffiti on walls and other inaccessible places are other forms of propaganda. A consistent propaganda . . . explaining the meaning of the urban guerrilla's armed actions, produces considerable results and is one method of influencing certain segments of the population.[35]

---

[35] Marighella, C. 1969. *Minimanual of the urban guerrilla: Armed propaganda*. http://www.marxists.org/archive/marighella-carlos/1969/06/minimanual-urban-guerrilla/ch31.htm.

A basic propaganda technique is controlling the information that is released about death in wars or terrorist attacks. Specifically, the reporting of the number of civilian deaths, as well as the circumstances of the deaths, are usually controlled. Terrorists have often used civilian deaths to further their own cause. This is done to show that Western countries hide behind the veil of democracy but are really terroristic. The stories of those killed are widely publicized to demonstrate this. Others purposely portray governments as deliberately targeting civilians.

The Western media often focuses on the number of deaths and sometimes on the demographics of those killed (e.g., age, gender, and nationality). Indeed, Cilluffo and Kimmage criticized the media for failing to reveal a narrative of the victims and for failing to offer any other form of information beyond the number of victims.[36] During a war, usually only the numbers of deaths in armed attacks by Western military are covered. The same control exists for the numbers and circumstances of soldiers' deaths. Indeed, the disclosure of information about soldiers is socially constructed in such a manner as to gain the approval of its audience. The death of civilians during a war must be accidental (collateral damage). If not, the country runs the risk of being labeled as terrorists who purposely kill civilians to achieve their goals. Too many accidental deaths can also pose a problem. To deal with this, authorities control (or at least attempt to control) the frequency of news reporting on the deaths of civilians and how reports are framed.[37]

Another tool that terrorists and governments use is narratives, which provide the proper spin (i.e., favorable construction) of an event. The key to an effective narrative is to gain widespread acceptance from the audience by providing a compelling line (whatever the terrorist or government is spinning). It seeks to provide an account of events, how they will most probably unfold, illustrate underlying issues, assign blame, and offer hope of success. These narratives have always been important. Their development has been challenged by mainstream media and the Internet through which there are currently many distinct sources from which information can be retrieved and analyzed. Accordingly, today individuals are faced with many different narratives of the same phenomenon. It is the mission of those developing the narratives to convince individuals to support their cause because it is "just."

A narrative must have a beginning, middle, and end. The beginning draws attention to a grievance, the middle provides indication for potential solution to the problem, and the end provides the solution or calls on individuals to resolve the problem themselves.[38] Quiggin provided an example of this. Specifically, one video

---

36 Cilluffo, F., and Kimmage, D. 2009. How to beat Al-Qaeda at its own game. *Foreign Policy.* http://www.foreignpolicy.com/articles/2009/04/13/how_to_beat_al_qaeda_at_its_own_game.

37 Papacharissi, Z., and de Fatima Oliveira, M. 2008. News frames terrorism: A comparative analysis of frames employed in terrorism coverage in U.S. and U.K. newspapers. *The International Journal of Press/Politics* 13 (1): 52–74.

38 Quiggin, T. 2009, August. Understanding al-Qaeda's ideology for counter-narrative work. *Perspectives on Terrorism* 3 (2): 23. http://www.terrorismanalysts.com/pt/index.php/pot/article /view/67/138.

showed a "Chechen mission commander . . . identify[ing] the problem (the Russian occupiers), outlin[ing] a plan of attack for his followers (ambushing a convoy), and then" showed the successful execution of an attack against a Russian convoy.[39]

Terrorists use propaganda and narratives to gain attention and notoriety for their cause. Al-Qaeda openly acknowledges the importance of the Internet as a propaganda tool:

> Due to the advances of modern technology, . . . it is easy to spread news, information, articles and other information over the Internet. We strongly urge Muslim Internet professionals to spread and disseminate news and information about the Jihad through e-mail lists, discussion groups, and their own websites. If you fail to do this, and our site closes down before you have done this, we may hold you to account before Allah on the Day of Judgment . . . .We expect our web-site to be opened and closed continuously. . . Therefore, we urgently recommend any Muslims that are interested in our material to copy all the articles from our site and disseminate them through their own websites, discussion boards and e-mail lists. This is something that any Muslim can participate in, easily, including sisters. This way, even if our sites are closed down, the material will live on with the Grace of Allah.[40]

Other terrorist groups have also taken advantage of the Internet to publicize their attacks and spread their messages. Cases in point are Hamas and the FARC. Hamas uses its website to claim responsibility for suicide bombings and other attacks. To reach a broader audience, the websites of Hamas and the FARC exist in multiple languages. In particular, the website of Hamas can be viewed in 6 languages (Arabic, Farsi, French, Malaysian, Russian, and Urdu). Likewise, the website of the FARC can be viewed in 6 languages as well: English, German, Italian, Portuguese, Russian, and Spanish.

To gain followers, terrorists emphasize historical Muslim conflicts and provide narratives on individuals who have fought for Islam and how in so doing, won honor and fame for themselves, their families, and God. The Internet is also used to communicate threats to the government and its population. The threats are also addressed to the public to scare the population into calling for change in government or pressuring the government to give in to the terrorists' demands. Terrorists also use the Internet to target children. Hamas has one such website, known as *al-Fateh* (the conqueror). This site is specifically designed for children, with cartoon drawings and colorful stories tailored to them. However, the stories provide children with adult messages. For example, one excerpt of a story on the website stated, "our expectations will not be fulfilled until we fight and kill the Jews, especially as we are standing east of the river [of Jordan] with the Jews still standing

---

[39] Ibid.

[40] Anti-Defamation League. 2000. *Jihad online: Islamic terrorists and the Internet*, 14. http://www.adl.org/internet/jihad_online.pdf; Weimann, G. 2006. *Terror on the Internet: The new arena, the new challenges*. Washington DC: United States Institute of Peace Press, 66.

> ### Box 12-2 Terrorist in Brief: The Case of Sheikh Feiz Mohammad
>
> Sheikh Feiz Mohammad, an Australian citizen who is currently residing in Malaysia, is considered by Australia as the "most dangerous sheikh" because of his connections to known and suspected terrorists.[1] Additionally, he is known for his ability to reach and affect Western jihadists online. He has several Facebook pages with thousands of fans. His lectures, which are in English, can be widely accessed from YouTube, LiveVideo, and PalTalk. In addition, his lectures are posted on the same websites as famous jihadist propagandists such as Anwar Al-Awlaki (now deceased) and Abdullah al-Faisal (a Jamaican-born Muslim covert and cleric, who was convicted in the United Kingdom for inciting his followers to engage in violence).[2] While not as well known as Awlaki or Faisal, Mohammad is rapidly gaining followers in the online environment. In so doing, he is able to reach individuals whom the traditional jihadists cannot due to language barriers.
>
> ---
>
> [1] Stewart, C., and Kerbaj, R. 2007. Muslim cleric a danger on paper. *The Australian*, June 30, 2007. http://www.theaustralian.com.au/news/nation/muslim-cleric-a-danger-on-paper/story-e6frg6n f-1111113856958.
>
> [2] Abdullah al-Faisal has since been released from prison and was sent back to Jamaica, where he currently resides. Jamaica has banned him from preaching at its mosques. He has not, however, been banned from worshipping in them.

west of the river of Jordan; and until the rock and the trees says, 'woe Muslim, woe subjects of Allah, here is a Jew [hiding] behind me. Come and kill him!'"[41]

This site also promotes suicide terrorism. For example, "in October 2004, the website presented a picture of the decapitated head of young Zaynab Abu Salem, a female suicide bomber . . . The text accompanying the horrible picture graces the act, arguing that she is now in Paradise, a 'shaheeda' like her male comrades."[42] Like Hamas, Hezbollah also targets youths. In 2003, Hezbollah promoted a computer game, *Special Force*,[43] which simulates terrorist attacks on Israeli targets.[44] As Weimann noted, this game also featured "a training mode in which participants practice their shooting skills on former Israeli Prime Minister Ariel Sharon and other Israeli political and military figures. A 'high score' earned a special certificate signed by Sheikh Hassan Nasrallah and its presentation in a 'cyberceremony.'"[45] Apart from attempting to gain followers and promote their case, propagandists provide their tactical and strategic insights online for all to view. Accordingly, by analyzing these sites and propagandists' lectures and publications, one can find effective strategies for countering terrorists' ideologies.

---

[41] Weimann, G. 2006. Terror on the Internet: The new arena, the new challenges. Washington DC: United States Institute of Peace Press, 83. See also http://www.al-fateh.net/.

[42] Weimann, 2006, ibid., p. 91.

[43] Hezbollah's New Computer Game. 2003, March 3. *WND*. http://www.wnd.com/news/article .asp?ARTICLE_ID=31323.

[44] Weimann, 2006, above n 41, p. 92

[45] Ibid.

COUNTERING TERRORISTS' NARRATIVES AND PROPAGANDA

Effective counterterrorist strategies should seek not only to divide a terrorist group but also to reduce the group's bases of support in each village, town, city, state, or country. The type of counternarrative or counterpropaganda used will depend on the target. It will be tailored differently toward operatives, supporters, and sympathizers. To quash terrorists' ideology, the power of the Internet should be leveraged to expose any and all distortions by terrorists and should draw attention to the consequences of terrorists' actions. Generally, terrorists seek to demoralize their targets, change public opinion, and legitimate their actions. Counternarratives and counterpropaganda should be aimed at countering these goals by discrediting terrorists' actions and undermining their authority.

Delegitimizing Terrorists' Actions

In a video he released on September 10, 2007, Abu Yahya al-Libi, a well-known al-Qaeda ideologue, offered the United States tips on how to combat al-Qaeda's ideology.[46] He stated that to weaken the ideological appeal of al-Qaeda's message, the United States should focus on stressing the cases of jihadists who have renounced terrorism and their ideological commitment to al-Qaeda's cause. Here, the most prominent figures with significant followings before renouncing terrorism should be highlighted. As such, these cases can, as Brachman argues, "sow seeds of doubt across the Movement and deter those on the ideological fence from joining."[47] Yahya al-Libi further recommended that "mainstream Muslim clerics . . . issue *fatwas* (religious rulings) that incriminate the Jihadist Movement and their actions."[48]

As mentioned above, a tactic that can be used to quash terrorists' ideology is to focus on contradictions in their ideology. One such contradiction is their killings of innocent civilians. Many well-known Muslim scholars and leaders have condemned the killing of innocent people.[49] Moreover, in a survey conducted by WorldPublic Opinion.org between 2006 and 2007, the majority of the Muslims in all of the countries surveyed believed that attacks against civilians were contrary to Islam.[50] Nearly the same number of individuals believed that attacks against civilians in the United States and Europe were also unjustifiable.[51] A counter strategy must

---

[46] Abu Yahya al-Libi, 93-minute video tape, produced by *As-Sahab* cited in Brachman, J. 2007. Abu Yahya's six easy steps for defeating al-Qaeda. *Perspectives on Terrorism* 1 (5): 9. http://www.terrorismanalysts.com/pt/index.php/pot/article/view/18/39.

[47] Ibid.

[48] Ibid., pp. 10–11.

[49] CAIR. 2009, September 4. CAIR's anti-terrorism campaigns. *Council on American-Islamic Relations.* http://www.cair.com/AmericanMuslims/AntiTerrorism/SheikhYusufAlQaradawiCondemns Attacks.aspx.

[50] Kull, S. et al. 2007, April 24. Muslim public opinion on US policy, Attacks on Civilians and al Qaeda. *WorldPublicOpinion.org, Program on International Policy Attitudes, University of Maryland*, 2. http://www.worldpublicopinion.org/pipa/pdf/apr07/START_Apr 07_rpt.pdf.

[51] Ibid.

be designed to draw attention to terrorists' killing of innocent individuals, including children. In fact, al-Qaeda has killed children in their attacks, clearly stating their intentions to do so. In particular, al-Qaeda declared that they "have the right to kill 4 million Americans—2 million of them children—and to exile twice as many and wound and cripple hundreds of thousands."[52] American children are not the only children targeted by Islamic terrorist attacks. For example, in 2009, two separate incidents occurred in Baghdad, Iraq (October 25 and December 8), involving multiple suicide attacks that killed 282 individuals, 36 of which were children. These incidents should be highlighted in the media. In addition, attacks on locations such as schools should also be highlighted. The Taliban engaged in such an attack on February 9, 2009, executing a mortar attack on a school in Darra Adam Khel in Pakistan, which killed 15 individuals, 11 of whom were children. According to data obtained from the Worldwide Incidents Tracking System (WITS) of the National Counterterrorism Center, between 2004 and 2010, some 27,191 civilians were killed in attacks executed by Islamic extremists, 2,255 of which were children.

To defeat terrorist propaganda and cause the group to decline in popularity, the emphasis of the media should be placed on terrorists purposely attacking innocent individuals. The Egyptian government engaged in just such a campaign. A case in point was their response to the assassination attempt on the Prime Minister Atif Sidqi. A car bomb was detonated by the Islamic Jihad as the Prime Minister's motorcade passed it. Instead of killing the Prime Minister, a little girl, Shayma, age 12, died in the blast. The Egyptian government "launched a media campaign claiming that Islamic Jihad had deliberately targeted Shayma and not the Prime Minister."[53] As Brachman and McCants noted, the United States should "harness the power of the 'Shayma Effect,' broadcasting images of jihadi attacks that have killed . . . children."[54]

Another way to defeat terrorist propaganda and cause a group's popularity to decline is to emphasize the public disorder they cause and the damage to critical industries (such as tourism). Individuals have condemned such attacks. Consider again the survey conducted by the WorldPublicOpinion.org between 2006 and 2007. This survey showed that the majority of respondents believed that "attacks on civilian infrastructure—even if no civilians are killed—are completely unjustifiable."[55]

---

[52] Jihad and Terrorism Threat Monitor. 2002, June 12. *"Why We Fight America": Al-Qa'ida spokesman explains September 11 and declares intentions to kill 4 million Americans with weapons of mass destruction.* http://www.memrijttm.org/content/en/report.htm?report=678; Weimann, G. 2006. *Terror on the Internet: The new arena, the new challenges.* Washington DC: United States Institute of Peace Press, 69.

[53] Brachman, J. M., and McCants, W. F. 2006, February 1. Stealing Al-Qa'ida's playbook. *Combating Terrorism Center (CTC) Report,* 11. http://www.ctc.usma.edu/wp-content/uploads/2010/06/Stealing -Al-Qaidas-Playbook.pdf.

[54] Ibid., p. 19.

[55] Kull, S. et al. 2007, April 24. Muslim public opinion on US policy, attacks on civilians and al Qaeda. *WorldPublicOpinion.org, Program on International Policy Attitudes, University of Maryland,* 11. http://www.worldpublicopinion.org/pipa/pdf/apr07/START_Apr 07_rpt.pdf.

A further method with which to defeat terrorists' propaganda and narratives is to draw attention to their actions that result in the deaths of Muslims. Critics of Islamic extremists point to verse 48:25 of the Koran as proof that attacks on Muslims are impermissible according to Islamic law. Specifically, this verse holds that

> Had there not been believing men and believing women whom ye did not know that ye were trampling down and on whose account a crime would have accrued to you without (your) knowledge, (Allah would have allowed you to force your way, but He held back your hands) that He may admit to His Mercy whom He will. If they had been apart, We should certainly have punished the Unbelievers among them with a grievous Punishment.

The source of al-Qaeda's credibility is derived from its actions in defense of Muslims, its perceived piety, and its care for its operatives.[56] Nevertheless, these are not reflected in al-Qaeda's actions. Drawing attention to this can call al-Qaeda's legitimacy and credibility into question. One key narrative that can be used to quash terrorists' ideology is that they are defending Islam. In fact, groups like al-Qaeda believe it is their "mission to be the vanguard of the uprising of the oppressed."[57] Yet, their actions prove otherwise. The actions of al-Qaeda and affiliates are not in defense of Muslims. In fact, even supporters of al-Qaeda have questioned their killing of innocent Muslims. For instance, as Trethewey, Corman, and Goodall noted, during a Q&A session with al-Qaeda supporters,[58] Ayman al-Zawahiri was asked,

> Many people in the Islamic World and the Land of Haramin in particular complains [sic] . . . that [the] Al-Qaeda organization was behind many operations that targeted innocents [sic] civilians and Muslims within the Islamic nations and many Muslims and children died as a result of such operations, do you think not that you are shedding prohibited and innocents [sic] blood (...according to the Islamic Sharia)?[59]

Al-Zawahiri was also asked by another supporter the following: "What's your opinion on the daily civilian victims of al-Qa[eda]'s bombings in Iraq and other Muslim countries? If the U.S. is your enemy, what have these civilians done to

---

[56] Helfstein, S. 2010, June 3. A third way: A paradigm for influence in the marketplace of ideas. *CTC Sentinel* 3 (6): 16. http://www.ctc.usma.edu/wp-content/uploads/2010/08/CTCSentinel-Vol 3Iss6-art5.pdf.

[57] Quiggin, T. 2009, August. Understanding al-Qaeda's ideology for counter-narrative work. *Perspectives on Terrorism* 3 (2): 20. http://www.terrorismanalysts.com/pt/index.php/pot/article/view /67/138.

[58] Al-Qaeda's No. 2 defends deadly attacks. 2009, February 11. *CBS News.* http://www.cbsnews .com/2100-224_162-3991206.html; Bliss, J., and Johnson, E. 2008, April 3. Zawahiri defends Al-Qaeda attacks that kill Muslims. http://www.bloomberg.com/apps/news?pid=newsarchive&sid =a6oe.B63j_Ek.

[59] Trethewey, A., Corman, S. R., and Goodall, B. 2009, September 14. Out of their heads and into their conversation: Countering extremist ideology. *Arizona State University, Consortium for Strategic Communication*, Report No. 0902, pp. 10–11. http://comops.org/article/123.pdf.

deserve this? Their loved ones grieve for their loss and they hav[e] nothing to do with this conflict. Aren't they monotheist Muslims?"[60] Moreover, at another meeting with supporters, he was asked: "Excuse me, Mr. Zawahiri, but who is it who is killing with Your Excellency's blessing the innocents in Baghdad, Morocco and Algeria? Do you consider the killing of women and children to be Jihad? . . . Why have you—to this day—not carried out any strike in Israel? Or is it easier to kill Muslims in the markets?"[61]

Trethewey, Corman, and Goodall noted that al-Zawahiri has spent (and continues to spend) a significant amount of time giving "complicated explanations about exceptions to the rules, and circumstances where it really was permissible to kill innocent Muslims."[62] Furthermore, according to Drennan, "Al-Zawahiri accepts a great deal of collateral damage in the form of 'innocents,' stating, 'we don't kill innocents: in fact, we fight those who kill innocents . . . it may be the case that during [the targeting of enemies], an innocent might fall unintentionally or unavoidably.'"[63]

Similar questions have been asked of other terrorist groups that engage in similar tactics. For instance, the commander of the military wing of Hamas, the Ezzedeen al Qassam Brigades, Salah Sh'hadeh, stated,

> we do not target children, the elderly, and places of worship, although these places of worship incite to murdering Muslims. Similarly, we have not targeted schools, because we do not give orders to kill children. The same goes for hospitals, although this is easy for us, and attainable. We act according to the principles of Jihad to which we adhere. Our motto is: we are not fighting the Jews because they are Jews, but because they occupy our lands. We are not fighting them because of their religion but because they have usurped our land. If we kill a child, it is not intentional.[64]

Even though al-Qaeda claims to defend Muslims, the majority of the deaths that they have caused have been those of Muslims. In his speech following the death of Osama bin Laden on May 1, 2011, President Barack Obama noted, "bin Laden was

60 Ibid., p. 11.

61 Al-Zawahiri, A. 2008. The open meeting with Shaykh Ayman al-Zawahiri. *Al-Sahab*, April 2, 2008; Drennan, S. 2008, June 15. Constructing takfir: From `Abdullah `Azzam to Djamel Zitouni. *CTC Sentinel* 1 (7): 1. http://www.ctc.usma.edu/wp-content/uploads/2010/06/Vol1Iss7-Art61.pdf.

62 Trethewey, A., Corman, S. R., and Goodall, B. 2009, September 14. Out of their heads and into their conversation: Countering extremist ideology. *Arizona State University, Consortium for Strategic Communication*, Report No. 0902, p. 11. http://comops.org/article/123.pdf.

63 Al-Zawahiri, A. 2008. The open meeting with Shaykh Ayman al-Zawahiri. *Al-Sahab*, April 2, 2008; Drennan, S. 2008, June 15. Constructing takfir: From `Abdullah `Azzam to Djamel Zitouni. *CTC Sentinel* 1 (7): 2. http://www.ctc.usma.edu/wp-content/uploads/2010/06/Vol1Iss7-Art61.pdf.

64 The Middle East Media Research Institute (MEMRI). 2002, July 24. *A 2002 interview with the Hamas commander of the Al-Qassam Brigades, Salah Shehadeh.* http://www.memri.org/bin/articles.cgi? Area=jihad&ID=SP40302; Weimann, G. 2006. *Terror on the Internet: The new arena, the new challenges.* Washington DC: United States Institute of Peace Press, 85, ft 62.

not a Muslim leader; he was a mass murderer of Muslims. Indeed, al-Qaeda has slaughtered scores of Muslims in many countries, including our own. So his demise should be welcomed by all who believe in peace and human dignity."[65] Studies have supported this claim. For example, Helfstein, Abdullah, and al-Obaidi revealed that between 2004 to 2008, a total of "85% of al-Qa[e]da's victims hailed from countries with Muslim majorities and only 15% came from Western countries."[66] Figures show that primarily Muslims (not Christians and Jews) have been killed in terrorist attacks (See Table 12-1). In particular, data from the Worldwide Incidents Tracking System showed that between 2004 and 2010, Islamic terrorists killed 5,179 Muslims and a total of 153 Jews and Christians. The total number of Westerners killed (American and non-American) during the same period totaled 226. "Killing Muslims—even when undertaking legitimate operations against members of an unpopular local regime or symbols of Western occupation—is damaging to the jihadi movement because it inevitably leads to a loss of support among the Muslim masses."[67]

Another area that has resulted in divisions among terrorists, their supporters, and Muslim scholars is the notion of *takfir*, which is used to declare another an infidel or nonbeliever.[68] To justify the killings of innocent Muslims and other civilians, terrorists have used the word *takfir* to describe those targeted. The use of this term has been heavily debated among Muslim scholars. Al-Qaeda's view of *takfir* differs from that of the majority of Islam scholars. Al-Qaeda has regularly used the term *takfir* to "discredit or disparage other Muslims who oppose them. By doing so, fellow Muslims are now turned into enemies."[69] The consensus among Muslim scholars, however, is that the use of the term to declare other Muslims as infidels or nonbelievers is strictly forbidden and that Muslims who use the term are believed to cast infidelity upon themselves.[70] Generally, "extensive formal religious training has led to a rejection of *takfir* altogether . . . the less religious training a jihadist leader has, the greater his proclivity to excommunicate and kill more categories of Muslims."[71] As Drennan noted, "given constant debate over

---

[65] Iftikhar, A. 2011, May 2. For Muslims, a reason to rejoice. *CNN*. http://articles.cnn.com/2011-05-02/opinion/iftikhar.binladen.killing_1_al-qaeda-and-bin-muslim-leader-cairo-university?_s=PM:OPINION.

[66] Helfstein, S., Abdullah, N., and al-Obaidi, M. 2009. *Deadly vanguards: A study of al-Qa'ida's violence against Muslims*. West Point, NY: Combating Terrorism Center; Helfstein, S. 2010, June 3. A third way: A paradigm for influence in the marketplace of ideas. *CTC Sentinel* 3 (6): 16. http://www.ctc.usma.edu/wp-content/uploads/2010/08/CTCSentinel-Vol3Iss6-art5.pdf.

[67] Ibid., p. 12.

[68] Quiggin, T. 2009, August. Understanding al-Qaeda's ideology for counter-narrative work. *Perspectives on Terrorism* 3 (2): 22. http://www.terrorismanalysts.com/pt/index.php/pot/article/view/67/138.

[69] Ibid.

[70] Ibid.

[71] Drennan, S. 2008, June 15. Constructing takfir, from `Abdullah `Azzam to Djamel Zitouni. *CTC Sentinel* 1 (7): 4. http://www.ctc.usma.edu/wp-content/uploads/2010/06/Vol1Iss7-Art61.pdf.

Table 12-1 Terrorist Attacks by Islamic Extremists Between January 1, 2004–December 31, 2010

Group Type Affected	Victims	Deaths
Buddhist	5	1
Christian	580	152
Foreigner	1,663	557
Hindu	129	29
Jewish	12	1
Muslim (Shia)	11,553	2,873
Muslim (Sunni)	3,542	1,386
Muslim (Unknown)	2,406	920
None	1,873	351
Tribal	3,641	1,559
Unknown	133,877	36,916
Western (American)	502	129
Family Member	950	481
Western (not American)	92	30
Total	**160,825**	**45,385**

Source: Data Obtained from the Worldwide Incidents Tracking System of National Counterterrorism Center.

the correct construction and implementation of *takfir*[72] and noting the decline of several movements due to their proclivity for killing Muslims,[73] *takfir* is evidently" detrimental to the movement.[74] Accordingly, the scholars' view of *takfir* should be highlighted to delegitimize al-Qaeda's cause.

A further contradiction involves the use of the term *martyr* to describe suicide bombings. Al-Qaeda's view of becoming a martyr (*shaheed*) differs from that of the majority of Islamic scholars. According to Quiggin, "al-Qaeda advocates becoming a shaheed or 'martyr' by the act of suicide bombing. This *istimate* (suicide act) is part of their *hirja* or migration to God. They believe that they will be

---

[72] Terror Free Tomorrow. 2008, January. *Results of a new nationwide public opinion survey of Pakistan before the February 18th elections.* http://www.terrorfreetomorrow.org/upimagestft/TFT%20Pakistan%20Poll%20Report.pdf; Kull, S. et al. 2007, April 24. Muslim public opinion on US policy, attacks on civilians and al Qaeda. *WorldPublicOpinion.org, Program on International Policy Attitudes, University of Maryland,* 9–10. http://www.worldpublicopinion.org/pipa/pdf/apr07/START_Apr 07_rpt.pdf; Drennan, S. 2008, June 15. Constructing takfir, from `Abdullah `Azzam to Djamel Zitouni. *CTC Sentinel* 1 (7): 4. http://www.ctc.usma.edu/wp-content/uploads/2010/06/Vol1Iss7-Art61.pdf.

[73] Drennan, ibid. As Drennan noted, an extreme *takfir* doctrine led to the demise of, for example, the GIA (Armed Islamic Group), al-Takfir wa'l-Hijra, and Abu Musab al-Zarqawi's organization.

[74] Drennan, ibid.

rewarded in heaven for this action."[75] Other terrorist groups advocate this too. For example, "on its websites, Hamas often cites the fatwas (Islamic theological rulings) of Sheikh Yusuf al-Qaradawi, [to] legitimize . . . suicide bombings based on its own radical interpretation of Islamic rules."[76] By contrast, Muslim scholars believe that

> suicide is an act that is strongly forbidden in the Qur'an and the Haddith. Allah has granted you a body. Only Allah can decide when the body will be taken back. There are no justifications for exceptions to this rule. Lives, be they human or others, are sacred, and must be honored. Whoever commits suicide will be considered eternally committed to hellfire. Once in hell, the individual will spend the rest of eternity dying again and again in the same way they committed suicide. Therefore, suicide bombers will spend the rest of eternity having their arms, legs and head pulled off.[77]

A final narrative that needs to be countered to delegitimize terrorists—and more specifically, al-Qaeda and affiliates—is their narrative, which holds that Western countries are at war with Islam. In 2006, Pope Benedict XVI "quoted a medieval text characterizing some of the Prophet Muhammad's teachings as 'evil and inhuman' and calling Islam a religion spread by the sword."[78] According to one report, extremists have stated that the comments of the Pope prove that the West is at war with Islam,[79] which is a belief that has been repeated by many extremists. For example, Azzam Publications, which has promoted jihad, stated that, "Muslims know that America only wants to fight Islam and to liquidate everyone who acts according to the Islamic Sharia, because America knows that the biggest danger to it and for the Jews is Islam, and its believers."[80] Many Muslims also believe that the West is at war with Islam. Consider again the survey by WorldPublicOpinion. org., conducted between 2006 and 2007, which revealed that an average 79% of the 3,752 polled in Egypt, Morocco, Pakistan and Indonesia believed that the U.S. goal was to weaken and divide Islam, "including a very large majority in Egypt (92% [of 1,000]) and large majorities in Morocco (78% [of 1,000]), Indonesia

---

[75] Quiggin, T. 2009, August. Understanding al-Qaeda's ideology for counter-narrative work. *Perspectives on Terrorism* 3 (2): 22. http://www.terrorismanalysts.com/pt/index.php/pot/article /view/67/138.

[76] Weimann, G. 2006. *Terror on the Internet: The new arena, the new challenges.* Washington DC: United States Institute of Peace Press, 83–84.

[77] Quiggin, T. 2009, August. Understanding al-Qaeda's ideology for counter-narrative work. *Perspectives on Terrorism* 3 (2): 22. http://www.terrorismanalysts.com/pt/index.php/pot/article /view/67/138.

[78] Al-Qaeda warns Pope that Islam will prevail. 2006. *USA Today*, September 19, 2006. http:// www.usatoday.com/news/world/2006-09-18-pope-qaeda_x.htm.

[79] Ibid.

[80] Weimann, G. 2006. *Terror on the Internet: The new arena, the new challenges.* Washington DC: United States Institute of Peace Press, 82.

(73% [of 1,141]) and Pakistan (73% [of 611])."[81] Other surveys show similar results. In fact, "there is ample survey evidence to show that many Muslims in the U.S. and the UK, as well as in Muslim countries, see the Global War on Terror as a war on Islam."[82] As Leuprecht, Hataley, Moskalenko, and McCauley noted, "so long as Western troops are deployed in Muslim countries, particularly Iraq and Afghanistan, a counter-narrative for the War on Islam will likely remain difficult to formulate."[83] The United States, however, is taking steps in this direction. In October 2011, President Obama declared that all U.S. forces would be withdrawn from Iraq by the end of the year, which has largely been achieved.[84]

Western countries have repeatedly declared that they are not at war with Islam. In his speech following the death of Osama bin Laden on May 1, 2011, President Obama noted, "we must also reaffirm that the United States is not—and never will be—at war with Islam. I've made clear, just as President Bush did shortly after 9/11, that our war is not against Islam."[85] Other U.S. officials have also sought to disavow the notion that America is at war with Islam. Specifically, in 2010, New York City mayor Michael Bloomberg stated that "Islam did not attack the World Trade Center—[a]l-Qaeda did . . . To implicate all of Islam for the actions of a few who twisted a great religion is unfair and un-American. Today we are not at war with Islam—we are at war with [a]l-Qaeda and other extremists."[86] Such a message needs to be repeated. However, the actions of governments and populations must also reflect this. Anti-Muslim statements only help Islamic terrorists' cause and fuel the belief that the West is at war with Islam. This became evident with the debate surrounding the "Ground Zero mosque." In New York City, a 13-story Islamic Center (not a mosque, as detractors claim) was built a few blocks away from Ground Zero (the site where the WTC towers once stood prior to 9/11). While the Islamic Center received support from the Financial District Committee of New York Community Board 1, others opposed it, and multiple demonstrations

[81] Kull, S. et al. 2007, April 24. Muslim public opinion on US policy, attacks on civilians and al Qaeda. *WorldPublicOpinion.org, Program on International Policy Attitudes, University of Maryland*, 5. http://www.worldpublicopinion.org/pipa/pdf/apr07/START_Apr07_rpt.pdf.

[82] Gilbert, D. et al. 2004, June. The Hamilton College Muslim America poll. http://www.hamilton. edu/news/MuslimAmerica/MuslimAmerica.pdf; Leuprecht, C., Hataley, T., Moskalenko, S., and McCauley, C. 2009, August. Winning the battle but losing the war? Narrative and counter-narratives strategy. *Perspectives on Terrorism* 3 (2): 27. http://www.terrorismanalysts.com/pt/index.php/pot /article/view/68/140.

[83] Ibid., p. 33.

[84] Wilson, S., and DeYoung, K. 2011. All U.S. troops to leave Iraq by the end of 2011. *Washington Post*, October 2, 2011. http://www.washingtonpost.com/world/national-security/all-us-troops-to -leave-iraq/2011/10/21/gIQAUy Ji3L_story.html.

[85] Iftikhar, A. 2011, May 2. For Muslims, a reason to rejoice. *CNN*. http://articles.cnn.com/2011-05 -02/opinion/iftikhar.binladen.killing_1_al-qaeda-and-bin-muslim-leader-cairo-university? _s=PM:OPINION.

[86] Shawn, E. 2010, April 24. Bloomberg calls allowing Mosque near ground zero "fighting terror with freedom." *FOXNews*. http://www.foxnews.com/us/2010/08/24/voices-rise-favor-moving -islamic-center-mosque-proposed-near-ground-zero-nyc/.

at the site have occurred protesting it. The Koran burning incident by Florida pastor Terry Jones on March 20, 2011, is another example. As President Obama stated, this incident is a "recruitment bonanza for al-Qaeda."[87] Interpol also warned of the impeding risk of violence in the wake of the Koran burning; and they were right. In Afghanistan, thousands of protestors, "stirred up by three angry mullahs who urged them to avenge the burning of a Koran at a Florida church, . . . overran the compound of the United Nations . . . killing at least 12 people."[88]

Subverting Terrorists

Terrorists should be discredited in order to limit their influence. In the past, attempts have been made to discredit and undermine known terrorist leaders' authority. A case in point is Abu Musab al-Zarqawi. The United States possessed a video showing al-Zarqawi's inability to handle a weapon. This video was distributed in order to deter would-be terrorists from serving under him.[89] Another way to discredit terrorists was posited by Abu Yayha, who recommended that the United States fabricate "stories about Jihadist mistakes and exaggerate real Jihadist mistakes whenever they are made."[90] Fabricating stories, however, should be avoided, because if the truth were to come out, it would have a detrimental effect on the country. Such stories run the risk of causing mistrust among the country's population and its allies. Yet mistakes of the movement should be highlighted. The importance of drawing attention to mistakes was stressed by Carlos Marighella when he argued that the best methods used by urban guerrillas include "exploiting . . . the mistakes and the failures of the government and its representatives, forcing them into demoralizing explanations and justifications" for their actions.[91] Terrorists are very quick to exploit government failures; governments should likewise exploit terrorists' failures. Yahya further noted that the government needs to emphasize that these so-called mistakes were actually the intention of terrorists.[92] As stated earlier in this chapter, for al-Qaeda and other Islamic terrorists, this means drawing attention the deaths of civilians.

---

[87] Gruber, B. 2010, September 9. Florida pastor cancels Koran burning plan. *Reuters.* http://www.reuters.com/article/2010/09/09/us-usa-muslims-idUSTRE68709M20100909.

[88] Najafizada, E., and Nordland, R. 2011. Afghans avenge Florida Koran burning, killing 12. *New York Times,* April 1, 2011. http://www.nytimes.com/2011/04/02/world/asia/02afghanistan.html?_r=1&pagewanted=print.

[89] Jacobson, M. 2009, August 12. Terrorist drop-outs: One way of promoting a counter-narrative. *Perspectives on Terrorism* 3 (2): 13. http://www.terrorismanalysts.com/pt/index.php/pot/article/view/66.

[90] Brachman, J. 2007. Abu Yahya's six easy steps for defeating al-Qaeda. *Perspectives on Terrorism* 1 (5): 10. http://www.terrorismanalysts.com/pt/index.php/pot/article/view/18/39.

[91] Marighella, C. 1969. *Minimanual of the urban guerilla: Armed propaganda.* http://www.marxists.org/archive/marighella-carlos/1969/06/minimanual-urban-guerrilla/ch32.htm.

[92] Brachman, J. 2007. Abu Yahya's six easy steps for defeating al-Qaeda. *Perspectives on Terrorism* 1 (5): 10. http://www.terrorismanalysts.com/pt/index.php/pot/article/view/18/39.

Terrorists have sought to impress other jihadists by fighting superpowers. In 2004, Abu Bakr Naji (a well-known al-Qaeda propagandist and jihadi leader) advocated for jihadists to provoke superpowers into invading the Middle East directly.[93] This occured in the aftermath of 9/11 with the war in Afghanistan and continued with the Iraq war. Naji believed that this would impress other jihadists, that they were fighting directly with a superpower, and show that the superpower was not invincible.[94] To counter this, governments and the media should stress the losses that terrorists suffer as a result of this fight.

In addition, governments should implement measures that make it more difficult for terrorists to execute attacks. The need for such measures is more pronounced on the Internet. Al-Qaeda and affiliates laud their ability to inspire Muslims and other followers in distant lands to take up arms and join the jihad. To counter this, governments should seek to implement measures that prevent the spread of extremism, especially online. One way in which this can be accomplished is by removing the information that can be used to plan and execute terrorist attacks. With regard to the removal of information, post-9/11, many government websites largely removed from online sensitive information and that which could be used to plot or engage in a terrorist attack. For example, "the Department of Transportation limited access to the national pipeline mapping system of the Office of Pipeline Safety, which lays out the network of high pressure natural gas pipelines throughout the nation . . . Access to these highly detailed maps of roads and utilities is now limited to federal, state, and local government officials."[95] In addition, terrorists are readily able to download manuals that provide attack scenarios and information on how to create explosives. Sites that house these items should be monitored for intelligence purposes in order to gain insight into who is visiting the sites and downloading information from them. Otherwise, these sites should be shut down.

Terrorists also use the Internet to demoralize the enemy. They frequently post footage of beheadings, executions, and bombings to frighten the target and its citizens. For example, al-Qaeda has posted the videotaped execution (termed "slaughter") of U.S. citizen Nicholas Berg as "payback" for the abuse of prisoners in Abu Ghraib.[96] To counter such actions, governments should publicize successful captures of known terrorists. Here, the counternarrative needs to high-

---

[93] Brachman, J. M., and McCants, W. F. 2006, February 1. Stealing Al-Qa'ida's playbook. *Combating Terrorism Center (CTC) Report*, 7. http://www.ctc.usma.edu/wp-content/uploads/2010/06/Stealing-Al-Qaidas-Playbook.pdf.

[94] McCants, W. F. trans. (2006, May 23). The management of savagery: The most critical stage through which the Umma must pass, 17–19 of Naji, A. B. 2004. *The management of barbarism*, 8; Brachman, J. M. and McCants, W. F. 2006, February 1. Stealing al-Qa'ida's playbook. *Combating Terrorism Center (CTC) Report*, 7. http://www.ctc.usma.edu/wp-content/uploads/2010/06/Stealing-Al-Qaidas-Playbook.pdf.

[95] Weimann, G. 2006. *Terror on the Internet: The new arena, the new challenges*. Washington DC: United States Institute of Peace Press, 194.

[96] Ibid., p. 72.

light the instances in which the government has infiltrated groups and disrupted terrorists' operations. For instance, in 2010, a group of government-supported hackers in Britain penetrated the computer systems of al-Qaeda in the Arabian Peninsula and inserted code (a list of cupcake recipes) into the first edition of their magazine, *Inspire*, thus delaying its publication for a few weeks.[97] Successful prosecution of terrorists and their supporters should also be highlighted. For example, in November 2010, Bilal Zaheer Ahmad praised Roshonara Choudhry, who was convicted for attempting to kill a member of the UK Parliament and called on others, in online forums, to emulate her.[98] In addition, Ahmad posted online a list of the names and contact information of UK MPs who supported the war, along with a link to buying knives at the online store Tesco.[99] He received a sentence of 12 years for this in the United Kingdom.

Terrorists further use the Internet to have their voices heard by individuals in other countries. They also seek to change public opinion about themselves and the government. Moreover, they seek to weaken public support for the regime. Consider the FARC's website, which contains information that "condemn[s] the Colombian government as illegitimate and fascist . . . denies responsibility for violent acts . . . [and] affirms [the group's] principles (including peace and democracy)."[100] It also presents itself as being "persecuted by the government and the United States, highlighting its heroic fights for 36 years to bring about democracy and social equality for the people of Colombia."[101] To survive as a terrorist group, popular support must be maintained. The failure of al-Qaeda in Saudi Arabia due to the lack of popular support attests to this.[102] Abu Bakr Naji argued that groups had failed in the past because the local regimes were able to turn public opinion against them.[103] What is needed, therefore, is an aggressive media campaign aimed at the defamation of jihadists.

---

[97] Gardham, D. 2011. MI6 attacks al Qaeda in "Operation Cupcake." *Telegraph*, June 2, 2011. http://www.telegraph.co.uk/news/uknews/terrorism-in-the-uk/8553366/MI6-attacks-al-Qaeda -in-Operation-Cupcake.html; Pantucci, R. 2011, September 26. The UK's efforts to disrupt jihadist activity online. *CTC Sentinel* 4 (9): 15. http://www.ctc.usma.edu/wp-content/uploads/2011/09 /CTCSentinel-Vol4Iss96.pdf.

[98] Pantucci, 2011, ibid., p. 16.

[99] Ibid.

[100] Weimann, G. 2006. *Terror on the Internet: The new arena, the new challenges.* Washington DC: United States Institute of Peace Press, 77.

[101] Ibid.

[102] Kull, S. et al. 2007, April 24. Muslim public opinion on US policy, attacks on civilians and al Qaeda. *WorldPublicOpinion.org, Program on International Policy Attitudes, University of Maryland*, 5. http://www.worldpublicopinion.org/pipa/pdf/apr07/START_Apr07_rpt.pdf; Hegghammer, T. 2010, February 25. The failure of jihad in Saudi Arabia. *Occasional Paper Series, Combating Terrorism Center, West Point.* http://www.ctc.usma.edu/wp-content/uploads /2010/10/CTC_OP_Hegghammer_Final.pdf.

[103] McCants, W. F. trans. 2006, May 23. The management of savagery: The most critical stage through which the Umma must pass, 17–19 of Naji, A. B. 2004. *The management of barbarism*, 8.

Websites, chat rooms, bulletin boards, newsgroups, and other Web forums could be used to create divisions among followers and promote disharmony. This can be accomplished by challenging propagandists' and leading jihadists' use and promotion of violence against Muslims and innocent civilians. In line with this reasoning, Abu Yahya recommended that the United States discredit influential thinkers and propagandists of the jihad movement. According to him, "not all Jihadists are replaceable: there are some individuals who provide a disproportionate amount of insight, scholarship or charisma."[104] Governments have implemented measures to do just that. The Check the Web initiative in Germany, which seeks EU cooperation in monitoring terrorists' websites, is one such example. Former terrorists, former supporters of terrorists, religious imams, and nongovernmental organizations should spread counternarratives and counterpropaganda. They should challenge extremists' ideology. Moreover, activists, entrepreneurs, media personalities, students, business people, and others can be used to counter terrorists' propaganda and narratives. A prime example of the use of nongovernmental organizations to counter terrorists' ideology is the Quilliam Foundation, which is led by former members of a terrorist group known as *Hizb ut-Tahrir*, and stresses that Islamic extremists' ideologies must be criticized and refuted whenever and wherever they are found.[105] A key component of a global counterterrorism strategy should thus be to deter the production of extremist materials and create a hostile environment for extremists' perspectives online.

Furthermore, hackers and other volunteers monitor the Internet for terrorist websites and notify authorities of their locations.[106] Indeed, Internet users are better placed to detect and challenge radical ideologies online than government officials are. Having realized this, many private groups have searched the Internet for extremists' websites and other forums. Independent groups of citizens have also sought to search the Internet for terrorists' websites. Once found, these websites are reported and eventually shut down by Internet service providers (ISPs). Terrorists have responded to these actions by threatening the groups that report their websites with violence, even death. One such example involved the Kataeb Mujahedeen. In July 2004, this group sent Aaron Weisburd, the head of Internet Haganah (which helped shut down more than 450 terrorist supporters' websites), a letter threatening to decapitate him unless he stopped and closed down his website.[107] Another group that seeks to shut down terrorists' websites is the Young

---

104 Brachman, J. 2007. Abu Yahya's six easy steps for defeating al-Qaeda. *Perspectives on Terrorism* 1 (5): 11–12. http://www.terrorismanalysts.com/pt/index.php/pot/article/view/18/39.

105 Jacobson, M. 2009, August 12. Terrorist drop-outs: One way of promoting a counter-narrative. *Perspectives on Terrorism* 3 (2): 15. http://www.terrorismanalysts.com/pt/index.php/pot/article/view/66.

106 Kohlmann, E. 2005. Al-Qaeda and the Internet. *Washington Post*, August 8, 2005. http://www.washingtonpost.com/wp-dyn/content/discussion/2005/08/05/DI2005080501262.html.

107 Weimann, G. 2006. *Terror on the Internet: The new arena, the new challenges*. Washington DC: United States Institute of Peace Press, 199.

Intelligent Hackers Against Terror (YIHAT). The goal of this hacking group, which was founded by the German hacker Kim Schmitz, is "to gather information on terrorists and [give] this information to U.S. authorities."[108] Another group is the American Antiterrorist Coalition (AAC), which, in April 2004, released "a database of terrorist websites and groups (with over 300 entries), focusing mainly on extreme Islamic groups."[109] To quash terrorists' ideology, therefore, online communities should be empowered to self-regulate and participate in governments' strategies to combat the spread of terrorism and radicalization online.

Governments should additionally create their own websites to lure actual and would-be terrorists. In particular, "honeypots" can be created. These are a form of intrusion detection/prevention. They are decoy mechanisms that are implemented to lure offenders away from valuable network resources and can help capture new and unknown attacks. Honeypots are a "security resource whose value lies in being probed, attacked, or compromised."[110] They are monitored and can provide detailed insight into how a specific exploitation occurred. To be effective, honeypots must be isolated from the network. If this does not occur, honeypots that have been compromised might be used to launch attacks on the real network. Additionally, honeypots should not be used for legitimate services or network traffic. Given that there is no legitimate reason for interacting with a honeypot, all activities that target it are considered suspicious. Furthermore, it is imperative that the honeypots created are able to record and monitor all activities.

Honeypots have been created to try to detect terrorists. U.S. and Saudi Arabian intelligence agencies have been known to set up such honeypots to lure terrorists. The intelligence obtained from such sites is invaluable. Honeypots help shed some light on terrorists' identities and their plans. Publicizing the existence of honeypots online (though not the specific sites) should be encouraged; so too should prosecuting individuals who visit these sites. This publicity is meant to instill fear and uncertainty in the terrorists or supporters of terrorists that their online illegal actions may be brought to the attention of authorities, for which they will certainly be punished.

To be effective, such websites should be plentiful. Additionally, each website should contain subtle pieces of misinformation. If enough websites exist with misinformation, eventually terrorists will learn to not trust what they read on the Internet. Kohlmann provided an excellent example of this: Azzam Publications, a former al-Qaeda website, criticized an English-language jihad information website, Jihadspun, as being a CIA intelligence-gathering site. Kohlmann added that this website sold videotapes online, which could be purchased with a credit card number, making the tracking of an operative easier (unless of course, a stolen

---

[108] Ibid., p. 198.

[109] Ibid., p. 192.

[110] Spitzner, L. 2003. *Honeypots: Tracking hackers*. New York: Addison-Wesley, 40.

credit card was used). These instances should be publicized as well to ensure that others are also skeptical about the veracity of websites.

HYPOTHETICAL SCENARIO

A new terrorist group has taken the Internet by storm. It is called Jihad 2.0 and adheres to an ideology similar to al-Qaeda's. This group has multiple websites. Members have created videos with sermons and distributed them on YouTube and other sites. Members also have Facebook pages with thousands of followers. Some of the members have engaged in terrorist attacks in various locations around the globe, resulting in 5,000 deaths. The majority of those killed were Muslim, and one-fourth of those killed (1,250) were youths.

1. What can governments do to counter this group's ideology?
2. What can the media do to counter this group's ideology?
3. What can private citizens and groups do to prevent this group from spreading its ideology online?

CHAPTER SUMMARY

Terrorists depend on mass media to promote their cause. Before the Internet, terrorists had to rely on television, radio, and print publications to transmit their messages and cover their attacks. When the demands of terrorists are broadcast, the media source that engages in this conduct becomes a willing tool of terrorist propaganda. The media has released information that governments claim has been detrimental to counterterrorism efforts. Discussions should be opened between news media and government representatives on the best way forward.

Propaganda and narratives are important tools for governments and terrorists. The counterterrorism strategy formed must be tailored to the audience. Even though al-Qaeda claims to defend Muslims, the majority of the deaths that they have caused have been of Muslims. Al-Qaeda has also killed children in their attacks. The counternarrative and counterpropaganda strategy should, therefore, stress civilian deaths by these terrorists, as well as the deaths of Muslims. The latter will be used to counter terrorists' claims that they are serving Muslim interests. In fact, several movements have declined due to their proclivity to kill Muslims. Accordingly, countries should draw attention to the victims of terrorists, more so than is currently occurring. In addition, the coverage of victims should not be limited to their numbers.

To quash the spread of terrorists' ideologies on the Internet, it is critical for online communities to be empowered to self-regulate and participate in governments' strategies to reach these ends. In addition, governments must deter the production of extremist materials and create a hostile environment for extremists' perspectives online. Furthermore, the power of the Internet must be used by governments to both call attention to all mistakes and distortions by terrorists and publicize the consequences of terrorists' actions.

REVIEW QUESTIONS

1. How does a terrorist's ideology spread?
2. Why do terrorists need the media?
3. If television news stopped covering incidents of terrorism, would terrorist groups cease to exist? Why or why not?
4. Can governments and the media work together to combat terrorism?
5. Choose a terrorist group. What are two examples of their propaganda and narratives?
6. How can terrorists' narratives and propaganda be countered?
7. What role do nongovernmental actors play in combating terrorists' ideologies?

chapter thirteen

Making Peace with Terrorists

This chapter examines other noncoercive approaches to counterterrorism, namely, negotiations and peace agreements (e.g., the Good Friday Agreement and Oslo Accords). Here, special attention will be paid to countries that have entered into successful peace agreements with their domestic terrorist groups. In addition, the agreements between countries and terrorist groups that have been unsuccessful will also be examined to determine what went wrong in those cases. Finally, this chapter explores the viability of the United States using such an approach to combat post-9/11 terrorism.

NEGOTIATIONS AS A METHOD OF COUNTERTERRORISM

Negotiations are processes during which two or more parties engage in open dialogue to resolve their differences and come to a mutually agreed upon decision on a matter (or matters) under dispute. Conflicts have been successfully resolved in the past via negotiations. Historically, negotiations have been used by international, regional, and national actors to stop the spread of genocide, end imperialist rule, and promote peace. When governments engage in dialogue with terrorist groups, it is often to end conflicts within the region and negotiate for peace.

Many countries have declared a blanket policy of no negotiations with terrorists. The belief is that if no concessions are made, then terrorists will realize that there are no rewards for engaging in terrorist activity and thus will be less likely to engage in such attacks in the future. As such, if governments refuse to concede to terrorists' demands, acts of terrorism would cease, or at the very least be significantly reduced. Even though most countries have a general policy of no negotiations with terrorists, in practice, this policy has largely not been followed. Countries have given in to terrorists' demands in the past, the United States included. For example, the FBI did not object to Ted Kaczynski's offer to cease his deadly attacks in exchange for the publication of his manifesto in a newspaper.[1]

A main argument brought forward against negotiations with terrorists is that it legitimizes the activities of these individuals. As Neumann posited,

> [t]he argument against negotiating with terrorists is simple: Democracies must never give in to violence, and terrorists must never be rewarded for using it. Negotiations give legitimacy to terrorists and their methods and undermine actors who have pursued political change through peaceful means. Talks can destabilize the negotiating government's political systems, undercut international effects to outlaw terrorism, and set a dangerous precedent.[2]

Terrorists are criminals, as they commit acts that violate national and international laws. Terrorists have also engaged in illicit activities to fund their operations. The political aspect of terrorism deflects attention from this important truth about terrorism. Engaging in dialogue with such individuals thus sends the message that governments are rewarding individuals for criminal activity. Surveys have showed that the public rejects negotiations with terrorists. For example, a study conducted by Angus Reid Global Monitor showed that in 2010, only 16% of Russians surveyed (256 out of 1,600 individuals) believed that it was necessary to negotiate with terrorists. However, the results of this survey are by no means representative of the public opinion of other countries. For instance, the majority of Palestinians surveyed by polling companies (JMCC, Near East Consulting, and WorldPublic Opinion.org) supported peace negotiations between Israelis and Palestinians.[3] Additionally, domestic and international actors have varied in their perspectives on the justifiability of negotiating with terrorists. A case in point is the significant disagreement among national and international agencies on whether to include the Colombian United Self-Defense Forces (AUC), which was formed to combat left-wing terrorist groups in Colombia (such as the FARC and ELN), in peace talks.[4]

---

[1] Blum, G., and Heymann, P. B. 2010. *Laws, outlaws, and terrorists*. Cambridge, MA: MIT Press, 151–152.

[2] Neumann, P. R. 2007. Negotiating with terrorists. *Foreign Affairs* 86 (1):128; Toros, H. 2008. We don't negotiate with terrorists!: Legitimacy and complexity in terrorist conflicts. *Security Dialogue* 39 (4): 411.

[3] WorldPublicOpinion.org. 2006, March 2. *Most Palestinians believe Hamas should change its position on eliminating Israel*. http://www.worldpublicopinion.org/pipa/articles/brmiddle eastnafricara/173.php?nid=&id=&pnt=173.

[4] Downes, R. 1999. *Landpower and ambiguous warfare: The Challenge of Colombia in the 21st century*. Carlisle, PA: Strategic Studies Institute, US Army War College, 19–20.

The most common argument brought forward against negotiation is that it encourages future attacks.[5] Particularly, if governments give in to terrorists' demands, this may encourage other groups to follow suit, as it gives the impression that this tactic is successful. Future terrorist attacks may also be encouraged because the willingness of a government to negotiate may be seen as a sign of weakness by the terrorist organization. By contrast, others argue that if governments do not negotiate, terrorists will escalate their actions if they are provided with no alternative means to voice their grievances.[6] Moreover, if governments do not negotiate with terrorists, then hostages may be killed or a terrorist may follow through with an attack.[7] A danger thus arises when governments do not negotiate with terrorists. This became evident in the refusal of the Italian government to negotiate for the release of an Italian politician Aldo Moro in 1978. As a result, Moro was killed by the Red Brigades. Dangers also arise when governments improperly negotiate with terrorists. Such an instance occurred with the negotiations of Italian Prosecutor General Francesco Coco with the Red Brigades, who had kidnapped Mario Sossi on April 18, 1974. Coco persuaded a court to agree to the release of prisoners pursuant to the demands of the terrorists. The condition for the release of the prisoners, however, was that the Red Brigades first release Sossi unharmed. The Red Brigades complied and released Sossi, after which the Prosecutor General convinced the government to renege on their agreement with Red Brigades. In June 1976, Prosecutor General Coco was assassinated by this group in retaliation for this incident.

Some proponents of negotiating with terrorists believe that such negotiations provide an opportunity for gathering information about terrorists and their organizations.[8] Intelligence gathering is a vital component of any effective counterterrorism strategy. Terrorists who have or want to negotiate with governments may be willing to provide insights into the inner workings and functions of their groups. It also provides governments with insights into terrorists' grievances that they would not have access to if they had pursued other counterterrorism policies.

Negotiations may reduce recruitment to the terrorist organization engaged in dialogue with the government. Individuals may no longer see the need to join the group. Negotiations also send the message that grievances can be heard and addressed through nonviolent means, discouraging future acts of terrorism. Negotiations have contributed to the disarmament of terrorists and their renouncement of violence in the following ways: "by opening an alternative way to change for [terrorists]; by strengthening the factions favoring talks; and by offering [terrorist

---

[5] Ibid., p. 139.

[6] Blum, G., and Heymann, P. B. 2010. *Laws, outlaws, and terrorists.* Cambridge, MA: MIT Press, 144–145.

[7] Ibid., pp. 143, 145.

[8] Ibid., p. 144.

organizations] the possibility to transform themselves into a legitimate entity."[9] Furthermore, according to Heymann and Blum, "there is a possibility that negotiation works, not only to resolve an immediate crisis, but also, more crucially, to transform the relationship between the government and the group."[10] History shows that this can occur. For example, in Uruguay in 1985, the government declared a general amnesty for Tupamaros prisoners, and subsequently the group reconstituted itself as a legitimate political party.[11] Reconciliation programs were also developed in Algeria. As a result, many Armed Islamic Group (GIA) terrorists surrendered to Algerian security forces; the remaining members were believed to have joined other terrorist groups.[12] As such, even though "negotiating with . . . terrorists . . . can indeed lead to their legitimation, [it is] through this very legitimation [that] . . . terrorists . . . [are offered] an alternative path and the chance to transform into nonviolent actors."[13]

PEACE ACCORDS

Many peace accords have been achieved through negotiation. For instance, through negotiations that were led by the Clinton administration, the General Framework Agreement for Peace in Bosnia and Herzegovina (the Dayton Accords) ended the Bosnia war in 1995. Similar instances have been observed in other wars and conflicts. For example, the Arusha Peace Accords, which ended the conflict between the Rwanda government and the Rwanda Patriotic Front, were carried out through negotiations led by the Organization of African Unity and the United Nations. In addition, in South Africa, negotiations between the South African government and the African National Congress (ANC) ultimately ended the violence between them and led to the release of Nelson Mandela (the leader of the ANC) from prison. Apart from wars and genocide, peace accords and agreements have been achieved between terrorist groups and governments. The Moro Liberation Front, a separatist group seeking to create an independent Islamic state in the islands of Mindanao and the Sulu Archipelago in the southern Philippines, is another group that signed a peace agreement with the country with which they were in conflict.[14] Another example is the Islamic Salvation Front, an Islamic terrorist

[9] Toros, H. 2008. We don't negotiate with terrorists!: Legitimacy and complexity in terrorist conflicts. *Security Dialogue* 39 (4): 416.

[10] Blum, G., and Heymann, P. B. 2010. *Laws, outlaws, and terrorists*. Cambridge, MA: MIT Press, 145.

[11] Henderson, H. 2001. *Global terrorism: The complete reference guide*. New York: Checkmark, 63.

[12] U.S. Department of State. 2001, April 30. Appendix B: Background information on terrorist groups. *Office of the Coordinator for Counterterrorism, Patterns of Global Terrorism*. http://www.state.gov/s/ct/rls/crt/2000/2450.htm.

[13] Toros, H. 2008. We don't negotiate with terrorists!: Legitimacy and complexity in terrorist conflicts. *Security Dialogue* 39 (4): 422.

[14] Henderson, H. 2001. *Global terrorism: The complete reference guide*. New York: Checkmark, 57.

group in Algeria that signed a cease-fire and amnesty agreement in 1999.[15] Moreover, the National Union for the Total Independence of Angola (União Nacional para a Independência Total de Angola, UNITA), which was a terrorist group that sought to overthrow the government of Angola, agreed to a cease-fire in 2002; the government, in turn, provided members of the group with amnesty.[16] Not all accords, however, have been successful in maintaining peace. In the next sections, successful and unsuccessful peace negotiations and agreements are explored.

Good Friday Agreement

The Irish Republican Army favored a united class struggle over armed conflict. Members who disagreed with the rejection of violence to further their goals splintered from the group. One of the groups formed was the Provisional Irish Republican Army (PIRA). After many years of armed struggle, in 1994, the PIRA declared a cease-fire. However, 2 years later they bombed the Canary Wharf financial district of London, causing £85 billion worth of damage, killing 2 and injuring 39. The Good Friday Agreement was signed in Belfast on April 10, 1998. The agreement called for the immediate disarmament of the PIRA. With this agreement, Sinn Fein (the political party of the IRA) received a seat in the Northern Ireland Council. Additionally, the agreement called for the release of the prisoners from the groups observing the cease-fire. Finally, this agreement repealed the Government of Ireland Act of 1920, which had split Ireland into two Irish states: Ulster, which consisted of 6 Protestant counties in the North, and Eire, which was composed of the remaining 26 Catholic counties of the South. Furthermore, one of the most important principles enshrined in this agreement held

> that it is for the people of Ireland alone, by agreement between the two parts respectively and without external impediment, to exercise their right of self-determination on the basis of consent, freely and concurrently given, North and South, to bring about a United Ireland, accepting that this right must be achieved and exercised with and subject to the agreement and consent of a majority of the people of Northern Ireland.

Not all members of the terrorist group, however, agreed with the terms of the Good Friday Agreement. As a result, splinter groups, such as the Real Irish Republican Army and the Continuity Irish Republican Army, were formed.

On July 28, 2005, the PIRA formally declared that its armed campaign was over.[17] Subsequently, the St. Andrews Agreement was signed in 2006. This agreement "set out a clear way forward for all parties to commit to the full operation of stable power-sharing government in Northern Ireland and to full support for

---

15 Ibid., pp. 52–53.

16 Anderson, S. K., and Sloan, S. 2003. *Terrorism: Assassins to zealots*. Lanham, MD: Scarecrow, 411.

17 Sanders, A. 2011. *Inside the IRA: Dissident republicans and the war for legitimacy*. Edinburgh, Scotland: Edinburgh University Press, 233.

policing and the criminal justice institutions."[18] The success of the peace agreement with the PIRA has not been repeated with others groups, such as the ETA, which is explored below.

ETA Ceasefire and the Possibility of Peace

Other terrorist groups have also declared a cease-fire; however, some have engaged in terrorist attacks afterwards. Consider the ETA, which declared a permanent cease-fire that would take effect on March 24, 2006.[19] And yet, following this declaration, it engaged in another terrorist attack on December 30, 2006, which targeted Madrid's Barajas International Airport. In particular, the ETA detonated a van laden with explosives in the parking lot of this airport. In the blast, 2 were killed, 26 injured, and millions of Euros worth of damage was incurred. Prior to the detonation of the explosives, anonymous phone calls[20] warned law enforcement agencies of an impending attack at the airport. In response to these calls, the police evacuated the areas of the airport that the calls warned would be bombed. The two individuals who were killed in the blast (Diego Armando Estacio and Carlos Alonso Palate) had been sleeping in their vehicles.

The PIRA and the ETA have certain similarities, which lead academicians and politicians to believe that peace accords can be successfully implemented with the ETA. The PIRA and the ETA began their violent struggle around the same time, used similar tactics (e.g., targeting government, military, and law enforcement personnel), and had been subjected to governmental abuse of their human rights. As reporters of *The New York Times* noted, "[t]ime and again the Basque separatists who called their cease-fire in Spain [on March 24, 2006,] identified with the Irish Republican Army and the eerie parallel between the two groups held up over nearly four decades, all the way to what seems to be their mutual oblivion."[21] There are, however, stark differences between them. While the PIRA sought to unify Ireland, the ETA seeks to separate from Spain and create an independent Basque state within providences in Spain and France. In addition, some of the issues enshrined in the Good Friday Agreement, such as the Basques becoming part of the political process by having their own assembly and elected representatives, are already in place in the Basque region. Others, however, are not. Specifically, the Good Friday Agreement stipulated the release of PIRA prisoners. A release of ETA prisoners has not been negotiated as of this writing. Many of the ETA's high-ranking leaders are still imprisoned.

---

[18] Irish Department of Foreign Affairs and Trade. 2011. *The Good Friday agreement.* http://www.dfa.ie/home/index.aspx?id=335.

[19] Council on Foreign Relations. 2008, November 17. *Basque Fatherland and Liberty (ETA) (Spain, separatists, Euskadi Ta Askatasuna).* http://www.cfr.org/france/basque-fatherland-liberty-eta-spain-separatists-euskadi-ta-askatasuna/p9271.

[20] It is important to note that the caller claimed to represent the terrorist group.

[21] Brothers, C., and Lavery, B. 2006. ETA walking a path first trod by the IRA. *New York Times,* March 24, 2006. http://www.nytimes.com/2006/03/24/world/europe/24iht-separatists.html.

Peace can be possible only if the ETA declares permanent cease-fire. Yet, such a declaration alone will not suffice. The ETA has a history of engaging in fruitless negotiations with Spain. In particular, in 1998, the ETA had declared an "indefinite cease-fire"; however, peace negotiations broke down 14 months later.[22] In 2010, the ETA announced that it would no longer engage in terrorist attacks. Subsequently, in January 2011, the group "declared a permanent and 'internationally verifiable' cease-fire."[23] Given its history of announcing cease-fires and then subsequently engaging in terrorist attacks, the Spanish government has declared that the ETA will need to hand over their weapons to authorities to show that they are authentically seeking to end their armed struggle. The Spanish government has repeatedly stated that until they do, there will be no negotiations with the ETA.[24]

In 2011, prior members of the IRA and its splinter groups met with members of the ETA and the Kurdistan Workers' Party (PKK) at a summit to encourage both of these groups to adopt a political dialogue and end the violent conflict.[25] With regard to the PKK, peace is sought between Turkey and this group as this group's armed conflict has resulted in approximately 40,000 deaths.[26] The PKK had sought peaceful negotiations with Turkey in the 1990s, albeit unsuccessfully. Specifically, in 1999, Turkish agents kidnapped the leader of PKK, Abdullah Ocalan, which disrupted the peace process.[27] Nevertheless, in 2011, the PKK agreed to a temporary cease-fire. The impact of the summit on the PKK and the ETA remains to be seen.

Peace in the Middle East: Is it Beyond Reach?

In 1947, Britain relinquished its mandate over Palestine and requested that the UN intervene to determine the creation of two states in Palestine. That same year, UN General Assembly Resolution 181 created a partition plan for Palestine into Jewish and Arab States (the UN Partition Plan). The UN Partition Plan called for the division of the territory of Palestine (except Jerusalem) as follows: approximately 56% of the territory would encompass the Jewish state, and the remaining 44% would encompass the Arab state. Each state had a majority of its own population within its own territories. However, as the numbers clearly show, the territory designated to Israel was larger than that allocated to the Palestinians. Conflict between the two states inevitably ensued.

---

22 Rainsford, S. 2010, September 5. ETA "ceasefire" all too familiar for Spain. *BBC News.* http://www.bbc.co.uk/news/world-europe-11192114.

23 Spanish PM Zapatero Hails End to Basque ETA Violence. 2011, October 21. *BBC News.* http://www.bbc.co.uk/news/world-europe-15398799.

24 Rainsford, S. 2010, September 5. ETA "ceasefire" all too familiar for Spain. *BBC News.* http://www.bbc.co.uk/news/world-europe-11192114.

25 Bowcott, O. 2011. Irish republicans to hold peace summit with Kurdish and Basque separatists. *The Guardian,* February 10, 2011. http://www.guardian.co.uk/uk/2011/feb/10/ira-eta-kurds-peace-summit.

26 Ibid.

27 Henderson, H. 2001. *Global terrorism: The complete reference guide.* New York: Checkmark, 39.

Both Israelis and Palestinians believe that the land currently allocated to Israel is rightfully theirs according to their religion and history. From 1948 until 1993, there was unrest between the Jews of Israel and the Palestinians. In addition, water was scarce in these regions. As such, the Arab-Israeli Conflict and the Israeli-Palestinian conflict also involved their fight for water resources. The shared water basin was located both within and at the borders of countries in the Middle East. Previous arrangements for water sharing (e.g., the U.S. Johnston Plan of the 1950s and the Yarmouk River Proposal in the 1970s) had failed. Their differing beliefs and fight for resources has led to over 60 years of conflict and several wars (e.g., the Civil War of 1948 and the Six-Day War of 1967). In particular, in 1948, the Arab-Israeli war erupted between Israel and five Arab states: Egypt, Jordan, Syria, Lebanon, and Iraq. The war concluded with the Armistice Agreement in 1949, establishing the green line, which is the armistice line between Israel and the West Bank (which at the time was under the control of Jordan). In 1967, another war erupted—the Six-Day War, from June 5 to June 10—between Israel, Egypt, Jordan, and Syria. By the end of the war, Israel took control of the Gaza Strip and the Sinai Peninsula from Egypt, the West Bank and East Jerusalem from Jordan, and the Golan Heights from Syria. Several months after the war, on November 22, 1967, UN Security Council Resolution 242 was passed. Included in this resolution was the "land for peace" formula, "which called for the establishment of a just and lasting peace based on Israeli withdrawal from territories occupied in 1967 in return for the end of all states of belligerency, respect for the sovereignty of all states in the area, and the right to live in peace within secure, recognized boundaries."[28] Moreover, Article 2 of Resolution 242 called for the "withdrawal of Israel armed forces from territories occupied in the recent conflict" and the "termination of all claims or states of belligerency and respect for and acknowledgment of the sovereignty, territorial integrity and political independence of every State in the area and their right to live in peace within secure and recognized boundaries free from threats or acts of force."

On October 6, 1973, the Hebrew Day of Atonement, Egypt and Syria simultaneously engaged in a surprise attack against Israel by entering the Sinai Peninsula and Golan Heights with their military forces (Yom Kippur War). UN Security Resolution 338 of 1973 was implemented at the onset of the war. Specifically, this resolution, which was passed on October 22, 1973, held that parties fighting in the Middle East must immediately "cease all firing and terminate all military activity" and begin negotiations to establish a "just and durable peace in the Middle East." Three days after passing this resolution, on October 25, 1973, the war ended. That same month, the Organization of Arab Petroleum Exporting Countries (OAPEC) declared an oil embargo. The embargo caused the 1973 energy crisis, causing oil prices to significantly increase, and the availability of oil to decrease due to OAPEC's curtailment of production and shipment to targeted countries such as the United States and the Netherlands. During that time the prices for oil skyrocketed.

---

[28] U.S. Department of State. 2010, December 10. Background note: Israel. *Bureau of Near Eastern Affairs*. http://www.state.gov/r/pa/ei/bgn/3581.htm.

The embargo lasted for approximately six months (between October 1973 and March 1974) and ended with a negotiated settlement between Syria and Israel.

Negotiations between Israel and Egypt occurred thereafter. As a result of these negotiations, on September 17, 1978, the Camp David Accords were signed by Israel and Egypt, in which both recognized UN Security Council Resolution 242 of 1967. These agreements called for the full implementation of the resolution and the establishment of a self-governing authority in the West Bank and Gaza Strip. Pursuant to these accords, Israel was to withdraw its troops from the Sinai Peninsula and its civilian settlers. In return, Israel sought the freedom of passage in the waterways of that region and a limitation on the military forces Egypt could place in that area. These peace accords were not without consequence. Egyptian President Anwar El Sadat, who promoted negotiations between Egypt and Israel, was assassinated in 1981 by individuals opposed to the peace accords.[29]

Major peace developments occurred in the 1990s. Of particular note are the signing of the Oslo Peace Accords, which were negotiated between the Israeli government and Yasser Arafat, the leader of the Palestine Liberation Organization (PLO). More specifically, in 1993, Israel and the PLO signed a Declaration of Principles (Oslo I), which "established an ambitious set of objectives relating to a transfer of authority from Israel to an interim Palestinian authority."[30] The following year, both parties signed the Gaza-Jericho Agreement[31] and the Agreement on Preparatory Transfer of Powers and Responsibilities, which were aimed at starting the process agreed upon in the Declaration of Principles for the transferring of authority in certain designated areas from Israelis to Palestinians. In this year, a peace treaty was signed between Israel and Jordan. In 1995, the Israeli-Palestinian Interim Agreement (Oslo II) was signed. Pursuant to these peace accords, the PLO, al-Fatah and other factions of the PLO renounced terrorism. Additionally, these agreements established the framework for future Israeli–Palestinian relations and negotiations.

In April 2001, the Sharm el-Sheikh Fact-Finding Committee wrote a report, commonly known as the Mitchell Report after George Mitchell, the former Senator who led the committee, on the Israeli–Palestinian conflict in which the committee recommended a cease-fire, the end of settlement activities, desistance from terrorism, and a renewal of peace negotiations.[32] Less than two months later, in

---

29 Abdelhadi, M. 2006. Sadat's legacy of peace and conflict. *BBC News.* http://news.bbc.co.uk /2/hi/middle_east/5412590.stm; Browne, J., and Dickson, E. S. 2010. "We don't talk to terrorists": On the rhetoric and practice of secret negotiations. *Journal of Conflict Resolution* 54 (3): 397.

30 U.S. Department of State. 2010, December 10. Background note: Israel. *Bureau of Near Eastern Affairs.* http://www.state.gov/r/pa/ei/bgn/3581.htm.

31 In the Gaza-Jericho Agreement of 2004, Israel agreed to withdraw its military from Gaza and Jericho and transfer authority over the region to the Palestinian authority. See Israel Ministry of Foreign Affairs. 2011. *The Israel-Palestinian negotiations.* http://www.mfa.gov.il/MFA/Peace%20 Process/Guide%20to%20the%20 Peace%20Process/Israel-Palestinian%20 Negotiations.

32 Council on Foreign Relations. 2011, April 30. *Mitchell report on Israeli-Palestinian violence.* http://www.cfr.org/israel/mitchell-report-israeli-palestinian-violence/p13836.

June 2001, with the Palestinian–Israeli Security Implementation Work Plan (Tenet Cease-Fire Plan), the Israeli government and the Palestinian Authority reaffirmed their commitment to the security arrangements embedded in the Mitchell Report.[33] Pursuant to this plan, both parties would cooperate on "measures to enforce strict adherence to the declared cease-fire and to stabilize the security environment."[34] In 2002, UN Security Council Resolution 1397 was passed, which called for the "immediate cessation of all acts of violence, including all acts of terror, provocation, incitement and destruction." It additionally required "the Israeli and Palestinian sides and their leaders to cooperate in the implementation of the Tenet work plan and Mitchell Report recommendations with the aim of resuming negotiations on a political settlement" and peace.

In 2003, under the auspices of the Quartet, which includes the United States, EU, UN, and Russia, the Performance-Based Roadmap to a Permanent Two-State Solution to the Israeli-Palestinian Conflict (hereafter Roadmap) was created. This Roadmap includes "clear phases, timelines, target dates, and benchmarks aiming at progress through reciprocal steps by the two parties in the political, security, economic, humanitarian, and institution-building fields." The Roadmap was to be implemented in three phases. Each party was to work concurrently in completing each phase. The Quartet was responsible for evaluating the performance of the parties at each phase. That same year, another UN Security Council Resolution was passed, Resolution 1515, which endorsed the Quartet's Roadmap. It also called on the parties involved to fulfill their obligations pursuant to the Roadmap and envisions two states—Israel and Palestine—living side by side in peace. Due to the lack of progress in peace negotiations and implementation of agreements and an increase in violence in the region, a further UN Security Council resolution was passed in 2008, Resolution 1850. This resolution reiterated the need for Israelis and Palestinians to fulfill their obligations under the Roadmap. It further mandated that "all States and international organizations contribute to an atmosphere conducive to negotiations and to support the Palestinian government that is committed to the Quartet principles and the Arab Peace Initiative" and to intensify "diplomatic efforts to foster . . . mutual recognition and peaceful coexistence between all States in the region in the context of achieving a comprehensive, just and lasting peace in the Middle East." The Roadmap had envisioned the settlement of the conflict by 2005; however, as of 2012, this had yet to be achieved.

Further complicating peace matters, a Hamas leader was elected as the Prime Minister of the Palestinian Authority government in 2006. However, the results of a public opinion poll indicated that this win may not have been because the public supported the Hamas' view rejecting Israel's right to exist and the group's goal of creating an Islamic state that encompasses territories that currently make up the

33 Israel Ministry of Foreign Affairs. 2001, June 14. *Palestinian-Israeli security implementation work plan—Tenet Cease-Fire Plan.* http://www.mfa.gov.il/MFA/Peace+Process/Guide+to+the+Peace +Process/Palestinian-Israeli+Security+Implementation+Work+P.htm.
34 Ibid.

State of Israel.[35] Indeed, the poll showed that two-thirds of the Palestinians surveyed believed that the "Hamas should change its policy of rejecting Israel's right to exist."[36] In addition, the poll revealed that "Hamas' victory [was] due largely to Palestinians' desire to end corruption in government rather than support for the organization's political platform."[37] The majority of Palestinians surveyed also did not advocate for violence. Indeed, in a poll conducted by the WorldPublicOpinion. org, 72% of those surveyed were willing to move beyond violence if Israel agreed to a settlement that called for the establishment of a Palestinian state.[38] Israelis surveyed would accept these terms if Palestinians, in turn, agreed to refrain from violence for an extended period of time.[39]

Shortly after the Hamas leader was elected, the Quartet "outlined three basic principles the Hamas-led PA must meet in order for the U.S. and the international community to reengage with the PA: renounce violence and terror, recognize Israel, and respect previous agreements, including the roadmap."[40] These terms were subsequently rejected by the Hamas-led PA government. As a result, the United States suspended its assistance to the PA, prohibited government contacts with them, and prohibited unlicensed transactions with the PA.[42] Some believe that the terms were rejected because they stood in stark contrast to the terms provided to the PLO. In particular, Mullin argued that the Hamas were required "to renounce violence, recognize Israel and recognize all previous agreements made between Israel and Palestinian leaders in the past, without requiring similar concessions on the part of Israel."[41] Hamas has actively sought to participate in politics. As such, the formal inclusion of Hamas at the national level is more likely to assist the long-term goal of peace between Palestinians and Israel. As Gunning claimed, "given that democracy . . . is believed to be one of the preconditions for a lasting peace . . . the inclusion, rather than the eradication, of Hamas appears to be vital to the future success of any peace process."[42]

---

[35] Stephens, A. 2006, March 2. Most Palestinians believe Hamas should change its position on eliminating Israel. *WorldPublicOpinion.org.* http://www.worldpublicopinion.org/pipa/articles/br middleeastnafricara/173 .php?nid=&id=&pnt=173.

[36] Ibid.

[37] Ibid.

[38] WorldPublicOpinion.org. 2002, December 9. Large Israeli and Palestinian majorities indicate readiness for two-state solution based on 1967 borders. http://www.worldpublicopinion.org/pipa /articles/international_security_bt/137.php?nid=&id=&pnt=137.

[39] Ibid.

[40] U.S. Department of State. 2011, September 23. Statement by Middle East quartet on Israeli-Palestinian peace. Office of the spokesperson. http://www.state.gov/r/pa/ei/bgn/3581.htm. (Distributed by the Bureau of International Information Programs, U.S. Department of State. Web site: http://iipdigital.usembassy.gov/iipdigital-en/index.html)

[41] Mullin, C. 2010. Islamist challenges to the "liberal peace" discourse: The case of Hamas and the Israel–Palestine "peace process." *Millennium—Journal of International Studies* 39 (2): 531.

[42] Gunning, J. 2004. Peace with Hamas? The transforming potential of political participation *International Affairs* 80 (2): 254.

As of 2011, negotiations have focused on creating two states—Palestine and Israel—on the 1967 Mideast War lines, which include mutually agreed upon land swaps between both parties.[43] Specifically, a U.S. news media source reported that "the Palestinians want to establish a state in the West Bank, Gaza and East Jerusalem, territories Israel captured in the 1967 Mideast war. They have said they are willing to consider minor border adjustments through land swaps that would enable Israel to annex some of the largest of dozens of Jewish settlements it has built on occupied territory."[44] Unfortunately, the agreement to create these two independent states was not reached at the UN General Assembly in New York in 2011. Nevertheless, President Obama brought up a very important point at the assembly, in which he stated that "[p]eace will not come through statements and resolutions at the UN—if it were that easy it would have been accomplished by now. Ultimately it is Israelis and Palestinians who must live side by side. Ultimately it is Israelis and Palestinians—not us—who must reach agreement on the issues that divide them: on borders and security, on refugees and Jerusalem."[45] Unless both parties are willing to make concessions, it unlikely that negotiations will finally bring peace to the region and end the conflict that has plagued the Middle East for over 60 years.

Sri Lanka and the Tamil Tigers

The Tamil Tigers seek to create a separate state in Sri Lanka for the Tamils, which would encompass those areas mostly populated by the Tamils, namely, its northern and eastern provinces. History shows that for decades, negotiations and peace talks between the Sri Lankan government and the Tamil Tigers (LTTE) have reached an impasse. Some accords were more promising than others. Consider the peace agreements from 1987 onwards. Specfically, concessions were made to some of the Tamil Tigers demands with the signing of the Indo-Lanka Accord in 1987. Some of the Tamils concerns included "devolution of [Sri Lankan] power to the provinces, merger—subject to later referendum—of the [n]orthern and [e]astern provinces, and official status for the Tamil language."[46] Even though the Tamil Tigers had agreed to a cease-fire, they viewed the 1987 Accord as unfavorable because it did not secure the independence of the northern and eastern provinces.[47] Another important

---

[43] Obama Insists 1967 "Basis" for Israel-Palestinian Peace. 2011, May 19. *BBC News*. http://www.bbc.co.uk/news/world-us-canada-13464427.

[44] Palestinian President Slams Israeli Prime Minister's Peace Vision. 2011, May 25. *Associated Press*. http://www.foxnews.com/world/2011/05/25/palestinian-president-slams-israeli-prime-ministers-peace-vision/.

[45] McGreal, C., and Sherwood, H. 2011, September 21. Palestinians ready to put statehood on backburner in favour of peace talks. *BBC News*. http://www.guardian.co.uk/world/2011/sep/21/barack-obama-israel-palestinian-negotiations.

[46] U.S. Department of State. 2011, April 6. Background note: Sri Lanka. *Bureau of South and Central Asian Affairs*. http://www.state.gov/r/pa/ei/bgn/5249.htm.

[47] Bouffard, S., and Carment, D. 2006. The Sri Lanka peace process: A critical review. *Journal of South Asian Development* 1 (2): 162.

criticism leveled at this agreement was that it was between India and Sri Lanka; the Tamil Tigers were not consulted nor involved in the negotiations. This may, in part, explain why the Tamil Tigers continued with their armed struggle against Sri Lanka.

In 1995, however, both sides agreed to desist from hostilities as a first step toward engaging in peace negotiations. Yet, this lasted only a few months before the Tamil Tigers recommenced attacks. Nevertheless, in 2001, both Sri Lanka and the Tamil Tigers declared a cease-fire. In 2002, both parties signed a cease-fire agreement and engaged in peace negotiations. The Tamil Tigers eventually dropped out of the peace negotiations, claiming that the government was marginalizing them. Specifically, the peace was disrupted in August 2005 when the Sri Lankan Foreign Minister Lakshman Kadirgamar was assassinated.[48] The Tamil Tigers denied responsibility. Violence subsequently ensued and in January 2008, the Sri Lankan government pulled out of the 2002 cease-fire agreement.[49] However, despite both parties agreeing to renew their commitment to the cease-fire agreement 2 years later, terrorist attacks resumed. It was not until May 19, 2009, that the conflict ended, but this was not due to negotiations or peace agreements. According to the U.S. Department of State, "the government declared victory over the LTTE as they reported the capture of remaining Tiger-held territory and the death of LTTE leader Velupillai Prabhakaran."[50]

Colombian Peace Process

Many groups have desisted from terrorist activity when provided with a legitimate opportunity to engage in the political process. The Farabundo Martí National Liberation Front (FMLN), an umbrella term for left-wing, Marxist terrorist groups in El Salvador, signed a cease-fire agreement with the government in 1991. By the mid 1990s, former leaders of FMLN had transitioned into politics and the FMLN became a political party.[51] Likewise, the Guatemalan National Revolutionary Union, which was an umbrella term for left-wing, Marxist terrorist groups in Guatemala, became a political party after they signed a peace treaty with the government (the Accord for a Firm and Lasting Peace) in 1996, which ended the group's 36-year-long insurgency.[52] In addition, the Movement of the Revolutionary Left, a left-wing terrorist group in Chile, agreed to peace with the government, disengaged from armed conflict, and became a legitimate political party.[53]

---

[48] Bhattacharji, P. 2009, March 20. *Liberation Tigers of Tamil Eelam (aka Tamil Tigers) (Sri Lanka, separatists)*.http://www.cfr.org/terrorist-organizations/liberation-tigers-tamil-eelam-aka-tamil-tigers -sri-lanka-separatists/p9242.

[49] Ibid.

[50] U.S. Department of State. 2011, April 6. Background note: Sri Lanka. *Bureau of South and Central Asian Affairs*. http://www.state.gov/r/pa/ei/bgn/5249.htm.

[51] Anderson, S. K., and Sloan, S. 2003. *Terrorism: Assassins to zealots*. Lanham, MD: Scarecrow, 124–128.

[52] Ibid., pp. 148, 151.

[53] Ibid., p. 264.

In Colombia, several amnesty and peace agreements were made with domestic terrorist groups, some of which were more successful than the others. For instance, the Movement of April 19 (M-19), a Colombian terrorist group seeking to overthrow the government and end U.S. imperialism, began to function as a regular political party after signing several peace accords with the government.[54] Additionally, in 1991, the Colombian government offered amnesty to members of the Popular Liberation Army (EPL), who had agreed to a peace treaty similar to that of M-19. The EPL subsequently became involved in the political process. However, like other terrorist groups in the past (e.g., the Provisional Irish Republican Army and the Palestine Liberation Organization), dissidents of the peace process either formed splinter groups or joined other existing groups.

Given its success with the M-19 and EPL, the Colombian government decided to engage in peace negotiations with the Simón Bolívar Guerilla Coordinator, which included the Revolutionary Armed Forces of Colombia (FARC), the National Liberation Army (ELN), and dissidents of the EPL. Peace talks eventually broke down as individuals on both sides—government and terrorist groups—were intransigent on certain issues. Following the breakdown of peace negotiations, the Colombian government launched an aggressive offensive campaign against terrorist groups operating within its borders. In 1994, a change in government occurred and the newly elected president, Ernesto Samper Pizano, actively sought to restart negotiations. Unlike his predecessors and other countries dealing with domestic terrorist groups (e.g., Spain and their response to the ETA), President Samper agreed to negotiate with terrorists without having them first agree to a cease-fire. The ELN subsequently declared its willingness to negotiate with the Colombian government and publicized its demands. The FARC followed the ELN with one important difference: the FARC's demands were not made public. The negotiations with the FARC and ELN eventually collapsed.

In December 2003, the Colombian United Self-Defense Forces (AUC) engaged in negotiations with the government and accepted a peace agreement "that has led to the collective demobilization of over 31,000 members. In addition, more than 20,000 members of the FARC, AUC, ELN, and other illegal armed groups have individually surrendered their arms."[55] In July 2005, the Colombian government also offered reduced sentences to terrorists who renounced violence and returned illicit assets, which would be used for victim reparation.[56]

The negotiations between the Colombian government, the FARC, and the ELN have not been so successful. According to Hanson, "in October 2006, the FARC issued a letter that clarified the conditions under which they would agree to a bilateral cease-fire and prisoner exchange. Since then, there has been some forward movement on the exchange of imprisoned FARC members for hostages,

---

54 Henderson, H. 2001. *Global terrorism: The complete reference guide.* New York: Checkmark, 61.

55 U.S. Department of State. 2011. July 13. Background note: Colombia. http://www.state.gov/r/pa/ei/bgn/35754.htm.

56 Ibid.

Box 13-1 Food for Thought—Repairing the Harm of Terrorism: A Case for Restorative Justice?

Restorative justice is a "process whereby all the parties with a stake in a particular offense come together to resolve collectively how to deal with the aftermath of the offense and its implications for the future."[1] Basically, it attempts "to make good the harm done and in so doing to shift attention from the culpability of the offender to the harms suffered."[2] The restorative justice process is aimed at restoring the victim, offender, and community to their precrime status. Here, victims (or families of deceased victims) are afforded the opportunity to reconcile with the offender and to negotiate reparation. Also, the community is provided with a role in terms of mediating the reconciliation. In addition, the offender is allowed to make amends to the victim and the community, and in so doing, righting the "wrong" that he or she had committed. Research findings reveal that the most decisive elements for victims to engage in a restorative justice process were the need for information, the need to tell their story, and the need to gain some sense of closure.[3]

Restorative justice, thus, moves away from state punishment and attempts to restore the harms done to the victims (and, by way of extension, the community) by the offender through various practices and techniques. For example, one of these practices is victim–offender meetings, in which the offender is encouraged to express remorse, to accept responsibility, and to apologize; in addition, the victim may inform the offender about how the crime impacted them and so on. Existing research reveals that victim satisfaction "with victim–offender mediation is consistently high for both victims and offenders across sites, cultures, and seriousness of offenses."[4] If victims do not want to engage in a direct face-to-face meeting with the offender, then indirect victim–offender mediation is possible. In these types of mediations, the victim and offender can communicate to each other through an intermediary.

Scholars have sought to determine whether restorative justice could be used for terrorism. Siemens conducted research on nine victims (two actual victims and

---

[1] Marshall, T. 1996. The evolution of restorative justice in Britain. *European Journal on Criminal Policy and Research* 4 (4): 37.

[2] Zedner, L. 2004. *Criminal justice.* Oxford, UK: Oxford University Press, 101.

[3] Zehr, H. 1990. *Changing lenses.* Waterloo, ONT: Herald Press, 26; Zehr, H. 2002. *The little book of restorative justice.* Intercourse, PA: Good Books, 14; Weitekamp, E. G. M., Parmentier, S., Vanspauwen, K., Valiñas, M., and Gerits, R. 2006. How to deal with mass victimization and gross human rights violations. A restorative justice approach. In *Large-scale victimization as a potential source of terrorist activities,* eds. U. Ewald and K. Turkovi , 230. Amsterdam: IOS; and Staiger, I. 2010. Restorative justice and victims of terrorism. In *Assisting victims of terrorism: Towards a European standard of justice,* eds. R. Letschert, A. Pemberton, and I. Staiger, 270. Dordrecht, The Netherlands: Springer.

[4] Umbreit, M. S., Coates, R. B., and Vos, B. 2004. Victim–offender mediation: Three decades of practice and research. *Conflict Resolution Quarterly* 22 (1/2): 287.

(continues)

Box 13-1 Food for Thought—Repairing the Harm of Terrorism: A Case for Restorative Justice? (continued)

seven family members of victims) of the Red Army Faction.[5] Some of the victims who were interviewed expressed the need to engage in a dialogue with the terrorists and to have their suffering acknowledged by the terrorist.[6] Other than studies, there have been individual cases of attempts at reconciliation between terrorists and the surviving families of their victims. A case in point is the reconciliation between Jo Berry and Patrick Magee. On October 11, 1984, Patrick Magee detonated a bomb in the Grand Hotel in Brighton, where the Conservative Party conference was held. British Prime Minister Margaret Thatcher was at the hotel at the time of the blast and although she was not harmed, the explosion killed 5 people, including Conservative British Member of Parliament, Sir Anthony Berry. Magee was released pursuant to the Good Friday Agreement in 1998. Jo Berry, Sir Anthony Berry's daughter, actively sought to come to terms with her loss and decided to engage in dialogue with Magee to obtain closure and move on with her life. Both parties have claimed that the process has been healing and helped them recover their humanity.[7]

Existing initiatives in Northern Ireland (LIVE-Programme) and Israel and Palestine (Parents Circle-Families Forum) further reveal that "reconciliation between communities is possible, even when the conflict is still ongoing or just resolved."[8] The LIVE-Programme (Let's Involve the Victims' Experience-Programme) was created by the Glencree Centre, which was established in 1974 in the Irish Republic. This program facilitates dialogue between victims and former combatants.[9] The Parents Circle-Families Forum (PC-FF) was also created in 1994 to facilitate and support dialogue and reconciliation. The founders, Yitzhak Frankenthal and Roni Hirshenzon, both lost sons in the Palestinian–Israeli conflict. PC-FF has offices in Tel Aviv and the West Bank and "is made up of more than 600 families, half Israeli and half Palestinian, who have all lost immediate family members in the conflict."[10]

1. Is restorative justice appropriate for all forms of terrorism? Explain.
2. Do you think a country's counterterrorism arsenal should include restorative justice? Why or why not?
3. If a country decides to integrate restorative justice in their counterterrorism strategy, are there any political, legal, or social barriers to its implementation?

---

[5] Siemens, A. 2007. *Für die RAF war er das system, für mich der vater: Die andere geschichte des Deutschen terrorismus.* München: Piper Verlag.

[6] Ibid.; Staiger, I. 2010. Restorative justice and victims of terrorism. In *Assisting victims of terrorism: Towards a European standard of justice*, eds. R. Letschert, A. Pemberton, and I. Staiger, 297. Dordrecht, The Netherlands: Springer.

[7] Ibid., p. 316.

[8] Ibid., p. 308.

[9] Ibid., p. 324.

[10] U.S. Department of State. 2011, October 26. Special envoy Hannah Rosenthal honors the work of Parents Circle Families Forum to fight hate. *Office of the Spokesperson, Washington, DC.* http://www.state.gov/r/pa/prs/ps/2011/10/176216.htm.

but no negotiations on a cease-fire or demobilization."[57] In 2009, the peace negotiations between the Colombian government and FARC stalled.[58] Hanson further noted that "the Colombian government has been engaged in a peace process with the ELN since May 2004, but as of October 2007, eight rounds of talks had yet to produce any results. The two parties disagree on the terms of a cease-fire, whether the ELN should end kidnappings, and the ELN's use of anti-personnel mines."[59] The ending of kidnappings has been on the government's agenda since the 1990s and has served as a point of contention between the government and terrorist groups. In an effort to prevent individuals from paying ransom—and in so doing, reducing the rewards terrorists obtain from kidnapping individuals—Colombia enacted Law 40 in 1993, which made it a crime for anyone to pay ransom for the return of an individual who has been kidnapped.[60] This part of the law, however, was later rendered unconstitutional by Colombia's highest court.

Why did only some terrorist groups in Colombia effectively negotiate and disarm? Negotiations and disarmament decisions are based on cost-benefit analysis. If the cost of resistance (e.g., the continuation of terrorist attacks) are set high and the costs of participation in negotiations (e.g., being offered amnesty, reduced sentences, a position in the political process, etc.) are set low, terrorists will favor participation. As Shugart argued, the government's "promise of a voice in restructuring the country's basic institutions gave [M-19 members] a stake in participating."[61] This holds true only if the primary objectives of the group is participation in the political process and a voice in civic affairs. Indeed, while political reforms were used to convince M-19 and EPL to accept a peace accord and disengage from future terrorist attacks, they have not been sufficient for the FARC and ELN. The failed attempts of the Colombian government to get them to accept peace agreements based on political reforms attests to this.

In reality, for these terrorists groups, illicit activities have become a way of life. Indeed, the FARC engages in drug trafficking, kidnappings, and extortion of legal and illegal businesses to fund its operations. The FARC also offers "protection" to cocaine laboratories and clandestine airstrips for a payment (money or trade of illicit items). The ELN similarly engages in drug trafficking to fund its operations, although according to the congressional testimony of the U.S. Drug Enforcement Agency, the ELN controls Colombia's opium poppy and cannabis growing areas.[62]

---

57 Hanson, S. 2009, August 19. FARC, ELN: Colombia's left-wing guerrillas. *Council on Foreign Relations*. http://www.cfr.org/colombia/farc-eln-colombias-left-wing-guerrillas/p9272.

58 U.S. Department of State. 2011. July 13. Background note: Colombia. http://www.state.gov/r/pa/ei/bgn/35754.htm.

59 Hanson, S. 2009, August 19. FARC, ELN: Colombia's left-wing guerrillas. *Council on Foreign Relations*. http://www.cfr.org/colombia/farc-eln-colombias-left-wing-guerrillas/p9272.

60 Blum, G., and Heymann, P. B. 2010. *Laws, outlaws, and terrorists*. Cambridge, MA: MIT Press, 150.

61 Shugart, M. S. 1992. Guerrillas and elections: An institutionalist perspective on the costs of conflict and competition. *International Studies Quarterly* 36:136.

62 U.S. Drug Enforcement Agency. 2002, April 24. Drugs, money and terror. *Congressional Testimony*. http://www.justice.gov/dea/pubs/cngrtest/ct042402.html.

The ELN is "less dependent than the FARC on coca and cocaine profits to fund its operations."[63] These groups' dependence on these operations serve as an impediment to the Colombian government's efforts to engage in successful peace negotiations with these terrorists. According to Boudon, "drug trafficking, in particular, may prove to be too powerful a motivating factor to keep at least some guerrillas at odds with the government. The peace process, if successful, may strip away the ideological veneer from the rebels, revealing the criminals for what they are;"[64] that is, more interested in maintaining their lucrative lifestyle through drug trafficking proceeds than promoting the interests of the public. Exposing this may cause terrorist organizations to lose popular support. The fate of Omega-7, a Cuban terrorist group that sought to overthrow Fidel Castro, attests to this. As Anderson and Sloan noted, "the increasingly criminal character of the group alienated members of the Cuban community and created internal dissension with Omega-7."[65]

PEACE AGREEMENTS IN THE POST-9/11 WORLD OF TERRORISM

Many scholars, practitioners, and government officials believe that negotiations and peace agreements with al-Qaeda members, affiliates, and those inspired by al-Qaeda's cause (e.g., homegrown terrorists) are unattainable. For instance, in 2003, President George W. Bush declared: "You've got to be strong, not weak. The only way to deal with these people is to bring them to justice. You can't talk to them. You can't negotiate with them."[66] The 9/11 Commission report also noted that individuals who are fully committed to Osama bin Laden's version of Islam "are impervious to persuasion."[67] Some believe that negotiations with these terrorists should never be pursued. As Neumann argued, "opening negotiations would be a counterproductive move: it would provide al-Qaeda with political legitimacy while undermining both moderates across the Muslim world and the negotiating governments themselves."[68]

Others argue that negotiations with al-Qaeda are impossible due to the structure (or lack thereof) of the organization. Al-Qaeda was forced to decentralize after 9/11. With its nontraditional structure and loosely affiliated (if at all) network of cells and like-minded individuals, with whom does a government negotiate? Who will speak for these terrorists? In addition, the current threat of terrorism is by

---

[63] U.S. Department of State. 2002, March 13. Terrorist groups increasingly linked to drugs, officials say. *Washington File: Experts Testimony Before US Senate Subcommittee.* http://www.au.af.mil/au/awc/ awcgate/state/epf304.htm.

[64] Boudon, L. 1996. Guerrillas and the state: The role of the state in the Colombian peace process. *Journal of Latin American Studies* 28 (2): 297.

[65] Anderson, S. K., and Sloan, S. 2003. *Terrorism: Assassins to zealots.* Lanham, MD: Scarecrow, 299.

[66] Toros, H. 2008. We don't negotiate with terrorists!: Legitimacy and complexity in terrorist conflicts. *Security Dialogue* 39 (4): 407.

[67] See Kean, T. H., and Hamilton, L. H. 2004. *The 9/11 Commission report: Final report of the National Commission on Terrorist Attacks upon the United States.* New York: W.W. Norton, 37.

[68] Neumann, P. R. 2007, January/February. Negotiating with terrorists. *Foreign Affairs* 86 (1): 136.

Box 13-2   Security Brief: Terrorist Groups Engaging in Organized Crime Activities

Terrorists have been involved in different types of organized crime activities, the most prominent of which are money laundering and drug trafficking. With respect to the latter, many terrorist groups have sold drugs to finance their operations. The U.S. Department of State lists Hezbollah and the Shining Path (Peruvian terrorists) among the groups believed to engage in drug trafficking to fund their operations.[1] Particularly, the Shining Path has been known to benefit from the taxation of drug cultivation in the region over which they have control.[2] Another group engaged in drug trafficking is the Taliban, who manufacture and sell heroin to fund their activities. Indeed, Afghan heroin has been a substantial financial resource for not only the Taliban but also al-Qaeda and its affiliates.[3]

Terrorists are also working with organized crime groups. In 2008, a member of the FARC, Raul Reyes, met with an associate of Semyon Yukovich Mogilevich, a member of Ukrainian organized crime, in Bucharest, Romania, to purchase uranium.[4] Moreover, Baz Mohammad, an Afghan drug lord linked to the Taliban, was extradited to the United States in 2005. According to his indictment,"between 1994 and 2000, the Baz Mohammad Organization collected heroin proceeds in the United States for the Taliban in Afghanistan. In exchange for its financial support, the Taliban provided the Baz Mohammad Organization protection for its opium crops, heroin laboratories, drug-transportation routes, and members and associates.[5]

The indictment further noted that Baz Mohammad had stated that "selling heroin in the United States was a 'Jihad' because they were taking the Americans' money at the same time the heroin they were paying for was killing them."[6] In addition, the FARC has also enlisted al-Qaeda groups in West Africa for assistance and protection in trafficking cocaine through the region to Europe.[7] Moreover, the Islamic Movement of Uzbekistan (IMU) is believed to have profited by the drug trade in Afghanistan

---

[1] U.S. Department of State. 2002, March 13. Terrorist groups increasingly linked to drugs, officials say. *Washington File: Experts Testimony Before US Senate Subcommittee.* http://www.au.af.mil/au/awc/awcgate/state/epf304.htm.

[2] Hutchinson, A. 2002, April 2. Narco-terror: The international connection between drugs and terrorism. *US Drug Enforcement Agency.* http://www.justice.gov/dea/speeches/s040202.html.

[3] Ehrenfeld, R. 2011, May 3. Drug trafficking, kidnapping fund Al-Qaeda. *CNN.* http://articles.cnn.com/2011-05-03/opinion/ehrenfeld.al.qaeda.funding_1_islamic-maghreb-drug-trafficking-al-qaeda-centr a l?_s=PM:OPINION.

[4] BBC Worldwide Monitoring. 2008. Terrorists, arms dealers use Romania as meeting point. *BBC,* March 18, 2008. Original report by Galca, B. 2008. *Ziua* (Romanian Newspaper), March 11, 2008. http://m.ziuanews.ro/.

[5] U.S. Drug Enforcement Agency. 2005, October 24. *US Extradites Taliban-linked narco-terrorist.* http://www.justice.gov/dea/pubs/pressrel/pr102405.html.

[6] Ibid.

[7] Nagraj, N. 2010. Columbian FARC rebels, Al-Qaeda joining forces to smuggle cocaine into Europe. *Daily News,* January 5, 2010. http://articles.nydailynews.com/2010-01-05/news/17943446_1_al-qaeda-smuggle-colombian-farc-rebels.

(continues)

> **Box 13-2　Security Brief: Terrorist Groups Engaging in Organized Crime Activities** (continued)
>
> and the drug trafficking through its territories to Europe and Russia.[8] Furthermore, information obtained by the U.S. Drug Enforcement Agency reveals that the PKK provides protection to drug traffickers (for a fee) and taxes drug shipments in the region within which they operate.[9]
>
> Leaders of terrorist organizations have been tried for crimes usually associated with organized crime figures. Shoko Asahara, the leader and founder of Aum Skinrikyo, was tried for several crimes, including drug trafficking.[10] Likewise, on November 9, 2011, the leader of AUC, Carlos Mario Jimenez-Naranjo, was sentenced to 33 years in prison by a U.S. District Court for drug trafficking.[11]
>
> ---
>
> [8] U.S. Department of State. 2002, March 13. Terrorist groups increasingly linked to drugs, officials say. *Washington File: Experts Testimony Before US Senate Subcommittee*. http://www.au.af.mil/au/awc/awcgate/state/epf304.htm.
>
> [9] Hutchinson, A. (2002, March 13). Statement of Administrator of Drug Enforcement Agency before the Senate Judiciary Committee, Subcommittee on Technology, Terrorism, and Government Information. *Drug Enforcement Administration*. http://www.justice.gov/dea/pubs/cngrtest/ct031302.html.
>
> [10] Green, S. 2002. Combating the cult next door: Japan. *The Age*, October 12, 2002. http://www.theage.com.au/articles/2002/10/11/1034222593525.html.
>
> [11] U.S. Department of Justice. 2011, November 9. *Colombian paramilitary leader sentenced in Miami to 33 years in prison for drug trafficking and narco-terrorism.* http://www.justice.gov/opa/pr/2011/November/11-crm-1475.html.

stateless enemies without any territory or population to defend. These individuals often pursue nonnegotiable objectives. As such, no peace talks are conceivable. Al-Qaeda and followers have made this clear in public statements through the media. In fact, in 2004, Osama bin Laden had stated, "take note of the ground rule regarding this fight. There can be no dialogue with occupiers except through arms."[69] However, it should be noted that both bin Laden and Ayman al-Zawahiri had offered cease-fires to the United States and Europe. The problem was that there was no guarantee that the members of the group and their followers would honor the cease-fire.

Despite this, proponents argue that negotiations can be fruitful for some terrorists. More specifically, individuals such as David Petraeus, the current Director of the Central Intelligence Agency, had, in the past, advocated for negotiating "with less extreme Taliban members."[70] Moreover, scholars such as Toros have stated that even negotiation with al-Qaeda is possible. Particularly, Toros noted

---

[69] Toros, H. 2008. We don't negotiate with terrorists!: Legitimacy and complexity in terrorist conflicts. *Security Dialogue* 39 (4): 418.

[70] Blum, G., and Heymann, P. B. 2010. *Laws, outlaws, and terrorists*. Cambridge, MA: MIT Press, 158.

that "[a]l-Qaeda's layered structure may offer multiple points of entry for negotiations . . . allowing for the possibility that separate peaces be made, reducing the network's global reach."[71]

Currently, no official policy is in place for negotiations with terrorists nor has the issue of peace agreements with al-Qaeda been addressed. The efficacy of such a process remains to be seen. Peace negotiations have been successful in the past. However, such processes have involved groups with an easily identifiable structure. Nonetheless, it may indeed be possible to make peace with factions and members loosely tied to the organization. This recommendation should not be dismissed outright. It may prove beneficial in creating divisions among followers and cause dissension and distrust among individuals subscribing to al-Qaeda's ideology. Such a measure may assist governments in quashing terrorists' ideology by providing certain followers the opportunity of having their opinions heard through means other than violence.

HYPOTHETICAL SCENARIO

The United States has decided to negotiate with al-Qaeda. You have been tasked with developing a plan for implementing this policy.

1. With whom should the United States negotiate? Why?
2. With whom should the United States avoid negotiation? Why do you think so?
3. How would this plan be implemented?
4. Are there any obstacles to its implementation? If so, what are they?

CHAPTER SUMMARY

Negotiations can be successfully achieved through consultation and mediation. In the past, international, regional, and state actors have successfully used negotiations to promote and maintain peace. Negotiations should be used to end conflict, settle territorial disputes, end terrorism, and restore peace. Dangers can arise when governments do not negotiate, or improperly negotiate, with terrorists. There are also arguments against negotiating with terrorists. Negotiations can set a dangerous precedent as they can legitimize terrorists' methods, undermine government's political systems, and undercut efforts to prohibit terrorism.

Peace agreements between terrorist groups and states have been signed and enforced. Indeed, many groups have desisted from terrorist activity when provided with a legitimate opportunity to engage in the political process. This provides terrorists with a viable nonviolent alternative to have their opinions and voices heard. Several terrorist groups have continued their armed struggle even after a peace

---

[71] Toros, H. 2008. We don't negotiate with terrorists!: Legitimacy and complexity in terrorist conflicts. *Security Dialogue* 39 (4): 422.

agreement. As history shows, factions have developed within groups, and splinter groups have formed among dissidents of the peace process. Several peace accords have failed outright. The reasons for their failures have varied according to country and group. Concessions need to be made by both parties to the accord to ensure that the provisions of the agreement are willingly enforced.

REVIEW QUESTIONS

1. What are the benefits of negotiating with terrorists?
2. What are the negative consequences of negotiating with terrorists?
3. What might happen if governments refuse to negotiate with terrorists?
4. Which peace agreements between terrorists and governments have been successful? Why were they successful?
5. Which peace agreements between terrorists and governments have failed? Why did they fail?
6. For those agreements that failed, what could governments have done differently?
7. Could the U.S. government negotiate with al-Qaeda? Should it?

chapter *fourteen*

Thinking Outside the Box: In Search of the "Mitos" for Terrorists

On August 18, 2011, terrorists engaged in coordinated attacks on vehicles (a military vehicle, two private vehicles, and two buses) that lasted less than an hour near Israel's border with Egypt. The attack began with active shooters firing automatic weapons. Other weapons used were improvised explosive devices, mortar shells, and anti-tank missiles. Attacks on motor vehicles in Israel are not a new tactic, although usually such attacks are perpetrated by suicide bombers and not active shooters. Beyond Israel, counterterrorism discourse seems to focus extensively on bombings. What if active shooters are involved in the next terrorist attack in the United States?

Active shooters are a constant threat to the security of transportation areas, workplaces, public venues, government facilities, and schools. The shootings that have occurred in these areas in the past attest to this. Some examples include the following: In 1979, Brenda Ann Spencer (16 years old) used a scoped rifle her father gave her for Christmas to shoot employees and students at Cleveland Elementary School, killing 2 and injuring 9.[1] In 1984, James Oliver Huberty (41 years old) used an automatic weapon to kill 21 and injure 20 at a McDonalds in

---

[1] Ortmeier, P. J. 2009. *Introduction to security: Operations and management*. Upper Saddle River, NJ: Pearson, 262.

California.[2] In 1993, Colin Ferguson (35 years old) opened fire on passengers of the Long Island Rail Road, killing 6 and injuring 19.[3] In 2009, Dimitris Patmanidis (18 years old) shot and killed 3 people (1 student and 2 passers-by) at a vocational training college in Athens, Greece, before killing himself by a single, fatal shot to the head.[4] In 2011, Jared Lee Loughner (22 years old) opened fire on a crowd attending an open meeting by U.S. Representative Gabrielle Giffords and her constituents at the parking lot of a Casas Adobes Safeway supermarket near Tucson, Arizona, killing 6 and injuring 14. Among those critically injured was Rep. Giffords herself.[5]

Several recent thwarted and materialized terrorist attacks on U.S. soil have involved active shooters. One such example involved Rezwan Ferdaus, a U.S. citizen and homegrown terrorist, who was arrested in Framingham, Massachusetts, on September 28, 2011, for plotting to attack the Pentagon and the U.S. Capitol Building. He had first planned to use radio-controlled model airplanes filled with explosives to bomb the targets. After attacking the facilities, he had planned to use rifles and grenades to kill people as they evacuated the buildings. Another example involves the November 5, 2009, attack at Fort Hood, Texas, by Nidal Malik Hassan, a U.S. Army officer stationed there. During the attack, Hassan shot and killed 13 and left 30 wounded. And 2 years later, another Fort Hood attack was thwarted: Naser Jason Abdo, a 21-year-old U.S. Army soldier who had gone AWOL (i.e., absent without leave) from his duty station (Fort Campbell, Kentucky), was arrested in Killeen, Texas, on July 27, 2011. He was suspected of planning to attack military personnel by disguising himself as a soldier stationed at Fort Hood to gain unauthorized access to the base, its facilities, and personnel. When authorities searched his hotel room, they found a uniform with Fort Hood patches, jihadist literature, firearms, ammunition, and several items that could be used to make explosives. What is the appeal of Fort Hood? It is one of the largest U.S. bases and prepared armed forces personnel for deployment to Afghanistan and Iraq. Should more attacks be expected at Fort Hood? What can counterterrorism officials and researchers learn from these attacks?

History can provide insight into appropriate counterterrorism measures. Looking at past practices and potential measures for the future, this chapter

---

2 Granberry, M. 1989. A 77-minute moment in history that will never be forgotten. *LA Times*, July 16, 1989. http://articles.latimes.com/1989-07-16/local/me-5818_1_san-ysidro-boulevard.

3 Barron, J. 1993. Death on the L.I.R.R: The overview; Portrait of suspect emerges in shooting on L.I. train. *New York Times*, December 9, 1993. http://www.nytimes.com/1993/12/09/nyregion/death-lirr-overview-portrait-suspect-emerges-shooting-li-train.html?ref=colinferguson.

4 Gatopoulos, D., and Paphitis, N. 2010, April 10. Gunman shoots up Greek school, injuring 3 and killing himself. *Huffington Post*. http://www.huffingtonpost.com/2009/04/10/gunman-shoots-up-greek-sc_n_185537.html.

5 Lacey, M., and Herszenhorn, D. M. 2011. In attacks' wake, political repercussions. *New York Times*, January 8, 2011. http://www.nytimes.com/2011/01/09/us/politics/09giffords.html?pagewanted=all.

Box 14-1   Food for Thought—Hospitality Security: A Forgotten Item in the U.S. Counterterrorism Arsenal?

On November 26, 2008, a group of 10 terrorists hijacked a ship off the coast of Mumbai, India, killed 3 crew members, and ordered the captain to guide them into Mumbai. Once near the shore, they killed the captain. After landing, the terrorists attacked targets popular with tourists, including the Taj Mahal Palace and Tower Hotel, the Oberoi Hotel, the Chhatrapati Shivaji train station, and the Nariman House, an ultra-Orthodox Jewish center. When the attacks were over, approximately 170 people had been killed. The terrorists were members of the Pakistani-based Lashkar-e-Taiba, a group affiliated with al-Qaeda.

Fast forward to June 28, 2011, when a popular hotel among foreigners and government officials in Kabul, Afghanistan, the Intercontinental Hotel, was attacked by 9 Taliban militants. Ten civilians were killed along with the terrorists (some died from suicide attacks, others from security forces). These attacks illustrate the current vulnerability in hospitality security. The latter hotel was one of the most heavily secured locations in Kabul, and yet still terrorists were able to attack.

1. Are hotels in the United States high-risk targets for terrorism? If so, what is being done for hospitality security in the United States?

---

searches for the "mitos"[6] in counterterrorism policies worldwide; that is, a measure (or measures) that can efficiently and effectively aid authorities in finding their "Minotaurs"; namely, terrorists. To do so, it first covers alternative measures with which to detect and combat terrorists—for example, speech profiling, behavioral profiling, and new technologies in the field. It then introduces new terrorist threats and the measures needed to combat them. Finally, this chapter seeks to incorporate measures that were successfully used in the past into a counterterrorism strategy that can be used to combat terrorists and terrorist groups worldwide.

ANTICIPATING THE NEXT MOVE

In 2010, two female suicide bombers engaged in attacks against Russia's subway stations (Lubyanka and Park Kultury) in Moscow. These attacks, along with others preceding it, illustrate the worldwide need to secure transportation systems from terrorist attacks. Prior to this incident, several attacks had occurred on commuter trains and subway systems. For instance, the Madrid and London bombings in 2004 and 2005, respectively, both targeted transportation systems. In 2008, a

---

[6] In Greek mythology, no person, except Theseus, ever made it out of the Minotaur's labyrinth alive. Theseus succeeded in doing so with the help of a "mitos" (a golden spool of thread), which was given to him by Ariadne. He tied the thread to the entrance of the Labyrinth and used the spool to make his way through it. Using this mitos, he was able to find the Minotaur, kill it, and make his way back to the entrance of the Labyrinth.

homegrown terrorist, Bryant Neil Vinas, an American citizen of Peruvian and Argentinean descent with prior U.S. military service, was charged in connection with plans to attack the United States. Vinas informed U.S. law enforcement officials that he had provided al-Qaeda with information about the New York transit system and that al-Qaeda planned to blow up a Long Island Rail Road commuter train in New York's Penn Station. In 2009, terrorists plotted to simultaneously blow up Manhattan subway trains on lines 1, 2, 3, and 6, days after the 9/11 anniversary. One of these terrorists, Najibullah Zazi, was arrested for his role in this plot and is currently awaiting sentencing in the United States. These attacks and plots illustrate that transportation systems are a desirable target for terrorists. Accordingly, these targets need to be hardened by precisely the types of measures that can forestall an attack.

To be effective, counterterrorists must keep abreast of emerging trends in terrorism and terrorist attacks. International organizations and public and private national partnerships are tasked with providing risk assessments and level of preparedness of specific areas in the event that certain types of attacks should occur. One such example is NYPD Shield, a public–private partnership with the goal of protecting New York City from terrorist attacks. NYPD Shield provides terrorism assessments that not only include analyses of international and domestic terrorism or other security-related incidents, but also consider how these events may affect the security of New York City.

Additionally, an effective counterterrorism strategy must have measures designed to successfully anticipate the terrorist or terrorist group's next move. The catastrophic harm that may result if a terrorist attack materializes is potentially too great for governments to respond to only after it has occurred. It is thus imperative that measures are in place that can foresee future acts of terrorism. As such, in the following sections, particular emphasis will be placed on introducing and evaluating measures that are designed to anticipate terrorists' intentions and actions (e.g., targets and tactics) such as profiling and certain new technologies in the field.

Profiling

Profiling involves the process of extrapolating information about an individual based on traits. Profiling is a highly contested practice, although the challenges brought to this practice depend on the type of profiling that occurs. One of the most challenged profiling practices is racial profiling, which occurs when individuals are targeted for law enforcement, transportation agency, and/or government action based on race, ethnicity, national origin, or religion. Such a practice is extremely discriminatory. Moreover, such a practice is counterproductive in counterterrorism, especially with respect to homegrown terrorists. As shown elsewhere in the text, there is no single, identifiable profile that can be used for homegrown terrorists.

There are many different types of profiling, some of which are better known than others. Criminal profiling is the process by which the traits of individuals responsible for committing criminal acts are inferred.[7] It does not assist in identifying a specific suspect. Instead, it provides "a general psychological description of the most likely type of suspect, including personality and behavioral characteristics suggested by a thorough analysis of the crimes committed."[8] This form of profiling relies on a group of characteristics that are believed to be associated with specific types of crimes. An example of this is the drug courier profile, which consists of a list of identifying characteristics and behaviors that law enforcement agents associate with drug couriers.[9] However, there is no single, universally recognized drug courier profile. In *United States v. Van Lewis*,[10] the drug courier profile that the U.S. Drug Enforcement Agency (DEA) used included the following characteristics: "(1) the use of small denominations of currency for ticket purchases; (2) travel to and from major drug import centers, especially for short periods of time; and (3) the absence of luggage or use of empty suitcases on trips that normally require extra clothing; and (4) travel under an alias." The profile, however, includes more characteristics. In *United States v. Sokolow*,[11] DEA agents used a profile that not only included the previously mentioned characteristics but also the nervousness of the individual and the fact that he had not checked in any luggage to justify stopping him at the airport. Specifically, the following justification was provided by DEA agents for stopping the individual:

> (1) he paid $2,100.00 for two airplane tickets from a roll of $20 bills; (2) he traveled under a name that did not match the name under which his telephone number was listed; (3) his original destination was Miami, a source city for illicit drugs; (4) he stayed in Miami for only 48 hours, even though a round-trip flight from Honolulu to Miami takes 20 hours; (5) he appeared nervous during his trip; and (6) he checked none of his luggage.[12]

The drug courier profile has been used as a means for establishing reasonable suspicion that someone is engaging in drug trafficking. Nevertheless, the reliability of this profile has been heavily debated in U.S. courts. Some courts, such as those in *United States v. Mendenhall*[13] and *Reid v. Georgia*,[14] "found the use of drug

---

[7] Turvey, B. E. 2008. *Criminal profiling*, 3rd ed. New York: Elsevier, 2.

[8] Greene, E., and Heilbrun, K. 2011. *Wrightsman's psychology and the legal system*. Victoria, Australia: Wadsworth: Cengage Learning, 142.

[9] Cloud, M. 1985. Search and seizure by the numbers: The drug courier profile and judicial review of investigative formulas. *Boston University Law Review* 65:847.

[10] 409 F. Supp. 535, 538 (E.D. Mich. 1976).

[11] 490 U.S. 1 (1989).

[12] 490 U.S. 1, 2 (1989). Kadish, M. J. 1997. The drug courier profile: In planes, trains, and automobiles; And now in the jury box. *The American University Law Review* 46:757–758.

[13] 446 U.S. 544 (1980).

[14] 448 U.S. 438 (1980)

courier profiles unreliable in determining reasonable suspicion."[15] In fact in *Reid*, the court noted that the DEA drug courier "profile could also be used to describe presumably innocent travelers."[16] Other forms of profiling, including speech and behavioral profiling, will be explored in further detail below.

Speech Profiling

The investigations of realized (e.g., 9/11 attacks) and attempted attacks have revealed that the threat of terrorism in the United States is posed by terrorists who have uncertain capabilities and intentions. Research is thus required to fill this knowledge gap and assist government, law enforcement, and intelligence agencies in making known the capabilities and intentions of terrorists. Speech profiling seeks to do just that by utilizing the validated and reliable methods used by political psychologists over many decades to measure the personality of political leaders at a distance (through their speeches and interviews) to understand their behavior. Personality can be measured by analyzing an individual's spoken and written words, as these can reveal the psychological state of the individual. Several studies have conducted such measurements, although none have focused on terrorists. Specifically, studies have assessed the personalities of novelists,[17] heads of state,[18] American presidents,[19] EU commissioners, and UN Secretary Generals.[20] This body of research has shown that personality traits are good predictors of behavior.

This research can be translated into the context of terrorism. In fact, research that is being conducted by Charles and Maras focuses on speech profiling of terrorists.[21] In particular, their research seeks to predict the behavior of al-Qaeda's leadership based on their personality traits through an assessment of their written and spoken words (speeches and fatwas). Understanding the behavior of these high-value terrorists by measuring their personalities—as anchored in the situations they face on the run—and observing the patterns of their behavior using verifiable information from multiple sources, can assist U.S. government agencies

---

[15] Cogan, M. R. 1992. The Drug Enforcement Agency's use of drug courier profiles: One size fits all. *The Catholic University Law Review* 41:955.

[16] Ibid.

[17] McCurdy, H. G. 1947. A study of the novels of Charlotte and Emily Bronte as an expression of their personalities. *Journal of Personality* 16 (2): 109–152.

[18] Hermann, M. G. 1980. Explaining foreign policy behavior using the personal characteristics of political leaders. *International Studies Quarterly* 24 (1): 7–46.

[19] Donley, R. E., & Winter, D. G. 1970. Measuring the motives of public officials at a distance: An exploratory study of American presidents. *Behavioral Science* 15 (3): 227–236.

[20] Kille, K. J., & Scully, R. M. 2003. Executive heads and the role of intergovernmental organizations: Expansionists leadership in the United Nations and the European Union. *Political Psychology* 24 (1):175–198.

[21] Charles, C. A. D., and Maras, M-H. (forthcoming). *Measuring the personalities of al-Qaeda leadership at a distance: Personality, terrorist behavior and counterterrorism.*

in understanding terrorists' objectives and methods of operation and their inclination to attack. Similarly, understanding the personality–situation interaction of al-Qaeda's leadership can provide useful insights into their motivations as well as their behavior toward unanticipated setbacks. Understanding the behavior of these terrorists also allows for the modeling of counterterrorism strategies in response to this behavior. The personality assessment of selected terrorists and their likely behavior on the run can be placed in agent decision-making models to determine their behaviors based on their preferences. The resultant terrorist profiles can then be used to develop counterterrorism measures for terrorists on the run. Specifically, the likely behavior of each terrorist can be placed into a game theory model to determine how each terrorist, individually or in a group, strives to maximize gains by choosing particular courses of action. This study, therefore, seeks to predict terrorist behavior and make possible the incorporation of its results into actionable policies with which to combat terrorism. This research can be applied to all forms of terrorism. As such, Charles and Maras are planning to conduct their research on other forms of terrorism as well.

Behavioral Profiling

In August 2009, Abdullah Asiri attempted to kill the head of Saudi Arabia's counterterrorism operations, Prince Mohammed Bin Nayef, by detonating explosives that had been hidden in Asiri's rectum. In December 2009, Umar Farouk Abdulmutallab managed to pass through airport security in Nigeria and Amsterdam with explosives in his underpants and board a U.S. passenger jet, Northwest Flight 253. This event triggered the proliferation of "Whole Body Imaging" devices, which, using x-ray technology, provide security personnel with a detailed image of a person's body revealing any weapons, contraband, or explosives that he or she might have hidden in their clothes or on their person, and their use in the airports of the United States. To ensure that such technology respects passengers' privacy rights, it cannot store, retain, copy, print, or retrieve images, nor can the screened image be linked to the person being screened. In addition, the person who analyzes the scanned image must be in a separate location from the person being screened.

Currently, the only security measure at U.S. airports that can prevent an Asiri-type terrorist from boarding an airplane are the Whole Body Imaging devices. However, these devices are not used at all U.S. airports; and where they are, passengers can either choose to opt out of the screening (the alternative is a rigorous pat down that would not be able to detect the explosives hidden inside the body) or simply take a flight out of an airport that does not use these devices. The United States has thus spent millions of dollars on an airport security measure that is easily evaded by terrorists. Are these devices at least designed to deal with another Abdulmutallab? The answer to this question is no. The airport security of the United States did not fail in the case of Abdulmutallab. Even if all U.S. airports had this technology (which currently they do not), a similar attempted Abdulmutallab-type attack could not be prevented. Why? The proliferation of this technology distracts security officials from one important truth: U.S. airport security did not fail in Abdulmutallab's case, international security did. Accordingly, no matter what the United States does to enhance airport security, it would not prevent another Abdulmutallab from boarding a plane bound for the United States with explosives in his underwear. The use of this technology tries to prevent Abdulmutallab -type terrorists only from leaving or traveling within the United States, not entering it.

Furthermore, on November 14, 2011, the European Union prohibited the use of x-ray body scanners at European airports. The European Commissioner who is responsible for transport noted that:[22]

> Security scanners are not a panacea but they do offer a real possibility to reinforce passenger security. Security scanners are a valuable alternative to existing screening methods and are very efficient in detecting both metallic and non-metallic objects. It is still for each Member State or airport to decide whether or not to deploy security scanners, but these new rules ensure that where this new technology is used it will be covered by EU wide standards on detection capability as well as strict safeguards to protect health and fundamental rights.

Why were they banned? The x-ray body scanners use ionizing radiation, which, according to an investigation by ProPublica/PBS NewsHour, have significant health concerns for individuals.[23] Specifically, ionizing radiation was shown to damage DNA and cause cancer. Even though the amount of radiation that passengers are exposed to is extremely minute, several studies indicated that a small number of cases of cancer may result from the millions of passengers scanned each year.[24] Now, the only types of body scanners that can be used at EU airports, other transportation systems, and border checkpoints are those that do not use x-ray technology. There exists another type of body scanner, one that uses radio frequency technology, which can be used and has not been shown to have significant health implications. In particular, airports will use "millimeter-wave scanners that utilize low-energy radio waves,"[25] Currently, the United Kingdom has trial x-ray technology deployed at its airports. Pursuant to this new EU rule, the United Kingdom will remove the x-ray technology body scanners from the airports when the trial is completed.

The U.S. Transportation Security Administration (TSA) has lauded the ability of x-ray body scanners to effectively detect weapons and contraband. To support this claim, the TSA has provided statistics showing "that since January 2010, more

---

[22] EUROPA. 2011, November 14. *Aviation security: Commission adopts new rules on the use of security scanners at European airports.* http://europa.eu/rapid/pressReleasesAction.do?reference =IP/11/1343&format=HTML&aged=0&language=EN&guiLanguage=en.

[23] Grabell, M. 2011, November 15. Europe bans x-ray body scanners used at U.S. airports. *ProPublica.* http://www.propublica.org/article/europe-bans-x-ray-body-scanners-used-at-u.s.-airports.

[24] Ibid.

[25] DiSalvo, D. 2011. Europe bans airport body scanners for "health and safety" concerns. *Forbes Magazine*, November 15, 2011. http://www.forbes.com/sites/daviddisalvo/2011/11/15/europe-bans -airport-body-scanners-over-health-and-safety-concerns/.

than 300 dangerous or illegal items have been found on passengers as a direct result of using x-ray body scanners."[26] Test trials using this technology at airports in certain Member States in the European Union did not render similar results. In fact, before the European Union passed legislation banning the use of x-ray technology in security scanners for use at airports, Germany decided to not deploy them. Instead of citing health concerns, they noted that these devices produced too many false alarms.[27] Italy followed suit by removing this technology on the grounds of its inaccuracy.[28]

It is important to note that something that has actually kept individuals safer at airports are vigilant passengers and flight crew members. In 2002, an airline attendant noticed a passenger (later identified as Richard Reid) trying to light explosives in his shoe. In December 2009, a passenger's quick-thinking response prevented Umar Farouk Abdulmutallab from lighting the explosives that were hidden in his underpants. These events demonstrate that airport security technology did not identify these terrorists—ordinary people did. What does this mean for airport security? Is there a way for airport security measures to address suspicious behavior? An answer to this last question can be found by looking at the security practices of the Ben Gurion Airport in Tel Aviv, Israel (one of the safest airports in the world). Even though Israel has been the focal point of violence in the Middle East and is under constant threat of a terrorist attack, the Ben Gurion Airport has not experienced a serious terrorist incident for over 30 years. Instead of subjecting each passenger to extensive security screening (as the U.S. does), the security focus at the Ben Gurion Airport is on using unseen techniques with which to screen their passengers. Key to this security is the use of behavioral profilers at the airport. Only those deemed to be high-risk passengers (i.e., suspicious individuals) by the profilers are subjected to intensive security screening.

Airport security measures based on behavioral profiling have also been implemented in the United States. The TSA already uses behavior detection screeners at airports to spot terrorists and other dangerous travelers through subtle clues in the way these individuals act. Specifically, the TSA's program Screening Passengers by Observation Technique (SPOT), in place since 2003, employs federal agents who are trained to closely observe travelers' faces in order to determine if they might pose a security risk. Behavioral profiling programs rely on the Facial Action Coding System (FACS) developed by Paul Ekman and Wallace Friesen. FACS is a "comprehensive, anatomically based system for measuring all visually discernible facial

---

26 Ibid.

27 NewsCore. 2011. Body scanners scrapped from German airports after error-filled trial. *Herald Sun*, September 1, 2011. http://www.heraldsun.com.au/travel/news/body-scanners-scrapped-from -german-airports-after-error-filled-trial/story-fn32891l-1226126966777.

28 EPIC. 2011, September 2. *Whole body imaging technology and body scanners ("Backscatter" x-ray and millimeter wave screening)*. https://epic.org/privacy/airtravel/backscatter/.

movement,"[29] standardizing "a method of deciphering facial behavior for cues of deception."[30] This program is used at airports and mass transit systems.

As part of the SPOT program, over 3,000 Behavior Detection Officers (BDOs) have been deployed throughout airports in the United States.[31] Pursuant to this program, BDOs "observe airport passengers for certain physical and physiological characteristics and reactions."[32] They determine whether an individual should be subjected to more intrusive questioning, pat downs, and/or baggage inspections based on an assigned numerical score tallied from a set of criteria that contain 30 possible suspicious behaviors (each with their own numerical scores).[33]

In the United States, BDOs are recruited from routine TSA security screeners, which requires only a "high school degree, GED, or its equivalent, and a criminal background check."[34] In addition, SPOT program training of BDOs consists of 4 days of classroom instruction on behavioral observation, behavioral analysis, and questioning techniques.[35] Personnel are subsequently required to undergo 24 hours of on-the-job training at airport security checkpoints. By contrast, behavioral profilers in Israel undergo significantly more training (a 9-week qualification course) and those selected for the program are highly trained Secret Service–type operatives.[36]

Behavioral profiling is a much more complex task for the United States. Israel's airport security operations are considerably smaller than that of the United States, which requires significantly more rigorous training to deal with the task at hand. Currently, however, this is not occurring. Indeed, the Government Accountability

---

[29] Rosenberg, E. L. 2005. The study of spontaneous facial expressions in psychology. In *What the face reveals: Basic and applied studies of spontaneous expression using the facial action coding system (FACS)*, eds. P. Ekman and E. L. Rosenberg. New York: Oxford University Press.

[30] Herbert, L. 2007. Othello error: Facial profiling, privacy, and the suppression of dissent. *Ohio State Journal of Criminal Law* 5:82.

[31] Pawlowski, A. 2011, August 2. Boston airport expands behavior detection program. *CNN.* http://articles.cnn.com/2011-08-02/travel/logan.airport.behavior.detection_1_behavior-detection -greg-soule-isa ac-yeffet?_s=PM:TRAVEL.

[32] Frank, T. 2005. Suspects' body language can blow their cover. *USA Today*, December 28, 2005, p. 3A; Florence, J., and Friedman, R. 2010. Profiles in terror: A legal framework for the behavioral profiling paradigm. *George Mason Law Review* 17:426.

[33] Karp, J., and Meckler, L. 2006. Which travelers have "hostile intent"? Biometric device may have the answer. *Wall Street Journal*, August 14, 2006, p. B1; see also Herbert, L. 2007. Othello error: Facial profiling, privacy, and the suppression of dissent. *Ohio State Journal of Criminal Law* 5:82; Ekman, P. 2006. How to spot a terrorist on the fly. *Washington Post*, October 29, 2006, p. B03; Florence, J., and Friedman, R. 2010. Profiles in terror: A legal framework for the behavioral profiling paradigm. *George Mason Law Review* 17:427.

[34] Harcourt, B. E. 2006, August 20. *Behavioral profiling at U.S. airports*, 3. http://www.law. uchicago.edu/files/files/Harcourt%20OpEd%20Behavioral%20Profiling%20Longer%20 Version.pdf; Florence, J., and Friedman, R. 2010. Profiles in terror: A legal framework for the behavioral profiling paradigm. *George Mason Law Review* 17:428.

[35] Florence and Friedman, ibid., pp. 428–429.

[36] Harcourt, B. E. 2006, August 20. *Behavioral profiling at U.S. airports*, 3. http://www.law.uchicago .edu/files/files/Harcourt%20OpEd%20Behavioral%20Profiling%20Longer%20Version.pdf.

Office, in its report on airport security, found the training of BDOs to be deficient. Among its many recommendations were:[37] providing BDOs with more real-world videos for training; providing recurrent behavioral observation and analysis training through online videos; having BDOs spend more time training on the job; and including more role playing and scenarios in the classroom training (this will help them practice their conversation skills).

New Technology in the Field

Technology has become an integral facet of security. Counterterrorists are increasingly using new technologies that seek to identify terrorists before they institute attacks. The following sections will focus on two of these technologies, namely, brain fingerprinting and Future Attribute Screening Technology.

Brain Fingerprinting

The brain fingerprinting system is designed to mathematically analyze brain waves and make a determination as to whether or not information is present or absent in the brain.[38] According to Dr. Lawrence Farwell, "the human brain emits a characteristic electrical brainwave response, known as a P300, and a MERMER (memory and encoding related multifaceted electroencephalographic response), whenever the subject responds to a known stimulus."[39] Measured brainwave responses that contain a MERMER indicate that the information is present. Brain fingerprinting, therefore, tests for specific information about a terrorist attack or crime. It does not include locations, people, or events that individuals would know for other than nefarious reasons. It is specifically designed to focus on aspects of a plot or executed attacks that only those involved in such acts would know.

Put simply, brain fingerprinting is designed to test whether certain information is present or absent in the individual's mind. To determine this, a computer shows the person images and words and the person is made to listen to sounds. After the presentation of the data, the electrical brain responses of an individual are measured in a noninvasive manner (a headpiece with sensors). How can this technology avoid implicating an innocent individual? The answer is simple: the technology is designed to "read" activity in the part of an individual's brain that stores information. If that area is active when the person is shown information that only the suspected terrorist would know, then this indicates that he or she was involved in the plot, attack, or is (was) engaged in other terrorism-related activity.

---

[37] Government Accountability Office. 2010, May. Aviation security: Efforts to validate TSA's passenger screening behavior detection program underway, but opportunities exist to strengthen validation and address operational challenges. *Report to the Ranking Member, Committee on Transportation and Infrastructure, House of Representatives.* http://www.gao.gov/new.items/d10763.pdf.

[38] Brain Fingerprinting Laboratories. n.d. *Brain fingerprinting testing helps bring serial killer to justice.* http://www.brainwavescience.com/GrinderSummary.php.

[39] Brain Fingerprinting Laboratories. n.d. *Brain fingerprinting testing ruled admissible in court.* http://www.brainwavescience.com/Ruled%20Admissable.php.

The validity and reliability of brain fingerprinting in the United States has been established. In *Harrington v. State of Iowa*,[40] the judge ruled that evidence derived from brain fingerprinting was admissible in court. Specifically, standards have been developed to determine the validity and reliability of technology and thus its admissibility in a court of law. The most notable of these standards are the *Frye standard, Coppolino standard* and *Daubert standard*. In *Frye v. United States*,[41] the defendant tried to submit evidence of expert testimony on the systolic blood pressure deception test, which was an early version of the polygraph test. Frye wanted to show his innocence by introducing evidence that he passed the test. To do so, Frye wanted to admit expert testimony to explain the test and the significance of the result. The court rejected his request on the grounds that the systolic blood pressure deception test had not received general acceptance in the scientific community. This standard, however, does not leave much room for admitting novel but valid tests that have not yet received general acceptance within the scientific community.

Some courts rejected the Frye standard and instead used the Federal Rules of Evidence to determine the admissibility of evidence and admit novel but relevant evidence in court.[42] The Coppolino standard did not follow a similar path as the Frye standard. In fact, the Coppolino standard rejected the "general acceptance" test that was prominent in the Frye standard. Instead, in *Coppolino v. State of Florida*,[43] the court held that a novel test may be admitted if its validity could be proven, even if the general scientific community was unfamiliar with it. Similar to the Coppolino standard, the Daubert standard also allows novel tests to be admitted in court, albeit with different criteria. According to *Daubert v. Merrell Dow Pharmaceuticals Inc.*,[44] the four criteria that are used to determine the reliability of a particular scientific theory or technique are:[45]

1. Testing (i.e., has the method in question undergone empirical testing?)
2. Peer review (i.e., has the method been peer reviewed?)
3. The potential rate of error (i.e., error rate in the results produced by the method)
4. Acceptability (i.e., has the method received general acceptance in the relevant scientific community?)

---

[40] 659 N.W.2d 509 (Iowa 2003).

[41] 293 F. 1013 (1923).

[42] E.g. *United States v. Downing*, 753 F.2d 1224 (1985).

[43] 223 So. 2d 68 (Fla. Dist. Ct. App. 1968).

[44] 509 U.S. 579 (1993).

[45] *Daubert v. Merrell Dow Pharmaceuticals Inc.*, 509 U.S. 579, 593-595 (1993); see also *Kumho Tire Company, Ltd. v. Carmichael*, 526 U.S. 137, 145 (1999).

The Daubert standard requires an independent judicial assessment of the reliability[46] of the scientific test or evidence. In the *Harrington* case, the judge held that brain fingerprinting met all four criteria and thus was valid scientific evidence. Specifically, the judge stated that brain fingerprinting testing is based on the "P300 effect," which "has been studied by psycho-physiologists . . . The P300 effect has been recognized for nearly twenty years. [It] has been subject[ed] to testing and peer review in the scientific community. The consensus in the community of psycho-physiologists is that [it] is valid."[47]

Furthermore, evidence derived from brain fingerprinting has helped law enforcement officers close cases. Most notably, in the case of serial killer James B. Grinder, the results of brain fingerprinting testing were instrumental in attaining a confession and guilty plea. Grinder was shown details of the crime scene that were not released to the public. The only person or persons who could know these details were the officers who investigated the crime scene and the suspect or suspects. Grinder's brain wave responses to these images "contained a MERMER, indicating 'information present' which means that the details of this crime were stored in his brain."[48] Technology similar to brain fingerprinting has been deployed at border and transportation system checkpoints.[49]

Future Attribute Screening Technology

U.S. government officials, TSA agents, and security professionals have entertained the idea of implementing WeCU Technologies (get it?) at the airport. These technologies, developed by an Israeli company and implemented at the Ben Gurion Airport in Tel Aviv, claim to be able to detect passengers' suspicious behavior by measuring heart rate and body temperature to detect elevations that might occur when a person sees a trigger picture. Individuals provide emotional and physiological responses to certain images if they are familiar with them. Biometrics sensors designed to measure the reaction of the traveler are hidden. The responses of an individual are evaluated by a computer program. Some critics claim that these technologies are reminiscent of George Orwell's "thought police" in his novel *1984*.

Other technology that claims to be able to detect suspicious traveler behavior is MALINTENT. It "uses a series of sensors and imagers that measure body temperature, heart rate, and respiration for unconscious signs of bad intentions that escape

---

46 Reliability concerns when a measure "yields consistent scores or observations of a given phenomena on different occasions." See Bachman R., and Schutt, R. K. 2003. *The practice of research in criminology and criminal justice*, 2nd ed. London: Sage/Pine Forge, 72.

47 Brain Fingerprinting Laboratories. n.d. *Brain fingerprinting testing ruled admissible in court.* http://www.brainwavescience.com/Ruled%20Admissable.php.

48 Brain Fingerprinting Laboratories. n.d. *Brain fingerprinting testing helps bring serial killer to justice.* http://www.brainwavescience.com/GrinderSummary.php.

49 Rosenblatt, D. 2008, December 2. Behavioral screening—The future of airport security? *CNN.* http://articles.cnn.com/2008-12-02/tech/airport.security_1_airport-security-cutting-edge-security-security-screening?_s=PM:TECH.

the naked eye."[50] MALINTENT, which is still in its testing phase, "searches your body for non-verbal cues that predict whether you mean harm to your fellow passengers" and is designed to read "body signals terrorists and criminals may display in advance of an attack."[51] This technology is part of what the Department of Homeland Security has called Future Attribute Screening Technology (FAST), which seeks to read nonverbal cues of suspicious behavior by deploying "a range of 'innovative physiological and behavioral technologies' to pick up 'indications of malintent or the intent or desire to cause harm.'"[52] Specifically, this project seeks the use of sensors and cameras designed to read heart rates, breathing, body temperature, eye movement, and the fidgeting of an individual.[53] FAST purports "to use objective, scientific criteria to identify dangerous people by analyzing their facial movements, voices, blood pressure, sweat levels, heart and breathing rates, and even brain waves."[54] The Department of Homeland Security envisions using this technology at airports, border checkpoints, and special events that require security screening.[55]

NEW THREATS

There are certain threats discussed by academicians, politicians, policymakers, and practitioners, that have not yet come to fruition. One notable exception is chemical and bioterrorism attacks by governments and certain terrorist groups (e.g., Aum Shinrikyo). The next section explores two of these threats: cyberterrorism and weapons of mass destruction (WMD) terrorism.

Cyberterrorism

Cyberterrorism may be defined "as the politically motivated use of computers as weapons or as targets, by sub-national groups or clandestine agents intent on violence, to influence an audience or cause a government to change its policies."[56] A cyberterrorist may hack into U.S. critical infrastructure in order to cause grave harm such as loss of life or significant economic damage. Such attacks are aimed

---

[50] Barrie, A. 2008, September 23. Homeland security detects terrorist threats by reading your mind. *FOXNews*. http://www.foxnews.com/printerfriendlystory/0,3566,426485,00.html.

[51] Ibid.

[52] Elsworth, C. 2008. New airport screening "could read minds." *Telegraph*, September 23, 2008. http://www.telegraph.co.uk/news/worldnews/northamerica/usa/3069960/New-airport-screening -could-read-minds.html.

[53] Benson, P. 2009, October 7. Will airports screen for body signals? Researchers hope so. *CNN*. http://edition.cnn.com/2009/TECH/10/06/security.screening/index.html.

[54] Florence, J., and Friedman, R. 2010. Profiles in terror: A legal framework for the behavioral profiling paradigm. *George Mason Law Review* 17:424.

[55] Elsworth, C. 2008. New airport screening "could read minds." *Telegraph*, September 23, 2008. http://www.telegraph.co.uk/news/worldnews/northamerica/usa/3069960/New-airport-screening -could-read-minds.html.

[56] Wilson, C. 2003, October 17. Computer attack and cyber terrorism: Vulnerabilities and policy issues for congress. *US Congressional Research Report*, 4. http://www.fas.org/irp/crs/RL32114.pdf.

at wreaking havoc on information technology systems that are an integral part of public safety, traffic control, medical and emergency services, and public works. While this type of attack has not yet materialized in real life, the world of film has depicted it (for example, *Live Free or Die Hard*) and academicians, practitioners, researchers, law enforcement agencies, and politicians have entertained the possibility of it occurring. Additionally, computer security experts have created mock cyberterrorism attacks to expose America's weaknesses in its critical infrastructure during a war game titled "Digital Pearl Harbor," hosted by the U.S. Naval War College in 2002.[57] These attacks illustrated that the most vulnerable systems were the Internet and the computer infrastructure systems of financial institutions.

In the United States, certain aspects of cyberterrorism are dealt with in Title VIII of the USA Patriot Act of 2001. The most relevant section of the Patriot Act to this crime is Section 814, which deals with the deterrence and prevention of cyberterrorism. It prohibits and provides penalties for cyberterrorism offenses. For instance, an individual violates this section if he or she causes physical injury, loss of life, or in any way threatens public health or safety as a result of damaging or gaining unauthorized access to a protected computer. It also covers damage to a computer system that the government uses in the administration of justice, national defense, or national security.

Terrorist groups have been known to target government websites, flooding them with attacks that take days and (sometimes weeks) for the sites to become operational again. The Internet Black Tigers (who are affiliated with the Tamil Tigers) have engaged in such attacks against foreign government websites.[58] These attacks, however, cannot be classified as cyberterrorism. Cyberterrorists seek to attack the critical infrastructure systems (such as water, energy, communications, etc.) to intimidate or coerce a government for ideological, religious, or political reasons. Cyberterrorists may seek unauthorized access to critical infrastructure computer systems to:[59]

- Disrupt air traffic control, public surface transport (e.g., trains), and/or emergency systems;
- Shut down electric utilities and/or damage gas utilities;
- Contaminate water, food, or medicine supplies;
- Block communications systems.

---

57 Wilson, C. 2008, January 29. Botnets, cybercrime, and cyberterrorism: Vulnerabilities and policy issues for congress. *US Congressional Research Report*, 20. http://www.fas.org/sgp/crs/terror/RL32114.pdf.

58 Dick, R. L. 2001, April 5. Issue of intrusions into government computer networks. *Testimony of the Director of the FBI National Infrastructure Protection Center before the House Energy and Commerce Committee, Oversight and Investigation Subcommittee.* http://www.fbi.gov/congress/congress01/rondick.htm.

59 Collin, B. C. (n.d.) The future of cyberterrorism: Where the physical and virtual worlds converge. *11th annual International Symposium on Criminal Justice Issues.* http://afgen.com/terrorism1.html.

According to a report by the Working Group on Unlawful Conduct on the Internet,[60]

> the Department of Justice has encountered several instances where intruders have attempted to damage critical systems used in furtherance of the administration of justice, national defense, or national security, as well as systems (whether publicly or privately owned) that are used in the provision of "critical infrastructure" services such as telecommunications, transportation, or various financial services.

An example of this occurred in 1997, when a teenager from Worcester, Massachusetts, hacked into the public telephone switching network, disabling telephone service for a number of residents, the fire department, and the airport control tower in the area.[61] U.S. air traffic control systems have been targeted many times since 1997. One of these incidents occurred in 2009, when individuals hacked into the air traffic control mission-support systems of the Federal Aviation Administration (FAA) and stole the personal information (e.g., names and social security numbers) of current and former FAA employees.[62] Authorities believe that such threats can soon spread, through network connections, from the support systems to operational systems that process real-time flight information and communications.[63] The consequences of terrorists disabling operational air traffic control systems could be devastating. However, such attacks are only possible with interconnected systems; today, most critical systems are separated from administrative networks and/or the Internet.

Critical infrastructures have also been targeted overseas. There is only one known case in which an individual has used a computer system to cause significant environmental harm. In 2000, Vitek Boden hacked into the computer system of an Australian sewage treatment plant and leaked hundreds of thousands of gallons of sewage into rivers and parks near the facility.[64] That same year, an individual hacked into a Russian computer system and gained control of natural gas flow.[65] Hypothetically, this hacker could have easily increased the gas pressure until the

---

[60] This agency was established by Executive Order 13133 (August 6, 1999) in order to evaluate the extent of cybercrime and the tools and capabilities of law enforcement to deal with this threat. See Working Group on Unlawful Conduct on the Internet. 2000, March. *The electronic frontier: The challenge of unlawful conduct involving the Internet.* http://www.justice.gov/criminal/cybercrime/unlawful.htm.

[61] Elmusharaf, M. M. 2004, April 8. Cyber terrorism: The new kind of terrorism. *Computer Crime Research Center.* http://www.crime-research.org/articles/cyber_terrorism_new_kind_terrorism/.

[62] Whitney, L. 2010, March 31. IBM, FAA partner on aviation cybersecurity. *CNET News.* http://news.cnet.com/security/?keyword=FAA.

[63] Mills, E. 2009, May 7. Report: Hackers broke into FAA air traffic control systems. *CNET News.* http://news.cnet.com/8301-1009_3-10236028-83.html.

[64] Schneier, B. 2003, June 19. The risks of cyberterrorism. *Computer Crime Research Center.* http://www.crime-research.org/news/2003/06/Mess1901.html.

[65] Elmusharaf, M. M. 2004, April 8. Cyber terrorism: The new kind of terrorism. *Computer Crime Research Center.* http://www.crime-research.org/articles/cyber_terrorism_new_kind_terrorism/.

valves broke, causing an explosion. This did not occur in this case. Yet, this case illustrates the ease with which access to critical infrastructure systems can be gained and what could be accomplished. Moreover, in 2007, researchers at "Idaho National Laboratories identified a vulnerability in the electric grid, demonstrating how much damage a cyber attack could inflict on a large diesel generator."[66]

SCADA (Supervisory Control and Data Acquisition) systems are the computer systems of most of the critical infrastructure industries in the United States. According to a Congressional report, SCADA systems "are often placed in remote locations, are frequently unmanned, and are accessed only periodically by engineers or technical staff via telecommunications links."[67] This report further stated that in order to increase the efficiency of SCADA systems, they have been connected to administrative networks and/or the Internet.[68] This, however, has made the systems susceptible to an attack from cyberspace. In 1998, a teenage boy hacked into the SCADA computer systems that controlled the Roosevelt Dam in Arizona. Authorities stated that the hacker had gained complete control of the dam; however this claim has been contested. It was estimated that he could have flooded two towns with a total population of one million people if he had opened the floodgates.[69]

Credible intelligence exists which reveals that al-Qaeda has a significant interest, capability, and intent to engage in cyberterrorism. Computers seized from al-Qaeda operatives in Afghanistan contained information on U.S. computer systems controlling critical infrastructure.[70] Al-Qaeda and its allies have also expressed interest in learning about the U.S. water supply. Specifically, a seized computer of an al-Qaeda affiliate had numerous items concerning the structural engineering of dams and other water-retaining structures in the United States.[71] Recently, a water utility system was targeted in the United States. In particular, a cyberattack was launched on the control systems of an Illinois water system in November 2011, which burned out a water pump. This attack was discovered when workers at the water plant observed a malfunction in the SCADA systems. Upon reviewing thelogs, it was revealed that someone had hacked into the system. According to the

---

[66] Finkle, J. 2011, November 18. US investigates cyber attack on Illinois water system. *MSNBC News.* http://www.msnbc.msn.com/id/45359594/ns/technology_and_science-security/t/us-investigates-cyber-attack-illinois-water-system/.

[67] Wilson, C. 2008, January 29. Botnets, cybercrime, and cyberterrorism: Vulnerabilities and policy issues for congress. *US Congressional Research Report*, 21. http://www.fas.org/sgp/crs/terror/RL32114.pdf.

[68] Ibid., pp. 21–22.

[69] Gellman, B. 2002. Cyber-attacks by Al Qaeda feared: Terrorists at threshold of using Internet as tool of bloodshed, experts say. *Washington Post*, June 27, 2002. http://www.washingtonpost.com/wp-dyn/content/article/2006/06/12/AR2006061200711.html.

[70] Elmusharaf, M. M. 2004, April 8. Cyber terrorism: The new kind of terrorism. *Computer Crime Research Center*. http://www.crime-research.org/articles/cyber_terrorism_new_kind_terrorism/.

[71] Public Safety Canada. 2002, January 30. Terrorist interest in water supply and SCADA systems. *Information Note Number: IN02-002.* https://www.publicsafety.gc.ca/abt/index-eng.aspx.

Illinois Statewide Terrorism and Intelligence Center, those involved in the cyberattack may have stolen information that would allow them to gain access to other water control systems in the United States.[72] The Department of Homeland Security and the Federal Bureau of Investigation later stated that there was no evidence of any malicious activity in the water system.[73]

Furthermore, there have been instances of malware being introduced into industrial control systems with the intent of damaging and obtaining information from them. Stuxnet, a computer worm, "is believed to be the first known malware that targets the control systems at industrial facilities such as power plants. At the time of its discovery, the assumption was that espionage lay behind the effort, but subsequent analysis by Symantec uncovered the ability of the malware to control plant operations outright."[74] According to reporters of *The New York Times*, Stuxnet "also secretly recorded what normal operations at the nuclear plant looked like, then played those readings back to plant operators, like a pre-recorded security tape in a bank heist, so that it would appear that everything was operating normally while the centrifuges were actually tearing themselves apart."[75] In 2011, Symantec reported that a new form of malicious software—Duqu—was discovered by CrySyS (a lab at the Budapest University of Technology and Economics). This form of malware seeks to surreptitiously gather information from industrial systems (e.g., water treatment facilities and power plants). It is a Trojan Horse that enables remote access of the infected system. Attacks involving Duqu have been launched through means as innocuous as merely opening Microsoft Word attachments. Experts say that the Duqu computer virus is based on Stuxnet. One important difference between them is that Stuxnet was designed to cripple industrial control systems, whereas Duqu was designed to gather data. Even though these forms of malware target critical infrastructure and industrial control systems, they cannot be classified as a form of cyberterrorism. Regardless, from the analysis above, it is clear that measures need to be implemented to better secure critical infrastructure systems both within and outside of the United States to prevent cyberterrorist attacks from occurring in the future.

WMD Terrorism

Weapons of mass destruction (WMD) is a term used to denote nuclear, radiological, chemical, and biological weapons. WMD terrorism refers to the use of one

---

[72] Vijayan, J. 2011, November 25. DHS sees no evidence of cyberattack on Ill. water facility. *ComputerWorld.* http://www.computerworld.com.sg/tech/security/dhs-sees-no-evidence-of-cyberattack -on-ill-water-facility/.

[73] Goodin, D. 2011. FBI: No evidence of water system hack. *The Register*, November 23, 2011. http://www.theregister.co.uk/2011/11/23/water_utility_hack_update/.

[74] Mills, E. 2010, October 5. Stuxnet: Fact vs. theory. *CNET.* http://news.cnet.com/8301-27080 _3-20018530-245.html.

[75] Broad, W. J., Markoff, J., and Sanger, D. E. 2011. Israeli test on worm called crucial in Iran nuclear delay. *New York Times*, January 15, 2011. http://www.nytimes.com/2011/01/16/world /middleeast/16stuxnet.html?pagewanted=all.

or more of these weapons to inflict mass casualties for ideological, political, and/or religious reasons. Terrorists seek to engage in this form of terrorism because of the public panic that would ensue, economic losses that would be incurred in the target society, and the magnitude of the devastation caused in terms of deaths, injuries, and property damage. Other chapters in this volume have revealed that intelligence reports indicate that terrorist groups like al-Qaeda have sought to engage in attacks with weapons of mass destruction.

Nuclear terrorism involves the use of nuclear materials or attacking nuclear facilities with the intention of causing significant harm to persons and property. While nuclear facilities have been targeted, thus far, these instances have not occurred with the intention of seriously harming individuals and/or property. In addition, of all of the forms of WMD terrorism, nuclear terrorism is the least likely to occur, particularly because nuclear weapons are extremely difficult to acquire. Moreover, the elements needed to create a nuclear weapon (e.g., plutonium and highly enriched uranium) are very expensive and hard to obtain.

Radiological terrorism involves the spreading of radioactive material in a terrorist attack. This material acts as a toxic chemical, seeking to contaminate individuals and the environment. A well-known example of radiological terrorism is when an individual uses an explosive device with radiological material (a "dirty" bomb). Intelligence shows that the Taliban and al-Qaeda have sought to obtain radioactive material to create a radiological weapon.[76] Also, Jose Padilla, a U.S. citizen and prior detainee of Guantanamo Bay, had plotted to engage in a dirty bomb attack against the United States. A further example involved Dhiren Barot, an al-Qaeda operative who in 2006 was convicted in Britain of planning to detonate a dirty bomb and launch an attack on London's subway system.[77] Nevertheless, to date, no successful radiological terrorist attack has occurred. However, several terrorists (including those previously mentioned) have been arrested and tried for attempting to use a dirty bomb in an attack.

In contrast to nuclear and radiological terrorism, bioterrorism and chemical terrorism attacks have been executed in the past. The biological and chemical weapons used in these attacks can be distributed as gases, liquids, or aerosols. The first use of these types of weapons in the United States was in 1984 with the attack by the Bhagwan Shree Rajneesh cult in the Dalles, Oregon, in which 751 individuals were poisoned with salmonella at restaurants in order to influence a local election.[78] A further example involved a British white supremacist right-wing

---

[76] Director of Central Intelligence. 2002, February 6. *Testimony before the senate select committee on intelligence*, as cited in Bowman, S. 2002, March 7. Weapons of mass destruction: The terrorist threat. *CRS Report for Congress*, 3. http://fpc.state.gov/documents/organization/9184.pdf.

[77] Muslim Convert Who Plotted Terror. 2006. *BBC News*, November 7, 2006. http://news.bbc.co.uk/2/hi/uk_news/6121084.stm.

[78] Chalk, P. 2004. Hitting America' soft underbelly: The potential threat of deliberate biological attacks against U.S. agricultural and food industry. *RAND National Defense Research Institute*, 29. http://www.rand.org/pubs/monographs/MG135.html; Monke, J. 2004, August 13. Agroterrorism: Threat and preparedness. *CRS Report for Congress*, 5. http://www.fas.org/irp/crs/RL32521.pdf.

terrorist, who, in 2010, pled guilty to the production and preparation of a ricin toxin for use in a bioterrorism attack.[79]

Information on the science and technology required to build biological weapons is readily available. Particularly, there has been certain information published in scientific journals that could be used for nefarious purposes. One recent example involves research that uses the genetic code sequence of the H1N1 virus to generate a virus identical to the Spanish flu virus of 1918, which caused the worst pandemic in the 20th century, resulting in millions of deaths. The findings were published in the journal *Science*. However, a review by the National Science Advisory Board for Biosecurity (NSABB) concluded that the benefits of the future use of such information (e.g., the development of new vaccines and therapies to protect against a pandemic of this nature) in the academic community outweighs the risks involved in its publication.[80] Terrorists could use this research to reconstruct extinct virulent pathogens for use in biological weapons. Such published research can also aid in the development of novel, virulent pathogens (for which no vaccine exists) and the engineering of pathogens to avoid detection and delay diagnosis; this could cause significantly more deaths in consequence. Currently, national and international laboratory experiments dealing with such pathogens pose great safety risks, especially because research has shown that facilities that conduct this research are not adequately secured.[81]

Chemical terrorism involves the use of toxic chemical agents that are deliberately introduced into air, water, and food in order to cause catastrophic harm. Chemical agents are easier to control than biological agents. There are four types of chemical weapons:[82]

> choking agents, such as chlorine and phosgene, which damage lung tissue; blood gases, such as hydrogen cyanide, which block the transport or use of oxygen; vesicants, such as mustard gas, which cause burns and tissue damage to the skin, inside the lungs and to tissues throughout the body; and nerve agents, such as tabun, sarin and VX, which kill by disabling crucial enzymes in the nervous system.

Aum Shinrikyo has engaged in both chemical and biological attacks. Some notable examples include the following: In the fall of 1994, using the nerve agent VX—a weapon of mass destruction according to the United Nations Security Council Resolution 687 (1991)—Aum Shinrikyo killed approximately 20 of its own members.

---

[79] Sims, P. 2009. Police smash white supremacist terror plot to poison ethnic minorities with ricin. *Daily Mail*, June 6, 2009. http://www.dailymail.co.uk/news/article-1191148/Police-smash -global-plot-poison-non-whites-lethal-toxin.html; Galamas, F. 2011. Profiling bioterrorism: Present and potential threats. *Comparative Strategy* 30 (1): 86.

[80] Kaiser, J. 2005. Resurrected influenza virus yields secrets of deadly 1918 pandemic. *Science* 310 (5745): 28–29; Enemark, C., and Ramshaw, I. 2009. Gene technology, biological weapons, and the security of science. *Security Studies* 18 (3): 637.

[81] Enemark and Ramshaw, ibid., 2009, p. 626.

[82] Falkenrath, R. A. 1998. Confronting nuclear, biological and chemical terrorism. *Survival* 40 (3): 47.

That same year, law enforcement agencies in Matsumoto, Japan, dismissed evidence of sarin gas use by Aum Shinrikyo. Instead, they believe that "a former chemical salesman had accidentally mixed the poison gas that killed seven people."[83] The following year, Aum Shinrikyo engaged in chemical attacks in a train car on the Keihin Kyuko rail line traveling between Yokohama and Tokyo. In this attack, on March 5, 1995, at least 19 passengers in the subway of Yokohama experienced symptoms similar to those of the subsequent attack on March 20, 1995, in the subway of Tokyo. In the Tokyo attack, 5 members of Aum Shinrikyo punctured 5 plastic bags inside 5 subway lines, disseminating the nerve agent sarin. A total of 12 people died and approximately 1,039 were injured. Two months later, on May 5, 1995, the cult attempted to release a chemical agent, hydrogen cyanide, but the device failed. In principle, the attainment of toxic chemical agents is not difficult, especially as compared with other forms of weapons of mass destruction. Some types of chemical agents that can result in mass casualties can be manufactured in someone's home; basic laboratory equipment and commercially available precursor chemicals can be used.[84] The most toxic chemicals, however, require sophistication, scientific knowledge, and specialized equipment.[85]

Many measures have been taken domestically and internationally to combat WMD terrorism; the most notable of which is crisis management and disaster preparedness (otherwise known as emergency management). Emergency management involves the development of policies and management of principles and concepts such as organization, administration, and planning as applied to emergency situations. Its purpose is to minimize the loss of life by protecting people and properties and aiding affected communities in rebuilding after a natural or man-made disaster. Emergency management includes four basic phases: mitigation, response, recovery, and preparedness. The first step, mitigation, focuses on lessening the effects of emergencies in the event that they occur and reducing vulnerability to potential future disasters. This step differs from the remaining three because it seeks to implement long-term risk-reducing solutions.[86] When dealing with the threat of an attack with weapons of mass destruction, effective intelligence gathering strategies and surveillance measures that can diminish the impact of the threat are examples of mitigation tools.

As part of the mitigation strategy for WMD terrorism on the international level, the nonproliferation regime should be strengthened. Radiological sensors have also been placed in key entry/exit points of countries to detect radiation

---

[83] Quillen, C. 2000. State sponsored WMD terrorism: A growing threat? *Terrorism Research Center*, 6 http://babylonscovertwar.com/Terrorist%20Groups/Weapon%20Systems/Quillen%20WMD%20Terrorism.pdf.

[84] Falkenrath, R. A. 1998. Confronting nucelar, biological and chemical terrorism. *Survival* 40 (3): 48.

[85] Ibid.

[86] Haddow, G. D., Bullock, J. A., and Coppola, D. P. 2008. *Introduction to emergency management*, 3rd ed. New York: Elsevier, 75.

Box 14-2 Terrorist Threat in Brief: Agroterrorism

Agriculture production is at risk of a terrorist attack because it is often geographically located in unsecured environments. Attacks leveled at agriculture production are known as agroterrorism, which involves the introduction of zoonotic and human pathogens or toxins in the food supply.[1] More specifically, it "is defined as the deliberate introduction of an animal or plant disease with the goal of generating fear, causing economic losses, and/or undermining stability and disruption of consumer demand."[2] Al-Qaeda has also made public its intent and capabilities of engaging in such an attack. In particular, as Chairman Collins said before the Committee on Governmental Affairs of the United States Senate,[3]

> Osama bin Laden himself has considerable knowledge of agriculture. He controlled sunflower and corn markets in Sudan in the mid-1990's and may have used his farms to train terrorist operatives. This horrific page is from *The Poisoner's Handbook*, an underground pamphlet published here in the United States that provides detailed instructions on how to make powerful plant, animal, and human poisons from easily obtained ingredients and how to disseminate them. It was found in Afghanistan in the hands of a group known to support al-Qaeda.

Agroterrorism is not a new phenomenon. Historically, there have been incidents of such attacks by both state and nonstate actors. For example, in 1979, Palestinian terrorists sought to sabotage Israel's economy by poisoning some Jaffa oranges, which Israel exports to Europe.[4] For chemical and biological terrorist attacks targeting the food supply, existing prevention and deterrence strategies include "international treaties and standards (such as the International Plant Protection Convention, and those of the [International Office of Epizootics]/World Organization for Animal Health), bilateral and multilateral cooperative efforts, off-shore activities in host countries, port of entry inspections, quarantine, treatment, and post-import tracking of plants, animals and their products."[5]

---

[1] Breeze, R. 2004. Agroterrorism: Betting far more than the farm. *Biosecurity and Bioterrorism* 2 (4): 251–264; Cupp, O. S., Walker, D. E., II and Hillison, J. 2004. Agroterrorism in the U.S.: Key security challenge for the 21st century. *Biosecurity and Bioterrorism* 2 (2): 97–105; Turvey, C. G., Onyango, B., and Hallman, W. H. 2008. Political communications and terrorism. *Studies in Conflict & Terrorism* 31 (10): 947.

[2] Runge, C. F. 2002, August 25–28. National security and bioterrorism: A U.S. perspective. Prepared for the 8th Joint Conference on Food, Agriculture and the Environment, Red Cedar Lake, Wisconsin, as cited in Turvey, C. G., Onyango, B., and Hallman, W. H. 2008. Political communications and terrorism. *Studies in Conflict & Terrorism* 31 (10): 948.

[3] Collins, S. M. et al. 2003, November 19. Agroterrorism: The threat to America's breadbasket. *Hearing before the Committee on Governmental Affairs, United States Senate, 118th Congress, First Session*, 2. http://www.access.gpo.gov/congress/senate/pdf/108hrg/91045.pdf.

[4] Sprinzak, E., and Karmon, E. 2007, June 17. Why so little? The Palestinian terrorist organizations and unconventional terrorism. *International Institute for Counter-Terrorism*. http://www.ict .org.il/Articles/tabid/66/Articlsid/246/currentpage/5/Default.aspx.

[5] Monke, J. 2004, August 13. Agroterrorism: Threat and preparedness. *CRS Report for Congress*, 29. http://www.fas.org/irp/crs/RL32521.pdf.

materials. These have proven quite effective in detecting such materials. While it would be ideal to place radiological sensors at every airport, seaport, and border crossing, the cost would be prohibitive. There are currently no cheap detectors that are reliable enough for countries to use in screening individuals and cargo. In an attempt to prevent bioterrorism and chemical terrorism, the proliferation of biological and chemical weapons have been outlawed. In particular, "with the ratification of the Biological and Toxin Weapons Convention in 1972, many countries, including the United States, stopped military development of biological weapons and destroyed their stockpiles."[87] Likewise, the Convention on the Prohibition of the Development, Production, Stockpiling and Use of Chemical Weapons and on their Destruction (Chemical Weapons Convention) of 1973 banned the production, stockpiling, and use of chemical weapons.

In 2001, the European Union established the Health Security Committee, which consisted of representatives of the Health Ministers, in order to promote cooperation in combating bioterrorism. The committee agreed to a program that called for the cooperation of EU Member States on preparedness and response to chemical and biological terrorist attacks (BICHAT). The BICHAT program required: the creation of a database to detect and identify all agents that could be used in terrorist attacks; the creation of a database that contains information on "medicines stock and health services and a stand-by facility for making medicines and health care specialists available in case of attack"; and the drafting and dissemination of "guidance on responding to attacks from the health point of view and coordinating the EU response and links with third countries and international organisations."

The Commission on the Prevention of Weapons of Mass Destruction Proliferation and Terrorism, which is responsible for addressing the threat posed by the proliferation of weapons of mass destruction to the United States, published a report in 2008, World at Risk, which included recommendations on how to prevent bioterrorism attacks. This commission recommended the following domestic measures to prevent bioterrorism:[88]

1. Conduct a comprehensive review of the domestic program to secure dangerous pathogens
2. Develop a national strategy for advancing bioforensic capabilities
3. Tighten government oversight of high-containment laboratories
4. Promote a culture of security awareness in the life sciences community, and
5. Enhance the nation's capabilities for rapid response to prevent biological attacks from inflicting mass casualties.

---

[87] Monke, J. 2004, August 13. Agroterrorism: Threat and preparedness. *CRS Report for Congress*, 3. http://www.fas.org/irp/crs/RL32521.pdf.

[88] Commission on the Prevention of Weapons of Mass Destruction Proliferation and Terrorism. 2009, October 21. *The clock is ticking—A progress report on America's preparedness to prevent weapons of mass destruction proliferation and terrorism*, 26. http://www.teachingterror.net/resources /MDR-Final.pdf.

On the international level, the commission recommended that the United States should "press for an international conference of countries with major biotechnology industries to promote biosecurity, . . . conduct a global assessment of biosecurity risks, [and] strengthen global disease surveillance networks." [89] With regard to the latter, disease surveillance needs to be strengthened on the domestic and international level. To do so, the World Health Organization should be notified immediately of outbreaks. Furthermore, to prevent bioterrorism and chemical terrorism, domestic and international agencies need to keep abreast of emerging threats, such as "new agents, toxic industrial chemicals, improvised agents, and delivery systems."[90]

The second step, response, seeks to effectively respond to an emergency in order to save lives, protect property, and meet basic human needs. Domestically, volunteer groups as well as local, state, and federal agencies are involved in emergency management. The severity of the hazard will dictate who will be involved in the response stage. For a less severe threat, only local agencies would be involved, such as emergency medical service (EMS), fire, law enforcement, and public works personnel. First and foremost, first responders are tasked with providing medical assistance, setting the boundaries to the disaster or hazard incident and removing all nonessential personnel from the scene. Local emergency managers are responsible for developing, maintaining, and overseeing the implementation of local emergency management plans. The state intervenes when local authorities cannot deal with the threat by themselves. Each state and territory of the United States has a state emergency management office. As far as disaster response, state emergency managers use the National Guard, which provides "personnel, communications systems, and equipment, air and road transport, heavy construction and earth-moving equipment, mass care, and feeding equipment, and emergency supplies such as beds, blankets, and medical supplies."[91] Assistance may be rendered on the federal level if state resources are overwhelmed or when the interests at stake are federal. Volunteer groups also provide assistance wherever needed. Internationally, there are many agencies involved in emergency management. Some of the agencies include the Food and Agricultural Organization, World Bank, International Telecommunications Union, World Health Organization, and World Food Programme. Additionally, the North Atlantic Treaty Organization (NATO) is responsible for providing both support to national agencies during emergencies and protection against the affects of weapons of mass destruction. The United Nations acts as the coordinator for emergency management on an international level.

The third step, recovery, involves restoring the disaster-affected area to pre-incident conditions by repairing damages. This step of the emergency management

---

[89] Ibid.

[90] Kosal, M. E. 2008, September. Chemical terrorism: US policies to reduce the chemical terror threat. http://www.dtic.mil/cgi-bin/GetTRDoc?AD=ADA486309&Location=U2&doc=GetTRDoc.pdf.

[91] Haddow, G. D., Bullock, J. A., and Coppola, D. P. 2008. *Introduction to emergency management*, 3rd ed. New York: Elsevier, 107.

process focuses on assessing the damage that has occurred (directly and indirectly) as a result of the hazard to individuals and property (both public and private). How long this step lasts depends on the magnitude of the devastation caused by the incident. Another aspect of this step is emotional recovery. After 9/11, many citizens suffered from Post-Traumatic Stress Disorder (PTSD) and required mental health assistance and counseling. The emotional distress caused by traumatic events must also be factored into the recovery process.

The fourth step, preparedness, requires communities, cities, and nations to get ready for disasters that will or may happen in the future. In the United States, the National Incident Management System defines preparedness as "a continuous cycle of planning, organizing, training, equipping, exercising, evaluating, and taking corrective action in an effort to ensure effective coordination during incident response."[92] Public education is also required. Preparedness for disasters should also be the responsibility of individuals, families, and businesses.

To prepare for a WMD attack, the United States has implemented several programs; the most notable are Department of Health and Human Services' Biomedical Advanced Research and Development Authority (BARDA) and Project BioShield. BARDA "leads an integrated, systematic approach to the development and purchase of the necessary vaccines, drugs, therapies, and diagnostic tools for public health medical emergencies."[93] Project BioShield "funds medical countermeasures against biological, chemical, radiological, and nuclear agents."[94] In the United States, the Project BioShield Act of 2004 allowed the stockpiling of vaccines that have not been tested for safety or efficacy in humans because such testing cannot occur without exposing humans to the biological, chemical, or radioactive threats being treated. While there are at least a dozen critical biological weapon threats, there are only two vaccines for them under Project BioShield.[95] As Mauroni noted, "for the 270 cities in the United States with a population of more than 100,000, only thirty-odd cities have Project Biowatch detectors. It's a very expensive project to sustain against a wide variety of potential threats."[96]

For biological and chemical attacks, eradication measures exist both in the response and preparedness phases of emergency management. However, mass eradication is quite controversial. For instance, in response to the foot and mouth disease[97] outbreak in 2001, the United Kingdom burned the carcasses of infected

---

92 Federal Emergency Management Agency. 2010, August 11. *Preparedness.* http://www.fema.gov/prepared/index.shtm.

93 Commission on the Prevention of Weapons of Mass Destruction Proliferation and Terrorism. 2009, October 21. *The clock is ticking – A progress report on America's preparedness to prevent weapons of mass destruction proliferation and terrorism,* 12. http://www.teachingterror.net/resources/MDR-Final.pdf.

94 Ibid.

95 Mauroni, A. J. 2010, September. Homeland insecurity: Thinking about CBRN terrorism. *Homeland Security Affairs* VI (3). http://www.hsaj.org/?fullarticle=6.3.3.

96 Ibid.

97 FMD is a fatal viral disease that affected cloven-hoofed animals.

animals that had died from the disease.[98] In 2004, the H7N3 virus was found among chickens at poultry farms in the Fraser Valley community in British Columbia, Canada. In response to this contagious virus, the Canadian government decided to kill millions of poultry in the farms.[99] Such instances of mass slaughter and carcass disposal have led to the demand for the scientific community to seek alternatives to these practices. These alternatives consist of implementing measures to try to prevent mass outbreaks. In addition, confinement measures exist both in the response and preparedness phases of emergency management. Consider Severe Acute Respiratory Syndrome (SARS). Several countries adopted stringent measures to screen and control visitors coming from SARS-affected countries. Thermal imaging technology was installed at airports and other entry/exit points to scan passengers for fevers. If fevers were detected, travelers were subjected to medical screening to determine if they were infected with SARS. Those with SARS were quarantined. Along with quarantine and traveler screening, travel restrictions were placed to SARS-affected countries.

A vital step in both response and preparedness is communication of the threat to the public and the appropriate authorities. Information concerning the threat must be correctly communicated to the public. All affected communities must be promptly informed of the impeding emergency and the steps that public agencies are taking to deal with it. Actually, the public must also be informed during all four phases of emergency management. Common communications plans must be developed and interoperable communications equipment, processes, and standards must be used by both public and private agencies to ensure the accurate and timely flow of information during the emergency and all four phases of the emergency management process.

In the event of a bioterrorism attack on food markets, "communication and education programs would need to inform growers directly affected by the outbreak, and inform consumers about the source and safety of their food."[100] Usually, biological attacks may not be immediately apparent. Indeed, biological attacks might potentially be misdiagnosed as a natural disease outbreak. This occurred with the attacks by the Rajneeshee cult and Aum Shinrikyo. Experience shows that early detection, diagnosis, and containment of a disease outbreak is crucial. While not a bioterror attack, the handling of SARS provides an excellent example of what not to do during an outbreak. By the time SARS was contained, 8,300 individuals were infected and close to 800 individuals had died in 28 countries. The outbreak started in China. However, the Chinese government delayed responding to SARS and notifying the international community of the outbreak. When the

---

[98] Monke, J. 2004, August 13. Agroterrorism: Threat and preparedness. *CRS Report for Congress*, 32. http://www.fas.org/irp/crs/RL32521.pdf.

[99] Ibid.

[100] Monke, J. 2004, August 13. Agroterrorism: Threat and preparedness. *CRS Report for Congress*, 35. http://www.fas.org/irp/crs/RL32521.pdf.

World Health Organization was notified, the disease had already spread across borders. Early warning and communication of the threat is thus critical.

THE WAY FORWARD

The aim of this text was to evaluate existing counterterrorism measures and the threats they were designed to deal with. For new catastrophic threats such as cyberterrorism, the security of critical infrastructure systems is paramount. This also requires better security at the facilities that house these systems. For WMD terrorism, effective emergency management policies at the international and domestic levels are required. New technology in the field must be implemented only if it respects fundamental rights, is in accordance with the law, and does not adversely impact the public's health. New counterterrorism practices, such as behavioral profiling and speech profiling, must also be used only if their validity and reliability has been established.

The evaluation of counterterrorism practices seeks to shed some light on the consequences of measures currently being implemented to combat terrorism. Additionally, it seeks to try to prevent—or at the very least deter—the recycling of ineffective counterterrorism policies. There are existing measures that constitute a real "mitos" because they have aided in the detection, investigation, and prosecution of "Minotaurs" (i.e., terrorists) in the past. Accordingly, it is these practices that can and should be applied to terrorism. In line with this reasoning, there are also practices that should be used only in limited circumstances and only if they are in accordance with the law. Furthermore, there are practices that need to be abolished outright due to their illegitimacy and ineffectiveness. Each of these is explored below.

Counterterrorism practices to be maintained:

- intelligence gathering (as long as it is in accordance with the law and respectful of human rights);
- the use of undercover agents and informants;
- the prosecution and incapacitation of terrorists through the ordinary criminal justice system;
- rehabilitation practices (wherever needed and appropriate);
- limiting (within the constraints of the law) terrorists' access to the media and preventing them from spreading their messages and obtaining information that could be used to create bombs/weapons and plot attacks on targets;
- leveraging the power of the Internet and other media sources to expose any and all distortions by terrorists and draw attention to the costs of terrorists' negative actions;
- developing and monitoring honeypots, which have been created within the limits of the law, to identify terrorists; and

- engaging in negotiations and peace agreements with terrorists (if required and only if this practice is suitable to the terrorist or terrorist group in question and after having weighed the costs and benefits of doing so).

Counterterrorism practices to be used only in limited circumstances, as a last resort and if they are in accordance with the law: If absolutely necessary, targeted killings, closed borders and blockades, and sanctions can be used as countermeasures. The frequency in the use of the latter will depend on the type of sanction. Specifically, individual sanctions can be used more often than collective sanctions.

Counterterrorism practices to be abolished:

- the use of torture to obtain confessions and elicit information from suspected terrorists by government agents, law enforcement officers, intelligence agencies, and military personnel;
- the use of illegal coercive interrogation tactics to obtain confessions and information;
- the use of the death penalty as a form of punishment for terrorists;
- the use of house demolitions as a form of deterrence;
- preventive detention for terrorists;
- housing terrorists in Guantanamo Bay and similar facilities;
- trying suspected terrorists in military tribunals instead of through ordinary criminal justice channels;
- the restriction of fundamental rights of suspected terrorists housed in detention facilities; and
- counterterrorism measures, such as mass surveillance measures, which violate the rule of law and civil liberties.

Terrorism aims at striking at, and destroying, the fundamental values of a democratic society. The only effective tool to combat terrorism is one that respects fundamental freedoms. As Sergio Vieira de Mello[101] declared before the Counter-Terrorism Committee of the Security Council, "the best—the only—strategy to isolate and defeat terrorism is by respecting human rights."[102] While terrorism is precisely the case whereby affording individuals (terrorists) the liberty to plan attacks and evade detection can threaten the security of the majority, it does not follow that in order to deal with terrorism, civil liberties must be sacrificed. Likewise, if the measures of democratic societies do not take place within the framework of the rule of law, they have allowed terrorists to destroy the very foundations

---

[101] The late UN High Commissioner for Human Rights was killed in a terrorist act when a truck filled with explosives was detonated at UN headquarters in Baghdad on August 19, 2003.

[102] Statement of UN High Commissioner for Human Rights Sergio Vieira de Mello to the Counter-Terrorism Committee 2002, October 21. www.un.org/Docs/sc/committees/1373/HC.htm as cited in Flynn, E. J. 2005. Counter terrorism and human rights: The view from the United Nations. *European Human Rights Law Review* 1:31.

of their society.[103] In sum, it is simply wrong to assume that democratic societies *must* abandon their commitments to the rule of law and human rights in order to deal with the threats posed by terrorism. The counterterrorism measures that need to be abolished are those that represent just such an abandonment.

Terrorism can be eradicated only through universal countermeasures. The (in)security of one country affects the security of another. Technological advances and the erosion of borders (which allowed the free movement of persons and goods), and lax border control and security not only create opportunities for individuals to engage in terrorism and terrorism-related activity but also make such activity difficult to detect. Security is indeed only as strong as its weakest link. The lack of coordination of countries worldwide on measures with which to combat terrorism affords terrorists the opportunity to avoid and subvert detection and capture by authorities. Accordingly, security from terrorism truly requires a unified, international effort. Only then can an effective counterterrorism strategy be achieved.

HYPOTHETICAL SCENARIO

In Barneveld, New York, with a population of roughly 330 people, 50 individuals were hospitalized after attending a town fair. The individuals hospitalized exhibited two or more of the following symptoms: shortness of breath (dyspnea), loss of consciousness, and/or seizure. Upon further testing, lab results revealed that these individuals had been exposed to soman (a nerve agent).

What should the town do first? What should they do afterwards? Please explain each step that should be taken in your response.

CHAPTER SUMMARY

New technology in the field of counterterrorism should be used only if it is valid and reliable. Not all existing technologies used in the field have met this requirement. In addition, behavioral profiling, while a promising counterterrorism measure in theory, has proven somewhat ineffective in the United States in practice. This may, in part, be due to the lack of appropriate training and qualifications of those tasked with engaging in behavioral profiling. Another novel counterterrorism practice, speech profiling, is still being researched, but its potential for predicting terrorist behavior is promising.

Two forms of terrorism can cause harm of greater proportions than other forms of terrorism, namely, cyberterrorism and WMD terrorism. Cyberterrorism, to date, has not materialized. However, given that its perpetrators seek access to critical infrastructure systems with the intention of causing catastrophic harms to

---

[103] Goldstone, R. 2005. The tension between combating terrorism and protecting civil liberties. In *Human rights in the "war on terror,"* ed. R. A. Wilson, 166. Cambridge, UK: Cambridge University Press.

individuals, property, and the environment, it is of great concern to counterterrorists. To protect from cyberterrorism, critical infrastructure systems and their facilities must be properly secured. Unlike cyberterrorism, WMD terrorism has occurred in the past, although not all forms of it. For WMD terrorism, a comprehensive emergency management plan on the domestic and international level is required.

Counterterrorism is multifaceted and currently involves an array of practices both beneficial and detrimental to the security of nations worldwide. Counterterrorism practices that result in the abandonments of the rule of law and human rights must be abolished. Efficient and cost-effective measures that have enabled governments to detect, investigate, capture, prosecute, and incapacitate terrorists, along with rehabilitation practices and peace agreements (wherever appropriate), should be the only measures included in a counterterrorism strategy.

REVIEW QUESTIONS

1. What new measures and technologies have been implemented to combat terrorism?
2. Has an act of cyberterrorism occurred?
3. Which type or types of WMD terrorism have been successfully implemented in the past? By whom?
4. What measures should governments use to respond to WMD terrorism?
5. What measures should a successful counterterrorism strategy maintain?
6. What measures must be abolished?
7. Which counterterrorism measures should be used only rarely? Recall your readings of previous sections. Why do you think these should be retained for limited use?

appendix

Selected International and National Terrorism Incidents

June 5, 1968: U.S. presidential candidate Robert F. Kennedy is assassinated by Sirhan Sirhan, a Palestinian who is motivated by Kennedy's pro-Israel positions.

June 9, 1970: The Palestinian Liberation Organization (PLO) attempts to assassinate Jordan's King Hussein.

September 1970: The Popular Front for the Liberation of Palestine (PFLP) hijacks planes in the Netherlands, Switzerland, and Germany, killing more than 400 passengers. In response, Jordan attacks Palestinian neighborhoods, which results in more than 20,000 deaths.

May 11, 1972: The Red Army Faction bombs the U.S. barracks in Frankfurt, Germany, killing 1 and injuring 13.

July 21, 1972: The Provisional Irish Republican Army (PIRA) sets off 22 bombs, killing 9 and injuring 130 individuals (Bloody Friday).

September 5, 1972: Black September, an Islamic terrorist group, kills 9 Israeli athletes at the Olympic Games in Munich, Germany.

September 10, 1973: The PIRA sets off bombs at London's Euston Station and King's Cross Station, killing 21.

December 20, 1973: The ETA assassinates Prime Minister Admiral Luis Carrero Blanco in Madrid, Spain.

February 4, 1974: The PIRA detonates an explosive device on a coach carrying approximately 50 individuals from Manchester, England, along the M62 motorway to an army base in Catterick, North Yorkshire. In this attack, 12 people are killed, including 8 off-duty soldiers and 2 young children.

October 5, 1974: Bombs placed at two pubs in Guildford, England, which are popular with British Army personnel, are detonated. In the blasts, 5 individuals are killed and 65 are wounded. The Guildford Four (Paul Michael Hill, Gerard "Gerry" Conlon, Patrick "Paddy" Armstrong, and Carole Richardson) are subsequently convicted and sentenced to life imprisonment. Approximately 15 years later, their convictions are overturned.

November 21, 1974: Explosive devices are detonated in two central pubs in Birmingham, England, which killed 21 people and injured 182. The Birmingham Six (Hugh Callaghan, Patrick Joseph Hill, Gerard Hunter, Richard McIlkenny, William Power, and John Walker) are accused of carrying out the attack. About 16 years later, their convictions are overturned.

April 24, 1975: The Red Army Faction sieged the West German embassy in Stockholm, Sweden, and blew it up.

December 23, 1975: 17 November assassinates CIA Station Chief Richard Welch outside his residence in Athens, Greece.

July 30, 1977: The Red Army Faction shot and killed the head of the Dresdner Bank, Jürgen Ponto, after a failed kidnapping attempt.

March 16, 1978: The Red Army Faction kidnapped Italian politician and former Prime Minister Aldo Moro, who is killed 55 days later on May 9, 1978.

July 29, 1979: The ETA bombs two railway stations in Madrid, Spain, killing 7 people.

November 4, 1979: Fifty-two U.S. diplomats are taken hostage by fundamentalist Islamic students in Tehran, Iran, and held for 444 days.

May 13, 1981: Pope John Paul II is shot in an assassination attempt by a Turkish assailant who claims PFLP membership.

October 6, 1981: Egypt's President Anwar al-Sadat is assassinated by Muslim extremists within the Egyptian army.

December 31, 1982: The FALN (Fuerzas Armadas de Liberación Nacional or Armed Forces of National Liberation) detonate explosives outside FBI headquarters in Manhattan and a courthouse in Brooklyn, injuring 3 police officers responding to the scene.

April 18, 1983: The U.S. Embassy in Beirut, Lebanon, is destroyed by a suicide car-bombing by Hezbollah, killing 49 and injuring 120.

September 25, 1983: Thirty-eight IRA prisoners shoot their way out of Long Kesh, a maximum security prison in England, killing 1 and injuring 6.

October 23, 1983: U.S. military barracks are destroyed by a truck-bombing carried out by Hezbollah in Beirut, Lebanon, killing 241 U.S. Marines and 58 French troops.

December 17, 1983: The PIRA detonates explosives in Harrods, a West London department store, during the Christmas shopping season, killing 6 and injuring 90.

January 18, 1984: The President of American University of Beirut is shot and killed by members of the Islamic Jihad.

September 20, 1984: The U.S. Embassy annex in Beirut, Lebanon, is bombed, killing 20 individuals.

October 12, 1984: The PIRA detonates explosives during the Conservative Party conference at the Grand Hotel in Brighton. Prime Minister Margaret Thatcher is in attendance but is unharmed in the attack. Conservative MP Sir Anthony Berry is killed, along with 4 others.

February 23, 1985: A bomb is detonated at a Marks & Spencer store in Paris, France, killing 1 and injuring 18.

April 12, 1985: A bomb is detonated in a restaurant in Madrid, Spain, by Islamic terrorists, killing 18.

May 14, 1985: The Anuradhapura massacre occurs in Sri Lanka, in which 146 Sinhalese civilians are killed by the Tamil Tigers.

October 7–10, 1985: The Achille Lauro cruise ship is hijacked by the Palestine Liberation Front. During this time, 69-year-old Jewish American Leon Klinghoffer, who is wheelchair-bound, is killed and thrown overboard.

December 27, 1985: Terrorists affiliated with Abu Nidal start shooting and throwing hand grenades at passengers at ticket counters in the Leonardo da Vinci-Fiumicino Airport outside of Rome, Italy, and the Schwechat Airport in Vienna, Austria.

April 5, 1986: A discotheque in Berlin, Germany, frequented by U.S. military personnel, is bombed, killing 3 (a Turkish woman and two U.S. servicemen) and injuring more than 130 (over 50 of whom are U.S. military). Libya is blamed for the incident.

April 21, 1987: The Tamil Tigers detonate a car bomb at a bus terminal in Colombo, Sri Lanka.

June 19, 1987: The ETA detonates a bomb in the parking lot under the Hipercor shopping center in Barcelona, Spain, killing 21 and wounding 45.

November 8, 1987: The Remembrance Day parade in Enniskillen, County Fermanagh, Northern Ireland, is bombed by the PIRA, killing 11 and injuring 63.

June 28, 1988: 17 November assassinates U.S. Naval Captain William Nordeen, an American diplomat and defense attache, in Athens, Greece, by remotely detonating a car bomb.

December 21, 1988: Pan Am Flight 103 explodes over Lockerbie, Scotland, killing 259 passengers, including American students and military personnel. The Libyan government and Popular Front for the Liberation of Palestine–General Command (PFLP-GC) claim responsibility.

September 26, 1989: 17 November assassinates liberal Greek politician Pavlos Bakoyannis.

November 5, 1990: El Sayyid Nosair, an Arab male with links to al-Qaeda, assassinates Meir Kahane, founder of the American vigilante group the Jewish Defense

League and head of Israel's Koch party, in the lobby of a hotel in Manhattan, New York.

May 21, 1991: A member of the Tamil Tigers detonates a suicide vest, killing the former Indian Prime Minister Rajiv Gandhi.

March 17, 1992: The Islamic Jihad bomb the Israeli Embassy in Buenos Aires, Argentina, killing 29 and injuring over 240.

July 16, 1992: The Shining Path is suspected of having detonated explosives in the Miraflores District of Lima, Peru, killing 18 and injuring about 140, and causing extensive property damage to a 10-story building and vehicles in the area.

January 25, 1993: A Pakistani national, Mir Aimal Kansi, uses an assault rifle on cars waiting at a stoplight in front of the headquarters of the Central Intelligence Agency, killing 2 and injuring 3.

February 26, 1993: A truck bomb explodes in the garage underneath the World Trade Center in New York City, killing 6, injuring over 1,000, and resulting in $500 million in damages. Ramzi Yousef and Sheik Omar Abdel Rahman, terrorists with links to al-Qaeda, are sentenced to life imprisonment on September 5, 1996 for their roles in the attack.

April 14, 1993: An assassination attempt on former U.S. President George H. W. Bush is foiled in Kuwait.

April 16, 1993: Hamas engages in a suicide car bombing attack at the Mehola Junction in the West Bank, killing 2 and injuring 8.

April 24, 1993: The PIRA detonates a truck bomb in Bishopsgate, London's financial district, killing 1 and injuring 44.

May 1, 1993: A suicide bomber of the Tamil Tigers kills Sri Lankan President Ranasinghe Premadasa.

October 4, 1993: Al-Qaeda militants destroy U.S. helicopters in Somalia, killing 18 soldiers.

March 1, 1994: A Lebanese-born immigrant, Rashid Baz, opens fire on a van carrying Jewish students on the Brooklyn Bridge in New York, killing 1 student and injuring 3.

June 28, 1994: Aum Shinrikyo releases sarin gas in Matsumoto, Japan, killing 7 and injuring approximately 660.

October 19, 1994: A Hamas suicide bomber detonates his explosives on a bus in Tel Aviv, Israel, killing 22 and injuring 56.

November 11, 1994: An Islamic Jihad suicide bomber detonates his explosives while riding his bike at the Netzarim Junction in the Gaza Strip, killing 3 and wounding 6.

March 20, 1995: Aum Shinrikyo releases sarin gas in a Tokyo subway, killing 13 and injuring over 1,000.

April 9, 1995: Two Hamas and Islamic Jihad suicide bombers detonate their explosives in Gaza, killing 8 and wounding 50.

April 19, 1995: A Ryder rental truck packed with explosives destroys the Alfred P. Murrah Federal Building in Oklahoma City, killing 168 and wounding 600.

The attack is carried out by Timothy McVeigh and Terry Nichols. McVeigh is executed for his crimes on June 11, 2001, and Nichols is sentenced to life imprisonment without parole on August 9, 2004.

June 11, 1995: The FARC bombs a music concert in Medellín, Colombia, killing 22 and injuring over 200.

August 21, 1995: A Hamas suicide bomber detonates his explosives on a bus in Jerusalem, killing 5 and injuring 100.

January 31, 1996: A Tamil Tiger suicide bomber detonates explosives at the Central Bank in Colombo, Sri Lanka, killing 90 and injuring approximately 1,400.

June 25, 1996: The Movement for Islamic Change detonates truck bombs outside the U.S. Air Force Khobar Towers housing complex in Dahran, Saudi Arabia, killing 19 and wounding 515.

July 1, 1996: A Kurdistan Worker's Party (PKK) suicide bomber detonates explosives in Tunceli, Turkey, killing 6 and wounding 30.

July 24, 1996: The Tamil Tigers bomb a commuter train in Sri Lanka, killing 57 passengers.

October 22, 1996: A female PKK suicide bomber detonates her explosives in Sivas, Turkey, killing 3.

February 24, 1997: Ali Abu Kamal opens fire on the observation deck of the Empire State building, killing 2 (including himself) and wounding 6.

March 21, 1997: A Hamas suicide bomber attacks a café in Tel Aviv, killing 3 and wounding approximately 50.

September 4, 1997: Three Hamas suicide bombers detonate their explosives in Jerusalem, killing 5 and wounding 180.

October 4, 1997: The Tamil Tigers attack the Hilton Hotel and Parliament in Colombo, Sri Lanka, killing 17 and injuring 100.

January 29, 1998: Anti-abortion terrorists, the Army of God, bomb a health clinic in Birmingham, Alabama, killing 1 and injuring 1.

August 7, 1998: Al-Qaeda coordinates truck-bombings of U.S. Embassies in Kenya and Tanzania, killing 224 and wounding more than 5,000 Africans.

August 15, 1998: The Real IRA detonates a car bomb in a crowded shopping area in Omagh, Northern Ireland, killing 29 and injuring approximately 220.

December 18, 1999: A Tamil Tigers suicide bomber detonates explosives at an election rally in Colombo, Sri Lanka, killing 23 and injuring over 300. The target of the attack is former President Chandrika Kumaratunga, whom the terrorist fails to kill.

June 7, 2000: A Tamil Tigers suicide bomber detonates explosives during a War Heroes Procession at Golumadama Junction, Ratmalana, Sri Lanka, killing 22 and injuring 60.

August 1, 2000: The Moro Islamic Liberation Front is suspected of detonating explosives at a carnival in the Philippines, killing 3 and wounding 36.

October 12, 2000: Al-Qaeda operatives ram the *USS Cole* in Aden, Yemen, with a boat laden with explosives, killing 17 and injuring 39 American military personnel.

March 4, 2001: The Real IRA detonates a car bomb outside of the BBC's main news center in London, injuring 1 person.

September 11, 2001: Al-Qaeda operatives crash commercial airliners into the World Trade Center in New York City and the Pentagon in Arlington, Virginia, killing an estimated 3,000 and injuring approximately 16,000 civilians.

September 18, 2001: Letters containing anthrax are sent to 5 major U.S. media outlets, killing 1 civilian. A second batch of anthrax letters is sent on October 9, resulting in 4 deaths and 17 injuries. The FBI claims that the anthrax letters are sent by domestic terrorists, but no terrorist group has taken responsibility. On August 6, 2008, the Department of Justice announces that Dr. Bruce Ivins, a government biodefense researcher who committed suicide on July 29, 2008, is the likely perpetrator.

December 13, 2001: Lashkar-e-Taiba and Jaish-e-Mohammed launch an attack against the Indian Parliament in New Delhi, killing approximately 12 and injuring 18.

December 22, 2001: Richard Reid attempts to ignite a bomb in his shoe aboard a transatlantic flight. He is subdued by flight attendants and passengers.

January 27, 2002: A female member of al-Fatah engages in a suicide attack in Jerusalem, killing 2 and injuring 140.

February 1, 2002: Daniel Pearl, the South Asia Bureau Chief of the Wall Street Journal reporter, is beheaded by members of Lashkar-e-Jhangvi, a group affiliated with al-Qaeda.

February 16, 2002: A Popular Front for the Liberation of Palestine suicide bomber blows himself up at a pizzeria in a shopping mall in Karnei Shomron, Israel, killing 2 and injuring approximately 30.

March 9, 2002: A Hamas suicide bomber kills 11 and injures 54 at the Moment Café in Jerusalem.

April 11, 2002: An al-Qaeda terrorist drives a truck laden with explosives into a synagogue in Tunisia, killing 21 and wounding more than 30.

May 8, 2002: Jose Padilla, a U.S. citizen, is arrested for plotting a "dirty bomb" attack.

June 29, 2002: 17 November engages in a failed attempt to detonate explosives at the port of Pireaus in Athens, Greece.

July 4, 2002: An Egyptian gunman opens fire on the El Al ticket counter at Los Angeles International Airport, killing 2 and injuring 3.

September 13, 2002: The Lackwanna Six, Sahim Alwan, Yahya Goba, Yasein Taher, Faysal Galab, Shafal Mosed, and Mukhtar al-Bakri, are arrested in Upstate New York for providing support to al-Qaeda. All six individuals are U.S. citizens of Yemeni descent.

October 12, 2002: Al-Qaeda members destroy nightclubs in Bali, killing 202 and wounding more than 300 people.

October 23, 2002: Chechen terrorists seize Moscow's Dubrovka Theater and take the attendees hostage. In the rescue attempt by Russian Special Forces, approximately 170 are killed and over 700 are injured.

May 1, 2003: Iyman Faris, a naturalized U.S. citizen originally from Kashmir, pleads guilty to charges of providing material support and resources to al-Qaeda and conspiracy for providing this group with information about potential targets in the United States.

November 28, 2003: Nuradin M. Abdi is arrested for planning to blow up a shopping mall in Columbus, Ohio.

December 9, 2003: A Chechen female suicide bomber detonates her explosives belt on Mohovaja Street in Moscow, Russia, killing 6 and injuring 44. This incident is known as the 2003 Red Square bombing.

February 27, 2004: Abu Sayyaf executes the world's deadliest attack at sea by detonating explosives on Superferry 14 off the coast of Manila, Philippines, killing approximately 120 people.

March 11, 2004: Al-Qaeda operatives explode bombs on 3 commuter trains in Madrid, Spain, killing 190 people and injuring approximately 2,000.

August 3, 2004: Dhiren Barot, the leader of a terrorist cell, is arrested for plotting to attack the New York Stock Exchange and other financial institutions in New York, Washington DC, and Newark, New Jersey.

August 4, 2004: Yassin Aref and Mohammad Hossain, leaders of a mosque in Albany, New York, are arrested for planning to purchase a shoulder-fired grenade launcher and use it to assassinate a Pakistani diplomat.

August 27, 2004: James Elshafay and Shahawar Matin Siraj are arrested for plotting to blow up the a subway station near Madison Square Garden in New York City before the Republican National Convention.

September 1, 2004: Chechen terrorists storm a school in Beslan, Russia, and take 1,100 people hostage, ultimately killing 334 hostages, including 186 children.

November 2, 2004: Theo van Gogh, outspoken critic of Islam and descendant of the 19th-century painter, receives numerous death threats before being brutally assassinated in Amsterdam by Mohammed Bouyeri, a member of the Hofstad group.

July 7, 2005: Four al-Qaeda operatives explode bombs on London Underground trains and a London city bus, killing 52 and injuring more than 700.

July 21, 2005: A homegrown terrorist cell attempts to bomb London's public transport system. The attack fails because only the detonators explode on the devices.

August 17, 2005: Approximately 500 homemade bombs exploded at 300 locations in all counties of Bangladesh (excluding Munshiganj), killing 2 and wounding more than 100.

October 29, 2005: Multiple bombs explode in New Delhi, India, killing 62 and injuring over 200. Indian authorities believe that Lashkar-e-Taiba is responsible for the attacks.

December 5, 2005: Michael C. Reynolds is arrested for plotting to blow up a Standard Oil refinery in New Jersey, a Wyoming natural gas refinery, and the Alaskan Transcontinental Pipeline.

June 15, 2006: The Tamil Tigers detonate two claymore mines targeting a bus carrying civilians, killing 68 and injuring approximately 60.

June 22, 2006: Seven individuals are arrested in Miami for plotting to bomb the Sears Tower in Chicago and other buildings in the United States.

July 11, 2006: A series of bombs are detonated over a period of 11 minutes on the Suburban Railway in Mumbai, India, killing 209 and injuring over 700. The Mumbai train bombings are perpetrated by Lashkar-e-Taiba and the Students Islamic Movement of India (SIMI).

July 31, 2006: In Germany, bombs are placed on two regional trains near Cologne in an attempted coordinated terrorist attack.

August 21, 2006: An al-Qaeda plot to destroy airplanes en route from England to the United States using liquid explosives is foiled and 21 terrorists are arrested.

September 5, 2006: In Denmark, individuals of a homegrown terrorist group, who had allegedly planned several terrorist attacks on undisclosed targets in Denmark, are arrested for their procurement of materials to make explosives.

December 6, 2006: Derrick Shareef, an American citizen and Muslim convert, is arrested for planning to set off explosives in the crowded Cherryvale Mall in Chicago, Illinois, during the Christmas season. On September 30, 2008, Shareef is sentenced to serve 35 years in prison.

December 30, 2006: The ETA detonate a van loaded with over 200 kilograms of explosives in the four-story parking garage of Madrid's Barajas International Airport, killing 2 and injuring 26.

April 11, 2007: Al-Qaeda members detonate two car bombs in Algiers, Algeria, killing 33 and injuring 222.

April 11, 2007: Christopher Paul, a U.S. citizen from Columbus, Ohio, is arrested for conspiring to use weapons of mass destruction in Europe and the United States.

May 7, 2007: A plot to attack the U.S. Army base at Fort Dix, New Jersey, is foiled. Eljvir Duka, age 23; Dritan Duka, age 28; and Shain Duka, age 26 (ethnic Albanian brothers who were illegal immigrants); Mohamad Ibrahim Shnewer, age 22 (a U.S. citizen who is born in Jordan); and Serdar Tatar, age 23 (a legal U.S. resident from Turkey) are charged with conspiracy to murder U.S. military personnel. The men are arrested right after two of them purchased weapons from an FBI informant. On April 28, 2009, Dritan Duka, Shain Duka, and Eljvir Duka are sentenced for the 2007 Fort Dix terror plot, receiving life imprisonment without the possibility of parole. Mohamad Shnewer and Serdar Tatar are sentenced the very next day, receiving life imprisonment plus 30 years and 33 years in prison, respectively.

June 30, 2007: Al-Qaeda plots to attack Glasgow International Airport in Scotland and sites in London are foiled, resulting in 8 arrests.

December 27, 2007: Al-Qaeda terrorists murder Benazir Bhutto, former Prime Minister of Pakistan, and kill 20 innocent civilians, escalating the war on terror.

May 22, 2008: Nicky Reilly, a 22-year-old Muslim convert, attempts—but fails—to engage in a suicide attack at the Giraffe cafe and restaurant in Princesshay, Exeter, United Kingdom.

September 5, 2008: Suicide truck bombs kill 35 and injure 70 in Peshawar, Pakistan.

November 26–29, 2008: Terrorists attack hotels, a train station, a Jewish community center, and other targets in Mumbai, India, killing approximately 170 people.

January 28, 2009: Bryant Neal Vinas, an American citizen of Peruvian and Argentinean descent with prior U.S. military service, pleads guilty to terrorism charges in court. Vinas planned to attack a U.S. military base and informed U.S. officials that he had provided al-Qaeda with information about the New York transit system, and that al-Qaeda planned to blow up a Long Island Rail Road commuter train in New York's Penn Station.

April 3, 2009: Hassan Abujihaad is sentenced for leaking classified information about the U.S. missile destroyer *USS Benfold* and other ships within its battle group to terrorist supporters.

May 20, 2009: Four men, James Cromitie (the leader of the group), David Williams IV, Onta Williams, and Laguerre Payen, are arrested for attempting to bomb synagogues in the Bronx and shoot down military aircraft with missiles.

July 27, 2009: Daniel Patrick Boyd, a Caucasian U.S. citizen and homegrown terrorist from North Carolina, is charged with providing material support to terrorists and conspiring to kill, kidnap, and injure individuals overseas. Boyd's children, Dylan and Zakariya, who are also charged with crimes, are planning to engage in suicide attacks in Israel.

September 19, 2009: Najibullah Zazi, a 24-year-old Afghan, is arrested for his role in plotting to engage in suicide bombings in the New York City subway system.

September 23, 2009: Michael Finton, a U.S. citizen, is arrested for attempting to detonate a car bomb filled with what he believed to be explosives outside of the Paul Findley Federal Building and Courthouse in Springfield, Illinois.

September 24, 2009: Hosam Maher Husein Smadi, 19-year-old Jordanian, is arrested for attempting to plant a bomb in a skyscraper in Dallas, Texas.

October 16, 2009: Colleen LaRose (a.k.a. Jihad Jane) is arrested for conspiring with other terrorists to kill Lars Vilks, a Swedish cartoonist who drew the head of the prophet Muhammad on a dog's body in 2007. In February 2011, she pleads guilty to federal terrorism charges. As of this writing, she has yet to be sentenced.

November 5, 2009: Nidal Malik Hassan, a U.S. Army officer stationed at Fort Hood, Texas, kills 13 individuals on base and leaves 30 wounded.

December 25, 2009: Umar Farouk Abdulmutallab manages to pass through airport security in Nigeria and Amsterdam with explosives in his underpants. Due to vigilant passengers, Abdulmutallab fails to ignite the explosives in an attempt to blow up the U.S. plane he is on.

March 26, 2010: Raja Lahrasib Khan, a naturalized U.S. citizen from Pakistan, is arrested for providing material support to a foreign terrorist organization in Chicago.

March 29, 2010: Two female suicide bombers detonate explosives in Moscow's subway system, killing approximately 40 and injuring approximately 60.

May 1, 2010: Faisal Shahzad, a 31-year-old Pakistan-born U.S. citizen, attempts—but fails—to bomb Times Square in New York City.

June 5, 2010: Mohamed Mahmood Alessa and Carlos "Omar" Eduardo Almonte, Muslim U.S. citizens, are arrested at JFK International Airport in New York City for planning to travel to Somalia to join al-Shahab, an al-Qaeda-linked cell, and charged with conspiracy to kill, maim, and kidnap people outside the United States.

October 17, 2010: Farooque Ahmed is charged with planning to attack the United States. Specifically, he plotted to conduct a coordinated terrorist attack on the subway system in Ishington DC.

November 26, 2010: Mohamed Osman Mohamud, a Somali American, is arrested after he attempted to detonate what he believed to be a car bomb during a Christmas tree lighting ceremony in Portland, Oregon.

December 8, 2010: Antonio Martinez (also known as Muhammad Hussain), a Muslim convert and U.S. citizen, is arrested for attempting to detonate what he believed to be a car bomb at a military recruiting center in Maryland.

January 4, 2011: Emerson Winfield Begolly is arrested in Pennsylvania for distributing information on explosives and weapons of mass destruction and soliciting others to engage in acts of violence. He is a moderator and supporter of an Islamic extremist web forum, Ansar al-Mujahideen English Forum (AMEF).

January 22, 2011: Abu Khalid Abdul-Latif and Walli Mujahi are arrested for plotting to attack a military recruiting station in Seattle, Ishington.

February 23, 2011: Khalid Ali-M Aldawsari, a Saudi Arabian college student in Texas, is arrested for buying explosive chemicals for use in terrorist attacks against several targets, including dams, nuclear plants, and the Dallas, Texas, home of former U.S. President George W. Bush.

May 11, 2011: Ahmed Ferhani and Mohamed Mamdouh are arrested in New York for attempting to purchase weapons (guns and grenades) and ammunition for use in plots to attack synagogues and the Empire State Building.

June 28, 2011: The Intercontinental Hotel, a popular hotel among foreigners and governments officials in Kabul, Afghanistan, is attacked by nine Taliban militants. Ten civilians are killed along with the terrorists (some die from suicide attacks, others are killed by security forces).

August 18, 2011: Terrorists engage in coordinated attacks on vehicles (military and private, and two buses) that last less than an hour near Israel's border with Egypt. These individuals begin their attack by shooting at their targets with automatic weapons. Other weapons used are improvised explosive devices, mortar shells, and anti-tank missiles. In the attacks, 23 people are killed (including 10 attackers) and 40 are injured.

September 28, 2011: In Framingham, Massachusetts, Rezwan Ferdaus, a U.S. citizen and homegrown terrorist, is arrested for plotting to attack the Pentagon and the U.S. Capitol Building. He first planned to use radio-controlled model airplanes filled with explosives to bomb the targets. After attacking the facilities, he planned to use rifles and grenades to kill people as they evacuated the buildings.

November 20, 2011: Jose Pimentel, a Dominican-born Muslim convert and Manhattan resident, is arrested by NYPD for plotting to build and detonate bombs in New York City. Pimentel is a lone wolf and maintained a website, which contained bomb-making instructions taken from al-Qaeda's *Inspire* magazine. Unbeknownst to him, a person with whom he is in contact is an NYPD informant who recorded their conversations. This informant invited Pimentel to his apartment and videotaped him building a bomb.

December 7, 2011: A parcel bomb is sent to Deutsche Bank in Frankfurt, Germany. Authorities believe that an Italian anarchist organization, Federazione Anarchica Informale (FAI – Informal Anarchist Federation) is responsible.

December 9, 2011: A letter bomb attack occurs at a tax collection agency in Equitalia, Italy. Authorities believe that the FAI is responsible.

December 13, 2011: Nordine Amrani, a 32-year-old male of Moroccan descent, using an assault rifle and explosive devices such as hand grenades (one of which actually kills him), murders 4 and injures approximately 125 in a busy square in Liege, Belgium. The motive of the active shooter is currently unknown.

January 1, 2012: Al-Shabab terrorists open fire on New Year's revelers in two bars in Kenya, killing 5 and injuring more than 28.

Name Index

Subject Index